THE FIRST AMERICAN NOVEL

The First American Novel

Part I
The Journal of Penrose, Seaman
by William Williams

Part II
The Author, the Book and the Letters in the Lilly Library,
by Terry Breverton

ISBN 1-903529-20-4
ISBN 978-1-903529-20-1

Printed in Wales by J&P Davison, Trefforest

THE FIRST AMERICAN NOVEL

PART I
THE JOURNAL OF PENROSE, SEAMAN

William Williams (1727-1791)

PART II

THE AUTHOR, THE BOOK AND THE LETTERS IN THE WILLIAMS COLLECTION, LILLY LIBRARY, INDIANA

THE JOURNAL OF PENROSE, SEAMAN

EDITOR'S PREFACE

The manuscript, in Indiana University's Lilly Library, is written in 18th century copperplate handwriting, and has been marginally updated to make it more accessible for modern readers. The literal transcript of this original, by Dickason in 1969, is extremely difficult to read, and thereby has no 'flow' for the modern reader, detracting from the acceptance of the book.

Over the course of over 200 years, changes in writing style, paragraph and sentence construction, spelling and terminology have made such a transcript almost unreadable. Thus sentences, paragraphs and spelling have been amended for the modern reader, and the 18th century practice of capitals for certain words within sentences has been changed. Dickason made a tentative attempt to explain some of the words, terminology and context, but this edition has been far more extensively annotated, to demonstrate the validity of Williams' factional novel. I have altered archaic spellings, thus *scheem* becomes scheme, *welth* is wealth, *conscent* is consent, *intirely* is entirely and so on. In some cases Williams spells 'received' as *recieved* or *recived*, and again modern spelling is substituted. In other cases, words like *barrowcooters* and *guanos*, used throughout, are transposed into barracuda and iguanas.

Some of Williams' original paragraph construction has been kept, but all conversations have been italicised, for the sake of clarity. The first two pages of the manuscript are reproduced exactly as in the original manuscript, to demonstrate the complexity of the editing process. The original *Journal* is written in 338 pages, followed by one and a half pages of Paul Taylor's '*Account of the Journal*'.

Chapters have been placed in the book, with relevant titles added, unlike in Williams' manuscript. As the reader progresses, Williams' terminology and phrasing becomes easier to understand. The first edition was published in four volumes (in 1815, twenty-three years after Williams' death) but this work has been kept intact in one volume. I must thank the Lilly Library of Indiana University for granting me a *Helm Fellowship* in September 2003. This greatly assisted with the expense of researching Williams's manuscript and associated letters at the Library. Dr Breon Mitchell and Ms Penny Ramon of the Lilly Library helped me every step of the way.

This book is a fascinating and extremely valuable contribution to the literary canon, with its anti-genocide and anti-slavery message coming a century before its time. The description of one of the most remarkable places on earth for flora and fauna, the Nicaraguan rainforest, is equally remarkable. What most shines through is the author's absolute enthusiasm, his passionate curiosity in the new world around him. There are around 700 footnotes which explain some of the phrases, flora and fauna in the original transcript, authenticating Williams's stay on the Miskitu Coast. Unfortunately no publisher or agent has as yet expressed any interest in this wonderful piece of literature, but it is hoped that its publication in this small edition will encourage the interest that the first novel written in America so truly deserves.

the Journal of Penrose, Seaman.

If ever the following lines should reach my dear country,
the Reader is not to expect to meet with any persuasive
Arguments to enforce belief, or language to adorn
the story, as the Author never received more learning
than what a common country school affords.
In the first place, I shall give the reader a faithful
Narrative of every occurrence within my memory.
from the day of my birth, unto the time I first left
my native shore, to cross the Atlantic.

Lewellin Penrose is my name. I was born near
Caerphilly in Glamorgan shire, in the month of
May, anno dom 1725. My father who was a Sailor,
was cast away in a Ship belonging to the city of Bristol,
called the Union Frigate commanded by a certain
Cap.t Williams (who was his own countryman) in the
great January storm, at the Texel in Holland,
where every soul perished of a fleet consisting of near
60 sail of Vessels, only one Dutch Dogger which
lay without, riding it safe the whole time.
My Mother being left a Widow, with two children (Viz)
my self and a Sister five years younger, after a time,
married a School-master, and removed with him into
Worcestershire, thence into Monmouth shire and after
that into Wales. This man, I may justly remark, at
least in my own opinion, proved the innocent or rather
obstinate cause of many hardships I have since his days,
undergone, as I learnt a few years after of his death.

THE JOURNAL OF PENROSE, SEAMAN

Page 1 of the original manuscript

If ever the following lines should reach my dear country, the Reader is not to expect
to meet with any persuasive Arguments to enforce belief, or language to adorn the
story, as the Author never received more learning than what a common country school
affords. In the first place I shall give the reader a faithful Narrative of every
occurrence within my memory, from the day of my birth, unto the time I first left my
native shore to cross the Atlantic.

Lewellin Penrose is my name. I was born near Caerphilly in Glamorgan shire, in the
month of May, anno dom. 1725. My father who was a sailor, was cast away in a Ship
belonging to the city of Bristol called the *Union Frigate*, commanded by a certain
Capt. Williams (who was his own countryman), in the great January storm at the
Texel in Holland, where every soul perished of a fleet consisting of near 60 sail of
Vessels, only one Dutch Dogger which lay without riding it safe the whole time.
My mother, being left a Widow with two children, (viz) myself and a sister five years
younger, after a time married a School-master; and removed with him into
Worcestershire, thence into Monmouth shire and after that into Wales. This man, I
may justly remark, at least in my own opinion, proved the innocent or rather obstinate
cause of many of the hardships I have since his days, undergone, as I learnt a few
years after his death.

And pity it is that parents take such notice of their own Children's budding genius, speaking of them with such Adulation in their infancy, yet when a Youth becomes of an age capable of receiving an Education suitable to the talent the Almighty has bestowed on him, Every delight shall be snatched from him at once, Because perhaps an Uncle, Cousin or neighbour has acquired some little wealth by this, that or other calling. Now Jack must be placed under a Master, at once, as to the natural bent of the boy, such a thing becomes entirely out of the question, as being by no means a competent judge of that matter.

This was truly my case, In short, nothing would suit, but that I must be placed with a Lawyer, and that without the least inclination on my side.

My poor Mother; always sided with her Husband, and thinking his advice the best, gave me so many lectures, day after day, that I grew quite wearied out as I detested the Profession, and now I determined to follow the seas.

When they found me so averse, they took another method with me, as thus. They came to a consent that I should go on a voyage, but this as I found afterwards, was only in view of weaning me, now when I had been on three or four small trips, they again renewed their dissuasions, this only aggravated my mind, and as it was now War-time, I entered into a new scheme with a companion of mine, this young Lad's name was Howell Gwynn, and to run away we were resolved, We conducted our affair so artfully, that no soul knew, or had the least idea of our elopement.

And here let me beg the kind Reader's permission to let fall a few tears, as it brings to remembrance a kind and tender-hearted Mother.

CHAPTER 1

Running Away to Sea

If ever the following lines should reach my beloved country, the reader is not expected to meet with any persuasive language to enforce his or her beliefs, or language to adorn the story, as the author's learning only derives from a common country school. In the first place, I shall give the reader a faithful narrative of every occurrence in my memory, from the day of my birth, until the time I first left my native shore to cross the Atlantic.

Lewellin Penrose is my name. I was born near Caerphilly in Glamorganshire, in the month of May, 1725. My father, who was a sailor, was lost in a ship belonging to the city of Bristol, called the *Union Frigate*[1]. It was commanded by a certain Capt. Williams, who was his countryman. This was in the great January storm[2] at Texel in Holland, where every soul perished in a fleet consisting of near 60 sail, only one Dutch Dogger[3] which lay without, riding it safe the whole time.

My mother, being left a widow with two children, myself and a sister five years younger, after a time married a schoolmaster. She moved with him into Worcestershire, thence into Monmouthshire and after that into Wales. I may justly remark that this man, in my opinion, proved the innocent (or rather obstinate) cause of many of the hardships I have undergone since those days, as I learnt a few years after his death.

And it is a pity that parents take such notice of their own children's budding genius, speaking of them with such adulation in their infancy. For when a youth reaches an age capable of receiving an education suitable to the talent the Almighty has bestowed upon him, every delight shall be snatched from him at once. This is because perhaps an uncle, cousin or neighbour has acquired a little wealth by this, that or another calling. Now Jack must be placed under a master, at once. As to the natural bent of the boy, that is entirely out of the question, as he is seen as no competent judge of the matter. This was truly my case. In short, nothing would suit except that I must be placed with a lawyer, and that without the least inclination on my side.

My poor mother always sided with her new husband, thinking his advice the best, and gave me so many lectures, day after day, that I grew quite wearied. I detested the profession of lawyer, and now I determined to follow the seas. When they found me so adverse, they took another method with me. They consented that I could go on a voyage, but as I found out afterwards it was only with the view of weaning me away from the idea.

When I had been on three or four small trips, they again renewed their dissuasion. This aggravated my mind, as it was now wartime[4], so I entered into a new scheme with a companion of mine. This young lad's name was Howell Gwynn, and we resolved to run away. We conducted our affair so artfully, that no soul knew, or had the least idea of our elopement. And here let me beg the kind reader's permission to let fall a few tears, as it brings to remembrance a kind and tender-hearted mother.

Alas! To think now on the wickedness of that act chills my blood. Notwithstanding it may be reasonably judged, the ocean seldom softens the passions. I observe this here as a note of caution to any young fellow whom, if God so please, may come to read my singular story.

I say then, having found no means to convey our clothes and other trifles away, and with no more than four shillings in money, in the month of September 1744 we very early in the morning quit the houses of our parents, without the least remorse or conscience, to make the best of our way to Bristol. We took care to evade all enquiries, slept in barns and stables, now and then asking for a piece of bread and cheese on the road, saying that we had been cast away, and to make our money hold out the longer. As we went through a village called Pile[5], a young fellow met us who was returning from a cruise, and advised us by all means to return back to our parents, he having been unsuccessful. But the reflections we thought to meet with, should we do so, determined us to proceed until we got the whole length of the journey with only three halfpence left in store.

The first thing we did was to march to the quay, where by chance we met with a young fellow who was a kind of relation to me, and a sailor also. He no doubt was pleased to find I had taken such a turn, and undertook to get us berths. The city of Bristol then swarmed with numbers of privateers' men[6]. My cousin took us to a rendezvous on the quay, the sign of *The White Lion and Horseshoe*. We had not been long in the house before my companion Howell was persuaded to enter service as a privateer, but as I had a greater mind to become a good seaman, than to commence being a hero all at once, I evaded all their temptations. Now, as I was in a strange place without money, I took my friend's advice. My companion Gwynn took his leave of me to go down to Hungroad[7], and from that day to this hour we never met more. I remained all the evening with my cousin, who I found to be a hearty cock and never flinched a can of grog[8]. Now, being in no way inclined to liquor, I left him in company and went upstairs to sleep on a rush-bottomed couch in the fore-room.

In the midst of my sleep, I was roused by the most sad outcry of a boy, as I thought, under severe discipline. This alarmed me greatly, as it was accompanied by most horrid imprecations from some man. Being but a stranger in the house, and finding that the man was downstairs, I determined to make my best way downstairs also, in order to find my relation. There was a small light, which gleamed into my room. On I pushed, but as I went along the passage I heard a soft voice call to me, begging me to come into a room on my right hand. No sooner did I enter, but I saw a charming creature, stark naked before me. I was for passing on, but she laid hold on me, and made me sit on the bedside with her. She began to tell me that her husband, the landlord, had beaten her most cruelly in a fit of drunken jealousy. No mortal was ever much more alarmed than me in that situation, dreading her husband's return.

She showed me the gooseberry bush he had beaten her with, and indeed he had curried[9] her to some purpose. Now it happened the candlestick fell down. This was a lucky stroke for me. I directly offered to go downstairs and relight it. To this she consented, but I took care not to go back with it. And well for me, perhaps, for shortly after the husband went up the stairs again and gave her the second part of the foregoing tune, and played it well. I groped my way into the fore-parlour in order to rouse some of the snoring tars[10], but I might as well have spared the trouble. They were all so snugly moored in *Sot's Bay* that it was out of my power to trip one of their anchors. At last I ran foul of a man in the entry, standing in his shirt. '*Who are you, messmate?*' said I.

'Oh, cousin,' he cried, '*Is it you?*'

'*For God's sake, let us get out of this house,*' said I, '*at any rate.*'

2

Shortly after this we heard the Watchman pass, when we took our courage and hailed him. *'Go to sleep if you are drunk,'* he said.

We then called through the keyhole and shouted *'Murder! Knock at the door, man!'* He then called two more and they thundered at the street door. We then drew back into *Sot's Bay* when down came Mr Bean, the furious landlord, with the candle and opened the door. No sooner did he do it, than out we pushed, and insisted on their taking us off with them, as we greatly feared the fellow would murder his wife before morning light. This was about three o'clock. After this we marched the streets until six, when we entered another house called the *Champion of Wales*. There we got breakfast and proceeded down to the Gibb, where his boat lay. He took me down to Pill on the next tide, where he purchased a few articles for me.

The wind coming round to the East, we stood down the Bristol Channel the next day and took in a load of coal at Neath[11], from whence we proceeded to Cork. On the passage I learned that my cousin had been the cause of the landlord's jealousy, and that the landlord had given him a fine basting before I awoke.

Now it happened as I was standing on the quay on a day, before the bow of the vessel, a man seized me by the hand, and clapping my thumb between his teeth threw me over his shoulder, and in this position carried me into the next public house, where he called for a quart of ale on my head as a new import. I was greatly amazed at first, but some of our people, following and laughing, told me it was the custom among the porters. This man's name I can well remember was Billy Vane.

One evening after this, my cousin needed me to go on shore with him to look out for a brute, as he used to call the *ladies of pleasure*. He was then in liquor, and remembering the Bristol adventure, upon the whole I refused. He then began to upbraid me with what he had done for me, but as I dreaded the consequences, I persisted to remain on board. He then told me that I might as well march on shore, and shift for myself. He had not been gone more than two hours, when I left the vessel and repaired on board a snow[12] bound for London. There I begged my passage, in exchange for work.

After my coming to London, I directly entered on board a privateer, having not one shilling in the world. I followed it up, playing the same game as other sailors do when on shore with Prize Money[13]. After this time I was pressed[14], and shifted from one to another until I found means to make my escape, going under different names as it best suited my purpose. Thus I spent my time until the year 1746.

I then shipped myself on board an old Indiaman called the *Harrington*[15], bound for Jamaica and at that time lying at the Red House, Deptford[16], with one Hunter as commander. With what little cash I had left, I purchased a few shirts and trousers, a jacket, scotch bonnet[17], a pair of shoes and a small seaman's chest. After this the ship sailed down to Gravesend, from thence to the Downs, and there I experienced the first thunderstorm I had ever been in, on salt water. The rain and wind were so violent off the shore that she was soon on her beam ends[18], as we were then getting under way. The flashes of lightning were so quick that I could scarcely keep my eyes open, but it was of short continuance. After this we proceeded to Spithead, there to wait for the convoy.

In three or four days we put to sea, being about one hundred sail, bound to different ports. Our convoy was a ship called the *Old Chatham*[19], of 50 guns. Our own ship mounted 20 guns. With a Letter of Marque, we parted company in the Bay of Biscay and proceeded alone. Nothing of note happened on our passage, except some of our maintopmen[20] who, during the time we were exercising the great guns, chanced to set the mizzen topmast staysail on fire as they were busy in the main top; but it was soon happily extinguished. Nevertheless it put all hands in a great hurry, as no misery can equal that of a ship on fire in the main ocean.

After this we made the islands of Antigua, Montserrat, Nevis and St Christopher's (St Kitts), and passed between them. Here we spoke to the French, under a flag of truce. A few nights after, we ran onto the Isle of Vache[21], off St Domingo on a very dark night indeed, but saw it in enough time so as to receive no damage. The next day we came abreast of the White Horse Cliffs on the Jamaica South Shore. Here, the pilot came on board, and we got safely into Port Royal. And here I shall observe that our first captain did not voyage with the ship, and a certain Mr. William James, then chief mate, took the command at Spithead.

During our stay here, Admiral Davers[22] died; and as all the ships in the harbour were firing minute guns on that occasion, when it came to our turn one of the guns on the larboard side discharged before its due time. I happened to be standing on the gangway, and saw a young fellow of the name of Palmer, sinking. The blood flew from his head and arms like a spout, and a piece of his skull I found in the main chains. This unhappy young man had been sponging the gun and had left some of the old cartridge on fire within. When he rammed home another cartridge, it took fire and blew him to pieces, at the same time blasting the fingers of the coxswain, who at that time held them in the touch-hole.

About the latter end of November, having our full lading in, we set sail for London; but the Almighty was pleased to frustrate our intentions and to disperse us in a wonderful manner. We beat to windward for several days, to little purpose. At length the storm carried away our foretopmast, top and all; two of our hands went over with it, but saved their lives.

Our commander then proposed to bear away for Blewfields[23], to repair our damage. After we had got up a new top and topmast, we put to sea and bore away for the Gulf of Florida (Gulf of Mexico). Some time after this, on a blustery night, we almost ran ashore on the Isle of Pines. However, we wore out the storm and stood off again. From this time the weather proved very hazy, with a little rain, and it stayed like this until Christmas Eve. Every mess (kitchen) was now busy in making puddings, but alas, now began the prelude to our future troubles.

A squall arose, about the second watch, and all hands were called out. It blew for about half an hour. After this we jogged on, under an easy sail, until break of day. Little did I think at the time, that it would prove so fatal a Christmas Day to me.

Our Chief Mate, Mr Ramage, shortly after he came on deck, spied a sail right ahead of us. Directly all hands were called to quarters, as she was lying to, not two miles from us. Just as this happened, we discovered the *Morro Castle*[24], quite plain under our lee. Now, as the enemy was astern, we could not discover their force. Nor did she seem to take the least notice of us, and as we were in no kind of fear about her, we *stood on* and waited for her to overhaul us. Shortly after this, as we came almost abreast of her, we plainly perceived her to be a ship of force. She then bore down into our wake, hoisted Spanish colours, and began to fire several random shots at us. Directly we ran out our two stern chasers, and crowded all the sail we could. However, in a short time, away went our maintop gallant mast, and as she quickly gained on us, our captain ordered our ensign flag to be hauled down.

The ship we struck to was a Spanish man-of-war, called *El Fuerto*, mounting 50 guns and commanded by one Captain Mahoney, a good-natured old Irishman. We were carried into the Havannah, and there our crew were divided on board two men-of-war,

4

The Dragon and *Conquistador*[25]. Thus I well remember that my Christmas dinner was changed from plum pudding to horse beans and poor jerked beef[26].

In this place we remained prisoners and had the grief and mortification to see flags of truce come in and go out every day, it being a practice in those times for flags to visit the Spaniards from North America[27], laden with flour and other articles; and this was supported through the sneaking contrivance of their bringing and taking away one or two prisoners at a time, so that this low, cunning game might last the longer, while hundreds of His Majesty's loyal subjects were detained to labour at the Morro Castle, in the abject condition of carrying stones to repair the enemy's fortifications against their will.

Our employment on board these two ships was the picking of oakum[28], pumping the ship, hoisting in their water, and the like. We had our berth allotted between two great guns on the lower deck. It was then proposed by the elders of our brothers in captivity, that we formed a set of laws among ourselves, for our better keeping of peace, and also so not to annoy the enemy. We in the first place concluded never to mention the word Spaniard but to substitute that of *hoopstick* instead. By this method we could talk about them freely at all times, as none of them understood English. Another law was to strictly observe the hours of 10 in the morning and 4 in the evening, for the ridding of the vermin with which we greatly abounded. The law was so strictly observed that if anyone was found to transgress; he was directly brought to the gun where he received a good copping, alias ten and a puss on his posterior with a barrel stave[29].

The Spaniards took much pleasure in hearing us sing, or play at cards. But there was one thing which I never thought was commendable with the English, which was deciding their foolish quarrels on shore in a boxing bout, to the great derision of our enemies and their own shame; the Spaniards never failing, on such occasions, to call them '*perros Ingleses, English dogs.*'

We were served every day with fresh beef from the town, but as poor as carrion; yet we had bread enough so that we used to sell a part to the marines on board. They took our money on shore and bought roots or greens for us, so that we did not fare miserably.

They duly served divine service, every day, after the Catholic manner. In the meantime, our jack tars, far from thinking alike, used to assemble below and fall to singing, for which they were often reproved. But there was one refractory chap who was every now and then laid in the stocks. Their way is to lay the person on his back, with his neck inside the hole and a block under the head.

While we were there, news came in of the accession of Ferdinand to the throne of Spain[30]. There was great rejoicing on the occasion, for several days. Medals were struck and thrown to the populace. Bells jangled the whole time. A '*castle*' was erected, in order to be attacked by an '*English ship*', drawn through the town on a carriage. On her quarterdeck was placed the figure of Admiral Vernon[31]. Her rigging was hung with all sorts of fireworks, so that when she came to engage the '*castle*', she soon became on fire, when poor Vernon fell a sacrifice to their rancour. But, by the by, this was a farcical pantomime of their own.

Every evening, all the churches, castles and batteries were finely illuminated, but our desire to see those curious sights almost cost some of our people dear. Now, as we were never suffered to go on shore on the town side, in the evenings we used to get up in the ship's tops to behold the sights on shore. One night as we were innocently aloft, and the '*hoopsticks*' under us at prayers on the forecastle, no sooner had they finished that they ran up on each side of the shrouds, and fell to paying (started hitting) the poor English as fast as they could come at them. Some ran down the stay, others fought their way down the shrouds the best they could. None could understand the meaning of this treatment or what it meant. As many as could do so, hid between decks. At last we found out the story to be thus.

In the foretop was a small hurricane house for the Captain of the Top to sleep in. In this place was a small model of a ship, in which some of our people, through laziness, had '*watered*'. Unfortunately for us, she had a small hole in her bottom, and the urine ran down on the '*hoopsticks*' as they were at prayers. But the whole thing blew over next day, as we all declared none intended it as an insult.

We had been there about six weeks when they thought it best to send us away in an old leaky sloop. The appointed day came, and she came alongside to take us all on board, and proceeded to Jamaica as a '*flag of truce*'. There were on board this vessel some 5 or 6 Spaniards with an Irish captain, who knew no more of the sea than a parson, and to the best of my memory about 70 of us.

We proceeded to beat through the old Straits of Bahama under a ship's nurse[32]. The sloop worked so well that she had her wake ever on the weather crutch, her pump constantly going. This, added to our pilot's ignorance, made them at last give the ship into the charge of our mate, Mr Ramage, to navigate her to the island of New Providence[33].

We met with two sail, which took out a few of our people. Now the rest, by some means or other, found some cash hidden in water casks and the like. This discovery was imparted to but a few; and to defend the booty, they made bludgeons to guard it. This the Spaniards found out, but I cannot say whether Ramage was to be rewarded for his labour by the Spaniards or not. But just as we came to Rose Island, near New Providence, he broke the matter to them, to return the money, but they peremptorily and boldly denied its existence. At this time the wind had died away, and the moneyed heroes insisted on having the longboat hoisted out to go on shore, thinking that it was New Providence itself. Away they went, by force, and left us to sink or swim; but providentially the wind sprang up, or we would have certainly foundered. This breeze brought us into the port just as the heroes were crossing over from Hog Island[34] to the town.

The captain immediately laid his complaint before Tinker[35], who was at that time Governor and as great a trickster as those the captain laid his charge against, as the report then went. Some of them were taken up, and examined before his Excellency, but they had all found the means by which to secrete the cash away, except for a certain Frank Harris, upon whom some of the dollars were found. This poor young fellow was by the Governor's order clapped into the fort and compassionately forced to become a grenadier, after he had obliged him to ride on the *wooden horse*[36] repeatedly.

In this place we rambled up and down half-naked and all friendless, without any means of support. And here I shall give the reader a rough draft of my garb as I then appeared, viz. a long pair of ragged and narrow Spanish trousers, a fragment of an old blue shirt (not enough to pass under my waist-band), a remnant of an old red handkerchief around my head, without either shoe or stocking on my feet. I still had my old blue bonnet. Now, this place being full of privateering, we all '*entered*' in one way or another; as for my part, I was full in for it, by way of retaliation on our enemies.

And now, in serious mood, let me acquaint the reader who is not yet convinced of my folly by the hard sufferings I had hitherto felt. On a fatal hour I entered on board a schooner called the *Recovery*[37], of which James Strike was the Commander, anno 1747, on a cruise – against whom? Alas, against my poor self. I obtained a few dudds, as sailors term clothes, from the skipper, which were to be all paid out of our prize money[38]. Now as I was going with a people who act with some difference from the Europeans, I conducted myself accordingly, and got hooks and lines for my profit as well as pleasure on the cruise.

We sailed out of the East End[39], as they termed it, and after a short time came to, at an island called Andross[40]. Here we stayed but a short time, then stood away for an island called the Bimini about 100 miles west of Providence. Here the bateau, or canoe, was hoisted out, and all hands became full of high spirits. Some of our officers went on shore with fowling pieces; in the meantime some of the crew fell to fishing. This new mode of life agreed well with my mind. In the evening our people came down on the shore and the boat went and brought them off, but not in so good a condition as they left us.

For it happened that one of them rambling about by himself, and not being perceived by another who was then taking a sight at a bird, received part of the shot in his posterior, as he was discharging a point of necessity. The smarting drove him mad for a time; but where there were people around him who had little feeling of the tender passions, it all turned to ridicule and diversion. However, when he was brought on board, the doctor restored him in a few days.

From hence we crossed the Gulf for the Florida Keys, and on one of them our people shot three birds, such as I had never seen the like of in my life. They were when erect six feet high and red as vermilion, the neck and legs being extremely long but the body no bigger than a fat hen. We had plenty of rum on board, but I observed that there was not the least economy among our crew; and indeed I had learned to relish it very well myself by this time.

I shall give the reader a specimen of our frugality. At Key West, where there is plenty of water, we got into a notion of spending a few hours at the *Sign of the Fountain*, as we called it. In order to do this, some of our most potvaliant (those made brave by drinking a 'pot' of alcohol) heroes took on shore flasks of rum and sugar, and seating themselves around the well, discharged the rum and sugar into it. Of this bowl I partook. When our mighty bole grew weaker, we replenished it, until most of us, by whooping and singing fell asleep. NB These wells are casks sunk into the sand, with holes bored through them.

In the meantime, while several lay snoring on the grass, the man at the masthead cried, 'A sail, ho!' We all hurried on board, and what was very extraordinary, in a few minutes every man appeared to be quite sober again, so great an effect this fresh alarm had on their spirits. The sail appeared to the southward, and we gave chase under all the large sail we could crowd on. We chased her the whole evening without gaining the least upon her; the next morning we saw no more of her, she having altered her course in the dark. We then hauled our wind and stood inshore again. Shortly after this, we discovered some savages on the shore, but as they proved too shy to come on board we ran in closer, where some of our '*valiant gents*' took the whim of firing on them. This I thought was cruelty indeed, to take a few naked poor creatures as a mark, out of mere sport, to be shot at.

While they were at the game, the schooner ran aground. Now the skipper began to rave, and ordered all the tallest overboard to shove her off again. And I could soon see that their mighty courage began to ebb, fearing to be wrecked on that inhospitable shore; but they soon hove her off again. The next day we saw two sail in the offing, and gave chase. These we came up with in the evening. They proved to be two small sloops of no value. These we took the hands out of, and set them on fire. The wind fell and it became a dead calm, so it was amazing to see what towering columns of smoke ascended from them. After this, we stood away for the west coast of Cuba and there landed our prisoners.

In this latitude we cruised for some time, when one day the man cried 'A *sail on the weather bow!*'[41] We directly gave chase, but as she was going large, we soon got the wind of her. The chase then began to crowd on all the sail she could make, but we overhauled and got within cannon shot of her, at about five in the evening. She proved to be a Spanish ship of fourteen guns, and engaged us for about two glasses.[42] This ship killed three of our men and wounded seven. When she shot away our jib stay and two of our shrouds, this affair nonplussed us for the present, and during the time it took in getting stoppers on them, she hauled her wind and ran for it. We soon made after her, but lost her in the night. On the morrow she could not be seen from the masthead. This day we were in the Latitude of Seventeen north.

We had now been out for a full month and had taken nothing of value, so that our crew began to murmur greatly, and begged the captain to cruise on the Spanish Main. He objected, in that our provisions would soon run short. Nevertheless, I could find a general discontent reigning amongst the people. Now I wished heartily that I had never come amongst them, and as we had some of the true descendants of the buccaneers amongst us, did not know what they might intend. At last they privately drew up a Round Robbin[43]; the major part of the crew signed it, but I declined putting my hand to the paper. The officers, finding this, were obliged to comply and away we shaped our course for the Main shore.

A few days after this, the wind came to blow fresh at north, and increased so that we were often forced to lay to. At length it became more moderate. We were now in the latitude of 15, and in the night one of our hands cried out, '*Breakers ahead!*' We tacked immediately, but only had just time enough, and that was all. As the wind died away, we let go the anchor in 8 fathoms, and thus waited for day. When the morning came, a morning I never longed for more in my life, we found the vessel surrounded with rocks and shoals. Not above two of our hands knew where we were, and those were not determined in the same opinion. At last they agreed it to be those dangerous shoals called '*Quita Suenno*' or '*Prevent Sleep.*'[44]

A new concern fell on my mind as thus – what a pitiful state we were really in, a small vessel full of people and no more than one poor canoe to help us in case of extremity. One of these quondam pilots advised us to stand away for Santa Catalina[45], where we arrived two days later, took on shore water casks, and boot-topped[46] the vessel. Here, the 'sons of noise' took it into their heads that they should have no luck, until they had finished all the remainder of the rum on board. And after the water was all on board, the play began; and matters were carried to such a height that it became one round of gunning, fishing, drinking, fighting and uproar. And now I began to think that I had truly experienced a taste of piracy, saving that we had a good commission[47] on board.

The next day we stood away to the southward, and on the next a sail hove into sight. We chased her the whole day long, gaining but little upon her. On the morrow, we saw her right on the lee bow; we had the wind then northerly. The chase was now renewed and we seemed to come up with her hand over hand, when she altered her course before the northerly and left us like the wind. About sunset we saw land and took it for the Main, so kept an easy sail all that night. On the morrow we found that she had given us the slip, and that we had been pushed nigh on the shore by a great current. We stood in for a few hours, and then ran along the shore at a distance of about four leagues[48] until the evening, when we fell in with the soundings in thirty fathom. Shortly after, it shoaled to 16 fathoms with patches of rocks.

Here we hove to, and all hands fell to fishing, with good success. While we were all busy at this sport a tortoise[49] swam alongside. They called for the *grainge*[50] (a type of harpoon), and three of us jumped into the canoe then alongside and pushed after it, but without success, as it was now almost dark. When we came back, they veered the canoe astern of the ship and I remained in her, where I was much the worse for liquor, as we had that day finished the last drop on board the vessel.

CHAPTER II

Marooned!

THE MISKITO COAST – THE FIRST YEAR
JUNE 15 1747 – JUNE 14 1748

How long I slept I knew not until the great motion of the boat awoke me; and as I was rubbing my eyes, to my great wonder I missed the schooner. The consternation soon sobered me, and what to do or how to act, I knew not in the least. My condition was now horrible, as the wind freshened up more and more. At last I saw a flash and heard a gun go off, but a great way away. But for me to pretend to gain the vessel again was impossible, so at once I gave up the thought. Thus I drove (rowed) and baled as I drove, in a sort of despair until the dawn of the day.

I was now close inshore and put into a small beach where I ran the canoe on shore, jumped out, and hauled her up. I could just discern the privateer in the offing, a great way out. Now, as I was standing thus, eagerly gazing about, I saw a large brig stretching out, as in quest of our vessel. She was near enough for me to see that she was a cruiser. Thus I marched about, sometimes seating myself on the gunwale of the canoe. It is impossible for me to give a just idea of the state of my mind, but thus I remained until I lost sight of both the vessels. I now looked around and could see nothing but a wild country of palmetto trees and shrubs, but if inhabited or not – as being an utter stranger in this part of the world – I knew not.

Now, I sat musing over what was to be done next – having no more than a sailor's frock over my shirt, a pair of petticoat trousers, my knife in one pocket, and my fishing tackle with a few hooks in the other, and my bonnet on my head. These items, with the canoe, paddles and grainge were all my store in this state of desolation. Thus the first thing I did was to get a stone for a killick[1] for my boat. This thought naturally made me cast an eye on the painter[2], and I found it had slipped the belaying[3]. Thus I spent the day in doleful dumps.

A reef of rocks ran out at the end of the bay, where I had landed. Now when I was gazing every way around me, to my great surprise I beheld a man standing on the shore, and could discern him to be naked, holding a kind of oar in his hand. I directly concluded he was a savage, he being not two hundred yards away from me. I directly laid myself flat on the rocks and sand to observe his motions, undiscovered. Shortly after this, he began to walk towards me, looking out now and then. My heart now beat in my breast, and whether to speak to him or not was the case. The prospect before me had now become dreadful, either to starve for hunger, or to fall into the hands of merciless savages, who perhaps would rid me of all my troubles.

However, committing myself to the hands of Providence, I determined to make myself visible as he was now within 60 yards of me. Up I got and stepped down on the beach. When he first saw me, he halted. I then hailed him, and made signs for him to come on. The first salutation was that he clapped his hands over his eyes, leaning forward, and then spread them abroad. I then did the same. Upon this he stepped up to me and then held out his hand. I received it, and then he looked me full in the face and said 'Christianos?' I answered, 'Si, Senor' or 'Signior'. He then stooped down and made a cross with his finger in the sand, and then laid his hand on my shoulder, and made as for me to follow him. I did so, and we walked along the shore. He talked to me the whole time, but I could make out nothing.

At last we came to a small inlet. Here was his canoe, and in it sat a stark-naked woman, and a little boy about three years of age with her, in the same state of nature as herself. She seemed to be greatly alarmed at the sight of me. I found the man, who seemed to be about 50 years of age, used all manner of means to clear her of her doubts. Upon this, I went to the side of the canoe and patted the child on his head; this pleased the man much, I found. He then gave me a piece of half-roasted turtle out of his boat. I was quite ravenous, having not had one morsel since the time I went adrift.

Now the man gave a sort of a cry, as to a person in the distance. I looked and saw a boy run among the high grass. The Indian then gave me a sign to stay by the canoe, and away he went after him. Upon this the woman opened her pipes and began to bawl to some purpose, the child also bearing his part. This brought the Indian back again, and he took me along with him. He went in amongst the grass and by much ado brought out the other boy, but the poor lad was so much frightened that I imagine he had never seen a white man before.

When we came back, the woman began afresh. I observed that they had several articles in the boat, such as turtle, eggs, iguanas and the like. Their boat was not above two foot wide, although she was above 16 feet long. After this, the man and boy got into her and I naturally thought that they would give me a seat with them. Now as the wife still went on with her clamour, the man handed me out a large calabash[4] with a string, and pointing to a place, said 'Agua, agua.' I understood he meant water, and ran off to fetch it, but after searching for some time, could find none. Now the reader will be surprised when, on my going to return, I saw the Indians paddling off as fast as they could, and they were by now about 50 yards from the shore. I stood like a man thunderstruck for a time, but they soon got round a point of rocks and left me to shift for myself as best I could.

The sun was now set and I had to ramble back to the canoe. Now, as I was on my return, it came into my head that my late new friend had certainly handed me the calabash as a stratagem in order that he might gain time to escape. As I supposed by the woman's behaviour, she would not consent to my going with them, through some fear of my ill behaviour to her or hers. At last I got back to the canoe, and seated myself in the stern sheets. I then hauled the boat up as high as I could and pulled off my frock, then lying at length in her, covered my breast with it to ward off the dew which falls so heavy in these parts, and then fell to reflecting within my mind, but in hope that I should see the schooner next day. But, alas, I never did see the *Recovery* again.

When I fell asleep I do not know, nor did I awaken until the sun was high. Directly, I turned around to look in the offing, but to no purpose. I was forced to cut off a bit of lead from my poor sinker (rope) to chew, as I was almost choking with thirst. After this, I marched along the shore to hunt food, and found plenty of whelks. These I broke against the rock stones, and took them to my boat where I sat down and ate four raw as they were, with the tears of true sorrow trickling down my cheeks. And now, had I my hat full of dollars, they should all have gone for one stick of fire.

The next thing was to go in search of water. I wandered around for above an hour, and returned without finding any. In this ramble I found that I was on an island, as I conjectured by its position, or else a long point. After this, I began a new route and in this march came very near to the end of my tether, on a point terminating with rocks and a small reef. I then came back and took out a paddle, went away toward the point, and finding a clear place of sand, fell to digging. This work cost me an hour's hard labour, but still no success. I then threw down my paddle and then myself upon my face, not caring whether I lived or died; but after some time I got up, thinking to return, launch my boat, and put along shore the other way.

But as I stooped to take up my paddle, to my unspeakable joy water had sprung up in my well. Instantly I stooped down and tasted it with my hand. It was brackish but tolerable. This was a great relief, and on all fours I drank my fill. After this, I returned to the canoe. Thus kind Providence in so short a time provided me with both meat and drink, such as it was. Now I became easier in my mind, being out of dread of immediately starving. I then went back to fetch my calabash to fill it, brought it back, and fixed it to the boat. After this I took a walk along the shore westward. In this march I found a conch, and with a stone returned, sat down on the bow of the boat, and worked around the crown of the shell until I had drawn out the fish, and as it is of a sweet taste, found it very pleasing to my palate. In the evening I prepared to compose myself to rest, and slept soundly the whole night. I arose next morning by daylight, and walked away along the shore as far as the little creek[5] where the Indians had forsaken me.

Here, I finished the remains of my conch, then tramped on through the creek about two miles further. Here I could see plainly the full extent, and that it was indeed an island. Upon this discovery, I mounted an old, dead tree to look out, and to my great sorrow found it to be not above half a mile across. I presently became alarmed at judging it to be no place of any great succour to me. Now, as I thus explored the places around, I saw at about the distance of five miles or so, a more promising shore, being a much bigger island, or perhaps the Main (mainland) itself. Down I hurried and made back for my boat as fast as I could, being determined if the weather proved moderate, on the next day to take leave of this place. The rest of the day I spent preparing for my departure.

I never failed to keep a sharp look-out for the schooner, as I was far from giving her up; but finding that she did not appear again, came to this opinion, that the brig I had seen stretch out for her had either sunk her or taken her. If not so, they had concluded to shape their course some other way, not caring to risk seeking me or the boat again. At other times I would imagine that they had returned to those Maroon[6] Islands again, and had either bilged on them or foundered at sea. Thus agitated, betwixt hope and despair, I passed my lonely hours. I could not sleep for the great hurry on my mind.

About midnight it began to rain hard and lasted so long that I was drenched, and much water was in the canoe. At last it began to hold up, and the day came on as still as a clock. I then got out, took my frock and wrung it out, then threw it on the grass. I did the same with my shirt and trousers, and then put on my frock that it might dry on my back, and in this trim began to bale out the boat. I then took the calabash to drink from it, and found that the rain had so freshened the water that it that it quite raised my spirits. After this I clapped on board my killick, and when I had got her afloat I replaced my calabash. I then took a walk along the shore, gathered about 20 whelks, and then threw them into her. By this time my shirt and trousers were tolerably dry, and I put them on and then prepared for my departure.

I paddled away along the shore, passed the place where my well was, and then

12

ventured out to double past the reef of rocks. I then stood away north on my new venture. The deepest water had seemed to be about 3 fathoms and it was often not even one. After I had been on my voyage for about three-quarters of an hour, I observed on a small key (island) some odd white spots. Thither I turned, but as I drew nigh an incredible number of birds of many kinds arose like clouds. Their noise almost made me deaf! Here I landed and found those white things to be King Conches. These shells are so large that some of them will contain three quarts (six pints) of water. I put five of them in my boat, and then began to gather eggs. While I was at this work, the pelicans would brush by my head, so as to almost knock off my bonnet.

After this, I put off for my new shore, and in about an hour got close in under the land. Here I found it bluff too, then a beach, the land overgrown with trees. Now, as I paddled along I spied a kind of creek, about a pistol shot away; I put in, and found the water to shoal at about 4 feet. I was so delighted with these new scenes that fear never entered my noddle. I found the land on both sides to be about the height of a boat's mast; but as I advanced in further I found it to be a lagoon or a lake. Here the mangrove trees hung over my head, laden with oysters like traces (bundles) of onions. The lagoon abounded with fish of diverse kinds in great abundance. The spoonbills, galldings[7] and cranes sat on the trees without taking much notice of me, as they were seldom used to the sight of men. At length I came to an opening. Fortune directed me that I should take to the left; this brought me to another branch, where it opened wide all at once. Here I found a small sandy shore. I then threw out my killick and jumped on shore.

It was now about meridian, as I judged the sun. Here I walked up the bank and found the soil bare, with rocks for about a hundred yards around; and as I stood viewing I saw a gap at some distance among the trees. I walked there, and when I came to examine the place, I found to my surprise another branch of the lake, and that I was on a small precipice with a pretty, sandy place beneath me. I then looked out for some way to get below. Now, as I was doing this, I saw plainly over the trees the island I had left in the morning. At last I got down onto the sands below. Here I found a cavern cutting into the rock; into this place I went and found it to be about 15 feet deep. There I halted to look around. The mouth was, as I judged, to be about 10 feet in height and 18 feet wide with a gravel bottom. Here I seated myself, and found a piece of wood carved in the form of a mask. Now, I thought to myself, I am not the first of mankind to have visited this place.

After this, I returned to my boat, being resolved to find out a way by water to this place, if possible. When I came with the canoe to the point of opening, I there cut a branch of the mangrove, and hung it up perpendicularly, in order to know the place again. I then took to the other arm of the lagoon, and in a short time found that it took me round to the cave, and there I resolved to take up my abode for the present. Then I carried on shore all my little matters – my whole furniture consisted of my lines, grainge[8], the calabash, and the 5 shells. After this was done, I seated myself on the ground, fell to on my raw whelks, and took a draught of water, then laid me down and fell fast asleep.

About 5, I awoke, when the dread of my wants in future took such impression of my mind that I got into my canoe, and away I went around to the place where my new signal branch hung, and from there paddled out to the mouth of the creek. After this, I ran her on shore and threw out the killick, and went on shore in quest of food, but only found three whelks. This threw me into a heavy quandary. Now, as I thus moved with my face to the ground, my ears were struck with a soft murmur, as of water. I directly followed it; when going up into a small opening between the trees, to my unspeakable joy I beheld a pretty little linn[9] of water falling over a shelf. This was an estate worth more to me than the whole Bank of England. I ran back to my boat, paddled away as fast as I could to get my calabash, and returned forthwith, with two of my largest shells also. These I filled, then chocked them up with stones and returned to my cave with them, intending to go out no more until morning. At the close of night the mosquitoes and sand flies began to annoy me much, which took off many hours' repose, but I had no remedy for it without fire. I then crawled into the back part of the cave, and covered my face and hands with my frock, and rested middlingly well until day.

At first in the morning I went to get some Panama[10] shells as they are called, and with these I concluded to keep my reckoning of the days, so concluded to put them in one of the conch shells, and laid it in the back part of the cave. This done, I went in quest of conch bait with a view to fishing, then returned into the lagoon and there came to. I saw fish in great plenty, but was in such dread of losing a hook that if any larger than ordinary fish came near the bait, I instantly drew up my line. Here I caught 7 or 8 grunts[11], and with them went to the cave and ate part of them raw. This was my daily practice. At length I found my strength diminishing daily, in a gradual manner due to my way of diet, as I thought. I grew lean, and judged that if my body became no better used to this course of living, that my days would be short in this land of desolation. This made me spend many a day in black melancholy, thinking that this cave or some more exposed place would soon become my Death Couch.

After I had been there for about a month, I began to give the schooner up for lost; nor had I seen one thing in the form of a vessel, since the Indian canoe. One evening the clouds began to gather very thick, and it came on to rain very hard with terrible thunder and lightning. I was just at that time returned to the cave from the shore with a few conches. This gust lasted above two hours, and I had just and great reason to be thankful that I had a dry house over my head, and it brought to mind a saying of my poor mother, when she would see me running to play in wet weather.

Early the next day, as I was walking by the seashore, all at once I observed a smoke rising out of the bushes. Directly I concluded there must be Indians near the place. How to act, I could not tell at first, but judging that inevitably I should not escape them for long[12], and as the man I met had already treated me well, I went resolutely up the beach and peeped among the trees. But what joy took possession of my soul, when I discovered it to be an old tree on fire! For a few moments I stood observing this old, dead trunk, and concluded that the lightning had done it.

Off I ran to my boat and placed a quantity of sand amidships; after this I gathered a parcel of driftwood and filled the bow of the canoe. Away I then flew and got some of that precious element (fire), and laid it on the sand and placed a few sticks over it. The joy I felt on this most happy occasion almost turned my brain. With an air of satisfaction I seated myself in the canoe, and paddled off with my prize for my cave, and became so proud that I seemed to want no more for the present. N.B. I never once returned my thanks to that compassionate God who had kindled it.

Directly on my going on shore, I transferred my fire under a shelving projection to preserve it from the rain when it might fall; and now having got me a good fire; I directly fell to cooking some fish. It was now a month since I had tasted a morsel of any food except raw. So grateful was this to my palate that I cleared all that I had at that time caught. Now, after my meal, a thought popped into my head in regard to the manner of continually keeping my fire burning. I knew the Popanack[13] wood would keep fire to the last bit; therefore wherever I found any, I never failed to bring it home. I had often tried rubbing two sticks together, but to no effect.

Seven weeks did I live thus, each day alike, keeping my account very regular by shells, when I took a fancy to explore the shore for some distance, by way of recreation. Now, as I was marching along the strand I observed something at a distance from me. As I came near, I soon found it to be a work of art, and then ran up to it. It proved to be a small, square chest, Spanish made. I turned it over and found it still locked and not very heavy. At a small distance lay a wooden bole (tree trunk). I clapped the box on my shoulder, and taking the trunk in my hand, returned to my boat and put them both in and returned up the lagoon. There I landed my little freight and then ran to my fire, found it in good order, renewed it, and fell to examine the contents of my prize. After I had got it open, I found in it 2 blue striped shirts, and one red and white striped, one pair of long striped trousers and 3 pair of canvas, 4 red silk handkerchiefs, a pair of shoes with silver buckles in them, two fishing lines and a small bag of hooks and sail-needles, a roll of tobacco for chewing, a small spy-glass in a wooden case, two clasp knives, and a palm[14] with a ball of twine. These things I could see were not English, by their make.

As for the tobacco, it was of no worth, but anyway was of no use to me, as I had never followed that custom. And the shoes I feared to wear, less they should make my feet tender again, having gone so long barefoot. How those things came to be there, without my seeing any part of the wreck, I could not judge at that time. All these things I placed away, with great delight, and then renewed my fire, when I turned in for the night. The next day I went out in search of bait, and returned in order to go fishing. I never failed to catch diverse kinds, and my new mode of eating soon recruited my strength and restored me to health.

Some time after this, I rambled along the shore and found a small yard[15], a boat's rudder, and an empty cask of little use. These proved to me that the box had belonged to some small sloop or schooner, wrecked on that shore some while past. While thus I observed this beach, I observed a track here and there of turtles. No sooner did I spy this than I followed one of the tracks up the beach; here I found one of them had been at work. Directly I fell upon my knees and began to turn up the sand, but soon found it to be a false place, as they are apt to do this to avoid a search, or because they did not like the spot. I then began on another and found myself right, but shortly after was surprised to see a parcel of young gentry, about the size of half a crown, dawdling over my fingers, all in perfect turtle shape. I must confess it alarmed me at first. Directly I left them to shift for themselves, and proceeded to another place. In this I got about 75 eggs in good condition, went back to my boat and laid them in, in two trips, in my calabash, and returned home. N.B. I always took home with me the driftwood that lay by my way, but this was not my only office in that way, for I, before that, used to gather all the brushwood I could.

After this, I sort of existed until the wet season came on, never seeing a living soul but myself. It was my way to wear but a few clothes, that those that Providence had bestowed, might last the longer. Often, I went without anything but trousers, but now I was forced to wear clothes, as it was rather cold at times. I used to make my fire within my cave, lest the continual rain should deprive me of that blessing, which would have been a loss indeed to a man in my forlorn condition. I daily laid up some small, dry wood, as it rained more or less for above a month, according to the best reckoning I could make. In all this time, I went no farther from home than to fetch palmetto leaves to make my bed, go fishing in the lagoon, and get water.

After this, the weather began to clear up again, and nature appeared in a short time, dressed anew to me. Now, I concluded in my mind to take a small trip abroad in my boat. I made everything ready, and leaving a good fire, I put out of the lagoon early in the morning. I stood over for the small Bird Key, where when I arrived I found conches and whelks in plenty. After I had thrown over a hundred of them into my boat, I went on shore and got a few eggs with three young birds, then put off. On my return, a very large shark followed me; as he swam with part of his tail and cobbler's knife[16] above water, I judged him to measure 14 feet in length. He followed the canoe for a good while, but on my throwing over a conch, he left me and went down after it.

On my arrival at the cave, I went to roast a conch. Now, as I was doing this, I observed a bit of spongy stuff, which grew on part of my fuel, to kindle and burn very quickly. I directly broke it off and put it out, then touched it at the fire, and soon found it to answer to the purpose of tinder. I well knew where there was plenty of a bastard kind of white flint pebbles along the shore; those I concluded, with my knife, would set me up to make fire. After I had eaten, I put it into practice. They were not so free as those of the dark kind in Europe, yet answered my purpose very well. I then went on a hunt for more of the 'punk'[17] and found that I could master that matter well enough, there being enough about the dead stumps of trees. After this, I prepared a shell as a tinderbox, and was never without it wherever I went, either afoot or in my canoe.

By my account, I had been on this shore about 9 months now, and a most solitary life I led. Sometimes the tears would burst out as I walked along. Such perturbations would take place at times that I most wickedly wished myself dead. Never did I once conceive it to be no more than my own deserts. My grief sprang from this – my being separated from those dear companions I had lost. If they had been fortunate, how much prize money might have fallen to my share, to have squandered away in madness and folly. Alas, little did I then think the kind hand of Providence was so carefully watching over me, rescuing me as I might say, from the power of the Devil, to place me here in a state of innocence, if I could but conform to the will of God. But I was young, and full of the vanities which attend a life of dissipation.

But to proceed. One morning I resolved to go along the shore eastward, and here I found the land to fall low, with many palmetto trees growing in a sandy soil. At last I came to a small kind of inlet. Here I went onshore, and after going about 20 yards up a sandbank, I found a fine salina, or salt pond. There I found a large company of soldiers, all ranged in their regiments, enough to have struck any single unarmed man with dismay, had I not been so well acquainted with their peaceful disposition, they being nothing more than a large flock of flamingos. And here, I had an opportunity of observing the way these birds breed. They raise up a pyramid of sand in the pond; in the top of it they make a pit; over this they sit to lay and hatch with their long legs hanging down on either side. N.B. Although those birds are as red as scarlet when old, yet their young are for a time an ash colour, growing red by age. This bird is of a very stupid nature. It will not move for the noise of a gun, so that if a person can keep concealed he may load and fire often before they will take flight.

Not long after this, I counted over the number of my shells, and found to the number of 315; and from that time until I had completed my whole year, I remained in solitude, seeing nothing to disturb my peace or give me hope in the least.

THE SECOND YEAR OF MY LONELY CONDITION – YELLOWBILL
June 15 1748 – June 14 1749

About a month after I had begun my second year, I had a very odd adventure, as thus. One evening as I was sitting on the shore, about two miles from my cave, when all at once I heard a great snort, as I thought, from the bushes. I jumped up and ran down to the boat as fast as my two legs could convey me. After my first alarm was a little over, I began to reflect within myself what this could possibly be; and in this mood I paddled along the shore towards my home, keeping a proper distance off shore, fearing a second alarm. But just as I passed a short bay, to my great astonishment I thought I beheld a troop of Indians marching along the shore, abreast of me. Now I was terrified indeed. The first thing I did was to lay down in the canoe lest they spied me, and thus observe their motion – but I was soon undeceived by discovering them to be a train of twenty-odd deer.

Now, as I lay with my head raised up a little, my foot happened to tumble a shell. This caused the foremost to halt, and stare directly at the canoe. On this, he gave two strong snorts, when they all scampered up the beach into the woods. Now all my fears vanished, and I put away for home, as fast as I could. Nothing but the deer ran in my head to several days together. However, I had no gun or ammunition, and I could not expect to succeed as a hunter, so gave all thoughts of a venison repast up, for that time.

There were two sorts of lizards with which I was often amused at times. One of these frequented the rocks above high water mark and, contrary to all the others I ever saw, had their tails in a curl on their backs, were yellow-brown, beautifully mottled with dark spots, and carried their heads quite erect, like little dogs. They were seldom above 5 inches in length. Hundreds of times have I seated myself, as knowing their way, when three or four of them would come around me, look me in the face. If I began to whistle they would first turn their heads to one side, and then to the other and listen very attentively; yet so alert were they that if I offered to stir they were gone in a moment, so that I could never catch one of them alive, with all my cunning.

The other sort is what they call in Jamaica the Woodslave[18]. These are larger than the other sort, and I remember that the first I saw one of them, it surprised me greatly. It was on the limb of a low tree and of a verdigris green, but during the time I had my eyes on it, it began to change its colour, turning to a fine golden yellow, then from that to a dead leaf colour with broad stripes down the side from head to tail; from this it changed to a deep brown, and lastly to a profound black. Some of these I caught now and then, by means of a small noose around the neck, and tying them afterwards around the loins with a small bit of twine kept them about my place for a week or more at a time. I could never see that they took any kind of food, except that they caught a fly now and then.

I went on in the same way for several months. In this interval of time I made a table and a stool; this I performed as follows. I cut twigs and wattled (interlaced) them after the manner I had seen the country people do at home, then fixed them on four uprights; and I cannot boast they were so strong as I desired, for I never ventured to cut anything very large with my knives, fearing to break one of them, the preserving of them being of the utmost consequence in my situation.

I shall digress here, to observe a singular circumstance, although not of great moment; yet as it was attended with drollery and a means whereby I got a companion, I shall recite it. One day, as I had been catching some land crabs, and having tied three of them together, I left them on the beach while I gathered a few of those kind of shells our silversmiths at home turn into snuff boxes, as thinking that should I ever get home, they might turn to some account. Now as I was busy at this amusement, I heard a noise over my head and looking up I saw a Fish Hawk[19] bearing off my bunch of crabs.

But it turned out otherwise for him, for he could not raise them, and soon came down to the beach, crabs and all. Although I could not be expected to be in any merry mood, yet the thing drew a smile from me; and of a truth it was the first time since my landing here. When I first came up to him, I found that two of those amphibious gentlemen had fastened on his leg. He soon began hostilities against me, fighting with his wings and beak. But to put the contest to an end, I took an opportunity and got him around the neck, knowing full well my other myrmidons[20] would not quit their holds. In this manner I bore the whole bunch to my boat, and there bound up his beak, then his leg, and thus brought home the whole body of disputants.

The first thing was to disengage them by putting fire to the crabs, which soon made them quit their hold. I then cut one of my new comrade's wings; after this I provided him with a small log to one of his legs. When this was finished, I cut the string from his beak, to enlarge him. During the whole business he did his best against me. I then gave him over to his future fortune. This bird was of a most beautiful plumage of mixed white, yellow, brown and black, yellow legs and bill, the long talons black. He was about the size of our English Kite, and his cry much like that bird.

I soon found my care for his running away needless, his legs being so short that he could make but poor way of the ground, those birds always devouring their prey on the limbs of old dead trees, from whence they sit and behold the fish with a keen eye. Add to this that the crabs had hurt his leg not a little, so that he was lame. After this I offered him some broiled fish, which he refused with disdain, nor would he taste one bit for two days. But on the third, I observed when I returned from my fishing, that his stomach began to crave. The fresh fish drew on an appetite, as I judged by his crying, and I threw him some garbage. He eyed it for a while, and then fell on it greedily, and gorged the lot in a short space of time. This so pleased me, that my mouth opened incontinently and I cried out to him, in the Welsh tongue: 'Much good may it do you, Mr. Yellowbill!'[21] And in fact, they were the loudest words I had uttered from the time the Indians had left me, until that hour.

In the course of a month we became very intimate, so much that when I came home, he would salute me very kindly, and I used to return the compliment, being proud of having anyone to speak to. After this, we became almost too intimate – he would haul the fish away without my leave or licence. At length this poor fowl became so docile, that I could do anything with him. In the evening as it grew dark, he would come in to the cave to roost by himself, so that I began to pity his dragging the log about and I took it off. He knew his name, and would come when I called Yellowbill. Whenever I seated myself, he would come and place himself beside me and remain, picking his feathers the whole time. This caused me to amuse myself quite often talking to him, or her, as I knew not its sex.

Now one day, as I sat fishing, I took a resolution for a small journey of discovery, and for this purpose concluded on my return to fix all things in order, and leave meat for my bird lest the night should overtake me. Accordingly, the next day I got some roasted fish and water into my boat, in case I did not soon find any, and put away out with my tinder tackling[22] also, towards the salina. There I left the canoe, and marched away over some barren soil producing nothing but Palmettos and Prickly Pears. Then I walked away toward a kind of grove, about a mile away. On my arrival, I found the shore was more rocky, and inclined more to the left, where it ended in a reef. Over these rocks I made my way. Here the land trended yet more to the left and I saw before me a great bay of sand, the country full of large woods. Shortly after I came to a kind of inlet and here I spied a large iguana. This pleased me highly, as I now hoped to find out their haunts, as they are good eating.

Up the side of the creek I went for near a mile, and saw thousands of fish in it; here I found the trees hanging over the water in many places. It now became difficult for me to pass on that way; therefore I took more into the wood, keeping the creek still in view. Here I saw many lime trees full of fruit. These were most pleasing objects to my sight. I plucked one of them and cut it, and although they are most sharp and acid, the taste was most grateful to me, and exceedingly refreshing. Now I found the creek was changing its course. Therefore I began to suspect that I might lose myself as I could no longer see the coast, so concluded to rest myself and take a short repast. Not far from this, on a small rising ground, I sat down and saw at its foot a small ripple of fresh water, with multitudes of Land Crabs about it. Down I seated myself and began to relieve my hunger, amidst numbers of birds of various kinds, some of which warbled most delightfully.

In this place I observed a most singular kind of bird called the Old Man[23], from its having the feathers of its crop of such a length, that when it perches it resembles the grey beard of an ancient person. After this, I arose and wondered whether to proceed or return, but at length curiosity gained the better and I went up a small height, where it became very level and full of brush except here and there. But I now fell upon a sight, which really was uncouth enough. At a small distance grew several Machineel Trees[24], whose fruit is deadly poison to man. The very juice of its leaves will raise terrible blisters, so as to deprive a person of his sight. – Now from beneath those trees, to my no small amusement, I beheld armies of land crabs marching off on my coming, with each an apple in his claw and many of them had two. The sight was truly droll, the more so since they carried them upright.

After this, I walked on for a distance of 100 yards, keeping a good observation of the sun. Here an odd appearance caught my sight. On a plain place stood a huge rock stone almost upright, about the magnitude of a small church tower, and as I judged, about 40 feet in height and almost a square. When I came up to it, I found many scratches on it made by some instrument or other, in the form of ovals, triangles, rude imitations of heads and the like. These I judged to be the work of Indians.

As I walked around it, I found many letters cut, as with knives. These I judged to have been done by Spaniards and others, perhaps pirates. Some few of them I took down afterwards for my own curiosity, and I shall give them a place here –

++E M+A. P+V. JL. E+S. L$^+$O. V$_+$M. R : +C &ccc.

I also observed four dates in different places added to names as thus,

I+E 1589. Bat S.^{8} 1605. A+A 1582 and W^m R 1673.

In another place was to be seen the following characters,

+TO ++cc. ^ ^.

N.B. Those letters having crosses between them I attributed to the Spaniards. The others

the Sun. here an odd appearance catched my sight, on a
plain place, stood a huge Rock Stone, almost upright, about
the magnitude of a small Church tower, and as I judged, 40
feet in height, and almost a square, when I came up to it,
I found many scratches on it, made by some instrument or
other, in the form of Ovals, Triangles, rude immitations of
heads and the like, these I judged to be the work of Indians. —
as I walked round it, I found many letters cut as with knives,
these I judged to have been done by Spaniars and others, perhaps
Pirates, some few of them I took down afterwards for my
own curiosity, and I shall give them a place here. —
M+A . P+V. ꝗL . E+S . L†O . V+M . R∴+C &ᶜᶜᶜ —
I also observed four dates in different places added to names
as thus, I+ E 1589. Bat 1: 1605. A+A 1582. and
Wᵐ R 1673. In another place was to be seen the
following characters, +To . ⳨ . ⊕ cc . ⅄⅄
N.B. those letters having crosses between them I
attributed to the Spaniards, the others were the mark
of Buchaneers or Pirates who had rambled over these
parts in former times. — — —
I now thought of returning home and arrived at my
small cove where the boat lay toward Evening, then
put away along shore for home and got in just in the
dusk. well pleased with my cruise, I found all safe
as I left it, and was kindly recieved by my new
Comrade, who expressed great joy, raising his large
Wings, stretching forth his neck, making a soft and
murmering noise, and rubbing his head and beak against
my bare leggs. — —
The following night I had a very troublesom dream
Occasioned without doubt, from my Excursion the
day before, In my sleep I thought that I was then
sitting by the aforesaid huge Stone I have mentioned,

were the marks of buccaneers or pirates who had rambled over these parts in former times.

I now thought of returning home, and arrived at my small cove where the boat lay. Towards evening, I then put away along the shore for home, and got in just at dusk, well pleased with my cruise. I found all safe as I left it, and was kindly received by my new comrade who expressed great joy, raising his large wings, stretching forth his neck, making a soft and murmuring noise, and rubbing his head and beak across my bare legs.

The following night I had a very troublesome dream, occasioned without doubt from my excursion the day before. In my sleep, I thought that I was then sitting by the aforesaid huge stone I have mentioned, when all at once from behind me I heard many voices approaching. Casting my eyes back, I beheld several men advancing toward me. The uncouth garb they were dressed in caused me to directly jump up. They came on, and hailed me thus 'Buenos Dias, Senor.' These men all had whiskers and were in armour. Then an old man asked me if I had seen anything of Manuel Guiterez that way. I answered that I had not seen any mortal man since my first landing on this shore, except three or four Indians. They then asked me how long and by what means I came there, to all of which I answered in good Spanish, as I then thought. Upon this, they all began upon me and said I was the King of Spain's prisoner, and laying hands on me, said I must go with them to the mines as a slave.

This, as I suppose, gave my whole frame such a shock that I awoke, hollering in a most fearful way. It so frightened the poor hawk that he flew into the water, and would certainly have been drowned, had not the sight of its distress brought me to my senses again. I ran away to save it, and then seated myself before the cave, where while poor Yellowbill was endeavouring to replace his plumage, I fell into a deep reverie. I took to thinking that perhaps this vision might be verified on me one day or another, and perhaps that day was not far off. Now I had good grounds for this fear, as I had learnt it to be the practice with the Spaniards in this part of the world upon Englishmen who should be caught on their coast through misfortune; and most certain it is that many a poor woman has lamented the loss of a husband, son or sweetheart as supposing them dead when perhaps they were at the same time in a far worse condition[25].

I became so greatly troubled by these ruminations that it caused a fever, which lasted three days. After this I got better again, and threw it all off as a mere dream. And now I determined in my mind sincerely to resign myself up to God's disposal, concluding for the future to be as placid under all my sufferings, as the nature of the thing would admit. Soon after this I went to my reckoning and found by the number of my shells that I had been here above one year and four months. I never omitted casting a shell every morning of my life, directly after I had turned out (got out of bed), having some provided near me for that end. And in this place I must observe one thing, as thus, I cannot be expected to give a just record of time and things at this distance, as then I was not possessed of (writing) materials for the purpose; so that the reader must be content with circumstances as they come to my remembrance.

After some time I came to the resolution of making a voyage westward, as I had nothing to hinder me spending my time in making one round of fishing, eating, drinking and sleep. So, fixing all in order at home with provision for Yellowbill, I put out on a fine morning expecting to return the next day. I kept along the shore for the space of two hours until I began to explore new scenes, the land running high here, low there, indented with fine, sandy bays. At length I opened up a fine lagoon. Into this place I put and proceeded up it for a good distance.

Everything appeared most inviting when, as I turned around a low, rocky point, I was struck with the sight of several human skulls, as I then took them to be. They were as white as snow. To shore I put, and went up to them. I now judged my opinion right, and that they had belonged to a gigantic race of people near this place. I saw there had been fire in time past, in some remains of ashes and burnt ends of sticks. Now, thinks I, this proves beyond all doubt that this place is, or has been, frequented by a wretched crew of cannibals. I then took up two or three of the heads and put them in the canoe, and determined to get out of that place as soon as possible. Away I went, needing no–one to drive me on, and put along the shore.

After this I spent so much time in viewing places, that night came on, and I put on shore. Not long after this, the clouds began to gather thickly all around; the rain came on with thunder and lightning. Here I hauled up my boat, high and dry. I walked up to get under shelter, but to little purpose. The flashes were so frequent and the thunder so terrible, that I thought that one of the claps had separated the whole mass of nature. I was so stunned by it that I stood motionless for some time, and as soon as I could well recover myself I ran down, and flung the skulls out onto the beach, through a foolish and idle superstition. After this, I marched about the shore until day began to peep, when it all dispersed and the sun rose fair and clear.

Now, I had not a dry thread about me. My fire tackling (the tools to make fire) and food was afloat in the boat. There was no help for it, and I fell to spreading out my duds (clothes) and bailing out the canoe, and thus I remained until the sun was about two hours high. Curiosity made me take up one of the skulls, and as I turned it around in my hands, I observed that it had no signs of where the teeth should be. I then examined another and found it to be the same, when it came into my head that they could not be human, but that they were the skulls of Loggerhead Turtles. After I was thus convinced, I got into my boat and like a poor convicted fool paddled away homewards and arrived safe, but should have been miserably at a loss for fire had I not been master of spare tinder in the cave, as the fire was totally out.

After this frolic, I stayed a long time at, or near, home and employed my thoughts to make my life as easy as I possibly could. And, indeed, to make honest confession, until now I had never felt a gleam of that true contrition a man in my condition ought to feel in his heart. But from this time I frequently called myself to account, when my thoughts yearned for the onions and garlic of my native shore. However, after a time, I so reasoned with my own heart, that I became quite resigned and easy-going.

Shortly after this, it came into my head why I did not endeavour to penetrate into the woods nearer home. Now this put my wits to work as to how to accomplish that end. I had neither an axe nor any other cutting instrument whereby I could be expected to gain my purpose, and to venture the use of my knives would be a sort of cutting against my own interests. Nevertheless I took it upon myself to put it in force, but with the greatest economy possible, and to this end looked out for the most convenient place to begin my incursion. I chose a place about half a mile west of my dwelling, and a few days later made a beginning.

In the first place I cut myself a large pole, which took up some time, as it was both hard and heavy. With this, after I had cut away with my knife, I beat down the bushes to get about twenty yards into the woods. At last I came across a huge yellow snake, and killed him with my pole. This animal measured, as I judged, a full six feet, and ten inches round. This made me begin to grow a little timid, and I also began to find that I had given myself a large task, and I could not tell to what great purpose, so had a mind to decline it when a thought popped into my skull, that I could try fire. Accordingly, waiting for a favourable wind lest it should draw towards my dwelling, I went to the place one morning, and with a load of dry brush set fire to it. It soon began to work with great force. N.B. I simply thought it would burn only the low bushes, but to my great surprise in the space of an hour, even large trees were on fire.

I retired down to the shore, and now I began to seriously repent of the deed, as the fire became dreadful, such amazing crackings I heard at times that were wonderful. After this, it burned for the whole day, but when night came it was awful indeed. I slept not a wink that night, as a thought struck me – what if the wind should shift, perhaps it would then come directly to my cave. But towards morning it became quite calm, yet the fire continued to burn for more or less seven or eight days. At last a glut of rain came and subdued it: nevertheless, a huge smoke ascended for above a week or longer.

In the time I thought the fire must needs be all out, I took a march over a part of this desert of ashes. The scene was truly odd. Every here or there, stood the trunk and limbs of a cedar or cotton tree, with other sorts I knew not. At last I came to a stump, which gave me great vexation – it was of the true Plantain tree, of which the Creoles use the fruit as a substitute for bread. Now, how did I grieve that there was no getting at them except by their destruction, a means flatly against my interest, and answered only this end to inform me that they grew in the neighbourhood.

I now began to turn my mind to the making of fishing lines. This I was informed how to do by an old Negro on our schooner, by soaking the leaves of the Corrittoo[26] or the Aloe, and working it into fibres. And I found it to answer my purpose so well, that I never wanted on occasion after. And in this manner I spent the day-by-day, being seldom idle. Had it been otherwise, I would have led the life of a mope. But here let me note that I had one kind of attendant who generally whetted my memory every two or three days, viz. a small insect called a Chigua[27] which, getting into the feet, there nestle and breed. These must be got out with a needle or the point of a knife. But after I became callous-footed, they seldom gave me much trouble.

THE THIRD YEAR – MISS DOE
June 15 1749 – June 14 1750

By my account, I found I had exceeded two years by some few days, for I cared not to reckon too often, as it generally gave me a melancholy fit afterwards. About this time as I was on my walk eastward, I had the curiosity to taste a Prickly Pear fruit, and ate three of them. I was then going in quest of iguanas. Now when I arrived on the spot near to where the Stone Tower stood, I had a call of nature, when to my great terror I saw my urine as red as claret.[28] The reader may judge my consternation before I recollected the true cause, as that it must proceed from eating those pears. Although I was not quite reconciled all that day, on the morrow all my fears vanished as I did not find any ill consequences to follow.

I shall observe that during the time of the wet season, I stirred little abroad except to catch fish, and I could not dispense well without them. In all this long period of solitude, I never had the sight of one vessel moving on the face of the ocean, nor did I open my lips to a fellow of my own form from the time I left the Long Key; yet I had learnt by this time not to repine at this, my desolate situation.

I shall remark in this place a circumstance, which always happened when any light shower of rain fell, which was this. Immediately a noise as of multitudes of chicken began, nor could I with all my industry learn what it might proceed from, although it would be frequently close by me – unless it were done by the lizards, yet I have kept my eye fixed on one of those animals without perceiving any cause to proceed from them. N.B. This never happened except in the woods. I could never learn the true cause as yet.[29]

I shall now give the reader an account of how my household affairs stood in regard to provisions, and the various methods I used at times. In the first place I never wanted for the three grand articles, Fire, Water and Fuel. Fish never failed – I had that kind of food in plenty and of great variety such as Groupers, Hinds, Porgies, Black and Red Snappers, Grunts, Rainbows, Parrot Fish, Coneys, Gillambours, Doctor Fish, Yellowtails, Pork Fish, Marget Fish, Cuckold Fish, Schoolmasters, Tango, Squirrel Fish, Sucking Fish, and Crayfish[30]. As for sharks and barracudas, I industriously avoided them lest they should rob me of too many hooks, as I valued them above pearls. Yet at times, I would run the venture with my lines made of Corritoo. I then went out in about three fathoms of water, perhaps a mile distant, by way of novelty. There I caught an Old Wife, Hogfish or perhaps a Small Jewfish. Nevertheless a shark would get the better of me at times and carry away a hook.

And here it may not be amiss to relate an odd adventure which I had, as I was at this amusement. The day was very still, and flat calm. Now as I sat very composed at my line hanging over the side of the canoe, all at once I heard a violent rushing, as of a cannon shot, through the air. Down I dropped into the boat's bottom, and so lay for about a minute. But when I raised my head I saw a large bird called a Man of War[31], rising up from the surface of the water, with the garbage of a fish I had lately caught, in its talons. Having caught a grouper who gorged my hook, I had opened it to recover the hook, and had thrown the guts overboard, and it had drifted away to some distance. Although this affair may seem trifling to you, yet to me – a poor, lonely creature – it was truly alarming, being never disturbed with any noise louder than the cry of a poor bird.

As to fruit and vegetables, I never touched those I was a stranger to. Sapodillas, Guavas, Limes, Mammees, Coco Plums, Cassia Fistula, and Sea-Grapes, Colliloo & co.[32] I made use of them, as I found them. Flesh, except for that of iguanas and a few birds out of nests, was what I seldom tasted. I found a way to catch the Ground Doves[33], as thus. I took notice, that after my great fire in the woods, numbers came thither to bask in the ashes. I took the hint, and now and then made fires in bare places, among the ashes of which I laid snares, and by this means caught many of them from time to time, which I roasted.

Now I well remember, as I happened to be after this game, chance brought me to the spot where lay a young fawn, about two or three days old[34]. I was eagerly going to take it up in my arms to take it home, when a thought came into my head – in what way should I feed it? This made me conclude to leave it where I found it, and thither I repaired every day to scrape its feet. Thus it remained for three weeks or more. I then got some corritoo twine and belayed it to a stump. The old one came always in the night to suckle it, I suppose, for I could never get one sight of her in the daytime. When it was about five weeks old, I brought it home to my place, and there made it fast among the low trees hard by. It soon became the tamest of creatures, and if at times I cast it loose, it still attended me. It was a female and I gave it the name of Miss Doe. It now fed anywhere around my dwelling, and at last became so familiar that she followed me like a dog.

One day I took a notion to have a trial with her, so made her fast, then got the boat round to the beach. I then returned and cast Miss Doe loose. She followed me to the seaside. I then got into the boat and she jumped in also, gazing around wildly: but no sooner did I put off and she felt the motion, than out she sprang in an instance to a good distance, and there fell to capering like a mad thing. After this, I put along the shore and she stood with her head erect gazing after me, but on my whistling she began to frisk along the sands after me. Now, as I could not coax her into the canoe, I put to and got out. She then ran to me, reared her forefeet on my shoulders, and then fell to licking my face.

And here I must needs observe that this was a scene of real pleasure to me, reflecting in my mind how the Divine Providence should thus throw in my path this poor inoffensive animal, as an innocent amuser of my disconsolate hours. Some time after, she became so used to the boat that she would jump in, the moment I took my seat, and went with me anywhere. About this time there appeared on the coast numbers of whales. I saw them first in the morning as I was sauntering along the shore. They remained in sight, blowing and playing the whole day, and on the morrow they were still in view. As I was every now and then casting my eye that way, I saw one of them raise its body about half out of the water. At other times, their tails came out seemingly very high. Thus they kept blowing and sporting, in sight for three days, and then went away to the southward.

But to return to my household matters. In the turtle season, which was generally about June, July and August as I judged, I feasted sumptuously but found my body to break out in large blotches, after eating them for a long time. But it had this effect, that I always became healthier afterwards. At times I cut the lean parts of them into long narrow strips, and laid them in brine, and then hung them up in the sunshine where they became hard and dry. These strips I boiled at times with some colliloo in a large shell. My fish I cooked, either boiled, roasted or stewed, but this last was my general way. But I must observe that I had one way, especially when in haste, which was to cover up a fish just out of the water, under the hot embers, where it remained about ten minutes. After it was done, I then took off the skin entirely, opened the belly and took out the internals. Thus I obtained the true flavour of a fish, as the sooner they can be cooked, the better.

I must not omit to observe that by frequent boiling, my shells grew crazed, which obliged me to look out for more. I took the utmost care of all my European articles. Now, my head became full of making baskets, and I resolved to make a trial. I sought out the most favourable twigs, but to my great disappointment, few that could answer my end. This put me on my old work of wattling again. I first made the bottom, then fixed upright at the four corners, and then wattled up between them, and thus I formed an ordinary kind of basket, which would hold about half a bushel.

Some time afterwards, as I happened to be out in my boat near the Bird Key, and going over a very shoal place, I saw a large fish close, alongside the canoe. It was the first I had ever seen of the kind. I struck it on the head with my paddle, when it began to flounce at a most high rate. The water was so shallow that it had not depth enough to swim. At last, as it was endeavouring to get around, it got its long saw over the gunwale of my boat and played away at no small rate. At last, I jumped out on the off side with my paddle, and began to pay away at it; but it soon got out of my sight. This fish seemed to be about ten feet in length[35]. Had I at that time my (grainge) harpoon with a line, I could have caught it with ease.

I shall in this place take notice of an affair which often gave me much uneasiness, I being not altogether free from that wretched prejudice, imbibed by the generality of children, concerning apparitions. This they suck in with their nurses' milk, and often from their own simple mothers' tales. I say this had never left me, and it gained as I travelled, having it renewed by the constant repetition of sailors, a set of men by no means clear of such imaginations. N.B. My present uneasiness proceeded from a noise I often heard late on moonlit nights. This was a hollow treble tone, as thus: *Yaoho, Yaoho,* repeated perhaps three or four times together. Some other like sound always answered this at a distance; this was always to the westward of me in the high land and at a great distance[36].

Now the chief cause of my terror originated thus. While I remained in Providence Island[37], I had frequent converse with an old Negro man, a native of the Island of Jamaica, who in his younger days had been acquainted with many of the buccaneers, had sailed with them, and knew many of their haunts, but had come in by the Queen's Act of Grace[38]. He then followed the piloting trade, or went out to hunt after wrecks about the coast. This white-headed old fellow, although he could read and write and was well-versed in the Scriptures, had been in England, France, Spain, and all over the coast of the Spanish Main, but was yet full of superstition. Now this old man, whose name was William Bass[39], related to me among other stories one concerning a sort of Nocturnal Animal, who walked upright as a Man and the same size, that they were black and wonderfully swift of foot, and that they sucked the blood of all the animals they caught, and left them dead. He observed also that by the track of their feet, one would think that their heels were placed foremost, and that their cry was as above related. He observed likewise that nothing but a bullet made of silver could kill one of those creatures, such credit did he give those romantic notions. Now, although I did not care to credit him too far, yet when my own ears became charged with the like sound, I thought verily I should see them, and perhaps too soon. But as they did not visit me, I became the less concerned, unless the sound seemed to be nearer than ordinary.

Thus time went on with me until the wet season[40] was coming on, and I prepared to lay up a store of wood, brush, conches & co. The latter I could keep by me for a long time, by making a small fence around them in the water, and by this means had my bait generally near at hand. About this time I had a most dreadful dream indeed. Methought it was the wet season, and that the whole country was overflowed, and that I was obliged to quit my cave in my canoe. Like a second Noah I wandered about for land, but could see only one small hummock at a distance, for which I paddled with all my force. This dream so wrought on my spirits, that my striving woke me, and glad was I to find that it was no more than a dream. Little I thought then, that it would be verified so soon after, as it was in some degree.

The rains came on, and so great was the fall of the water day by day, that it overflowed the lagoon quite up to the entrance of my dwelling. And now I was forced to bestir myself with all diligence, hurrying away with all my poor articles to the high water mark, and covering them as best as I could. Here I was obliged to remain, quite exposed to the weather, for two days, when it abated. In this, my great hurry, I had forgotten my poor bird; as for Miss Doe, she stuck by me. After this, I ventured to visit my cave, where I found that the water level had fallen a great deal, and that had I but retired into the back part with my things, they would all have been safe. I then began to look around for my poor Yellowbill. At last I found him up in a low bush, stone dead, as he had had no food for three days or more.

Now I began to call a council within myself, as thus. Fire and water are no friends to man unless under a strict limitation; therefore I resolved with despatch to erect a hurricane house, to which I might remove on the shortest notice. Soon after I had removed my things back to the cave, I began this work and made it in the form of an awning closed at one end, and a door at the other, thatching it well with palmetto leaves. After I became a little settled again, I began to think about my poor bird; and had not the fawn supplied its loss in some measure I should have found myself more solitary than ever, so great a consolation is any companion in any place, a recluse from the rest of the busy world.

One day, as I happened to be out in deep water fishing, I spied a sail in the northeast quarter. She came away large, and in about an hour I perceived her to be a small sloop; but she kept a great offing and stood away in the southward. Yet I kept my eyes on her for as long as I could perceive her, until she ran the horizon down, this sight being so great a novelty to me that it brought back a kind of retrospect. I longed, and that earnestly, for to be once again removed among men. But when I reflected that she was certainly a Spaniard with whom I had no desire to associate, in a few days my craving began to vanish. Nothing from this time, worth remembrance, came on until my reckoning I had begun another year.

THE FOURTH YEAR – PENROSE SHELTERS AYASHARRE AND YALUTA
June 15 1750 – June 14 1751

Fourth year commenced, and as far from any expectation of relief as ever, I endeavoured to make my mind as easy as possible. Now I frequently used to make a party at hunting at this period, and the reader may be surprised at how I brought this to pass. It was thus. Of a morning I used to prepare things ready in my boat, with my mate Miss Doe, for whom I had made two small bags for her to carry on her back and a trifle of a load. Thus equipped, away we went along shore for the east Lagoon where I landed and walked overland to Towers Field, as I termed it in my mind. At this spot I used to unrig my companion and then light a fire. From thence we proceeded to a sandy plain, a great resort of the iguanas. Those creatures have burrows in the ground like our rabbits, and can run very swift. Yet now and then I proved too hard for them, knocking them down with a short stick.

But if they ever got so far a start as to gain their holes, in that case I made fire over their burrows. This seldom failed to fetch them out, when I was sure of them. Now having been often out on this business, I shall observe a droll piece of entertainment Miss Doe gave at times, as thus. When she would perceive me in full chase of an iguana, off she would fly and be up with it in a trice, where she soon beat the creature dead with her forefeet. Such a sight as this could not fail to divert many of our English sportsmen, to see a man hunt with a deer instead of a dog.

I now began to think the cause of my never seeing above one vessel, in all the time of my abiding here, must proceed from their knowing the coast to be dangerous, full of shoals, banks and reefs, and that possibly it might be long ere I should see another. I conjectured that those who chanced to fall in with the land in the daytime knew it their best way to keep a good offing, if possible. But a few days after I had been thus forming my conjectures, a large ship hove in sight, standing to the northward. She was about four leagues out, and this threw me into a fresh relapse again; and when I parted sight with her I could have laid me down and given up the ghost. But time works strongly on the mind of man. After a few weeks had elapsed I again returned to my usual tranquillity and then resolved, that go fate as it would with me, I would repine no more. But as the most sagacious men are but idiots in the Eye of God, how then should such poor worms be able to forecast what shall be most fitting for them? Yet we must arrogate to ourselves a judgement as we wish; and if the thing meditated falls as we desire, then our God is forgotten and we claim the applause. Now I lay this all to my own charge, as thus – what an eager desire I had to be off in that ship which passed by the other day. If so, perhaps we had never gained any port, but all have perished on the vast ocean. Oh! The ways of the Omnipotent, are they not hidden, and all things come to pass as He wills them to be? This I have all the reason on earth to believe, by what followed soon after.

According to my account I had been on this shore about three years and two months, and I had not been abroad for many days, as the wind had been very fresh at south, with frequent rain and thunderstorms. Now after it had settled for a day or so, I concluded to make a trip over to the Bird Island after conches and whelks. Accordingly off I put the next morning, very early, but I had not got far out before I spied a canoe about a mile to the westward of my dwelling, with two people on the shore. Directly I put back, thinking they had not seen me, and hauled up my canoe. Then I ran along the shore and got to a convenient place behind some trees.

There appeared to be no more than two persons, one standing, the other sitting near the canoe. I saw them both retire up to the bushes; after this they came down again and both looked into their canoe. After this, they began to run about the strand making many odd motions, then threw themselves on the ground and acted like people beside their reason. At length I determined to get nearer to them, as I knew there could not be above three or four of them, by the size of their boat. At length I approached them so near that I could plainly perceive one of them to be a woman. I could see them now and again caress each other most lovingly, then in a moment they would fall into the most extravagant frantics, throwing the sand over their heads and crying in the oddest way imaginable. At last I resolved to show myself. I had nothing on at that time but my bonnet, a rag around my waist, and my paddle in my hand, and thus I sallied down onto the beach. They were at this time not 60 yards from me. No sooner did they get sight of me, than away they ran among the bushes. I hollered to them, but they never once cast an eye back.

I then marched up to the canoe, where I beheld a very aged man in her bottom, seemingly at the very point of death. I took him by the hand, but he never opened his eyes. I then spoke loud, whereupon he lifted his eyelids and seemed to look on me. I then began to call after them. At length the lad came out; I beckoned to him but he stood stock still at first, then came on again, and then continued to do the like until very near me. At last he threw himself at my feet, taking one of them and placing it on his head, returned it and did the like with the other. Upon this, I lifted him up, clapped him on the back, and shook him by the hand. He now stood before me like one under conviction. I then smiled in his face; this gave him some courage and he went to the canoe side, spoke to the old man, but soon he closed his eyes and died away. I then made signs for him to call the woman, which he did. She then advanced, but in a manner that plainly indicated her great fear of me – but by my repeating my civilities she came and did the very same tokens as the other had done. Now while these things were transacting, the old man gave one deep groan and expired.

Now when I found that the old man was absolutely dead, I made signs for them to get into their canoe and paddle along shore as I directed them. They readily obeyed, and the lad guided her along shore abreast of me as I went. Thus we went until we came to the spot where lay my boat. I then launched mine and made signs for them to follow me. This they did in profound silence until we arrived at my own cave. When I landed, I invited them on shore in the most friendly manner. They now began to cast their eyes around them, seemingly with much concern, now and then giving a sorrowful glance at each other. I then produced fish and placed it before them, but they shook their heads and declined it, seemingly very melancholy.

I now had an abundance of business on my hands, to have new tenants and a corpse to bury, all in one day. And now the reader may be curious to learn what kind of company I had got, and their characters. I shall therefore describe them in the most intelligent way possible. The girl seemed to be about the age of 17 perhaps, about the height of 5 feet 3 inches, her complexion that of the nut brown or rather lighter, her eyes black and the whites of them a China cast inclining to a blue, a small nose and mouth, her teeth even as dice, her neck, shoulders, arms and legs most finely turned, her hair like jet parted before and curiously tied behind, hanging down in plaitings (plaits) united together with strings of beads of many colours to a great length. Around her neck, arms and legs she wore three rows of teeth belonging to the tiger[41] or some such animal. Round her hips ran a narrow piece of woven cotton, replicating the fig leaves of our first parent Eve.

The lad seemed to be a year younger but stronger built. As to his head of hair, it hung over his forehead and shoulders after the order nature had disposed it, in which she had by no means been sparing. As to dress he was completely to be seen in his birthday suit, without any manner of disguise by art. Sometimes I thought them to be twins as they were both of the same height, and so much resembled each other in features that it seemed impossible for it to be more so.

The rest of the day was spent in endeavouring to gain them over to a good opinion of me, after the best manner I was master of. Now as they both continued to behave in a melancholy strain, I attributed it to proceed from a twofold cause, first the death of that aged person who I took to be their grandfather, and the other their being so unexpectedly discovered by me. The tears constantly flowed over the girl's breast, whenever she cast her eye toward their canoe. The lad's trouble seemed to be of a more manly kind.

But as there was at this time much to do, I could not spare the time for condolence, as I had lodging to provide in the first place, and then the funeral to be ordered. Therefore without any loss of time, I took part of my own couch and carried it to my hurricane tent, and spread it the best I could. I then showed them where to turn in for the night. They both obeyed in a condescending way, showing at the same time their gratitude. I slept little the whole night. Into my canoe I got by the peep of the day and went out fishing, then returned in about two hours, where I found them both sitting in their own canoe, weeping. I called them out, and cheered them the best I could, and began to kindle my fire. When this was done, I fell to cooking as fast as possible. After this, I made signs for them to come and eat with me. The lad came directly but the girl declined it. I then went to her, took her by the hand and brought her to the table, and bade her to sit down. I then gave each of them a roasted fish. Hunger now gained the day over grief and they both ate heartily, which pleased me much.

After breakfast, I made signs for them to wait on me to the canoe, and then I took the corpse up by the head and shoulders, pointing for them to take the legs. They did so, and we carried it to a distant place and laid it down. I then began with a paddle and dug a sort of grave, then made them help to lift it in. I then went and sat down to rest myself, watching their behaviour, but they seemed only to be waiting my motions, so then I got up and began to cover the corpse in sand as fast as I could. Now the lad began to assist me, and the girl threw herself flat on the sand, weeping exceedingly. When we had made up the grave, I then took them back with me.

I must observe in this place, immediately upon the appearance of my new guests Miss Doe absented as being frightened of strangers for the first day, but the next morning saw fit to follow us at a distance.

In a day or two, my new friends became a little more free in their behaviour. This gave me reason to think my conduct had made them entertain a good opinion of me. Nothing could be softer than their speech, yet it seemed to me very difficult to attain, as they drew the words in with their breath and then uttered them from the throat. I found the girl extremely modest and bashful, especially whenever I looked on her, she never failing at such times so as not to see me; yet with the glance of an eye I could every now and then catch her viewing me when she found an opportunity. In about 7 or 8 days we became more sociable together, but I could observe that whenever we were on the shore, they would be pointing to the southward, and the sighs would escape the girl's breast frequently. The lad would point that way with his finger and say a great deal to me.

Now I had one great difficulty to master, as this. I could by no means whatever learn their names, for whenever they spoke to each other there would be some kind of change in the words, so that I could not fix on any as appellatives. The method I took was this. On a day that the girl was washing some fish out of the canoe, and knowing that the lad was out of sight, I made signs for her to call him. But here I was deceived again, for standing up she began to cry in a small, shrill voice, 'Hoo, oo, oo, ahea!' He soon came up, and I was quite nonplussed. I put him to stir up the fire, as a pretext for having called him. But as we were sitting at victuals, I pointed to my own breast and said, 'Penrose'.

Directly the lad understood me, and nodding his head looked at his sister; then pointing at his own breast said 'Ayasharre, Ayasharre.' Then, directing his finger to the girl said, 'Yalut-ta, Yalut-ta'. Now, thinks I, it may not be yet what I would be at. Therefore some time after I took an opportunity to call 'Ayasharre.' He came running, and smiling at me directly. After this, I took occasion to go into the cave and called the girl as best I could. She came at once, and I gave her a shell to bring me some water, as a sham. Now, thinks I, this is enough; but I repeated the lad's name so often that at length I had brought it to Aharry, so resolved thence forward to call him Harry; and the same method I took for the girl, calling her Luta for shortness.

Hitherto, I had not meddled with anything I saw in their canoe, although I saw there was much trumpery[42] in her. Now Harry, as I called him, went into her and among the things he grabbed out was a yam, and he ran eagerly to the fire to roast it for me, as I judged. This sight made me run, and snatch it out as soon as I could, it being the most precious jewel to me. This caused them both to wonder, but I soon made them understand that I would plant it in the ground. With that, he ran down to the canoe and brought up 3 more. I felt such a joy on the occasion that I became transported. After this, I went with them and examined their freight, and this is the invoice of the cargo: two very neat paddles, bladed at each end; two small harpoons fixed with lines and staves; a bow with several arrows headed with sharp stones and stringrays' bones; a small silver bell; half a roasted turtle; eggs; and part of a dead dog or some other animal resembling it. The two latter articles I made them throw into the lagoon as they stank like carrion. Several sorts of fruits and roots – these we used and planted a part of them.

But what transcended the whole cargo in value to me was a clever small hatchet, good as new. On this hatchet was stamped the maker's name, as follows: '*Pedro Munoz, Cadiz*'[43]. By this I knew they had traffic with the Spaniards. It was with the greatest difficulty that I could keep my legs in this canoe, yet they had a small mast and a matt sail, which they could ship and unship as they had occasion. Yet I many times afterwards saw four tall Indians stand and paddle them with great dexterity, when I am certain that the most expert of our seamen could not have kept his balance in them.

I now began to learn them a few words of English at times, and the first word in English that Harry caught was '*Come*' as he heard it so often repeated by me. As for the girl, she betrayed a very great reserve whenever I aimed to instruct her. But one day as we were sitting together, the deer coming up to her, she said '*Miss Doe*' as plain as I could speak it myself. The method I took with them was this. Every morning I showed them two or three objects and named them, they aiming to say the like. At last, Harry would ask me the name of a thing that he had forgotten, when the girl would never fail to set him right. By this I found that, although she did not speak as often as her brother, yet she retained words much better in her memory. These poor, innocent young creatures became every day more and more the delight of my mind, being always eager to obey me in all I desired or directed them to do, and I industriously strove to gain their regard by every means I could study. Nevertheless, I carried myself so as that they should regard me as a kind of superior wisdom.

Harry was so delighted by my method of striking fire, that he would ask me for my knife every now and then to be at it, and would even put the fire out for the purpose of lighting it again, so I was often forced to refuse him. Now it happened that I was going to take Harry with me one day, to take a view of the burnt ruin I had made. The girl perceiving it, began to weep; this moved me to know the cause. Upon this she threw her arms around her brother's shoulders and whispered some words. Upon my wanting to know the meaning of it, he was put to it for an explanation, but began thus, '*You go, me go, Yalut-ta go not, never come, dead, sick, die.*' Upon this I took her by the hand and made her go with us, as I could not think of giving her cause to complain.

So off we went together, Miss Doe in company, but when we came to the spot, I was much surprised to see what a great change had appeared. Multitudes of things had sprung up afresh, and even blossoms were to be seen on many shrubs. This made me determine to plant my yams here, at any event. Now, as I had never seen one deer, for the space of the whole time since my burning of the woods, I concluded they had forsaken these parts. Here, Miss Doe, perceiving the great space before her, would set off and race away to a great distance, yet immediately on my whistling she would bound back to us, swift as an arrow. The next day, I made them take the yams to the same place, and made them plant them, and from those we obtained sufficient for our use forever after.

Some months passed on thus, in perfect harmony, when an accident occurred of great moment to me, as thus. As I went on a time to my reckoning, I found that I had more shells than I ought to have, or that I was much deceived. I pondered it in my mind, but said nothing, as I knew my reckoning was totally marred, and it gave me a great deal of uneasiness, as I suspected in what way it had happened. The affair proved according to my conjecture. Some two or three days after, I observed Mr Harry to bring in a few shells and throw them into the basket in front of me, certainly out of good will to oblige me. Now, how to return him thanks for his great service, I knew not, but burst into a fit of laughter and so turned it off, as it was a folly to pretend my reasons for what the shells were intended, so told him I had enough of them.

Now I became obliged to invent some new plan whereby to keep my time, and for this purpose determined on the following, (viz.) to cut it out on the trees with my knife, 50 days at a time; and for that purpose I looked out a large cedar, or rather fig tree, whose bark resembles in texture that of our beech bark, and on one of those trees I cut the date of my full time as near as I could possibly conjecture. It was just 3 years and 2 months when I first found them on my shore, and they had at that time been with me perhaps 4 months, so that I fixed the period at 3 years and 6 months. From this period, I continued to add by fifties, giving Harry a strict charge not to touch the marks, on pain of my anger. Now, as these marks appeared to him a kind of conjuration, he studiously avoided even touching the tree.

Having mentioned this fig tree[44], I shall give the reader some account of its singular qualities. N.B. This tree does by no means resemble that of our tree of the same name in Europe. The manner of its first acting in its infant state is thus. It grows perhaps to the height of 9 or 10 feet, at which time it becomes so weak that it stands in need of succour. It is to be observed that it seldom fails to spring up some 2, 3 or 4 feet from a stately cedar. At this height, seemingly as from instinct, it parts into two arms tending towards the cedar tree, where it clasps it as with two arms, being so weak in its own nature that it would fall to the ground unless thus supported. After it has thus obtained succour it begins to grasp and climb, growing daily higher and higher; and I have observed frequently that although other trees would at times intervene, it would shun them in order to better come at the cedar tree. And thus it proceeded to gain strength and magnitude until it attained the very top branch of the highest tree in the forest[45]. At the same time its body, having the same kind of adhesive quality, extended itself in such a manner around the bark of the cedar that it totally enveloped its kind benefactor, unless in some few places the cedar could still be perceived through. And thus in the process of time the whole external appearance became an ample fig tree, or a grand counterfeit. The reader may rely on this as a matter of fact, as I have been a witness of it over a thousand times.

N.B I have frequently called them in my own mind 'Ingrates', comparing them to such kind of men who in adversity will abjectly fawn and wheedle themselves into the honour of any, the very meanest of company, so as to obtain relief in adversity. Yet if fortune but once smiles on them, they prodigally reject and shun their very benefactors. This I may with the strictest propriety charge my own soul with, as thus. Did I not, and without the slightest provocation on her part, slight that tender-hearted parental cedar-tree, my own mother, whose arm had so kindly and tenderly supported my infant fig-tree state until I attained to that strength as to stand erect? I say, did I not suffer her then to wither and dry away as the sap from the cedar in weeping for my folly, while I plumed myself in all the extravagances of a mad-headed fig tree among the thorns and thistles of this world? But let me hope that I have made some atonement for that great act of ingratitude by the dire contrition I have since felt, and the mortifications I have since that day undergone.

One evening, as Harry and I were walking on the shore I chanced to hear the Yoho's cry[46]. Upon this, I bade him to listen and asked him what he knew concerning it, expecting some odd account or other. But to my no small confusion he laughed as he said, *'That Birry.'*

'What is Birry?' said I.

'Bird' said he. *'Go all nights, bite bird little.'* Then, clapping his hand to his mouth, he made exactly the same noise. That was enough for me. I at once concluded it to be an owl or some such nocturnal bird, and called myself an owl or an ass for implicitly

swallowing down such idle tales recited by credulous fools. N.B. These anecdotes are not supposed to have fell out exactly to the very time as I recite them, but in or near as best I can remember, my having no use of pen, ink or paper until the time the Dutch ship was lost.

In order to divert the time I used to play at quoits now and again with my messmate Harry, and this he learnt to such perfection that he soon became my match. And often when we were at this sport, which was always on the beach, Luta – as I called her by way of an abbreviation – would seem much elevated whenever I won the game. This I found never failed to cause much sniggering in my friend Harry, but as it always passed in their own language, they thought I disregarded it. But sometime after this, as they were with me in the cave, Harry came and stood before me and said *'Where you come?'* This I knew meant from whence I came. It put me to a great stand, as I knew they had not enough English to comprehend my full information, so I pointed to the sea, made as though I slept often on my journey in a canoe, and arrived on their shore.

This I found made them very thoughtful, and the girl wept much, but to pass it off as well as I could, I began to instruct them in words. Now, as Harry observed me to be much pleased with his sister's pronunciation, he leaped at once to his feet and taking Luta by the hand, put her hand in mine. Then he fell to shouting, hollering[47], whooping, dancing and making his obedience to us after the manner I had learnt him, crying, *'Eat it, drink it. Eat it, drink it. Catch it, have it. Catch, get Luta!'*

And thus he went on, like one frantic with joy. I then gave Harry to know that I understood him very well, showing by my look that I was pleased with his proposal, it being a matter that I could by no means be against, as she was a young creature of so charming a disposition, and so ready to administer in her kind services on all necessary occasions.

I then asked Luta if she was willing to sleep with me, as having no other address whereby to convey my intimation of making her my wife. It is natural to suppose that the ladies, if ever these lines should reach their hands, may be curious to learn what kind of answer this fair one made me. It was this: *'Penoly'* – as that was the nearest they could sound my name at first – *'Penoly not go out,'* pointing to the sea. *'Me make fire all days,'* directing her finger to the ashes. This I conceived as a figure of conjugal love.

I told her that she and I would have to make a new fire for every morning. At this speech she fell on her knees and kissed my feet. I then lifted her up. When her brother saw this, he ran and clapped us both around and fell to dance, sing, and whoop louder than before, uttering all the English he was master of in the most confused way; yet I could plainly understand the true meaning that it was the joy of his very soul, and I must confess by no means against my own inclination, as I had imagined a thing of that nature would infallibly unite us as one. But I kept all such thoughts aloof, leaving it all to time lest I should perhaps disgust them.

Here was a wedding indeed, but without a parson. Yet trust me when I aver that there never came together a young couple on more equal terms. Our love, interest, fortune, desires and intentions were one, (viz.) that of becoming a helpmate to each other; and that kind Providence had given us the power to perform even in this wilderness. This happened just 3 years and 7 months after my first landing on the Spanish shore (as I learnt it afterwards to be, although at that time I thought it was an island). I now proposed to Harry that he should go to sleep in my bower. This he readily gave into, and slept there afterwards; telling him that when he could find out a wife for himself, I would be very glad.

Sometime after this great affair was settled, my new brother and I went over to the Bird Island after conches and eggs. When we came on the shoal, and hauled our boat near a clump of bushes, there seemed to be a great stir beneath them, and observing, we found a multitude of shellfish or rather amphibious gentry called Soliers or Soldiers[48] from their red colour. And as the nature of those beings is always singular, I shall give the description according to my own knowledge. (Viz.) They are always to be found inhabiting small shells of various kinds, but the whelk is the largest they seem to dwell in. The forepart of this small animal resembles the lobster when boiled; the after part within the shell is so delicate a nature that it cannot suffer the least injury. They come out of the sea most certainly, or go thither for their shells. But what is most remarkable, soldier-like they frequently commence hostilities and join in combat; and in these warm contests they beat each other out of their tents, never failing to take advantage of an empty house. Immediately on the others leaving it as they grow larger, they shift from one shell to another yet larger. They are good eaten roasted on the coals, leaving the shell directly as the fire touches them. They begin to bite as soon as caught, and that sharply with the claws.

After we had gathered about half a peck of those soldiers, I took a walk around a point where there were many pelicans, and some so young that they could not fly. But I had not been long on the spot before the old ones, taking a circuit round, gliding on the wing, would return with such slaps on my head that I was forced to defend myself with a paddle as I retreated. After I had gathered a few eggs, I returned to the canoe where Harry showed me a large fish, called a Ten-Pounder[49], he had struck with his dart. These fish are shaped like a mullet, exceedingly swift of fin, but very bony; but it served to show me the great dexterity of my new brother, he having struck it on its full career, as a good shotsman would a swallow on the wing. After this, we hunted out for a few large shells and between us found 5 whole ones. Now as we were at this work, Harry took up a trace of an odd kind of stuff, the like of which I had kicked before me often on the shore. This he showed me was young conches, and on his breaking one of the parts it proved to be so, there being about 40 young ones in the cell, all completely formed. This trace of stuff was at least two yards long, and must have contained thousands, as the joints were close together, in form like the House Leek plant and of an odd texture, in colour resembling sandy yellow.

Now this leads me to a remark seldom taken notice of by most seafaring men, (viz.) that shellfish, as they increase in age and magnitude, retire into still deeper water and this is the reason why we so seldom find shells with the fish in it of great size, when such numbers of the small are frequent. The large shellfish never come into shoal water, except when worked up by tempestuous storms. And this I think I am clear in – as I once sat fishing in about ten fathom water there came up with my hook a monstrous shell with the fish in it alive, of the Helmet species. Now I had seen thousands of them along shore, but not one of them a quarter the size of that I found, it weighing at least 10 or 12 pounds.

After we got about 50 yards from the shore I spied a small Chicken Turtle[50], on top of the water. I showed it to Harry, who, snatching up his dart, bade me to paddle slowly for it. I did so, and he struck it in the back. The staff dropped out and away she towed us, he tending the line which was fastened to the dart until she grew tired and we got her in, being about 20 pounds. We then returned home and had a feast with it. This adventure determined me to set about and make a strong line for the very purpose, and accordingly I ordered Harry to prepare stuff for that end. After this we often got a turtle;

and this put my brain to work afresh, which was to endeavour by the help of my brother Harry to contrive to make a small Turtle Crawl to confine a few of them as we caught them, and by dint of labour we finished it to our satisfaction.

Now finding they understood English well enough to comprehend me, I sounded them out about their country. I asked Luta how far off their place was where she came from. She shook her head and said, '*About 3 Sleep and 3 Walks*,' meaning about three days' journey; but Harry tartly said that it was more than '*4 Sleep*', he was certain. I asked her then, who was the old man who died in their canoe? She said he was her Mother Father (mother's father) called Coduuno, that their own mother was dead, and their father put dead by the fighting men[51], and that she and Harry lived with the old man, having two brothers and two sisters who were married to men and women like she and I were. I then asked them if ever any white men came among them. They said not every day, but once in many sleeps; that she had never seen but three old men of them long ago when she was but so high.

I asked her what they did when they came. They brought crooked sticks[52] with them, she said, and made the women tell everything. I asked her then if they did not exchange things with them. '*Some small, all for good*,' she said – but that her people did not like to walk with them.

'*Why?*' I replied. Because, she said, they used to kill all her old people when the old trees were but small, as she heard the old folks say. But as they were now everywhere, her people had no way to get away from them, and they could not push them into the sea. I then asked Harry if their people did not eat men when they killed them in fight. He gave me a sneer and spat on the ground, saying, '*No, no, no, never not!*' – but said that the oldest men had heard that such things had been done when the Moon was a little star.

After this, I asked Harry how they happened to come to my place. To this he made answer that they came out to fish and catch turtle, but after they had been out two days the old man fell into a fit, as I understood him, which he was much subject to; and that the wind came off the shore so strong that they could never regain it; and finding the old man to grow still worse they had at length gained my shore after being out 9 days, drifting away with the current quite out of their knowledge, having never been so far from home before. '*Should you be willing to go back?*' said I.

On this they both eagerly cried, '*Go, yes, go! You go, you go!*' I told them I would go when I found the way thither, and dropped the matter.

Thus things went on until my fourth year ran out.

CHAPTER III

The Fifth to Seventh Years

THE FIFTH YEAR – THE FIRST VISIT BY INDIANS
June 15 1751 – June 14 1752

Fifth year commenced. One evening as we all three were sitting together, I reassumed the subject of their going back again. On this they both caressed me fondly and said, *'yes, go, one, two, three!'*

'No,' said I, *'If I should go, your folks don't know me and so would have nothing to say to me. But there is your canoe – go when you please, and I can remain as you found me.'*

Upon this, a kind of sullen silence ensued, and I observed the tears to fall from the girl's eyes. Upon this I took her in my arms, and told Harry to observe his sister. He then fell to blubbering and said, *'I never go, Penoly, without you and Luta.'*

In the midst of this affecting scene all at once I felt a thing sting me on my thigh sharply. I got up and found a huge centipede[1] under me. In a short time it became almost intolerable, and gave them so sudden an alarm that it quite dissipated the other passion. Harry ran and killed the insect, and pounding it with some wet dirt laid it on my thigh, and Luta[2] bound it up the best way she could. I then retired to lay down, was in a fever for above an hour with my head in the girl's lap, weeping over me in the most tender manner; and thus I fell asleep. How long I lay I know not, but when I awoke I was almost choked with thirst. They gave me some fish soup, and by the morning I felt not the least uneasiness. But when I began to show myself as was usual, Luta said to me softly, *'I never go, Penoly, no go. But Penoly go, and Harry too.'*

I now began to reflect within myself that there can be no true pleasure proceeding from giving pain to others; and as it was but a wanton kind of trial in me of their affection, I was but fitly served and had met a very just cheque for my wanton inquisition.

I began now to consider Harry my Chief Mate in all undertakings; and one day as he returned from gathering wood he brought a large yellow snake[3] with him. I had seen them before, also a small green sort with another like a barber's pole, one sort of black and long, another yellow as saffron. I asked him what he would do with it. *'Eat it,'* he said. *'Do so,'* said I, *'if you can stand poison.'* He then cut off the head and skinned it, after this gutted it and laid it on the coals, and when it was done he brought it to me to taste, but I declined it. Then I asked Luta if she liked it. She said yes, and *'it very good.'* So when I found them falling to it, I tasted it and must confess it to be as tender as a chick, and of a fine relish.

Another time he brought home a prodigiously large calabash[4] on his head. I was then in the cave, and Luta called me out to see it, and I must confess that it was the largest production of any fruit kind I ever beheld. To speak within reason, it could not weigh less than a quarter of a hundredweight.[5] Harry cut it in two, and then seated himself to scoop it out. Certainly when it was made hollow, each part would contain above a gallon of water. This monstrous pair of shells he laid by in the shade to harden, and when so, they became of very material use to us, standing always in the cave full of water for our use, by way of serving as buckets.

Shortly after this, as being now become better and able, I determined to revisit the new lagoon where I found those turtle skulls I have mentioned. Therefore I bade Harry to get ready both the canoes, and the next day we dressed a few fish and filled one of the large shells with water, and left the cave, Luta and myself in my canoe, Harry and Miss Doe in the other. We had no interruption on our passage, but arrived at the place of the skulls with ease, then proceeded up until we came to a place full of mangroves.[6] Here we saw a great multitude of mullet and other fish, with plenty of Whistling Ducks, Cranes, Galldings and other fowl of those kinds. The Bald Eagles, Fish Hawks, & co. were in greater numbers than I had seen before, which was a sure sign of much fish in the lagoon.

There was a channel about four or five feet deep all the way to the mouth of it, but at the entrance the water deepened to about two fathoms in most places, until we came up it at the distance of half a mile, where it shoaled by degrees. The whole length of this lagoon is about 1 mile or perhaps more, with its entrance so shut in by a point, that at the distance of 100 yards, it is not perceptible. Now, when we got to the head of it, we found a large and spacious place with a beautiful fall of water coming down from a cliff, seemingly about forty feet high, with fine trees overhanging the cliffs. This water had its course to the lagoon head, down a fine lawn, mixed with patches of gravel. This lawn gently descended to the falls for about 100 yards. Nothing could exceed the beauty of this fine view. It formed a kind of half-circle, measuring by computation about a mile, everywhere environed by groves and thickets except on the right as you advance, where you may walk up among the trees until you gain the summit, where you may have a view of the whole area, the lagoon and all, seeing out to sea for a vast distance.

I now told Harry to make fast our canoes, and then we all proceeded up the lawn to the waterfall; and as we advanced a large flock of parrots flew over our heads, making the most confusing outcry. This made me halt a little; as it was the first time I had ever seen any of those birds wild. As I was thus gazing around me, I perceived a kind of vacancy at a distance among the rocks. Thither we bent our course, and on a nearer view we discovered a fair cavern with its entrance oblique to the lagoon and, as it were, facing the run of water which came from the falls. It is difficult for me to give any exact description of its form, unless I say that the entrance was like a kind of high arch resembling some of our cathedral doors, about 20 feet perpendicular but irregular and about 30 feet wide; all of a ragged kind of rock and the floor being fine gravel and small stones. I then told them to follow me, being determined to explore the place.

As we advanced the echo was so great that our common words sounded very loud. When we were in to the distance of 5 yards, I found that the roof was more lofty than at the entrance. At this place, I thought it proper to return, and bade Harry to gather some sticks and kindle a fire. This he did, and after it had burnt for a time, I concluded to go in further, with firebrands in our hands. Now while this work was doing, I discovered many marks and letters cut on the rock on both sides of the entrance, in like manner with those I found cut in the Tower Stone, as before mentioned. By this time, I knew full well that many had been at the place before my time. It is needless to give any description of them, as they are similar to what I have given a sample of already, except that I remark that two of the marks contained the names of perhaps two very great villains, and are as follows: Martin Fletcher and George Needham 1670[7].

Each of us now took a brand in our hands and advanced forward. We got in, about the length of 8 yards, when it then contracted on all sides to about half the magnitude, and inclined much to the left, so that a total darkness would have ensued, had it not been for our lights. Soon after this, we heard a strange bustle within, which put us all to our heels in a moment; and we were soon followed by such a posse of harpies that we were out in the blessed light of day in a trice, with numbers of fluttering fiends in our vanguard. These were huge bats[8], whose ancestors had inhabited that old mansion for many ages for ought I knew.

After this alarm was a little over, I told Harry to get fresh light and make another search. This he did boldly, contrary to my way of thinking. All the time he was gone, I could not refrain from laughter, as expecting him to return again in the same way. At last he came running and whooping out, with a whole legion of those nocturnal gentry before him, crying, 'Poo, poo, poo, poo!' and laughing at no small rate, whisking the firebrand over his head like a crazy fellow.

'Well, what now,' said I, 'Harry, have you found the end?'

'Yes, yes,' he said. 'I hand me put there, too.'

'And how is it?' I said.

'Very dark, very little short,' he replied. By this I knew he had been to the end of it.

Soon after this, Harry pointed and showed me a very fine Plantain tree[9], and I directly spied two more. This so charmed me that I shortly turned round to Luta and asked if she would like to live there. She said yes, if I would like to come and live there too. Upon this I came to a full resolution of moving without further delay, being so taken with the place that I never once reflected on those necessary obstacles which then stood in the way of retiring, so far from our yam patch, and becoming quite land-locked from the sea. But when I once reflected on that, it put me to a sort of standoff. Yet when I came to measure the great gain on the other hand, such as we should be quite safe from storms and inundations, together with many more advantages, and that we could with the help of a hatchet clear a way up the cliff, and there have a more grand view of the sea than from the beach below, I gave wholly in to it, at all events.

Here we spent the remainder of the day, and then went into the great entrance and prepared to sleep there for that night with three large fires burning before us, without any disturbance until the next morning, except that now and then a bat would fly into the place.

At the break of day, we prepared to set off, and got home to our old place in good order without anything happening, and found all was safe on our arrival. Now my mind began to run strongly on my new situation, and I communicated my thoughts to Harry on the matter. He seemed to like my proposal but made objections I had never thought of, (viz.) we should be far from our Turtle Crawl, the iguana grounds, and that we could find no driftwood there. That was all true, but I observed to him that the place was far more to our comfort in all other respects, that I was determined to remove, and that very soon; and that in regard to our iguana ground and plantation, it was just going further to them on occasion; and that after we were settled we would plant afresh nearer home, and make us a new 'crawl' for our turtles at the most convenient place we could find. And so far we all agreed.

We had fixed the next day as our leaving the cave, when shortly after in the morning, as Harry was out after wood on the shore, he spied a canoe and came running away to us almost out of breath, crying, 'Boat! Boat! Canoe boat!' Away I ran with him, Luta in the greatest fright after us, not understating the meaning. When I came on the beach, I saw a canoe standing right in for shore, about a mile off, with three savages standing quite erect in her with their paddles, intending to land about half a mile below us, as I judged. Upon this, we all three retired into the bushes. What means to take in this critical moment I knew not, but concluded firstly to observe how they would act. Now I found that Harry and Luta became uneasy, although they had been so much for my going with them before, but I spirited them up the best I could, and thus we waited their landing.

They soon came to shore and hauled up their boat. Soon after, one of them pointed to our dwelling and then they began their march toward us. Now, thinks I, they have certainly seen us or our smoke, so resolved to meet them at all hazards; and in this I was the more bold as I could not entertain an evil thought of them. After they came within 200 yards of us, I asked Harry to go down on the beach, and I then took Luta by her hand and followed, she trembling with fear. We were all three naked, in a manner, as those we were going to face, except that I had a pair of striped trousers on and my bonnet upon my head. The instant they perceived us they stopped short. Upon this, I hailed them and they answered me. Then, to show I was in no kind of fear, I advanced boldly up. Then an elderly person called out, 'Espana?' I answered, 'No, Inglese.' On this they all said to me, 'Senor Capitano, bon, bon!' Now, I took care to style myself an Englishman, from what I had learnt from Harry and his sister. I then made signs for them to follow me.

After I found them to be friendly, I asked Harry to try to see if he could understand them, but how much I was struck when I saw young Harry fly up to one of them in such a transport of joy, and call him by name. They all three got about him, but to give any just description of their transport is beyond my power. He then pointed to his sister. Here I had no need to enquire in any way about the matter. The true language of the heart displayed itself amply, for I at once saw them to be old acquaintances. I could see during the heat of the conference that they cast a look of great esteem on me. At last I could contain myself no longer, but joined their company when Luta, throwing her arm around my shoulder, gave them to understand that I was her husband. Then all three saluted me kindly in their way, and made a regular survey of me, remarked that I was larger than themselves, they being all three, light men but well proportioned.

The reader may guess of my wanting further information, and I told Harry to invite them home with us. I cannot but remark their great wonder and amazement when they heard Harry and Luta talk English to me. They would often lift up their hands over their heads betokening admiration, crying, 'O wah, wah he!' As we went on, I asked Harry what and who they were. He told me that the elderly man was Komaloot, his sister's husband's brother, and that the taller of the other two was Futatee; but as to the third he did not remember his name because he was not much acquainted with him. This pleased me highly, and shortly after we brought them to our cave. I now bade Harry and his sister to sit down with them and talk over everything, and Luta soon became full of chatter. I found her topic to be on her own affair of being lost; and then I bade Harry prepare a sort of mess[10] for them. This he flew to obey with speed. – I remarked one thing peculiar to these people, (viz.) that they all showed their teeth much, never closing the lips in conversation, except rarely.

Now I wanted to learn if accident or design had led them to out habitation. Therefore I put Luta on that enquiry and she related to me as thus, that there had been a great canoe lost lately, and that their friends had been out in the great water to it, to see what they could find. I told her to enquire if any of the people were saved. She said no, but they found four men dead, and they buried them; but if this was true, no one could tell. I then enquired whether they were English or Spaniards. They replied that that were the latter by their clothes and little wooden crosses around their necks, saying that they knew the English threw such things away unless they were made of gold or silver, as they said that the English did not use wooden goods because they thought them of little worth. This made me smile. Upon this, Luta said something, which made them all laugh also, and on enquiry she had told them that I had no God at all that she ever saw. I asked her how she could tell that, when she made me such an answer that it closed up my mouth, (viz.) if I had one, I had never showed Him to her.

But to return, I asked Luta what they said concerning Luta and Harry being lost in the canoe. She told me she was informed by them that they had been out all along the coast, and had given them over (for dead) long ago, thinking that they had perished at sea or that some vessel had taken them up and carried them away; that the old man's wife was also dead, also one of her (Luta's) sisters called Niuxa[11]. When she mentioned her name, I could see the tears fall. One of those Indians enquired whether I was not afraid to live there, on account of the rainy times. I bade her tell him that I was going to remove to another place, and I would show it to them before they went home again, if they would stay a day or two. Harry told me that they said they would, and were going to make a small hut to sleep with us for a while. Then we all began to eat of such things as we had, and after this Harry and one of them went and brought around their canoe.

When it came, I observed that they had collected many things out of the wreck, by which I knew she had been of the Spanish nation. There were 3 pair of uncurried[12] leather shoes, 2 small brass kettles, a large roll of sailcloth, some woollen frocks and trousers, a good firelock but no powder or shot, a great number of spikes and small nails, a parcel of knives (without springs like our clasp knives) but open with a back stopper behind, about 20 balls of twine, 6 hatchets, some chisels, 3 saws with plenty of fish hooks and a pair of shark hooks, a dozen fish grainges tied together quite new, two felt hats and above a dozen new ones made of straw, a bag of fine Lima beans, four hammers and one mallet. But there was one thing that gave me some concern (viz.) a bloody shirt. This gave me cause to suspect their honesty, but possibly they were innocent notwithstanding. I did not care to meddle with their booty, so what might be hidden underneath I knew not. Mr Harry made very free to examine their cargo, and I curbed him as fearing that they might take a pet[13] and leave us, and anything of that nature would have given me much concern

I had been on shore about 4 years and 3 months when these Indians discovered us. After this they began to cut down stuff for erecting a temporary hut for themselves. Harry lent a hand and myself also, which pleased them much. During this they enquired, in particular, how I was cast on their shore. Now, as I had found that they had got some knowledge of it from Luta, I bade her give the whole relation to them. In about three hours the tent was finished close to that of Harry. After this, they prepared to rest for the night; and on the morrow I proposed for Harry and two of the Indians to go out striking[14] fish (viz.) Futatee and the other, keeping Komaloot with the girl and me. I ordered it thus as a precaution, but my suspicions were groundless as I found afterwards. They returned with some fine fish, and then I ordered some to be cooked for our voyage.

The next morning we all put off and had a pleasant trip of it. When they arrived on the spot, they all concluded that it would suit much better than the old habitation, but that I must expect to be bothered now and again by tigers and woodcats[15], and that Harry must keep a good look-out after the Peccaries and Waris[16], or they would devour our yams and other things. This was a new hint, for I had never once thought of anything of the kind, having never seen any in all my time there. Nevertheless, I was determined to settle on that spot, and I observed to them that I had never seen tigers while I lived down at the other place. They told me that this was very likely as those creatures never frequented the low mangrove grounds, being much disturbed at the noise of the ocean, and finding little game in such quarters. But they observed that whenever any visited us, we should show them some fire and they would soon run off, observing that the very smoke continued for a length of time seldom failed to make the tigers quit that quarter; then, pointing to the deer, observed that she would be apt to draw tigers about us. But I was determined to stand the chance, as I was passionately fond of the place.

We took a general viewing of the place, while Harry prepared some fish, and after dinner we all got into our canoes and returned to the old habitation again. On the morrow, I proposed to go after turtle, and off we went. The party consisted of Futatee, his companion, Harry and myself, leaving Komaloot with the girl at home. We turtled for two days, in all of which time we only caught but 6 tortoises, alias turtles. I reserved but three of them for ourselves; the others they roasted in their own slovenly manner on coals, for their use as they returned home to their friends.

They now began to talk of departing. I then put Luta upon begging them to bestow some few articles out of their canoe, as we had no means of providing the like in our poor condition, intimating that we should be very ready to assist any of their people, should they come our way in any distress. Upon this they held a council together, than asked what we desired and they would exchange with us. As to any exchange, I bade her tell them that they could plainly see that I was very poor. Then Komaloot took me to the canoe and asked Harry what I wanted. I then pointed to the hatchets, kettles[17], twine & co., but what I seemed most to require were the very things they were the most unwilling to part with; but he took up the shoes and offered them. Upon this, I gave them to know that I was now an Indian like themselves, and that my wants must be similar to their own. This put them on a fresh consultation.

At last, Komaloot and Futatee spoke a great deal to Luta, which she thus delivered to me – that they advised for us to go and reside amongst them; and that they were certain everyone would treat me with kindness as I had been some good to Luta and Harry. I now began to think this was an evasion so as not to part with any of their ill-begotten goods, as I suspected, and acquainted them that it was quite uncertain if I did go to dwell among them that I might through ignorance give them some cause to be offended with me, and that I did not choose to be within the knowledge of the Spaniards. So it was best for me to abide where I was, but that I should always be glad to see any of them at my poor habitation when I was removed to the other place, observing that if Harry had any mind to return with them to his friends, I would by no means desire to detain him. But in regard to his sister I had all the reason in the world to think that she did not desire to leave me, as we lived in great love and harmony. Upon this they observed that they had no room for Harry if he would go, their boat was so full.

Then Luta reported on them sharply that, although they had so much, they would not part with anything to her. This caused a loud laugh, and after jabbering amongst themselves they took her by the hand and brought her to the canoe to show what she wanted. On this, she laid her hand on one of the kettles and they gave it to her. Then they asked me what I chose. I told them Harry wanted an axe. They gave him one, and then I observed that they had many knives and we wanted some, and they gave us three with some of the twine. I then asked for a few of the Lima beans to plant; and of those they gave us readily as many as we would have. And now finding them in strain to give us more, I asked for some sailcloth; that we had also. But it was with much difficulty that we could extract a few spikes and nails; because they valued them greatly. They also gave us 5 sombreros, or straw hats. Some time after this, I took it into my head to see what flattery could do, and advised Luta to intimate what a great fondness I had conceived for Komaloot. The bait took, and before they went he gave me a shark hook and two of the new fish gigs[18]; these I valued much. Also they gave me a hammer and a saw, with a parcel of the small fishhooks.

The next day they prepared to leave us, but when Harry found this he took Luta aside and desired that she would entreat with them to procure him a wife. This caused much mirth; but as Luta and I had joined in the petition, they said that when they got home that they would advise the people. They then observed that if they came, we must expect them in canoes, as they had never been to our place by land. After this they took their leave in a friendly manner. We went down to the beach to see them off, and remained there for over an hour; and it was wonderful to see with what expedition[19] they paddled away, full as the canoe was, so that I could not have trusted a favourite dog in her unless he could be near enough the shore to swim for his life.

While they remained with us I used every art to learn what part of the coast I was upon, but without effect, except that they told me I was on the continent and not an island as I conjectured. Sometimes they would mention Carthagena[20] and a few other places. They told me that no Indians lived within 4 days journey of me. They said there were a great many Indians to the northward of me, with whom they never talked or walked.[21] When we returned to the cave I was surprised to find the shoes and gun among the mangroves, but judged that the Indians had gone and forgotten them. Now Luta and Harry became very dullened and remained so for two or three days.

It happened soon after, as I went into the cave I saw on a ledge 3 dollars. This surprised me and I asked Luta to enquire about it. She told me that she had them out of the canoe from under the sailcloth, and that they had as many as would fill a wooden bole. This concerned me little; as such an article was of no use to me, as being too far from any market.

The next business I took in hand was a thing of such a nature that I believe few of my own countrymen are accustomed to do, (viz.) no less than making my lady a petticoat out of the fragment of sailcloth, and by help of twine and a sail needle I finished it, then showed her how to put it on. She was so highly pleased with it, as I told her my own country's people wore the same, that for two or three days she was constantly viewing it as she walked along. She was so awkward that I could not refrain from laughing, the shortness rendering it the more comical as it did not fall above a foot below her waist. If ever any of her own sex should read this, they will excuse me when I plead the want of stuff to make it longer. One day as she was advancing towards me, I took it into my head to learn her to make a curtsey[22], and Harry to make a bow. Now, as I knew so little how to instruct her, she did it in such a diverting way that I laughed immoderately. After this, whenever she observed me to be a little duller than usual, she would be every now and then dropping a curtsey before me until she forced me to smile.

In the next place, I determined by the help of my tools to fit my canoe as a sailing boat. I cut the old boat's rudder and made a thwart[23] to fix amidships, then cut me a small mast, not lanky[24], as my store of sailcloth was but little. When my sail was made, I cut me a bowsprit[25] for it. When the mast and sail were ready, I took a small trip in her with Harry and his sister, and she worked very well. The next matter was to examine her bottom, and for this purpose we got her capsized on the beach. After this Harry and I pegged up all the worm holes[26] with pegs, then we covered her over with a large quantity of boughs to stop her rendering[27] while we went in quest of a shark[28] or two. Accordingly, the next day we went in the small canoe on a hunt and it was a long time before we succeeded; but at last we hooked a shark, and after we had killed him, we towed him home, rendered his liver in our little brass kettle, and then paid all the canoe's bottom[29] with it. Some of this oil we used to burn in a shell at times, but they soon cracked and became unfit for further use. But Harry and I knew of a kind of wood, which burnt like a flambeau,[30] which we made use of at times.

Now, being on our removal I took care to mark it down and found my account to stand thus at our departure – 4 years and 6 months. We carried all our movables thus – Harry had the deer and a few other things, the rest I stowed in my large canoe and then took in my lady, bidding him to paddle away ahead, as I had a large wind. But I soon forereached him and got there first, where I landed my spouse and awaited his arrival. He came in about half an hour after. We then carried up all our materials to the Castle, as I intended to term it, and then gave up all to go striking fish. Harry was a dab at that work; we were not long before he struck a fine snook[31] fish, enough for two meals for us all. When the evening came on, we made three large fires before the Castle gate as a guard against the tigers; and when this was done we got a few palmetto leaves out of my canoe and laid them as a bed for the night. Then we retired within the entrance, but had little sleep the whole night, the place being strange to us, but nothing disturbed us in any other way unless a bat now and then flew out and in.

Early in the morning Harry and I went down to the lagoon and cut a way into the mangroves, leaving a good shade overhead. There we docked our two canoes. The rest of the day we employed in putting all our matters in order; yet it was a full week before I could reconcile myself to my new habitation, the thought of wild beasts ran so strongly in my mind. But my two companions slept well enough; their native innocence protected them.

The first thing we went upon at our new dwelling was to make a stool for each of us to sit on, and a new table. N.B. These were to be made of boards, but those boards were first to be procured. I then put Harry to felling a few small trees, such as we could best cope with. These I undertook to cut in lengths and then saw through. Much labour it cost me before the work was finished and, although rough enough they were when made, they served us well enough. I chose the inner part of the castle as our bedchamber, and to that end made fire in it, lest any damp should annoy us, and to banish the bats from it. The outer part was for Harry, so that we lay some distance asunder and hidden from each other's view. And thus we went on, without any interruption for above two months. I was quite charmed with the dwelling.

But one afternoon we heard an unusual noise. Harry ran out but soon came running back to me, bawling like a mad fellow. No sooner did I get out than I beheld poor Miss Doe flying home with a tiger cat sticking fast between her shoulders[32]. Rage possessed my mind at once. I snatched up one of the hatchets and flew to her aid. Harry was soon up with me and we soon brained the tiger, but the poor deer was so mangled that at once I knocked her in the head. This made Harry look at me in a strange manner, but I soon gave him to know my reasons for so doing, as I then saw that she was so torn that she must needs die of her wounds; and by my putting her out of pain and misery it would prevent a like disaster in future.

All this time Luta kept a distance, and indeed I was surprised at my own ferocity, when the affair was over. Harry said he was not timid in the least, as he had a bow and arrows in his hand; and his merit in that way was greatly certain, having seen him hit small flying birds, iguanas and lizards running, and that at a distance of 30 yards. We were now provided with a venison feast when we least expected it, so fell to work in skinning her. All the time this operation lasted, Luta did nothing but weep. Indeed we were all three concerned at the loss, as she was so diverting a creature, so cunning and tame to the degree of a spaniel dog. However, what must be must be; and we ate off her carcass until it was no longer fit for our use. The rest I told Harry to throw into the lagoon for fish meat.

Some time after Luta observed to me that it was a bad omen, and that we would have been better remaining at the cave. I laughed at her, for by this time I had got the better of all superstition, so gave myself little concern on that heading. What gave me most concern was how to fall on the best means to keep off those Devils (tigers) for the future, and for this purpose we made it a rule to build up a large bonfire twice a week. This answered our purpose so well that we seldom saw any more for years.

After we had been here a considerable time, we went out one day along the shore to the southward of our lagoon. Here we found the water to be very shallow, with a small current setting north, and as we were paddling along I spied a long range of a small kind of red rushes in the water, as I thought, but on better examination found them to be the horns of multitudes of crayfish[33]. We then put the canoe close in amongst them and grabbed handfuls of their horns, plumping them into the boat; we could have fully loaded her if we had been so disposed as they were not very shy. These crayfish are of a light freestone[34] colour spotted with black and yellow; and some of them Harry has since struck often weigh perhaps 4 pounds apiece. The discovery of these fish proved afterwards of great service to us as a variety of food. We returned home greatly pleased with our cargo, and continued to live quite happily together.

The deer skin, Harry cured Indian-fashion, and I took a notion to make me a kind of jacket from it with the hair outwards, without sleeves as I was not tailor enough for that part of the work, but I finished it after a fashion. I was not a little proud of it, as it spared what little duds I had with me; for I had one great annoyance when naked of such a nature that I could ill withstand, which was a sort of fly called a Doctor Fly[35]. This insect is about the size of a hive bee and shaped much like it, but its head is of a bright Saxon green. No sooner do they find an object than they dart at it, and instantly make the blood fly forth like a lancet's touch.

I shall in this place give the reader a short view of the usual dress we appeared in, (viz.) in the first place a huge sombrero or broad-brimmed straw hat on my head, my deerskin jacket without sleeves reaching to my hips, a piece of striped cloth around my waist below that, Mrs Penrose in her short canvas petticoat and a straw hat, lastly Mr Harry with a straw hat and a scrip[36] around his waist.

By this time Mrs Penrose was far advanced in the way of increasing our family, and on that account I took more than ordinary care of her. Her brother was so proud of it, that he would ever be talking on the subject, asking me what name I would give the child if boy or girl. And now we began to clear us a good road up the hill with our hatchets so that we might better come at the top of the cliff over our Castle entrance. This we did by spells, a day now and then, until my reckoning proved that I had now been another complete year on this shore.

After we had cleared around the top of the cliff, we could survey the whole coast far and wide, and I plainly perceived the great danger ships of burthen[37] would be in if they approached too near – nothing but rocks, sandbanks, reefs and currents with eddies and breakers to be seen all along the coast, so that I wondered no more, that I saw so few vessels pass by.

One day I took occasion to ask Harry if he could tell me what his name meant in English. This put him to trumps a little. At last he consulted his sister on the thing, and they agreed that Ayasharry signified a *'Swift Runner'* or a light-footed person. I then bade them translate Luta's name, and they said it signified a *'Green Grove'*; that Komaloot meant a *'Finder'* or *'Searcher'*; and Futatee a *'Bald Eagle.'*[38] I then asked what Codu-uno meant (viz.) the old man who died in their boat, and they said that it signified a *'Man of Great Strength'*.

One day as I ascended the hill to look out, as was my usual way, I thought I saw something like boats off a point to the southward. On this, the spyglass came into my mind, so I returned down for it. Harry was at that time gone out fishing. We both returned up the hill and I saw them plainly to be boats or canoes. We then came down and stayed until his return, which was soon after. When I told him of it, he ran away and soon came hurrying back, saying that Komaloot was coming with three canoes. Upon this I revisited the eminence, but could see no more than two, he having exaggerated the thing out of earnestness; and I laughed him almost out of countenance by observing that one canoe was large enough to bring him a wife. This made him shake his head, saying he believed that they would not do him that service now that his father, mother and old Codu-uno were dead. Some time after, they came around the end of the Long Key and put right away for our new dwelling. By this time, I could count 8 people, then we all three got into my canoe and went down the lagoon to meet them. As soon as we got out, we landed and made up a fire. This they soon saw, and when they came within hail we gave a good shout. They answered us; and then I bade Luta and Harry to both dance and sing like me. This I did, in order to show them how very glad I was to see them.

The first man who jumped out was Komaloot. He ran to meet me, and I him. After embracing he said, *'Yallut-ta?'* I pointed to the fire where she stood; he then ran and took her in his arms, and shook hands with and hugged Harry. By this time all the rest were landed. Now a fine scene represented itself to me[39]. They all ran together[40] in a cluster, and fell to weeping, laughing, hugging and even to bite each other. This I well knew betokened friendship, and I kept singing and dancing at such a rate that had any of my own countrymen beheld me, they would have thought me as much a savage as the rest (but this is by the way). I knew it to be my province so to do, it being of the greatest moment to me as a poor stranger.

My visitors were as follows: Komaloot and his brother called Vattequeba – this person was the husband to Luta's sister; his wife Lama-atty; Owa-gamy – this man seemed to be a sort of principal; Futa-tee, who had been here before; Dama-Sunto and Zula-wana; and lastly Cara-wouma with a little boy in her arms aged about two years called Quearuva.

We all then embarked again for our Castle and arrived soon after. When they were all landed, I made signs of the great joy their presence gave me and then led them all up to my Castle, where I told Harry to tell Komaloot to place them before me, according to their dignity. When he understood this, he took Owa-gamy by the hand and seated him first. I then bade Harry to bring me a few flat stones, and with the point of my knife I scratched Owa-gamy's name on it. After this I asked Harry what it was in English; he told me it was 'Traveller'. This I wrote beneath and placed the stone in Luta's lap. The next that came was Zula-wana; they told me his name meant a 'Good Canoe-Man.' This I put down, and delivered the stone. Then came Vattequeba, alias an 'Excellent Fisherman'; Futatee, alias the 'Bald Eagle'; then Lamaaty, alias 'Transparent Water'; Carawouma[41] or a 'Beloved Darling; and lastly the boy Quearuva or the 'Counsellor'. The whole time this was going on, they all sat very serious, and looking fixed at me. But as soon as I had done it, Owagamy enquired the reason in a very earnest way, and Harry told him I did it on purpose to learn their names. This pleased them all, so that Owagamy, pointing to them all, told me their names over again.

After this, Komaloot stood up, and took the young woman called Carawouma by the hand, then began a long harangue to me, now and then turning to Owagamy and the rest, who all answered in one tone like an Amen in the church. When he had finished his speech, he sat down, leaving the girl standing. During this time, Harry would smile and look at his sisters, they nodding their heads in return, so that I gathered enough to inform me of what was the theme. Then I desired Luta to give it all to me in English, the best she could, and she began thus:

'Komaloot says when he went back to my people, he told them that they had found my brother and I, no more dead, because one white lost man who had a heart as big as a great friend, had lifted up our lives again, and covered over the bones of their old friend; that Penoly had made one of three people; so they all agreed I was a great-hearted man, and that made Owagamy come with them to drink clear water with me. And out of the great love they bore to Ayasharre they had brought him Carawouma for a wife, she being willing when she heard that he was come alive again.' When she had finished I took the girl by the hand and called Mr Harry forth, then made them join hands in the presence of the whole company.

I now began to think it a high time to refresh my visitors, but was forced to bid Luta inform them that they must excuse us, as their coming so early in the day had prevented our making a provision suitable for them, so that I must beg that they would help my brother Harry in catching a few fish. Immediately two offered their service, and I told Harry to take them away among the crayfish, so off they went. While they were absent, by my advice Luta showed the others around, and I showed them our manner of living and sleeping. Owagamy observed many things to her in regard to our future happiness. This she interpreted to me, and put me in mind that I should get water, and drink with the men, as it was their custom with friends. I then told her to fetch me a calabash, and I then went to the stream and fully dipped it in, then took Owagamy by the hand and drank to him. This pleased him, I found, and he received it from me. After this, I tasted it with all the rest. No sooner had this ceremony passed than they all began to sing, dance and laugh with me, in a much freer manner than hitherto.

Soon after, the canoes returned with plenty and they fell to cooking, and when ready, all hands[42] sat around and got their fill. As for our liquor, it was the pure stream, which ran from the rock. After we were all refreshed, I bade Harry to sing them an old song I had taught him, (viz.) 'Welcome Brother Debtor,'[43] as I used to chant it frequently when I reflected upon my own condition. They all seemed very delighted and were very desirous to know the true meaning. I then told Luta to give them the sense of it in their own tongue; this she did after her fashion. Then Owagamy made this remark, that he believed that Alexander the Great must have been a Spaniard by his travelling so far, and one of those who first came into the country to murder his old fathers[44], but that he must have been a great boy to cry, because he could not kill them all. For had it been so, their sons could have had no Indians to murder in the mines – at this time expressing some words I knew not, with great bitterness. After this they all got up, and took each other by the hand and fell to singing and dancing after their own rude way, which I thought to be barbarous enough. I took notice they had but little motion, being no more than a gentle trot, stopping now and then to give a kind of whoop. This being passed, they all went and fell asleep in the porch, as I may term the cave entrance.

I took so great a liking to the little boy that he began to play with me, but whenever he chanced to touch my beard he would shrink back to his mother again. This made her ask Luta why I did not pluck it out as their men did. She told her it was not the custom of my country to do so, but that the white men used to cut it off with sharp knives, but I had none of them fit for this purpose. On this Lama-atty observed that she would not like to feel her husband's face so. Luta laughed at her, and said she must take great care never to touch her husband's head either, but that she was then with her cheek on the head of her child.

Luta said her sister informed her they had brought some things in their boats for us, which I was glad to hear mentioned, and told me also that Lama-atty said that she was glad to find her with child, for that would make me love her harder. 'But,' she said, 'I told her that could not be unless you were to eat me.'

This made us laugh so loud that I awoke the men, and they all came out to us. Shortly after, Lama-atty said something to Zulawana, and away they went down to their boats and brought up to us a bundle of Bass rope[45], 4 earthenware pots made of a very fine red clay, about half a peck[46] of Lima beans, a kind of very small peas, rotten oranges[47], long sweet potatoes and other sorts of roots, about three handfuls of Indian corn, mammees, avocados, cashew nuts, squashes, pumpkin and gourd seeds all in the planting way. They also gave us 5 coconuts and some cottonseed, with several other things I knew not by name.

Now I had my eye on two dogs they brought with them, differing very much from our English dogs. They were of a middle size; coloured like rusty iron, with their ears erect and broad-faced, having sharp snouts and stump tails. I could have been very proud of one of them, but could not venture on begging one, as I did not care to appear greedy. But Owagamy, perceiving my fondness, made me signs that I should have one when they went away, to drive away the wild beasts.

I shall now observe the odd behaviour of Harry toward his new lady. Every now and then he would take her by the hand and lead her off from the company, and when he got out of our sight, as he thought, he would caress her with fervency, so that he soon brought her into a pleasant mood.

The Indians now began to talk to Luta about planting and gave her advice about it. I then asked them concerning my planting a sort of fence around our abode to guard us from tigers, & co. This they strongly objected to, saying that the more trees we had around us, the more mosquitoes would annoy us. I took their good council; and they continued with us for the space of 5 days, when they began to prepare what could be gathered for sustenance on their return. I gave them what I could spare, doing everything in our power by way of recompense[48]. Just as they were upon leaving us, Zulawana took and tied one of the dogs to a stump for me. Then they all took boat and we accompanied them out to the bay, whereon their parting I made Harry give them the song again. After he had done, they all sang in their turn. Now just as we were on parting, and hearing the dog howl all the time, I took occasion to ask how we should feed him, as we got so little flesh. They laughed, and said he would eat fish and fruit as well. Then I desired to know when they intended to pay us another visit. They said, after many moons, when they could walk by their neighbours with good countenances. By this I judged they were at war.

The observation was very apropos for me; and I desired Harry to tell them that they would never communicate my being on this shore to the Spaniards, as my nation was ever at war with them, lest they should catch me and they should send me to the mines, and I should be forever lost to them and Luta. They then one and all made signs that they would rather be burnt with great fires than betray me; and I verily think that they were truly sincere in what they said. We kept company as far out as the Long Key and then took leave among much lamentation among the women, especially poor Luta – she wept bitterly on parting with her sister.

And indeed I was much moved myself, the cause being truly reasonable (viz.) Here I was to part, perhaps never more to meet, with some of the most disinterested mortals, a people who out of common humanity had done their utmost in their way to be generous relievers of my wants, and had come so many leagues without any expectation of reward. And this I blush to own was not done by European Christians but by men we are pleased to call Savages. So I may with justice remark, where is the advantage they have gained by the Spaniards' discovery of this New World? Have they not done all manner of evils among them, destroying and enslaving under the colour of exchanging one idol for another, while they committed such crimes among them which ought really to point themselves out as the most infamous and inhuman savages on earth? I say, had not those poor creatures been in a much better state to have remained, until God should have been pleased to have brought about their Redemption in, or by some more Apostolical means?[49]

After our return, our first business was to make some wooden shovels to turn up the earth withal. These we were forced to make out of the solid limbs of trees, the best way we could. Now I began to counsel Harry as to his conduct towards his wife. I insisted that he should behave in all respects to her, as he should observe me behave to his sister. As he observed me to be remarkably serious, he made me a reverent bow and said he would do all the good to it as he could think of. After I had finished, he brought Carre-wouma before me and desired that I would give her a new name, as I had done to his sister and himself. Upon this I told him that we would call her Patty. He asked me what that was in English. Now, that being the first name that came into my head, I was at a standstill, so told him it meant a Fine Girl. That pleased him very well, as perhaps any other would. And now my family was increased to five including the dog.

The next business was our planting. This I considered would be best at the old burnt ground near the old cave. As I did not know how much we might be troubled by the wild beasts, and I had never seen any on the low coast near the sea, I judged that the most promising of success. These things took us up above a fortnight; and now we found the turtles draw in for the shore, their time of laying being near. After this, we went out striking every day, taking the girls with us, until we had caught eight. And then it came into my mind that we need not be at so much trouble, observing to Harry, should we watch them when they came on shore to lay, it would save us much trouble, and by that method we should get all females, the males at that season being very lean. This practice we followed soon after, and turned onto their backs so many that we were obliged to desist.

While we were at this sport on a fine moonlit night, Harry was too impatient for the turtle to fix herself to nest. Upon that she spied him and was making back for the sea again. He, observing that, ran and got astride her back, and grasped the forepart of her carapace[50]. I, seeing that, ran and got behind Harry, and Patty came and clung to my waist. Nevertheless, the turtle was so large and so strong that she scrabbled us fairly into the sea. The girl tumbled off backwards, I slid on one side and lost my hat, but Harry stuck on her until she sunk him, up to his chin, before he left her. We had much laughter on the occasion, and Luta she enjoyed the scene all the time, from the beach. After I had regained my hat we returned home for that night; and the next day we returned to the scene of the action and by hard labour got them all into our turtle crawl, being eleven in number, the smallest of which weighed near three hundred[51]. We had at the same time eight Chicken Turtles. We now and then got Sea Grass for them with conches and whelks, and it was a surprising thing to see with what ease they cracked the shells, although they were as hard as flint.

My lady now became near her day, and we had the sad misfortune for Harry to fall sick. Patty was very tender over him; and how to act in this case I could not tell, but he took to his poor bed of leaves and was in a high fever. The girls had some knowledge of herbs and made a kind of tea. I prepared weak soups for him, but he would be now and then light-headed. At such times, he was for going a-fishing, or to see his sister Lama-atty. All business now lay on my shoulders, so that I was now obliged to go to the old cave for yams and turtle alone, also a-fishing.

Now as I was going on one of these errands one morning very early, no sooner had I got out of our lagoon than to my great alarm I beheld a sloop at anchor off the end of the Long Key. I plainly saw men walking who had a sort of sail tent on shore. Now, thought I, what a fine pickle I am in, but I had the thought to put back directly within the point, being pretty sure that they could not see me, being so close under the land. I directly put up the lagoon, and the first thing I did was to put out the fire. My girl, seeing me much gravelled[52], needed to know the cause, but I waived it. Yet when she saw me get out my glass and run up the hill, she asked me if any people were coming. That was enough – out came Harry, ill as he was, and would follow me. When we got up to the top, I could plainly see 5 or 6 men fully clothed and that they were Spaniards by their broad hats. While I was thus viewing them, they kindled up a large fire. Some of them went off on a ramble, and I saw the smoke of a gun. Now I was sure they were not Indians, which was enough for me, being determined to have no manner of concern with them if I could in any way avoid it. I was quite amazed to see Harry – he acted as if nothing ailed him, and wanted for us to go to them.

But as I was eagerly looking out, and carelessly leaning over a crooked stump of tree, it gave way by the roots and off I went down the declivity for some yards, until a rugged rock brought me up, much scratched and hurt, so that I lay quite helpless. The stones tore my leg and back. Harry went and called Patty, and between them they conveyed me down the hill. Now I was laid up, unable to move much. Patty gathered medicinal herbs and my wife boiled them, and then they washed my wounds, Luta being also very near laying down (giving birth). Harry gave me trouble, lest he should relapse, and the enemy at the door – all these things added together, becoming a great load on my mind. But contrary to expectation, either by my fall or the sight of the Spaniards' sloop, Harry kept his legs. After the girls had bathed my wounds, I found my spirits recruit, and that I was not hurt so much as I then thought. I bade him to go and hunt the glass, and keep a good lookout. He came back with it, and the strangers tarried there all day.

The next morning, he went up very early and said that they were still there, and going about in a boat. I had no longer patience – up I got, and found my right leg to be very stiff so that I could hardly put it to the ground; yet I must needs hobble up the hill supported by Harry and Patty. When I arrived, they seated me; I then took the glass and found they were striking their tent. We had eaten nothing from the time that they first appeared. We then ate a few dried turtles' eggs. The Spaniards remained there all the next day, and we spent the second night like the first; but on the morrow Harry came down and said that they were all gone. Away I went, with my best leg foremost, and could see no more of her, but found her soon after by the help of my glass, standing close-hauled to the eastward. And who they were, and on what errand I never knew to this day, but was glad enough of their departure.

This happened about 5 years and 3 months after my landing on this shore. And the next day Luta had a son. I gave him the name of Owen[53], this being the name of my father. The following day was remarkable also by my spying a large ship in the offing. When I first observed her, she was a great way out, standing to the westward. We soon lost sight of her, as she never neared the shore. This was the first large ship I had seen near the coast in all my time.

A few days after this there began an aloe to bloom directly before our dwelling, and it was surprising to see the great progress it made in a short time. I had taken notice of them before, but never had one so fair within my view. In the space of a fortnight or twelve days it grew to the height of thirty feet as I judged, full of the most glorious tufts of yellow flowers, and scented the place around. The humming birds, bees, wasps and flies were feeding all the days on its sweets, so that it became a perfect habitation. In particular there came one sort of humming bird, which had two feathers in its tail, three times the length of the bird. In one point of view it was profoundly black, but in another shone like green gold[54]. Harry knocked one of them down with a blunt arrow, but struck away one of the long feathers out of its tail. I kept it by me for a long time, until some vermin ate it away.

It happened one day as Harry was out on his rambles he chanced to see a green parrot[55] fly out of a hole in an old palmetto tree, and found two young parrots, which he brought home scarcely fledged. These birds he took good care of, and raised them on guavas and other wild fruits. At last they would eat yam and plantain, we having got access to several of that kind in the woods; and Harry had planted several from suckers. We also had plenty of good squashes and pumpkins coming on, for everything seemed to thrive rapidly.

Patty came on in her English very fast, and as to her own person she really was a 'fine girl', taller than Luta and of a lighter colour but not as full fleshed, and as I judged her, somewhat older. Whenever we went abroad anywhere Luta had a broad piece of tree bark to fix her child on, as though in a trough; and this I know, it cost me a pair of trousers for baby linen with which she used to wrap him up, so as to carry him on her back. We lived after the same way as usual for a long period of time, never seeing one soul, save our own family. We ate, drank, lay down and got up as we listed (wished), without the least disturbance. Each day was a kind of copy of the foregoing. Add to all this, we were blessed with a good share of health; and my companions knew no other mode of life.

Yet I must needs own that I could have been much pleased, to know how the world went on, and to have the enjoyment of a good companion of my own country. But as this perhaps might have cost me some unforeseen trouble, it gave me no great anxiety, as I knew myself at this time, by experience as that if I was taken from the joys of this busy world, I was amply recompensed by being removed from the reach of rancour and malevolence. And now I found to my great comfort that a young man might live, if so disposed, without vice; and I am certain, I had gained so much over the vanity of my own heart, that I verily think I should never have dipped again into such a scene of dissipation. So, that finding myself the gainer, I became quite easy, nor had I a desire to return for any reason whatever, except for the joy I conceived in beholding my dear mother's face once more.

I took a great distaste to the parrots, as their noise was the most ungrateful to my ears, but as I found them diverting to the girls, I put up with it, they being fine birds to the sight. Yet when they began to chatter, I could not help talking to them at times. Luta, observing me, would divert herself sometimes with them at my expense, as thus. Getting one of them on her hand she would talk to it thus: 'Cut it off! Cut it off!' – meaning my beard; then say: 'Where is your father, your mother, Penoly?', 'Where do you come from?' and the like.

All this, the birds learnt pat, and also responded to their names. And if at any time they grew dull, we had no more than to give each a bunch of goat or bird pepper[56], when they would both begin to prate at no small rate, so that I would be glad their tongues would cease. And if at times Luta found me dull, she would threaten to give the birds a pepper.

Some time after, Harry came home and reported that he had seen wild beasts, and a great many more than a hundred. This surprised me, and caused me to ask how he had escaped them. He replied that he was not in fear of them. I then wanted to know what kind they were. He told me they were a kind of hog with white faces. Therefore I imagined them to be what I had heard called waris. 'Why did you not set the dog to hunt them?' said I.

'No, no,' said he, 'too many. If the dog catch one, all the rest will bite him to death.' I knew Harry to be the best sportsman, so gave up the point, but I was determined to contrive some scheme or other to trapan[57] them. Now in all this time I never saw above two tigers, and Harry one. We found that setting up a loud shouting made them turn tail directly, so on their account I became a little easier in my mind, but took care never to suffer the girls to wander far in the woods alone.

One day Patty brought home some of the candle fruit or cassia fistula. They are about the length of a foot, and when green hang dangling like myrtle candles from the tree; but when ripe they resemble black pudding in colour. She told me they were good put in hot water against pains in the bowels or costiveness[58]. The substance within resembles tar and is very sweet, so that I used to dilute a small quantity of it in water and squeeze a lime amongst it. This made a tolerable beverage, in colour resembling coffee.

We had not tasted an iguana for a long time; there were none frequenting our quarter, the soil being in no way sandy. The next thing was a voyage to Towers Field on a party to hunt iguanas. We took all the whole family to prevent harm (in our absence). We fastened in the parrots with plenty of victuals in their rude cage we had made for them, and then put away down the lagoon. My wife, child and self were in the large canoe. Harry, his lady and the dog were in the other. Thus we proceeded to the old dwelling; there we went on shore and took a repast.

Now as we were all out together, I took the notion to visit the Key opposite where the Spaniards had been lately. When we arrived on shore we found the marks of their tent, with a boom of an old oar made of green heart[59] and exceedingly heavy. At some distance we found an old jar, which would hold about three gallons, made of a coarse earthenware, and round at the bottom. Harry picked up a case with a knife and fork in

51

it, very rusty, but I took care to scour it so as to become fit for use. I found that they had been so generous as to sink a barrel into my well, as a legacy to those who should touch shore there in future times. We shipped our things, and just as we were putting off I picked up a good fishing line and sinker with hook. When we got over to the other side, we stood alongshore and got to our hunting ground. There, our dog ran down four iguanas and we gathered a parcel of limes, then put back for our old dwelling where we all slept that night, and the next morning set out for home where we found all was secure. But the joy the poor parrots showed on our return was wonderful – they talked the whole day long.

Now, as a man is never too old to learn, I got Harry to make me a new bow that I might learn to shoot at marks (targets) with him, as thinking it would be of use to me. What spurred me on to this was, Harry the day before had shot a duck as she flew over our place. Our dog hunted well, although he had no likeness to a spaniel, and took to the water freely. I gave him the name of Swift. This dog never barked, but in the night would give a long howl at times.

Nothing of note happened from this time except the rains, until I found that I had now been there 5 years and 9 months. At this time we kept much within doors, as I may say, although we really had no door at all. And now the beauty of our fine cascade became quite changed to a great cataract of red water, thick and muddy[60], and continued so, for above a fortnight. Therefore we used to fill or large jar and the calabashes and set them by to settle[61]. Providence never failed us, and we had either a boil or stew, and at times a roast. (Viz.) We had the duck roasted. Harry made a wooden short spit and stuck the bird on it; this spit he fixed in the ground inclining toward the fire, turning it around in the ground now and then until it was done. As for our iguanas, we always stewed them.

After the wet season was passed by, Harry proposed to go out and strike some stingrays, telling me that they had bones in their tails which were good for arrowheads. As to those bones, I had seen them, having been catching those fish before. And as it is a fish little known in England, I shall give it a description here. They are formed much like those fish called thornbacks. I have seen them weighing above 200 pounds. Just at the dock of its tail are fixed those bones, one above the other. I have seen them with three, point behind point. These bones are very sharp at the ends with exceedingly fine teeth each side (barbs) as they lay flat on the tail. Those teeth are in a contrary direction to their points, so that when the fish becomes vicious it erects the tail and darts these stings into its enemy, tearing out flesh wherever it strikes, and leaves a great anguish in the wound for a considerable time afterward, as I felt by experience. Their skins are sharp-grained, like unto a shark.

There is another species of that animal whose skins are exceedingly hard and tough, and are transported to Europe for the use of our cabinet-makers. This fish is called a rasp-ray. There is yet a third sort of these flat fish called the whip-ray[62]. This fish differs from the rest, having the head almost resembling that of a tortoise. The back is bluish with small white circles all over it, with the skin exceedingly smooth and shining, with a tail black as jet and of such a length that a fish the size of a common thornback shall have one perhaps six feet in length.

After those fish, Harry went in his own canoe and was out almost the whole day. He came home with about 7 bones, having struck three of those fish. What had detained him so long was this, he said that the last fish was a very large one, and as he struck it the staff slipped out of his hand, and the fish made away into deeper water with it sticking in its back; and had it not returned again for the shore, he should have lost the whole, and that was what we could ill spare.

THE SEVENTH YEAR – MATTY IS BORN AND TOBY ARRIVES
June 15 1753 – June 14 1754

This year commenced with an ugly stroke of fortune for me, as thus. We all took a small trip to the cave after yams and sweet potatoes, and while I was there I took a notion to wash myself in the sea but I paid heavily for it. As I was about to come on shore I felt something dart into both my feet, attended with instantaneous pain. I directly swam to shore, but was obliged to fall down on the sand. Harry ran to know what was the matter with me, and found both my feet full of the darts of sea eggs[63]. By this time I was in such an agony that I expected to faint. He directly ran for the girls and they got me into the canoe, put on my clothes, and then hurried me home as soon as possible. By that time my feet were swollen so much that I could not budge, and they were forced to carry me up to the bed and they laid me down. After this Luta got prickly pear leaves and split them, then toasted them at the fire and applied one to each foot, binding them on. From that time almost until the next day, I remained in a high fever. When it abated she took off the leaves, and my feet appeared as though they had been boiled, but the thorns came away with the leaves and I felt quite easy. But I could not walk for three or four days, my feet were so tender; but they soon came to order again.

These sea eggs are of that class of beings, which never move from their first stated fixture. They are of many different sorts, shaped like an orange, divided with curious lines of partition, and spotted with green, black, yellow, red and brown. Some have no thorns at all, but the sort from which I received my injury have darts four or five inches long which are black. These darts, they have the power to play about in the water, directing them as a man would point with a sword, any way as they lie.

Soon after this we were entertained with a very diverting scene. One of the parrots had got away to a distance and was perched on a cashew tree, where she sat refreshing herself, and a parcel of wild parrots passing over spotted him or her. Upon this, they all came and settled in the same tree. Patty saw them first, and came to call us out to share the diverting farce, and indeed it was a scene truly comic.

They would walk sideways up to her and place their heads parallel to her, then give her a peck. Another would get over her head in the meantime and do the like. Ours would hold up her foot, so as to ward off the blow. Others would take a slap at her with one wing. At last they gathered, as by consent, all around her and fell to paying (hitting) her at a sad rate. Upon this, the poor thing began to call out, 'Harry! Harry! Owen! Little Owen!' as fast as possible. But no sooner did she speak plain English than they all flew off, screaming like so many mad things and quite frightened, no doubt. Directly, our parrot began a loud laugh and flew home; but when she got into the cage she began to prate away to the other as fast as her tongue could go, the other bird saying, 'Hey, hey, hey!' as though it understood the relation. This diverted Harry to so great a degree that he rolled on the ground laughing.

Shortly after this Harry expressed a desire to go after flamingos and I consented, so off he went with the dog next morning in a small canoe. He did not return that day, but as I knew it to be a good distance I was in no way uneasy as he had fire works[64] with him, and that made an Indian at home everywhere, either by day or night. The next morning was ushered in with a new adventure; it was thus. I called Patty to rise and make up the fire, saying her man would be home soon. This she went out to do, but she had not been out long before she came running in to us, crying that there was a great dog-like thing fallen down by the fire, from the top of the rock over her head. What this could mean was quite beyond my comprehension, so I got up and ran out, but just as I came to the fire down came another. This amazed me, but I picked up my courage and went to examine them and found they were peccaries, both of them disembowelled. Now, thinks I, this must be a piece of messmate Harry's gamut; but as the dog did not come in first as was usual, I could not think what or how it could happen.

At last a loud laugh began above our heads. Directly I ran in and snatched an axe, being determined to stand my ground. When I came out, I heard a voice call down from the cliff, 'Yallut-ta, Yallut-ta!'

Upon this I cried, 'Come down, you scoundrel! Come down. Let us have no more of your dog's tricks!' And indeed I was at that time very angry with Harry, as I thought. My spirits were so hurried, that I never adverted to the pronunciation or difference of voice until an Indian showed himself, and called down to me. Immediately I saw it to be Komaloot. Upon this I called out to the girls, quite overjoyed. I then made signs for him to meet me and away I ran up the hill. There I found Komaloot, Owagamy, Zulawana and a young Indian I had never seen before called Sama-lumy. I saluted them all, and they returned it. They were all four armed with bows, arrows and machetes or cutlasses. When we got down to the house, great joy commenced immediately. Komaloot took the child in his arms and hugged it. They then asked after Harry, and Luta told them what he was gone after.

I then enquired how they came so secretly upon us, and said that they had scared us not a little. Owagamy then told Luta a story as follows – that they happened to be out after game when they came to a fine open country, and there Komaloot made a proposal to find out our place. To this they agreed, but that they had gone past our place; this they learnt by getting up a large tree from whence they discovered a smoke on the right, near the coast. This they concluded must be the place of our abode, and they turned off for it. Shortly after, they fell in with a few peccary hogs and killed two of them, and gutted them and cut out their navels, intending to bring them as a present to us. N.B. The navel of this animal is on its back, and if it is not cut out as soon as the beast is dead, the whole carcass taints soon after. He said they discovered us at last by the great smoke that the girls made, for Sama-lumy was then got up a tree not far from our habitation. They soon after got sight of our place, where they called a counsel and concluded to proceed after the manner they had done, lest their sudden appearance should alarm us too much. I told Luta to return them my thanks for their good conduct.

While Patty was preparing a little of what food we had, the dog came running in. I then knew Harry was not far off. The poor animal was quite transported at the sight of his old masters. At length messmate Harry made his odd appearance, dressed in scarlet from head to foot with his flamingos, his great straw hat on his head; in one hand he held his bow and arrows and in the other he had a fine hand of plantains. But as soon as he saw our family thus increased, he made a full stop. I called him to come on, and as soon as he found whom our company were, down went his cargo all at once, and much joy came on.

Harry enquired after their canoe. When they told him they all came overland, he asked how many tigers they had seen. This question made them send the young Indian off, who soon returned with the skin of a tiger on his shoulders, they having forgotten it where they first saw the girl. The skin Owagamy presented to me. There was such a piece of business between our dog and the two they brought with them, that he led them all over our grounds. Now we began to ask after their families. They told us Lama-atty had another child, a girl; and that they had made friends with some other Indians after a long variance.

I then asked if the young Indian who came with them was a captive or not. They said no, that he was a relation; but that he was under some trouble and that they wanted to bury him. I could not judge the intent of this dark speech, so put Luta to enquire of them what they meant by it. Then Komaloot took Luta on one side and held her in talk for some time. After this Luta told her brother to take the young Indian and show him all around the place, so away they went together. When they were gone, Luta told me that it was the desire of her friends that I would consent for their leaving Sama-lumy to live with us for a time, as they had a great reason for it, that my consenting would show that I had a true regard for them, and that they should ever be willing to oblige me in all things, and that Sama-lumy would serve me even to the hazard of his own life. Now what to think or say I knew not, but in the first place I desired Luta to request that they should be plain with me in regard to the subject in hand.

Owagamy then took me by the hand and gave me a look most powerful, and then proceeded to talk nervously to me for a time, then bade Luta interpret the same. (Viz.) She told me that as her friends understood that I was in much dread of the mines, and that they were so far from discovering me to the Spaniards, that they would sooner suffer death than betray me. Therefore, as Sama-lumy was now under the same terror at this time, they had thought it best to bring him off to me that he might be concealed until such a time that it should be forgotten. As he was young, they thought he would grow out of the Spaniards' knowledge.

Directly I took them by the hands, and by Luta's help told them to confide in me as their sure friend in need. They thanked me, and then I told Luta to give me a relation of how the misfortune happened. She then said that they told her that Samalumy had been to visit some of his relations who lived among the Spaniards, and that by ill luck he had made free to hang around his neck a string of beads with a cross on it; and as they were all playing together he had the misfortune to break the cross by striking another with it, on the back. This was perceived by a little girl who ran and informed a padre who was not far off. The padre came and reviled him, calling him 'Perro Salvaje,' (savage dog) for presuming to meddle with it as being unbaptised; and that he would soon find him better employment in the mines, and then left him in great anger. This so terrified Samalumy that he took the first opportunity of slipping away to his friends, who on his information had shifted him from place to place, until they thought of this scheme to bring him to us.

Now I fathomed out the whole drift of the land visit, and think that they played the part of good politicians on me. Owagamy told me that whenever any of the padres fell out with those who had nothing to pay for an offence[65], they never ceased pursuing them by all their arts until they had obtained their revenge – and yet pretended great pity. But as sure as they were taken hold of by an officer, they never then saw the priest's face any more, nor was it in their power to withstand it unless at great risk.

This was a miserable subjection, where every poor Indian is obliged to carry an insolent priest on piggyback[66]. Surely nothing can be more aggravating, especially to a people who have received all the reason in the world to hate and detest them, as the Devil hates holy water. All this I know of a certainty, whatever others may report to the contrary. And many barbarous stories are related of them – I mean the Natives; and in truth, they may make their report good (believable) among people who know no better. But let us first enquire who were the aggressors – I have resided so long amongst them that I know the error to fall on the Christian side. I myself have been an eyewitness along the coast of Florida when Indians have been wantonly shot at, because they were in dread of coming on board our vessel. And never was there greater truth than this spoken in the world – but this is enough on that matter.

When Harry and the young fellow returned, they had the affair laid open to them. Harry became marvellously pleased to have a companion, and the young Indian came and made me many signs of thanks for consenting to his stay. I then asked Harry to get me a flat stone, as I wanted to set down the translation of the lad's name. When he brought the stone I asked what Sama-lumy meant, and Luta conferred with Harry, saying that it was a 'Mountaineer'. I then wrote it down and ordered the stone to be placed away among the rest. After this, they asked how our seeds came on, and were informed that we had most of the things now in plenty, except the oranges and cocoa nuts. Owagamy said that there would be many, many long moons first. He then directed his discourse to the young Indian, and as I was told, charged him to mind all my directions and to be my true friend, and to be sure to oblige the women. This he did, and they took their farewell, saying they would come once again when they had time.

After the Indians were gone, I began to think that I had brought an old house over my head by having this Indian left with me, fearing that if the Spaniards should come to the news of it, they might use me very ill; so I determined that if such a thing should happen that they found me out, in that case he should be gone out of sight. This was hinted to him, and he promised to obey me in all things.

One day, as we were all shooting at a butt, Harry told me Sama-lumy wanted a new name, by which he might be thought of as one of our family. I told him that was but right, and that he might call himself Toby if he pleased. He enquired if that was a good name. I told him that it was, as it was the name of a young man who took great care of an old blind father. This was sufficient for him, and we called him Toby from that day.

We lived on very friendly for a long time together, and our little one began to daddle[67] about. Mrs Harry became bulky and threatened to add another to our family, which made her spouse very proud. Mrs Penrose commenced being a Schoolmistress, and nothing could be more innocent than to see her sitting with them at learning. At times Harry would contradict her; she would then appeal to me, and what I said was a law among them so that all disputes ended on my saying a word.

I now had no trouble on my hands to care about the family provision, unless I went out now and again for my own pleasure. Now one day as the lads were on the lookout, they came down and reported that they saw a vessel out at sea. When I came to examine with my glass I saw three, one without the other; they appeared to be standing in for the land with the wind at west. As they came inshore, I found two of them to be schooners, the other a sloop[68]. But they put about soon after, and we saw no more of them until evening when they stood in again, then tacked and left us for good. I made a memorandum of it on the side of the rock, with my knife.

About this time I put my two mates on digging pitfalls, for catching the wari and peccary. This they laboured at for several days together. They dug six of them and we baited them with plantains, yams, potatoes and the like. Now and then we used to catch one, but we were obliged to knock it on the head before we dared go down, they were so fierce and courageous.

56

I shall now observe one circumstance, which led us to a good discovery. I happened to ask Harry if he had ever seen a lizard with two tails[69], I having been informed that there were such seen at times. He said that he thought he had, and enquired of Toby. However, one day as Toby was out on his rambles, he imagined he saw such a thing run under a bush, but in going to poke his head under the bushes, he met with a sad disaster. I was the first who saw him when he returned, but he was so altered that I scarce knew him. He was stuck full of lumps of red clay, one on his cheek, another on his leg, two on his thighs, and one on his breast. Some of them he had bound up with a long sort of grass. He cut such a strange figure that I called the family out of the Castle to behold him. This made him laugh, but then the scene became heightened beyond all description. His eyes were almost closed up, and his under lip swollen bigger than five lips, showing his teeth so oddly that they all laughed at him immoderately; but as I was ignorant of its true meaning I could not laugh so much at him. However, he made a shift to inform us of the whole adventure, and then the girls made use of the old recipe[70] for him, and by the next day he was as well as ever again.

But to hear him relate the affair in broken English was droll enough. The poor fellow had thought that he had seen a two-tailed lizard run under a bush, and in satisfying his curiosity he ran his head into a wasps' nest or that of hornets, where they had peppered him to some purpose. His description ran thus: '*Twotail go in go. Toby good look, bush. Maum come. Maum maum bite Toby. Run Toby, run Toby. No see two-tail tomorrow!*'

Whatever pains he had been at, to find this clay, I know not, but am certain he paid for it. Nevertheless I found our burning it in the fire proved that good earthenware could be made from it, could we but shape it into any sort of vessels. But this was a kind of manufactory I little understood. I now resolved to set my two messmates to work on the clay, and they lugged home a parcel of it where I made them temper it; and the first trial we held was thus. I got one of the large calabashes and oiled it around, and then palmed clay all around it without, and by this means made an ugly sort of Yabba[71]. After it had stood by to dry for a time we burnt it, and it answered very well to hold our water, and would boil things very well had it not been so unwieldy. After this, we made several other utensils for our purposes, fitting enough for our use.

About this time, I made a fresh calculation of time and found by my best judgment that it was 6 years and 5 months or more. I every day became more composed in my mind, studying to subdue the passions as much as in me lay, so that by this time my spirits were so calm that I never fell into any kind of hurry, except the time I mistook the Indians for Harry. A few days after this, Mrs Harry brought forth a girl.

I was by this time tolerably skilled at the bow, but never could attain to the nicety of either Harry or Toby's judgement. For instance I saw Toby one day hit a small hummingbird as it was spinning on the wing before a blossom, at 20 yards' distance. If this be not credited, how shall I advance that they could knock down the butterflies as they flew? Yet, the reader is left to think as he is pleased. Yet before I drop the subject, let me make one or two remarks. I know that there are those who implicitly credit every romantic tale told by travellers, be they ever so absurd; when on the contrary others will presume to deny that things known and attested by men of real veracity could never be, or have existence, because they had not seen the like, or because Penmaenmawr or Cader Idris in Wales did not produce such things, nor had they been heard of among the wonders of Derbyshire[72].

Considering this, I may gain but small credit with some folk by my description of the Pudeling Wythe[73], a kind of vine which, after it has aspired to the top of the proudest tree in the forest, drops down perpendicular a number of bell-ropes all of a thickness until it comes down within 4 feet of the earth, when it sprouts out resembling the tail of a horse, but on touching the ground takes roots afresh and re-ascends as before. Also the shrub called Flying Prickly Pear[74] whose minute thorns are so subtle that when the wind blows, and any person is to the leeward of them, they will insinuate through his skin imperceptibly at a distance of 20 or 30 yards. N.B. I advance nothing but what has been demonstrated to me, through the testimony of my own senses.

About this time we became annoyed by a most disagreeable smell. The wind was then northeasterly and the stench at times became very offensive. I enquired if they had left any fish garbage about but could find none. At last it came on to such a degree, that I was determined to find out the cause. Therefore I went with Toby in the large canoe along the east shore, but when we got beyond our old dwelling the smell became intolerable in puffs. At last I thought I saw something on a point right off Towers Field, as I termed it, resembling a ship's long boat, bottom upward. But we had not gone much further before there came such a strong hogo (stench) [75], directly into our mouths and noses, that I began to suspect the true cause, therefore made a stretch out in order to weather it[76]. When we got to the windward side of it, I found it to be a dead whale laying on its side.

When we drew near, thousands of birds were flying in all directions about it. The fish were as numerous below. I saw some of the largest sharks I ever beheld measuring 15 or 16 feet. There were snappers, barracudas, cavallos[77] and many of other kinds in abundance. The whale measured, as I judged, above 60 feet. I then asked Toby if he had ever seen so large a fish before. 'Not up,' said he, 'but much, out in the big water. Blow water like wind blow.' It was the same with myself, having never seen one so plainly before. The mouth was wide open and gave me the opportunity of learning that what is termed whalebone among our tradesmen lies around the roof of the mouth, supplying as I judged the place of gills, or as a kind of strainer whereby to retain their prey.

Having thus satisfied my own mind at the expense of my nose, we returned and made our report at home. I now and then sent the lads out to take a distant view of it, and we had this ugly hogo for above a week longer, when the breeze stood our way. It was above a month to be seen above water. In a short time after, I paid it another visit but the scene was quite changed: all the ribs were parted and most of the fish were gone.

Some considerable time after this the youngsters[78] went to Towers Field after iguanas and limes; although we had lime trees already planted around our place. Now as they were fond of sailing they took a stretch out to the remains of the whale, and as they were thus satisfying their own curiosity they saw a vessel wrecked away to the northward. On this, they made their best way home to inform me. I enquired if they saw any people. They said no. Now, how to order things at home was the problem, as I guessed it to be at least 5 leagues by their account. At last I came to this resolution, to leave Harry at home, and to set out the next day well provided, with my second mate Toby. Accordingly, the next morning I took leave and away we paddled down the lagoon. After this, I stood directly out for a considerable stretch, and then fetched almost beyond our old dwelling. The next tack was fetched almost as far as Towers Field, and thus we proceeded until abreast of the Whale Point, from whence I could see over to the wreck.

It was evening before we got there, and she proved to be a brigantine[79] and appeared to have been lost for some time. Her bows were sunk in the sand. Her main, fore and foretopmasts were still standing, but the main topmast gone; the bowsprit was gone also. Part of her foresail was yet fixed to the yard; the boom hung over the starboard side with part of her mainsail yet hanging in the water over the starboard quarter; her hatches were gone and I saw much sand in her hold, through which I perceived chimes of barrels[80]. Everything was gone from the quarterdeck, even the doors of the companion-way. The caboose[81] lay sunk under the bow. This vessel seems to have been about 70 tons burthen[82]. She had a black stern and on it was written in white letters Sant Pablo.

I then asked Toby if he would go down into the cabin, as she was but a little beneath the surface abaft. This he did, and brought out a well-stoppered jug of a long shape. Then he went down again and brought up an old hat, the third time a small sheet. I then cut away the fore braces and one sheet, and then put to shore where we remained for that night, exposed enough. The next morning we went off to it again; it was then quite calm. I then cut away several pieces of her sailcloth and left her. We were now forced to paddle for it, and did not get home until the third day, in the forenoon. We found all well, and they much rejoiced at our return. I then tasted of the bottle and found that it contained some fine agua ardiente.[83] I then laid it up as a reserve in the case that anyone should fall sick; and this was the first liquor stronger than water that I had tasted for above 6 years, nor did I like it in any shape.

Our young lime and orange trees came on finely, and two of the coconuts had burst out of the ground to the size of flour barrels, and had shot forth most ample leaves. The guavas came up wherever we dropped the seeds. After this, I sent the lads away on the wreck, giving them charge to make the best observations they could along the bay for anything which had drifted on shore, and to bring what they could home with them, if of any use. They were gone for three days, and on the fourth came in about noon. They had a barrel in their boat which on sight I took to be containing pitch or tar, more of the smaller rigging, a wooden bole, part of the companion-way, two small boards, a bag of nails, with an oar. They had rambled along the shore and been at the labour of parbuckleing[84] the goods into the canoe, although they did not know the use of them at this time.

The next day Harry went fishing in the lagoon and came back to tell me that he had hooked a monstrous fish, and that it had carried away his hook. 'It is a shark,' said I. 'No, no,' he replied, 'it was a large brown fish.' I then judged it either to be a Rock or a Jew Fish[85], and away we went with three conches for bait with the shark hook. When we got to the place he showed us, I threw over the bait and it was not long before the gentleman took it. Away he towed the canoe up the lagoon until he was quite spent. Our shouting brought down the girls so that they were present at the sport. It was a rockfish that weighed at least 60 pounds. We got a paddle into his mouth and then reaved[86] a rope through his gills and tied him fast to the mangroves. Harry recovered his hook also.

Just as this sport was over, Toby told Harry to listen. We all stood in suspense for a few minutes, and then we all heard the tooting of a conch shell, as at a distance. Away the lads ran and were on the cliff in a minute. There they fell to hollering out, 'Yo, yo, yo! More canoes coming!' We directly got the glass and up I went, where I could count 7 canoes all under sail and standing right in for the lagoon. This I thought rather over many, but as I had found them to be ever faithful, I plucked up my spirits. I then got into our canoe with Harry and went out to meet them; there I lay by for them. As they came in I hailed and they all then began to sing. We then stood away ahead until they entered the lagoon; I then hailed them again. I was answered, 'Amigos, Senor!' from my good friend Komaloot; and I could not help smiling to hear him salute me in Spanish, as I judged he had not many words in their language, or he had greatly deceived me.

Our ladies were waiting their landing with their children, and when they came on shore I could have wished half of them back again, they being no less than 25 in number, male and female. We showed them a kind reception and took them all up to the Castle, where such greeting began amongst the women that there never was the like. They admired my son for his light colour; and I found this to be a visit of downright curiosity to see in what way we went on.

Our Harry ran away directly to the brook, to fetch me some smooth stones to scratch down their names. Upon this my friend Komaloot ordered them all to be seated, and he then stood as spokesman. He first presented me with his wife Inna-tary, and Luta said it meant 'Yellow Flower'. Then came Owagamy and his wife Lama-atty, her cousin called Quali-rema or 'Tall Vine'; then came a brother of Mr Toby whose name was Yova-wan or 'Paddle Maker', Nocana-bura or 'Commander', a girl called Ina-linca or 'Mellow Fruit', Noonawaiah or 'The Dreamer', Razua-bano or 'Great Hunter', Kona-sove or 'Basket Maker', Futatee here before, Matta-linea or 'Red Fruit', Soro-teet or 'Crab Catcher', Gatto-loon a 'Forecaster', Latto-gamy or 'The Returner', Shoa-tate or 'Bird Catcher', Wayatuza or 'Comptroller', Zulawana here before, Gayna-sunto a 'Bewildered Person', a boy called Faribeed or 'Singing Bird', another called Muzzo-gayah a 'Fighter', a third called Koura-coon or a 'Spy', a girl called Vuna-qusta or a 'Favourite', and one yet younger aged about 13 years and called Jasa-wina or 'Honey-Sucker'.

After this, I ordered all their names to be laid up safe and they looked on it as a great honour paid to them. Our visitors were dressed and painted in a very gay manner according to their taste of things. Owagamy had a string around his head, stuck full of macaw feathers. Over his back hung the tail of a fox; at each ear hung a racoon's tail;[87] around his waist was wrapped the skin of some beast, and a large bunch of sharks' teeth at his breast with other things I knew no name for at all. Komaloot's garb was much after the same sort, except that he had a piece of looking glass dangling at his breast by a red string. The ladies had little ornament on their heads except a fine tuft of cotton on each side, but around their necks hung many strings of shells, beads and the like, also around their arms and legs; and every one had small wrappers of cotton stuff around their hips. The men each had a piece of baize, the young boys not anything.

Komaloot ordered one of the Indians to go down to the canoes and fetch up some things, and among the rest was a valuable article indeed – no less than a pair of scissors and they were presented to Luta; a piece of looking-glass; and a few rattles made from calabash shells for the child. Owagamy gave another machete. They gave us half a dozen mats, such as they use for sails and for to sleep on, some very fine shells, arrowheads made of a very hard green stone,[88] a few fish darts, one small hatchet, a few paddles, and a macaw bird of most noble plumage. For all this I returned them great thanks, observing that I was sorry we had nothing to give them in return. Upon my saying this, Owagamy laughed and said, 'What we give to our brothers and sisters, we never ask for again like children.' Upon this Lama-atty asked the name of Patty's child, and on being informed it had not a name as yet, she desired we would call it her name, which was concluded upon, and from that time it went by the appellation of Matty.

I now began to take notice that a young fellow whose name was Soro-teet alias Crabcatcher kept constantly by my Harry, and held him in talk. This made me ask if he was not a relation of his. 'Up the side,' he replied, but said that this Indian remembered me very well, having seen me a long time before. This put me on the enquiry where he could have seen me. Harry then made me understand that he was the same Indian's son I found on the Long Key at my first landing there from the schooner – all which might be very true, but he was now grown quite out of my knowledge. I then bade Harry to ask him how they came to run away and leave me to starve for want. His answer was the great fear that his mother was in that I might ill-treat her, as I looked so fierce. – So that here I had the Christian represented fiercer than the Indian savage.

I then told them that the Great One had sent us a fine fish just for when they arrived, and sent Harry and Toby to fetch it up. I then had the handsome pots or yabbas of our making brought forth, which caused some mirth. They then fell to cook the great fish, cutting it into chunks for a stew, roasting plantains and yams & co. Two or three pots were put on for our beans, peas and the like so that we made out tolerably well, although the company consisted of more than 30 people. Mr Toby waited at the table, which was the bare ground, except the place where the ladies sat; this was by way of a compliment as they had the mats under them.

When we were all satisfied, Owagamy told Toby that he might return home again with them, for that Padre Bastano was dead, and that he had never been enquired after at all. Toby, hearing this, gave me a sort of sideways look. I then told him that as his abiding with us was only during his own pleasure, he was free to return whenever he wished. Upon this Toby, casting his eye on a young girl in the company whose name was Matta-linea or 'Red Fruit', asked whither she had a husband or not. The girl looked like a fool, got up, and went to the fireside. Upon this Toby cried out, 'No man! No man!' I asked him then if she chose to become his wife, would he then choose to stay with us. Upon this he went down on one knee and began a speech in his own tongue, in order, as I judged, that they all should understand him. I then told Luta to translate it, as I saw them all well pleased, and she began thus: '*I protest before all these my people you to be my good friend and brother. When the Sun gets up and goes to sleep, when his sister the Moon comes after him to give light in the night, when blackness covers the trees and the wide sea, when I am dead in my sleep, sick or lame, and while I am able to shoot with an arrow, hunt or catch fish, dig yams or potatoes, fetch fruits, &co, &co, &co, let me remain with you. But if you, Penoly, say go, then Sama-lumy goes with his people.*'

All the ladies were in tears the whole time. Now it became my turn to speak, so I told Luta to inform them that I desired nothing more, as I liked the young fellow well. Upon this they all gave a kind of 'Hah!' as liking what I said. They then interrogated Toby and he said he should be glad to stay if the girl would stay with him as a wife, for then he could always be by me, learn my talk, and hear me speak about the strange things beyond the great water. But if the girl would not have him, he was willing to go back with them to speak for a wife. Komaloot said they could not answer if she were willing to give herself away, as she had a good father and mother, but they would represent the matter when they returned home, if the girl thought well of it. Luta then called her and put the question to her. She said she would go home first. Finding her very pleased, I asked Toby if he would go with her. He answered, 'Yes,' and thus the discourse dropped for that time.

Among the things they gave us was a piece of rough stone resembling our grindstone, which became of great use to us in sharpening our tools. And now there were so many men with us that I expressed the desire of making up a kind of shed, by way of a kitchen. This they all came into, and soon after fell to the cutting of uprights with one accord, desiring that I would direct how I would have it – so I concluded that we were hands enough to have it large enough. I then laid out the ground about 40 feet by 30 feet. After this was done I ordained Harry, Toby and 4 of their people to the fishing department and the women to stand as cooks. When all was settled we all went to work, and in about 5 days we got it completely thatched in with palmettos. My turtles went to pot freely so that there was no want all that time. There was a doorway at each end, and two places

61

open at the top for the smoke to pass out.

After all was complete, they began to prepare to return home after being with us twelve days, and Toby went with them. We went out as far as the Long Key with them. But when we came to part, Luta said she had entreated one of the young girls to tarry and live with her, but she was ashamed to ask the men. I then told her that she should have told me of it before, if the girl had a desire. Very much, she said, for she had no mother or father. I then hailed Owagamy off the point and bade her mention it to them, as my desire. Directly on their finding the child willing, she was put into our boat and returned back with us. This was Jasa-wina or the Honeysucker. We then wished them all safely home, and brought home our new maiden. I soon found the girl as glad to be with Luta, as Luta was to have her; and thus matters stood with us. We gave this young girl the name of Jessy afterwards.

We had not seen upwards of a dozen monkeys[89] in all the time of my living here, but after we had the Indian Corn[90], the matter became much altered, especially while in its green and tender state; and then we were playing a fine game ere we found out. This discovery was at a time when we were harvesting squashes at the old ground. We saw perhaps 30 of those geniuses make off and mount the trees. This was a difficulty to surmount, but as soon as I got home I went to work and contrived a sort of wind clapper to fix on a pole. This took the desired effect – not one monkey was seen for some time after; but I determined to plant some corn at home, lest we should be totally deprived of all.

It was not a little diverting, nevertheless, to see those little toads sit on the limbs of trees with an ear of corn in their hands and husk them as dexterously as we could do it. There was one truly diverting scene. I once observed an old monkey seated on a limb with two young ones; to these she gave a corn or two as they sat on each side of her. Others handed it over their shoulders to the youngsters on their backs, so conformable to the human species, that I could scarcely begrudge them a portion.

We had no account from the Indians for a long time, so that I began to think that Toby had quite gone off from his intended measures, or that something extraordinary had happened. But one day, as Harry and I were on the look out, we heard a noise as of people in the distance in the woods, and talking very loud. Harry asked me if he should halloa out. 'By no means!' said I, observing that if they were coming to us they knew the road, so I ordered him to follow me down. In a short time after Mr Toby and two other Indians arrived, one of them his brother called Yova-wan or the 'Paddle Maker', and Noona-waiah or the 'Dreamer', who had both been here before. They brought two iguanas with them, and a sort of bird unknown to me. They then asked for the girls, who all came and welcomed them. We then got victuals for them, and I observed to Toby that I thought he was dead or had determined never to return to us again. Upon this, he shook his head and then laying his hands to his knees, said, 'Toby here now, know all trees here grow. I want to see them one more time.'

'But where is the wife?' said I.

'Oh, she see one tomorrow time.'

Now, as I was thinking him a little in the dumps, I left speaking and took myself off, as thinking that Luta would soon pick out the cause of her not coming with him. After this, Luta told me that Toby had informed her that when they got back the old folks called a counsel and were all well disposed for it, but her father would not give his consent for her to leave home. But, as they found that the young pair had got a great mind to each other, to prevent further trouble they determined to give her to another, and accordingly did so. That this affair made Toby grow very sick, until it happened that a few neighbours came to visit them, among whom was a very fine young girl called Rava, with whom he fell greatly enamoured, she being much bigger and handsomer than the other. And that she had by her friends' consent agreed to be his wife, if we would allow her to return now and again to visit her friends. That Owagamy had given his word for that, and they had promised to bring her in canoes the next time, observing that his brother and Noona-waiah were to tarry with us until their arrival. I then desired to know when he expected them. 'See,' said he, *one moon and half a moon when cotton was done.'*

'Now,' said Harry, *'we are strong to go on the dead ship.'*

'You are a fool,' said I, *'She is all gone to pieces before now.'*

Nevertheless he was all for it, and in two or three days away went he, Toby, and his new messmate Noonawaiah, leaving Yovawan to tarry with us. They were absent 4 days and now the girls began to be a little clamorous. But on the 5th day I saw them coming round a point, to my great joy. It was not a wonder that they were so long away. They told me that when they came there, they could not find her; that the two trees (masts) were gone out of her, but the long tree which hung over the side, was driven on shore in the bay. They said they found ten barrels on the shore and hid them in the sand. This I liked very well. After this I sent them again and they brought home four barrels in two trips. As to the rest, they remained there.

The next thing we went upon was to pay[91] both the canoes' bottoms, and then remained in expectation of seeing or hearing from our neighbours. The lads kept a sharp look out every morning. I now caused 5 of our tortoises to be turned adrift, they becoming extremely lean through want of proper food, reserving but two against the coming of friends. And thus we went on day by day. The lads supplied plenty for our table every day by striking or with line. And now my year wanted but a few days of expiring, and we spent it in common and usual occurrences.

CHAPTER IV

The Eighth to Eleventh Years

THE EIGHTH YEAR – THE FIFTH VISIT BY INDIANS, YALUTA DIES AND SOMER ARRIVES
June 15 1754 – June 14 1755

Having now been on this shore some 7 years, I told Luta that we would have a sort of feast, so concluded to kill one turtle, and this was done. After it was brought home, I had them get everything ready, such as yams, plantains, pepper, salt & co., and made a good large feast on the next day. I then sent them out for a good mess of fish, for I expected we would have company enough tomorrow to help see it off. This I spoke as a joke, not thinking that it would really prove so. But the next day as two of them were out fishing, they spied canoes coming. Away they pushed with the glad tidings, and now Toby became quite another man, having been on the droop for a time before. I then took my glass and went up the hill, and soon saw three canoes coming in. I directly ordered our sailing boat out, and for them to get the mast and sail ready, and then dressed myself in my best attire, (viz.) first my sombrero on my head with two fine macaw feathers stuck in it, my tiger's skin then made into a jacket, the hair-side out; round my waist a belt of bass rope[1] in which hung my hatchet, at my back my bow and arrows, with a machete in my hand; and in this garb I seated myself abaft, with Harry and Noonawaiah as my two mates.

When they came nigh I bade Harry to sing; directly they began the answer. I now found them to be 6 men and 3 ladies. They proved to be Owagamy, Futatee, Nocana-bura, Komaloot, Ruzuabano, and Gaynasunto, Owagamy's wife Lama-atty, the girl called Vinaquota, and Rava the bride. The ladies were painted and dressed wondrous fine, especially the bride. We escorted them all up the lagoon, and they were mightily glad to see our ladies waiting on the shore to welcome them. They were all landed, and we then took them up to the house. Great comfort this, certainly to Mr Toby – he took the young lady by the hand and spoke a few soft things to her; and while this was doing I had a full survey of her person, and must needs own that she was the finest Indian girl I had seen as yet.

After they had been in conversation about an hour or so with our women, I then enquired of Komaloot if all parties were fully agreed, and I was answered that they were. I then told them through Harry to assemble in a circle around me, which they did. I then called Toby to me and asked him to take the girl by the hand; this he did. Then I enquired her name and was told that it was Rava Ocuma or Ravacuma. On this I joined their hands, and bade Luta to tell them that I should always esteem them as man and wife. Upon this, they all fell to clapping their hands and shouting. This done, I bade Harry to fetch me one of our brooms, and I caused them both to jump over it[2]. Now Harry, observing this, very politely stepped up to me and asked why I had not done the like with his sister, so to please him I took my partner by the hand and did the like. Upon this, he snatched hold of Patty and they repeated the same, to the no small diversion of them all. Owagamy wanted to know the meaning of it, and I told him that it was a common custom among my people when they had a mind to marry. After this, we all went to feasting and spent the remainder of the day quite happy. The young couple were put to bed in the kitchen, and the next morning they turned to and built themselves a small wigwam opposite our dwelling. The party remained with us for above a week, and took their leave of us in a very friendly manner, to return home.

Now my family stood thus: myself and Luta with our son Owen, Mr Harry and his wife Patty and daughter Matty, Mr and Mrs Toby and the girl Jessy, nine in number, and we all lived in love and true good fellowship until about 6 weeks after, when fortune began to envy our happiness. Luta was at this time nigh her time, and soon after was delivered of another son, but she survived only a few days. This I thought would have gone near to breaking my poor heart, and especially as she left me a young babe to bring up, I knew not how. Patty still had milk, so was forced to become a nurse afresh. This child I called Morgan, which signifies born of the coast[3]. We had lived together upward of 4 years in strict conjugal love, and never had man a more loving partner.

As soon as I could summon up my spirits, I was under the hard necessity of ordering the funeral myself, with a leaden heart, and at last called the two lads to me, poor creatures, who were seemingly both in as much trouble as myself. Patty became almost mad; she would not leave the corpse for one moment. I signified to them that they should dig a grave among the orange trees, after the best fashion they could. I was forced to oversee it myself. They dug down about 5 feet, and then came to the hard rock, so were forced to desist. Now the reader may picture to himself a scene moving enough, to behold me sitting at the head of the corpse in a stupid sort, with my son Owen asking me when his mam[4] would get up. Patty stood on one side with her child in her arms silently weeping over the body, and Rava Ocuma with Jessy were like two creatures quite lost to all sense, especially Jessy. This poor wretch did nothing but look on me, and howl, for she loved her mistress greatly as the deceased had shown great respect to her.

Before she died, Luta desired that I would sit down by her, and I took her by the hand, which she squeezed, and said she was going to the Old People of long times, and that it was her great desire when she was 'fast asleep' that I would return back to my own country with her two children, if the Great One would let me go; and if I did, to say to my country-women not to be angry with her for keeping me there as she was sure, had I been so much beloved by one of them, she should never have heard of me at all, for that I should then never have come so far to get a poor Indian wife. All she desired, I told her I would perform if God pleased, and then was forced to go out to vent my grief. In about half an hour after, she expired, leaving her hand in the same position as I had left it.

After she had been dead about thirty hours, I was forced to give order for her burial. Patty and Ocuma bound up the corpse a little as they could, and then I told Harry to go to the head and Toby to the feet, then they lifted up the corpse. I took my poor boy in my hand, and the three girls came behind with the children in their arms. After the body was laid in, I made signs that they should cover it up with the earth. But now was my poor heart rent with the outcry of my little Owen when he saw his mother covered with mould; therefore I told them to take the children back to the house. In all this time none of them spoke a word to me, but now it brought on a general lamentation. I then returned, fell flat on my face in the entrance and gave full scope to my passion. I lay thus for over an hour, but finding no end likely to this clamour I got up, and called them all before me and thus began:

'You very well know, my good friends, the great regard my poor Luta had for you all, and you certainly must be truly sensible to what a great loss such a good woman must be to your friend Penoly; but you know that we must all die. The Great One has now taken away from me what I most loved, on purpose to see how you will use me when I am troubled. Therefore I hope you will all do the best in your power standing as my friends as long as you are with me, that you will show by your best endeavours that you will make up my loss the best way you can. Love my children for you know they have no longer a mother to look upon.'

Hitherto Harry had never spoke one word to me or anyone else from the hour of her death, but now they all declared that they would stand my friend even to life and limb. I thanked them, and then resolved to compose my mind the best way possible. A short while before her death I had determined to clip my beard with the scissors, but now determined it should continue to grow.

Harry and Patty would frequently go and seat themselves upon the grave for an hour or two, conversing together. I became so indifferent after this happened that I cared little how things went, except I took good heed to my two children, and I must say Patty and Jessy used their best endeavours to discharge their duty toward them. Ocuma, being as yet incapable of speaking English, could do no more than silently bemoan the children and me. About a month after this had happened, Patty lost her daughter Matty in a kind of fit, and we buried her by the side of Luta.

The place now became quite melancholy, so that I went out more often than before with one or other of the lads, and it was on one of these trips that we found a large lump of ambergris[5], as I judged it to be by its strong smell, although I had never seen any of it in my life. It weighed 150 pounds or so. We laid it on a shelf by the rocks and laid aloe leaves about it, as I found that some sort of insects ate it. This stuff was of a dark grey colour and of no manner of use to me, but as I thought, if it was really the true thing it must be of much worth, could it be transported to Europe.

One day, as I returned from fishing with Toby, on my entering into our dwelling I found Harry and the girls, very earnest, over those stones I had inscribed, for I had placed them on a row above the child's reach in order to preserve them, and had added one for my poor Luta. On enquiring what they were about, Harry said they were learning them to talk.

'How so?' said I.

'Oh,' said he, 'we know who they all are very well.'

That cannot be, I thought, but on my making trial I was astonished to find that they could call them all over distinctly by name. I could not but wonder at it, but it plainly showed that they were capable of remembrance, so as to be able to learn all those stones by some distinct mark, colour, shape or magnitude; but it came into my head that they must have learnt them as they were arranged. This I was determined to know, and told them all to withdraw while I changed their places. This I did, and then called them in again, but to my confusion they were still as perfect as before I moved the stones.

Some time after this we had a few days of very dirty weather, with the wind from the southwest and great thunder, lightning and rain. Now it chanced as Harry went to look out, after it had lulled for a time, he came driving down to me open-mouthed and said that there was a great ship coming at us. This put us all in a flutter. Up I ran and saw plainly a large ship heeling on her larboard side on the Key Reef, with her head to shore, and running her colours out as a signal of distress. I then got my glass and could perceive as I thought, Dutch colours, she being about 6 miles from us in a direct line.

How to act, I could not tell, as I was not certain of her being a real Dutchman, but the cause was to do good if I could. In the meantime, the wind shifted and fell more. Now, thinks I, go I will somehow or other, and ordered them to get ready the boat, with fire tackling. I then got out a shirt from my poor store, and in I jumped with Toby. When we got to the point of our lagoon, we made up a good fire and I fixed up my shirt (as a flag). Soon after, we perceived a boat put off directly for us. On this, I got into our boat, thinking that now I was 'in for it', and I would give all up to Providence; and back we hurried as fast we could.

When I got home, I dressed myself as I had done when the Indians last came, and took my little Owen in the boat with me. Harry, seeing this, said they would come too. 'Well, then, first get your arms,' said I. He was not long before he came down to the point after us, bringing the poor girls and children also. This vexed me highly, but as I plainly saw he did not know what he was doing, I held my peace, having enough on my head at that time. When we all showed ourselves at the fire, they had showed a white flag abaft, then a Dutch flag then a white flag again. Now I was strongly agitated between hope, fear and desire.

As they came near, I told Harry and Toby to follow me and do all they saw me do. Then we left the women and children by the fire and away I marched with my two messmates behind me to meet them. When they came abreast of us, a man stood up in the boat and hailed us. I clapped my hands to my mouth and answered, 'Hollow!' On this they pulled in for the shore, and there they lay on their oars to view us. I could now plainly see that the boat was Dutch-built, and that there were nine men in her. Seeing them thus in suspense I called out, 'From whence came ye?'

They answered but I could not make it out, and then came in, to land. Now a man jumped on the beach and, saying something to me, they put off from the shore again. The man left on the beach then called out to me, pulling off his cap at the same time. I returned the compliment, but could not understand him, After this, I went up to him and held out my hand, saying, 'An Englishman.'

Upon this, he shook me heartily by the hand, and told them all that they might come on shore, as I judged, for so they all did, gathered all around me in amazement, then shook me by the hand. My lads seeing this did the like, but what to make of us was their greatest wonder, for not a soul of them could speak English. But I gave them to know, the best I could, that I was cast away like themselves, and had been on this shore for above 7 years. I found that they could understand 7 years, by their aiming to repeat it. Then they surveyed me from top to toe, lifting up their hands and saying, 'Ah, boor Mon!'

Now I found that they began to fret, because they could not understand me. But a lad said 'Godart Somer Engels spraken en der schip.'[6] This put them in a good humour again, and I invited them to walk with us to our fire. This they complied with, so far as to accompany us in their boat. Here three of them landed again. No sooner did any of my people see them, than off they ran, but I called them back and they came, trembling with fear. One of the men asked me if they were my 'vrowen,'[7] as I thought. Then they said that they would go 'on the schip bring Godart Somer comen on lant' with them, but I made signs for them to go home with me. This they declined, but concluded that one should stay with me. As a man offered to stay with me, we all shook hands then, and off they put for the vessel.

After they were gone, I asked this man his name and he said it was Jan Brill. Now, finding the time growing so heavy on our hands, for the want of understanding each other, and as he appeared quite disconsolate, I told Toby to go with the small canoe to fetch some victuals. In the meantime, the man and I walked to and fro along the beach. He held me now and again in talk, but as I could not understand him, it was of little purpose; and thus we remained until Toby returned. Now, Harry and Toby were so full of it that they would have fed the poor man. Harry would now and then take him by the hand, and say he was like me, meaning cast away.

Some time after, we saw the boat go alongside, and about dusk they returned and brought Godart Somer with them. They had not been landed long before it came into my head, that I must for certain have seen the young fellow before, as his countenance appeared familiar to me. I enquired from whence they came. He told me the Texel, and that their ship's name was the *Dertroost*, and that they were bound for Buenos Aires.

'*Did you ever sail out of England?*' said I.

'*Yes,*' he said, '*three voyages.*'

I then asked him if he ever sailed on a ship called the *Harrington*[8] out of London. He paused awhile and then replied, '*Oh, no, neet! Over Ick vas on bord dat schip. I been gon on shore en der Gravesend.*' Directly, I found him to be the person I took him for, as he was one of the supernumeraries put on shore at that place. They were all pleased at this, and began to grow impatient for him to ask me questions as to whether I knew the coast well, and tell me that their skipper desired that I would come on board with them.

I told him that I was so far from knowing anything of the coast, that I knew not where I was myself, but if they wanted to be informed about the shoals near my habitation, I was at the captain's service; but as to my going on board, it would be of no manner of use except to oblige him, and told him that I did not care to go with them as I expected another squall from the same quarter. And as for their impatience, it was my opinion that she would never more be got off from that place, because she would sow[9] down in the sand and perhaps was bilged now. But they would not think so, and begged that I would come off as early in the morning as I could, to show them some channel, if they could haul her off by any means. Now it came on to rain again, and we soon lost sight of her. Shortly after, the wind chopped round to the southward, and freshened up and increased, so that I did not choose to remain where we were with our little family. I then told them that I must return home, and if they chose to go with me they were most welcome, as I thought they could not pretend to get on board that night, without danger of filling their boat by the great sea, which would soon set in if the wind should increase. But they chose to make the trial and we parted.

All this time, the wind strengthened, and when we got round the point we were as safe as in a mill pond. They laboured at their oars for some time, while I remained within the point, much troubled in mind as thinking that should it come to a gale, what an unhappy condition those poor souls would then be in. But a few minutes after, the wind increased so strongly that I saw them pull round for the shore again. Directly, I landed Harry and told him to run along the shore and wait for them, then get into their boat and pilot them in. Soon after, this was the case, and away they came in after us, and soon after we all went on the shore as wet as drowned rats. I showed them into the kitchen and got a large fire made up, to dry their clothes for them. They all looked much cast down, as if they were expecting a miserable account of things next morning.

I took John Brill and Somer up to my lodging, thinking they might want to have some counsel with me, for sleep never once visited us all that night. Thus, we sat and talked, but Mr Brill wept much. At last we got up and went to look out, visited the kitchen, and found them all fast asleep and snoring as though no trouble had befallen them. I then called Ocuma and told her to order some torches and bring them in. After Toby had fixed them, he kindled the fire. And now the wind abated. At length towards morning it fell stark calm. Then I proposed to Somer that we would awake the people and go in quest of the rest, as I told them that we might depend on the fact that they had never stayed with the vessel, for I was certain that the sea had made a fair breach over her on that reef. This Mr Brill and Somer agreed to, but when we came to arouse the crew, they were so ignorant of their situation that they acted very foolishly, running against the thatch walls and asking nonsensical questions, as Somer told me. But the trouble soon brought them to reason, and I ordered Harry to get our canoe ready, to go with me.

This was about 4 in the morning and away we all went, leaving Toby with the women. When we got some distance out, we saw the ship had swung round and lay on her beam-ends. No boat appeared to be near her. Mr Brill then wrung his hands, like a man in despair. Somer told me he wanted me to go on board with him, and to go into their boat. This I did, and we put the canoe to a killick.[10] We then rowed away for their vessel. Soon after this, Somer called out in Dutch that he saw a longboat. I soon saw her, and people walking on a point above the Old Cave. When we came in from the beach, I saw 5 men who all ran and showed much gladness to see their shipmates again. Mr Brill then asked for the skipper. They said he insisted to abide with the ship with 5 more, and they knew not whether they had survived that dreadful night or not.

Now there was no time to be lost, so off they put for the ship, but soon returned saying that there was not one soul left alive anywhere on board. I then asked Somer which was the mate, and he pointed to him, and I went and shook hands with him. I then desired Somer to inform him that I desired that they should all return back with me to my place, and there we should hold a consultation on what was first to be done, as the ship was lost past all redemption. While I was speaking I observed one man who went up the beach and seated himself on the grass to bemoan his wretched fate, as I judged, but to my great surprise saw him very deliberately draw out of his pocket a pipe and a pouch of tobacco, then fill his pipe. After this, he drew out a tinder horn[11], struck fire and lit his pipe, then with much composure clasped his two arms around his shins and began to puff away, without any seeming concern at all.

They soon came to a conclusion and away we all put for the Old Cave. There we landed and got a parcel of roots and the only turtle we had in store. After this, we all put away, and put Harry on board his canoe, and so returned to our place where 14 of them landed, being all who were left alive. Now, I had enough on my head to have so many mouths to feed, and knew not for what length of time. And should they take it into their minds to have full possession (of our family and home), we had no power of resisting.

Then I asked Somer what was the mate's name, and he told me it was Jacob van Tulden.[12] Upon this, I welcomed him to my poor habitation as an asylum, and desired him that he would favour me so far as to be a friend, in endeavouring to protect our girls from any insult which might be offered them. This, Somer told him in Dutch privately, and he then took me by the hand, promising to do all in his power on that score. As these men talked a language unknown to all my people, the girls kept aloof, being not a little afraid of them. Mr Van Tulden, observing the colour of my children, asked if one of the girls was not my wife, but I gave Somer information and he told him of the loss of my wife, and that two of those were wives to my two friends. After this, the cookery began, and we all ate together except the females and children.

I then made Godart Somer my interpreter, speaking always through his mouth, telling him that it was highly necessary for them to appoint some to go fishing with one of my men; otherwise we should soon come to a starving condition, being so many. Van Tulden and Brill, who I found to be the boatswain[13], said it was a just observation. The next thing was to order others for fresh gangs, and after a while it was settled thus: the mate, Somer, myself and 5 others to go away in the longboat for the vessel; some to cut wood; Mr Brill to have Toby with him to guard the girls and children; while Harry went with others after our food. When things were all adjusted, we prepared to go off to the ship. The weather was as calm as a clock, so that we got alongside of her in a couple of hours.

The first thing that struck my eye was a yellow cat[14], running along the windward side, mewing in a sad manner. The ship we found bilged, with the entire lower tier under a foot or two of water. Then the mate sent some of them down into the steerage, where they remained for some time. I now bade Somer to inform the mate that, as I was certain that there were no inhabitants except Indians along this coast, I could advise him of nothing better than to get what they could out of her, for their own use. Otherwise I was sure that the natives would come and plunder all, as soon as they spied the wreck. This alarmed him; and then we got down into the cabin, where we found that everything had all gone to leeward and was capsized in a confused manner; but what was singular, that little water was to be seen abaft. This I attributed to her being so high abaft, and she was more by the head also.

The rest of the hands I found, were got into the hold, and as they came on deck were all 'in liquor'. As as now they were all become masters, there was 'nobody left to throw the water out of the longboat'[15] as the sailors term it. I had not a word to say. The mate found a keg of gin in the steerage and took a small sup, then handed it to me, but I declined it. Just then, casting my eyes around, I spied one of those precious things called a biscuit. Eagerly I snatched it up, and said; 'God be praised!' then took a bite, tasting bread once more after being above 7 years without one morsel. Now, observing Somer to become a little intoxicated, I made bold to chide[16] him, saying they knew not how precious their time was, and that if they did not bestir themselves with speed, perhaps all hopes would be forever cut off. This he took kindly, and told the rest what I had said. They seemed to be a little more on their guard after this, and Somer told the mate that there were two of their people dead in the forecastle, as they told him. These were two of the hands who had perhaps done that miserable folly, as seeing death before their eyes, and had taken their fill of liquor to forget death. He said that their names were Verwilt and Poersen.

After this, I happened to ask Somer to beg the mate to look for some paper for me, if there was any there. 'Paper,' said he, 'dare is more as (than) a boat load on bord de schip.' Nothing could have pleased me better. I then asked him to mention it to Mr Van Tulden, who as soon as he was sensible to my desire, took the hint, and running forward by the mast, clapped his hands on a vast bale of it. Seeing me so elevated, he took out a knife and began to cut away, and soon discovered me paper enough, then going aft into his cabin produced me a bottle of ink as I thought. These articles I took plenty of, and got them into the boat. He then went to work in the cabin, and got out a parcel of clothing, several guns and pistols, some bedding and other things, and then he brought out a quadrant[17]. I then took out a compass, as it seemed only to be unhung; and all these we got into the boat. The people got out two barrels of beef[18] with three kegs of gunpowder, brandy and gin; and then we put off for the first time and got back safe to our company, where I found that the girls were become more free. This was owing to Brill's good conduct.

Now the mate reflected that he had forgotten to hunt for the logbook, and to bring shot, bullets and other things of material use. So away they went next morning by daylight for the wreck. I remained at home. About the same time in the evening they came back, chock full. This they did daily until they had brought off a prodigious quantity of things, until the wind came around to the north and then blew fresh, so that the sea soon beat in on the vessel's upper works. – I forgot to observe that the cat jumped into the boat when we made the first trip, but no sooner did he land on shore that he fell so greedy on the fish garbage that he became unable to quit the place, until Nature, being so over-charged, threw it off again or it must have died.

After they had got everything from the ship which could be got at, they began to consult what was the best step to be taken next. This I could have no hand in, as I knew no more of the coast than a child, so left them to their own counsel for that.

Now, while matters were thus in agitation as to how they should act for the future, we had much trouble to encounter, as thus. Although Mr Vantulden and the bosun used every method to keep good order while on shore, there was plenty of liquor, so it was totally out of their power to keep the people sober. Then Somer acquainted me that if I did not provide to secure some of it for my own use, it would soon be all gone, and privately conveyed by Mr Vantulden's order, four anchors[19] of brandy and some few kegs of gin away by the assistance of Harry and Toby, while they were all sleeping.

After, they concluded to go to the southward in the longboat and to leave the yawl with me. I asked them where they intended first to touch at, and they told me at Portobello[20] if they could reach it, and that they intended to keep inshore along the coast. I then desired them to inform me what latitude they thought we were in, and they said they judged about 11d and 30m north[21]. Then I enquired what name the country bore, and they said that they believed it was Costa Rica.

I desired Mr Vantulden to leave the date of the year and day of the month, as I was quite ignorant as to any certainty about it. He then asked me for the bottle he had given me, and I told Harry to fetch it, and I then expressed a desire that I would contrive some sort of a pen. This I was under the necessity of being beholden to one of the parrots for, and made a sort of pen with one of her feathers. He then bade Harry to get a little water in a small shell, and when it was brought he took the bottle and emptied forth a powder of a grey colour and then with his finger produced ink, being the first ink powder[22] I had ever seen. He then told me that Somer should speak it in English, or I should not understand his writing, so I had best write it myself. This was done, and I found out that it was thus: Anno 1754 and the month of August the 5th day; so that by my own account I had missed in my reckoning about six weeks, somehow or other, but it was a matter of no great moment to me.

Now, there were two fellows among them who were absolute brutes, and void of all grace or generosity, by name Claus Deckker and Adam Brandt. These two hellhounds, for they deserve no better title, took occasion to pick a quarrel and demanded the liquor that they said was missing. All argument had no effect on them. Brandt went about cursing and raving like the devil that he was. I offered it back again, but all the rest insisted I should not return it by any means, for I had been a true friend to them all. About half an hour after this, as Mr Vantulden and Brill were sitting at victuals with me, we heard a pistol go off. Up we jumped. I snatched a machete and each of them took a pistol and out we ran. The noise came from the cook-room as I thought. The girls were running away with the children up the hill, screaming like they were distracted. Now my blood began to mount and away I flew to the kitchen. But just as we entered, off went another. We then ran back and stood together, not knowing what to do, when out rushed Somer like a fury, with a pistol in his hand.

We then all three stood on our own defence, but he called out to me saying, 'Never mind, Skipper, never mind! Dat divil is gone pon Hell now!'

'For God's sake,' said I, 'Somer, have you gone mad too? What is the matter at once, or I will cut you down!'

'Vel, dan, dat divil Brandt he vill say Toby hites da chin. He say neet him do ut. Dan dis Hell's son he shoot him in van minuet. Out dan I rones and plows out his pranes, and dat is all.'[23]

We then ran into the kitchen and found Toby rolling in blood. I stood like a man thunder-struck. And now all became confusion and noise. The mate and the boatswain then called Somer and me out to them, and then demanded who were on their side, when one and all came over to us – even Deckker himself, as through fear now his colleague was dead. After strict enquiry we found that there was no kind of plot at all, but that all had taken place from that wretch's own jealousy of my poor Toby, poor fellow, who innocently lost his life by it, to my great grief.

Everyone highly commended Somer's action, and after all became a little quiet again, I gave orders for the burial of my poor, unfortunate, faithful friend, and they laid him by my own wife, on the other side. Ocuma would not be seen but shut herself up, and all my pleadings could have no power over her, for she remained in the back part of my dwelling for two days, without being seen at all. At last, by much entreaty, we got her out so emaciated, that it was wonderful to see her in so short a time. But I was forced to let her have her own way, as I knew she had lost so great a friend, and I as fine a fellow as ever was born.

Now some of them talked of burying Brandt, but I absolutely refused it, saying that no murderers should be laid anywhere near my peaceful habitation. Then the majority said he should be taken and sunk off at sea, for sharks' meat, and this was done accordingly.

They then began to talk of leaving my place, and made me an offer of a place in the longboat if I had any desire to leave the place I was then in. But I thanked them for their kind offer and said that as I had two young children left me to take care of, I thought it my duty to stand their true father, as perhaps should I leave them they would become mere savages – and that would remain on my spirits the longest day I should live.

The mate, soon after matters became reconciled again, called me aside and told me that Brill and Somer had been talking with him on an affair of much concern to him, meaning Somer. 'Well,' said I, 'can I be of any service in the matter?'

'Yes,' said Somer, 'I bin saying met Mr Vantulden, as you vil ick sal stay hare und liven met you, as I ben feared for Deckker he vil go put me pon chail ven ick sal comen en Oland, as you knowen for vat.'[24]

'Is the mate willing?' said I.

'Yes, besure,' said he, 'all mine people sayen so, it is petter for me.'

I then asked him if he had a wife; if so, I thought it more expedient for him not to remain with me, but to return to some other part of the world, where there was a probability of providing for his family.[25] But he answered that he had none to care for but himself, and that he was no way inclined to run himself into danger, while it was in his power to prevent it.

'Come on, then,' said I, 'Old shipmate, and I shall be proud to have you for my companion, so now you may let them all know that you and I are one, and that you are fully out of Deckker's power (to harm you). Now you can bid him defiance.'

Then the mate called Brill the boatswain and they both shook me by the hand, then told Somer that whatever they had no direct call to carry with them, was for our use. I told them that we must certainly acknowledge this as a great favour at their hands. They made answer that they were all certain that I owed them nothing but good will, and that they should take care to report my Christian-like behaviour to their owners, if ever they lived to return to Holland. Mr Vantulden then told Godart Somer to call all the men together, and then retired into the house where, seating himself at my table, he took pen, ink and paper and drew up a sort of petition[26] in Dutch, then read it over to them, and they all with one accord signed their names to it.

The substance of which was that after the loss of the ship under Captain Meert, with part of the crew, that a certain friend, a subject of Great Britain shipwrecked or cast away on the coast some years before and there residing, had through the kind assistance of Providence been greatly aiding, and did everything in his power toward their immediate relief. To which he asked them all if they were free and willing to put their names. They all answered, 'Yaw, yaw, yaw,' and kindly shook hands with me all around. The names of those who signed are as follows: Jacob van Tulden, Jan Brill, Adam Oest, Harman Byvank, Wouter Meyer, Abert Dubbels, Godart Somer, Claess Deckker, Peter Bylert, Cornelius de Man, Teysen Willems, Davit Oert, and Joust van Drill, a boy.

I then begged that Somer might translate it for me, that I might have a copy of the same to keep by me, and they told me to do so, which I did. Mr Vantulden then mentioned to them the affair of Somers remaining with me, and they all agreed that they thought him much in the right to do so. Nevertheless they all said that what he had done was no more than common justice, as they thought that the taking of Brandt's life was ridding the world of a great villain. After this, they made all ready, as fast as possible, having fitted up the longboat to the best advantage for the run, and got on board all they could conveniently carry. The carpenter Adam Oest had caulked[27] her afresh, and now they only waited a favourable wind. About three days later, it came around to the northeast, and then they began to muster all hands, being 12 in number.

I then told Somer to speak to the mate, and tell him that it was my earnest request that he would do me the favour of not mentioning anything concerning me being here, when they should come amongst the Spaniards, as he knew my reasons, and that he would not fail to forward my letter to my mother by all means possible. All this he faithfully engaged to do, if he lived to get home again. And now, as they were just on the go, I summoned all my folks. Mr Vantulden then kissed the girls and children with tears floating in his eyes, shook hands with Harry and all the crew followed the example, then turning to me, offered to put a few pistoles[28] (gold coins) into my hand. But I bid Somer inform him that I should think myself almost as bad as Brandt should I dare to take it, knowing that it could not be of any use to me as I was so situated, but that it might prove of great benefit to them where they were going.

He then laid his arms over my shoulders and said, 'You ben wan goot vrind, mine hare,' then turning to my old shipmate said something in Dutch and dropped on his knees. This I took (understood) directly and as they all knelt, I made a motion to my folks and we all joined them, and by his behaviour he seemed to me very devout. They then began to sing a psalm, or rather a sort of hymn as I thought. When they had done, they all got up and took their leave of me and all the rest in a most hearty way; but just as they were stepping onboard I called for a large bottle they had given me, and made them all take a parting drop of brandy with me. Then they shoved off and we gave them three cheers. After this ceremony was passed, they began to row away down the lagoon, and we all ran up the hill to see them out. When they got out so as to give the reef a good berth[29], then they bore away before it, and about two hours later, we lost sight of them as they doubled a point.

They were with us from the first time of their landing about three weeks, and took their departure on the 30th day of August, anno 1754. And now I must make my candid declaration that Vantulden, Brill, Bylert, Oest and indeed all, except that fool Deckker, behaved to us in all respects like honest men. During the whole time they remained with us, I made all the three girls sleep in the internal part of the dwelling, as I judged that precaution best, finding some of the men a little too fond of Jessy; but Ocuma kept a keen eye on her, by my direction.

I now began to think it necessary to keep a new sort of regulation in the family, as Toby was dead, and another in his room (place) who it was possible would not be quite so tractable as the other, to my mind. And soon began a serious conversation with Somer, as that his stay with me being absolutely his own choice, I begged he would take my advice in all respects, knowing as I had been here for so long a time, I said that I for certain knew the natural tempers of the Indians better than he possibly could; and that if he strictly studied to be my friend, that I should use all my best endeavours to make all things as easy to him as lay in my power. That he had won the love of Harry, I was positive by the noble part he had acted, in revenging the death of Harry's countryman and friend. Somer said that he should abide by my council, as I knew full well he was a stranger. I then told him that he might fall to, and Harry should help him to fit up a good berth in the kitchen to sleep in; and then they went about it.

Now I resolved to take Rava-Ocuma to myself as a wife. This I had the greater mind to do, as thinking that perhaps Somer might pay his address to her. And for to put it out of all hazard, I took an opportunity to give Patty notice of my intentions, and to mention it to her in their own language, as Rava-Ocuma had not enough English to understand me. After this, in about an hour Patty came and called me aside, and told me that Ocuma had said that she must do all things, as I would have her to do if I thought her good enough, and that she would willingly serve my children and me with all her heart. 'Then tell her to come into the house with me,' said I, and away Patty went and brought her. I then told Patty to call messmate Somer and the rest in. When they were all assembled I took Ocuma by the hand, and declared before them all that I took her as my wife, and mother to my children. Nothing could go beyond the joy they all expressed on the occasion; and thus I became a married man again, as I may say.

The ship showed herself above water for a long time after this, and Somer went off to her with Harry now and then, bringing back what they could come at, as they found opportunities. I had now been here approaching eight years, and everything proved quite agreeable. My new friend acted in all respects as became his condition. But one morning early, Godart came in and informed me that he saw 5 Indians coming down the hill, and caught up his gun. 'What are you at?' said I, 'don't terrify yourself, they are all my friends; you may be certain of that. But go and call Harry and his wife here.'

Now, when the Indians observed that I had another white man in my company, they halted until I beckoned them, when they advanced, saluting me in a very kind way. These Indians were Vinniquote or the 'Smoker' and brother to Ocuma, Selacato or a 'Joyous Person' – these two strangers were conducted hither by Owagamy, Futatee and Noonawaiah, my old acquaintances as I may say.

Owagamy asked directly for Luta. Upon this I withdrew to a distance, leaving Harry and his wife to recite the whole melancholy story, which took up almost an hour. All this time, I kept out of sight, to give them the opportunity. After this, I returned and seated myself alone, but no sooner had I done so than my three friends all came to me, and showed the greatest tokens of compassion in plain and unfeigned consolation. They then all hugged Somer as though they could have eaten him. They told Harry that they were well pleased to learn that I took poor Toby's widow for my own wife, as it showed the true regard I had for him, as they also did the like amongst good friends.[30] They told us that they had seen a boat full of white men pass by their shore. Harry told them they were messmate Somer's friends. When they learnt this, they said had they known that, and had they landed among them, they should have used them as well as ourselves, observing that if I used their people so favourably, it was their duty to do the like by mine – drawing this parallel.

Owagamy told Harry that firm friends should be compared to a strong man whose two arms assisted each other to fight, and defend the body from injuries; while his two legs were the mutual supporters of his body while he ran, leaped & co. I answered that Mr Somer and I were greatly beholden to him and his people, and should use our best endeavours to continue the old friendship. Owagamy then desired me not to be cast down, saying that as to my loss, he thought that I was well recompensed for the Spirit of Luta was now centred in the heart of Ocuma, and that of Toby in the Soul of my new friend, pointing to my shipmate Somer, saying that if he had not possessed as good a Spirit as Toby, he would not have revenged his death. Then Owagamy observed that we did not perhaps take the same conduct as the Indians did whenever they took Fool-Water[31]. For on all such adventures it was their standing rule to lay aside their arms, and to order a certain person to take care of the true things, lest when they should become as foolish as the water was itself, and they should revenge the deaths of their Old Fathers[32] a thousand moons ago.

The Indians stayed with us four days, and I gave each one of them a piece of woollen cloth that we had got from the wreck. Somer desired Harry to ask if they would bring some tobacco with them, when they should next visit us, and they said we should have enough. Then they departed. Shortly after they were gone, Ocuma asked Harry if Somer was not younger than me. I told him to let her understand that he was my elder, and that she would soon see his beard become long also from want of a razor – and this remark put me on trimming my own with the scissors. I had humoured my whiskers so that they turned up finely. As for brother Harry, he plucked his out by the roots after his own country's fashion.

It was wonderful to see what a quantity of goods we had got together from the wreck; it took us two days to stow things away for my own advantage. We could now dress ourselves in Dutch clothes, which I did at times to divert the Indians. We wanted not for strong liquors, yet at times I could have wished not to have had one drop, as my friend Harry had got too great a relish for it.

This put me on a scheme to wean him, if possible at once. I took a good time, when he was absent, and conveyed a measure of Groupar Slime[33] into a bottle, then filled it with brandy and gin mixed, then hid it for my view until a fair opportunity. Soon after this, he asked for some. I then took occasion to tell him that if he loved it so much, it would cause him to hate all his best friends, saying it was not made to make men mad, but to use when they were sick[34]. So a drop served for that time; but before night Harry told me that he was sick.

'Are you very sick?' I replied.

'Yes, yes, very!' said he.

'Oh, then you shall have enough of it Harry, to be sure; and when you have taken what *quantity you like, go to sleep.'* This took[35], and I gave him the bottle. He took it off, quite pleased, to his lodgings, and was not long without a very good suck[36], undoubtedly.

Now, as we did not see him for some hours, I sent to enquire after him. They found him fast asleep, nor did I see him all the evening. But after we were all gone to bed, Patty came to waken us, crying that Harry was sick, sick. Now as she stood with a torch of pitch burning in her hand, and showing a most dismal face, it put me in mind of the midnight operations of witchcraft. Nevertheless, we got up to save appearances, and I showed much seeming concern. The poor girls were all in tears, so that Jessy ran to call Somer. No sooner did he come, than like a true Dutchman he cried, *'Oh! Dat felow is tronken, he is trunk, dat is all.'*

And indeed the poor fellow had taken such a quantity that I began to dread the consequences. He had almost finished the bottle, and it had worked him fore and aft at no small rate[37]. The next morning, he began to come to a little, but was very stupid and sick. No reason was to be got from him all day. I told them to inform him how vexed I was, and to say that if he had died, his friends would lay his death at my door. Soon after he came to me, and begged pardon, saying that he would never have one more drop in his life. I then told him that if he was resolved to go after poor Toby, he could not lay his death to me, having been informed of alcohol's true use before, but that he would not take my advice.

'What would you have had to say,' said I, *'if it had made you as mad as the white man Brandt, and you then had shot me?'* This was enough.

'No, no, my good brother Penoly! The Great One made me sick on purpose!'

'Well, then,' said I, *'do you want any more of it? There is enough left.'* But off he ran, and not one drop more would he ever taste. As for the girls, they could not be brought to taste it at all. This turned my shipmate against it, so that we had it in plenty, without much use.

It may not be much out of character if I mention the odd behaviour of our Indians when they first saw me begin to write my Journal. They would gather round me and whisper to each other, and if they chanced to crowd me too much, if I did but put my pen towards them, they would jump back as much terrified. And one day, as I was reading it over to Somer, Harry said that now he was sure that I was a very cunning man, because I could make all my old words speak again quite new, and that I could make dead people talk. *'How so?'* said I.

'Did I not hear my sister Luta talk to Mr Somer,' said he, *'just now? And she is yonder in the grave,'* pointing that way. This made me smile and I observed to him that I would make little Owen do so soon. *'Ay, ay,'* said he, *'when he has got a beard as long as yours.'* Sometimes he would touch the nib of the quill pen, and say no wonder birds could learn to talk, for he supposed it all came out of their wings. – I met with great difficulty in getting a knife sharp enough for pen-making. My pens, too, they were of a brittle kind of quills, as of Turkey Buzzard[38] and from Hawks and Bald Eagles.

After we all became well settled I asked Somer one day where he was born. He told me Middleburg in Zeland[39].

Do you not remember Peter Cass and George Nielsen, your countrymen, on board the Harrington?' said I[40].

Yes,' he said, *'very well.'*

I then told him that Cass had died at Kingston, Jamaica, that same voyage. This discourse carried on, and talking of the war, he observed to me that it was peace now between England, France and Spain. I asked him for how long. He said that in the year

1748 peace was made[41]. I was glad of the news, as thinking that should the Spaniards find me now, perhaps I might meet with more favour from them.

I had been for a considerable time at my Journal, day by day, before I could bring it down to this period of time; and as to what preceded, it has all been collected as I could best remember. But I persuade myself that nothing of any note has escaped, remembrance having been careful to retain all I thought in any way worthy. But I must observe that in regard to Indian information, spelling their names and the like, I do not affirm them to be exact, as a man must be born among them before he shall be able to give a true pronunciation, or be able to copy their ideas and manner of conveying sentiments.

THE NINTH YEAR – SOMER WANTS A WIFE, AND JOB IS BORN
June 15 1755 – June 14 1756

Ninth year commenced. We had much business on our hands over the last year, much interest and much trouble, and now it was June 15th, anno 1755. When Mr Somer and I were both sitting by the light of a torch reciting over old adventures in former travels, a monstrous beetle[42] struck him in the face, and gave him a terrible black eye. These beetles I have seen frequently in the woods in the evenings. I have found them as large as a hen's egg and of a dark green colour. They have a long kind of forceps like the claw of a crab set with teeth, and a black polish, so nothing could be finer looking. With these forceps they lay hold on young twigs of trees such as they can grasp, then expanding their wings begin to whirl around the branch with great force or velocity, and by that means cut the bark through to the sap; then by hanging under they suck it.

Our girls used at time to produce a sort of music with two or three of these insects, as thus. They made them fast, as our children do chafers[43] at home, by long strings, and then hung them up in the cavern passage and left them to spin around; and it was surprising to hear the sound they made, even like the deep pipes of an organ. Sometimes, according to the magnitude of their wings, they would strike chords most sweetly. Messmate Somer's eye happened to be of the discord order, and was not well for a week or more, but we took Indian methods for the cure of it, and it was at last quite restored again.

I shall now, being on this subject of insects, describe a kind of ant in this country. They are of a dirty white colour and shaped quite differently to other ants. They build their nests on the limbs of trees, stumps of old trees and rocks. Their nest is as large as a beehive, and of a consistency resembling coarse brown bread. From this nest, or general Commonwealth[44], they have generally three or four high roads made of the same sticky substance. These roads are arched over and about the size of a man's little finger, so that all their works are deeds of darkness. They never fail to have one of these paths leading to water; and if at any time accident should damage this causeway, which they lead up and down upon the bodies of trees, rocks and the like, they never fail to repair the breech again; but the matter of which they compose is not the same colour as when new, being then grey. Should you break any part of this road, you will soon see that two or three make their appearance, but retire back again as informers; then incontinently forth comes a multitude in the greatest hurry and confusion imaginable.

Yet if you watch, they all forsake it again, leaving the breech as it is; but if you go thither next morning you shall find it fully repaired. But then should you take a fancy to break it down a second time, in that case they will not repair it as before, but they carry it around circular or in a large curve but join it as before. The Indians say that the nest burnt to ashes is good for many disorders. As to that I can say but little; but that they destroy wood is most certain, having eaten off an upright of my table in one night's time. They bite intolerably, so that whenever they took a notion to lead a road our way, we were under the necessity of routing them with fire.

But Oh! How often I have been soothed in this solitude when the Divine Works of nature have insensibly drawn me into deep contemplation. Then I have sinfully and anxiously desired to have my youthful associate Bill Falconer[45] to be with me to explore these real beauties and record them in his sweet juvenile verses. But alas for me, and I hope well for him, it was not to be his lot. No, I parted with him in old England and there may his bones rest in peace, where I am perhaps never more to set foot. Come, Fate, then, deal me out that portion which is to be my share and let me particularly submit to the blessed will of Providence with all my due resignation.

My messmate Godart often expressed what a loss he was at, for a pipe and tobacco. This was a thing not easy to surmount. I had some old stuff by me, but of no use through length of time; but a pipe was the difficulty. He observed that there were pipes aboard their ship, but we never saw any. I told him that if he and Harry could find some substitute for tobacco, I would soon make a pipe by hook or by crook. We then consulted Harry, as his people smoked frequently when among us, but they smoked it in rolls, like the cigars used by the Spaniards. Harry said he would soon find a plant that his people used when they were out, and without 'tobacco of the right sort', as he called it. This leaf he soon produced. Then I told Somer that if he would cure the leaves, I would undertake to make pipes[46]. I then bade Harry to knead up some clay very finely, and rolled it around a wire. This was by way of a stem. Then I botched up an ugly bole (trunk); these I joined together by raising a mouse[47] of clay over them.

After this I ran the wire through it again, and after it was dry we burnt (fired) it. This put Somer's genius to work; he made a good kind of mould with his knife, and after this we never wanted for pipes.

Seeing Godart so pleased when all this was accomplished, and observing him to talk with more spirit when he had his pipe in his mouth, I then began to practise it myself, so that we all three soon became good smokers. And indeed the girls did too, in a short time after. As the stuff we used was sweet and in no ways disagreeable, I indulged them in the notion, for we were never visited by any very polite company, so it was no inconvenience. And now you might have seen the whole family quaffing together of an evening at no small rate. Now and then Somer and I indulged ourselves with a drop of liquor, but very sparingly although we had a good quantity by us, as I had very cogent reasons for so doing.

I now began to think of instructing Owen in the alphabet, and these letters I made with my pen in the best way I could. And during the time I was showing him, the rest would sit by so they all learnt together. And now I would have given a thousand dollars for a Bible, had I been worth them. The little fellow could say the Lord's Prayer as well as I could, and perhaps was the first of the Indian natives who had ever done the like on this coast, in the English tongue.

And after this matter[48] I used to amuse myself with my time, now and then with my gun, but this was seldom as we had not plenty of shot; at other times writing, fishing and the like. Somer employed himself in making a mast and sails for the yawl[49], and when we had done, we got her keel up and paid[50] her bottom with pitch, tar and sand, as thinking it would warn off the worm[51], and found that it answered (the problem) middling well.

And now, notwithstanding that we were in far better circumstances, I began to find my peace of mind disturbed not a little, as thus. Somer began to alter much in his carriage (manner). He would get his pipe and retire to some distance and remain for an hour or two, yet he never showed any ill blood to me. Yet it gave me much uneasiness, situated as we were then in this vague part of the world. I had observed this behaviour for some time, before I chose to mention it to him, but as I found the man to continue in the same mood, I took it into consideration and resolved to have a serious talk with him. Therefore one evening I said, 'Mr Somer, suppose that you and I should take a trip over to the Long Key, perhaps we might find some things have drifted on shore from the wreck.'

With all his heart, he said.

'Well, then, Harry shall get the boat ready for us tonight. We will take our guns and lines, and Swift shall go with us.'

This pleased me very well. Accordingly the next morning off we put, with our pipes in our mouths. I put some brandy in the boat also. I left Harry as governor, and told him that if anything should chance to happen, he was to hoist a piece of old ensign, being part of a Dutch ensign from the wreck. Now it happened, soon after we arrived at the Key and were walking towards the point, Somer cried out with an oath, 'Dare is von schip comen!'

'Avast[52] swearing, shipmate,' said I. 'Show me her.'

'Dare, met mine fenger,' said he.

'Well, pray, don't be so hurried,' I cried, then taking out my glass perceived her to be a small sloop standing to the westward. 'There, let her go, and a good passage to her!' I said.

'Oh, that is not the thing,' he said, 'I want that she shall come in here, come here!'

'What do you want with her, pray? She is some Spaniard bound down the coast, I suppose.'

'Oh, that is the thing always with you,' he said, 'You don't want to leave those Indian women. You are no more a Christian man. You will live here, all your time.'

Now, thinks I, this is a fair slatch[53] for me to begin, better late than never. But just as I was about to begin, he took notice that our signal was out at home. I then proposed to return, thinking that the vessel was perhaps not the only cause. When he found this out, he said, 'What, you will go then?'

'For certain,' said I.

'I thought that you can't wait to see how the ship steers.'

'Not I, indeed. I know she never means to speak to us, being certain they know nought of us.'

'I suppose Harry got drunk again,' said he.

I chose to put up with it all, knowing there was no other help but patience. So away we went. When we were seated, 'Mr Somer,' said I very calmly, 'I now perceive plainly that you cannot reconcile yourself to the blessed will of Providence, and it gives me much concern indeed to think that you cannot conform like a good Christian to the will of your God.'

'Oh, vat you vil say!' said he, 'Dare is neet broode, neet flais, neet oder dings.'[54]

'How can you talk after such a manner, Godart?' said I. 'Do you want for anything? How could your case have stood, had you been cast on this shore as I was, with nothing but shellfish to support Nature and those to eat raw, without a fellow mortal to converse with, expecting every moment to be knocked on the head by savages? Think on this, my good friend. How differently has the Almighty dealt with you. Has He not spread you a table in this wilderness, a thing you had no right to expect? And was it not your own choice to remain with me, rather *than run the risk of being executed for taking the law into your own hands?'*

This all touched him a little. *'That is true, mate,'* said he, *'but I am not used to it like you are. I think I shall not live here as long as you have.'*

'As to that, no man can foretell what he is to go through in this life. But let me advise you to be fully resigned to God's will, as it is my determination so to do. If you only take this resolution every morning at your first rising, you will soon find your heart more at ease. This is my daily practice. Nothing is more certain, that should Providence so order that I should see my native country again, I would be thankful. But if I am to remain where I am, or wander to the day of my death, I am still resigned. My name is 'Content' in this matter.'

'Well, say no more, Mr Penrose,' said he. *'If I must die in this country I cannot help it. The same God is in every place. You are my good friend; and so knock it off, knock it off, and I will think better.'*

When we got home, we found company had arrived there. We found Mr Owagamy, Komaloot, and Vinnequote, the brother of Ocuma. Now commenced great joy on all sides. Somer put on a more placid air than lately, and we entertained them with the best we could. Now I must observe to the reader an odd turn in Somer's humour, as this. He took me aside and desired that I would treat with Owagamy to procure him a wife. This I promised to comply with. And now I thought within my breast, what a poor, fluctuating creature man is; today he passionately hugs the very thing he totally rejected yesterday. But, as I concluded that this step might prove greatly in my favour, I desired Ocuma to mention the thing to Komaloot and the rest. Whereupon they returned this answer: that if Somer desired such a thing, he should go and look for a wife along with them, for that it was not the custom among them for the girl to go about to hunt the man, as men went out to hunt deer in the woods.

This brought on a laugh at poor Somer's expense, but he was pleased to join and follow their opinion. Upon this, I observed that such a thing would be a great difficulty for us, as we knew not the way to their home. Komaloot then archly asked whether we desired them to bring all the girls of the nation for him to choose one from the whole body; and if they came up, they would eat up all we had before my new friend could find one to please him.

I desired Harry to tell Komaloot that I thought his remark very just, and that we had no other way than for my messmate to return with him and make his own market the best he could, and that Harry could go along with him, on condition that Vinniquote, my new brother, stayed here in his stead until they returned. In about two hours, the thing was agreed upon, although not to the satisfaction of Patty, she being near her time of giving birth.[55] Somer now began to act a new farce, between hope and despair, but I bid him to keep (his spirits) up, and never fear, because my friends would treat him civilly on my account.

The day came when they were to set out, and I was for the first time to part with my good friend Harry, and that with reluctance as I truly esteemed him. But off they went, well armed. My shipmate was dressed in a very odd garb, a pair of Dutch breeches with a little short jacket, and one of my sombreros on his head. At their departure I gave Owagamy a piece of cloth, and some trifles to the rest; this was by way of sweetening their tempers.

Now I was in a different plight to any I had been in before. As for Patty, she was all in tears, the poor children calling after Harry, and myself not in the best of tempers, fearing some disaster should befall them; but I was obliged to bear all with patience the best way I could. Now I was forced to go with Ocuma's brother on all errands, as he knew not one word of English. After this matter, we remained the same for a whole month.

Now we began to keep a sharp lookout as we expected them by sea if Somer succeeded. In their absence we got one wari; and another time Vinnequote, being among the traps, spied a tiger[56] devouring a peccary in one. He ran to inform me. Directly, I got my fire-piece charged with two musket-balls and soon dispatched him. No tumbler could have showed better postures that he did, but Vinnequote soon put an end to his gamut.[57] He then drew him out (gutted him) and dragged him home, where we skinned him and put him out to dry.

Five weeks had now passed, and no signs of our quality.[58] This made me grow very uneasy, thinking often within my own mind, Oh! how much happier did I live, when I had none but Harry and his sister with me. But those days are now passed by, and what the future may bring forth, God only knows. When I first landed on this forlorn coast, what I would have given for the consolation of a companion! Since that day, I have feared less I should be overcharged; and now, whether I have too much or too little was the question. Thus are our poor souls never tied to one stay, tossed about on this ocean of human life, ever greedy for this or another change like the child who soon grows weary of his plaything; and the last use he makes of it is to be satisfied in knowing what it is composed of – when that is done, he throws it aside and becomes anxious for a novelty.

This reflection brings back to my memory the observation Somer made, on a certain day he saw me playing with Ocuma.

'I wonder how you can be so fond of those yellow women,' said he.

I made him this reply, 'When a man is in Rome, he must comply with the Roman custom or he will lead a miserable life there, Somer.'

'But I can leave those Indian girls to themselves if I do not like them, I suppose,' said he.

I told him that he need never stand in any great dread of being ravished by any of them, either awake in his sleep. But what a change took place! My poor messmate had the natural frailty of man working strongly within him, and knew not that to be the principal cause of all his uneasiness. Could he have had only one of our fine blooming girls transported to our habitation from Europe, all perhaps would then become Elysian Fields to him.

Alas, how little do we know what we are, thought I; and now is my messmate gone to look for the very thing that he so much despised – So have I rejected dainties at my mother's table, but want brings us to a due sense of things, and we eagerly jump at the rejected crust which we so lately despised, and heartily thank our gracious God for it. And sure I am that he who studies to make any state of life which shall fall to his lot easy, even though it were at the very gate of despair, yet by due reflection he may obtain comfort if he will but zealously put his confidence in God his Maker, by daily imploring His divine aid, He being Omnipresent.

I had contrived to make an angling rod and line with which at times I used to amuse myself at the head of the lagoon, with the small fish there. Now, as I was one day at this sport and in one of my contemplations, I heard the sound of a conch shell being blown. Directly I acquitted my sport and turned up at the house to inform them of it. I then got out our colours and my glass and mounted the hill. I soon perceived three canoes coming around the point of the key. I then came down and put on a suit of Dutch seaman's clothes, and told Ocuma to put on my Tiger jacket. I then gave a piece of red cloth to her brother, and a blue piece to Patty, and thus we got into the yawl and went down to the lagoon to meet them, leaving Jessy with the children. They soon came into the lagoon and met us, blowing their shells.

No sooner did they draw near than I heard my old shipmate Somer begin a Dutch song, display his hands, and show every token of joy. So, so, thought I, you are pleased again, I hope; and I waited to see the 'marketing' he had brought home. Shortly after, Harry began his song. This was all my desire, but poor Patty burst into a mad fit of crying for joy. Soon after this, we landed and they all came in. The first man who jumped on shore was Harry. He ran with open arms to hug me, then his wife and all the rest. Then came forward Mr Somer and shook me by the hand, most heartily. I observed that he was now a doubloon[59], I hoped.

'Oh, yes, yes!' said he. 'Over I vill show you mine pretty young vife, Wanee.'

Our company consisted of Komaloot, Futatee and four more Indians who had all been here before, and 4 ladies, Mrs Komaloot, Mrs Owagamy, the bride, and another young woman. As soon as we got up to our dwelling, Mr Godart brought his lady by the hand and presented her before me and said, 'Dare is Madam Somer, as you bleases.' She was a good, jolly dame aged about 18, as I judged. 'Well, now, I hope you are cured of the Mully Grubs,'[60] said I.

'Vas is dat, dan?' said he.

'Why, had you not been feeding on chopped hay for a long time before this?' I said.

'Vel, over all, Mr Penrose, dare is neet comfort for man if he bin out von goot kirl, unt dat is drue!'

I then welcomed them all, and desired Komaloot to send away a gang to strike fish, as we were not provided for a wedding. Upon this, Harry cried out they were married already.

'That is not to my purpose,' I said. 'I am determined to have it celebrated here anew.'

'Dat is right,' said Somer. 'Come on, dan!' This was made known to the whole company, and all whooped for joy. I then went and made up a brave bole of grog for them, and we enjoyed it with our pipes. The ladies soon after retired into the house, to chat by themselves. As for my shipmate, he was now become quite a new man. No long, silent puffs of tobacco – his tongue ran to me the whole time on the reception he met with when among them, and of their manners and customs.

After this, we spent the time talking until our sportsmen were all returned with plenty of fish and fowl. Now evening came on, and I told Harry to make a good parcel of torches. By the time all our sportsmen had drank around, they had swallowed down 5 great pans of grog[61], which was at least 7 or 8 gallons – yet none were drunk, for I kept a tough hand that way, lest the sport should be spoiled. About 6 in the evening I ordered a broom to be brought out, and now the Indians knew what next was to come on. Then the ladies were called forth and we made them both jump over it. After this I saluted the bride and all the ladies; this was followed by all the rest, to the no small mirth of the whole company. I then bade Harry to tell Komaloot to make all as merry as possible, which he soon put into practice. After supper, we all fell to dancing, singing and playing until the sun rose on us. At last, all became so weary that we were glad to turn it to rest, not a man being much the worse for liquor. Thus ended Messmate Godart's wedding, and I must own this, I was never merrier in all my days. What gave me such spirits was to see my comrade so much altered; and he afterwards declared that he believed his whole melancholy proceeded from his being, as it were, a bird alone without a mate. So Nature is the same throughout the Universe.

The company tarried but 4 days with us, then took Vinniquote away with them. Mrs Somer and my lady soon became sociable, and everything was now in a fair way again. But Harry told me that I had forgotten one thing, which was to give my wife and Mrs

Somer new names in English. *'Well, then,'* said I, *'in the first place what is the young girl's name?'* Somer told me that it was quite a long one, and he could not speak it very well. Then Ocuma told me her name was Mattanany, meaning *'Sweet Taste'*. I then desired her husband to call her what he thought proper, and he called her after a sister of his own, Eva or Eve. *'Well, then,'* said I, *'we will call Ocuma after my sister also'* – which was Betty, which names became established.

I now told Somer that it was high time for us to think of turtling, the time being come; and we followed it up with good success for a time. And on the 7th day of January, Patty brought forth a son to Mr Harry. Full of joy he came to me with the news, but it was all smashed at once – little Morgan was missing and could not be found. At last I had the melancholy news brought in that he was drowned in the lagoon, having been with a stick aiming to catch fish, and had been dead perhaps an hour. I took this misfortune as coolly as patience would let me; and after the burial was over Harry came over very innocently, to know what name I would give his son. This coming so abrupt on me, I said, *'Call him Job,'*

Job,' he said, *'what is Job?'*

Patience,' I told him.

Well, that is a good name,' said he.

Nothing now happened worth my notice for some time, so that I but seldom went to my book, and we all lived together very friendly. We were now nine in number and Jessy grew to be a fine young woman, quite obedient in all things, and would have sacrificed her life to serve either my wife or myself. So that I now enjoyed my full peace of mind, nor had I once a wandering thought in my heart. And thus I closed my year as to the state of my own reckoning.

THE TENTH YEAR – THE PIRATE TREASURE TROVE
June 15 1756 – June 14 1757

One day, I stood leaning against the side of our kitchen with my face towards our dwelling when I was so struck with the scene that I imagined in my mind, if some ingenious artist had a sight of it, it would have certainly made a curious picture, as thus. First was to be seen the mouth of a large cavern, somewhat resembling a very high cathedral door except the arch was much wider. On the right hand was to be seen my Betty, with Patty sitting behind her braiding her long black hair. A little without the cave entrance was to be seen my young Owen taking aim at his Uncle Harry, who stood on the other side of the entrance, with his back against the rock as a kind of butt for him, and catching the arrows as they came into his hand; Somer sitting against the side of the rock within, with his red pipe in his mouth, tailoring, with an old Dutch cap faced with fur on his head; Eva receiving a bowl of stewed fish from young Jessy before the door. N.B. We wore but little clothing when within the doors, the girls seldom any more than a short breechcloth.

Myself (would be pictured) sitting about the centre within, at my table, writing, the table covered with a piece of sailcloth; Patty with her young child slung at her back with a scrap of cloth; the two dogs and cat before the doorway; and our parrot cage on one side of the cave, but the birds on top of it in general, the cage oblong and square. From a chink in the rock projected a long stick, with another sloping towards it, whereon Moggy the Macaw was in general to be seen. Over the cavern were to be seen huge rocks overhung with trees, except a place where stood our flagstaff, the flag about 7 feet long and 5 deep consisting of only two stripes, the upper blue and the under white.[62]

Now it came to my head to ask Somer for a regular account of the journey, when he went a female hunting. He told me that now and then they caught land crabs[63] and roasted them. The Indians killed two monkeys, upon which they feasted. Then they went over one very long and high hill with little wood on it, and then descended to a large pond or inland lake. Here they walked 5 miles, as he judged, and in it he saw large numbers of large and very frightful animals, both in and on its banks. These I judged to have been alligators. He said that travelling hard had made his feet full of blisters, so that his guides were forced to walk at his rate, and were ever willing to halt whenever he showed the desire. On the 5th day in the evening they came to a place where some plantain trees grew, and there seating themselves, ate all they had in store. But instead of making up a fire according to custom, they got up to set forward, which dismayed him not a little, finding that Harry had known no more of the way than himself up until now. He then enquired whether they were going to travel all night. 'No, no,' said he, 'we are now come,' and in a short time, they heard the crowing of cocks.

Presently after that, they came to a large wigwam. Here the Indians seated themselves and began to make an odd noise, with their hands held hollow before their mouths. This brought forth two Indians who they directly knew, and they all entered the wigwam; and here they slept until day appeared.

At this time, a number of voices was heard, with conches blowing & co. Soon after this many Indians from all quarters came, and saluted them, among them both women and children, gazing with much curiosity. Then finding himself in the midst of them, he offered to shake hands with some of them, but none of the younger sort would touch him by any means. Then Owagamy came and took Harry by the hand and led him about from house to house, as a great curiosity or lost sheep found again; but in a day or two they behaved more freely and would gather around Harry and him to hear him speak English, with which they were highly delighted and frequently aimed to repeat the words after them.

Somer said that it was above a fortnight before they took the least notice of the affair he came upon, and that Harry advised him that Komaloot should be pushed on, in the affair. This was done, and his answer was that he did not perceive the girls to run away from him. Soon after this, Harry told him that there was a girl at the next wigwam with whom he had conversed, and that she had expressed a sort of desire to live with Ocuma; so that if he was but to get her brother once to consent, he was sure she would have him, as he had given her great encouragement in regard to the love Penoly had showed his own wives.

This he did, and soon after Owagamay and the rest assembled on the occasion; and Harry told Somer, so they managed the affair by representing me to such an advantage that her brother gave full consent. He then begged Harry to ask the girl before them all if she was willing to go with him, as he desired that they should all be thoroughly satisfied before they took their departure. The girl then had the question put to her, to which she answered in the affirmative. As this all became settled, the brother took her by the hand and delivered her to him, saying, as he was told by Harry, 'You are now my brother flesh.' Here ends Somer's account of his journey and reception among the Indians.

I had suspected my new lady to be pregnant before she became mine, and now found it really so, but an affair soon happened which reversed the matter. Harry happened to be chipping at the flint of his gunlock, and the piece went off. As his own wife sat very

84

near him, he almost shot her. This so terrified my dame that she was soon forced to retire, and thereby lost her child. She remained quite ill for above a week, and on this account we procured her every little article of nourishment in our power.

Now it so fell out that as she was sitting one day before the door, with a little crab soup before her, she called to me and desired I should take notice of what a large iguana there was on the green among the lime trees. Upon this I called to Harry and said, 'See, there is a fine mark for your bow and arrow.' He then took them in hand and shot, but missed the mark, as it just at that interim passed behind a bush. On this, he snatched up a machete and gave chase to it, and soon after called out, 'Here he is.' Upon this I followed and came up, just as he had killed it.

The iguana had got into an odd kind of nook covered with bushes. Now, as I was thus surveying the place, I perceived through the bushes further in, a heap of stones piled up like a kind of pyramid, about the height of 4 feet. 'Here has been some Indian buried,' said I to Harry.

'No, no,' he said, 'we don't do it that way.' However, being flushed with curiosity, I told him to go and fetch Somer, and I showed it to him, to know his opinion. He said that he could not judge what it signified, and stooping into the bushes drew out the bottom of a glass bottle, and said he thought it was the grave of some Christian person. 'Well,' quoth I, 'let us move away the brush and make a search further into the affair.'

'Oh! no, no!' he cried. 'Don't offer to disturb any man's bones!'

'Never mind that,' said I. 'Come, Harry, let us begin.' So, to work we went. After we had been employed for some time I told Somer, laughing, 'You shall have no share in the prize if you don't turn to, and lend a hand.' Upon this, he began. After we had worked for a considerable time, we came down to a thick plank. 'Now,' said I, 'let us lift it up.' When we had removed it, we found part of a skeleton beneath, with its head almost entire but much decayed. Now Godart would have no more to do in the business. Then finding it lay in between three other boards, I told Harry to move the bones off to another place. As he was at this work, I took up the skull in my hand and found a cut on one side of it, as made with an axe or sharp weapon. I showed it to Somer, saying that this had been foul play at some time or other. When all was cleared off, and the under board removed, I perceived the neck of a large bottle above the ground, and closely stopped with a black pitch-like substance. This I bade Harry to dig up with his machete. By this time, they were all gathered around to satisfy their curiosity.

This bottle I carried away with me up to the house, and there seated myself, then taking out my knife, cried, 'What say you, Godart, will you go shares with me?' – and began to work around the neck of the bottle.

'I think you're a man of strong heart, Mr Penrose,' said he.

'Well,' said I, 'here goes!' But I found that unless I broke it, the business would prove tedious. I knew it did not contain any liquid, by its weight. Upon this, I got a stone and prepared to knock off the neck, but when I came to the breaking part, Somer serving as an example, they all left me and ran off to a good distance unless some hobgoblin should escape and devour them all. This made me laugh, as it was impossible to refrain. With a machete I soon clinked off the neck[64] and found the contents to be a roll of paper. Then I bade Somer to draw near, but he absolutely refused to do so.

I then determined to overhaul it myself and found three rolls of paper, one within the other. The first contained the contents of what the seamen term a Round Robbin, and as thousands may not be acquainted with the full meaning of such a thing, I shall give it the most simply that I can. Whenever a conspiracy is forming to carry any scheme into execution, either on board or on shore among seamen, whereby to gain the point intended, then the ringleaders form a circle on a piece of paper around the margin of which they sign their names, causing the rest of the conspirators to sign their names around in rotation until the whole be filled up, by which means it becomes imperceptible to the spectator which person first put his hand thereto. This being done, they then bind themselves by oath to stand by each other, whatever difficulty arose to oppose the undertaking, even to life itself if it was a thing of desperate consequence.

The second paper contained a most infernal oath devised by some of the Devil's own principal agents, undoubtedly. This was accompanied with some of the most horrid imprecations ever uttered by man against any who should presume to disturb that place, unless he had their own infernal right to do so; also against anyone of their own party who should dare to betray the secret to a stranger or any who were not proper claimants thereto, unless they previously knew the rest of their diabolical fraternity to be dead and gone.

The third paper contained some very odd characters mixed with readings, yet not so artfully contrived as to put it wholly out of man's power to unravel the secret. Had it indeed been otherwise, I am certain that many of those ignorant reprobates would have been far enough (away) to seek in any length of time; but fate ordered that their hellish plot and booty should remain unmolested forever.

After I had thoroughly examined these papers and formed the best conjectures I could concerning them, I then called to my friend Somer telling him that he need not give himself to any superstitious conjectures about the matter; that it was some of the Devil's manufactory (doing) was certain, but he knew God to be above him; and as he saw I was in no way moved about it, he as a man should never give way to any such idle ideas. This brought him to me, saying, '*Vat you have gotten dare?*' I then gave him the papers to look at but found that he could make nothing of them.

Now, I should have been all of a piece (agreed) with him, had I not learnt while in the Island of New Providence many odd relations concerning that detestable class of people denominated as pirates. Therefore, to render everything concerning that execrable set of people as clear to his understanding as it was in my power to do, I told him that nothing was more certain than the very things I held in my hands had previously been the darling scheme of those abominable wretches. And then, to give him a thorough taste of what man can say, write and act once he has rejected his Maker, I recited over the second paper, but with no great desire as to my own will. When he had heard its contents, he cried '*Put ut to da Divle!*'

'*That I shall soon do,*' said I, and then rammed it into the flames before his face, saying, '*Go and follow up your cursed inscriber as fast as you can post!*'

I then told him that it had been an old custom among those odd wretches, when chance threw any large treasure or booty in their way, then fearing to carry it about with the vessel, they used to hide it on islands, keys, and in secret places along the coast, using a most diabolical ceremony at the interment of their accursed riches, as thus. After they had in the first place signed their Round Robbin[65], they, instigated by the Devil, decreed privily to sacrifice some poor unfortunate Spaniard, Mulatto or Negro and there to bury him, leaving his Spirit as a kind of guardian or sentinel over their ill-begotten wealth until such time as they should return. And then it was they drew up those detestable articles of their faith, and buried the whole in a bottle with the corpse and riches, to preserve it from moisture or any other injury of time.

After I had well considered the affair I went in and laid the papers up in a safe place, as Somer seemed no further curious about it. So then I took Harry back to the spot, and we threw all the bones together again, and dug a hole on one side where we deposited the bones. And thus this uncommon adventure ended for that time; yet I thought I was clear in thinking that money or some other things of value were there hidden.

The Round Robbin is exactly transcribed from the original manuscript, as faithfully made out as the badness of the characters and blindness of the ink would admit. N.B. Those names to which crosses were added were such as could not write, as I judge; and I take note that there are Negroes' names among the rest such as Sambo, Cudjoe, and perhaps others of them were of the mixed breed, as the principal character necessary to become one of such a banditry was that of being an approved reprobate. If he could once recommend himself capable of robbing father, brother or relation, force a rape on a maid, wife or widow, swear black was white or the contrary, or even stow a poor unfortunate man in Davy Jones's Locker[66], he was the man fit to be sworn in as what they styled 'a *good fellow*'.

ROUND ROBBIN AND NIMROD'S PORTION

Cornelius Adams+
Richard Quin
John Marata
Gabriel McCombe+
William Lemon
Edward Evans
Daniel Watkins+
Patrick Dailey
George Bristow
Gilbert Dickinson
Simon Richards+
Owen Flinn
John Fletcher+
Lewis Peters
William Waterman+
Sambo+
Charles Rankin
Jacob Carter
Charles Prince+
Jeosepi Renato
Joseph Simnel
Thos Current+
Alan Snowden
John Curtis
William Wood
Joseph Hartman+
Darby Keaton
Robert Atkinson
Cornelius Rian
Andrew Bunce+
Rod.* McLeran

the *Round Robbin* Exactly transcribed
from the Original Manuscript, as faithfully made out as
the Badness of the Characters and blindness of ye Ink, would admit.
N.B. those names, to which crofes are added, were such as could not write.

as I judge, and I take notice, there are Negroo names among the
rest, such as Sambo. Cudjoe and perhaps some others of them, were
of the mixed breed, as the principal character necefsary to become
one of such a Banditty, was that of being an approved Reprobate.
If he could only recommend himself, capable of Robbing Father
Brother or Relation. Force a Rape on Maid, Wife or Widow.
Swear Black, was White or the contrary, or even Stow a poor
unfortunate Man in Davy Jones's Locker, he was then the
man fit to be Sworn in, as what they Styled a good Fellow.

A faithful Representation of the Third Paper, as to the matter
and due forms, with what I deem to have signified Watch Words.

Nimrod's Portion.

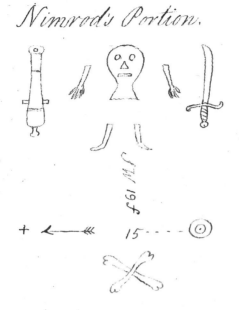

£ 191

+ ⟵ ≪   15 - - - ◉

Now this Paper was what I conjectured to contain the whole secret,
nevertheless I kept the affair to my self, Knowing full well, could it make
us as Rich as ten Jews, it could by no means render us one farthing the
happier in our condition. I often pondered on the thing, in my mind,
Night after Night, did I dream nothing but Pirates, either that
we were digging, and beset by those kind of People, that the Ghost of
the murdered Victim was petitioning us to relieve him, or we were
Sharing money, so that frequently, I raved and started in my fits
of agitation, And heartily have I wished, Harry, had never gone
after that Guano, then thought I, we might ever have remained
in total Ignorance, and been yet as happy as heretofore ——
But after a time, those Idle visions vanished, as we talked seldomer
or the Subject Yet I cannot say, but a great desire, would at times
rise in my heart, to satisfy my own curiosity, and had not Somer
been so backward and Indifferent on the matter, we should not
have been long ere we had made the trial ——————

Skinner Peers
Peter Fleming
Jacob Rupert+
Michael Murphy
William Meadows
Henry Ward
Job Watkins+
Patrick Sullivan
Andrew Voto
Cudjo+
Thos Davis+
Abraham Tobin
George Simmonds
Roger Grant+
Thos Timmins
Jasper Cary
David Ruddle+
Peter Marks
David Roberson
Mark Watkins

This is a faithful representation of the Third Paper, as to the matter and form, with what I deem to have signified Watch Words.

Now this paper was what I conjectured to contain the whole secret. Nevertheless I kept the affair to myself, knowing full well that although it could make us as rich as ten Jews, it could by no means render us one farthing[67] the happier in our condition. I often pondered on the thing in my mind. Night after night did I dream of nothing but pirates, either that we were digging and beset by that kind of people, that the ghost of the murdered victim was petitioning us to relieve him, or we were sharing money, so that frequently I raved and started[68] in my fits of agitation. And heartily have I wished that Harry had never gone after that iguana. Then, thought I, we might ever have remained in total ignorance and have yet been as happy as heretofore. But after a time, those idle visions vanished, as we talked seldom on the subject. Yet I cannot say but that a great desire would at times rise in my heart to satisfy my own curiosity. Had not Somer been so backward or indifferent on the matter, we should not have been long ere we had made the trial.

Some time after this, I proposed to shipmate Godart that we would take a voyage along the coast eastward, to which he agreed, in order to make some further discovery that way. I was put on this, by his desire of seeing the great stone that Harry had told him about at Towers Field. Harry was to be left as guard to the women, and when we had laid in necessities, off we put down the lagoon in the yawl, and stood along the shore until we got to the Old Cave. There we landed and got some yams. From thence we stood out about an hour, then tacked and stood away for the next bay, and after a time got the length of the creek, where just as we were going to land, Swift jumped on shore after an iguana and he soon killed it; then we put in.

We then took through the bushes but missed the true tract, so that I could not find the Stone for my life. Now, as we remained thus in suspense, our dog at a distance began to howl, and we were sure that he had the sight of something or other. We followed him, cutting our way with our machete, until we opened into a large pond. Here we heard noises resembling the murmurs of young whelps or puppies. The place was overgrown with large reeds, and my messmate cried out there were some of such *'Divil creatures'*[69] he had seen when travelling with the Indians. Directly I called off the dog, who, poor toad, trembled much. I verily think we saw above twenty of them. We directly quit that repository of greedy devourers, of which many lay sunk beneath the surface of the water with only the nose out. After we got off, I could not help thinking how happy had been my lot to be landed where I had so long resided, without knowing such monsters were so near to me. But as I knew those animals seldom quit the ponds to ramble into the uplands, I was not much concerned.

After this we returned, and I struck as near as I could for the Rock and by chance soon found it. We then took a good survey of it, and Somer took it for the remains of an old tower, but when I observed to him that there was not the least signs of any cement or mortar to be seen, he gave over to that opinion.[70] As we came away, he observed that that place had also been frequented by pirates. *'Undoubted,'* I said, *'as they were acquainted with the whole coast, it being their general maxim to lurk within a lagoon, creek and the like with a man posted either on a tree, hill or masthead. From whence they could espy a sail from a great distance when, waiting a proper advantage, they popped out and captured the poor culprit by virtue of those laws themselves had made.'*

After this we went to the palmetto grove and caught three more iguanas, then stood away for Whale Point as I termed it, but saw no more than the skull and some ribs sunk in the sand. When we got round, we landed, and kindling fire we roasted one of the iguanas and had a good meal of it and a yam. Next, I proposed we should range the long bay, which now lay before us perhaps 5 miles in length, thinking that we might find something had drifted there. Some time after, we came up with the brig's boom; farther on we found 3 barrels of tar sunk in the sand by our own lads, perhaps; and thus we trudged for above 4 miles as we judged, being more ground I had gone over at one time, than for several years before. We now concluded to return, finding nothing worth stooping for. After we got back to our boat I proposed to explore around the next point. Godart agreed, and we were forced to give it a large berth as there was a shoal and surf running out from it. When we got round, we found the land trended away to the left for about two leagues, then fetched a compass round more eastward as far as the eye could see.

Now as we were exploring these new scenes I observed a large smoke to ascend, about 3 leagues, right ahead of us. *'There are people,'* said I, *'yonder, of some sort or other.'*

'That is nothing to us,' said Godart.

Then did I retort on him, *'How long since you fell into this way of speaking, Landsman?'*[71] Directly on speaking, I descried a sail in the offing to the southward, right before the wind, so near in that with my glasses I saw she was a very large ship. *'What say you now?'* said I, *'Shall we stand and show ourselves?'*

'No, no,' he said, *'let us take down the mast and lie snug.'*

This we did, and got her in behind a parcel of low bushes. Here we remained for some time, and saw another fire yet nearer. *'Now,'* said I, *'Somer, I am certain they are Indians or Spaniards, for if they were folk in distress, one fire would be sufficient as a signal.'* The ship kept her course and after she had passed by about an hour, we got into our boat, stepped our mast, and put away around the point with a flowing sheet[72]. After we got abreast of Towers Field, we hauled inshore and landing there, concluded to sleep under our sail for the following night.

The first thing after turning out next morning was getting a fire made, and after we had refreshed ourselves with a good meal we went in quest of some limes, and then stood alongshore homeward, put into the old plantation and gathered a parcel of yams, potatoes and co., and then put off for the Castle and arrived about noon. But how amazed we were on our landing, to find our kitchen had burnt to the ground.

They all came running down crying and clapping their hands, full of joy at our return; but I stood like a mope, not knowing how the thing could have happened. But finding them all alive, I took my wife in one hand and Owen by the other, walking up to the house in silence, seated myself, and then enquired how such an affair could happen. Harry then told me that Owen had gone into the kitchen, and got playing with the fire, as he had innocently told them. Soon the whole was in flames but that Harry, with the women's help, had saved all the valuable things at the great hazard of their lives. 'Well,' said I, '*I am heartily glad things are no worse.*' But the loss of our kitchen was a matter of concern to us all as we had been so long used to it, and for its being a hall of reception when any visitors came among us.

The next thing to be thought of was rebuilding our kitchen, and we had one thing much in our favour as they had dragged down the thatch where the fire would let them, so quickly that all the uprights remained unhurt, being of a very hard kind of wood. Now Somer and Harry were employed in fetching home palmetto for our thatch; and after this we went cheerfully to work, but it was a full fortnight before it was complete, and at the last did not equal the Old Temple seen in former days. Nevertheless, although it was not quite so shipshape[73], as is the sailor's term, yet it answered our purpose well enough.

Now, as I expected a long series of rain, I proposed to Godart that we should lay in a good store of roots and other things of that kind, as this conduct had hitherto been much neglected. And I determined to lay them in the back part of our dwelling, lest another kitchen blast should take place. And now speaking of these long rains, I shall observe that they come on twice a year, but mostly about October[74], and then hold on with but few intervals, 3,4, or 5 weeks more or less. And on an evening when the rain would hold off a little, myriads of fire flies then swarmed in the air twinkling like so many stars. And on a serene night when all was hushed, I have heard things grow. Several times Somer has cut a tuft of grass for that end, and we have found that it has sprung 3 inches in perhaps 30 hours time. The most disagreeable thing at this season was a kind of tree toad[75] whose noise was the most doleful that can be conceived.

We remained chiefly within doors during these times, our employment being chiefly making pipes, pans, pots and ordering our tobacco. The girls spun thread after their way and sewed also with sail needles. Sometimes we took a bout with the bow and arrows at marks, at other times played quoits.

But at last my good messmate Somer fell bad of the rheumatics, and became so lame in both his arms that he could not feed himself, so that his poor wife was under the necessity of doing that office for him. It then left his arms and fell into his legs. Now I was forced to undertake a new task, (viz.) making a pair of crutches for him; and assisted by these he would hobble down to the boat where he would sit and fish with his pipe in his mouth by the hour. For to give him his due, he ever hated idleness if he could possibly stir.

He remained in this condition above three months and then got better every day until he threw away the crutches; when, like a true Dutchman, he must begin some employment and this was no less than making a tub. I thought it beyond his skill, but to my great wonder he made it after a fashion, for it was suited to hold water and became of great use for many things. We had nothing worth notice from this time forwards, but the sight of one sail[76] which passed by to the eastward, until by my account I had completed my tenth year and began the next, in the same constant bond of harmony.

THE ELEVENTH YEAR – KOMALOOT DIES, REES AND HANNAH ARE BORN, AND THE INDIAN ALBINO VISITS
June 15 1757 – June 14 1758

Eleventh year began. Now it chanced on a day as I was at my table writing, and Somer with his pipe standing behind overlooking me, he took it into his head to ask where I had put that *'Divil's paper'* we found in the grave. This was what I expected would come out one day or other, having concluded it should rest so until it came out of its own accord. I then closed my book and turning around, arose and said, *'Here is the paper safe enough, but let us not go about things rashly. Let me light my pipe first and then you and I will take a walk, and have some conversation on that affair.'* So off we walked and seated ourselves down among the orange trees, where I began thus: *'Godart, I think in regard to this paper, it imports there is a sum of money hidden in, or near, the place where we found it.'*

'Oh, you dink so? You ben choakin (joking)?' said he.

'No, no,' I replied, *'I have no bone in my throat.[77] I think I speak clear enough and think I have found out the whole secret, too. Observe here'* – showing him the paper – *'you are to observe here two words. These are the Watchwords, which none were privy to, but the very parties concerned. In the next place observe the man's head represented and there his arms and feet. This means the person buried here, whom they killed, to be as a Spirit to guard over the treasure there hidden.'*

'You dink dat?' said he.

'Yes, I verily do,' I said. *'As to this gun and sword perhaps they were what figures they carried in their colours, as also these cross bones.[78] But now take notice. Here is 19 feet southwest, and thence 15 feet to the very spot or else the same distance as this dart directs; and within such a circle lays the cash I dare say, if any may be there; and this is my judgement.'*

'Well,' said Somer, *'suppose we should make a trial of it?'*

'With all my heart,' said I, *'if you have the courage to undertake it, messmate.'*

'Oh, I am neet feeren da Divle,' said he.

'Come on then, we will fall to. But now I think it will be better to postpone it a little longer, until you gather more strength.'

'Youst as you vill for dat,' said he, and the thing was dropped for the present.

Soon after this we had a visit from the natives. They brought with them an Indian albino white as a horse and seemingly very purblind.[79] I soon found our people were well acquainted with him, and as such a sight was an odd object to Somer and me, I desired Harry to give us his account of it. He observed that now and then, but very seldom, such objects were born; but as to the cause he could give us no better information than that they called them Moon-lights, and that people said they were conceived at the minute the moon was at the full.

'Then,' said I, *'one might think you might have some more of them.'* But he could say no more except that they were not beloved among them; none would wed them; but that they lived and died as they were, as being of no service unless on Moonshine nights and that then they were as brisk as other Indians, seeing very sharp, going to fishing with

their darts when other people could not see at all. I observed that his eyes appeared to be inverted as to ours like an inverted crescent, keeping them much closed in the daytime. This Indian's name was Erreawa or 'White Shiner'. The Indians who had called to see us, had brought him at his request on the visit. They were Muz-gayo, Damasunto and Vattequeba. They remained with us for about 5 days, and in that time made a perfect cure of Somer by means of roots boiled in water with which he was bathed; and I told Betty to learn the true knowledge of them before they left us.

Soon after they were gone, and finding Godart began to stand stronger on his pedestals, we took a new voyage westward on the discovery. We took our departure from the point of Long Key and stood down along the coast about 3 leagues, when we came to a bluff headland. About this place there were multitudes of mullet, with porpoises in pursuit of them; they were so thick that we knocked several on the heads with our oars. These mullet have often in their company a fish of a much larger size called a Calipiver[80], differing little in form from the true mullet.

After a short stay, we put off again down along the shore, with the wind easterly, until we saw a long sandy bay, at the farther end of which ran off rocks, with a small hummock directly off that. This we rounded, and then ran into a little cove where the water was about three feet deep. Here we landed again and Godart shot a White Poke or large kind of White Crane.[81] These birds are so exceedingly white and tall that I have many times mistaken them for a sail, especially when they have been standing out so far from the shore on a flat with the sun shining strong upon them, as at such times they have loomed exceedingly large, and when nothing but the margin of the horizon could be seen behind them. And certain I am at such times that I have perceived them at the distance of 3 leagues until, either by flight or a sudden move, they have undeceived me.

In this place we spent that evening, but on the morrow the wind came up fresh at South, so that we came to a determination to go no further and put back right before it, until we got the length of our Long Key. After we had got round the reef, the wind fell and it soon became a dead calm. We then turned to and rowed, getting into our lagoon in the evening not a little fatigued, without either profit or much discovery, and thus ended our cruise.

After we had been home about three days, we got the notion of examining our Pirates' Corner. Our Indians could not think what our designs were, but we got the shovels and marched to the spot. In the first place we cleared away all the low brush, then I cut a stick nigh to a foot in length and got to measuring the ground. When this was done, I told Harry to begin digging. He worked for some time with such poor wooden tools as we had, but to no purpose. Now and then we had hard roots to cut through with our machetes. However, we worked down about 3 foot and then desisted for that time, finding nothing.

Then Somer began to laugh at me and said, 'All de Monix is dare I vil put in mine eye, and dan Ick sal see, too!'

'Well,' said I, 'now we will begin directly so far on the other hand, and if that fails we will then begin in a line from the foot of the skeleton.' Then to work I went myself, then Harry took his spell, and Somer joined him. But they had not gone down 18 inches before Harry discovered some hard surface. I then began to joke Somer in my turn, saying, 'Here is the prize, my Soul!' – being at the same time just upon giving the whole affair up. I then bade Harry to clear away the dirt and we discovered a smooth surface like lead. 'Huzza, Somer,' cried I, 'here it is, here it is!' We then fell hard at it until I plainly saw a round circle. We soon got up the prize and found it to be a huge chamber stool pan.[82] Directly on this I took out my knife and began to scrape it, and found it to be good silver.

By this time, Harry had got to work at something more and found it to be two more lying on their sides; these we lugged out also. After this, we found 17 dishes of various sizes all of the same metal, 4 large and 26 oblong plates, 6 basons[83] that would hold 3 quarts each, and above 50 things for table use. Beneath this we found cups or cans and then came to a vast body of Cob Dollars[84]. And as we were thus viewing it, Harry observed a thing of another shape among them but could not stir it. We then fell to and cleared away and found 7 large candlesticks above 4 feet long, these were all doubled to make good stowage[85]; 10 more about half that size; and after we had got out about one half of the dollars we came to a very large bason with 4 rings to it, and within it was a large sum of gold coin. This bason we found stood on terra firma so that we then desisted, all three in a copious sweat. 'Now', said I, 'Messmate, lend me your hand. You are by far a richer man than when you turned out this morning, if money can make you so; and I heartily wish you had a part of it safe lodged in the bank.'

Some of the plate had rich raised work on it with coats of arms displayed, lions heads, chevrons, shells and stars; and on the feet of some of those candlesticks was the name: *Isabel Rubiales D. 1605.*[86]

Now, after we became possessed of this vast booty we really knew no more how to dispose of it than so many idiots. Many arguments Somer and I had about it, as to think of enjoying it was to us absolutely vain, it being not of the least worth to us. It was true I could have trusted Owagamy or Komaloot with the secret; but the matter was how they could conduct the thing in such a manner as that the affair should never be traced to its first origin, as the Spaniards would easily discover it to have been their property. Sometimes we thought of melting the vessels down, and thus it went on for such a length of time that it became a matter of little concern to us. There it lay just covered over, useless and no more regarded than if we had never found it, except we kept out a few of the gold coin wherewith the women adorned themselves and the children.

I then made Harry plant a parcel of lima and guava seeds before the place, which in a few months time threw a mask before the whole. After this was done, we gave all our Indians charge never to speak of that affair before our visitors, lest by that means we might all be involved in trouble before we were aware of it. This they all promised steadfastly to observe. And many times have we diverted our hours in acting the part of dealer, contractor and purchasers. Sometimes Somer was the merchant and contracted with me as a carpenter to build him a ship of such a tonnage or burthen. At other times I purchased large tracts of land from him. And in this way we amused the time with little variety, until we had a visit from the Indians.

These were Owagamy and three more and they informed us that Komaloot was dead. This threw us all into unfeigned sorrow for the loss of so good a friend, which made me observe that although he was now gone and could never more pay us his kind visits, yet it was our earnest desire that they would not think of dropping us on that account. Owagamy then gave a sudden start and replied that he knew a friend from an enemy by the feel, and that he did not leave touching him until death had made him too cold. I returned him my hearty thanks for his good opinion of us.

He then took occasion to enquire where we got the gold he saw on our wives and children. I told him we found it by chance on the sands by the seaside. He then said he supposed it to be some of the money my merry countrymen had hidden when they had come along the coast to plunder the Spaniards in his old fathers' time. He observed that when he was a little child there died amongst them a very old white man who had been one of those people, and he remembered his name was Yaspe.[87] Moreover he said his father when talking with him, heard Yaspe tell that he had been at the plundering of churches and getting great riches; and that on a time he with a number more had buried some once on the coast to the northward of their dwelling, where they belayed[88] a young mulatto fellow to keep watch over it. That his father and some of the other Indians, among whom was old Coduuno who died in the canoe with me, proposed to go with him in search of it; but that Old Yaspe told them in case he was to find out the very spot he nor they could be anything for the better for it, as it would, on their digging, continually keep sinking lower into the earth. On their enquiring the reason for this, he told them that the Spirit would sink it as knowing he had no title to any part of it because they, on a quarrel with him, had landed or marooned him with a curse so that it rendered him totally incapable of being in any way a partaker. This was the superstition of that old vagabond.

On this I directly got Harry to pronounce to me that old fool's name but it could be brought no nearer than Yaspe; and on going to my paper I found one of the men's names who signed the Round Robbin to be Jasper Cary, who undoubtedly was the very person Owagamy signified. Our friends stayed but three days with us, and then departed for their own home. We all desired that they would bear our sorrow away with them to our friends at home, on the death of Komaloot.

About this time shipmate Somer had a daughter born which he was pleased to call Anauche or Hannah; and three days after, Betty brought me a son. Him I called Rees[89]. Now we were become eleven in number, a little society hid away from all the world as I may say, perfectly happy if we could but be content, for we wanted for nothing, but such things as we could well do without. For instance, we had a large bank. If at any time our ladies were a little out of order we could on such a pressing occasion procure a duck, diver[90] or some other fowl; yet this was attended with rather too much expense – our ammunition growing short – as I valued one charge of powder at the rate of ten dollars, and could well have given 50 of them for 5 pounds of that infernal composition.

I shall in this place take notice of a diverting scene we were every now and then entertained with. (Viz.) The Indians when last with us brought with them a very young monkey as a gift to Owen. This little creature, being but lately taken from its dam, became much taken with our dog Swift, so that whenever he lay down the monkey would get on his back and place itself between his shoulders. This came on at first, by the child putting it to play with the dog. From this time forward it was ever on its back, go where he would, the dog never offering to snarl or refuse. This was what in future opened the ball, as I may say.

Harry would call the dog by name, then set off as hard as he could run, the dog after him with the little monkey sticking at its back. By frequent trials the monkey rode to admiration. At length Somer made him a little cap and whip. Now and then Harry would go privately among the woods and then call eagerly for Swift, when off would set the dog and rider at full speed, who was to become so great a horseman that he never once fell. But what went beyond all the rest was to see the great address he showed when the dog would push him through a thicket, for then he would dodge his head first to one side and then to the other, with such care that I would defy the best huntsman to push through a brake[91] better.

If ever we attempted to send the dog into the water, the monkey would be off his back in an instant, let us take all the precaution in our power at such times. Nothing could be more diverting than to see the little toad run home with his whip in hand and cap on his head. No sooner would he arrive but he would go up to my wife, get on her shoulder, and there begin to chatter as though he related his grievance to her; but such tricks would make him quit the dog's back perhaps for two days.

I think it quite unnecessary to recite over all our ordinary customs as they are in general one and the same round, in order to avoid being too tedious. And now another year had revolved since I first came on this foreign shore, but I am content.

CHAPTER V

The Twelfth to Fourteenth Years

THE TWELFTH YEAR - CAPTAIN HORGAN IS ENTERTAINED
June 15 1758 – June 14 1759

Twelfth year began. On a day as Somer was going through the trees he told me how he had been beset by a small bird; and as these birds are somewhat remarkable I shall mention their nature in this place. It is called by some the Hanger[1]. There are several sorts of them, but all fine feathered. They are about the size of our starling and make their nests to hang down from the outer branch of a tree by a string. The nest is oblong, like a cabbage net. Many times as I have passed any, where near to one of their nests, the bird has at once darted down from a limb full into my face, flew back and then returned in a furious way as it would pick out my eyes, so that I have been forced to beat them off.

These birds are fond of a particular kind of insect[2], which is altogether singular in its way. I always found them on the cedar, cypress and such kinds of trees. The insects make themselves a kind of house resembling the shape of a ship's buoy, and of a substance so tough that it is impossible to break it with a man's finger. They fortify this buoy with particles from the same tree in a very curious way. At the upper end of this buoy the insect appears, about half its body out, where it is constantly spinning its threads, lowering itself down and then hauling itself up hand over hand, as is the sailor's term, with great dexterity. I have seen above a thousand of them hanging from one tree like so many bobbins. It is curious to see how dextrously the Hanging Bird catches them as he flies, then putting the insect under his foot on the limb of a tree, disengages it at once.

We often found land tortoises.[3] These Harry told me were choice good eating; otherwise I should never have thought of such a thing. Of these we made excellent soup. It is almost incredible to think how long those animals will retain life after the head has been taken off. I have known them to move 10 or 12 days after that operation if kept in a shady place. This is an absolute fact.

One day this year, being out about half a mile back from our home, I proposed for us to make our way back into the country to see what we could discover, and on the next day we armed ourselves for the purpose. For some time our passage proved exceedingly hard and difficult. At length we made our way so far that we came to an opening of the ground well grown with fine lofty trees, and after that to a bare country. There we spied three deer running swiftly; our dogs put after them but soon lost them. We then came to a place where there was a kind of morass, on the other side of which was to be seen a long range of broken banks. Here we saw multitudes of wild parrots flying over our heads.

Now, as the scene was quite new to us, we were the more curious, and Somer observed at the foot of the bank a monstrous skull of some beast or other. It was as much as he could lift. The jaw teeth were many of them yet in the head, quite sound, but could be drawn out easily. Going a little further on, I pulled out of the bank a rib of monstrous size. We then found more bones pertaining to the same kind of beast. Now what species of animal it could be I knew not, but Somer insisted it must have been an elephant, having seen one, but I never had[4]. However, we came off with three of the teeth, and we found that all the bits of wood, or sticks, that had fallen into the water were petrified. We made a shift to mount the bank, from whence we could see far around us. After we had so far satisfied our curiosity, we returned. When we got home a council was held again about the teeth, but all were ignorant. Only Harry had heard the old folks say that they had found such when hunting. And thus it rested, nor could we make any more of the matter.

Shortly after this, Somer proposed that we should have a general day with the whole family in the boats, it being fine weather. Accordingly, the next morning, everything being got ready, off we went in two boats. And thus we proceeded – Somer, wife and child, my wife, children and self in the yawl; Harry, his wife Jessy and child with the dogs in the great canoe. Our voyage to the old plantation was very fine. From thence, we put off for the end of the Long Key, and there we landed the women and children. I stayed with them and kindled a fire, while Somer, Harry and Owen rambled along the south shore. In about an hour Harry came back and informed me that they had found a very large boat like that in which Mr Somer's brothers had gone away to the South, but that it was full of sand, and that he desired that I should come along to see it. I then went with him and found it to be an English longboat with a bilge in her prow[5], on her starboard side, painted black and yellow, and seemingly not old but weather-beaten. We left her as we found her, for some time.

I returned to the girls, and they went after the birds. When I got back I went to work with my line at throwing out, and caught a couple of fine Mutton Fish[6]. These, with a few Redshank and Scaup[7], they brought back with them to give us a plentiful meal, under an awning Somer and Harry raised for us with our sails. After this we comforted ourselves with a little toddy[8] and our pipes, and in the evening returned to our Castle again in high spirits.

Shortly after this, Somer and I undertook to go and clear out the boat we had discovered. This cost us some trouble but we patched her up so as to make her swim home very well. The next thing was to get her up shore.[9] This we accomplished by the help of rollers when all hands were mustered; and she was got up so that Somer could get at her very well, for he was a carpenter, sail-maker, caulker and cooper on all occasions. The getting up of her cost us much labour, doing it by spells inch by inch.

Now, as I observed my shipmate to be so very earnest about putting this longboat into repair, I asked him one day wherein lay all the necessity for the great labour and pains he was at, as when she was refitted we could have little or no call for her, as we had two sailboats and a canoe already. But he said it was a diversion to him, and for that reason I held my peace. But when he had done, I told him that he and Harry had only created a new job for themselves.

'As how?' he said.

'Why, now you must fall to, and build a shed over her, or else she must be launched again; otherwise the sun will soon do for her.' And in order to preserve her from the worm they built a shed over her. After this, she remained where she was.

The next thing we fell upon was melting down our silver plate, as thinking that by that method we might some time or another get it off.[10] For this purpose we dug a large hole. Harry was employed for some time in cutting billet wood. When all was ready we made up a kind of cross pile and laid all the different things thereon, and Harry and Jessy were to stand as stokers; and after the whole was completed it formed a huge pyramid. But although the fire was well kept up, it was above 5 or 6 hours before the whole was run down, and then we left it to extinguish itself. In a day or two we cleared away all the ashes and got a noble mass of plate, which ran into many odd shapes. These we were forced to reduce into smaller pieces, and it cost Harry work enough, but he had time enough on his hands. By bending and the application of an old axe he reduced it all. We then buried the pieces in a private place against a time (if ever) they might also become of use to us.

Nothing of any significance came on until I proposed that Somer and Harry should take a trip alongshore southwest of the Long Key. Accordingly, they took the large canoe and left us the next morning. After they were gone, I took a march with my gun among the traps, not daring to go too far in their absence. In one of the traps I found an odd kind of beast of a brown colour. It had been there so long that it was in a state of decay, so that I left it there until such a time the boat returned. This day also I shot a beautiful kind of parrot, which was quite white as snow except for a fine crest of yellowish feathers on the head[11]. This bird I showed to my wife who said it was an Auckco, but observed that they would never talk much.

My two friends did not return that night, and I began to grow very uneasy on their account, fearing that they had met with some disaster. That night I slept not, as the wind blew offshore. Thus did I wait in suspense, until the next afternoon when to my great joy I saw them coming around the east end of the Long Key. They brought home a very large kind of shark, such as I had not seen before. This fish had no teeth, and its skin was exceedingly rough to the feel. They also had in the boat a good lump of ambergris, differing in colour from that which we had already. I then enquired what kept them out all night. They told me that they had ranged the shore above 5 miles, where they found a cask that they imagined to be either beef or pork, but had left it safe on the beach until I should go and pay a visit. That shortly after, they saw a vessel standing to the southward, upon which they unshipped their mast and retired among the trees, but that in about an hour she tacked and stood out to sea. And by this time it had grown late, which made them conclude to remain there for the night, as there was a pretty small creek running up about 40 yards, at the head of which was a charming run of fresh water where they had stayed all the night, plagued to death by the mosquitoes. I could not think how that vessel had escaped my sight, except that she was too far to the southward for my eye.

After this, I took Harry to the trap and showed him the animal I had found in it, and he lugged it out and gave me this odd account of it. He said those creatures live chiefly by catching ants[12], saying that they will creep slowly on towards a nest, laying flat on their bellies, then put forth their tongues to a great length, which never fails to attract multitudes of those insects upon it. When the beast finds by their strong biting that he has got his freight, he then whips in his tongue and swallows them, and then begins the same process. The tongue of this animal when Harry drew it forth was exceedingly long, narrow and round.

It happened one day as Somer and I were walking by the shore near to some low flat rocks, we had a curious scene of an amour between two sea crabs, and as there are not 2 in 2000 who ever happen to see the like, I shall touch upon it. (Viz.) I was sitting on a long stone perhaps 20 feet by 15 feet in length, when a crab came up the side of it, and marched slowly to the middle of it and there squatted down. About one minute after that, up came another on the opposite side. Directly as the first crab saw the second, it erected itself on its legs as tall as possible. The last comer then advanced very slowly for about three feet toward the other in the centre and there made a full stop, the other facing it. The second crab then began to move in an oblique direction, but slowly to a very wide angle, from right to left so as to form a kind of curve or semicircular motion to the crab in the centre. This he repeated for a considerable time, and making his regular advancement by retracting his curve, increasing in velocity as he advanced, so that by the time he had made about two thirds of his progressive motions, his velocity became so exceedingly quick that the eye could not catch the motion. The centre crab constantly moved at the same time, as if it was fixed on a swivel or pivot, until the male crab became very near, when in an instant the female became willing to sit still, and a union commenced.

Godart's attitude the whole time was very expressive of admiration. He stood with his two arms before him and hands clenched, then burst into the following expressions: 'How crate is our Got make all dem tings, shipmate, He is here, He is dare al over da vorld, unt dat show us He bin in dis lant mit us, dis minute.'

'Most certain,' I said. 'His almighty eye never slumbers. Therefore should not you and I watch also, messmate, that we may not forget we are ever in His holy view wherever may be our lot to be cast in this life?'

This naturally leads me to make some remarks on the other sort, called land crabs. They are of an amphibious nature, but their chief residence is on land. There are two different sorts or colours of them, the one of a chocolate colour, the other that of a mulatto. The dark sort are reckoned the best and are to be found even so far upland as some miles; yet they have their annual time of coming down to the sea which is in the breeding time, about March. What is very wonderful, is that when they are on a march they never turn either to one hand nor the other, but if a huge stone, log or trunk of a tree chance to lie in their passage they mount over it, and that they do, should it be as high as one storey of a house. At which seasons they come down from the high country by thousands; the males are so vicious that they have frequent battles and fight furiously, giving each other such blows with their great claws that the sound may be heard twenty yards away, as their claws are much larger than those of the Sea Crab, especially one of them. When one of them finds himself rather the master, he will strive to seize the other by one of his large claws, and thus holds him for such a length of time that his antagonist, finding no other means of escaping, gives such a sudden snap with the joint next to his body that he leaves the whole member to be devoured by the other and thus makes his escape.

This sort of crab devours everything indifferently as it can come at it. They burrow deep into the earth, having generally two holes, the one for to make their escape by, perhaps, or for some other reason. If a corpse should be buried without a coffin, as is many times the case abroad, they never fail to find it out and devour the whole flesh from the bones. They are so swift that it is out of human power to overtake them, if they have a fair field for the chance. These crabs differ in bodily shape from sea crabs, being of a round and compact body. The lizards take particular care to avoid them, knowing by instinct that if they come within but a snatch of their claws there is no redemption.

My friend Somer from this time fell into a kind of melancholy, and one day I asked him the cause of his dullness.

'Oh, my good friend,' said he, 'I am thinking on my wickedness.'

'So should we all,' I told him.

'No, no, Mr Penrose,' said he, 'you have not been so great a sinner as me. Did I not shoot

Brandt?'[13]

'*Pray don't give your heart so much trouble on that account,*' I said, '*for it is my real opinion that you were appointed by the great Judge himself as his instrument to be the end of that wretch. Know ye not that it is His divine decree that whosoever sheds innocent blood, by man shall his blood be shed?*'

'*That is true,*' he said, '*but then I sent him to hell without my giving him a chance to ask pardon.*'

'*Leave that reflection alone to the great Author of our being, and pray let us drop the subject.*' So to divert him from it, I asked him when we should go and examine the cask that they had found.

'*Tomorrow,*' he said, and we went accordingly.

Away we went next day in the yawl. When we came to the spot, I scuttled[14] the cask to examine its contents and we found it to contain hams. We then got it on board and returned home, but when we came to examine them, to our great surprise we found that they had lost all their saltness in a manner. We hung them in the sun to dry, and dry they did, sure enough, becoming hard as sticks. Our Indians would never taste it after the first time, so that they hung by for a long time, except Somer and I now and then cut a piece and ate it by way of a novelty.

And now I shall give the reader a sample of my own courage when put to the test. One evening Mrs Penrose and Harry took it into their heads to divert themselves a little at my expense. She knew me to have a custom to cut off a bit of those hams in an evening, to eat with a plantain, and I usually sat on a stool outside the cave. Now as I was sitting with my pipe smoking, Betty took occasion to ask me why I did not take a bit of the ham for my supper.

'*I think I will*' said I. Now they hung back in the cavern, so up I got and opened my knife for that purpose and marched in to that intent. But when I came to advance towards the place, whistling as I went, all at once I was struck with one of the most horrid sights that I had ever beheld. Back I ran much faster than I had entered, and was making for my stool with my hair standing on end. My wife, observing me to be so much alarmed, burst into a great fit of laughter. This brought me to myself a little. She then told me the secret and rallied me not a little, saying she wondered that white men could be frightened at such trifles, who were not dismayed at the winds and great waters.

When I had recovered my thoughts again, I went in with her to get a fair view of it, and yet the sight was truly odious. It was Mr Harry who had got 4 of those Fire Flies I have mentioned before; they are nearly as large as chafers. These he had fixed, two of them between his teeth and one in each socket of his eyes, then placed himself in a dark corner, the green-ness of the light casting such an infernal gleam over his face, together with his mouth and eyes appearing to be all on fire, that I defy the bravest heart not to be daunted should he come upon it as unaware as I did.

Somer happened to be then down by the waterside, and Betty when she saw him returning told Harry to place himself again as before. When he came up I asked him if he should get a bit of ham for each of us.

'*With all hearts,*' said he.

'*Go, then, and cut a bit for each of us,*' said I.

In he went freely but in a short time we heard him holler, but he did not run back as we expected. But out ran Harry in a great hurry, calling to us. We ran in and found him lying in a strong fit. I bade them run and get a torch directly, and it was nearly an hour before we could get any sense from him, when he was so far recovered as to converse. I got him some gin, and asked what was his disorder, when he began: *'Oh, Donder, Donder! Ich sal never liven much longer!'*

'What has terrified you, man?' said I. *'You stare like one quite mad.'*

'Oh, shipmate, I have seen von spook for Brandt.'

'Pshaw,' said I, *'don't be foolish, man! You have fallen in a fit. You are subject to them, I suppose.'*

He said he had never had one in his life to his knowledge. Now I would have given a thousand dollars for this trick never to have been played. The poor Indians were all terrified to death, and how to contrive the matter I knew not. I advised him to go to sleep, strictly charging his wife to watch by him, and that he should not know anything of it until the next day. The next morning he seemed quite recovered. I then told him the real story, and that they had served me in like manner. But he could not be persuaded, until it was repeated the next evening, and then it was all passed off in a joke, the best way we could.

Few young people give themselves the time to reflect on the dangerous consequences attending a great fright; yet how frequently they practise the thing, although thousands in the world have been rendered useless to society by it, to the grief of many a family.

It was now about the middle of July when, as Somer and I were on a hill looking out to seaward, I thought I saw some kind of vessel in the offing, and therefore called down for my eyeglass. When Eva brought it up to me, I found it to be so, but what to make of her we could not tell. She was as we thought under no sort of sail, and too far out to be at an anchor. It was about noon when we first discovered her, and there she remained all that day. The next morning I went up again and found that she had not drifted half a mile from her first station. This put us on disputing – Somer was for going out to reconnoitre her, but the move did not suit then with me, as not knowing how things might turn out. This I found gave messmate Godart uneasiness, so I told him that if she remained that way two hours longer I would consent to go out with our yawl and get a more satisfactory view of her. He observed that, as he was convinced that she was in distress, our duty called on us to save life.

'What would you say should it prove a sort of decoy?'

He then made me this reply: *'Don't you always beg me to hold fast on the Divine Providence, and where are you now, man?'*

'Say no more,' I replied, *'but let Harry get the yawl ready, and in God's name we will go.'*
By this time, the whole family were interested, and we kept a constant eye on her.

Now as I found my wife not fond of my going, I told Somer that he and Harry should go, giving them strict charge not to go too near her, unless they saw absolute necessity to do so. So away they went with a light wind, leaving me full of concern until their return. Every now and then I took a fresh lookout. At last I saw them lie to. Some time after this I saw a small thing put out from alongside the vessel and join ours; and as I was thus under my cogitations I saw both boats go alongside the vessel, and I hoped to some good end. The reader may easily think what a state I was in, while they remained on board her. When I went up again, I saw that they had put off, and stood right in for our bay. I waited with impatience for the upshot of the affair. At last I could perceive my own people in her; but no sooner did they come in than I ran eagerly down, crying, *'What news? What news?'*

'Oh, give me some water to drink!' said Somer, *'and then I shall tell you all.'*

'How came you to be out of the water?' said I while they were drinking.

Then he began and said it was a sloop from Santiago in Cuba[15], in great distress; that they had been struck by lightning which had carried away their mast about 6 feet above the partners[16], with two hands struck dead; and that they had not one drop of water left when they came onboard them, having finished the last the day before; that they drank off all that they had carried in the yawl at once.

'How did you come to understand them?' I said.

Somer then told me that he believed the captain was an Irish man, for he could speak English very well and his name was Dennis Horgan[17], and that he earnestly begged my kind assistance if possible.

'How many hands are they?' said I.

'Only 3 men and a boy.'

'Well then, come on. Let us in the first place carry off some water in one of our empty kegs, for we can pretend to do nothing further until she is had in to anchor.'

'I have told them to go for water to the point of Long Key,' said he.

'That was right,' I told him. We then got in some of our provisions and put off directly. As we got out of the lagoon, we saw their boat heading for the Key point. We hurried off to them as fast as we could, and when we got alongside the captain stood crossing and blessing us, making bows to me. I jumped on board directly, when he came and eagerly kissed me, saying that we were Jewels of Angels sent from the Holy Powers, to be sure, to save their lives.

'How long have you been in this distress, captain?' said I.

'18 days, my dear,' said he, 'and out 29 days.'

They had not one spar left. They first got up the square sail yard to the boom as a mast or rather jury mast[18], and lost that three days after, being carried away in a gale of wind, and now had nothing more left, saying that if they had, they had become so exhausted in strength that they could not make any hand of it. I told him that we must first get her inshore to an anchor if we could, and then we would try to cut him a small tree down and endeavour to get it stepped for him, according to our strength. Then he asked us down below and offered us some aquadienta, but I told him it was thing we were not used to, so begged him to excuse us.

'Oho', said he, 'my dear children, you are the first sailors I ever knew in my life who don't like a drop of the silly cratur.'

I told him I would inform him more on that head, another time.

Now as we were thus sitting in conversation I took up a book, which lay on one of the lockers. Curiosity made me open it, when I found it to be Spenser's *Faerie Queene* in English. 'This is the first book I have seen in many a long year,' I said.

'And is it, troth?' he said. 'Why then, honey, I could gratify your desire by the fist full, if that be all, but first let us be getting the sloop in to an anchor, by your laves.'[19]

'As soon as your boat returns,' said I. Some time after this we turned to, and towed her into 12-fathom water and there came to, it now becoming almost evening. I then took my leave of them, as I did not care to remain on board her all night, lest something happened at home. I asked the captain to go on shore with us, but he did not choose to leave the sloop.

I slept but little that night, but about three in the morning roused Harry and told him to call Somer. We then put off down the lagoon, and were obliged to row to her as it was flat calm. They were all turned out, waiting our arrival.

'Good morning to you, my sweet babes,' said the captain. 'Long life to you!'

We then jumped on board and he took us below. I observed one of his hands to be a Spaniard, the other two Negroes. The captain then took out a bottle, and holding it up to the light said, *'Well, now, what may your name be called, I pray?'*

I told him Penrose, at his service.

'Penrose,' said he. *'Was you ever on board of the old Namur, young man?'*[20]

I answered in the negative.

'Well, true and faith, then; I was well acquainted with one Davy Penrose on board of that ship in the year 38.'

But you must understand,' said I, *'those days are too old of date for me.'*

Faith, and that is true for you, I believe,' he said; *'but however it's the same thing, maybe he was your elder brother.'*

Some relation, perhaps,' I answered.

'Oh, then, by my Shoul you don't gain great credit by your kin, joy; for he would be after milling and pilliareing any one's Dudds[21] he could lay his hands on, so that some of our knowing lads would be after remarking dat he was one fisherman's boy, each of his fingers a fish hook. But that is neither here nor there. Take a bob a piece of this, children,' holding out the bottle and glass to me – *'as you would not take any before.'* So to humour him we took a little of it.

After this we returned and got up the anchor, then leaving the skipper at the helm we got three into each boat, and began to tow her further in. While we were thus employed the old man asked me if I knew a good berth, to bring her to in. *'I have not been here so many years not to know that,'* I told him. After we had been towing for about the space of an hour, he called the boy Perico on board, and ordered him to cook us a good mess[22] of chocolate. The sound of chocolate revived my heart. Shortly after we all took about a pint with a good Spanish biscuit each, and then brought her safe to anchor opposite our old plantation, where she lay in two fathom water, snug enough.

When matters were brought thus far, I gave the captain to know I should be glad of his company at our poor habitation. He said with all his heart, so leaving the boy to look after the vessel we came away together. As his two people and Harry rowed, we 3 sat, and I then ran over my story in brief to him. During the time the old man would cry, *'Salve Domine!'* At length we came to our Barcadera[23], when I took Captain Horgan by the hand and bade him welcome. The rest of our family had gathered round to meet us, but no sooner did they fix their eyes on the Negro man whose name was Rodrigo but away ran the children, and the girls began to move also, as it is my opinion that they had never seen an African before.

Now I told this kind old Hibernian that without any more ado or ceremony he was free to make use of our place as he listed[24], and that Mr Somer and I would give him all the assistance in our power; that we had plenty of those things needful towards the support of human nature, but as to dainties we had long since learnt to live without them; and that when we were a little refreshed we would take a hunt among the trees after some sort of a mast, and Mr Somer generously undertook to make it. I now took the opportunity to ask him how much powder he had onboard.

'Indeed,' said he, *'it is not long since I was in great dread I had too much of it on board, when we had the misfortune of the lightning.'*

I then observed that we had a fine lump of ambergris by us, and should be proud to make an exchange with him for powder.

'Oh,' said he, *'you shall have what I can spare, for nothing, joy,'* since we were so civil to lend our help in his distress.

I then told Harry to bring the women and children to me. They came and I presented them to the old gentleman, and he received them cordially; and as the Negro fondled the children they became more free with him.

After we had dined, Mr Somer and Diego the Spaniard took a walk in search of some sticks to cut for a pair of sheers[25], while Mr Horgan and I hunted out a tree fit for a temporary mast. After this we returned and chatted over our pipes, he observing that he had not done the like for 5 years, as he always made use of cigars. He then said that he would present us with some tobacco, with a little sugar and chocolate. I then began to ask about twine, needles, nails & co. or anything he could well spare, most of which we afterwards obtained in some degree.

The next day they went to work and felled the trees, then Somer and Diego went to work on them and in about 5 days they formed a tolerable sort of mast. Now what is surprising, as the captain told me, was that they never once had sight of any vessel during the whole time, being frequently becalmed for days. He also told me that two casks of water were stove in by the thunder in the hold, and 5 long bars of iron were fairly melted; that when they were first struck he imagined all his people to be dead as they were all down below, but that Pedro Gomez and Martin Galvan never came to, so that they committed them to the deep the next day.[26] I then enquired whither they were bound, and he told me a port called Madalena[27], and that he owned half the sloop himself. She was about 60 tons burthen, quite old and much out of repair.

The next day the captain and I, with Harry and the Negro, went away to the sloop, taking some yams and beans for the boy's use. Now while we were on board, and having leisure, I asked him to give me a sight of some of his books. He then called Perico to get out a square box. When it appeared I was struck with an odd circumstance. The lid had the following directions on it, done in black paint: 'To the care of Mr Aron Manby, Kingston, Jamaica.'[28]

'This has been prize goods, I suppose,' I said.

'Indeed it was all that,' said the captain, 'They have laid a long time at St Jago in an old store, unheeded as few or none could read them, so I bought them, child, for a trifle.'

I then said 'What will you take for them by the lump?'

'Why, as to that, honey, I don't care to part with them at all, do you see, because I know some of my acquaintance where I am bound who will give me a good price for some of them, as we never have any English books come among us but by the wheel of fortune, as I may say.'

'Come, then' said I, in a word will you take the value of 50 pieces of eight, as you say you gave but a trifle for them?'

'Indeed, Mr Penrose, I can deny you nothing at all, at all. And now, faith and soul, if you will give me 70 dollars you shall have them, and cheap enough, too.'

Now, I thought, you are an old fox, that is flat.[29] 'Well, then, I will give you in good solid silver the full value of it. Is it a bargain, or not?'

'Show me the money,' said he.

'As to money,' said I, 'where should I get cash? But you shall have it full weight in silver when you come on shore.'

'Are you on honour, my love?' he said.

'For certain,' I told him.

'Well then, my jewel, you may have them, so say no more but take them with you when you go.'

And then to mend the bargain, he gave me a bottle of cordial. I then called Harry and he with the Negro boy got the box into our yawl. I was now become so eager to be on shore that I knew not where I stood. Now just before we were going to put off, I was surprised to hear the Negro fellow talking English with my Harry, and laughing.

'What makes you so merry, Blackie?' I said.

'Master, I was saying to your man that the old fellow was well paid for those old books.'
How so?' I replied.

'Because I was with him when he paid for them, and he gave but 5 pieces of eight.'

'Never mind that now,' said I. 'Pray, where did you learn English?'

'I was born in Spanishtown, Jamaica[30], and was carried off by a privateer from Old Harbour[31] about 13 years ago when a boy.'

'Are you a free man now?' said I.

'Yes, sir,' he replied. 'My wife bought me free. She is a Spanish mulatto of Rio Madalena.'

After we came on shore I told the captain that I should convince him of my honour, and then produced a quantity of plate in pieces and bade him examine it well. He then began to cut it and ponder upon it[32]. At last he said: 'By the Holy Saint Columb, it is good plate, sure enough. And where did you find this, now?'

'By chance digging for turtle eggs,' said I.

'Well, then, by the blessed St Patrick you were a very fortunate man, Captain Penrose, to find turtles that laid silver eggs.'

'Now how shall we weigh this said plate?'

'Oh, leave that to me, honey,' said he.

Yes, but I hope you will let me have a hand in the affair, captain, too,' I answered. Then taking up a piece I asked him what he valued that at.

About 8 dollars,' he said. When this was done, I wrote a receipt and he signed his name to it, Dennis Horgan.

After this, we went to visit the mastmakers, and brought them down to the house, where I made them a good yabba of toddy out of our little store. And then I sent out the canoe striking fish, and in about two hours they returned with a fine mess, which was directly cooked. And as we were eating, the old man took occasion to ask me if I were a Catholic or not. I answered in the negative.

'Ah, that is your misfortune,' said he, 'but no matter, honey, if you are to be saved, you are; It is no meat of mine, child, only it is a great pity and an error of judgement among your people to be quitting the true and only Old Mother Church.'

'Never mind that,' said Somer. 'Don't you see how the goot Got mack his sun shine pon all? You vill neet call us for da Divel when we mack you von goot mast wan dime more.' And thus it ended. Then the pipes were called for, with some of our friend Horgan's choice tobacco. After this, the old man went up the hill with Somer and Diego to see to the work.

In the meantime I took the opportunity to examine my purchase and found the contents as follows: *The Faerie Queene*, *Pope's Essay*, *Spectators*, *Seneca's Morals*, *Chaucer's Tales*, *Don Quixote* and *Ovid's Epistles*; then *Josephus*, *Anson's Voyage*, *Ramsay's Songs*, *Foxe's Book of Martyrs*, and a fine large old Bible with great clasps, the *Spectacle de la Nature*, some of *Baxter's* works, with *Virgil*, *Homer* and *Horace*, and many unbound pamphlets.[33] These books had lain so long neglected that the worms had passed through them, but had not hurt them so much as to spoil them. Nevertheless, I thought the old captain well paid for them, although I would not have returned them for double the money, as I looked on it to be a chance among thousands for me to meet with anything of that kind in this place. And so highly proud was I of them, that I stowed the box away with the greatest care imaginable, valuing it as an inestimable treasure.

The next day we sent off the sheers and small boom to the vessel. As for their other boom, they had in the first place cut it, in order to make it suitable to the strength they had to raise it, for a kind of jury mast. And when the new mast was finished we mustered all hands and with rollers and handspikes got it down to the lagoon in two days, from where it was towed alongside the sloop. After this was done, I mustered all our whole force that could be spared, from the shore. I sent off Patty, Eva and Jessy, so that now they mustered nine in number. On the morrow Harry and the boy came in and told me that Mr Somer had got the mast in, and that the captain desired that I would let him and the boy go out striking fish for them, while they got up the shrouds[34] and other things. Accordingly I despatched them away with some roots and what I could spare.

It was above a week after this, before Mr Somer had got her any way in readiness; and then they had her mainsail to cut less, to suit her mast, as it was neither so taut or tight as the former.[35] But in about a fortnight they got her in the sort of condition with which to proceed, and then we made a kind of frolic on shore, and were as merry as so many poor people could be expected to be on the occasion, and the old gentleman was as liberal to us as he could well spare, like a true Hibernian.

They remained with us for almost a month, living chiefly on provisions from our plantation, fishery and gunning. In the meantime, while they remained with us, we got about 30 pound weight of gunpowder and about a hundredweight of bar lead. The captain gave our women some boxes of marmalade. They had a quantity of dry goods on board of several kinds; I got above 2 dozen Barcelona handkerchiefs, and a variety of ribbons for our girls with which, like true females, they afterward dizen'd[36] themselves out. Mr Horgan presented me with a small pocket compass, a thing that gave me great joy. He gave Somer a wood-plane and a pair of compasses. Harry for his share got an hour-glass, which pleased him to such a degree that he would now and then lay himself flat on the ground with it before him, and watch the whole sand run down, frequently striking the glass to cause it to run the faster, as he foolishly imagined. We got a store of twine, thread, hooks, needles, pins, two penknives and many other articles we stood in need of. And the time grew nigh that they were about to go, and the old man and I settled. I paid him for almost all we had, as we scorned to take anything for our labour, as Mr Somer and I looked upon it as no more than our duty to relieve the distressed – having received sufficient example from the poor savages, our sincere friends.

After all things were settled, the old man asked me to take a walk with him in private, when he began thus: 'Mr Penrose, how is it possible that you could live so many years here among these savages? If you will but leave them and go with me in my sloop, you may there become a very happy man. We have several holy men with us who will be proud to bring you into the true way, I mean the bosom of our Holy Church. What can you expect to be, after spending your life in this wilderness?'

I made him this reply – that as to my living among savages I had sufficiently found to my account, by their faithful services, that they were my true and experienced friends; and in regard to my situation I was so well content with my condition that I would not by choice change it, unless such a thing should come to pass that I could be once transported with my wife and two children in some English ship to my own country again, and I well knew my removing among the Spaniards could never prove fortunate to me, being determined never to change my religion; and that I was well assured that my friend Somer was steadfast of the same mind, saying that if we did not enjoy the superfluities of the busy world, we were over and above made amends by living in a state of innocence, and in no great dread of wanting what was sufficient to support us, could we be anything else but content.

'Well, then, my dear jewel,' said he, 'I shall have no more to say.'

'Now,' said I, 'Daddy, I have one petition to beg of you which will cost you no more than the keeping of a secret, (viz.) that you will never discover this our residence to the Spaniards of your acquaintance, as our being on this shore can never prove in any way detrimental to them, being in no way concerned with others, nor have we evil practice in our hearts.'

He then grasped my hand and declared by the Holy Spirit that he would ever be silent on the matter, and that he would manage the affair so that none with him should be the means of being so discovered.

A few hours later, he proposed to go off, and we waited on him to the sloop. When they had got up the anchor, I then stood pilot until we saw them clear of the Long Key and then bade them a good voyage, returning back safely to our old mansion. And I hope that we discharged our duty by them; and perhaps on the whole they made a saving voyage, for they got both pieces of ambergris, which must be of great value. And thus ended this new adventure.

We were now become so happy as to read and hear the Scriptures, a thing which proved of much comfort to us. Now after they were gone, I repented that we had not sold the longboat to the captain, but Somer observed that it could never have answered their need, as they could neither hoist her in or out, and to tow her would impede her way too much.

'Let her be,' said he, 'who knows how soon we may want her for ourselves?'

Some months after this, my messmate Godart became much out of order, with spitting of blood; and I thought his great application to reading might be the occasion of it, as he became so fond of it after I had learnt him to read, that he would be at it hour after hour. I therefore begged him to refrain, and that I would read myself whenever he had a desire, advising him that as we now had powder, to go out with the gun or fishing with Harry at times. This he complied with, and soon became much better.

THE THIRTEENTH YEAR – NORMAN BELL JOINS THE FAMILY
AND LUTA IS BORN
June 15 1759 – June 14 1760

It now became the latter end of June, and time rolled on after the old sort. Nothing happened of note, only my School advanced apace. My son could now read middling well and Harry almost as well, as I kept them at it daily, each in their turn; so that I had six scholars and all were very zealous.

One day, Somer and I took a notion to count over our treasure, for hitherto the whole had remained as first we found it. We began with gold and it amounted to 557 pistoles and the silver to 7,944 dollars[37] – a brave sum to be divided between two poor Jack Tars[38]. 'Now,' I said to Godart, 'suppose you and I had shared all this from a prize in England, how do you think we should have behaved with it?'

'I think,' said he, 'it would all have been shared among whores, fiddlers, pipers and public houses.'

'How so, messmate,' I replied. 'Do you think we should not have found out some more honourable way?'

'Look you[39], mine goot vrindt,' said he, 'we are not now such mad, skipping drunken fools as we were in those days. We are now men. The great God has disposed of us another way. It is nothing more than the work of the devil himself when men act after such a manner, Mr Penrose. He has always his friends ready to instruct others, so the boys learn it from the men.'

'That is very just, messmate,' said I. 'The Devil is never at a loss for an agent.'

'But now what do you say,' he replied, 'to privateering itself? Is it robbing the honest trader of his goods, if you please?'

'Do they not act after the same sort by us?' said I.

'Yes, that is true. But nevertheless you may plainly see by the way we and many others live, that men, if they were truly just, could live without cutting each others' throats, and plundering innocent people who would live as harmless as we do now.'

'All this is very good,' said I. 'And yet, shipmate, I do remember the day when you had a strong hankering for the public world again. And what was all that for, but to indulge your vicious will again?'

'Ah my good man,' said he, 'at that time I was more at the Devil's service than now.'

'Pray, Somer, be plain and honest. Would you not of a choice rather live in Holland, provided that you could at will convey what money you are master of, to there?'

'That I should prefer living among good Christian people and to be above want is true, but not to lose my good state of mind, for the whole world.'

'Well,' said I, 'make our heart easy. We are likely to remain as we are. But I could have left this place with Captain Horgan if I had been that way inclined, as he made me the kind offer.'

'And by this time, you would have been begging.'

'It may be, perhaps, so indeed,' said I. 'So how do we know but whatever is, is right, as Mr Pope says in that book we were reading last night?'

'Very true,' said he.

'Yet I would wish to know whether my poor mother be yet alive,' I said.

'What good would that do you?' said he. 'I have no father or mother to mourn for me, for they are both dead.'

'So, let us drop it, and learn to live so that we may never be in dread of the day when God shall call us off.'

The dialogue, whose topic began with us counting over the dross[40], ended as we returned from the place, leaving it in its native soil as we found it first, and made no more account of it for the future – leaving all to the divine will of God, and making ourselves as cheerful every day as we should, in innocent amusements of some kind or other, such as shooting at marks with bows and arrows, playing at quoits, setting the girls and children to run races, making utensils, singing psalms, and sometimes jumping at distances.

In a short time after, as Somer and I were talking on a few lines I had been reading in Josephus, I took it into my head to propose a sort of worship on the Sabbath Day. This he seemed much to like. Upon this I proposed that it should be his province, strictly to observe the day of the week. This he took upon him; and I ordained that every Sunday after breakfast we should say at my table the Creed, Commandments and Lord's Prayer, then the first chapter of the Bible, so to be continued in rotation as they came, and to conclude with a psalm after the best way we could. As to myself I could sing but one, which was that of the 104th tune[41]; but Somer could sing several Dutch tunes, a few of which we adapted the best way we could. And thus our form was settled, to begin the next Lord's Day.

Accordingly, when the day came, I told Harry to collect the whole family, and when they were all met, I took my place and gave them all strict charge that they did not make any noise. During the whole time, the most profound silence was kept as I read, until Somer and I began to sing the psalm. The parrots then began to hoot and sing at such a rate, that we were forced in future to remove them to the kitchen when Sunday came, to avoid being pestered with the screaming. And indeed we found the need to do the like with one of our dogs. This would set the other to work often, so that at times we were forced to put the whole disorderly crew in durance[42] together. Nothing could be more singular than the behaviour of the women when they were at this service. Their looks were so profound and seriously innocent, that it gave us much pleasure.

The next thing Godart went upon was to make a kind of desk for me to read at. And thus we kept irregularly on, unless some unforeseen thing hindered us. And here I must remark that once on Sunday as we were in the midst of our psalms there came three Indians by land and walked up towards the cave, where they halted and stood in a very serious attitude of attention until we had finished our ceremony.

These Indians were strangers to me, except one who had been here before and was called Gaynasunto. Another of them was named Owasotas and was a kind of half-brother to my wife, 'by two fathers' as he expressed it. These Indians brought seeds of tobacco from Owagamy, and a peccary that they had shot. This was dressed afterwards, and we made a plentiful repast with our friends.

I shall in this place take notice of something singular in regard to the old Bible, which I purchased, from Captain Horgan. On the first unprinted leaf of this book was the following memorandum: '*Samuel Shaddon was born May 4th anno 1670. Joseph Shaddon, his son, was born in Westminster on the 12th of August, anno 1701. Mary Shaddon was born on the 9th of October, anno 1703. Nicholas Shaddon was born on the 23rd of November, anno 1705. Elenor Shaddon was born on the 2nd of June, anno 1708.*'[43] Then on the inside of the cover was thus written in another hand the following lines:

'*Thomas, this is the last favour you can possibly expect to receive from my aged hands. Take notice and remember that it is my earnest request that you strictly peruse this book, and the more this world frowns on you, open it the more often. If you truly examine its contents you will find consolation, the one thing needful, for no man knows the severe trials in this life. Never part with it if possibly you can avoid it. But rather, when you and yours have by frequent using of it rendered it necessary to be rebound, reserve the old binding in your own family for the sake and remembrance of the donor who wishes you all happiness. James Rogers, 1719.*'

About this time as my wife and I were walking on the other side of the plantain walk, I took notice of a small bird, telling her that we had a bird in my country much the same size which we called a wren. Nothing can exceed these pretty creatures. They go always in pairs. Their shape and magnitude, together with their actions, are much like the bird above-mentioned, but their colour exceeds the parrot in greenness, and under the throat is a large spot equal to the ruby in colour. They are not very shy, seldom mounting above the high shrubs. She told me they called them *Manune*, which word I could get no better impression of than '*Mutual Love*'[44]; and, well adopted, I thought, as they are ever together. When one flies, the other does the like. When or wherever the one pitches, the other alights close by its side. They frequently bill like pigeons. This conjugal love, so apparent in diminutive creatures, renders them highly to be admired and imitated.

But now shall I draw the sorrowful scene which we both soon became witness of? I observed one of those little innocents begin to flutter its wings and chatter much, then run along the spray of leaves and return to its mate. This I at first took to be a kind of courtship, but shortly after as it flew down to the ground, Betty pointed to a long and very slim yellow snake[45] which was coiled up, with its head in the centre erected, and playing its tongue at a great rate. The little bird would run to and fro, fluttering its wings and making a sad noise, then fly up to its mate again. Every time it came down, it drew still nearer to the snake. At last the snake threw itself at its length, but still kept its head directed towards the bird. Betty then told me I should soon see the snake open its mouth very wide, and then the bird would run and play close before it, when the snake would give a dart with its head and take it in.

'How can that possibly be?' said I, 'seeing the head of the snake to be no bigger than the end of my finger?'

But she insisted that it could take the bird in whole.

'But that shall not be,' I replied, 'if it is in my power to hinder.' Then with some warmth I cast my eyes around, and finding a kind of twig I ran and gave it a stroke athwart[46] the neck which soon spoiled its enchanting power, and by that means restored the poor little innocent to its disconsolate mate, who sat all the time on the limb, crying chirp, chirp and trembled at a sad rate.

I then turned to Betty and recited over the circumstance of our first mortal crime in the credulity of our Mother Eve. Upon this, she said that I was very big in cunning, for I could tell her anything I pleased as it happened on the other side of the great waters. But she was sure that such a thing had never happened in their country, because whenever any of their women chanced to spy a snake, they ran from them, or it, as knowing they would poison them, and they would not wait to hear what they could say to them if they could talk.

One day as I was passing into our dwelling I took notice of a white circle on the underside of the archway of the cave, and as I had not observed it before, I was a little the more curious about it. But on a nearer view I saw now and then a kind of brown wasp come in with a bit of the same matter, and fix it thereto. This circle was about the size of a quart bottle, and in the course of a few days they had formed it into the shape of a small punch bowl. Thus they went on, until they had got it to the size of a large bottle, when they began work to contract its bulk so as to bring it to the likeness of a neck, still working downwards, so that by the time it was finished it was almost a foot in length, leaving only a small hole sufficient for one to enter at a time. After this, they went daily to and fro during the hottest hours. The girls wanted to knock it down, least they might sting the children, but I forbade them. When I found they had all forsaken it, I told Harry to carefully cut it down with a large knife; and when I came to examine the internal parts, nothing could be more curious. The cells were arrranged[47] circularly one within the other, so that it formed one complete spiral line. As to the substance, it resembled our sort of coarse white paper but much stronger, and did not weigh above an ounce or so at least.

There is a sort of insect here of a very odd form, being in length about four inches yet so slim in one part that it is not much thicker than a small thread. It has eight very long legs and two horns, 6 inches in length tapering to such a small point that it is as fine as any cobweb in appearance. The whole insect, wings and all, is of the fine (metallic) hue of a watch-spring, but what makes it singular is its smell, as no rose can have a finer scent. It has the power to fold up these horns as in joints, or can at pleasure lay both horns backwards in a direct line.

There is another sort, which resembles a wasp, but three times its size and in colour like amber with a yellow head[48]. I never could see above one of them at a time. The manner of its life differs from that of all other insects of that class. It burrows into any dry and sandy place, to the depth of a foot or more. To this receptacle he brings all his prey, being very furious after all sorts of flies and the like, which he catches either on the wing in full pursuit, or by stratagem when they are on a leaf. He has two legs much longer than the rest; and as he always carries his prey between his feet, he by a movement of the joints of those two long legs poises the load, if it proves rather heavy. When he brings home his prey and has descended below, you shall hear a kind of noise the whole time, like a person drawing the fiddle stick over the smaller strings. When this noise stops, you may expect his return. Directly on his coming up, he then proceeds to work with his two long feet backward, and in a short time covers the entrance so curiously that the place is not to be observed; and should you make any alteration so as to deceive him, yet he has the sagacity to find it out, without fail. I have opened these repositories and have found at the bottom several small cells, in each of which were stowed numbers of insects of different kinds.

This leads me naturally to another sort of being with which we were amused at times, a kind of large beetle of a black colour. This insect, whenever it finds the dung of any animal or other kind of pulpy offal, it there takes up its residence until the whole is consumed.[49] But as the manner of its providing for itself is the most curious part of the story, I shall inform the reader. They always fly by night or in an evening. They have a most powerful knowledge in the finding out of any of the above-mentioned stuff, even should you lay it in a very secret place. When they first find it out, and if the surface of the earth be not of too hard a texture, they begin to work down through the centre of the mass to a considerable depth, bringing up the loose earth as in their arms. This they lay all on one side until the business of that sort is finished. They then begin to gather up arms full of the matter, just as one would do with hay or straw. When it has cleverly got up as much as it can grasp, it then walks backwards to the edge of the hole and throws itself backwards, load and all, and thus tumbles to the bottom of its pit or cell, then returns again and acts in the like manner until it has industriously collected the whole.

If you dig down some time after, you will find the whole mass curiously made up into a round ball, and very closely packed together. But when you break this ball, in the centre is to be seen its young embryo; and as that comes on to maturity, it has a sufficiency ready provided. It then begins to eat on the internal part. The old one does the like externally, so that by the time they have eaten up the whole, you young one has become capable to provide for itself. But if it should prove too small a quantity, the old one goes in quest of more and flies home to the cell with it in her arms, as I may say. And this she continues to do until her young one is fit to go abroad. When that time comes, she brings the young black bantling[50] up in her arms and there leaves it to itself.

About the latter end of August, Harry had a daughter born, and he chose she should be called Luta, after his sister who was my first wife. And as Somer and I were passing a joke concerning making out fortunes for our children, we happened to mention the word dross, meaning the money those sons of Jolly Roger[51] had buried.

Now, my young Owen chanced to stand by us at the time and said, *'Father, there is dross in the great Bible book.'*

'I know that, child,' said I, thinking he meant the clasps.

'No, not the clasps,' he said.

'Go along, you blockhead, and hold your tongue,' I cried.

'Indeed, daddy,' said the boy, *'there is dross in the boards of it.'*

'Come, Somer,' I said, *'let us see what he will be at.'* When we came to open the Bible, the child at once showed us a place within the cover where appeared a piece of some shining stuff, and on examination I found it to be a piece of coin. Upon this, I went to work and got it out and it proved to be a moidore[52] sunken deep inside the cover. And on further search, I found there was a range of them. We then turned to the other lid, and found it the same. Somer then looked at me and I on him; but after this pause I said,

'Now do I discover what the author of those lines, written on the cover, intended.' After this I laid it in all fair again, the best way I could, and observed to Godart that if old Horgan had discovered the secret, he would never have let me make the purchase. Upon this, Godart, taking up his pipe, went out of the house in the most extravagant fit of laughter. It was some time before I could get him to share the mirth with me. At last he said that he saw Old Mother Fortune standing right up against him, and making a game at he and I.

'In what shape?' I said.

'Vat shape? Shapen as two nunuchs (eunuchs),' said he.

'How so?' I replied.

'Why, she is given us monix like as von mountain, unt she know frall dat we been neet petter overall.'[53]

'Well said, messmate. That is a comical observation, indeed.'

Now, as I had good reason to think both covers were full, there could not be less than 60 moidores in each. And then we fell to rumination on the cause or intent thereof, when I came to this way of thinking. – That this book had been presented to a person who had perhaps been some great spendthrift, and that the good old author had ingeniously taken this method to supply his wants, as thinking that he would be in a better state of mind to receive so good and great a relief while frequently perusing this Holy Book. But alas, his Godly design miscarried and perhaps had gone through several hands, until by the wonderful turns of fortune it came into this remote corner, and into the hands of those who must needs prize the book far beyond the riches of its binding.

Soon after this discovery, I remember Harry and I were walking in the woods, and I observed to him a kind of vine growing up a large tree, and hung full with a kind of bean. I asked him if they were fit to eat. He said that the Indians ate them at times. The pods of these beans were a foot in length, and about the breadth of our Windsor bean but much flatter, and the bean small in proportion to the pod. As they were nearly ripe, we gathered a handful or two off the vine, and carried them home where we stripped them and stowed them in a locker Godart had made. Now it chanced that a few days after this I happened to sit myself on this box, when on a sudden a loud report went off, so that I got up and ran out, quite surprised. The girls ran in to know what noise it was. But on Harry's lifting up the lid, the beans all began and fired away at a brave rate. Some of them jumped quite out of the box, and before they had done, we had more than a Royal Salute from them.[54]

On the 4th of December, as Patty and Jessy were out on the hill looking for some leaves to burn, they came down and informed us that there were many large boats out on the waters. Away we ran up the hill and saw 7 large vessels with 3 others of a smaller size, all standing to the east. They being so far out, I got my glass and found some of them to be large ships, others of two masts. As the wind was at West, and but little of it, they remained in sight for several hours, and in the evening we heard a gun. Harry and I then took another look, and found them all huddled together. Early the next day, we went up again and could but just perceive them with the glass, and in about two hours we lost sight of them. That it was a squadron of the King's ships is my real belief, and belonging to Spain probably. The next day we saw a large sloop standing the same way, which was one of the same squadron's ships.

Somer now took a most romantic whim, (viz.,) that perhaps they were on the search for us, saying that it might be the Irish captain or some of his people had informed against us.

'That is a most ridiculous imagination,' said I, 'Can you be such an idle man to entertain a notion that we are of such great note or consequence that the Viceroy should fit out a squadron for no better purpose than to rout a couple of jack tars? Let not such vain thoughts enter your mind. For if the case stood that they did know of us, they need do no more than send a small armed launch, and she would sufficiently do our business, should they think it worth their time. So think no more of that, messmate.'

Nevertheless, when I first saw them huddled together when the gun was fired, I must own I became a little flurried, until I let reason take place. For, I thought, what could induce them to make it a point to rout a couple of poor seamen who had committed no crime, but landed there merely to save life. Yet I make no doubt had they but known of the cash we possessed, they would not have failed to visit us, for no other intent but to leave us as naked as when we landed. And should this prove the case, we could have spared it and have then remained as happy as before.

Once or twice a year we were visited by numbers of pigeons of two sorts, (viz.) Bald Pates and Sprig Tail[55]. I should have given a hint of them long before this, but as I could never command any of them for want of ammunition, they flew by unheeded. The Bald Pate, as I call them, do not breed about us as I never observed any of their nests. This bird is small and, what is not very common is quite black except the scalp or poll, that being quite white, feet and bill crimson with red circles around the eyes. The Sprigtail is a fine bird about the size of the English Wood Pigeon or Quist and much resembles that species. When they fly, the tail appears as terminating in one long point. This bird is so swift of flight that it is my sincere opinion that they can fly 7 miles in one minute. I do not advance this as a rodomontade[56], but by ocular judgment, having at times stood on an eminence as a large flock has been coming; when no sooner have they hove in sight which could be not less than two miles, yet before I could cock my piece they have been right over my head. Nay, the Indians as I was once observing this to them, insisted that they could fly above a thousand miles in the course of 24 hours without once resting. And this I really can credit. Owagamy's reason for it was sufficiently convincing – he saying that his people had shot them with a kind of red berries quite fresh in them early in the morning, which berries do not grow within two moons walk of them, going away to the south-west as he directed with his finger.

Now, as I am speaking on these birds I shall mention another species of Pigeon or Partridge, as it seems to partake of each kind. This bird is in size about that of a partridge, but in regard to its colours I have not words to express its great variety, many parts of being of the changeable kind.[57] The Indians call it a Deceiver, and with great propriety. They are never to be seen in any exposed place, but always in hilly country among rocks and bushes. Their flight is of but short duration depending much on running; and so exceedingly subtle are they that if they are pursued they squat and will not stir although you should tread close by them, but on your passing they artfully run back again with a flutter, by which means they are often betrayed. If by chance they can get no shelter when pursued, in that case they will squat behind any small stone on the off side, so that you may know to an inch where the bird is, yet cannot shoot it. Therefore they must be taken either on the run or the wing; all other means will prove to no effect. These birds are excellent dainties to eat.

About the end of December my beloved shipmate began to fall off again, and he declined so fast that he became skin and bone. Now what to do for him I knew not, it being totally out of my power to give him any relief. At last I proposed, by Harry's advice that they should take a journey to visit the Indians, thinking the change would prove of

115

some benefit to him. This proposal he seemed to like, and soon after undertook the journey, having become a little stronger. I was loth to part with a man I so much valued, yet my heart yearned so much towards his happiness, that I would have given all the treasure then in our power for his health.

When they came to depart, for Harry was to accompany him, he earnestly requested that if he never lived to return, that I would be a father to his child. And early on the morrow they prepared to depart, not without much concern on all sides. I now proposed that he had better take Eva his wife and her child with him, as perhaps she might prove of service on the journey. This she was glad enough of. Accordingly off they went; and enough had I left on my hands – Patty and Job in lamentation, and my son howling after Somer and Harry, for there never was a greater veneration between mortals than between them.

Now we were left to shift for ourselves, the best way we could. The whole business fell to my lot, and after they were gone we seemed like lost sheep. My heart was frequently heavy, as I was thinking I might never see the face of my esteemed friend any more. I then began to repent that I had made such an idle proposal, pestering my thoughts day and night that he might die in the woods, being in so weak a state. My wife administered her best consolation, yet I laboured the harder in my breast.

Thus I was forced to drag the time along, Patty ever in the dumps as she had the young children. And as I expected to hear from them or that they would return in about a month, when that time elapsed I became very uneasy, as thinking that Somer certainly must be dead. The thoughts of his departing among the savages almost drove me wild, not that I once had a notion of their neglect, but to think myself the author and the very hindrance of my discharging my dutiful last office in laying him under ground.

Now it happened very late one evening that my wife woke me, and said that she had heard a conch being blown. Up I got and ran to light a torch; I then called Patty. I then asked my Betty if she had not been dreaming. She said no, and that she was certain. I then got a shell and gave a strong blast. Shortly after, it was answered at a great distance. Now the ugly thought struck me that the sound might not proceed from my friends, and when this had once took possession I marched about like a man in a state of stupidity. But soon I heard the sound again. Well, thinks I, what will come, will come. I am now determined to stand the brunt; and I then gave another blast.

By this time the morning began to peep, which gave me new spirits. '*Make a good fire up*,' said I to the girls. On this, the shell sounded, and I knew they were not far off. Before the fire we stood for a time, and then I sounded and was answered from the lagoon. On this I gave a shout and was answered by Harry's well-known whoop. Then we all ran down to the landing place and waited until they all came in. The first man who jumped on shore was Owagamy. By this time it was light enough to see plainly. '*Where is my dear shipmate?*' said I with a loud voice.

'*He is here!*' cried Harry. Then came on shore my poor Godart. I took him in my arms and led him up to the house. But before I could well recover myself, I saw another white man, and a Spaniard, as I thought. This startled me much, but I was so overjoyed at my friend's return alive that I took no further notice at that time. Somer then told me he had been much worse or he would have returned before, but nevertheless he was resolved that if his time was not long, he would die with me, his friend.

Now, thought I, the secret burst at last. The Spaniards know of our being here, and farewell to all future comfort perhaps. Yet I determined to keep up my courage the best I could, and said, '*Harry, how many of you are in company?*'

'Ten,' said he.

'*Welcome all*,' I said. '*And pray who may this stranger be?*' – taking him by the hand in order to clap a good face on the matter.

But how astonished was I when in plain English dialect he said: '*A poor, unfortunate wanderer long lost from all comfort in this world.*'

'*The more welcome to me, messmate*,' cried I. '*This is a pleasant mistake indeed. I certainly took you for a Spaniard. But think yourself at home, friend. And pray what part gave you birth?*'

'*I am a subject of Great Britain born in the shire of Buchan.*'

'*Oh, you are a Scotchman I presume; and pray what may be your name, my friend?*'

'*My name is Norman Bell, at your service.*'

'*Make yourself as welcome as you please*,' said I, '*and if I can by any means contribute towards your future happiness, command me as you please, with all my spirit, messmate.*'

I had now got into such an odd mood that I knew not how to behave, so divided were the passions of my poor heart. On one hand stood Patty and Job quite overjoyed; on the other hand poor Eva with Jessy recounting her troubles, while the tears fell from her face; my new friend gazing around him like a man on enchanted ground; in another place Owagamy and the others chatting with my wife and Owen; Harry with the rest in another knot; so that the reader may paint the scene to himself if he can.[58]

When it was daylight[59] I told Patty to get water in one of the yabbas, and then I made some weak toddy for my poor fellow pilgrims and another for the Indians. But when I presented it to Bell he declined it, saying that he had not used the like for a long time. But by my desire they drank, and then Betty made them up our bed, being both of them weak. Bell and Somer slept for about 5 hours, where they rested well. In the meantime I told Harry that he must be in the necessity of going into the crawl for a turtle. Away he and another Indian went, and when they returned it was killed and dressed for our entertainment.

When my two friends awoke I joined them, and had them out to the Indians, as I chose to give them my company as much as possible, less they grew jealous by my paying more respect to my own sort than them. Mr Somer said that he found himself in a greater flow of spirits than for a long time past. This was good news to me; and after our meal we all enjoyed our pipes, and were the largest company of puffers I had had together since my first landing. I asked Mr Bell how long he had been among my good friends the Indians. He said not above three weeks, and that he had enjoyed more comfort in that time by the conversation of Mr Somer than for some years past. He was pleased to say that my friend had delivered himself so much in my favour that he thirsted to be with me.

I then took the opportunity to ask Owagamy his opinion concerning the teeth that we had found, and after the Indians had handed them from one to the other, and conferred notes together in their tongue, Owagamy told Harry that both he and his father had seen them, and that they knew of a deep valley wherein there were many of them, but it was far to the south. That he could never learn if any of their old people had seen one of those animals alive, saying they knew those creatures had long white horns as long as an Indian, for that some old people related that they had seen them – instancing old Wariboon, a great hunter, had kept one of them a long time by him, but as they lived a great distance from him they had never seen it.

Upon this, an Indian whose name was Kayoota, and present at the time said his father had seen it so many times – holding up his fingers; from all we gathered the beast then talked of must have been an elephant[60], and that those horns he mentioned came with the teeth of the animal. But how the whole race became extirpated remained to us a riddle unless the natives, in time out of mind, had unanimously joined to destroy them. Yet one should imagine that the task was of such a copious undertaking that they could never have succeeded; or as the continent being so extensive, all the natives could never have joined by mutual consent as they were separated thousands of miles asunder, and quite unintelligent of each others' existence. But I leave it to the learned to put what constructions on this great mystery they think proper.

THE FOURTEENTH YEAR – SOMER DIES, BELL MARRIES HIS WIDOW, AND THE TWINS AMERICA AND SOMER PENROSE ARE BORN
June 15 1760 – June 14 1761

Nothing worthy of recording happened from the time my new friend Bell came to reside with us, and it was now become the month of June and by my computation I had been here for a complete 13 years, not much within or over. And by permission of my new acquaintance, I shall relate a short account of his life from his own remembrance. (Viz.). He says his father, Angus Bell, was both in West Lothian and had followed the pedlar's[61] calling and died when Norman was but 10 years of age; and some time after that he was placed with a carpenter. From the carpenter he ran away when about 15 years of age, and got on board a vessel which traded up the East country. After that he went on some trips from Aberdeen to London, and there left the vessel. In the war time he went out on several cruises, and was taken and carried into St Malo in France, where he lay in prison for a long time, but during that space he learnt to play on the German Flute[62], from a certain fellow prisoner whose name was James Alexander, one of his countrymen.

After this they were exchanged and he came again to the City of London, and then got on board a ship bound for New York. That on his return he went to learn the French horn and trumpet, but by a foolish prank of wrestling got a kind of hurt in his back, so that rendered him unfit to follow the seas at that time. And some time after this he chanced to fall in with a set of puppet show folks who, finding that he understood the trumpet, engaged him; and soon after that he commenced Merry Andrew[63] with these people. Then on the rove[64] he travelled over part of England, Wales and Ireland.

His next connection was with a quack doctor with whom he travelled for two years, and took every opportunity to study his arts, saying he had ever been addicted to mimicry and could with ease take off the French, Dutch, Irish, Welsh[65] &co. But as he had long since got perfectly cured of his strain and coming to the city of Bristol, he took a fresh notion of going to sea again, shipped himself and was taken by the French and carried into Leogane[66], where he lay so long in prison that in order to obtain his liberty he engaged with one Captain Ruiz, a Spaniard then bound for Cartagena[67], and he procured his discharge with him. With him he sailed for some time, and went afterwards to Maracaibo[68], from which place he used to follow the coasting business.[69]

And there chance brought him acquainted with an old man who had been born in Dublin, by name McGill; and as he had constantly used his best endeavours to obtain the Spanish language, he could speak it with a little fluency. Now this old fellow told him that he could recommend him to a match of good advantage, if he could fancy the person, and that he was sure that he would succeed, as he knew full well, having her express as much one day when he was sounding her out with Pantoja's trumpet.[70]

Bell said, '*I suppose you mean Maria Bela, the mulatto girl?*' '*Yes,*' he said, and that she was possessed of four or five slaves, a good house, and money also.

Upon this, he determined to follow the old man's advice and soon after married her. And he lived well with her for about 5 years, until he became daily plagued by one of the padres on the score of religion. This man left no stone unturned to draw him from his first principles; but although he had led a very abandoned life, as he said, yet he was proof against all his art. But little did he think what a scene of trouble was coming on at that time. One day he returned from his little bark[71] or sloop he had purchased, and found matters to appear too glaring not to suspect his lady's honesty; but as he had found sufficient cause long before to think Father Martin and she were too close[72], he took no manner of notice at the time. It was lucky he had no children then alive. But when a fair opportunity came, he gave her a gentle reproof, saying that he wondered how any man in the state Father Martin was, could think of converting him when he so highly stood in need of conversion himself; and for his part he thought it a strange kind of religion, indeed, which forbade the marriage of priests, yet indulged them access to ladies at all times, even when all others were quite excluded, under colour that they were father confessors.

But to make short, from that time he never enjoyed one moment's comfort, as the unfaithful hussy[73] had communicated all his sentiments to the old rascal, as he called him. Martin from that time carried a higher hand than ever and one day, being in a kind of pet[74], said, '*Senor Bell, I am sorry you would never be advised of my kind council. Therefore if any evil befall you it is of your own seeking. I think you should have left the Church alone, by all means, after being so well received among us.*'

He wanted no stronger hints, he said, knowing that fire and hot fury was at his heels, and that he must either implore Martin to cuckold him or undergo Catholic resentment and persecution.[75] From that time, he became miserable, until he resolved to leave those parts to wander he knew not where. But for some time before he put the scheme into practice, he soothed the scoundrel in the most abject manner, and when he had softened him down a little, he determined to make his flight. But as he could find no fair slatch[76] by sea, he was forced to take his land tack onboard, leaving behind the following lines to his wife – that as he found his life lay at Father Martin's mercy he had bade them an everlasting adieu, being determined to live no longer.

After this he wandered away in the night with but nine pistoles and a few little articles in a pack on his back, being determined that when he got beyond all knowledge of them to turn lunatic or buffoon; and after that manner he wandered above a thousand miles to and fro. By this method he had evaded all suspicions, passing for an Italian, and he gave himself the name Giovanetti saying that he put on the air of a slighted lover ever singing love sonnets or telling merry tales, so that he never wanted relief wherever he came. And thus he rambled for the space of 4 years, until chance brought him among our Indians where, finding my friend, he determined to pay me a visit and to take up residence if agreeable.

'*Well,*' said I, '*you have padded the hoof to some purpose, and have had a large draught of this intoxicating world.*'

'*Mr Penrose,*' said he, '*I have sowed my wild oats long since, I have laid all my follies aside, I can assure you.*'

I then took an opportunity and observed that he must have collected divers nostrums[77] in his travels, and that poor Somer stood in great need of his help, if he had any drugs.

119

'As to that part of the speech,' he said, 'I think him in a deep decline, and before many weeks he will no longer be our companion in this life.'

This gave me much pain, as he seemed to pronounce his doom, as it were.

'But,' said he, 'I know the virtues of several American plants and roots and will use my best endeavours to administer all the comfort that I can. But this I know, that he will linger away gradually, changing at times so that you may be flattered into a conceit of his recovery. But he will go off at once, when you may not expect such a thing.'

Mr Bell soon became a hale[78] man, but my worthy shipmate wasted away daily. Yet he was ever of the opinion that he would weather it, saying now and then, 'When I get a little stronger I will do this and that.' Nevertheless every day he grew weaker. At last he became a real object of pity, walking around like a living skeleton. The colour of his skin became dark brown; his trousers would hardly keep on him; his eyes became so exceedingly hollow with a fixed stare; and his lips shrank in such a manner that he became a terrible object to behold. Whenever he drank, we could hear the liquid rattle inside him. His poor stomach became so depraved that he would long to eat things unfit for the food of man or dog, yet he continually walked about.

At last he left his darling pipe and grew exceedingly fractious, although he was ever much to the contrary when in health. There was nothing we could procure to please him; but we took all this with generous patience, and whatever he wanted he had, if going miles could procure it for him. At last he took a notion for me to make him some fish broth; this I went heartily about doing. When I took it to him he raised up in the bed, and fell to feeding heartily, saying that he liked it much, and finished above a pint of it. He was then on my bed in the cave. I then asked him how he found himself. He made me no reply, but he fixed his eyes against the other side, as though he saw something, and in an instant threw the spoon against it with great force and, falling back, gave an odd kind of hollow sound and expired.

Upon this I turned out of the cave and went to incline my head against the rocks, as none were by. When I came out, they knew not the cause, but Bell coming up and seeing me thus, soon suspected the cause and went in. When he came out he called Harry, and told him that they might not disturb me. But soon the information circulated and a general din of lamentation began; and if ever true grief was expressed in its full scope, it was then – so I need not be prolix on that head.

My most worthy and true-hearted messmate departed this life on the 21st day of August, anno 1760, having lived with me in perfect brotherly love above 6 years, and was as much my brother in a sentimental way, as though we had been born twins. Thus did I lose my darling partner and fellow sharer in all my difficulties and advantages, one who out of a true sense of reciprocal regard, had continually made it his study to concur with me, in every social interest and occasion. Godart Somer was a man of true fidelity.

Chance had brought us together in England. Our first meeting was on board a ship at the Red House, Deptford[79], but as that time strangers, little intimacy passed between us; nor do I know that we ever held a conversation, as at that time he spoke English very indifferently. On our ships dropping down to the Nore[80], he with several others was discharged and put on shore at Gravesend as we were above our complement of hands; so that Claus[81] only made a kind of visionary appearance, as I may say. And although our junction was at that time but short, yet Providence had ordained it that, let us make whatever traverses we could upon the Main[82], we should meet again at a certain period of time, to become the mutual comforters of each other. Shall we say that this is Fate or Chance?

Another thing similar to this has happened to me in my time. I once was going out of Bristol in a snow[83] called the *Swan*; this was in my early time at sea. Now it happened as I was walking on the Gibb[84], I went into the shop of a block-maker[85]. Seeing a young fellow there at work, my intent was to ask the favour of him to touch my penknife on the lodestone[86]. This he complied with, and asked me among other things what ship I belonged to. I told him the *Swan* snow; and that I intended to bind myself next day to the captain as he had no younker[87] at that time.

'*I fancy you are wrong*,' said he, '*young man.*'

But I insisted to the contrary. He then told me that wrong I must be, for that he had been bound to the same man that morning, and that he was sure that he would not have two apprentices. On this I made enquiries and found the thing to be so. This circumstance made us become a little acquainted, and I took my course another way soon after. Yet notwithstanding he had fairly outed me, as I may thus say, of that berth, still we were to meet again another day, as thus.

Long after this, when I was taken in the *Harrington* and carried into the Havannah, as I came on board the *Conquestador*[88], to which ship we were committed as prisoners, I observed a young fellow sitting forward on the windlass[89] in a sickly condition, whose face appeared familiar to me. And as he was dressed in a blue woollen frock and trousers I turned to one of my shipmates and said, '*There sits my old friend Jemmy Fishers - Revenge!*'[90]

'*Who is it that knows Jemmy Fisher?*' said he.

This made me stare, as until now I had concluded that the person was a real Spaniard. '*Did you not belong to the Swan snow once, messmate?*' I said.

'*Yes,*' he replied.

'*Then I am such a person*' – mentioning my name. With that, he shook me by the hand, and turning out a round oath swore he was heartily glad to see me. '*Well,*' said I, '*you see I have fetched you up with a wet sail at last, so that the difference lies only in the departure. But as to the latitude, bearing and distance it is the same; so that if you can recollect the last subject we were upon when on the Bristol Gibb, we have time enough now to finish that discourse.*'

This young fellow told me that he had been a prisoner at that place for over two years, during which time I had rambled to and fro many ways, and after all found myself safe moored alongside him. Such are the great frolics Miss Fortune is pleased to divert herself with, now and then, with us poor mortals of the wandering tribe.

I now looked upon it as going to begin a new course, as the natural drift of Mr Bell's temper I was yet a stranger to. And I had enough on my mind. All the family took on unfeignedly so that, with their sighings and my son's innocent remarks on the actions of the deceased, I for some time went about with a dagger in my heart. Norman and Harry prepared a resting place for my beloved friend's remains, and we conveyed him to the grave, where he was laid to rest among those who had preceded him. After this I returned up to the house, and they all came and seated themselves in very melancholy postures around me.

After some pause, I broke silence to Mr Bell, ran over the many good qualities of my departed friend, and intimated that I then looked up to him as his successor appointed by Providence, as he had so very opportunely been directed to my habitation. I said that as one island had given us birth, I hoped that he would never fall from that integrity which was so long held by a man who was not my countryman, but had learnt by a proper feeling of misfortune to know himself, and to show a true Christian benevolence to his fellow under the like circumstance. He then made me this answer, that he should always think it his duty to concur with all my desires, as I had so generously treated him on his first arrival, saying he well knew the stress of a forward fortune, and that he should seek all opportunities to render my life easy and agreeable to the utmost of his power.

Godart was a man possessed of a generous soul, faithful to his friend so that he gave me the most convincing proof any man could. And when his poor worldly passions were once subdued, he became a most valuable and constant creature to me and to all with whom we were concerned. His soul ever desired to do good, so that idleness was a torment to him. His genius was always busy, and the many things he made fit for our purposes are too tedious to mention here, as one circumstance will be sufficient to convince the reader that he never gave up a point, when once taken in hand. I shall observe that a few months before his death he undertook to make two chairs for us; and although many things stood strongly against him, yet he went through with it, and completed the work with only such tools as we had. But how much commendation do I owe to the memory of so valuable and worthy a man! He is no more.

We passed our leisure hours chiefly in reading for some time, and I found my new companion a very agreeable and sensible man, so that by degrees I recovered my spirits. But Eva soon became sullen and sad, and would separate from us, so I knew not what to think of her. But as my girl and I were one day alone, I asked her what possessed Somer's wife; she refused to be comforted. She then said, 'I have picked out the secret from Patty at last. She tells me that if Mr Bell will not take her for his wife, she is resolved to go back to her own people again, because the Vine of Unity has become broken now, and that we will all look upon her and her child as a Dead tree, with her young branch withering away as of no more use.' [91]

'So, So!' said I. 'Here is a fresh piece of work cut out for my hands. But how can you or I do anything in an affair of such a nature, unless Bell should broach such a thing himself? And perhaps such a notion has never entered his brain.' But soon after this Bell talked of going out with Harry to catch iguanas, and as I knew the matter would take up some time, I told Betty to give Harry this lesson, to sound Bell out when they were abroad together. This was done, and when they had fairly laid the plan, Harry proposed going off the next day, and went accordingly.

Two or three days after they had been home, I asked Betty how the theme took. She informed me that Norman was determined to have no manner of connection with Eva, having told Harry that he had sufficient reason against taking a wife, and desired him never to say any more to him on the subject.

'Then it is all an end,' said I, 'for I am resolved my friend shall use his own discretion. So let me hear no more about it. And if I find her still obdurate, she shall return with the next canoes, when they may come, for I am resolved that no-one shall remain here unsatisfied on any account.'

Some time after this I found messmate Bell becoming very serious, and on mentioning it to him, he told me what he had learnt from Harry, and that he must own up that it fretted him not a little, as it perhaps was a thing I desired, saying he was ready to oblige me in any reasonable thing, but he hoped that I would not insist on his taking Somer's widow for a wife, as he had more than enough experience of a woman's infidelity.

'Mr Bell,' I replied, 'you may rest assured that I never promoted anything of the kind. Yet I know the girl would be fond to have it so, but I leave it wholly to your own self to act as you think proper. She shall return to her kindred at the very first opportunity, so pray make yourself easy on that score.'

Now, when Eva found the thing was past all hope, she continually honed for her departure. My lady, finding her remaining in that obstinate humour, began to take up the cudgels and told her one day, when she refused to come to victuals, that she thought her very greedy indeed, and a great fool into the bargain, to want a man without a heart, saying that she thought Jessy had the most right to such a favour, but that she had patience enough to wait until the man brought her the basket of love flowers (an Indian Custom). This vexed her to a high degree, so that she became from that time quite dumb.

I must in this place make one remark, lest I forget it. Some time before my friend Somer's death, a few days, several large birds of the vulture kind came and settled on a large old dead tree in our neighbourhood. The nearer his end approached, the more birds came thither and there remained until the hour of his death. But no sooner was he departed than they all took wing and kept floating in a circular manner until night, then alighted again. But when the body was buried they all left the place, to a bird.

These birds are of such a voracious disposition that their sagacity is hardly to be credited. Nothing is more certain than that they smell a body when death has seized it, from miles away, and this is proved to be thus. On any such thing happening, should the body be on a plain without a tree nearer than a league[92] or two, they never fail to be in the area at the time, although none are to be seen anywhere before that period. Now the reason we assigned for their visit was this: my poor friend for some time before his exit became very offensive in his breath, so that at times we could not well bear it.

This bird is in size about the magnitude of a young turkey[93], of a black colour, and has those odd excrescences around the neck like that fowl. They never kill, but patiently wait until an animal is dead, and as they know the time to an instant they drop down from the tree, if any be near, when the master of ceremony begins first and eats the eyes and fundament[94], then leaves it and the rest fall on. They never quit the place until the whole be consumed. I have been informed when in Jamaica where there are plenty, that a law was enacted with a penalty of £5 against the shooting of one of these birds as they are found serviceable in clearing off all carrion. I once made Harry shoot one in order to have a fair examination of it, as he had said that their stomachs were very full of very large worms, and found it really so. But what is surprising, when I came to lift up the bird, to my great wonder it did not weigh more than a pound, being no more than bones and feathers. Another thing is singular, in that it has no tongue.

As I happened to see Eva one day sitting on the grave of her husband, I went to her and found her weeping. 'Pray, child,' said I, 'let me beg thee not to renew my trouble thus.'

Upon this, she held up her child and said, 'Take it, for I know you intend it.'

'What has put this whim into your brain?' said I.

'I know it is white blood,' she replied, 'and you will not let me have her away with me, when I return to my people.'

'Who filled your head with this nonsense?' I cried.

'Patty says she knows you will not suffer me to take her away to my country, because you loved her father so much.'

'Do tell Patty she is a fool and that I am very angry with her for giving you so much grief. Do you think I am worse than the wild beast of the woods, to go about to rob you of your young one? No, Eva, you shall take your child home with you, when your friends next visit us. Yet I must acknowledge that I should have been pleased for you to have been the wife of my new friend Bell, but as he says he has had one very wicked woman already, he is resolved never to have another.'

Upon this, she flew into a rage and began to twist and drag her hair like a distracted creature, saying, '*Am I wicked, wicked?*' The poor child began to scream, and this brought my wife and Jessy. I told them to settle her rage the best they could and left them. And this was the greatest feud that we ever sustained in all our time, but I gained one piece of experience by it – this giving me a fair opportunity of learning the natural genius of these people when chagrined, and I found that they can be as implacable in their rancour as they are steadfast in their friendship. Such tempers as those should be used with delicacy. A while after, they brought her up to the house somewhat more composed, when Mr Bell began to cheer her up the best he could, telling her he did not reject her person as he liked her very well; but as he had been very unfortunate with his other wife he chose to remain single, and that she could easily obtain another man among her own people when she returned.

Things remained thus for some time, until the arrival of 4 Indians who had been out on a journey, and paid us a visit on their return. These were Vatteqeba, Gattaloon, and Wocozomany with a youth called Outaharry, his son. The last two had never been at our place before. We received them in a friendly manner, and the next day I put Betty and Harry on broaching the affair concerning Eva. After a time I found them to grow very serious, and some time after, Harry came to me and said that Gattaloon wanted to make a speech to me. '*Tell him I am ready,*' said I.

Upon this, he advanced up to me, as in a hostile manner, and throwing out his right arm with one leg advanced, he began to deliver his discourse, or rather, oration. This took up a long time, and his behaviour all the while was quite in the heroic strain. Every now and then he would appeal to his comrades, who all answered with one short word as one voice. I then desired Harry to give me the substance of his speech, the best way he could, and this he did, (viz.):

'*You far water stranger, your skin is whiter than ours, white like the moon shining in the night. Can you expect our actions to be whiter than your own? What are the things I know, I hear and see? Has not the wind of voices gone through the trees and by the side of the shore, that my brothers and sisters have given their flesh and their blood for a mixture with yours? Show me more friendship than this and we shall own it is whiter than ours. Now we hear the voice in the wind saying "Oh, the blackness is coming off the bird which devours the dead." Must we all not go to sleep? Are you not picking off the flesh from the bones? Our sister here must return without a covering of love, because her love is gone to sleep. Could she keep him awake any longer? Or tell us, did she put him to sleep? You will say, "No, no!" Awaken his Spirit again, as it is in your power, that she may find joy and laughing hours, lest the winds carry the sound of black sorrow among our people and they should forget their way to this place.*'

This was a thundering broadside, and I then thought should once my friendly connection with those people be broken, then farewell to all future comfort. The whole time Harry was giving us the interpretation, my friend Bell stood with his arms folded and his face to the ground; and when it was finished he turned round on his heel and marched to and fro. But on his discerning the great trouble in my countenance, he came up to me and said, '*Let me not be the cause of my friend's disquiet, no, not for a moment of time.*' Then going to Eva, he took her by the hand, and leading her up to Gattaloon, also took his hand, and thus advanced up to me, when he began thus:

'*Observe me well. I here declare before all you present that to wipe away all animosities, oblige my worthy friend Mr Penrose and all those with whom he holds friendship, I do now take Eva as my wife.*' He then kissed her and said, '*Tell these good friends, Harry, that I will use my best endeavours to blow away all the blackness they expected, by rousing the Spirit of our departed friend, for the comfort of their sister, in my own person.'*

Directly I bade Harry to run over what Mr Bell had declared, when joy illuminated every countenance and I took my messmate by the hand, saying I was much indebted to him, as he could never show me a higher token of his veneration than in this generous act. *'And now in order to disperse all those black clouds of impending troubles, let us show ourselves as merry on the occasion as we well can, before our friends.'* Then Harry flew away for his broom, and we made them perform the old ceremony, to the great mirth and satisfaction of the Indians. And thus was ended an affair which I greatly dreaded would terminate in trouble and vexation for me.

The next day the Indians took leave of us, and went away in good spirits. It was now the middle of December, and Bell proposed that it would be much better to make a new crawl for our turtle within the mouth of our home lagoon, before the next season came on. This I much approved of, and he and Harry went to work about it. This piece of business took up a fortnight of their time.

One day, while my two messmates were down at the new crawl, I took a notion for a peep into Mr Bell's little budget[95] or kit, and the contents were a clasp knife, a razor and hone, a lancet and some other trifles. But there was a small rag, made up very curiously, but I did not care to cast it loose lest it might give him offence, so left it as I found it. When he came home, I asked him what he had so curiously bound up in the piece of linen among his gallitraps.[96]

'Did you not see it?' said he.

'Not I', I answered.

'Then I know no reason why you may not,' and he went for it and after he had taken some time to undo it, showed me a stone about the size of a common sleeve button and said, *'This is a very valuable diamond,'* and that he had purchased it from an Indian from the River Plate[97] for 15 pieces of 8. There were in the bag 4 more, not a quarter of its size. Now as I had not seen anything of the kind in its natural state, I should have put small value on it, but he told me they were worth above one thousand pounds sterling.

'Well, then,' said I, *'you are nominally a rich man, not worth one single farthing.'*[98]

On this, he gave a Spanish shrug with his shoulder and made use of a common phrase among that people, (viz.), *'todo uno, tambien'*[99] or suchlike. And I must remark that I should never have suspected him to be any other than a real Spaniard, as he had been so long among them that he had contracted all their gestures and manners of speech. Add to this his hair being long and black, it gave him the very look.

One day, as we were all sitting at victuals and being in a good mood, I said, *'Well, messmate Norman, I hope you like your new wife, as I find she seems pleased again.'*

'Ask her that question,' said he, which I did.

She smiled, and said, *'How much did you like Luta?'*

'A great deal,' I told her.

'But she is gone to sleep now,' said she; *'and how do you like Ocuma Betty? Here she sits with her eyes open, then.'*

'Oh, you can all see how much I like her every day.'

On this she burst out into laughter and echoed me: *'Oh, you can see how much I like my new flesh also, if you have a mind to peep!'*

This made us all very merry, and I observed that nothing could make me happier than to find our family restored once again to its old state of love and tranquillity, saying we should have found affairs in a poor condition, had we incurred the ill blood of our neighbours.

About this time I had a mind to learn whether Somer or Harry had ever communicated about the secret of our treasure to Mr Bell or not. For this purpose I began about the bush[100], as is said, concerning piracy and of their hiding money, etc. He said he had learnt enough about them from the Spaniards, but I found he was quite ignorant as to my drift. So one morning as he was busy with his razor and hone, for he shaved himself, I asked him what he would take for his diamonds in ready cash. On this he gave me an odd smile, saying, *'Do you know any jeweller in this city who chooses to purchase?'*

'Yes,' said I, *'I do. Suppose I am the jeweller, what would you value them at?'*

'Ay, ay, that will do well enough,' he replied.

'Will you let me have them on paying down 500 dollars?' I said.

'I should be glad we were safe in England with as good a sum each,' he replied.

'No trifling, are they mine or not?'

'Yes, yes,' he cried, and put them into my hand saying, *'Down with your dust.'*[101]

'Come away with me to my counting-house,' and I took him by the hand.

'What game comes next?' said he. *'You are in a flow of spirits, I think, today.'*

But, to make short, I disclosed all my treasure to him, and when he cast his eyes on it, he became as fixed as a mast.

'The diamonds are mine, messmate,' said I. *'There is cash sufficient to discharge the contract.'*

'Troth, man, I believe it is true; but if it is, pray how came ye by it?'

I then gave him the whole story at large.

'Weel, by the Cross of St Andrew it winnelskews[102] me, and I can hardly believe my own sight.'

'Friend Norman,' said I, *'call for your cash as soon as you please.'*

'Troth, man, it is as safe in yere bank there as in onny other part I can remove it to, so let it remain.'

'Well, now I think I have safely laid my anchor to the windward of you,' said I.

'Not in the least,' he said. *'Go take your jewels to market and make the most of them!'*

'Come, come, take and put them up in your pack again,' I said. *'What is mine, is yours.'*

And then squeezing my hand he said, *'And mine yours, reciprocally, with all my soul.'* – And thus ended another piece of drollery for that time.

On the 9th day as I think, of February, Betty my wife brought me a couple of fine children at one birth. The girls were all three so highly pleased with the novelty that they got round me, and hugged and clung about my shoulders in such a manner that I thought they would have gone wild for joy. A day or two after, a small altercation came on among them, as to what names they should have, one being a boy and the other a girl. Upon this I said I would do my wife the honour to call the girl after her country, (viz.) America. When she found this out, she seemed much pleased, and said if I were willing that she would give the boy a name she knew would surely please me. On my asking what that might be, *'Somer,'* she replied.

'Thou are a good creature,' said I, *'Nothing could ever be adapted more to my liking, for certain. Oh,'* said I, *'let his good name remain among us to the end of our generations, henceforth.'*

Now I had taken it into my head to contrive a kind of addition before our entrance, and for this messmate Norman happened to be out in the wood cutting a few large poles, when a large tiger seemed to be after him. He came flying down the hill in a great fright, crying and bawling out, *'Harry! Harry!, Messmate!'*

Out I ran and said, *'What is coming on now?'*

126

'Oh!' said he, 'here's the Deel coming down the brae as fast as the wind.'[103]

I ran and snatched up my gun and said, 'Where is it?' By this time Harry was running with his machete, and the women scrambling away the children. 'Come, come,' said I to him, 'take up that little hatchet and follow us.' So away we went up the hill, but could discover nothing. 'Where is your Deel, Norman?' said I.

'I am sure I saw a terrible leopard or a tiger.'

'How do you know what it was?' I answered. 'Where did you ever see any of these creatures that you know them so well?'

He had seen them in shows of wild beast, he said.

I asked his pardon, and said, 'But this proves a vision, I think.'

But all at once Harry cried, 'Yonder he is, over the cliff behind the grove!' I ran and fired at him, but to little purpose. I then ran down and got up a conch shell; they did the like, and he soon quit the field when we began sounding; and we saw no more of him, nor had we seen one for a long time before.

Now as this flurry was going on, Harry said he was sure that he had heard the sound of a shell at a distance. This I thought to proceed from the great hurry he had been in, but he was positive, as he said. 'Then go and take a look,' said I.

He soon began to cry out: 'Boats! Canoes!' We then went up and plainly saw three canoes.

'This is a visit from Owagamy as sure as we are living, on the old affair,' cried I. 'So now you must put on every art to treat them with the greatest civility. And you, Norman, pray lecture your lady the best you can.' I then ordered the yawl to be got ready and hoisted our colours, then leaving the women, down we went to meet them, and in the first place gave them three cheers, in the next place we began our old song. They answered, but not so heartily as in times past. However, we preceded them up the lagoon, and there landing I received my old friend Owagamy in the friendliest way I possibly could. Messmate Bell and Harry did the like and did the same with them all around.

They were nine in number, and all armed, which was not their general custom. After we had given them some drink out of what little remained in store, I called for our pipes, but they declined the offer. I now began to tremble, as thinking on future consequences. After some short time Owagamy, beginning to survey the place around him over each shoulder, asked some questions of Harry. I now got a little warm-tempered and boldly bade Harry to let me know what was the thing that Owagamy enquired after. He said it was whether we all lived in love and peace together; and that he had informed him that we have never been more so, and that Owagamy replied that was well. 'Tell Eva to stand forth,' said I, 'and if she has any sort of grievance on her mind let her declare it before them all.'

Now I had never seen an Indian then present, who was her brother, before; nor did she take the least notice of him the whole time. Owagamy then questioned her with a few words, when I observed him cast his eyes on Norman and smile.

'Now, now, merry well,' said Harry.

'How so?' said I.

'Because she says she knows Mr Norman loves her.'

'Well, come,' said I, 'Betty, give your friends the whole account of the affair from first to last, and also my friend's objections at the first, and I suppose they will then be all reconciled, if they have any reason left within them.'

She then began and I could see much confusion in Eva. When Betty had ended her narration Owagamy burst out into a fit of laughter; all the Indians did the like. Upon my enquiry into the cause Owagamy led up Eva's brother to me and my friend Bell, and

127

made us join hands in good fellowship. I then asked Harry what caused that horselaugh.[104]

He then replied: '*Owagamy says Eva made all the cold blood herself; that she should have let Mr Norman alone to choose the plantain himself*[105] *and not begin so soon after her husband was dead; but that he judged that she liked the white flesh so much that she grew mad, fearing young Jessy would snatch it from her, and therefore she took care to bespeak him as soon as possible; and that she should think herself much obliged to him if he gave her two children every year, so that her family might never be without the breed; and that he would take good care to fasten her well by him by having them remarried in their presence, if I pleased.*'

Up I jumped and cried, '*Harry, go fetch the broom.*' I then turned to Norman and said, '*Now, Bell, if ever you were a Merry Andrew in your life, I pray turn out and show us something or other by way of diverting away this dull gloom, which has hung over our heads for so long.*'

With that, he ran and took his wife by the hand and in an instant had her on his shoulder, when he fell to capering and sung the following lines from an old Scots ballad:

'*Fye, let us 'a to the Bridal*
For there will be lilting there,
For Bell's to be wedded to Eva,
The Lass with the Coal Black Hair.'[106]

After this he cut such odd freaks over the broom that it amazed me, and much more the Indians; as he was a man fully six feet, and she was but light in person, so he made no more of her than a feather. Now all faces wore new aspects, and my friend Owagamy was the first to call for pipes and we all sat down to smoking together. Then Bell rose and desired a ring should be made, when he began his pranks again, and of all the mimics I ever beheld, I never saw the like of this fellow. He then said he would show them a specimen of his sleight of hand, with a small stone.

For this purpose, he stripped himself to the buff[107], then put the stone into his mouth, and in a short time produced it from under his armpit, and thus he conveyed it from one part of his body to another, to the great amazement of the Indians. He then tumbled, walked on his hands, and the like. Now as he was doing this, Eva ran and caught hold fast on him, as dreading he should fall. This made Owagamy laugh and say she was in terror lest he should break into two pieces, he supposed, as she knew if he were spoiled there was never another white man who could fall to her share.

I thought the Indians would have eaten him up alive. They then said they supposed I could do the like, if I pleased, but I bid Harry inform them to the contrary. They kept it up the whole day, and thus ended the wedding, to my great comfort. The next morning I thanked Mr Bell for carrying the thing off so well, but as he had been for many years out of practice, he was so stiff in his joints that he could scarcely walk.

Now the Indians gave us to understand that another of the men in their company, called Loosoyamy, was brother to Eva. I asked why they had concealed that matter when they first came. Harry said it was because they thought that we were turning black[108], but I bade him to inform them that they should never find any blackness to proceed from our side; that the whole mistake had proceeded from Eva's imagination and that I had intended to send her away from us. Owagamy then told Harry that they could stay no longer, as they had other affairs to transact when they returned, and took farewell the next morning accordingly.

The day after, Harry brought me the skin of a snake almost entire, as a curiosity. This put Harry on giving us to know that at the time these reptiles want to discharge themselves of their old coats, they go on the hunt until they can find any old knot of a tree or some such aperture. Through these holes they pass, and by that means leave the old coat behind them, after which they are obliged to keep retired for some time, as their new skin is still too tender for travelling. At one season of the year in breeding time, I have seen multitudes of snakes gathered near some run or other of water, in bunches or masses, and twisted into such strange combinations that it is wonderful to see.[109] And thus they tumble and roll about, at which times you may approach them as near as you please without dread nor harm, they being in no way capable of separating. I have seen perhaps a dozen in one bunch thus, and of different kinds.

CHAPTER VI

The Fifteenth to Seventeenth Years

THE FIFTEENTH YEAR – THE BURNING SHIP AND THE
TWO-HEADED SNAKE
June 15 1761 – June 14 1762

My new friend had resided now for about a year with me and we had become very happy together. And soon after, we took a ramble with our guns in the woods. Now, as we were going, he took a plant, and showing it to me observed that it was a fine 'narcotick', as he termed it; and after this he showed me others, saying, *'This is a very fine styptick, that a diuretick.'*[1]

'You deal much in ticks, messmate,' said I. *'But if you had once about a dozen such thumpers[2] as I have seen our Harry pull off our dogs at times, well fixed under each of your arms, you could not make so ready a conveyance of them, as you can with a small stone with all your sleight of hand – you have a great knack at your Scots songs,'* said I.

'Did you not observe a book of them amongst my things?' he asked.

'Oh, you have a fund of humour, then, I can assure you,' I responded.

'If you have such a thing,' said he, *'it is a good cordial for the spirits '*

'If I could read them,' I answered.

'I can do that for you,' he said.

'Well, pray then, let us have at it now and then,' I answered.

He then said that as Harry and he were one day at Towers Field, he saw plenty of large reeds growing; and that with a little patience and contrivance, he imagined that he could form some sort of German Flute[3] with them.

'Pray take good heed that your music doesn't bring you mourning,' said I, *'for that place is full of alligators, my friend.'*

'Never fear,' he replied, *'we will find out some way or other to get some of them. Tis but to make up a good fire and they will all retire.'*

'Ay, ay,' said I, *'and that work may bring on such another bonfire as I made soon after my landing here, which verily I thought would never be extinguished again.'*

'Well, leave all that to Harry and me,' he replied.

Soon after, they went to fetch home salt, and while they were away got some of those canes, which they brought home. After this, nothing but making flutes was done, and Bell got me to make a round iron in order to burn the holes. This I contrived out of a spike nail. After many unsuccessful trials, he produced a sort of German Flute, but for want of knowing how to adapt the holes according to the bore, they proved false in tone. But error taught Bell experience, and he at last made one tolerably good and true. The next thing was a book to put down notes in, as he said.

'And pray where are the tunes to come from?' I replied.

'Let me alone for that,' said he, 'I have a method of my own, and that you will see.'

The book was made, and every now and then he would be at it, 'pricking' as he termed it. Now as I understood music as much as the goose does conjuring, it all appeared mysterious to me. Nevertheless by his strong application, our wild forest became acquainted with, and learned to echo the charming melodies of 'Tweed Side,' 'Ettrick Banks,' 'Invermay,' and many other such tunes; and many an hour has his pleasant pipe charmed away for me in this forlorn place.[4]

Harry became so enamoured with music that he was forever tooting. This made messmate Norman instruct him, and he soon came on to a great degree. Our girls caught the sounds and learnt all the tunes they played. The Indian women have a charming natural sweetness of voice, and often joined in accord with them. The children took it from them, so that it was common to hear Owen, Hannah and Job chanting every day. And now may I truthfully say, we lived in perfect harmony together; so that the Lord was graciously pleased to raise me up to a new consolation when so recently severed from my worthy Somer, for whom I had so great a veneration.

Thus time went on until the middle of August, and as one day we were out after tortoises, I spied a vessel in the offing, standing away to the northeast. Now messmate Bell observed to me, what was there to hinder us leaving our place?

'As how, pray?' I said.

'Why could we not go off in that longboat?'

'And provided we could, where would you propose to go? Surely you cannot think of keeping the seas out for long, in an open longboat.'

'Could we not keep to the shore always?'

'But where bound?' I cried.

'Why, I think we might get to the coast of Carolina well enough in her.'

'What, to round all the bays, points and reefs, my friend? Only consider the vast bays of Mexico and many others, and all the unthought of difficulties besides.'

'Well,' said he, 'but you must consider that if we but once surmounted what you object against, we then should horse[5] through the Gulf of Florida in short time.'

'Don't reckon without your host,' I replied. 'Let me hear in the first place how you would lay your plan in order to achieve such a grand undertaking, and then, if feasible, well and good, friend.'

And thus he began: 'I would raise her a strake[6] higher, make us a snug cuddy[7] forward, with lockers abaft.' [8]

'And this would take time,' I told him.

'Hoot, hoot, what then?' as if he did not begrudge the labour.

'Well, admit matters were come thus far,' said I, 'then comes her suit of sails next.'

'We have enough canvas for that,' said he.

'That is all settled,' I cried. 'But there is the grant but yet to come, shipmate – provisions, my friend.'

'Oh, as to that matter, have we not enough of several kinds and plenty of water?'

I then became more serious and said, 'How long do you think such vegetables and things that we use daily would last? And where is the room to stow so much of our water necessary for the voyage, as there must be room for family, certainly?'

As to that, he said there would be no need to carry 'more than your wife and children' with his own girl.

'So,' said I, 'and how would you dispose of all the rest?'

'Let them return to their own people again,' said he, 'as I suppose they would prefer that, to going along with us.'

'Do you not know that I look upon Harry as part of myself?' I replied. 'Have I not had his sister as my wife, by whom I had two children? How then in conscience, think you, can I be guilty of such an extravagant piece of cruel infidelity to such an honest and faithful poor creature, who would at a word of mine brave the whole Ocean, to bear me company throughout the Universe? Pray, have you so soon forgotten that fine lecture the Indian gave us some time ago? Let us beware that we become not black, as he figured it to us, in the character of the vulture. Let us not forget that we have been once baptised and, as he observed, Nature had made us whiter than his race and, as he observed, the more we should show ourselves white in all our actions and deeds. But laying all this aside, I know that such a scheme would prove abortive.'

'But self-preservation, messmate,' said he.

'Are you not preserved already?' I replied. 'For it is evident to me that the method you propose must inevitably bring about our utter destruction, unless some miraculous act of Providence should bring us to a safe deliverance. And after all, perhaps, we should not find our account[9] by the change of conditions. You think this, that as we abound in worldly trash, that would give us the command everywhere. But pray consider, my good friend, how many temptations we should become liable to, amidst strangers. Let me beg that you will give yourself five minutes time to reflect on so important a matter, and then let us have a fresh conference on the subject.'

I continued, 'I daresay it has originated from the anxious desire you have to once more revisit your native soil. This is a natural and worthy thing in all degrees of men; but if we cannot afford to do so in a commendable and easy way, then let us abide where we are, in God's holy name. Know you not those homelings in our country who have never experienced the cold, heat and unheard of hazards of travel, often in penury and want and frequently naked also – I say that they, having never been far from the smoke of their own chimneys, expect all travellers to return home rich. The reason of which is this – they seldom hear anything else but the rich being bruited[10] abroad on their return to their respective homes. For those who have been prudent and unfortunate have rather chosen to remain and end their days where they were, rather than return in poverty among their old friends and relations, whose kindness can never be long trusted, lest you should become burdensome.

And certainly should that be any poor fellow's case, reproach ensues. They will then query, "How did you spend your time for such a length of years? And what is to be expected next? You have been either a drinker, gambler, or a very idle and inconsiderate man at any rate." And lest your cup of mortification should not fill to the brim, they will in that case gall your spirits with recounting that such and such left home later than you, and returned with a large fortune, and during his absence was continually supplying his poor relations. But you may every now and then hear by the slant that you were neither of any worth, Egg or Bird.

But alas! Let us see how many of these rich, honest and brave fellows return to spend the remainder of their days in ease and plenty. Oh, how few are they when compared to the vast multitude of those poor unfortunate objects who have perished abroad, throughout the globe, by one kind of death or another, and quite unregarded as unworthy remembrance.'

'Avast, take a turn there, and belay that, messmate if you please,'[11] said Bell. 'I must confess nothing, but the natural and longing desire a man has to see his country, before he dies, prompted me to what I have advanced. I now can see farther than before, for I don't think you can be averse to seeing your country again more than myself, were all things agreeable to that end.'

'You have said nothing but what is absolutely true,' I replied; and thus we were finished, belaying our argument for that time.

It was now about the middle of October, and about 10 in the evening there came on such a terrible gale of wind, that within two hours it was blowing a hurricane all around the compass. Every small article was blown down; and had we not been sheltered by a large grove of trees in front, forming a wall as it were, and a strong shelter two-thirds around us behind, I know not how we should have fared. For the wind would come with such an eddy and whirl around our place, that I ordered all our fire to be extinguished, fearing it might be blown among the thatch and so fire our kitchen again. But about three in the morning the wind fell, and Eva called me out of the cave to come and see.

'See what?' said I.

'The great blaze in the clouds,' she said.

When I got out, Bell called to me and asked what I thought of it. 'I can't imagine,' I replied.

'Let us endeavour to mount the hill,' he said. We were forced to bawl as loud as we could, for the wind was still so strong that we could hardly keep on our legs. But when we got up, we could plainly see a most dreadful fire at sea, as I judged about three leagues away. Upon this, we knew it must be some poor unfortunate vessel all ablaze, knowing that the fire could proceed from no other cause. And thus she burnt for two hours longer, and how long before we knew of it, we could not tell. And as the day came on, we saw no more of her. About noon it fell quite calm, and left our appurtenances all scattered about.

'Well,' said I to my friend Bell, 'were we not provided for this last dreadful night, think you? And what would those poor souls who belonged to that vessel have given to have then been among us?'

'Alas,' he replied, 'either fire or water has been their destruction before this hour.'

'You may be pretty well assured of that,' said I, 'for I am sure that no boat could live. And is it not a standing warning to us, messmate, to be content with our lot as thus instanced? Suppose now the case had stood, that you should have proposed the affair of leaving this place about a month or three weeks ago, and I had come warmly into that risk – You nor I could have never known of this hurricane at that time hidden in the hollow of the Almighty hand. And should we have been at that time, on the ocean in a poor open longboat full of one encumbrance or another, what would then have been our dreadful condition, think you? Ask your own conscience and say you have no need now for the space of five minutes reflection, to make me an answer on that head. You will naturally reply, "To have been back at our old Mansion again," without dispute.'

'Messmate,' said he, 'one ounce of due consideration is more in value than fifty pounds weight of folly.'

'Let this dreadful example then remain imprinted in full and evident characters on our souls,' said I, 'my fellow pilgrim. And henceforth let us never repine at what we may call Fortune; for we know not, poor short-sighted[12] creatures, for it may be Fate. Let learned Casuists[13] compose volumes to support pro and con arguments if they please; it is no study of ours. I am determined to remain steadfast and resigned to the Divine Will, and I judge by the feelings of my own heart His will is the only thing that can bring me off in my last hour.

What does not a man undertake or undergo to obtain a portion of the very articles with which you and I abound copiously? Does this not show the man of true content what a small portion would suffice to make him happy? Witness your diamonds and my dross which lies yonder in a useless heap, and why, truly, we do not want it.'

Mr Bell is in no measure chagrined at my writing thus, knowing that I mean nothing more than generous advice in regard to our common good and the interest of the family.

And here I observe, as he stands by me and may have hourly access to my journal, anything that I write or note down, if disagreeable to him, he has my free consent to erase the same, if he may imagine it in any way prejudicial to his credit should our book ever fall into the public's hands.

The next day we proposed to take a run out and examine the shore, thinking that by some favour of fortune a remnant of the ship might be found and saved. So we got the yawl and went away to that end, but were forced to return without the least discovery, finding nothing. And who they had been, or whence they had come we could never learn. Not a stick of her ever came on shore sufficient to indicate anything to that purpose. Staves we found at times, half burnt; these we knew undoubtedly had belonged to her.

About two days after this melancholy affair, as our Harry was away at the old plantation in the canoe, a poor dog came creeping up to him, almost starved to death. He brought him home with him, having lifted him into the canoe, as the poor thing was not able to do the like, for want of strength. This dog is a black and white spaniel of the largest breed[14] and perhaps much valued by his owner as he seemed, although in so low a condition, to have been very handsome. This poor beast had certainly belonged to that unfortunate ship; but in what manner he came to land we could not think, as the sea ran so exceedingly high, unless the crew had happily made their escape and had either left the dog behind them, or he had been lost before their departure. But if that really were the case, they must have landed away around Whale Point, as we could have no sight of them.

'Who knows?' said Mr Bell, 'but they may yet be there?'

'God only, and themselves,' I replied, 'but if so they stand highly in need of relief as I know by my own experience.'

He then declared it was his desire to go and satisfy himself as to be certain whether or not. 'Go, by all means, my friend,' I cried. 'Let us save life if possible.' I then told him that Harry must stand as pilot, as my friend had never been that way before. And I proposed that they should take the spaniel along with them, thinking that if perchance any folks were there, the dog would soon find them out. And away they went, early the next day, and did not return until late the next evening. The first thing I saw was the spaniel, which came to me with great joy. On this, I ran away down to the landing and called out, 'Yo, ho, there!' When they answered, I asked 'What news?'

'None at all of any service,' said Bell. They then came up to me and reported that they had examined the whole coast, even into Boom Bay as I called it, and as they were on the beach the dog put off and ran away ahead, to a thing they saw at a great distance. They followed him, and when they came up, found the corpse of a young fellow; and said that he at first intended to bring it home in the boat's bottom, but the smell forbade it. And as he found it so, he and Harry had stripped the body and buried it in the sand, bringing the clothes with them, saying they were certain that the dog had a knowledge of the deceased, as when they were digging the grave, the creature sat looking on the whole time. But when they came to strip the body and remove it to its place of interment, the poor animal began to howl and whine sadly. When they had covered it up, he went and laid down on the spot and stayed there, looking after them until they had walked away about 50 yards; that they then called him and the poor toad then got up and followed them freely to the boat.

Mr Bell described the corpse thus: that he took him to have been a young man aged about 20 or upwards, middle sized with sandy hair, his dress a striped fine shirt, petticoat trousers of a good white linen, with a jacket of the same kind to which his hat was fastened by a lanyard[15]. He had a pair of white fustian[16] breeches on under his trousers; and in the left pocket he found a clasp knife and a small bunch of twine, in the other a note from which we learnt his name was Richard Green. And in one of his trouser pockets was the following song in manuscript, '*Early one morn a jolly brisk tar etc.*'[17] by which we judged they were English, or at least we were certain that the youth had been a subject of Great Britain. No more could we learn of the matter.

We took pains to find out this dog's name, and by calling it numerous names discovered it to be Rover. And in about a month's time he was so well recovered, as though he had never been reduced to the degree we found him in. And I believe nothing but distress of hunger brought him so soon to relish fish.

About a month after this my son Owen shot a snake of the Barber's Pole sort[18], and came to me in a great hurry to inform me that he had shot a snake with two heads.

'*That can never be, child,*' I replied.

'Hoot, hoot,' said Bell, who was then standing by, '*the boy is winnelskewed. As I thought myself when ye showed me a' that gear yonder in the nook.*'[19]

'*Pray, Bell,*' said I, '*explain me that word if you please.*'

'*Why, it is a saying among our people in Scotland, whenever they mistake one object for two, that the moon is in the halyard[20], or clouded, and at such times they are winnelskewed or their eyes deceive them.*'

Upon this Harry went with Owen and they brought it up to us on a stick, when to our great amazement the thing became verified. This snake was not above 2 inches round, and in length about 4 feet. About 5 inches from the natural extremity of a single head, there began two necks branching out, terminating with two fair and perfect heads complete, capable of performing all the necessary functions. And this we were all witness of, as the creature was not yet dead, but opened each mouth and played with both tongues alike. This wonderful phenomenon I made Harry skin with the strictest care, and we have it by us as a proof to advance if any traveller should by chance pay a visit. I asked Harry if he had ever seen, or been informed of the like before, but they all agreed they were ignorant and that they had never seen the like before in their lives.

Nothing came on from that time, until it was December 23rd by our account. I took notice to Mr Bell, as I well remembered that my mother always took care to have a goose at Christmas Day[21], that we would have something like it, if possible, on that day.

'*Where will you buy it?*' said he.

'*We must try for a substitute,*' said I. '*You and Harry may go away to the Bird Key with your guns, and there you may find game of some kind or other.*' So away they went the next day and brought home 3 boobies[22] and 5 redshanks. '*Now,*' said I, '*Bell, if we can catch a couple of fine Red Snappers[23], I think we shall we be provided for a good Christmas dinner.*'

'Come on then,' said he. We then got our lines and away we went down the lagoon, but had not the success I hoped for, when as we were returning my Harry caught a large barracuda[24]. Now I observed to my messmate that those kind of fish are apt to be poisonous, and asked him if he knew how to prove them. '*Well, then,*' said I, *when they go to cook it, boil it alone with a clean piece of silver, and then we shall be sure.*' This was done the next day, and the fish proved to be good. Otherwise it would have turned the silver quite black, by their feeding on the mineral bank, as is imagined[25]. And that day we all dined together, which was not our usual custom, as Mr Bell and his wife usually dined with my wife and myself.

The next thing that happened was the loss of my friend Godart's orphan daughter

Hannah of a fever. My messmate used all his skill in his way, but to no purpose, and we laid her alongside those who had left our little society before.

About a month after Christmas Messmate Norman became lame in one of his hands. He had been out to fish alone in the Indian canoe, and among other fish that he caught was one that is called a Doctor Fish[26], from a sharp bone it has on each side of the tail. This bone is not perceptible to a man unacquainted with that fish, as it has the power to lay it close to its side or to erect it a its pleasure; but this bone is so keen that no lancet can be more so, and much resembles it in form. The whole fish is of a purple brown and about the size of a middling Haddock.

He brought home at the same time two others of a peculiar kind and construction. The first is called by our seamen a Parrot Fish[27], and with great propriety as I think, as the whole fish is green, except the fins, which are red. It has very large scales, but its bill or mouth is not formed like that of a common fish, having a pair of bones resembling the beak of a parrot, with which it mashes or cracks small shellfish. The whole roof[28] of its mouth is also one hard bone.

The other or second kind is almost a copy of the above-mentioned, except that instead of its being green, on the contrary it is a perfect blue and is called in Providence the Gillambour[29]. Whence they derive the name I know not, except from the Spanish.

Mr Bell's hand remained bad for over a fortnight, and at times gave him great pain. At last my dame took it in hand, and proved the more successful doctor of the two. She cured it in about 5 days by applying the juice of herbs to it. When it was well, I joked to him about the Doctor Fish that two of a trade seldom agreed.

'I shall take care in the future,' said he, when one of them pops his nose into my shop, to let him know that I will be master.'

On a day soon after Harry brought in from his traps a very curious little animal, the like of which I had never seen, but my messmate knew it at once and called it an Armadillo[30], saying there were numbers of them away to the southward. This animal was of a light ash colour about the size of a young suckling pig, and resembled that creature, only much slimmer and the tail much longer. But what makes it most remarkable is that they seem to be absolutely in an armour of shells. I asked Harry if they ate them.

Yes,' he said.

'Cook it then,' I said, 'and let us taste it.' Bell said no chicken could be finer, and I found it so in reality.

Now I proposed to Norman that we should turn up our yawl and large canoe, in order to examine them thoroughly and repair them the best way we could. This we went about, and I found my poor old canoe like a honeycomb. Upon this I set Owen to peg making, and with those we pegged all over her bottom. But she was now become old, and much worn by the waves by the length of time I had had her in my possession. As for the yawl, she was full of the worm also, but still in a much stronger state of preservation than my poor old Ark of preservation. But I found that mixing plenty of sand with our pitch and tar was of service, and we did all in our power towards their preservation.

After we had completely fitted up our two boats and mended their sails, and made a pair of new oars and some tholes[31], I proposed that we would make a day of recreation for the whole family; and accordingly when the day came we all mustered with what was necessary, and put away down the lagoon. Myself, my wife and three children were with Harry in the yawl; Mr Bell, his wife, Patty and Jessy in the great canoe; and Owen, Job and Luta in the Indian canoe. Owen was boatman and now could paddle very well, as he was now between 9 and 10 years of age, but when a little wind sprang up I took them in tow, and thus we arrived at the old plantation safe, where we left the ladies with their children, with Harry to guard and attend them.

After this, my messmate and I and little Owen went out into deep water in order to catch a few grouper and the like, in our yawl. We laid her to, in about 12 fathom of water, and let her drive over the patches of the rocks, as you can see the bottom distinctly at that depth in these parts of the world. We had not been long on the grounds, before fine sport came on. We hauled in and baited as fast as we could; but it happened that as I was bound with a large grouper, a shark came in full chase after it. I pulled as eagerly as possible, but he caught hold of it before it came near the water's edge, and left me no more than its head on the hook.

Now, as we were thus contending which should have this fish, another shark in chase of it at the same time, by mistake in the great scuffle bit his antagonist. In a few minutes after this, as we were all very merry at the circumstance, Norman put the laugh on me for catching no more than the head of a fish. He then at once became bound with a witness; and as he was not so much used to the sport as Harry and I were, we cried, 'Hold on, messmate, and play him well.'

But through eagerness, he fell down backward in the boat, crying, 'Hoot, hoot, mon! What for sort of sort of muckle horned Deel is dealing with us now, that's just lugging us aboot?'[32]

For by this time, I had got hold with him. Owen laughed to that degree that he lay down and kicked his heels. But soon after, we tired the fish, and he sheered alongside. I then took up an axe and soon gave him his quietus, and it proved to be the very shark that had snapped away my fish from the hook. The other had bit him into the bone through a part a full 7 inches thick.

After we had caught as much as we wanted, which we did in less than an hour, as had we been desirous, we could have filled the boat, I then gave the line into Owen's hand, he being like all children, full of novelty and ambitious to do great things. But he soon began to holler[33] out, 'Oh Daddy, Daddy!' I then took him around the waist and bade him to pull with all his might, but he soon began to cry lustily, and quietly resigned the line to me – otherwise he would have inevitably have been pulled overboard. I hauled the fish in for him, and then we stood in for the old place where we had left our ladies, and there found a rousing fire blazing, my wife saying that she had got it ready against when we came, as she could see plainly with the glass that we had had good luck.

We had not long landed when we heard Jessy cry out lustily. I sent Harry to know what the cause was, but he soon came back, and snatching up his machete, he flew off like a dart, and we ran after him. There we saw Jessy standing with a load of dry wood on her head, and Harry chopping at a large black snake[34], which lay right in the narrow path. This snake was at least 6 feet long and not venomous in the least, as Harry said. He brought the snake with him to the fire to roast and did so, offering a part to us but we declined it, keeping our stomachs for better fare.

'Well, well,' said he, 'he had no business to frighten Jessy, and I would serve forty of them if they came in my path.'

'Deel stick ye weem!' said Bell.

'I forbid that,' said I, 'so belay that speech, messmate.'

'Hoot, hoot!' said he. 'These Indians wad devoor the auld Whaapnab[35] himself, gin he were weel cooked, and sup his broth after that, I'm thinking. Foul fare on such beast.'

'Why Norman,' I replied, 'you don't know that I have eaten them before now with him, and really, they taste well enough.'

'Weel, then, ye had better, the next ye find, be getting one of them muckle tree paddocks[36] for sauce for ut,' said he.

In the evening we all embarked[37] and got home safe to our abode. Our stock of liquor had now become very low, so that we seldom touched it except in a case of necessity. The next thing that came on was to repair the damages we sustained in our thatch in the late tempest, and this business took up some length of time. Our plantain trees had suffered also. After this time, matters went on in the old channel, with little variation of circumstances, until such time as I had competed another year.

THE SIXTEENTH YEAR – THE EARTHQUAKE, EVA IS EATEN BY TIGERS AND BELL REMARRIES
June 15 1762 – June 14 1763

Sixteenth year began. It happened, as Harry and Owen came in from fishing they brought me a curious bunch or whipp of some living substance much resembling catgut, and of the same hue or yellow colour.[38] It was so interwoven that we could not by any means separate it, neither could we discover either end so as to find head or tail; yet it kept continually in motion, appearing like a handful of animated thread, and might as we judged be about 12 fathom long. I had seen one of them before, which I found in the stomach of a grouper, but if it bred in the maw[39] of the fish or was taken in as food, we knew not, as this that I am now describing came up on the hook.

This singular insect leads me to a description of one I found in the woods one day, about 4 years ago. It was lying on the ground, and as its shape was a little peculiar, I took it up to examine it and found it to be of a hard substance and black as jet, and in the true form of our barbers' curling pipes, and in length and bulk of that magnitude. It seemed to be composed of a range of scales, and at each end had a small aperture, and when on the ground could advance slowly with either end forward, and that with ease. There were neither eyes or mouth or any detached member to be seen.[40]

Many extraordinary things, which are absolute curiosities of Nature, have escaped my memory, especially such as fell under my observation in the first years of my residence here, for want of means to record them, as in those days I little expected to become the master of materials for that purpose. Yet whatever came within reach of my speculation never escaped my inquisitive inclination, having being from a child ever taking much delight in prying into the works and wonders of Nature. Now, whatever I have advanced or shall advance, I declare has passed within my view; and as thousands have passed or traversed across many parts of this vast continent, they may confute me easily if I advance falsehoods. But where could a man, situated as I am, expect to receive a benefit from, by imposing untruths on the world? Especially as I have but a scant expectation that what I write may ever fall under the inspection of my own nation and brother tars, for whose information chiefly I thus amuse my time. As to the learned, I stand not in any dread of their censure, being a man of no education myself, and therefore beneath their scrutiny and envy. Yet I may venture so far as to think they will not carp at what may be honestly advanced by me, who am but an illiterate sailor.

I make this digression on account that perhaps many things, which in the great length of time that I have resided here, have been seen and described by my pen, may have never been noticed by others before.[41] The reason is obvious: they keep moving from place to place and perhaps give themselves little concern to explore the beauties of this

Universe; when on the contrary I remain as a man consigned over to such a purpose, with time sufficient to answer all ends.

One evening, about 5 o'clock as messmate Bell was reading over some of the Scotch songs to me, and giving me the explanation of some of the old words in them, all at once the earth began to lift us up and down, twice. Upon this, we began to stare at each other wildly. Bell threw the book down, crying, '*It is an earthquake. Bring away the children from the side of the hill. Perhaps it is not over yet, and some of the stones may give way.*'[42]

Just after this, we had another motion, but much weaker. I had never felt the like in my life before, but my messmate said that he had felt several since he had been in this country, and had been shown large hills and cliffs split from clew to earring[43] (as we sailors call it) by them – saying that there was little danger where we were, as there were no volcanoes in our neighbourhood that he knew of. And as I found that our Indians heeded it not, it passed off, they carelessly observing that it was only 'a sign of heat', [44] which really was the case soon after.

The butterflies[45] now became more numerous than I had seen them in all my time before, and now I have mentioned them, it may not be improper to say something concerning them. In the first place they all differ from any I know in Europe, and are much wilder and swifter, generally flying up over the tops of the loftiest trees in the woods; but as to describing their plumage it would be an endless task, there being so many different sorts. But I shall remark that I have seen some fully as broad as the palm of my hand and many much larger, and I have often found pods of the silk-work sticking in crevices of the rocks and in clefts of trees. But there is one sort we find at times fixed to the limb of a small twig 5 times the size of the ordinary pod, and in colour a dark brown resembling oakum[46].

These pods are so strong that it is hard to rend them asunder. The butterfly that produces it, is as broad as a man's hand and of a beautiful variety of colours, grey, red and white, with a pair of fine yellow feathers in front of its head. There is yet another sort, of a brimstone colour with a circle in each wing, which is transparent as glass, with the after parts of their wings tapering away to a swallowtail. We sometimes see a sort, which are yellow, with bars running athwart in a very regular manner of black; another kind is green with black bars transverse to the other sort.

But I must observe one thing truly remarkable and beyond my comprehension, as follows. At times we found a kind of Brown Wasp which, falling foremost to the ground from the trees, there takes root, from whence springs up a small plant through their bodies. Mr Bell's opinion was that it proceeded from some kind of seed they swallow which intoxicates them, so that when the wasp falls to the earth, those seeds take root and immediately spring up again.

A single canoe now visited us from our friends. In it came Soroteet or the Crabcatcher, Yewarrabaso and Kayuza; the two last had never been at out habitation before. These Indians came out of curiosity to see us, and brought with them a pair of young fowls as breeders, saying they were as a present from Owagamy with his heart, as they termed it; and that he had had them sent to him from over the great hills. Nothing could have delighted me more. Among other things they informed us that they had another of those people called 'Moonlights'[47] born, a female, but that she had soon died, which they were all very glad of. After they had been with us for about three days they left, but after Soroteet had got on board the canoe he reminded Harry of a flute he was to make for him, and I gave him to know that he should make it.

Some days after the Indians were gone, we heard a great noise among the fowls in the kitchen. Eva sent Job to see what might be the cause, when he came running out and said that Jakko the monkey had got one of the new birds in his arms, and was pulling out the feathers. This fired my blood and off I ran. When I got in, there sat Mr Monkey with a fowl in his lap, picking out its feathers one by one. Directly, he held out the fowl to me. On this I took the fowl in one hand and him by the head in the other, and thus brought them out. The fowl was not much hurt, but to prevent his doing the like, we tied the monkey up, and with a small switch I made Owen flog him, while Job held the fowl's feathers to his nose. After this discipline, he was dismissed, but he grew so shy from that time, that whenever one of the fowls happened to come near to him, he was off in an instant. But when one of the young cocks began to crow, the monkey would rave and run into the first corner he could find, and there clap his hands before his face, which caused much diversion[48] among our youngsters; but he never touched them afterwards. Yet to give him his true character, he acted the downright skulker[49] on board a man of War, always at hand when anything was to be shared.

But among the multitude of his tricks, I think one of them merits recording. One day I observed his impship very busy down among the graves, and sent Harry's little daughter Luta to learn what he was at. The child came back and said that Jakko had got a heap of round things in a hole there. On this, I went down myself and found a hole wherein he had deposited 50 dollars or more. Although it was true we stood in no need of it then, yet I thought that some day or another we might have a call for it. I then bade them call Norman, who was then down at the boat. When he came, I showed him that Jakko had found a treasure likewise.

'Ay,' said he, 'and yours is grown less, I dare say.'

How he came by the discovery I know not, but he must have seen us at it, as he had been at labour to remove many stones before he could get at it. But to prevent the like, messmate Bell and Harry removed the whole in the night, so that no one knew where it was, except we three.

About the middle of August we had a most tremendous gust of thunder, lightning and rain, but no rain, scarcely, during which the large tree whereon those vultures lodged, at my friend's death, was split from top to bottom so that it parted like a pair of shears. I had all the family within the Cave the whole time, not above three quarters of an hour; and all becoming calm we ventured forth again. 'Well,' said I, 'we are all safe, thanks to kind Providence.' But shortly after, as my little Rees was running about, he came and told his mother that one of our Indian dogs was so fast asleep that he could not get up; but when Jessy went to see it she said that the dog was quite dead, struck by the lightning as we supposed. We could perceive no mark of violence externally, yet he was stone dead.

It was not long after this, that we had a dismal stroke befall us, attended with fatal consequences to us all, as thus. While we men happened to be out in the bay after turtle, the cursed monkey overset a yabba as it was boiling on the fire, by which my son Owen got one of his feet scalded. This so greatly alarmed them all, as they knew how much I prized him, that my wife packed Eva off into the woods after certain roots, to stew as a remedy. The poor creature went off with speed, although then with child. My wife said that Eva had been gone a long time after herbs or roots, and wondered what detained her so long. I took no notice at that moment about her, but ordered the monkey to be drowned at once, being determined that it should never be the cause of more mischief; and Harry settled that point with a stone about its neck in the lagoon.

Now as the evening advanced Mr Bell grew uneasy about his wife, saying that perhaps she had rambled beyond her knowledge, and had lost herself.

'How can that be? She has been all over the wood divers times,' said I. 'But you and Harry had better go off in quest of her, with one of the shells.'

And away they went and did not return until sundown, but without any tidings. Now I began to be much alarmed and advised that they should get torches without loss of time, arm themselves and set off again at once, dreading her being alone in the forest after nightfall, as I had no doubt that she would be devoured by morning. We heard them almost the whole time, tooting and shouting. I ordered Patty to make up as large a fire as she could, as a direction for them to get back again. Every now and then I blew a conch, and thus time passed until midnight. Now all were in tears about me; and if I did not hear their sound now and then, my soul filled with horror lest they should all three be lost.

At length, at about two o'clock they came in. Mr Bell was almost frantic with distress. No Eva could they hear or see. I now became sensibly touched, both on account of the woman, and my disconsolate friend. I put on all the most favourable circumstances, and used all my skill to keep up his spirits, yet I feared greatly that we should never see her alive again. Thus we remained until the dawn, and then I proposed to go in quest of her myself. I took Harry with me, and left Norman with the women as he was in so much trouble. We scoured the woods in the strictest manner until high noon without any discovery, and then returned.

Now I began to reflect heavily on my own neglect so as to leave the women at home without a guard, but I was by that time become self secure, as I may say.[50] Poor Norman, observing me to fret at such a rate, said with his eyes full of water, 'My friend, let me entreat you not to charge yourself as being in any way the original cause of this my sad disaster, for had you stayed at home the misfortune might still have happened.'

'Pray let me have my opinion,' said I. 'From henceforth nothing shall ever delude me so far from my reason as to neglect a thing of consequence.'

'My good brother,' said Harry, seeing me in such a perturbation, 'perhaps she has gone home to see her brother.'

'Blockhead! Fool!' said I, 'could she go so far without victuals, and alone?'

'You don't know what the Indians can do when the great ugly Spirit is on them,' he said.[51]

'I cannot be brought to think such a thing unless messmate and she have differed lately.'

'We never have as yet,' said he. 'Yet who knows but she has took some mad fit in her head, and may be gone off thither. But such a thought would not have taken place with me, had not Harry hit on it.'

'I shall be glad when you find your tongue true,' said I, 'with all my soul.' – Yet at the same time I could not entertain such a mad notion.

And thus our time passed on in a dolorous way for three days longer. Now Harry said to me that if Bell was so minded, he would go overland with him to their people. 'Go and call him to me,' I said. When he came I mentioned what Harry had hinted. Upon this he said it was highly needful, he thought, as otherwise we did not know what construction the Indians would put upon the matter. 'That is a very just observation, indeed,' I said. 'Therefore if you are willing, pray go; you have my approbation to do so.'

He came at once into motion, and arming themselves, they went off the next day with a few trifles of provision and the dog Swift with them. I charged Mr Bell to have his eyes about him, and strictly to follow Harry's advice as he best knew the country; and if in case they found her there to bring her back by water, but if it proved abortive in that case, to return as they went, by land, as by that conduct we should be better prepared on their arrival. I then said, 'I give you a fortnight, and if you do not return in that time, we shall be wretched.'

141

After they were gone, I formed many conjectures about the girl, as sometimes thinking that some strange Indians had found her and taken her off with them, or that she might be drowned in some pond. Again, that she had roved so far beyond her knowledge that she had starved to death for want. But the chief thing I dreaded was that wild beasts had destroyed her, and the women joined in that opinion.

Thus we remained betwixt hope and fear, day after day. I never left home once, further than to go down to the lagoon to catch a few Grunts and the like, living chiefly on a vegetable diet. About a week after this, about 9 at night, Owen cried out that he had heard somebody holler. We all ran out to listen, but could hear nothing. A short time after, he said he heard it again, and we soon heard one of those birds I had mistaken on my first landing for a Yoho. This threw us quite aback again, and we all turned in again with heavy hearts. And thus it went on, until the whole time had elapsed for their return, and still no appearance.

About 5 days after this, Swift came running into the cave. 'Here they are!' I cried in a transport[52]. Upon going out I perceived Harry and another Indian coming down the hill. My mind now misgave me at once, and I earnestly called out, 'Where is Bell?' When they came in, Harry said that they had left him there, being sick. Now, think I, Eva is not there, for certain. Harry said Eva never went there. 'What is the matter with my friend?' said I. 'Tell me at once.'

'He will return with some of our friends in a few days,' said he. I then told Betty to sound out Gaynasunto, who was the other Indian. She told me that after Bell and Harry arrived there, the Indians held a private council. When they had done this, they told Harry that they concluded that Eva was either taken off by some strange Indians[53] or eaten by tigers, saying that they knew me to be such a true friend that I would not give consent to showing any blood, as they could never find, by all their industry and diligence, so hard a charge against their White Brother in blood and flesh.

'Surely,' said I to her, 'have they then had spies to watch over us privately to observe our conduct? Tell me, I charge you, have you knowledge of any such proceeding?' She then frankly owned that some of their people had been deputed to come on such an errand, and had actually been at times so near our habitation as to get a fair view of all our behaviour. This news startled me, but as I know full well that they come for no other end than to make their observation as to what manner we treated their women, I soon became cool again. Yet I could not but wonder why they should take so great trouble merely to satisfy curiosity. But when I once reflected, from that source arose such a mutual friendship between us, I could do no more than highly commend them in so doing.

All this time Harry seemed to be reserved, as I took it, and I asked him the reason why he did not give me a full account of all that had happened during their absence. 'Oh,' said he, 'Owagamy told me to keep my mouth shut, saying that he will be the mouth when he comes back next time with Mr Norman, and then Gaynasunto is to go back with him.'

'What occasion,' said I, 'can they have in giving me so much uneasiness? If Eva be there, let her return with her husband.'

'No, no,' said Harry, 'she has been meat for tigers long ago, or starved to death.'

'Then if it be so, why did he not return with you?'

'Owagamy sent me off with that man,' said he, 'as thinking you would grieve, but they will come soon, and that is all I know.'

Well, thought I, if he has taken a conceit to reside among them, in God's name I must reconcile myself to my first manner of life, the best I can.

Above a fortnight elapsed, and no news of Bell. Then an odd notion popped into my head that perhaps the Spaniards had got knowledge of him, and the Indians had given him up. Then I thought that such a conjecture was dealing unjustly by my friends. But about two days later, as Harry was coming out of the bushes, he spied about three canoes coming into the bay. 'Hoist our colours,' said I. We then got the boat ready and went down, to have them entertain the better opinion of us, as I knew not how matters had changed from the time Bell left me. Only Gaynasunto and I were in the boat, as I had charged Harry to abide by the girls.

We met them at the mouth of the lagoon. Now, observing women with them, I began to think they had some sort of sport to play, and intended to surprise me with a sight of Eva again. I gave them a salute, and put away in before them. When we landed, Owagamy and Bell jumped on shore and saluted, which overjoyed me. I saw two women in the canoe, but strangers to me. When they came out, I led them up to the house. After some talk, I asked my messmate who those ladies might be, as my Betty knew them not. Then taking one of them by the hand, he presented her to me as his wife. 'O ho,' said I, 'if that be the case, much joy to you!' He thanked me and said that my friend Owagamy and his council had conducted the whole business, and that he had condescended not from choice, but as knowing that should he decline the proposal, it might prove of ill consequence in future and involve us in much trouble.

'You were very prudent, messmate,' I replied, 'and I am heartily glad that the matter has come to so pleasing a conclusion.'

I now gave the order that things should be provided that we might show them every civility possible. They were all in high spirits. Owagamy desired that the ceremony should be repeated, for he said that they had done 'the broom work' at their place already, to the great mirth of all the Indians; and it was repeated accordingly. I then learned that the bride was a widow. She seemed to be about 25 years of age and named Aanora, or 'A Thing Desired'. Mr Bell satisfied me the next day as to why he had stayed so long with them, as follows: That after they had weighed the matter well, they called a council and they took him to it, in a large wigwam, and after they all got together he was placed by Owagamy's side. Then a profound silence held for the space of about half an hour, during which time about 12 of them kept smoking.[54]

At last an Indian got up and spoke to Bell in Spanish, saying that his people desired Gattaloon (meaning himself) to be the one mouth and voice, through which he was to hear them all. That they all knew of a certainty that he was a fair and true man, and that they saw his heart through his eyes. They knew that he had lost his wife some days before he came to visit them, and they were much satisfied in regard to his coming to them on that account. Otherwise they would have entertained a far different opinion of him; but now knowing such a sad misfortune to have befallen him, not of our own seeking but of an oversight, their council had – finding him grieving so much for the loss – determined to keep him among them until they could find a proper plant for his cure, but that it took them some time to find it out, but that they had now found one. It was a little drooping for want of nourishment, as it had been a dry time lately where it grew.

Then an odd kind of noise was heard, and there came three women to the door, one of which was called in and Owagamy, rising, took her by the hand and said: 'This is a woman not of our nation, but our friend. She has lost her nourisher, and we give her to thee by her own consent. Nourish her as thou hast so done by Mattany our sister, now lost from life. We think it hard that you should be without a woman, as you know so well how to respect one. We sent our valuable brother Gaynasunto with Ayasharry lest our great heart White Brother Penoly should stand in need of friends in the meantime. We will return with Aanora and thee *to thy friend as soon as convenient.'*

I bade Harry return them our most hearty thanks for their love, and the great care that they had shown in salving the great wound my friend Bell had received. I had no liquor to treat them, now in store. This they were informed of. Owagamy answered that all things decayed in time except the Sun, Moon and Stars, so that he wondered not at it, in the least. After they had been with us about 5 days they took their leave. Before they went, I distributed some pieces of blue cloth among them, but the moth over time had much eaten all things.

When I was about to take my farewell of Owagamy at the boat, and saying what great friends he and his people were to me, he smiled and told Harry that I had one thing yet to do to convince his people of my faith. Upon this, I insisted to be acquainted in what way I could show them the great trust and confidence I had ever in him and his people.

'You have many times looked towards the place where we reside, in the long time of your being here, but you have never put one foot willingly before the other to visit me and my people. You know not the path through the wood yourself,' said Owagamy, *'but Ayasharry can lead you by the hand when your mind turns so, towards us.'*

I told him that the sole reason of my never doing them that duty, was owing to the great charge I had on me to preserve these his blood and flesh consigned to my care, but that he might acquaint his people on his return, that I now made it my firm resolution to pay them a visit on the first fair opportunity. Upon this, they all shouted, and we went down to the lagoon to see them off.

I shall in this place observe that both Harry and myself could speak at this time as much Spanish so as to be understood, as I had desired the favour of Mr Bell to take all opportunities to learn enough of that tongue to be able to converse, thinking it would prove of infinite service in future, as we knew not what might come to pass. And this he did very willingly. I came the sooner on to learning it, as I had got a smattering before, while a prisoner at the Havannah.

It now came into my head, as thus. I consulted messmate Bell that I was determined to study Spanish with a full resolution, and as I knew that he understood marking people's skins in characters, he should mark a Cross on one of my hands, and that I would get him to shave my beard and plait my hair after the Spanish mode. He laughed at me, saying how could I ever pretend to pass for one of those people when my tongue would soon betray me.

'Let me alone for that,' said I, *'I have got my own plan.'*

'As how?' said he.

'Thus,' I replied. *'I can report that I am a native of Barcelona[55], went into the service of an English gentleman at Venice when a boy, and remained with him and others after I came to England, for many years, by which means I lost my mother tongue to a great degree.'*

'Troth,' said he, *'that move will do, if you can carry it off well. And your name? How will that answer?'*

'I will fix on one for the purpose with your help,' said I, *'sounding as near to my own as possible.'* This motion being determined on, messmate Bell shaved off my beard in the first place, and ordered my hair, but when we put it into practice it was done in the Cave, and Harry was at that time down the lagoon. My wife and the girls were extremely diverted at my transformation, saying that I had gone back many, many moons and had brought back a pretty little young head with me. My messmate then put one of the old sombreros on my noddle, and making me a low bow, welcomed me to his abode in the name of Senor Luiz Penalosa.[56] *'That will do,'* said I. *'Bless me, my face feels as though half*

my chin was carried away,' said I. We had a kind of berries whose pulp washed away equal to soap, and these we always used for such purposes.

Soon after this, I missed Owen. I enquired after him, and they said that he had gone with Harry. When I saw them coming, we all kept our countenances the best way we could, but to see the behaviour of Harry and Owen on the occasion is beyond my skill to describe. No sooner did Harry see me sitting so altered, that he fixed his eyes on Norman, and looked so confoundedly simple that a man would think he had turned into a downright fool, but poor Owen burst into a flood of tears on hearing me speak. I called him to come to me, but he ran and got behind Patty, clung to her, and there began to bellow at a sad rate. Upon this Bell took hold of him, to bring him to me, but he resisted with all of his might, saying it was not his father. At last, I called to Harry, to come and shake hands with me.

'*O!*' said he, '*I know it is you, a little not you, sideways one way, but Mr Norman has cut your face and made it so sharp that it looks like a young calabash now.*'

'*I thank you for your comparison, Harry,*' said I.

'*You look like a young Spaniard now,*' he said, '*and you always was afraid of Spaniards. Now you make us all fools.*'

'*Never you mind that,*' said I. '*Mr Bell and I have done it to cheat them if we can.*'

'*Ay,*' said he, '*but you will never do so with my Indian people, for we can smell the difference well enough.*'

Now Owen began to smile a little and asked Bell what he cut his father for. But the thing pleased my wife highly, she saying every now and then how pretty my new head looked; only she thought it quite too small. I told her it would soon grow larger; yet I was a singular object among them for few days.

The next thing was to mark my hand, and this Norman did with two small needles tied together, and he filled the punctures with wet powder. It cost me both pain and patience before he had done. His own arm had had a crucifix drawn on it long before. I then proposed that we should make some small crosses to wear at our breast occasionally, and for this end Bell went to work with a dollar, out of which he cast two or three small ones. And thus we were completed as two counterfeit Spaniards.

After this, I said to Mr Bell that we should give his lady another name, as it had become our stated custom.

'*Troth, give her the name ye like best,*' said he.

'*Not at all,*' I replied, '*you must do that yourself.*'

'*Well, then, we will call her Janet if you like.*' And Janet was her name. I then told my wife to inform her of it, and she became mightily fond of it herself.

About the latter end of March, as Bell and I were out fishing in deep water, a prodigious large shark came ranging along, close in view. My messmate said it was very different from any he had seen before.

'*Let us bait the shark hook,*' I said, '*perhaps we may catch him.*'

Directly, he ripped out the bowels of a fish and hung it on the hook, then threw it out right before his nose; but he flew like a dart from it at first, yet returned immediately and took it in. We let him have time, and had the gentleman fast. He gave us brave sport for a time, sheering down below with great strength. At last he became tired out, and let us haul him in. When we got a fair view of him, we found that this fish had a piece of three inch rope in a knot just above his tail, and that it had been on him a great length of time. The fag ends[57] were about a foot long and had been longer, as we thought; they had become white as flax. The fish was about 16 feet in length, and the largest we had ever seen, having many rows of teeth, and had been an old cruiser in his time – perhaps had followed some ship from the coast of Africa after the dead slaves[58], was caught by one of those ships and had been let go again or had made his escape, as he was a true Tiger Shark[59] of a blue colour with the tips of his tail and fins yellow. Fortune at length brought him hither to make his exit. We got several quarts of oil from his liver, which was of material service to us.

Speaking of fish, I must remark that at times we found an odd animal running over the bottom in shoal places, of a triangular form and about the size of a large flounder, carrying its head erect as a hen does, the back mottled in a curious manner. It has four feet or fins shaped like the back fins of a turtle with a tail resembling a fan. The tail and fins, or rather fin feet, were edged with yellow. This creature[60] can run along the bottom nimbly, but in deep water swims with ease. We never ventured to take them, as not knowing their quality.

We also found a sort or insect, or rather reptiles, creeping in the shallow waters, of a dark olive green with black circles[61]. This creature advances in the manner our slugs do, dilating and contracting after that fashion. But the most curious part of the story is that upon being touched once, they instantly emit a most glorious purple liquid all around them to the distance of a yard or more, so that the animal is no longer perceptible.

About the beginning of May, my wife asked Harry to procure her some sapodillas the next time that he went out into the woods. Now on a day soon after, Harry told me in private, that he knew what had become of poor Eva.

'Say you so!' I cried. 'How did you not come to tell me of it before?'

'Because I thought that Mr Norman should not know it,' he said.

'I don't know what you mean,' I said.

'When I was last in the woods,' said he, 'for sapodillas-'

'Well, and how then?' I cried.

'Come with me, Penoly,' said he, and he then took me up the hill, where in a hole under some bushes he showed me the remains of the poor duds she used to wear. My blood ran cold at the sight.

'Whence came these?' I cried in confusion. He then told me, that as he was on a ramble about two miles off, he came to a thicket where he first found a rib bone, and looking about found the skull and other bones with the rags, and knowing them directly to be Eva's, he said that his Great Spirit came on so strongly that had 5 tigers been present, he would have engaged them all.

'Well, let's keep it secret,' I said. 'I shall let him know at some proper time.' I then went down and privately informed my Betty of it, charging her never to presume to leave home, on any occasion whatever, without a guard. Soon after this I gave them the whole of the discovery when they were all together, and it proved sufficient warning from that day forward.

THE SEVENTEENTH YEAR – THE DEATH OF OWAGAMY AND THE ARRIVAL OF PABLO NUNEZ
June 15 1763 – June 14 1764

A few days after our new year commenced, Gattaloon came with 10 more Indians, all of them of our old acquaintance. When we went to salute them, they all appeared sad, seated themselves and remained silent for a few minutes. Then Gattaloon got up and held forth, in a mournful strain, a long discourse in Spanish to Mr Bell, but I soon found it fraught with the melancholy news of Owagamy's death. After he had finished, seeing me so very dejected, he took me by the hand and said, '*I am Owagamy*[62] *now, and I will stand by my friends as long as they or I live. Your friends shall be mine and I will be theirs, and my strength shall go forth against your haters.*'

Mr Bell became so enraptured with his speech that he clapped him on the shoulders and cried, '*Well spaken, Hardicanute!*'[63] We informed them of Eva's fate, and as they were in no great flow of spirits, they soon left us in two days time, saying that Owagamy had charged them to be friends to us, and they were all determined so to be; that they were glad that I had fell on the scheme of passing for a Spaniard, as it would take a great stone off their heads which they had carried for a long time on my account, but that they had borne it with willingness.

Owagamy had ever been a steadfast friend, from our first acquaintance, and was a man of great penetration and forecast, according to what might be expected from an uncultivated native. And I must own that the news of his death truly affected me, knowing full well that he had always been our best bower anchor[64] whenever storms arose; and he jointly with our good friend Komaloot was ever ready and willing to stand as our pilot in conducting us to the safest harbours of calm repose, so that we might remain entirely landlocked from any wind which might chance to blow. Whenever any of our poor little skiffs[65] chanced to touch the quicksands of inquietude, they made it their principal care to tow us off into a safe berth. And remembering all these good and generous offices that they had performed in the course of our acquaintance, I desired Gattaloon to signify on their return not to forget to send our unfeigned condolences to all our friends.

One evening, Owen came in to me as I was reading and said that Mr Bell desired that I would come out and see the great rainbow[66].

'A *rainbow in the night, boy?*' said I, as it was then about 10 o'clock. But as I knew something uncommon was to be seen, I went out, and in the northeast was a large dense cloud in colour like skimmed milk, much more distinct than any I ever saw given by the sun's orb. Norman said that he had seen one before, but it was a novelty to me as in all my travels I had not seen the like, but Harry was not so great a stranger to the like.

About this time our fishermen brought in two fish of a kind I have not yet described. One of them is called by some seamen the Ballahoo[67] if I am not mistaken. It is a long fish, round and slim, shaped much like the Garr Fish[68], but differs much in all but the body, the upper fly of the tail being short and the under 4 times the length; but few fins, and in regard to its mouth very singular as the under jaw, or mandible, projects to ten times the length of the upper, terminating in a very sharp point, so that it is impossible for it to seize prey as other fish do. But nature has given it such an address that when lying on the surface of the water, and perceiving its object it instantly darts as an arrow from a bow, piercing its prey with the lower bill, then sinking to the bottom, where it remains darting the prey until it becomes no longer able to escape, when it takes it in at its pleasure. And this fish is to be seen in shoal water.

The other sort of fish is constructed much like a Flying Fish, but grown to the size of an ordinary mullet[69]. It is curiously marked with blue, green, yellow, brown and red. The wings or fins are much longer than the body, tail and all, and almost transparent. When these wings are extended they spread broader than a man's hand, and are beautifully variegated with many colours.

I shall now give the reader some account of the vast variety of lizards that we see both frequently and seldom. The most frequent and common are those called the Lion Lizard[70]. They are most numerous abroad in the heat of the day, exceedingly fleet of foot, although they seem to go much on the belly. This belly is chequered much like our common English green snake[71], but its back is striped horizontally from head to tail with delicate broad strips of a brown and yellow colour, resembling velvet. The male is very vicious after the female, and much larger. Their conjunction is lateral; and it is to be observed that in their courtship when the male first spies the female he protrudes a large bag from beneath his throat, puffing it out, full of wind, and drawing it back at pleasure, so that when he is not thus employed, nothing of that bag is perceptible. This is common to the iguana and lizard tribes.

The Galliwasp[72] – this is another species frequenting the woods, which lurk in holes in the ground, in colour dark grey and black. They bite sharply, as the Indians say, but are not poisonous as reported in the Islands of the West Indies by the Negroes. They are of the largest kind of lizards, and if pursued take to their holes, but smoke soon dislodges them. They are also very indolent, remaining long in one place.

The Satin Lizard[73] – these are of a solitary disposition. You seldom find more than one in a place, and that always in the shade under a rock, or in the chinks and clefts of rocks, where they lurk day and night. I have known them to remain in one place for three days and nights, without once changing their position. They are striped black, brown, white and grey, and shine like satin as they move. But it has one quality differing from all the other kinds, which is, it has the power to make its body so flat that it can at pleasure adapt itself to any chink it chooses to lurk in.

I have mentioned that sort called the Wood Slave already, but it is beyond my power to describe the whole genera of them. Some are yellow, others black, brown, red, speckled etc. Some come forth mostly in the heat and the driest time; on the contrary some kinds are seldom to be seen but after rain, and so forth. In general they live on insects, and have the tongue forked as the snake.

Now it happened after the family had retired, that my Betty being awake shook me, and when I answered she told me that someone or other was sick, saying that she had heard a very sad moaning. I heard it myself and got up, called Harry, and finding him well, sent him to learn who was out of order. But on enquiry, all were well; yet every now and again we heard sad and deep groans. The dogs were called, but they were all well enough, and what to think we could not tell. Sometimes it ceased and then began again, now strong, then weaker, and thus it went on until fair dawn. None went to sleep the whole night except the younger ones.

Now Bell started this notion, that some strange Indians had perhaps discovered us, and it might be a scheme to decoy us among the woods, as the sound seemed to come from a part beyond the place where we had found money and plate.

'Po, po!' said I. 'They have been long enough in finding us out then, and this is a poor method for them, indeed, as should they have any disposition to annoy us they could do it in a more manly way if they were so disposed.'

'What if it should be the departed spirit of the victim they left as guard over the treasure?' said Harry.

This made us smile, and I said jokingly, 'By my troth, then, he has been very remiss or on some long journey thus to begin his objections[74] after so great a length of time.' But the women were sure that an Indian or some other person must be out there in a very bad way or dying, saying that perhaps it might be one of our friends much hurt, as he was on his way to our place. This carrying some weight, I told Bell that he and Harry might arm themselves and take along the dogs, to find out the cause.

'Come,' said Harry. They then loaded their guns, took machetes, and away they went boldly. In about 20 minutes they returned.

'What news?' cried I. 'Have you found it out?'

'Found it out?' said Bell with a very serious countenance. 'Ay, ay, and if you had been with us, you would have found it out also.'

'Make me acquainted at once,' said I, 'let the thing be how it will, for I must be satisfied.'

'It is one of the natives of a most gigantic size,' said he, 'and dying, as I take it, but not one of our friends as I never saw him come hither in their company. Nor do I think him of the tribe as he differs greatly in colour from our friends. He has not the least sense we could perceive, but groans heavily.' All this time, Harry kept aloof. The girls were all gathered around, and standing there with open mouths. As for my part, I saw Bell begin to look seriously on the ground after he had given his account.

I began to form strange notions in my brain, saying, 'He is not dead yet – I hear him groan still.'

Upon this, Bell burst into a monstrous laughter and holding his head up, cried, 'I am to windward of you now, my good messmate.'[75] Then Harry came up to help him, and after they had laughed their fill, Bell said, 'Come, come, what do you think it may be?'

'You have the game to your own selves,' said I.

'Well, to clear off all further conjectures it is yon great cotton tree which the lightning split. There is a broken limb, fell athwart another, and as the wind dies or freshens it rubs, more or less with a groaning noise. But when one is near it, the sound is above the tone of any dying person.'

After messmate Norman had played off this fit of the horror so well with us, I came to a determination to visit my good friends to the southward, and for the journey I got Bell to make us a knapsack each to carry our roasted yams etc. in. Harry was to stand pilot, and the company were to be Harry, Owen and myself with the dog Rover. When the time came for our departure, I told Mr Bell that I gave the whole charge into his hands, saying that I rested satisfied with his conduct in our absence, to be kind to my wife and all the rest. Then, calling all together, I charged them that they gave good heed to my friend's advice in every respect. And as it was a thing incumbent on me, and what I could not in fair play put off, they having been so many times to visit us, I took a sailor's leave of my wife and the rest, leaving them all in tears abruptly, and away we went. Owen wept out for his part. The novelty of the thing gave him spirits, though.

I need not mention a description of our road as this has been done, but we all three arrived in safety; but as the child and I were never used to go such vast lengths, our feet became much blistered. Now, as we drew near to their residence, which was about 5 in the evening, tired to death having been six days on the trampoose[76] – sleeping on the bare ground every night with a large fire around us, living scantly as we got no more than 4 parrots and one pigeon the whole journey. Harry had shot a duck in a pond, and as he could not reach it, he wanted to send the dog in – this I absolutely refused lest he might be devoured by the alligators.

When we had got thus far, I made my child sit down by me, and sent Harry into the town before me to find how the land lay, and inform them of our arrival. In a short time, we heard a confused noise of many people advancing towards us; and soon after we perceived a throng of men, women and children coming up with little bells, calabashes and imitations of German flutes, making a most confused noise, with Gattaloon, Harry and several other faces I knew well. We then arose and Gattaloon took me by the hand with a generous smile on his face, and gave me a most kind welcome. Such a pleasing aspect was to be seen on all their faces, mixed with a kind of admiration that I had never beheld the like of before, and it much raised my spirits after my fatigue.

Owen stuck close by me all the way, as we went into their ranges of houses or wigwams, and stared about him as one astonished, being the first time that the poor soul had made his appearance in public, as I may say, for the whole universe was to him one scene of wonder. I had rigged my Owen out in such a manner that he looked like a young Cupid with his sheaf of arrows at his back, and bow over his arm. We were led into one of their places of dwelling and at the entrance were met by Zulawana and others. There sat on the mat a very ancient woman to whom Zulawana led up my child, and she took great pains to examine him, being very dim-sighted. She then placed her left hand on his shoulder and muttered a few words, which I desired might be interpreted to me. It was to this effect: 'Let not an arrow hit him, let not fire burn him, a tree fall on him or the waters choke him. All you strong men preserve him from the hot spirit of those who would kill him while he remains in the days of tenderness.'

Now Harry observed to me that she was one of their good cunning women[77] and had told many strange things; and that an Indian had told him that they had expected us that Moon, she having foretold it to them for some days.

The young Indians gathered around Harry and by gentle usage coaxed him out, and when they got bows, began to dastardise[78] him with feats of activity. Owen, having Harry his uncle at his side, took courage and showed them some of his skill. Some of the children would gently touch him and look on their own fingers after it, as thinking his colour might rub off, as he was lighter coloured than themselves, although he looked much more the Indian than the European.

Now, after I had been among them two days, Gattaloon said that he was mighty glad that I had turned Spaniard, as there was at that time an old Spanish soldier come among them, who intended to come and see me in about two hours, being then absent with two of their people; but that he and his friends had taken care to spread the report that I was a Spaniard. This put me to trumps[79], so that I became under the necessity of acting my part the best way I could. Accordingly he came, and saluted me in the Spanish way. I returned the civility and a conversation commenced. Then I gave him my whole history – that I was a native of Barcelona but had as a boy entered into the service of an English gentleman who was at that time in Venice, and with him went to England, etc. That in the course of time, I had lost much of my mother tongue, and after a multitude of changes became a servant to a gentleman bound to England from Jamaica and was taken, carried into Havana, and put prisoner on board a Spanish man-of-war. That after many turns of fortune I became lost in a canoe on this shore where I had resided for many years, part of which time quite alone.

He seemed amazed at what I related, and said that he found that I could not speak Spanish fluently but that I looked very much like a Biscain or Biscayan[80]. He then asked my name and I said it was Luiz Penalosa. Now, as we were talking I happened to mention the passage of events, which happened from the ship's top when I was a prisoner. On this, the old man gave a start and said that he well remembered the affair, being then a marine on board that ship. I then enquired his name and he said he was Pablo Nunez, but as that class of men did not associate much with us, I could not recollect him at first. He mentioned to me concerning a man whose name was Nick Jones[81], that he had been placed as sentry over him while in the stocks for drunkenness – calling him Nico Yone – and said that he was a drunken mad English dog.

Now, as we were talking, I happened to call my Owen in English, and when the child came to us, Nunez took him by the hand and said, 'Good boy, *hablar Englise? Me hablar Englese tambien. What is your nama, boy?*'

Owen answered. I then interrogated the old man where he learnt English, when he told me that he had been taken by the English in the reign of Queen Anne, and said that he was a prisoner in a castle there, by Portsmouth. That on being released, he went to Sir John Norris's fleet, was up the Baltic with him on board a ship called the Boyne[82], and remembered Peter the Great[83] when on board the fleet, and recited a few things concerning him – as on the Queen's birthday Peter had refused to drink her health with the Admiral out of a silver pint can, but ordered a pipe[84] of wine on the quartedeck, then calling for an axe knocked in the head, took a mess can and dipped into it, then lifting the can to his head drank such a quantity that Norris could not venture to do the like. Also, that to please him, the Admiral ordered a sham engagement and that Peter took up a shot (cannon ball) in his hand desiring that the Admiral would make use of some of those, as such a game was but children's play without them; that the Admiral replied that he must beg to be excused as he could not make so free with his mistress's subjects.

In a day or two the old man became greatly taken with me, saying, '*Brother Englese, I have no wife or children. Neither have I any provision from the Crown now I am become old and no longer of service. I have been away from the old country for over 30 years, and should I return to Burgos[85], no one would know me there at this day. Without plata[86] I have been a fool in my time, and have now nothing left but rags and grey hairs.*' Then giving a heavy sigh, he said he had grown weary of time, having been put off so many times for a passage home, where when he arrived the poor portion allowed was not worth going for, in a manner. And that he had for some time followed the profession of a barber and maker of segares until he had rambled hither, thinking that he would end his days after the simple manner of the Indians as he had now no more care for this world, saying that he need not seek after friend or kindred, knowing that he had none in all the country.

The old man delivered himself in such plain, honest terms that I at once said to him, '*Padre Nunez, know ye how to keep a faithful friend when you have found him?*'

He then turned his eyes toward me and said, '*Where, child, shall such grey hairs as mine find interest in falsehood at this day? I am now almost 70 years of age.*'

'*Could you be content to reside at my place,*' said I, '*and fare as we do?*'

'*Peace and quiet, Señor,*' said he, '*with a little morsel in friendship is the utmost of my ambition. I will go with you if you bury me in love.*'

'*Swear, then, only this,*' said I, '*that you will never betray the confidence I put in you as a faithful friend, and then return with us to our habitation, with all my heart.*'

He then took me by the hand and swore by the Blessed Virgin to be true and faithful to me and mine, in the presence of all my friends. As soon as they understood it, they all gave a great shout, and thus he became elected one of our society.

After this was settled, I became uneasy to be gone, and mentioned it to my old friends who were by no means against it, as they knew my reasons. I then agreed with Gaynasunto to make me two stout canoes, for which I promised them 50 dollars, and he engaged to get them made and to bring them around to us in about 3 Moons. And observing hides amongst them, I proposed that they should bring us such, with cotton cloth and mats to be paid for by me, to which they agreed. After all was settled, I proposed that we should return by sea, as old Nunez could not travel well so far by land. We left then in 4 canoes after I had been with them about a fortnight, and our company consisted of Gattaloon as commander, Zulawana and 7 other Indians with ourselves.

151

We took the favour of a southwest wind and stood away large[87] after we got clear of their creek. This lasted us the whole day. We then put inshore and landed on a beach. The Indians soon made up a shelter of bushes and we composed ourselves for that night. Early at the peep of day we were off again; but the wind fell so much that they took to their paddles; sometimes they stood, at other times they paddled on their knees. We went at least 7 knots an hour. In the evening we put into a low headland full of trees, but as the moon arose soon after, we remained there just to eat and then put out again. I now found that they acted with great caution, speaking with a low voice; and thus we proceeded until about 12 o'clock, then put in again, took a small nap in our canoes, and about 5 they got a fair wind again.

I now found Zulawana began to grow a little uneasy, frequently spurring on the Indians whenever the wind fell. Upon this, I wanted to know the cause. They spake in their own tongue, so I understood but a little, now and again. At last they informed me that as the Moon was then going to turn sides, (viz.) change, there might come on a strong wind from the north bringing rain also, saying if so we must be forced to put in and perhaps remain there for some days. This was dull news, but as we were not master or pilots, I said nothing. This evening, Zulawana told me that we should see the Long Key by my place, the next morning, if they only went to sleep for a few hours. This was concluded on, agreeing to put out at about 5 again.

But we had not composed ourselves for long before I felt a cool breeze from the north. I then told Nunez that I did not like our berth, and proposed that we should put into a small bay on the other side of the small point we were then at. This was done, and we hauled up the boats, making shelters as fast as possible. And thus we remained for three days. My poor child shivered with the stress of the weather, as he had never been exposed to the like before, although it was not cold.

When we had eaten up all we had, I took Harry with me to try and shoot something, but while we were absent the Indians sounded a shell for us to return. We did so, and Zulawana proposed that as it was now almost become calm, we should push away for it, and away we went. The Indians began to work away with all their might. My poor boy was almost famished for lack of food. At last they all began to sing, Gattaloon showing the example. I asked the reason, when they told me that they should soon see my place. This I could not well credit, but about an hour after, one of the Indians called out and pointed with his finger, and I saw the point of a low spit of land where they said I lived; but on my standing up I found that they meant our Long Key. Upon this, I told my Harry to begin our old song, as I knew that would please. This gave them all fresh spirits and in about two hours we came in with it, and glad I was to my very soul, even as much as If I had been at that moment going to land on my native shore.

I now proposed that we should land and I would go off with my gun with Harry, while others went striking fish, giving the order that they made up a good fire in the meantime. After about 2 hours we all assembled and relieved our hungry bellies with what we had procured. It was now about 3 o'clock and we all embarked again. I looked out for our signal but saw none as they had not seen us. When we got within the bay, I took up a shell and gave my usual blast, soon after which I saw our rag flung out, which rejoiced me much. When we got within the lagoon I heard my messmate blow, as we all had a different mode for that purpose, whereby we knew each other's blast.

When we got in sight of the landing, we saw them all hands, dancing and singing. Owen jumped out, and swam to shore for gladness. But such greeting was there when we were all landed that I need not endeavour to describe it, only that I must observe that my Betty expressed her joy by a flood of tears. But to be short, Bell told me that all had been well in my absence, and that they longed every hour for our return. And now we were reinstated, we had been absent for more than 3 weeks.

We had left three dogs at home as Harry, being a mighty dog man, now and then got one from one of his friends. But as they were frisking about, Rover being glad of his return, I missed Swift and on enquiry was told that he had paid his debt to nature by the bite of a snake, 5 days after our departure.

My home was so transporting a place to me now that the old proverb was truly fulfilled, 'Home is home, etc.'[88] Daddy Nunez said that if I had told him I had been born there he might have believed it, as we had so vast a body of articles about us. I introduced him to messmate Norman in the fairest light, and he received him as a friend, giving him to know that whomever I recommended to him, he made it his business to esteem.

Our friends stayed among us for 4 days, and on the third Soroteet or the Crabcatcher was missing for a time. At last he came down the hill with a small basket of flowers he had composed in the woods. These he came and presented to Jessy to the great surprise of us all. She received it, which made us wonder much, and then they both came to me and Soroteet asked me if I would suffer him to remain among us if he chose her for a wife. I then asked Gattaloon if it was agreeable to them all as, if so, they had my free consent – supposing the thing had been made up between him and Harry while we were at their place, and I found it soon to be the case. All agreed, and they performed the ceremony among them directly, when they took their farewell of us in as much good humour as ever.

The first thing I studied was the building of two new wigwams as our family was now increased, and this they went to work about, as I proposed that Mr Bell and Daddy Nunez should live in one[89], and the new married couple in the other. When they were finished, they took possession, and we all lived very agreeably together as I made it now a determined rule that Bell, Nunez, my wife and I should always mess[90] together. And thus we carried matters on for the future, living on after my old fashion for the remainder of my seventeenth year without control.[91]

CHAPTER VII

The Eigtheenth to Twenty-First Years

THE EIGHTEENTH YEAR – TRADING WITH PRIVATEERS
June 15 1764 – June 14 1765

Soon after the commencement of this year, and about 9 o'clock in the evening we heard several heavy guns fire in the offing[1]. Norman ran up the hill but could perceive no flashes. This put us all on the wonder, but how to account for it, we knew not. But old Nunez observed to us that he supposed that it might be Guardacostas[2], saying that the Spaniards had several out to prevent contraband trade, since the late peace.[3]

'Peace,' cried I, *'that has been for many years unless there has been a fresh war.'*

Upon this he told us that they had only just then concluded a peace with the English, for there had been another war since that which he and I were concerned in – all of which we knew no more of than a new-born infant.

On the 17th day of July, as our people were busy making torches at about 10 in the forenoon, all at once we heard a gun fired, as from some vessel near to our shore. This was a novelty indeed, and what to think or how to act, we could not tell. Away ran Harry and he came down with the news that there was a fine ship standing right off with a flag out, not far from the Long Key.

'What, what!' said Bell. *'Come away, now, Mr Penrose,'* he cried, *'let us see!'*

When we had got up the hill, she proved to be a large sloop, quite inshore with our bay. *'This is new indeed,'* said I. *'How must we act in this case, think you?'*

We saw them douse their colours three times.[4] *'They want to speak to us,'* I cried, *'and have discovered us by the great fire we have had this morning. And now, how we must proceed, I am sure is a mystery to me.'*

'Get the glass,' said Bell. When that was brought, I could plainly perceive she had up a St George's jack.[5]

'They are English!' I cried, *'or if Spaniards, they have discovered us at last, and have come to learn what we are here upon.'*

'Well,' said Bell, *'suppose they are. If you are willing, we will go off to them. It is but to know the worst, and let it come. What would they do to a couple of such forlorn fellows as we are?'*

'How will you order the affair?' said I. *'Suppose you and old Nunez go off to them. You can act the Spaniard to a notch.'*

This we fixed on. Now all was in confusion, but we told the old man our intention, and he complied. The yawl was got ready, and off they went without arms or anything except water. After some time I saw them, out clear of the lagoon. I had given Bell and Nunez their cue at their departure, so they knew how to carry the thing out. When I saw them getting alongside I said to my own heart – now is this day big with some important event or other, and how it may go, none can devise as yet. But I determined in my mind to keep up a spirit. I worried every hour of the day while they were absent, but in about 4 hours they returned and gave the following account of the expedition.

Bell said he found her to be a Bermudan-built sloop[6], which had guns[7] and looked much like a smart privateer with a bottom as white as a hound's tooth; and as they drew near her, he plainly heard, 'A rope for the boat!' called, with a 'damn me' tacked to the end of the charge.[8] When he got on board he asked from whence they came and was answered from Gillicrankey.[9] This, he said, seemed odd to him, as knowing that place to be in his own country, but he soon found they were English.

'Well,' said I, 'what brought them hither? It is my opinion that they are pirates, as Nunez says the war has been over for some time.'

'No, no,' said he, 'they are what you may call fair traders[10], and we can purchase some flour off them if you think proper.'

'That's the mark,' said I, 'and how did you come on with them?'

'They know no more than the dead, but I am a true Spaniard,' said he. 'I have told them that we live 5 miles up the country and that we would purchase from them if they stayed a day or two, upon which they asked where they could water, and I have directed them to the point of Long Key. So, now I think that I have done my part so far, messmate.'

'Well, then,' I replied, 'we must in the first place get out a parcel of our dollars and boil them in hot water and ashes to get off their blackness. But what may they ask per barrel?'

'Only 30 pieces of 8,' said he.

'Oh, that is but a trifle to us,' cried I, 'but money enough, God knows, to some folks. How many will they spare us?'

'As much as we want, for seeing our signal of smoke as they thought, was what made them bring to, and fire that gun'

'What do you really take them to be?'

'Why, they are people from North America, either from Pennsylvania, New York, Maryland or New England, upon what they call the fair trade.'

Now I observed to Bell that we should be obligated to admit our new associate Nunez into the secret of our cash, as it was unavoidable.

'Well,' said he, 'he has sworn to you to be true, yet I think it would not be amiss to swear him again on our Bible to let him know also that we are Englishmen, as he will certainly come by the thing one way or another in the course of time. It is my opinion that he suspects it already by our talking English so much, and by small hints he lets fall at times.'

'Agreed,' said I, 'and as we have little time to spare let us both take him into the house directly, and you shall open the whole affair to him in brief, as you can best do it, in Spanish.' We then sent for him and Bell began with him, on my advice, to the following effect:

'Señor Nunez, my friend and I have sent for you in order to inform you of a matter greatly to your advantage. You are well acquainted that your coming among us was of your own free will and seeking, and that you have given my friend here your positive affirmation to be true to all his secrets. What say you to this?'

'Gentlemen,' said he, 'I am now but a poor old man dependent on your generous friendship. I shall steadfastly keep my word.'

'Ay, hold,' said Bell. 'Stop there. Are you content and free, provided we make you a richer man than you ever were before, to swear on this Sacred Book that you will inviolably keep secret what we shall now unfold to you? We are two plain and honest men, and have no evil in our hearts against you or any man on this earth.'

He then said, 'My friends, I trust you because I see no cause to the contrary. I am at your service.' I told him that the book then before him was none other than the Holy

Scriptures, and tendered him his oath with a cross laid thereon, and he took it in a very serious manner. After this, Bell gave him to know that we were both Englishmen, and of the money I had discovered, etc. As to our being English, he said that was no more than he had suspected, and in regard to everything else, we might rely on his fidelity, and thanked us most cordially for admitting him as a member of our interest. I then sent him, Bell and Harry to work with the dollars, but when the old man came to behold our treasure, he said 'Santa Maria!' in an ecstatic attitude, 'Mucho plato per cierta!' or a great deal of money for certain. 'Maravilosa!'[11]

After we had got this piece of business done, early the next day I sent off messmate Norman, Nunez and Harry in the yawl with a quantity of money, yams, plantains, potatoes, oranges, limes and beans to deal with them after the best way they could, and to present the officers with such of the truck[12] as they thought best; also to purchase anything they thought we were in most need of; and also to bring me an account of what the 'fair traders' had to dispose of. And away they went. I had given Harry his lesson overnight that we lived inland.

About 12 o'clock the boat returned. Bell told me that he had bargained for 12 barrels of flour, and a goat with young to be delivered to the old plantation; a barrel of gunpowder, shot of different sizes, a parcel of flints, nails, fish hooks, clasp knives, 2 saws, 6 chisels, 2 adzes[13], 5 hatchets, 3 axes and some other articles. He said that they acted with precaution and dispatch, and asked about the guarda costas, but he could not learn the captain's name. But as there were diver articles he advised me to go off myself, saying that I could pass for an Irishman, and then I could please myself, as I liked. Accordingly, I came to that resolution, and as my lady had never been on board any vessel, I determined to take her with me.

So early on the morrow off we went, my wife, Bell and I with Owen in the yawl, Nunez and Harry in the old canoe, leaving Soroteet as guard at home. When we came alongside, Bell went first on board and told them that I was a neighbour of his, in partnership with him, that I was born in Ireland but had resided many years in that country, and that the Indian woman was my wife and the boy my son. Now I had charged Owen to say that his name was Muskelly if he should be asked, but otherwise not to speak, for if he did in English they would carry him away with them, and he would never see me again. That was enough for him.

After we had been on board for some time, I asked how they came into these so remote parts, Gillicrankey being in Scotland. Upon this, they said that there might be more places of the same name, and if I did not ask too many questions, they would tell me fewer lies. 'Well, then, faith and soul,' said I, 'I know how to keep my breath to cool my pottage.'[14]

I bought off them a large grindstone, two watches, two dozen of white beaver hats, 5 pieces of striped linen, thread, osnabrigs[15] and twine. Bell produced his small diamonds and a little fellow who seemed to be a doctor was put to examine them, and they had them for the value of about 200 dollars in truck; but we observed that this part of the game was played off under the rose, or juggled up in the round house[16]. We bought a pair of good fowling pieces, another watch for our friend Nunez, needles, pins, scissors, razors, raven duck[17], a good telescope as that which I had was but a small inferior one, some medicines and lancets (these messmate Bell chose), penknives, with two large iron pots, cordage, a gander and goose with a drake and duck – and well did we pay for them, as they had as much melted silver from me as balanced with 18 dollars.

They tickled us up also in a few quart bottles and phials we purchased from them. We got also a serving mallet[18], two dozen sail needles, three marlin spikes[19] and a dozen small blocks[20]. Also, several kinds of small stuff such as ratline[21], marline, spun yarn, etc. Bell brought my notice to several red-framed looking-glasses, and it struck me directly that they would prove fit presents for our Indian neighbours, as well as a few for our own use and we bought 3 dozen of them as reasonable; a dozen table knives and forks, and many other articles I cannot mention.

After we had got what we wanted, they seemed uneasy for our departure, and we wanted their company just as little. But as we were putting off from them, some ragamuffin fellow called to me and said, '*Paddy, what will you take for your squaw?*' – meaning my Betty. Now, the chap happened to be redheaded, and Bell stood up in the boat to return him this answer.

'*Ye reed pow'd brute, she is now remarking ye to be the most ill faced Deel she ever beheld with her twa eine!*'[22] This turned the whole skit on him, and they directly set up such a laugh that the fellow began to blackguard[23] us by way of a foolish revenge.

But on my desiring that no answer might be returned, and pulling away for the shore, a man on the roundhouse spake to us with a small trumpet and said: '*Signior Sawny*[24], *you forgot to purchase some oatmeal. I say, your crawthumping*[25] *wife will flog you for that when she gets you home, you renegade.*' Upon this, the order was given, '*Come, run up our anchor and hoist the jib there!*' And away they went, close-hauled[26] with the wind at south, and we set off for shore, glad enough that they had paid us the visit, and as glad of their departure as we wanted no more of their company.

After we got our purchase[27] home safe, we became as busy as bees in a barrel of tar. We lodged our flour in the kitchen. I put a white hat on each of their heads, which made them all as proud as Lucifer. We fell to on making shirts, shifts, trousers and the like, so that in a short time we appeared all of another regiment, and had another of those fair traders have come upon our coast, we would have been a match for them.

We were often very merry on the occasion and my girl was continually on the new subject, as it was a matter all new to her. She called the vessel's roundhouse 'the little Wigwam of the Great Men'; the hold she called 'the long Kitchen of my country folks' but she thought they were very impudent for they had looked through her eyes when she offered to open them. Owen and Harry's remarks were how so many people could find victuals to eat, and how they could carry those great heavy shooters (cannon). Owen thought it strange to see them run up the shrouds and haul the ropes through the blocks. But the drum was what struck them most – how could they possibly put so much noise into that thing with no more than those two little sticks.

Bell asked the favour when on board to have a gun (cannon) fired to see what effect it would have on the Indians, and they had obliged with three. Harry ran to me, got behind my back, stared like a wildcat, and shook like a leaf, crying, '*Ow, ow, ow!*' Owen fell down and roared like a stuck pig; but it took a different effect on Betty. She stood motionless with her eyes closed, but after a time, when she came to, she desired me to be going, for she was sure that another such knock would shake her head off and split her heart.

The women each had a looking glass presented to them in which they were constantly looking, calling them Water Stones. But the watches became the wonder of them all, nor could we persuade them but there must be a spider or some small insect within them to make Owyooks[28] of, or what we may term witches, to keep them always moving and ticking. These we were forced to preserve by informing them that none must touch them, except those who had been to learn how to charm them on the other side

157

of the great water.

The scheme succeeded so well that not a soul of them would touch a watch on any persuasion whatever; and Harry with Owen, if they saw either of us go to wind one up, would immediately withdraw to some distance. This was just as we would have it; otherwise our watches would have been soon spoiled. But what is remarkable, my young Rees could not be brought to fear a watch in the least, so that we were forced to make fobs to carry them about with us, or hang them high in the evenings.

After a short time we made leavened and kneaded cakes, and our ladies were so exceedingly fond of them that I could have wished that we had bought more flour. But now I found this mode to be a kind of waste and proposed to Norman that we should contrive an oven. Now as this was a large undertaking, and of moment, I began to restrict them in their flour usage until the oven should be built. Norman proposed making bricks and burning lime from shells, but Nunez told us that we need not give ourselves all that trouble, saying we could make yabbas well enough, and that we could fall to and make a large deep oven of the like form, then make a good clay hearth for it to rest upon – which, when well burnt, we had no more to do than laying our bread on that well-heated hearth, and then whelving[29] the large yabba over it, covering the whole with a glow of coals occasionally.

This business was put in force and they happily succeeded in the process; and then Nunez got Harry to help him build a small thatched hovel over our bake house. In this oven they baked now and then, as my shipmate Norman thought best, he being steward. We commonly had bread 3 times a week, and about half a pound each. But one day as they were heating this oven, I observed that it would not be long before the oven would be useless for want of flour, as we had but a very faint view of getting more in the like manner. After this, at times we used to mix yams, plantains etc. with the flour by way of eking it out, and produced good bread for such as we needed.

Thus we lived in love and friendship, and as we were in a lonely and solitary place, we enjoyed a constant round of unmolested tranquillity. We wanted for no thing meet for the use of contented mortals, and we thanked God for our blessings. Nor could we in reason repine at our lot considering all things, as how could I possibly have imagined at my first landing on this shore that the Lord would so graciously spread me such a splendid table in this forlorn wilderness? Let every mortal on earth look inward and reflect, then ask himself, 'What do I merit, after all this disobedience?' This was truly my case, as when I landed first on this shore I was in a real state of reprobation, accustomed to all vice except murder and theft.

Now it happened one day Harry brought home half a dozen flamingos, and while the children were de-feathering them, Norman observed to me that for the sake of novelty he would make us a fowl pie, and to work went he and Betty. They baked it nicely in our fine oven, so that now we could command boiled, roasted, baked, stewed, barbecued etc. as we chose it.

About the latter end of September Norman and I went out on a party for recreation and to fish in deep water, taking Owen with us. Now as we got out of the lagoon, the wind came around to East and my messmate proposed that we should make some stretches into the offing as it was a fine turning breeze, and we did so until we got about 5 miles out beyond the East point of Long Key. This was the greatest distance I had been right out in my whole time. And now the wind began to die away, but we had expected to return with a fine leading breeze. Now I proposed to stand in again.

'As you please,' said he, and away we went before it for the space of half an hour, when it died away and became stark calm.

We now found a small current running to the Westward. 'How now?' said I. 'Here we are, but to get back is the question.'

'We must take to our oars,' said he.

'And a pretty pull we shall have,' I replied. 'We shall drive a league below the Key before we can get in again.' But we went to it, and in about half an hour got within the current's way, and then concluded to fall to fishing when the water would shoal. But while we were thus chatting, we observed a white ball on the surface of the sea, with something playing around it. In a short time after, it bounced above the water to a height of 3 feet or more. We lay on our oars for a time to see the curiosity and saw the thing repeated often. What it could be, we knew not, but concluded to row gently towards it. When we had got within about 30 yards we could discern it to be that sort of fish called the Hedge Hog or Globefish[30]. This fish has the power of blowing itself up so as to become round like a ball, being armed at all points with long and sharp darts. Now, around this fish were gathered about 3 or 4 dolphins, who every now and then would strike it out of the water with their tails. When the globefish fell back to the surface, it would paddle away with its underfin to some distance very swiftly, and then the game renewed. Thus we went on until Bell chanced to make too great a movement with his oar, when it sank at once like a stone, so that we concluded it to be a real sport intended, seeing the globefish could disengage itself from the dolphins at pleasure. Now this led me to a confutation of what many seamen hold, (viz.) that a dolphin is never seen within soundings[31], but I am certain to the contrary as at this time we had not above 18 fathom of water and were over patches of rocks.

A little after this, we fell to fishing in about 12 fathoms and soon had fish round us of many kinds, among which were the largest Amber Fish[32] we had ever beheld. Now as we were very busy at our sport, now and then there would follow up the fish on our hooks a fish such as we had never beheld in our lives before, but as he did not show himself high enough to give us his true shape, I shall give the best description I can. It appeared black as a coffin[33] when covered with velvet, with a monstrous lofty fin on the back, running its whole length. On the highest part of this fin, right over the shoulders was a long kind of whip some 16 inches long. The upper fork of the tail had the same kind of tag to it, and these he continuously kept playing. The whole fish might be about 4 feet in length. It semed to be very active among the other fish, driving every here and there, and seemed to be very voracious, yet it would not touch our bait nor could we perceive that it offered to snap at the other fish. I could have been glad to have caught him, as I am fully persuaded that these fish are rare to be seen.

Soon after, a small cat's paw[34] came in from seaward, and we got up our killick, set our sail and stood in for the bay with the wind increasing, so that we soon arrived with our cargo of fish. Among the fish were two sorts deserving description; they are called Morays[35]. They are commonly about 4 feet long or so from the head to the tail, which ends in a complete point. They are shaped like a sword, having fins running the whole length above and below. This fish is flattened and not round as an eel, but in other things acts like it, twisting itself in various knots, and bites sharply. One sort is green as a leek, but the other is so finely mottled with white, black and yellow that the leopard's skin cannot be compared with it for beauty.

By this time we had gotten several young fowls about us, and Old Nan the goat had brought forth two sons. They gave us our hands full of trouble at times, being so very mischievous that we were forced to keep a sharp lookout over what linen we possessed, for whenever they could they would chew and nibble it presently to a rag. At last they found a way to my poor store of paper, and as fair traders began to treat themselves to it. Now, as it was with great difficulty that I could keep the worm from it also, I determined that we should take some new method to ward off the impending danger. Now as we could all see the great necessity, so all joined willingly to prevent the danger. Bell, finding my wattling work so useful, took a resolution of making a sort of hovel for our goats and fowls, and we all went to work with spirit. This business took us up 6 weeks, before it was all finished to our minds.

This work we carried on thus. It was divided into 4 apartments, one for the goats with its own door; another for the fowls so that they could never get out in the morning without permission; one for the dogs, free of access for them; the 4th was our store room three times the size of the others and was allotted for our dry wood. As for our gunpowder, we kept that at a good distance off, under a cavern of the rocks in the earth.

I told Bell to build a kind of fence around the side of the stream of water for our geese and ducks, so contrived that they could with ease play in it without wandering too far away. It had a small house in one corner of the fence. And by the time the whole was completed, it formed a kind of farmer's dwelling; and by this method we preserved our livestock from the tigers or wildcats, but those gentry seldom troubled us now. And many mornings I have been highly delighted with the crowing of the cock and innocent noises of the goats, geese and ducks calling the boy to give them their daily sustenance.

Some short time after this, and about 12 o'clock in the day, one of our dogs took off up the hill at full speed. Upon this, Bell turned out with his gun. I told him not to venture too far from home, but away Harry ran after him, with his dogs. They did not return in less than two hours. When they came in, I told Bell that I thought them foolhardy going off with only small shot. They said that they had followed the dogs for three miles, as they were sure they had the scent of a deer by the dung they had found, and that on their return they had found a bees' nest in a tree, full of combs. I enquired how far off it might be. They told me not above a mile. 'Well,' said I, 'shall we contrive to take it?' My messmate said the evening would be the best time for the purpose. 'Then there let it remain,' I cried, 'for me, I shall not venture my carcase on such an errand at such a time.'

'Well,' said Harry, 'if Mr Norman will go with me, I will venture.' Bell came to a resolution, and off they went in the evening with fire and powder and each a gun and machete. I was in pain the whole time for them, but in about two hours they returned victorious with a fine parcel of honeycombs. I asked them how they went to work and they told me that they first made up a good fire, then they suffocated them with a squib.[36] When they were all at home, I soon found out that the women knew better what to do with the honey than to make bread.

Now as I happened to be out very early on the morrow, I perceived a large smoke to blow over our cliff. Bless me, thinks I, what can this mean? 'Now,' said I, 'you certainly left fire in the woods last night and we shall be ruined if the winds keep southerly.' We then went up and found it to be the case. The fire was spread far and wide, and a dreadful appearance. 'Now,' said I, 'you have found out a most infallible method to rid us of our tiger fears.'

'Weel,' said Bell, 'and so best.'

'Ay, but now you must be at a loss for fuel unless you go farther afield for it,' said I.

'Oh,' said Harry, 'it will not come down below to us.'

And I found it so in reality, as the fire left off when it came to the brow of the hill, but the smoke continued above 3 days. When I found the whole was over, we took a walk and found all the traps ruined. Everything was devastated, so that the place for two miles back and wide was quite naked and bare. Yet I must needs own, that I was not much grieved, as I was now certain that the harbour was broken for those rapacious beasts. But we lost on the other hand as it was very handy on several accounts; besides, the beauty of the place was all gone in a regard to prospect. This affair happened about the 27th of December, so that we had a rare bonfire to keep Christmas with.

Nothing happened worth notice for some time after this, but we became pestered with hawks after our chicken, so that the boys were fully employed. The cat also made bold with a chick or two, but by the boys tying him up and giving him a trimming with a bunch of feathers around his neck, he left off the game. The hawks we put in dread by fixing up a pole with a cross at the top, to which we hung the dead hawks we had shot.[37] No sooner had we found out this remedy than we became troubled with a sort of large snake which swallowed them whole, but Owen and Harry often shot them and Harry used to roast and eat them and at last tempted Bell and daddy Nunez to do the like.

One day, as I happened to enter our dwelling and casting my eyes on our child America, as she lay sleeping on a few plantain leaves, I saw a monstrous centipede extended athwart her throat. The sight much startled me, as knowing that should it sting the infant in that tender part, the agony it would throw her into might prove mortal. Now, dreading lest its feet, by a movement might awaken her, and that she might perhaps put her hand up to it, by which means it would either sting her hand or her throat, I clapped my hand gently down by it and with one sudden jerk cast it clear of her, when I killed it. I put it in a bottle of brandy we kept for that purpose, as knowing it to be the best antidote against the poison by rubbing the injured part with it – it never failed to assuage the anguish or reduce the swelling. These insects are of a yellow brown colour, and their general size from 4 to 8 inches in length, and in breadth scarcely an inch. They are scaled on the back, as in joints with a pair of forceps or pinchers at the tail, and when angry erect them in a curve forward emitting an enormous quality through small apertures into the wound, which turns the injured part quite livid and brings on a most excruciating torment, which lasts sometimes for three or four hours.

I remember on a day I was talking to Betty, and she leaning her cheek against a rock side, I perceived a large scorpion close by her face, whereupon I withdrew and called her aside. When I got her from the place, I showed it to her. We then took one of the phials with some of the brandy out of the other bottle, and Bell by an artful twitch got it into the phial. But it was not in long, ere it emitted a drop of some liquid, and he getting his watch we stood by it for a space of 15 minutes, before the spirit overcame it so we could say it was quite defunct.

The scorpions are not large, as we never saw one above 4 inches in length, most of them being 2$^{1/2}$ or 3 inches. They are shaped in the fore part somewhat resembling a lobster having claws, but differ much abaft as I may say, having a tail of several joints, in the end of which is inserted a hook. This they use after the same manner as the centipede. They are of a pale dirty yellow and carry their young on their backs, and our Indians say that if any of their young should by chance come before them, they will at once devour them. Harry one day showed me one, and told me that I should see him make it kill itself. He made a circle of burning coals around it, and the scorpion endeavoured to escape for a time; at length finding it impracticable it began to turn up its sting and in a few minutes wounded itself to death. This insect, as well as the centipede, frequents all kinds of damp and obscure places and never voluntarily approaches the light of the day or sunshine.

I shall in this place take notice of the spiders[38], but as to give a description of the many sorts would be too tedious. Yet as I think mentioning the characters of a few may not be disagreeable, I shall begin with that of the greatest magnitude, and I can declare of a truth that I have seen some which would spread the full extent of a man's finger and thumb when expanded. These are frequently seen, and make their webs exceedingly strong, but they are not venomous although they have sharp black teeth and bite if molested. They are seen at times with a large round and white belly, as may be judged about the size of half a dollar, but this is none other than a bag in which they carry about their young. This bag they can dismiss at its proper season, and then they lodge it against some shelf, from which the young come forth at their appointed time.

There is another sort that I give the name of the Tiger to. It has no settled place of abode, nor does it ever spin any web but keeps on a constant cruise after the flies. It is striped black and white, and nothing can exceed the craft of this insect when lying in wait for its prey. You shall see them on the side of a tree, rock or the like in any place where flies frequent. Here he lurks as if he is asleep, but as soon as any fly chances to fix within the distance of two feet or so of him, he directly with one sudden motion of his body faces about in a trice, and with his short legs advances very slowly towards him. But if the fly chances to move his position in the least, he then in an instant points the same way and squats concealed[39]. He then begins again to advance exceedingly slowly until such time he comes within the distance of about 8 inches, when he jumps at once on the poor victim and devours him.

Another kind, not large, which Bell called Red Poops[40] as they had their after parts as red as vermilion – these gentry keep in corners and the like. They are continually spinning threads and running up and down them. If by chance they spy an object such as a grub or the like, they drop down by a thread and give it a gentle touch which instantly kills, when they descend again and by fixing more lines to it they draw the body up by degrees, hand over hand as one of our jacks would draw a bucket of tar up into the main top of a vessel. We found it necessary to kill them whenever they chose to visit our cave, as they would at times drop down and give us one of their favourable touches, which instantly gave the patient such an inflammatory burning that he would be forced to run to the first oil he could come at, or the phial of insects which laid (soothed) the poison in a few minutes.

But at times we found a kind of large black spider back in the upland, which deserves a description. They frequent banks that face the rising sun, in which they have cells. Now on a day as I was out with my gun and Harry and Owen with me, the boy bade me to look on the bank and see the Great Spiders, how they stopped their holes. This made Harry call me to halt, saying that if I went slowly I should see a fine thing, which I would love (meaning a great curiosity). And soon after I saw several of those spiders run into their holes and slap to their doors after them. On this I drew out my knife and picked at one of them, and to my great surprise found it to work to and fro on its hinges. It was composed of a thick substance of web and of a circular form. After I had satisfied my curiosity thus far, I told them that we would all three withdraw to watch their motions, and after some time we could see one neighbour open his door half-way, then another, and so on until many threw their doors right back and came forth. But now, as we were intent on viewing this wonder of nature, Mr Rover espied them and soon drove the whole town into close quarters[41], and so spoiled our further interest of observation for that time.

Now it happened as daddy Nunez was out on the hill, which was usually his morning walk, he came down and said that he thought he perceived some small canoes at a distance to the westward. Upon this, I took my new glass and went up with Norman. We soon perceived two canoes coming. *'Now,'* said I, *'these are our new boats, I will lay any wager, so let us prepare some kind of repast for them for when they come in.'* In about an hour they came around the Key and I could then plainly perceive 10 people in them. *'Get our boat ready,'* said I. *'Norman, you and I will go down and meet them,'* so off we went and met them in the bay.

When we got within hail I called and they answered *'Amigos'* or friends. We then put off before them, up the lagoon, and they all came on shore – Gattaloon, Gaynasunto and 8 other Indians, most of whom had been at our place before. We all welcomed them after our wanted fashion, and Gattaloon told me that those were my two canoes, they had made for my use. They brought us 4 beef hides, matting, cotton pieces for our women, some cocoa and coffee seeds and other things. The canoes were 18 feet long 2$^1/2$ by the beam, as I may term it, and would carry 8 men with ease.[42] I presented each of them with a small looking glass and some of our remaining Dutch cloth, but it was of little value being much injured by moths and time. Bell gave 50 dollars into the hands of Gattaloon, desiring that the Spaniards would never discover the means of their acquiring them, unless they reported that they had found them as we had done. All this they promised to observe strictly, and we doubted not their integrity, having had the experience of their fidelity for such a length of time.

Gattaloon asked daddy Nunez how he liked his situation, and the old man told him that he had not known so much ease and content for many years past. He then enquired the same of Soroteet. His answer was that he thought the *Agago*, or as they translated it, *The Killing Spirit*, had never found the way to our place or had never heard of it, saying that could they not see the *Manoluvy* or *Manolubee* was always among us whenever they came, by the laughing in our faces at all times. (By this word they mean a general amity or concord among us.)[43]

In about three days, and after our little business was settled they took their leave to return home overland, having brought arms with them for that purpose, saying on their departure that there was a vessel cast away, about half a day's paddling from their place more to the West. We asked them of what people but they could give not give us that satisfaction, saying they saw none of the men dead or alive and that she was all in pieces, had a white bottom, one mast and some great guns – from which we judged it might perhaps be our 'Fair Trader' as the description tallied with her.

We had nothing remarkable happen from the time the Indians left us, which was about the latter end of March. But some days after they were gone, Harry told me that he had got a great secret from Soroteet to tell me.

'What may that be?' said I.

He told me that Gattaloon had informed Soroteet when last here, that we were discovered or known to be here by the Spaniards.

'Ay, ay!' cried I and directly called Norman. When he came, *'Now begin,'* I said to Harry, *'and whatever you have learnt, speak it, let it be what it may, either good or bad.'* For I must confess it discomposed me at first, but reflecting again that it was a thing which must come to their knowledge one day or other, I became more calm again.

And he went on, saying that Gattaloon told Soroteet that affair because he knew he could talk neither Spanish nor English, and the affair could not be well divulged to me while they were among us, lest we should take it ill. We might attribute the discovery to their treachery, but desired that we would not entertain so hard a thought of them, as those who were now dead had pledged their hearts with us. That they knew not by what means we were discovered, but that a couple of Spaniards from Maracaibo[44] had been lately among them, and asked if there were not two Englishmen married among their people, and living along the shore to the Northward. That finding we were known to be here, they thought it a folly to deny that they knew anything of us, but had confessed that they knew of a poor man who had told them he had been driven onshore in a boat, alone; but that I had been here many long Moons before they had found me out, and recited the circumstance of one of their canoes being driven ashore where I resided, by which means I obtained a wife.

That I was a good man and liked to live there with my Indian family, but that I should have travelled to find out some Spaniards, had I not been informed that they would send me to the mines[45] as being an enemy at that time; but that I was so far from being an enemy to mankind that I had since my landing there given my best assistance to two or three distressed Spanish vessels, and that they had heard me often say that could I but be confirmed in one thing – which was that they would not injure me – I could die in a true state of satisfaction. That in regard to the other man who lived with me, he had been cast away long since and came among them, but hearing of me he had travelled to find me out, and had got one of their girls for a wife also. That we lived by fishing, and were the most inoffensive men that could live.

'Well,' said one of them who was an old man called Perez, 'when you see them again, you must inform them that they need not be in any manner of dread or fear, as their condition is not to be envied; and if they are content to be voluntary anchorites[46], none will make it their business to molest or disturb them. But they are not Bon Catholics[47], we suppose.' But they told them we were, and that we prayed to the Book and Cross often, to which they answered, 'Star Bon.'[48]

They enquired how far it was from where they lived, and they told them above 7 days. And thus their enquiry ended.

In our hearts, we both thanked them for their good conduct. And how, or by what means, they came by the knowledge we knew not, unless from some of the fair traders who might have been wrecked, or from old Horgan's people. However, we now became entirely easy in our minds, as thinking that we had made a happy discovery, knowing by the tenor of the Spaniard's discourse that they would not give themselves the trouble to seek us out, because we were of no consequence to them, either for good or ill.

THE NINETEENTH YEAR – ATTACKED BY WILD BOAR, BETTY IS BORN AND A VISIT BY THE GUARDA COSTAS
June 15 1765 – June 14 1766

One day, as daddy Nunez and Harry came in from fishing they brought home in the canoe from the Bird Key a part of some animal substance in long round shapes of a brown hue, exceedingly smooth, and of a consistency like soft gristle. I asked Harry what it was and he gave me the following description, which I thought odd enough. The old man kept continually chattering at the same time to Bell in Spanish, but the matter was as Harry said. He got out of the canoe and was wading among the rocks after one of those kinds of fish called a Cuckold[49], with his machete in his hand. All of a sudden he felt something clasp him round his legs, clinging very fast.

On looking down, he saw a monstrous Lancksa[50], as he called it; that he directly called out to Nunez to come to his assistance, which he did; and by cutting with his knife and the machete together he got free, and that he had brought part of it home to show it to us, and then would roast and eat it, which he did. But the description he gives of this being is quite romantic to me. However, as I have not beheld the like with my own eyes hitherto, I must beg the kind reader to rest satisfied with Mr Harry's account of it.

(Viz.) He tells me that they are not very frequent, especially this grand sort, but there are three sorts of a less magnitude. That they are always found adhering to the side of a rock or a huge stone in someplace where there may be an eddy or current of water; that they expand forth several arms which are continually playing about in the water, and that in the end of each of those arms is a kind of mouth, as he expresses it, which catches all kinds of little living things, meaning marine insects. That these arms convey what they catch into one great mouth it has in the centre of its body, but that it has no eyes, nor can it remove from the place it is fixed on. But should any part of it be cut or torn away, in that case the part so moved or separated will soon cement itself to some other place and become a new Lancksa and act exactly in all things like the old mother it came from. That they will lay hold on everything that they can reach, and provided the article is too large for them to take in, in that case they suck the substance out of it and then let the husk or skin drop. All this story appeared wondrous to me, and I must leave it to the learned to determine of what class it may belong to, unless it may be that being called a Polypus.

Now I am on this subject, I must remark on another kind, which it is my belief may belong to the same tribe of marine animals. These we saw when Somer and I were once out to the Westward in a place among rocks and even under water. Through several holes in the sides of those rocks about 4 feet down, there seemed to grow small tufts of flowers resembling in shape our polyanthus, but of a pale rose colour, now and then tinged with yellow[51]. But on my running down a paddle to shove a bunch of them off, they would instantaneously retire into the rock. This drew on a wonder in us, and finding by repeated trials that it evaded all our art, Somer took it upon himself to detach one of them which projects forth from an angular corner, with an axe. And to that end, he got overboard and knocked the piece off, when he put it in my hand and came in again; then seating himself began to beat it to pieces, and in a small cell we found a substance like a thin membrane. But those parts that had expanded like so many flowers had become quite contracted, yet there seemed to be some small palpitation left, showing life remaining. I judged the violence of his strokes had been the cause of death, as knowing full well it must be some kind of animal being or other, by others we had caused to retire now became displayed afresh; but on our offering to touch them they incontinently withdrew. This natural curiosity would ever have escaped my memory; had not this adventure of Harry's come to at this time to revive it.

And now I am on the sensitive subject, I shall remark on some others of a terrestrial kind. (Viz.) There is a kind of long grass growing in these regions that, if you should only cast or wave a hand or even a small switch over it, instantly falls down flat although not touched or approached nearer than a foot[52]. There is also a species of the Yam which when you find it sprung above the ground, should you then fix a stick or the like in any point of direction within a distance of three feet, it will in a short time find its way to it. But should you remove the stick a short time before it had reached it, and shift it to the other side at any one point of the compass, it will soon find the way round, and begin to climb up it.

There is to be found on the sea beach a kind of vine[53] with a red stem, about the thickness of a goose quill, with small leaves growing in pairs laterally, and at the distance of two feet from each pair. But what makes the thing most remarkable is that when it has extended its stems as from one centre like a star, to about the distance of perhaps 10 or 12 feet, it there takes root in the sand and becomes a fresh centre proceeding in like manner; so that in some places the shore will be spread with them for 50 yards and all from one common centre. And so strongly do these red tendrils hold in the sand, you shall find them taut or turgid like any ship's stern fast.[54] There are some kinds of flowers also which have the quality of displaying their bloom after the sun is set, and keep so the whole night through until the day comes on, when they all close again. On the contrary, others open with the rising sun and close again as it sets in the evening.

It may not be derogatory to this subject if I should mention a thing that all the Indians hold to be a real fact, but this I do not affirm as to my own knowledge. But they have advanced to me that there is one kind of deer which have ears in their feet, by which means they know when an enemy is approaching, even at a mile's distance or much further. And once, when walking in the woods, Harry picked up the foreleg bone from one of those animals, and showing me a groove in the shin part proceeding from the parting of the hoof, told me that was the channel by which those animals heard to such a great distance. But I rather concluded that some nerve of a very subtle sensation had lain in that hollow groove, which gave the creature such a distant warning of danger.

There[55] grows a kind of small tree here which bears a large fruit shaped something like a Bell Pear, but much larger and flat on one side, full of soft thorny points. It is of a dark green inclining to a purple at the large end, which is of a full purple.[56] Its pulp is white, spongy and very full of juice, with many purple seeds within it. Now what is a thing much to be admired is a small bird who feeds on the seed of it. This bird in size is like our English Greenfinch, and of that kind of green. Its bill resembles the parrot's. And as the fruit varies or graduates from the green to the purple, so changes the bird in its hue exactly, from its tail to the neck and head which terminates in the purple, so that when the bird is actually on the tree limbs or fruit, you can hardly know unless it should move or shift its place.

How manifold are the wonders of our Divine Creator when our eyes behold these things. Should we not say, 'In the majesty of Thy wisdom, o Lord, hast Thou created them to the improvement of our understanding, and to lead us step by step to a proper idea of Thy omnipotence?' And how thankful ought I to be thus to have so much leisure to contemplate on them; and, as I have said, step by step may they bring me and all mankind to a proper sense of my own state and their own, so that in the end we may all become worthy members of His divine abode, through the merits of Him who descended from where eternal happiness flows.

About the 10th day of August, Mrs Harry brought forth a girl, and they gave her the name of Betty as a compliment to my wife. And Harry observed on the occasion that Soroteet had not hitherto been renamed, as was customary with us when any Indian joined our family. I then turned to my friend Norman and told him to stand as Godfather, and he thought proper to call him Rory or Roderick. And from this time we heard no other sound for two or three days from Harry, Owen and the other children than 'Rory, Rory, Rory,' – so much would any simple novelty play upon their innocent minds, arising from their contracted mode of life and never being enlarged by a sight of this great world's hurry and varieties.

At times Mr Harry would amuse himself with learning the boys to swim, by taking them on his back in the lagoon. Now it so fell out that as he and Mr Rory were down at the water with the children at this sport, with Norman, Nunez and myself looking on and smoking our pipes, daddy Nunez cried out, 'Un tiberoon!' or a shark.[57] This soon made them all quit the water, with surprise, as we had never seen one so far up before. But the Indians got bait and soon caught her.

This shark was not above six foot long, yet she had 8 young ones that would not leave her, so they were all taken. These young gentry, although they were not more 8 or 9 inches in length, yet were so strong that it was a great difficulty to hold one of them in a man's hand with a strong grip. It is well known that a shark brings forth her young after the manner of quadrupeds, but there is a great mistake among those who think her young in any sudden danger run into her mouth or down her throat, when the very contrary is the truth. For on any approaching danger they all secrete themselves in the womb; and this we had the fairest opportunity of observing, as the thing was transacted to our satisfaction before our eyes.

The Indians had brought with them when last here, a few pods of some exceedingly large beans of a full brown colour, having but two in each pod. These beans or kernels are about the size of a dollar, and of an excellent virtue for all complaints of the bowels. As they report, the mode of using them is to scrape a part of kernel into warm water or stew them, and so great is their efficacy that the quantity of 3 or 4 grains will relieve the most racking colic immediately.[58] This we have experienced now and then, as occasionally required. I have ordered a few of them to be planted so that we need never be without them in future.

One day Harry and Rory brought home a Hawksbill Tortoise weighing about 30 pounds, of whose shell our artificers in Europe make great use in divers kinds of ornaments.[59] Yet this kind of tortoise is not very agreeable to the taste, so we do not eat them. And as this gives me an opportunity to mention more on the subject I shall take notice that there are 4 or 5 sorts of this animal; nay, I might say 7 sorts great and small.

(Viz.) In the first place the Loggerhead Tortoise. This kind is most frequent on our coast and is so large that many of them run to 400 pounds in weight. They have a very round back and are rather longer in proportion than the other kinds, but there is no beauty in the shell. The second sort is what we call the Trunk Tortoise, as they resemble the form of our old coffers, being ridged. They grow big and rank and are not very agreeable to the taste. The third I may term the Hawk's Bill as their beak resembles the beak of that bird. Now the fourth is what they call the Green Tortoise and the most coveted, as their flesh exceeds all others in taste. These are known to grow to the size of 300 pounds also. The fifth kind is such as never go into salt water, but frequent ponds and muddy places. These are of a most odious appearance to any stranger. I have seen them of above 50 pounds in weight, and when one of them finds himself environed by enemies, so that he cannot make his escape, he will fight with a hissing noise; and should he once fix his jaws on any object he will never quit it, without bringing off the piece. They are black, rough, and have bright red eyes with circles of red so that they are of a most formidable appearance; yet the meat of these animals stewed is very rich, and agreeable to the palate.

The sixth kind are of a diminutive size and frequent ponds also, but never grow to any great bulk and are of no estimation except for the beauty of their shell which is generally either yellow boarded with black, or olive bordered with either yellow or red. The seventh sort never frequents the water but keep up in the woods and never grow to any great size, seldom above three pounds. At a certain season of the year they retire below the surface of the earth where they will remain for the space of three months without any sustenance.

All these several kinds are oviparous, and there is one peculiarity in these odd things that they can do, which is to retain life for many hours after the head is separated from the body. But in regard to the sort I was just mentioning, nothing is ever more true than we have known a body to survive for 12 days after the head was taken off and the body became putrid. I well remember a circumstance of the head of one of the Loggerhead tortoises being cut off about 10 in the morning and thrown away, by the head of the lagoon. Yet poor Eva, now dead and gone, happening to take it up on the next day in the evening, wantonly placed her finger within the mouth. It at once fastened on her finger, whereupon she began to run and whoop at no small rate; but on Harry's thrusting a knife between, she got released.

We had not explored our back territories since the accident of the fire, but messmate Norman proposed that he and Harry should make such an excursion, as he had a mind to make a tour for a day, and for that purpose they equipped themselves with arms, ammunition and provision. Accordingly, early one morning they took into the woods, or rather barrens; three dogs went with them. They did not return until about 6 in the evening, and to my great wonder they brought back home with them 2 small black pigs but had lost one of the dogs. They told the following story –

That on their first setting out, they found all the underwood burnt for the distance of a mile or more, and as Harry stood pilot he took him to the place where we found those huge bones. That they then mounted the bank, and proceeded south about half a mile, when they came to a wood of fine trees. That there they seated themselves and refreshed, but that they did not go much further before they came to a great savannah[60] which lay low, and they saw here and there a single tree growing. But on their going into this savannah they perceived some small black creatures running quickly through the grass, keeping their course directly for a large tree at a distance of one hundred yards or so. Now as they drew near to that tree, Bell plainly discovered two or three of the same animals and taking sight, shot one so as to cripple it, but on their coming up found it to be a young pig about 7 weeks old, as he judged. No sooner did he take hold of it, than it began to cry lustily, soon after which he said they plainly heard the grunting of hogs as when they are enraged, with a great rushing through the grass, upon which Harry immediately began to climb the tree, desiring him to follow his example. But before he could get his arm around it, a huge brown boar came furiously on him.

What to do he could not at first determine, but got on the other side and began to load as fast as he possibly could, keeping his eye steadfastly on him, and dodging round, now and then. The beast would make directly at him, bouncing at a great rate and chamfering his long tusks, with his mouth all white with foam. But now as he was in this horrid situation and just making ready to fire at him, Harry discharged his piece from the tree, and took him directly in the ear which at once lay him motionless, and gave Bell an instant deliverance. That Harry now came down and loaded afresh, saying that he must follow him as Harry had perceived other boars from his situation. Soon after, they came in view of a female with several young ones, and they both fired on them, when Bell killed another of the young. The old sow and the rest took off through the grass with the greatest expedition, but they declined the pursuit. They then returned to the tree and took a survey of the old senior boar, and Bell said that he had never beheld any boar of such magnitude in his life. His tusks were at least 8 inches in length, and about the head and shoulders he was of a monstrous thickness. This august animal had let out the entrails of one of the dogs in a moment, by whose death messmate Bell perhaps preserved his own life, as by that means he gained time.

We sent off Harry and Rory the next day to bring home a part of the boar together with his tusks, but they returned with no more than the tusks, as they found the carcase had been almost completely devoured by tigers or those of their own species, which was what we judged, and the Indians say they will do so constantly. They also advance that in case a wild hog becomes wounded, if he can but get away, he seeks out a kind of tree and then fretting its bark with his teeth and tusks causes its sap to flow, with which by rubbing he anoints his wound and recovers again. They told me that they were very numerous in that quarter by the amount of dung they saw, and that they judged that they found food in that savannah by rooting in the ground, and eating some kind of long nut, resembling our acorns, which fell from some of the tall trees. Whatever could be the cause I knew not, but during the whole time of my residing in this place I never saw one of those animals in our neighbourhood, but perhaps the food they are most fond of grows in parts more retired from the shore. Bell says that he thought the boar did not weigh less than 200 pounds. As for the two young ones they brought home, we barbecued[61] them and found them delicious.

The next piece of business we went on was to make masts and sails for our new canoes, but in regard to their sails we were forced to be sparing in canvas, as we had no great stock of that article. And as we had not been out once in them from the time the first came, we concluded to make a small voyage in them to the north-eastward; and accordingly Bell and I with Owen on a morning put off out of the lagoon in one of them which Bell distinguished by the name of 'Jannet,' and the other, which I called the 'Komaloot' was manned by daddy Nunez and our Rory. We stood away for the old plantation where I visited my old grounds, having not been there for a long time except on the shore when we brought away the goods we purchased off the Gillicrankey man. I went into my old cave, from thence to the part which I had set fire to so long ago; but all was now become a new forest of young saplings and bushes. Yet every here and there were to be found an abundance of those kinds of things, running rank and luxurious, which had proceeded from the original plantings, as we seldom visited the place for such truck, because most of the same articles now grow within our own vicinity. But as we were on the return, Bell having been rambling in the bushes, he called to me to come to him. When I got to the spot he showed me one of the most noble calabash trees I had ever beheld, and as it is a tree of a very peculiar growth, I shall describe it.

In height and size it resembles much the Codling tree[62] but the limbs, or rather the superior branches, grow horizontally from the tree very straight and have but few small leaves which grow on pairs opposite to each other, with a pair at the extremity of each bough and branch. But it is the fruit which is more to be remarked upon. They grow to the magnitude of a small bombshell[63], are of a pale green and full of snow-white pith. Contrary to most other kinds, you shall see one protrude from the very extremity of a limb, so that by means of its great weight the bough shall bend down to the ground in, or on, another limb. They may be seen to push out from the side, sometimes in a small crevice between two limbs by which means they become distorted as having been cramped in their growth. Nevertheless, whatever kind of obstructions they may meet, does not diminish them much in quantity, as they will push their protuberance wherever they have vent[64]. Sometimes you shall see one or more push out not one foot above the root of the tree; and as the stem is so short and slender, it appears to the stranger that they are excrescences of the fungus kind rather than its fruit.

After we had been there about an hour and I had shown my two friends all about my first habitation, we took the boat again and proceeded to old Towers Field, and there landing, went to dinner, after which Bell took up his gun and away he went with Owen and Rory, who was but newly acquainted with firearms. Owen had to have my firing piece also with him. When they were gone I took daddy Nunez with me to show him the large stone that I had discovered among the woods. On our arrival I asked his opinion concerning it, and he told me that it was his opinion that the first adventurers, either Columbus or those who succeeded him, had erected it in that place as a memorial. This made me smile, saying, *'I pray, daddy, how many men do you think it would require to raise this stone, provided there may not be much of it below the surface of the earth?'*

He answered 1,000.

'And do you think that such a number of your countrymen were ever on this spot at that early period?' said I.

His answer was that the Indian natives in those days perhaps assisted them, as by divine appointment it was revealed to them so that they might have the honour of first preaching the Gospel among those savages. I now began to draw in my horns, as I did not choose to contradict the old gentleman. He had never given me any cause of contention; therefore I let him feed on his own bigotry as it suited with his own opinion.

When we got back to the waterside, we observed our people to fire and run to and fro much, out on a point towards the Whale Point. What they could be after we could not think, but in about an hour they returned, when Bell reported that they had surprised three seals asleep between some rocks, and that Owen had shot one of them with my piece, but as he had only slightly wounded it, the animal had escaped, notwithstanding that they did their best to get to the sea side of him and pelted him with stones. 'Oh,' said Nunez, *'if you had but given him a small stroke over the nose with the butt of your piece, it would have been soon over with him.'*

We now began to think of our return and put off accordingly, but just as I was stepping into the canoe I picked up a small kind of cockle shell of a fine crimson colour, from the bottom of which and on the inside grew up a beautiful branch of white coral, of a texture smooth as glass, and resembling the horns of a stag and in length about 4 inches. At the extreme points were small studs resembling so many stars of light blue. 'Now,' said I to Bell, *'this is a real curiosity and would fetch a good price were it exhibited on some show box in a London shop window.'* I have it by me still, among an abundance of other articles. We got home safe without anything more occurring at that time, and found all well.

We had not been home long before I observed Mr Harry strutting about at a distance with an air of great importance, dressed up in a clean shirt of mine, my old Tiger jacket, a Beaver hat, and a machete by his side and mimicking the air of a Spaniard, the girls all tittering. 'Look,' I said to Bell, *'I wonder what new whim had entered the head of my Lord Henry today.'* On this, I called to him and he came towards us, with an air of great dignity, to be sure.

Bell held forth his hand to him with reverence, but he put his hands on his hips and with one foot advanced, said, *'Me un grande Cabalero.'*[65] Upon this daddy Nunez fell into a fit of hearty laughter.

'Come, come,' said I, *'this is enough for once Harry. You are a great don today, and tomorrow you will be no more than my poor Indian brother, I suppose, unless your fit of prodigality continues.'*

'Ha,' said he, *'I am a rich man now, as well as yourself, and I will buy me a watch talker too, when Gillarandy*[66] *comes again.'*

'You fool,' said I, *'leave off your nonsense. I am tired of it.'* On this, off he went and soon

came back with his two hands full of doubloons, the sight of which surprised both Bell and me. *'Where got you those?'* I cried.

'In the Dead Man's Hole,' said he, *'in the old Dead Man's Hole, alongside.'*

'And how came you to find it out, after we had examined the place so well, and after such a length of time?'

'Come see,' said he.

So off we all went and he ran before us, and getting there first held up a large kind of cup to us. When Bell took it into his hands, there might remain about 20 more doubloons in its bottom, and on our scraping the vessel we found it to be of pure gold, weighing about 20 or 22 ounces. Now, the place being left so long exposed to so many succeeding heavy rains was what brought this to light. He said that as he chanced to be there, picking a few limes, curiosity led him to take a view of that place, and he saw the brim of the vessel sticking out of the side of the old hole quite plainly, and that he got it out with ease, not two hours before our arrival.

'Well, Don Henriquez,' said I, *'you have had the weather gauge*[67] *of us all in this discovery, for certain. And now let us know in what way you intend to proceed with your money and gold cup.'*

'Oh, what is mine is yours, my good friends,' said he, taking us off in our behaviour to each other on any occasion. We returned him our thanks, and the stuff was placed in the Treasury, according to his own desire.

Soon after this we discovered a sail lying to, right off our place. This was about the 19th of March and in the morning. I got my glass and saw that she was a large schooner.[68] Bell proposed to speak to her, but I objected as she was at least 2 leagues out. *'Notwithstanding,'* said I, *'If you are inclined so to do, you and daddy Nunez may take Harry with you and go out in the yawl and show yourselves, if you are inclined. We know the Spaniards are well acquainted that we are on this shore now, and why need we be under any restriction on that account? The wind is favourable.'*

On this they came into the resolution, and off they went with a few pistoles and a parcel of yams etc. They had not got far out in the bay before I perceived a white jack hoisted, and the schooner stood for them. Now I knew that if they stood on that tack long enough, they would certainly run onto a ledge of rocks, but in a short time they hove to again and lay by for our boat, soon after which I saw them get alongside of her.

Well, thought I, this may be another fair trader or not. I kept on the hill constantly until they had been on board her for above an hour, when I saw them put off with another boat in company. Now, thought I, Bell is getting beside himself. What view can he have in bringing any of those people ashore here? But I soon became sensible of my error by seeing the other boat part company and row away for the point of Long Key, which I understood was to get water.

When they came in, Bell informed me that they were a guarda costa of ten guns from Carthagena[69], and that the crew was a medley of mortals composed of all the dips or casts[70] from the Spaniard down to the Indian and Negro. That the white flag, as we took it, was the Ragged Staves in the form of the St Andrews Cross; that the commander's name was Zayas; and that he found among them an old foul loon[71], a countryman, one Watty McClintock who had turned Papist and had been among them from the time of Admiral Vernon's being on the coast, from whose fleet he had run away.[72] He told me that observing exactly such a clasp knife in McClintock's hand as we had purchased from the fair trader, he interrogated him as to what means he had obtained it, when he told him he found it on a Maroon Key some few months ago, saying several of their people had one of them each.[73]

'They are English,' said Bell. 'Has any vessel of that sort been cast away lately, then?'

'Why, no,' said he, 'none that I know of. But you must understand that there are several vessels from the north which belong to the English Colonies, who are by chance driven this way by some fatality or another, and as they know full well we are out, they leave now and then a few trifles on the keys and other places, so that they may not be disturbed while they take in a little fresh water or so.'

'Shake hands, Devils,' said I. 'Any man may construe that. But have they any things among them such as you thought may be of use to us?'

'Not anything,' said he. 'They look more like a gang of thieves than anything else. I got a good whetstone or two off the lieutenant in return for a few yams or potatoes, that is all.' Soon after this we saw them stretching out to seaward, and before night lost sight of them. Thus ended the adventure.

About this time Bell and Nunez contrived a kind of board in order to amuse their time at a game called Draughts, and at this they would sit by the hour without speaking many words, with a cigar in each of their mouths. They frequently would be at me to play, but one game extended to the full limits of my patience, it being a game fitter for cripples and tailors than a man who had the full use of his limbs, as I thought. Nevertheless, it was agreeable enough perhaps to the first inventor, as undoubtedly he was an object of a very sedentary disposition.

Harry was every now and then bringing home one curiosity or another, as he knew that such things were what I frequently used to amuse myself; but in this article he was much out of his judgment, often fetching me trifles of no beauty or rarity. But now and then a real curiosity presented itself before my eyes. (Viz.) He brought a few days ago a sort of marine plant growing on a large stone of about 10 pounds. This plant was black as jet, and so hard that a knife would hardly penetrate it, in height about that of a cabbage. Nothing could be more curious than the multitude of twigs, some of them as fine as a horse hair and shining much like it, not in any appearance resembling leaves. Its growth is in the form of a cypress tree with its root so firmly connected with the stone that I may defy a mortal to perceive the least joining thereto. Sponges and sea fans or feathers also – some of these things are extremely pleasing to the sight. We have these fans much broader in leaf than any cabbage, and of all the variety of colours, also sponges in the form of cups, tubes, roses etc.

But I must not omit in this place to mention a tree of coral now hanging over the entrance of our cave. This curious plant came up with our killick as we were fishing one day, and Harry stowed it in the yawl's bows. It is white as snow, full of small stars and branching forth much like the horns of a stag or elk. It is of such a solid consistency that it rings when struck, like a bell. Toward the root it is as thick as the small of a man's leg, and in height 5 feet and upwards, weighing at least 50 pounds.

The Remora[74] or Sucking Fish has so often been described that I need not mention it, unless I hint that we have the skin of one of those singular fish stuffed, which measures at least 3 feet.

We have a bird here about the size of our starling, black, grey and white. This sweet animal we have given the name of Charmer. Its daily practice is to repair every morn, at the rising of the sun, to the utmost twig of some dead tree and there hold forth its enchanting melody for the space of an hour, never failing to do the same as that blessed luminary is sinking in the west. Its notes are so loud and various that it never cloys. This bird we hold in such esteem that none of our family ever in the least molests it.

We have another, much the same colour and size, but with a larger head. This bird is so inveterate against the eagle that he never perceives him on the wing without directly mounting after him, where he so worries him by beating on his head, that the eagle is under the necessity of quitting that quarter. This bird we call the Little Hero, and nothing is more curious than to see the means the eagle takes to shun it, now mounting aloft and then darting with the greatest rapidity towards the earth. Nevertheless, his enemy keeps close behind his head, making one continual noise. If by chance this sport should begin at some distance from the trees, it that case the diversion lasts perhaps a quarter of an hour.[75] It has the same malice against the Fish Hawk or any bird of prey, and it will sit on the top limb of a tree for hours as on the lookout, now and then flying up perpendicularly and returning to the same branch.

THE TWENTIETH YEAR – HOSTILE INDIANS, DISCOVERY BY THE SPANIARDS, & THE DEATH OF NUNEZ
June 15 1766 – June 14 1767

By this time, our young gentlemen Owen, Harry and Rory, had made such work of the Pirates' Pit or reservoir to discover more treasure, that they had extended the diameter of the hole to the breadth of 10 feet at least, but as yet all their labours have proved of no effect.

Yesterday, Rory came down from the hill to me, as I was sitting on our bed, and said in his broken English, *'No friends can come over Long Key now. Long smoke, fire make.'*

'What? Is the Key then vanished in the night?' said I to him. But, he, finding that I did not fairly understand him, went out to Harry directly.

I overheard him saying that he saw people; this was pronounced in the Indian tongue. I then called Harry in, and asked him what Rory was at.

'He says that there are people at Long Key with a great fire, and that they are not our friends.'

'Call the white men, then,' said I, and taking my glass, away I marched. When we got on the cliff we perceived about ten or twelve people around a large fire, about 100 yards from the old well, but could perceive no canoes, boat or vessel. But that they were Indians we knew, as none appeared to have any covering on the head. Many conjectures we had among us on the affair, but neither Harry nor Rory would say of a certainty that they were our friends, as by the many actions they observed, although at so great a distance, seemed to confirm in them that they were none of their tribe.

'Well,' said I, *'are you willing to go out and speak with them, lads?'*

'Do you think I will not go to God than the Devil sooner?' said Harry. *'It may be they are some of the Sancoodas*[76]*, and they would soon roast me.'*

Upon this, old Nunez lifting up his hands said, *'Le Diabola per los Sancoodas!'* and asked if the fire might be put out, showing signs of dread.

'Who are those you call Sancoodas?' said I. Nunez told me that they were the same as we called Moskeetos[77] and that they were the most inveterate enemies to all Spaniards, and that he was certain, should they come among us, that they would soon put him out of pain.

'If that be the case,' I replied, *'it shall not be said that we gave them an invitation,'* so ordered the fire to be diminished to prevent further trouble.

Neither Harry, Nunez nor any of our Indians would venture up the hill again, after this. Therefore it fell to Bell's lot and mine, and when we took the second observation, which was about noon, we saw them all busy at a dance, as we judged by their actions. But about two hours after, they all retired behind the trees on the south side, and in a short time after that we saw them all paddling away south with 4 canoes. And thus they took their leave of our territories, which was what most of our family heartily desired; and what brought them there, or whither they were bound, we could not conjecture.

After they were gone, I asked them what occasion they had to show so much fear, as I had been informed that those Indians were in friendship with the English; or perhaps they were not Sancoodas as they thought, but Indians of some other nation. Harry replied that he was sure they were not any of his people; otherwise they would never have come so near to our place and not have visited us. He said that they must be some other Indians with whom they never walked or had heard of, and that was full enough for him. This happened on the last day of July according to my account, as I calculated the time.

Some months passed on from this time, without anything worthy of our observation, when one day I observed messmate Bell prostrate on the green, and very busy about something or other. I was at that time sitting reading, but finding him still employed I got up, and went to satisfy my curiosity. When I came to the place, I found him scratching on a kind of flat stone with his knife.

'Can you judge what I am about?' said he.

'Not I, truly. What may it be?'

'Why, you must understand that I am trying to shape out the draft of our habitation, but I believe I shall make but a poor piece of work of it without your help.'

'Help?' cried I. 'How should I assist you when you know I can draw no more than a horse?'

'Oh, ho ho!' he said. 'Can you draw only as well as a horse? If you can, come try your hand.'

I took the joke, and replied that I perceived that he understood much more of the matter than myself, and that we would have it transferred to paper when he had done. This he agreed to, and in a few days, by alterations and amendment, he finished it, such as it was. And although Mr Bell values himself not on any skill that way, yet as to the general form of the place he is tolerably exact; and this made me hint to him that some day we would make a draft of our harbour, this being a thing I judged we could better succeed in, as we knew all the bearings and distances fully well, by long and frequent observations.

About the middle of December on a morning, as Bell and I were out in the bay on our plan that we intended, (viz.) making a kind of chart of our islands and coast, I observed that our signal was out at home. This made us lay aside all thoughts of proceeding further for that time, as we knew not what might have happened in our absence. When we arrived, we were met at the landing who informed us that four friends from overland were come, and that the women were crying about the Spaniards. What to make of this we knew not, so away we ran up to the house where we found them all huddled together as in great counsel. We knew them all and saluted them in the most friendly manner, but my impatience was so great that I desired Harry to recite the true cause of the sad wailing I heard, led it be ever so bad or deplorable.

His translation ran thus: That Gaynasunto, one of the Indians, informed them that they had been sent by the Old Man (Gattaloon) at home to give us timely notice that some Spaniards had been to visit them about ten days past, and said that they were strictly ordered to enquire among them concerning some English people who were settled on the coast and had much money among them, whereby they were suspected of being pirates, or had come there for no good intent one way or the other; and that the Commandant looked to them for information, as he had reason to think the Indians were privately corresponding with them.

I cannot say the news surprised me much, as it was what I long expected, but it was not so with my two friends Bell and Nunez. They seemed to express a great concern, and how, or in what manner to proceed, I knew not. The next thing I enquired was if they could inform me by what means the Spaniards came to discover us, and if their folks had acknowledged their being acquainted with us. They told me that when they found we were discovered, they could not but acknowledge the thing as we had people of their town living among us; but that they were ordered to inform me and that they could not understand by what means we had been discovered, unless we had disclosed our own selves; and if so it would be madness to deny it. All this was delivered in so plain and honest a way to me, that I could by no means charge them with infidelity, as I judged with reason that the Guarda Costa must have been the sole cause, they having in some way suspected us, although we strove so much to deceive them.

I now asked the Indians if the Spaniards had informed them when they intended to pay us a visit. They said in about two moons, as they learnt from their old folks, and that they were ordered to do us good if we wanted assistance. I thanked them and desired that they would inform my kind friends on their return that I was determined to stand or fall by my innocence, let what would happen. I could not think any people on earth who owned the title of Christians could be so barbarous as to ill treat a man in my circumstance and condition.

The Indians tarried with us for two days and then took leave of us. We promised to send them intelligence by Harry and Rory if matters went well with us or not, if the visit should happen as they expected; but if in the contrary they did not come, I should nevertheless contrive it so that they were informed if they were not disposed to pay us any more visits for a time. They then parted with us, perhaps forever.

Matters are now changed greatly; at this my once peaceful dwelling a general confusion reigns. But I am determined to steer with my helm a-midships and take fortitude for my pilot, and I trust to a due resignation to the Divine Will to end my days in peace. But as to how and where, it is now a thing of little or no moment, knowing a sparrow cannot fall without the knowledge of God.

To add to my perplexities my two friends Bell and daddy Nunez are come to a conclusion not to wait the Spaniard's arrival, as they declare that they have sufficient reasons to the contrary, and are determined in removing to some distance until time may bring about something more favourable for them.[78] Alas, I must condescend. They propose to seek out some place most convenient to build a habitation whither they intend to retire, and to return if things shall prosper well with me. But it is my opinion that Nunez will not survive for long, as he seems to fall off daily, being now become an aged man.

I have been with Mr Bell to see this place he has fixed on for his retreat. It is about half a mile directly back of our own residence, near a small pond of water and under a bank shaded with thick trees, where they have cleared a small square for erecting studs[79], which he intends to thatch after the best mode they can, and there to retire with a few of our articles until such a time as the enemy, as he terms them, has been among us. Thither I have proposed to convey what monies we have left, with my Bible and journal, as there are circumstances mentioned in the latter I should be unwilling might come to their ears. For this purpose we intend to contrive a small strongbox and nail them up in it, then tar the outside to prevent the worms or ants penetrating it. I propose digging a small cell in the back, aback of the house and there deposit them.

Notwithstanding all my fortitude, all my resolutions fail me at times; once while I charge myself with so idly spending such a series of years so unprofitable to mankind as I have done, when I could have left this forlorn place at the time the Dutchman so generously invited me, and again with Mr Horgan, so that I might justly charge myself that I had a choice. But then on the other hand, had I left those to whom I had pledged my faith, to wander I knew not where, or to what unknown events might have come to pass – perhaps to lead a reprobate life among those who would never give themselves concern about the welfare of my soul, being altogether as wicked as myself – surely then it is far better for me as things are. Or even if the Spaniards should choose to remove me hence to some place, where perchance they might permit me to revisit my native country, in that case I cannot see what it could possibly avail me.

For a man who has spent so many years in tranquillity and solitary freedom, as I may call it, where he might say all was directed according to his own will and where he lived quite independently – for such a man estranged from all the wicked arts and devices of the world to return from a scene of love, harmony and affection to join a crowd of utter strangers in busy life, poor in manner and friendless – In such case, what happiness can he expect even in his native land? For my part, when cool reflection takes place and intervals of solid reason come in to my aid, I prefer if I may be suffered to remain and end my life in this blessed retreat, among those in whom I know I can in confidence put my trust. And I think should I ever voluntarily forsake these poor creatures around me, out of a mad whim to explore novelty, I should think myself one of the abandoned villains in nature and draw down upon my head the vengeance of the holy Author of all creation. But I will not dwell more on so melancholy a subject, knowing it can never enter my heart to do so.

As the Spaniards have been informed of our cash we need not doubt their coming, were it only to that end and to satisfy their curiosity, perhaps. And to make matters run as easy as we can, Bell and I have concluded to produce a part of what money we have by us, to present them. This he leaves all to me. My son Owen is made privy to the manner of my bestowing my journal, so that if things do not turn out as I wish he may perhaps find a means one day or other to convey it into the hands of some subject of Great Britain, to whose care I charge him to deliver it unless Providence may direct his course that way himself. – Not that I entertain any thoughts of its material use to my fellow mortals, but it may show the world the manner I spent my time in, and what became of the *Recovery* and poor Lewellin Penrose. But if Providence so order it that I remain where I am unmolested, I shall continue my narrative as long as my strength and materials last.

Now I must lay by my subject, as we know not the hour they may heave[80] in sight. I have the faith to think they will not treat me ill, when they see the state of innocence we live in; nor are we so much at a loss this day as in the past, being enabled by Mr Bell's instruction to converse in Spanish, well enough to be understood. And as to any question they may put to me, I am determined to deliver my story in plain truth as far as reason shall guide me.

Twenty years had almost run out since my first landing on this shore, and having seen nor heard the least tittle[81] concerning a visit from the Spaniards, nor indeed from our friends the Indians, we much wondered at it, and often formed various conjectures on that head. At length my two friends returned to dwell at my place as usual, although they would often sleep, as it suited their fancy, at their new hut. And as the old man frequently retired in the daytime to sleep, or rather perhaps to ease his aged bones, it so fell out that messmate Bell missed him longer than ordinary, and on going to call him, found him expired and lying on his left side. When he brought us down the news in the evening, we were first struck with surprise, and the young ones began to set up their pipes (to wailing) as they were but seldom used to scenes of death. However, I gave orders that some should sit by the corpse during the night, and on the morrow prepared for the funeral.

THE TWENTY-FIRST YEAR – OWEN BREAKS A LEG, RORY DIES AND AND JESSY MARRIES
June 15 1767 – June 14 1768

We buried old Nunez in the grove among the rest of our departed friends, in the most decent manner our circumstances would admit, and began the New Year after the old fashion. Now my friend Norman advised me that he thought it proper that we should put ourselves out of further suspense, by sending Harry and Rory off on a visit to our friends to gain some kind of intelligence. I jumped into his opinion at once and concluded to put the question to them on the morrow. They both agreed with us that the motion was right, and concluded to set off. I told them I thought it best that they should go by themselves and not to take the women with them, as the thing did require dispatch. And as the women were at this day so well used to us that they were very placid on the proposal, off they went, furnished with what they thought proper for their journey, the next day. We had taken care to counsel them after the best manner that we could devise, before they left us.

About 4 days after the young men were gone, we had a sad casualty happened among us, as thus. In the morning Mr Bell and Owen set out on a march after flamingos with their guns; and as they went in a canoe I desired that they would stop as they returned, at the old plantation to bring some large calabashes with them, as the girls wanted some for their use. But how I was struck, about two hours after with the sound of a conch, and that of my friend Norman, as I knew full well by the manner. '*What can this be?*' said I to my wife. Down we ran to the lagoon and into the Indian canoe. But I had not gone far, when I saw our boat on the return with only messmate Norman paddling, without my son.

Therefore, as soon as he turned the point I hailed him. He made me no answer, only paddled the faster. But when he came up, and seeing Owen on his back in the boat, I cried out, '*What is the matter, shipmate? Speak, tell me at once!*'

'*Don't alarm yourself,*' said he. '*Your son has had the mishap to break his leg.*'

'*Oh, hard fortune!*' said I. '*Mr Norman, how shall we get the better of this terrible affair?*'

'*In the first place,*' said he, '*we must get him home with all speed and do our best, in God's name, after.*'

But when we got to the landing, I was at a loss how to manage, so I gave a toot with the shell. This soon brought down the women, but when they understood what had happened to my poor son, unfeigned grief broke out, and all became a scene of woe. But as there was not any time to be lost, I sent up to the kitchen for a board and we laid the poor soul on it, as gently as possible, and in great agony he was, nevertheless. It was the right leg, and about 3 inches above the ankle. But for a mere lad, as I may say, he bore it with a resolution beyond all our expectations. It swelled to a great degree; and happy for us it was to have a person of Mr Bell's judgement and skill as such a time. Therefore the whole proceeding was given up to his direction, and we got his leg fixed[82] up snug, or set, as they say.

Now it happened, as they informed me, after this manner. As they were running alongshore, Owen spied a monkey and they put in to get a shot at it, but as he ran with his piece cocked, his leg unfortunately slipped into a kind of crab-hole, and by the force snapped it at once. I now fixed his place of durance[83] just within the front of our building, and clapped a small awning over his head to shade the morning sun from him, so that he sat and lay in a sort of state, as it were. And here I must give messmate Bell all his due. He was ever studying some kind of amusement or other to pass the time or lull Owen's pains, and often has he sat with him during his confinement a full hour, playing on the flute to amuse him, for which he has my sincere thanks unfeigned. And as for Owen, there can be no esteem lost between them, nor has he wanted all kind love from the rest, as far as their poor powers extended.

Our lads had been gone above a fortnight, when on an evening we were all sitting relating former transactions, and the night air fair and clear, all at an instant of time such an explosion went off that it gave the whole of us sudden surprise. But my child, little America, cried, 'Look! Look!' – upon which we saw in the air a number of small globes of blue fire. As they were vanishing one after the other, Bell said he had seen such things often before; but we all agreed never to have heard so loud a noise attend the same. I had seen one of them myself[84], but never to half the effect of this. However, it sent us all into our dormitories that night without more ceremony.

After we had turned in, in a short time my wife observed to me that she hated those fireballs so very much. On my asking her how so, she told me she was sure that we should have much sickness upon us soon, upon which I laughed at her and bade her to go to sleep and forget it.

'No, no,' she said, 'all Old Men said so' – where she came from, and I should see it 'as plain and round as the Moon.' And thus talking, we fell asleep.

On the morrow morning one of our dogs called Sleeper, which had gone away with the lads, came running down the hill, and soon after down the hill came Harry and Rory we thought, but when they drew near we found Rory to be missing and a strange Indian in Harry's company.

'What news?' I said to Harry with a face of wonder, being quite impatient. By this time all had gathered around him, so that it had become a Dover Court (all speakers and no hearers)[85]. Now I was surprised Harry did not direct his discourses more to me. On this I called, 'Brother Harry, where is Rory, pray, that I don't see him?'

On this he came up to me and said, 'I know you have a great heart and won't cry if I tell you Rory is dead and behind with my people, and a great many more old friends.' Upon this, I begged him to be brief and to give a true and fair relation of all since his departure, and if Rory's wife knew as yet of the matter. He said no, as yet.

He says that they got thither without anything happening to them in four days and nights, when on their first entrance they met a women who told them that all were sick of the flux, as he says, and many dying every day – among whom Futatee for one, and others who had been on visits to our place. That two days after their arrival Rory fell sick and lived but three days, after which a few Indians came to him and said they would take good care to bury my friend, but as for him he should think to return back home again, as soon as possible, lest he should die also, and that they advised young Sappash to accompany him. And that when they came to my place to tell my good friends, meaning us, that I should take Sappash and make a husband for Jessy at once, as they were too sick to hear any more mad complaints from women; and to inform me that they had never heard anything from the Spaniards.

After my brother had satisfied Mr Bell and me as to all further matters, I sent for Jessy and when she came, desired that she would mind well what I was going to tell her. Upon her saying she would, I began: *'You are to know in the first place that your people have thought it proper to keep your husband among them for a great reason they have, and have sent this young man to be your husband in his stead. And what do you think of it?'*

On seeing her struck dumb, as it were, I thought it best to cut matters as short as I could, and told her that the Great One, that she had heard me talk so much about, had been pleased to lay Soroteet in the ground; and that her friends had sent that young man Sappash out of their love for her and me, and she must not make me angry if she could help it. Off she went, mute as a fish and weeping, to my spouse for a dish of condolence; and thus the affair remained for a day or two, when my wife informed me that Jessy desired her to tell me that she would be ruled as I thought best, but that she hoped Sappash would look to my wife and me, and learn to love her as her first husband did. I then sent for Harry and had him inform the young stranger that I intended to celebrate the wedding on the morrow.

Harry was much concerned for my Owen, and asked me if I ever thought he would walk again upright. I told him that I hoped so, but Mr Bell was the man who could tell most on that matter.

'Ay, ay,' said Bell, *'he'el be taking to his qats[86] ere long again.'*

On the following day the ceremony was performed and we all spent the time as merry as possible, allowing for Jessy's bashfulness on the occasion. The next day Harry requested to know what new name we should give Jessy's husband. I told him Rory as before. This pleased all around, especially his wife.

After this, my girl desired me never to say Indians were fools again.

'As how?' I said.

She said, *'Did I not tell you fireballs made sick for my people?'*

I knew not how to answer her, therefore contrived to alter the subject. And in regard to my poor Indian friends, I must needs say that the melancholy afflictions that have of late visited them, touches my heart greatly. But it is the work of the Lord, and I must hold my peace and wait patiently until I may hear more favourable tidings of them.

No great matters fell out for a long time after this, and my son now began to go on crutches freely. Mr Bell observed to me that although he had shown himself so dextrous as he pretended at the splicing of Owen's leg, yet he felt the contrary in his mind, having never assisted at such an operation except once before.

Soon after this our poor children fell sick of the flux. This gave a general alarm to the whole community, as we expected it to be of the same kind as that of our friendly Indians, and my girl prophesised that we should all die of it. This vexed me a little, and made me insist that she should talk no more after that sort, or I should be very angry with her. This she dreaded, as I never had words with her at any time in anger. But in about a fortnight they all recovered and came about again, to my great satisfaction after so dreadful a prospect before us.

Some time after this, Mr Bell proposed an excursion to the northward by land, if it were in any way agreeable to me. I told him that he might take his own pleasure but that in regard to myself I was not so very forward about it. Yet if Harry chose to go with him, they had my full consent, and in the morning they began preparing for their jaunt. Now while matters were getting ready, I begged Mr Bell not to venture more than a few miles or so from home, which he promised me to observe strictly; and on the day following they both marched off before we had turned out. They took 2 dogs with them, and my small spyglass.

In the evening Owen took a whim to go fishing with Rory, down the lagoon. He went away about 4 o'clock and while they were absent I took a walk up the hill in order to look out, as was my usual custom. I had not been there long before I descried two sail in the offing, and as I thought by my naked eye, standing right inshore. Now what to think, I knew not, but as they seemed to stand in rather from a northeast quarter, I had doubts in my mind whether they were Spaniards or not. They were both sloops, as I imagined at first, being so far out; but on one of them gybeing[87] her mainsail she proved to be a schooner. In a short time after, a thick mist came up on the horizon and I lost sight of them. Then I walked down the hill again and, lighting my pipe, walked down to the landing, waiting with impatience for about an hour. I did not throw out my signal for the lads to return as I knew it to be of no effect[88]; but in a short time after, they came in from fishing and I told Owen what I had seen.

'Let us go in again,' said he, which we did, but as night was then coming on and the air thick, we could perceive no more of them.

No signs of our travellers returning for that night, I sat smoking with my wife, full of cogitations until midnight, when we both turned in. I was up before the sunrise and on the lookout, but not a sail could I perceive anywhere along the whole horizon; and who or what they were, remains to this day an entire secret to us. Yet I must needs say that I could not refrain from many foolish conjectures at the time.

The next day in the evening arrived our two adventurers, weary enough, and we were all glad to see them safe again returned, and as they came in late and almost famished, the girls got them a good mess, and to sleep they went for the night. The next day messmate Norman gave us a brief of their journey, as thus. He says that after they had gone about 5 miles away northwest, mostly through woods, they observed the land to rise gradually and at length came to open country. There they both sat down to refresh themselves, and as they were eating remarked a tree of a most amazing size, but hollow, and so large that within the trunk he thinks thirty men could easily stand within it.

'From this tree we took our departure afresh,' says he, 'and took our course north with the ground still rising until we came to a small wood of lofty trees, and at this place Harry mounted one of them, in order to look out.' When he got down again, he said that they were then on a very high hill, and that the land fell away to a deep valley full of woods, but that towards the sea there was a hill of rocks and a great lagoon with much water. Upon this intelligence, they descended the hill, and as they went on, found the bones of several deer, but in all that time had seen no living beast. Now they concluded that they were at least 10 miles from home, and began to have thoughts of what was next to be done, when Harry proposed to ascend another tree, which he did and brought down word that he judged they were not over 5 miles from the Great Cliffs, but that they must keep more away towards the sunrising.[89] And on this, they both determined to set off for the place but found Harry's judgment out rather as to the distance, as it was evening before they could get to the bottom.

Here, being in a valley and the sun then far to the west behind the hills, it became very gloomy and they had thoughts of making a large fire for their preservation in the night. But soon after they found the trees to become fewer and could perceive light through them. This gave them fresh courage and they put on, when in about a quarter of an hour they found themselves at the verge of a wood, where a vast expanse opened to their view.

Here, he says, nature became very wild indeed, or perhaps an earthquake might have in former times torn or split a whole mountain, as there were massive[90] stones lying at all points of the compass and of the magnitude of large houses. And in between some of these they concluded to lodge for the night with a good fire around them. On the morrow they began to look around them, when on getting on one of the high stones they could see over the mangroves and the low country clear out to sea, which they judged not more than 5 miles from them. With this discovery, they returned without the least harm to bring us this strange report, as I may call it.

CHAPTER VIII

The Twenty-Second to Twenty-Fifth Years

THE TWENTY-SECOND YEAR – QUAMINO IS DISCOVERED
June 15 1768 – June 14 1769

I had been on this shore now for about twenty-one years and two months, when a very uncommon event came about, and I shall give it as faithful a narration as possible. On a certain day when messmate Bell and I were out in the bay fishing for our pleasure, he observed to me that it was a little odd that I expressed no desire to visit his new Northern discovery, as he was pretty sure it could be easily done by sea.

'*Why, as to that part of your speech,*' said I, '*Bell, I have half a mind indeed.*'

'*Well then,*' said he, '*when shall we go?*'

'*We go?*' I replied. '*Can that be good policy? Rather either you or me, and Harry, is best, as it is so far from our women.*'

'*Well then,*' said he, '*you and Harry can go. Let him stand pilot, as to the place.*'

I now came to a determination, and when we got in, told my brother Harry what I intended. He was glad of the voyage, and said that he could hit the place exactly. I then told him that he must get one of our boats ready, and all things necessary for our trip.

About two days after, we put down the lagoon and got the length of Towers Field by 2 o'clock in the afternoon, weathered Whale Point, and got the whole length of Boom Bay by evening, where I concluded to stay that night. In the morning we put out to sea to get around a long point, and opened a new scene of country. Along this shore we ran at the rate of about 5 knots an hour. Now Harry concluded that we must soon see the cliffs from the sea, but we coasted the shore until by my judgment we got 8 leagues from our own bay and I had thoughts of returning back, just as we were abreast of a high bluff full of high trees. Here we concluded to go on shore and stay for the night, to return in the morning. After we had got on shore and made up the fire, which was towards evening, Harry said he had a mind to climb a tree, which he did. He cried out that we were not above a mile from the lagoon, for he saw the cliffs and all, quite plainly.

'*Then let us make up a tent for the night,*' I said, '*and in the morning we go in around the bluff, if the wind stands.*'

The next morning, we got round by sunrise but not a sign of any lagoon could I see at all, until we had got about a mile further, when out on a point I observed a few White Poaks[1] standing fishing. '*If it be anywhere,*' said I, '*it must be there.*' When we got thither the mouth of the lagoon showed itself, and I should not have given myself the trouble to enter had not Harry spied the tops of the cliffs between the bushes.

We put in and found a narrow pass for the space of a mile or so, not more than a ship's length wide and very crooked, then it opened into a much larger space, and the water was above three fathoms deep there. Now another strait for a short while, and all at once we opened into a lake or pond at least a mile or more across, surrounded by a large, stony

182

flat shore. This ran back half a mile or more, then began to rise, a most tremendous mass of rocks, cliffs and fallen huge stones. Now as we were viewing this new sight, I was prompted to take up my glass and I had not had it long in my hand before I cried out to Harry, that I saw a black man or some wild creature moving among the rock stones. This startled Harry, and he begged the glass off me.

Now as he was looking, he perceived him to move to a clear place, and returning the glass to me said, 'It is a strange man, indeed, and let us be going back directly, brother, pray!'

I told him not to be in a fright, for were it the very Lucifer himself I was determined to speak to him if possible, before we returned.

'Then,' said he, 'if you are not afraid of him, I won't either be afraid, brother.'

We then put into shore and both got out with our guns, and marched directly for the place we saw him first, but found that he did not observe us. After we had gone some distance towards him, I sat down to take a fresh review, and then could see plainly as I thought, a tall old Negro man with his head and beard white as wool, and naked with a staff or club in his hand. We were at this time about half a mile from him, and found that he did not observe us as yet. Now all of a sudden we lost sight of him amongst the rocks. We then advanced apace, but could not get the least glimpse of him again. Therefore we ran back to our boat, dreading lest we might be deprived of her before we could reach her.

Soon after we had put off from the shore on our return, Harry spied smoke arise among the rocks and cried, 'There is the old devil now, again.'

'And there may he be and remain,' said I. 'Let us get out and make home as fast as we can, Harry.'

'Brother's afraid!' said he.

'Not I, but what would you have done, should there have been more of them come and run away with our boat, while we had left her?' I replied.

'Then we must have gone home by land,' said he.

'And starve on the way, without fire tackling,' I answered. But out we got and put away for home as fast as we could; and got home in two days by hook or crook after getting aground on Whale Point. Our people rejoiced at the sight of us, and Bell had the whole relation from me. But I must need confess when the object first disappeared, my former idle notions of the Yahoos began to return strongly, but I got the better of it when I perceived the smoke arise between the rocks.

Mr Bell said that he was determined he would go if I would permit Rory (Sappash) to go with him, and he would not return before he spoke to him, if he could find him in any reasonable time.

'With all my heart,' I replied. And accordingly about a week after, they set out by my odd chart I formed for them. And the following is Mr Bell's story:

They got there with ease, and after waiting a whole day without getting a sight of any living soul, concluded it to be a mere visionary affair as no smoke was to be seen. Yet he was bold enough to continue there in the boat all night, when Rory awoke him to show him smoke early on the morrow. Upon this, he said he told Rory to get out the two guns and follow him. They made right away for the place where the smoke arose, which was about a mile from them, up among the rocks. But as they were about two-thirds on their way, and just as they turned around a large high piece of rock, the grey dog they had with them gave a long howl. Then to his surprise a tall black wretch stood but a short distance from them, as going to turn off to leave them after the best fashion he could, being but feeble in his joints.

Upon this my messmate hailed him, but he seemed not willing for any parley. Upon that they both went up to him and stopped him, whereupon the old man fell down on his knees and began to beg for mercy in Spanish. Mr Bell told him that he need not show any fear on their account, as they intended no manner of harm in the least, and asked him how many there were of them in that place, seeing him appear so very ancient. But how greatly was Bell amazed when the old man told him that he had been there alone longer than he could remember well.

'But would you not choose to end your days,' said Bell, 'among people, than so? How do you live? What do you eat? Do any people ever come to relieve you?'

He answered no, nor had he spoken a word to any man from the time he first got thither, nor did he want to speak to any man nor see any man again for the rest of his days. He then asked Bell where he came from. When being told, he replied, 'Then go back to the same place and don't trouble a poor old man who stands not in need of any help. I have lived long, long quiet since I left the faces of the white men. I shall not covet to return among those who live upon poor black men's blood. But if I had a mind to return to them, they could get nothing but dry bones to suck at. Now I am so old; so, young man, be advised by me and leave me where I am. Maybe I shall die tomorrow.'

'And who would you have to bury you?' said Bell.

'The crows,' said he, and began to move off. But we followed him at a small length of distance until he got back to his fire, which was between 4 rocks in a very secret place. When the old man found they had followed him, he turned about to them, and fixing his aged eyes on Mr Bell, stamped his staff on the ground, then cried, 'White men, trouble me no more! Go! I hate you and all those of your colour in the world. I have no more blood for you to suck. Let me die quiet by myself.'

But messmate did not think to leave him, without being better informed of his story, and began with him as thus: 'Old fellow, let me tell you that there are thousands of white men in the world far better, perhaps, than any it has been your fortune to fall among. So pray, let us have fair play, however, on both sides. You are one of the verriest old churls[2] that I have ever met in all my days. I dare to say, had you spent a year or two amongst us at our place, your opinion of white men might take a turn; or you must have been so ill used by the whites formerly as to be past all cure of your temper.'

The old man then replied that he was now very old, and had not the least desire to be more acquainted with us, at any rate, for that it was his opinion that I spake only in favour of my own colour; but if that what I wanted to advance was true, he could tell such stories as would plainly prove that his cause was very just, as well as mine, ending with a disdainful laugh and uttering, 'White man good? No, no, no!'

Bell thought then that he would try what coaxing he could do, and remarked that it was true – he had observed when in the islands that the condition of the poor black men was very miserable; and for his part it was a practice he had not been concerned in, nor none of his relations that he ever had knowledge of; nor should he ever give into the like opinions, as he detested making any men slaves whom God made free at their birth. Upon this the old man asked him if he would blame him, for choosing to keep himself free. Now finding the old man had become more civil and complying, Bell took the opportunity to desire that he would give him some account of his life and how he came thither, for that he supposed he had gone through misery enough before he came to that place.

'True, true, man,' said the poor old wretch with a heavy groan. 'You see my head all white and no friend left to stand by me now at the last hours.' At this, he stopped short, and looking at Bell sternly said, 'How did you find me out? You are no Spaniard. I know very well what countryman are you.'

'I am a Scotchman,' he replied, 'but that's no easy matter. I will contrive to make your old heart more easy before you die, if you will but be advised and come with me to my place. I have a partner who has been for many long years continually doing good to his fellow creatures, although he has been unfortunate enough himself.'

'What countryman is he?'

'English,' Bell answered.

'All the same, no better for that,' said the old man. 'Where do you live? How far off?'

'About thirty miles,' answered Bell, 'to the southward. And if you go, we will give your old days rest, and my friends will kindly receive you if you can leave this forlorn place.'

Now the old man told him that if he would swear to be a true man, and to bring him back to his old place again if he should not like to remain among them, then on that condition he should go, as Bell said they all lived free men together, and did not keep black people in slavery.

All this discourse passed in Spanish but Bell observed to me that he could speak English once, too, before he had learnt Spanish, having lived long, long with them at Barbados and Jamaica. We had spent so much of our time now, that we began to grow hungry, said Bell. He told the old man that they would set off the next day early in the morning, and then pointed to where the boat lay, and they took their leave of him for that time.

When the morning came, they observed the old man on his way to the boat. They embarked with him, and put out of the lagoon, and arrived without any long delay. But before they came in, Owen came down from the lookout, and said that he thought he had heard a shell blow. This mustered us together presently, and we marched down to the landing, when soon after, the conch went again, not far off. But no sooner did they come in, than a third object was discovered in the boat, and I must confess myself somewhat surprised. Away flew the young fry[3] as fast as their legs could carry them.

Indeed, I was left alone, for my wife had also taken herself off. Now, after they had landed, we were obliged to assist the old man to rise. The long time he had sat in the boat, not being used to it for years, and his age together had quite cramped him, but we made a shift to get him up to my place and there seated him in the shade, my young family peeping from behind the kitchen and other places. And indeed, he cut a most odd figure, as he sat with his hands over his knees, and his chin on them.

In the first place, as they had brought him contrary to my expectations, I told Harry to get him a bed made up in the old shed, where old Nunez had formerly slept. And after I found the old soul had risen from his seat and was stumping about a little, I walked up to him and asked him in Spanish what was his name. He asked which name, for he had three – one Negro, one English and one Spanish.

'O ho, then,' said I, 'old daddy, you have been among the English, have you?' – for I had received that I have before related from Bell, soon after they landed.

'My name is Primus[4] in English, Master,' he said. 'The Spaniards gave me the name of Diego. But my first name was Quamino in Guinea.'[5]

I asked him then how old he thought he might be.

'I can't tell you for true, but I had a wife when I came from the Ibo Country to Barbados.'

I then bade him to try and remember who was the King of the English people at that time. Yes, he said, he knew very well. They said the king at that time was a woman and a great warrior, he heard. This must mean Queen Anne[6] most certainly; but be it anyhow, his appearance showed him to be very old, 80 at least as we both judged.

'But, old man,' said I, 'how comes it that you have got such a great hatred against the white man, as my friends tell me you have? I should be glad to hear your story, and then I can be a better judge. It may be that you have been a great rogue when you were young. What say you to this?'

He then said, 'The man who brought me back here to see you, and to hear you talk, promised to take me back when I wanted to go, and if you think I am a rogue, send me back when you please.'

I told him he was brought to a place where there was nothing but constant friendship; that I was master of the place, and if he thought good of it he was welcome to stay as long as he could desire himself; and that I should be glad if he would give me the whole story on the morrow.

Then he came and took hold of my hands and said, 'I believe you have learned to be a good man since you have come to live at this poor place in the woods and stones, like my place, and, master, I will tell you all what I can think on in my mind, if I live till tomorrow.'

Thus we dropped it, as I did not choose to trouble him too much.

I was surprised that a man of his years should not be bald. His head was as large as a thumb mop[7], by the quantity of white wool on it, and a most copious white beard. This, joined to a black skin, gave him entirely a new appearance to us. Quamino had been a very stout man in his younger days, at least six feet high, but stooped much by reason of age.

The next morning the old man coming to visit me, I desired him to make himself free and tell me his entire story, as much as he could remember.

He then sat down beside me and began as follows: 'I remember they put me on board a ship one morning along with three more. The ship was full of black people before I came there. My wife was there too, but I did not know it then, when I first came on board, until she spied me out. We were all made fast, down in the hold. And when we had been out about ten days at sea my wife, having liberty to go into the cabin[8], found out that there was much knives there in boxes, and told it to us privately. Upon this the men agreed, that if they could get at the knives to kill all the whites, they could go back to our country again.'

I asked him if he did not think it a very wicked and barbarous undertaking.

On this, he replied not at all, as they then thought, not knowing whatever became of all their country folks the ships took away, for that it was evident that they never came back again. Therefore it was nothing but right to kill those who would kill them. After, she conveyed about 5 knives among them, which they hacked against each other in the dark, to make saws intended to cut off their shackles. They sang all the time they were at this work so the white men should not hear the noise. A little Negro of the cabin, who had observed her steal away the knives at times, discovered the scheme and he informed the mate, and it was all blown.

'Then,' said he, 'they took my wife and tied her up to the mast of the ship by her arms and whipped her sadly to make her confess which of the blacks set her on the business, but she would not confess. Then the captain ordered them to whip her more, but I was down below and could not see it. Still she would not say anything about the men of the secret. Upon this the captain told them to whip her worse than ever, and they did whip her dead and threw her into the sea, and two of the men after that were whipped; and had they known the woman to be my wife they would have whipped me dead, also,' said he. 'I suppose that from that hour I have never loved white men since.'

I could not help feeling for the poor old soul when he had given me this first cause of resentment, but I did not choose to interrupt his story. After this happened and they came to Barbados, he was sold and bought by a fisherman, who treated him so heartily at his first coming to the house that he burnt his back with a hot iron. This he was told by other Negroes was to mark him as his own.

'My master was a mulatto man, and any good people would think as he was part black himself, he would love the poor slaves more than the white people did. But he was as hard hearted as any devil in the whole island, and I had not been with him a year before I got a most severe whipping only because I had not comprehended him right in a trifle, for want of understanding English enough.

After I had been with him some years and did all the service for my master in my power, yet I got several times whipped for his own humour, as it were, or just when the Devil put it in his head. For as sure as any white people happened to have words with him in trade, then poor Negro men must stand clear at home. But I got this from his hard hands on the account of my sweetheart, a young Negro girl, who lived 4 miles off from Bridgetown.⁹ I had leave to go and see her on a Sunday, and staying at the dance too late, did not go home all night. In the morning, knowing that I should have been out with the boat, I was afraid to return as I expected the whip. Soon after, a Negro called Joe came for me, and I went home. My master ordered me to be tied up and I got 30 lashes. This I could have borne with quietness, but he was not content with that and swore I should be branded on the cheek for a Runaway.'

And that was true. 'See here,' said he, showing the place. 'I then told him that he might kill me, if he pleased, for I would no longer live with him. He told me I might get a new master and be damned, for he did not care who had me if he had his money again.'

'I knew one Mr Freeman from Jamaica who liked me, and he bought me from my master and took me to Jamaica with him, but he died of a fever soon after, and I was sold again. My new master lived on the north side of the island and he, knowing that I had been a fisherman, kept me for that purpose so that my life was spent mostly by or on the water. I lived with this man for several years, and had a wife belonging to the same estate, by my old master's consent. We had two children, when one day as I was sitting under the rocks on a sea beach near a point of land, all at once three men jumped upon me and said, "Vamos! Vamos!"¹⁰ I stood amazed, finding them to be three Spaniards, and go I must. When they took me around the point, there lay a small picaroon¹¹ sloop, onboard of which I was ordered, where there were more of my colour they had plundered like myself. I was not grieved at my new change, but for my wife and children.

I knew I was but a slave still, but when I thought of my wife and poor children whom I never expected to see again, then I hated the white men more than ever. They took me to Santiago in Cuba¹², and there a rich old gentleman bought me. He, finding that I had followed fishing, gave orders that I should have the same employment under him. My old master never ordered me to be whipped, as I took great care now I had got among new people, to do all I could for the best. Now one day my master, after I could talk Spanish a little, asked me if I had not left a wife and children behind me in Jamaica. I said yes, but they were no more for me now.

"Never mind that, Diego," said he. "You shall have another if you want one. We have girls enough."

I thanked him, and I thought to give my heart a little comfort I would look out for a new wife, as I was sure that I would never see Benneba¹³ again. My master liked me better every day, and made me overseer of all the Negroes who had anything to do about the boats, and I lived happier than for many years before.

At last one day as we were at work on an old canoe to patch her up, master sent for me to come to him under a great tree where he was sitting and said to me, "Diego, do you know old

Maria's daughter, the mulatto girl Isabella?"

"Yes, master," said I.

"Very well, and she likes you, I find by report."

"I hope so, sir," said I.

"Then you have my consent," said he.

But, Oh man, that brought trouble enough on me. About 6 months after I had my new wife, my young master came home from the Havannah, where he had been for a good time while about business for master, and he behaved very ill-natured to me. I wondered at it, because he used to like me much, before he went away. But one day when my wife was alone with me, she told me she wondered what ailed the young master. He hated her, she was sure, he called her such bad names when he thought nobody heard him.

"Maybe," said I to her, "he wanted you for himself."

She did not know it, she replied. But soon after this she began to grow sick, and an old man of my colour told me he was sure she was poisoned and would never have a child, but that she would look like this as long as she lived. However, in about 2 years she died, and soon after her, an old Negro woman, when she was dying sent privately for me and begged forgiving, as her young master had employed her to do it. But I had no power of revenging myself for I had better thoughts than to murder at this time, so kept my mind to myself until time should bring me revenge.

And about a year after, when all seemed to be blown over, my old master, seeing me striving so hard at work, began to laugh and said, "Why, Diego, I think you have bad luck in wives. Have you got any woman?"

I answered him no sir, nor did I intend to have another, for I could speak freer to him than any of the rest.

"Why so?" said he.

I said his God gave me three wives but white men took them all, and I was resolved they should never take another.

"How was it," said he, "Diego?"

I then told him concerning my other wives, but "Hold, hold! Diego," he cried out when I told him the last was poisoned. "Say you she was poisoned? If you find out who did the thing, I shall have full satisfaction done."

"Ah master," said I, "she is dead and gone home."

"Who did it?"

"But one is alive now concerned."

"Tell me who that is," said he with a fierce look.

Upon that I went down on my knees, and begged he would let me keep it a secret as long as I lived. "You have been well used by me, Diego," said he, "and can trust me with your secrets, I hope."

I did not know what to say now, for he left me quickly in ill will, as I thought. And I grew very sorrowful on the occasion, but soon after two Negroes came and told me I must come to the stock house. I threw down the net I was at work on, and went with them, was laid on my back with my head in a hole, and left there for two days.[14]

The third day the master sent for me, up to the house.

As soon as I came in he said, "Well, Diego, you see I don't like for blacks to be too free with me. I know how to be angry sometimes, and if you don't tell me now who is concerned in the affair of poisoning Isabella, you shall be shot without delay and sent after her."

Down I went on my knees again and said, "My good master, if I tell you it is all the same to poor Diego. Young master Hernan will kill me when he comes home again from Veracruz[15],

188

because he made old Quasheba[16] poison my wife."

Master, when he heard this, told me to go back to my work again, and went into another room. Master took no more notice of me; but the white men about the house said I was got into a bad condition and would come to be hanged, they supposed. This threw me into sorrow of heart. And as they did not expect young master home in under 2 months, I came to a resolution of leaving them all and flying, I did not care where; for now I hated all white men as much as possible for me to hate them.

And it happened soon after that master ordered me to collect several things for to be sent away to a country house he had, about 5 leagues to windward, where he was to have much company to meet him. I let no man know what was in my heart, but put everything on board that I looked on that I should want for use. And with another Negro called Mingo I put off for the place. When we got thither, I bade an old Negro who lived there to collect yams and many other kinds of things to go with the boat's return. Then on the next morning I went down to the boat early and shoved her off, hoisted sail, and stood directly out on a wind until evening, when the land wind came and carried me clear of the coast, so that by morning I was so far out that I had almost lost sight of the shore. In about 5 days I fell in with the place Mr Bell found me at, and there I have lived by myself since that time. And there I expected to die if you or somebody else had not found me out at last."[17]

Quamino having finished his odd story, I asked him how long he thought he had lived at that place.

'Moons enough,' he said.

Now as he had not kept any reckoning of his time, I could form no other to estimate it but by the age he was at the time of his flight, which by his account I supposed to be about 45 or not much over or under; and at the time messmate Norman first discovered him he thinks him to be 70-odd perhaps. Yet notwithstanding his age, the old fellow seems active enough at fishing matters, and very strong except for his stooping.

I have since asked him how he lived and provided for himself. His answer was by catching fish and eating yams and other roots and fruits. I asked him how he obtained them at that barren place where he lived. From what he had first brought in his boat, he told me, for that there was enough good ground at the back of the cliff; and as to his way of sleeping and other things he would show me if I would go some day thither with him. Upon this, I asked him if he had a desire to return again.

Just as I pleased, he said – it was all one to him. What was an old man good for, when he was past labour?

'*But could you willingly go and leave company, to remain there alone again?*' I asked.

He said that he would rather that I should please myself as to that.

'Then,' said I, 'here are young ones enough to feed you, old man. You shall do no more than what your fancy leads you to, at any time.'

I had lived there almost twenty years when I fell ill of a '*violent sun headache*', as messmate Norman calls it, and I would not wish my greatest enemy to be worse afflicted than I have been for some time past. The nature of this disorder is that the pain comes on as the sun rises, so that the time of the meridian drives the person quite light-headed, and so great is the throbbing that the stomach becomes quite sick and casts. Messmate Norman had a remedy of a kind of large leaves bound around the head, which has wrought a cure.

THE TWENTY-THIRD YEAR – CAPTAIN VALDEZ ARRIVES
June 15 1769 – June 14 1770

Some few months after my headache had left me, I took a fancy of visiting the old man's former dwelling-place, and he seemed much pleased with my proposal; and accordingly I told messmate Norman of my intention. I proposed that my son should bear us company, as he longed so much for a ramble. Accordingly, in a few days off we went, the old man, Owen and myself. I need not be particular as to our voyage except that we found a fine piece of ambergris directly off Towers Field, on the strand. When we came in to the lagoon, the poor old man hove a heavy sigh and said: *'There is my hole, master. Trouble never touched me at this place until I saw a white man's face again. Then trouble came back to me, for I thought no less but that I should be forced away against my will, and that made me so cross to Mr Bell. For I could not think there were such white men, as I have found you to be, in the world.'*

'Now,' said I, 'yonder is the spot where I first saw you, old man, when I was here.'

'Ay, but that was not the place where I used to sleep,' said he. *'Now if you please, we will get the boat up to the head of the bay, and I will show you my canoe where she lays. I believe that you would hardly find her out,'* said he, *'unless you were directed how to find her.'*

When we had gone thither, there opened another inlet, which I had not seen before, it being entirely land-locked from my sight; and on our entrance we came up to some of the fallen cliff stones. And in a place formed by the fall of the stones into a kind of sharp archway overgrown with poppanack bush[18], there lay his canoe quite hidden from the rays of the sun. This boat, Quamino told me he had made himself, and I gave him credit for what he told me. Nor was she of the worse shape I had ever seen; she was small, about nine foot long and suited his purpose well enough. This put me in mind of asking him what became of the boat he had arrived in, at that place.

'Oh,' said he, *'she lays sunk a little way out yonder, quite rotten now. Now we will go to my old lodging,'* said he, and away we went over divers rocks and broken paths until a large grove of small trees appeared before us. 'That is the place,' said he. *'I set all that to grow myself.'*

When we got there, 'Now,' said he, *'Please to follow me,'* and we entered among the trees, when we soon began to descend among rocks to a considerable depth, until we came to a kind of level, walled up on each side by the accidental fall of the cliff. This place may well be the size of a large cabin. This he had covered over with limbs of small trees and thatch, and had made a very good place of.

After we had seen his bed, he asked us to walk and see his cook room. This was not above twenty yards from his bedchamber, and consisted of only a large shelving place among the rocks. From that we marched to his storeroom. This indeed was much more furnished than the other. Here were to be seen several articles such as fishing nets, old darts, paddles and a number of other things and some remains of his old sail. I observed several kinds of old Spanish tools, but quite worn out with frequent use.

'I have one more place to show you,' said he, *'but I did not make it my place to live because I could not look out from it.'*

So after we had been to dinner, he led us around the south side of the hill and showed us a very large opening in the cliff.

'Here,' said he, *'Men have lived in old times, I believe, or used to come to it at times, for there is marks that fires have been made many times, and there is a pond of fresh water below in the valley, where I found an old path and burnt sticks in abundance, with several things cut*

with knives and marked.'

I told him that I did not doubt that it was a place well known to the pirates formerly, as well as my place. After this he showed us where his yams and plantains grew, and where his usual fishing ground was. There he said he generally struck with small darts, or caught and killed at night with an old cutlass and torchwood, and that he had tasted hardly any flesh meat from his first arrival at that place.

Soon after this Quamino led me into the cliff pass, and I did now just then take notice that Owen did not follow us. As such places had in many respects a resemblance to our own home, it was not a curiosity to him, but he had clambered up the rocks to get to an eminence to explore the country more at large. Soon after we were in, I heard a voice as from my son, just as we came under an opening, from above our heads. This caused me to wonder at first, when looking up to my surprise I beheld my Owen standing on a high precipice over our heads, and saying he saw a sail in the offing.

'Bon voyage,' said old Quamino, *'Let them go their way. We are content without their company.'*

This put me on to asking him if he had not seen vessels now and then.

Yes, he said, he had seen them several times; that once in the night he had seen one on fire, as he thought.

'Ay,' said I, *'that is a long time now, since we had the same sight, daddy, at our place. You must have been a great length of time here,'* said I.

He told me he knew not how long, but that he judged he had been by himself almost as long as he had lived among people, and I doubted it not. Or not being many years short of it.

There being quite a large stone on the ground behind us, 'Come,' said I, 'Quam, *let us sit down and take a pipe together, for never was I in this place before, nor did you ever expect to see me here, much less to conduct me hither.'* Then filling, I took out my tackle to strike a light. As I was doing this, I said, *'Daddy, what a great pity it is that you have never been made a Christian, as you seem to me to show sufficient judgement, and reason on things very well.'*

'What good would that have done me?' said he. *'Would it have made white men love me the better? No! No! Don't they curse and damn each other, fight, cheat and kill one the other? Black men cannot do anything worse than what white men do. They go to churches and tell God they will never do any harm to any people, and the same day come out and kill, cheat and say lies again. They say black men should be whipped to make them good slaves. How can they expect blacks to be good and no Christians, when they who say they are Christians are worse than we, who know not the books of God's as they do? Young men learn to be wicked in our country as well as anywhere else, and when they are brought among the whites they learn to do their wickedness also.'* – That the whites did not care for the blacks more than for the use they were, to rid them of hard labour; otherwise they might all go to the devil who was their father, as he said.

Then he asked me if I could tell who was Cain Devil, for the whites said the Negroes were all his children, and how could they pretend to know who was their father, better than themselves. That for his opinion the thought the same God made them all, black and white. Did I not see many other kinds of things differ in colour on the outside, but are the same within? 'Mind,' said he, *'if you look at the inside where the heart is, you can find no difference between the white and black. I can remember on a time my master had a white horse died in Jamaica and the Negroes skinned him; and when I lived with my master at Santiago he had a black horse died, and when he was skinned the colour was the same as the white one. But the white men, when they go about to do good, always keep it from the blacks, for fear they should learn if ever they do any. But I can't think they do much, because they go to confess often and remain still as wicked as before. They often say, "Curse your colour" to poor black men when they have often been about blacker works themselves.'*

All this time I sat silently puffing, for indeed I had little to answer on behalf of my own colour, but told him I believed him a much better man than many thousands who called themselves Christians.

After Owen had joined us, we arose and returned to the old man's bedchamber, as I may call it, and lay down on his palmetto bed place, all three together for that night. In the morning I asked Quam if he did not find it very doleful to be so much alone, at first.

He said yes, but that he soon became used to it, as it was his chief desire so to be; but that there was one affair which especially surprised him much, at the first when he had been there about a year, as he took it – (viz.) a loud noise as if it were a body of men giving a great 'Huzza!'[19] and that he heard it above twenty times in the course of his being there, but never above one huzza at a time, and that it sounded sometimes from one quarter and then another.

I told him that I judged it to proceed from the wind in that large cave.

In the morning we prepared for a return to my old habitation, but just as we had proceeded about halfway out, a musket was discharged to seaward of us. This gave us all three the alarm. But as I had braved so many dangers I could give no way to terror in the least, nor was old Quam much disturbed at the novelty. So we concluded to push out without the least fear or dread, but it was not so with Owen. He was really frighted, as being so seldom used to strange faces. When we got out I observed a vessel at anchor, about half a mile to the north of us. Presently Owen pointed to three men sitting on the beach not far from us.

'Shall I hail them?' said I, 'or shall we take no heed of them?'

'Do what you please,' he replied.

Upon this, I determined to speak to them and put to shore. Then I jumped out and walked on the beach, until I got within about 40 yards, when I hailed them in Spanish. They all got on their legs and returned an answer, on which I advanced up to them. They were all three elderly men, and Spaniards who belonged to that schooner, they said, and had been looking for a watering place. I told them that I would show them a good place for their purpose, if they were bound down the coast. They told me they were. I then enquired from whence they came.

Campeche[20], they said, and their skipper's name was Joachim Valdez[21]. They asked me to go on board with them.

When their boat came on shore. I thanked them and made a signal for my companions to come up to us, which in a short time they did.

Now when they observed the different complexions of my comrades, one of the men asked me of what country I was, as he knew by my speech that I was neither Spanish nor Portuguese. I candidly acknowledged myself to be an Englishman[22] at once, as I judged it to be most proper at that time, rather than to be found out in any falsehood, situated as we then were. Poor Owen stood motionless before them and old Quamino kept his silence, fearing perhaps they were from Santiago and might recollect him. But to put him out of fear, I told him they were from Campeche.

Now while we were all sitting together on the sand, all at once one of the Spaniards, as I took him to be, the same person who had discovered that I was no Spaniard, said to old Quamino, *'Faith and soul, old Trojan! Sure you won't say you are a Spaniard too, will you? For by Heavens you look as though you were born in the days of Finn MacCoul.'*[23]

I was greatly struck at hearing this man speak to him thus, in English, and he as much when the old man answered him in English again.

'O, booba, booba, boo!'[24] cried he, *'We are all English together I find now. And pray what is your name, my honey? Are you anything of a seaman,'* said he, *'and what brought you here, joy, among this spotted clan?'*

I told him my story was rather too long for the present, but that my name was Penrose, if that was of any significance.

'Sure,' said he, *'May it be that Welly then was your name? Ever Welly Penrose, at all?'*[25]

'Who can you be?' cried I, *'that ever knew Lewellin Penrose who has been so many years lost from his country? – unless you mean another of my name.'*

'How never,' said he, *'did you or did you not once belong to the Flying Oxford?'*[26]

Certainly, I told him I had.

'And don't you remember me, then, now – the man who was washed overboard and washed in again in a gale of wind off the Bay of Biscay?'

I said I well remembered the circumstance but had forgotten the person's name except it was Tady. *'Oh, that's right, child! Tady Lort*[27]*, that's my name, joy. But what keeps you among these dung coloured like thieves?'*

'Old shipmate,' said I, *'as I find you have once been, many changes have I gone through since that day; and to make short of the matter now, as I see your boat is coming onshore, you are to know that lad is my son, and has never known what a thief means.'*

'Oh, Blood! Welly, I ask your pardon, young lad. My good fellow, gives us your daddle,'[28] said he, and shook Owen so heartily by the hand that he made him stare again. *'Ah, messmate Welly,'* said he, *'I knew you were no Spaniard by the true English brogue on your tongue. Begorrah, my dear!'*[29]

The Spanish boat now being arrived, they asked me on board with them, and I told Owen to come alongside the schooner with our boat, so off we went to her. When we got on board, messmate Tady took me aft to the captain and told him that he had found a countryman on shore who would show them a watering place.

Captain Valdez received me kindly and asked me many odd questions concerning my manner of abode and living. After I had informed him of the circumstances of my life, he was pleased to say that it became every man to treat me civilly, as perhaps God had placed me there to administer relief to distressed seamen, and that he was glad to hear I was so well resigned to my uncommon way of life. He sent a boy down for a glass of agua dienta and drank to me.

I told him as I was seldom accustomed to it, I would rather decline it. Upon this he laughed heartily, and observed to me that English and Dutch men never flinched the glass, he thought, and I must not plead any excuse. Upon that, I drank it off.

He then gave order for them to run up the cable[30], and we stood down along the shore, keeping a good offing as I told him there were many shoals on the coast. But as the wind failed us in the afternoon, we let go the anchor off the Whale Point and there remained for the night, as I did not care to charge myself with the risk of the schooner's loss, by any means. I now thought I would send off Owen and the old man to inform them at home what had happened in our absence.

Early on the morrow, the wind coming up at east, we stretched off and in a short time came abreast of the point of Long Key, where we came to again. Then we went onshore and I showed them the watering place. Then I asked the captain to come on shore with me and see my family and place of residence, as I expected my friends with our boat shortly. About noon, Owen and Mr Bell came to us from our place and saluted the captain.

Captain Valdez did us the favour to go on shore with us in the evening. When we got into our lagoon, Owen took up the conch shell and blew a blast. Harry answered it directly, from the shore. The captain, observing this, asked the reason. I told him it was our stated custom, that we all had particular ways of sounding, so that when a strange Indian sounded we were always ready to receive him, or them, when they came to visit us. When we came to land, our whole congregation flocked down to view the stranger. Captain Valdez, on seeing so many curtsies and bows from my brown crew stood amazed, and turning to me asked which was my wife. I showed him my lady and our children, and introduced Mr Harry as my brother-in-law. Mr Bell entertained the captain the best way he could, for he was obliged to take the office on himself, as speaking Spanish fluently.

In the meantime, Harry and Rory went off after some crayfish, and the women provided yams and other matters as I directed them. While this was doing, the captain, Bell and myself walked all round our habitation, showing him our burying ground and that of old Nunez, his countryman, also. But Owen, out of his simple honest good nature, asked me to show the captain the place where we had found all our treasure. Now as he asked me in English, it was happily lost on the captain, and by Bell's giving him a check, it soon stopped his gab.[31]

After supper, the captain asked us if we had not a desire to revisit our country again. I made him the following answer, that as for myself I was well content to end my days where I was, in peace and quiet, as I had been on the same spot for so great a length of time. And messmate Norman said the same, observing that he should prefer my company before that of all men, as he had thoroughly proved[32] me and knew my ways, saying we had all we wanted. Kings could have no more in human life.

I proposed my own bed for the captain to sleep in for the night, and we all turned in at about eleven o'clock. On the morrow I went off with the captain to the Long Key and there renewed my discourse with my old fellow sailor, Tady Lort.

He no sooner espied me than he gave me this reception: 'Oh, the Devil from me! Are ye there, Welly? Sure and I'm glad to see you again with all hearts. I have been telling my shipmates all about you, and where I knowed you first. Faith, and that's a long, long time since. This is the last turn, and we shall soon aboard, my soul, and then we'el have a small drop of the Crater[33] together, for ould acquaintance sake, honey.'

I thanked my old shipmate and went on board with the captain, and about half an hour later, the boat came alongside with the water. The captain proposed to take his leave of us that afternoon, or early the next day, when Tady came aft, and making his leg to the captain[34], asked me if I would not take a parting drop of grog[35] with him before I left the schooner, although he was but a poor foremast man; and perhaps I might have more money than he now, yet he hoped I would not forget old times.

'Forget?' said I, 'No. For the honour of Old Ireland, if it shall prove the last grog I shall ever drink, I'll drink with thee, my old boy, although I am not used to drink spirituous liquors.'

'Well, well, then, enough said. Shall I call you Captain Penrose? said he. 'I suppose you trade in some craft or other by this time. Come, here is a merry madness to all misers, Mr Penrose!'

I received the calabash from his hand and drank to all true hearts and sound bottoms.

But while I was drinking, 'Ad's Flesh[36], man!' said he, 'do you never send home to the ould country at all? Give me a letter and I'll be bound to deliver it at Surinam[37] safe on board some Dutchman bound home, and that you may be sure of as sure as that the Devil's in Ireland,

I'll be bail for that,' said he.

I returned him thanks, and promised that if they did not sail before the next day, I would send one off.

Just at these words a lad at the masthead cried, 'Vela! Vela!' This I knew meant a sail, and he pointed to her in the offing with his hand. Directly orders were given to hoist a St Andrews Jack, or what our seamen call a Ragged Staff. This was no sooner done than the word passed forward to run up the anchor. On this, I went aft to the captain to take my leave. He told me it was a sloop which sailed in company with them, and he would stand out to join them, as she was bound for Surinam with them, but had parted company in thick weather about 7 days ago. I bade Owen to jump into our boat, but had just time to shake hands with Captain Valdez when the sails filled and they stood out to sea, Lort waving his red cap and crying, 'Long life to you, Welly, Long life, my soul!'

We waited among the reefs, striking fish for some time, to observe their motions. At last we saw them contact[38] each other, and both stand away south, when we returned to our place of abode. We lived on after the old sort, without anything new happening until the year ran out, and by my own account I had been there full twenty-three years and better.

THE TWENTY-FOURTH YEAR – THE DEATHS OF QUAMINO AND BELL
June 15 1770 – June 14 1771

Messmate Bell observed to me on a day, as he and I were out in the bay together, concerning my son Owen, saying had I not remarked a sort of change in the behaviour of him of late? I answered that I had not, except that he grew more sedate, I thought, than before but I supposed it was owing to his time of life, being now grown almost a man.

'What age may he be? asked Mr Bell, 'at this time?'

'About 18,' said I, 'or thereabouts'.[39]

'What causes this curiosity?' said I to him.

'Because I think, messmate, the sooner you can obtain a wife for him, it may be the better for him as well as yourself, and indeed the whole of us, for there is not a soul among us but truly regards him.'

'As to that matter, messmate,' I replied, 'you need not doubt but that I could easily obtain a wife for Owen among our friends, and they would be proud to provide him one, or even give him the preference of any Indian girl belonging to their whole tribe.'

On this, Bell began to laugh and said, 'I find you quite ignorant of the whole matter, Mr Penrose; for your son is in love already, nothing was ever more certain, to my sorrow.'

'To your sorrow, in love already? My friend, what mean you, for God's sake?' cried I in a commotion. 'Not with your wife, I hope!'

'No, no, messmate. No, a far different object, I can assure you, one fairer than she by many degrees. No, no, pray don't give yourself the least uneasiness that Owen would once attempt the virtue of my dame. His amours are of a more refined taste, I can assure you.'

'Upon my soul, Bell, you stagger my understanding,' said I, 'Come to the point at once, my friend.'

'Well, don't be startled, then. What think you of the Virgin Mary?'

'Oh, pray, Bell, give over. You cannot be in earnest now, I am sure, or the boy is of a certainty losing his senses, unless it be in a spiritual way; and, poor fellow, he had never received edification[40] to work such eager love in his breast, I am sure.'

'No, no,' said Bell, 'it is all-carnal, you need not doubt. But to put you out of pain, don't you remember what a beautiful picture of the Virgin and Child he saw on board of Captain Valdez' vessel? It is that which has set his heart so on fire, as you may remember to have heard him speak frequently about it. And, indeed, you and I have been the innocent cause of all Owen's sad malady by our extolling the beauty of our own fair countrywomen, and the frequent repetition of their charms in the songs he has learnt. So I judge it a hard trial to bring his stomach to come to digest one of our mahogany coloured beauties, for some length of time at least. But when he finds that you are acquainted of the affair, he may be brought to some degree of reason, and think more reasonably of the thing, as I am sure he can not think of obtaining any object of that cast in this forlorn part of the world.'

When Bell had made an end, I said, 'let me alone to find out a method of cure.' So the subject dropped for that time, and we returned home with our game.

Some time after this, on a day when Harry and Owen were standing together, Bell observed that Owen was the tallest of the two.

'Ay,' said Harry, 'Owen big enough for wife now. But he won't ever have one here among our trees and rocks.'

This made me laugh. 'And pray where is she to come from, then?' said I, 'and who made you so wise, Harry?'

'Oh, I know,' said he, 'if one ship would come here with the fine white and red[41] women of your country, he knows you would not begrudge to give him some of the gold and silver we have hidden yonder in the hole, for one of them to be a wife for him, for I know he loves them quite madly.'

'What say you, Owen?' I said to him. 'Are you so mad to desire a thing that cannot be obtained? Pray, cannot one of our friends' daughters serve your turn as a wife as they have done for Mr Bell and your father before you?'

But they were not so white and red, he said, nor would I or Bell have any like his mother had we our own choice, in our own country.

'You silly blockhead, where did you gather all these whims?' I said. 'How can you be such a fool to fall in love with what your eyes never saw?'

He replied, did he not see the mark of one of my sort of women on board the captain's vessel?

I answered, true, that was the mark of one who was much finer than many thousands; but could he think that one of our countrywomen would ever condescend to marry such a black fellow as he was?

'Why, then,' said he, 'did you and Mr Norman marry black people yourselves?'

I said the reason was plain – we knew where we were, no other wives could be had, and therefore we were content to have such as God ordained for us, and he was not to aim to touch the clouds with his fingers, notwithstanding they lowered so much at this time. For the sky was at the time very much overcast, and it threatened to come up thick and dirty from the southeast. This was about five in the evening, when it began to freshen up smartly, so that it soon banished all matrimonial thoughts out of our minds, and we began to collect all our light gear and stowed it away the best we could.

About the shutting in of the night, the rain came in, attended with such tremendous lightning and thunder, that the like we never had heard in our lives. Add to this, the boy Job, now about eleven years of age, had got little Somer with him down the lagoon in the canoe, and what to think or do in that case none could tell, as it blew so strong that none could keep their legs by this time. Yet Harry would insist, as he saw what was a taking my wife was in, to endeavour to go and seek them; but while we were all in this distress the poor boy Job came in with the child, safe and sound to our great surprise. I asked him how far off they had been.

Not far, he said, but that on their return he could not keep the canoe clear of the mangroves, so that he and little Somer were forced to take to the water and swim to the landing, a task fit for few except Indians. The storm continued for the best part of the night.

About five in the morning, I turned out to see what devastation had happened, and soon had the sad scene of desolation open to my view. As for our kitchen, that was flat to the ground, I mean all the weightiest parts; for as to the thatch and lighter materials, they were all blown as far as the cliff would suffer them. Not a goat, dog or fowl was to be seen. I then took the conch and gave a blast. This brought forth all our family one by one, and I was well pleased to find all well.

Bell observed that had it been in a cold climate, in all probability most of us would have died, as the rain penetrated through every place except my cavern. We soon found several of our poultry dead, and the poor old macaw also.

A few days after, old Quamino showed signs that he would not continue long among us, and on a morning Harry came in to me and informed that the old man was departed in the night, and that he went off quite easily without groaning in the least. The truth is that he certainly died of old age, unless the last tempest had hastened him rather sooner. Perhaps it was the case, for he wanted for no kind of indulgence or care while he lived among us. However, he lived long enough to be convinced that all white men were not of the like turn of thinking, concerning the poor Africans.

After Quamino's funeral was over, which we conducted after our usual mode, we began to fall on repairing, with all the expedition possible as to what was most needful; but Harry, Owen and Rory did the chief part of the business. And after all things were tolerably reinstated again, messmate Bell proposed to take a trip out to explore the coast, for we had not been abroad for above six weeks. Accordingly, we all got ready and stood out for our grouper ground, which was about two or three miles from the mouth of the lagoon. Now it happened, as I was sitting with the glass in my hand, I descried away to the north a wreck, as I judged. I gave the glass into Bell's hand to look, and he was of that opinion also, but it was so far northward that we could only just make it. We continued at our killick (anchored) for about two hours, and then returned home, intending to send the lads thither on the morrow.

It was not until the third day that Owen, Job and Rory set off on the discovery, well provided with all necessaries for the trip. Owen was to be skipper. I gave him strict charge that if it did prove a wreck and any people were saved, in that case to inform them that they might have all the assistance from us that lay in our power, let them be of any nation whatsoever, if he could but understand them; and if not, to bring us notice forthwith as to how matters lay. With this charge, off they went and we saw them full well out, from the hill.

On the third day in the morning they returned, and Owen gave the following account of the voyage. He reported that it has been a vessel of three masts, but that the main one was gone down low, as he termed it, but that she lay a great way out in a sunken reef, and was very low down in the water, quite in the sand; but there was nothing to be found except some of the sailcloth and an oar which was stuck up on end on the shore, right abreast of her, with a bottle made fast to it which they had got with them. They saw no people either dead or alive, only a vast smoke at a great distance along the shore, more to the northward. I sent down for the bottle, and when it was brought up, Mr Bell undertook to examine its contents. When he had gotten out the stopper, there was within it a small note to this effect in Spanish:

'The poleacre Isabella[42] shipwrecked this coast August 29 anno 1769. Andreas Lopez[43] capitain. Nine drowned and seven including the captain left this coast in their boat on the 31st for the north.'

So that she was lost on that dismal night I have mentioned above, but if she had guns or fired any we could not know, as the wind was so strong and she was also too far away for us to hear.

In a short time after, Bell and Owen with Rory paid a fresh visit to her, and brought home all the sailcloth that was left, and it came in a good time as we wanted sails for our boats very much, but, God wat![44] not at the expense of any poor unfortunate people whatever. Some of her rigging also they got, which was of good use to us.

Bell says she appeared to him to have been a good stout vessel almost new, as he conjectured by some of her things, especially her blocks, and burthened about 200 tons. A saint was painted on her stern in a white dress.

We had nothing of moment from this time until about 5 months after when the Indians came on a visit, or rather were deputed to find how matters went among us. We were not a little surprised to find out how they learnt the way, as they were all 5 strangers, and had never been here before. But Rory informed us that they had travelled by the trees and the sun, as he interpreted it, and by sleeps.

Harry well remembered two of them, and told me their names were Atory and Manabo. I desired to be informed from them how it came to be, that they had neglected us for so long a time. They gave for answer that their Old Men thought it not proper to send so soon after the great sickness had been among them, lest we being fresh, it should break out anew among us; and that they were bid to tell us now we were grown men in our place and had all we wanted, we could the better live without them, than in the days of our first coming there.

I then bade Harry to inform them that I should be glad if they would think Mr Bell and myself their friends in every respect, equal with all those who had been here before them. They then observed that they had been informed that I had the custom to mark down the names of all my good friends on stones, but had not done so for them. Upon this, Harry went and got four stones and gave them to me, then he gave me the name of each Indian, one by one, Atory, Manabo, Rabaito and Pannee[45]; and when they were all inscribed they were placed among the rest.

After this ceremony we entertained them after our old fashion. They tarried with us a whole week, and in a very friendly manner invited Harry and Owen to go home with them, on their return. But Owen declined the going, saying that he had been there once before and that he would much rather go to Jamaica, if he could but ever get the chance. N.B. This he spake in English and I am glad it so happened; otherwise their backs would have certainly been up on account of his disdainful speech, but they parted in good friendship with us all.

And when they were gone, I concluded to have a serious conversation with Master Owen, for now I began to think on the matter in a more serious light. But after what way to treat it, I was yet a stranger, therefore determined in my mind to hold a conference with messmate Bell as to the point in hand – that to obtain the booby a white wife where we were situated, was next to impossible, and then what white girl could be so procured so indelicate as for to contaminate with an Indian?[46] And even this could not be obtained, exept by sending him off with the next Spaniard who should by chance touch[47] here, which might happen when God only knew. And then again, should he make any proposals to a Spanish girl, he must first be baptised a Catholic, and that would never go down well with me.

Some time after, Mr Bell and I being abroad in the woods, he observed to me, that he took notice that I was not so cheerful as usual.

I told him Owen gave me much uneasiness on account of the strange humours he gave himself of late.

In regard to that, he knew it was quite out of my power or anyone else's as we were situated, he knew. '*Oh, leave the whole matter to me*[48], *and I shall take a course with him that shall succeed, I'll warrant you.*'

'*You do me a very kind deed, indeed, my good friend,*' I answered, '*if you succeed, for I am truly too proud to let him see how much concern it gives me. Yet I love him as becomes a father, but not to madness, dear friend. Perhaps were he where white women are to be got at, what money I could give him might induce some giddy girl to think him fair enough, for a time. But such connections are of short duration.*'

After this, I heard no more of the matter for some months, and Owen seemed to be rather more sprightly than he used to be. But it chanced to come about, on the carpet among the women one day, when Bell's wife said she hoped soon to see Owen, now he was back from Jamaica[49], married to one of her own sort of women.

'*How so?*' said I.

'*Oh, ask my man and he will tell you all about it,*' said she.

I was now quite impatient to have a talk with Bell, and asked my girl what she knew of the matter, but she said she knew no more than that Mr Bell had quite cured Owen of the white red women, as she understood it, and if I asked Owen, to be sure he would confess the matter. But I rather chose to have it from Bell at the first convenient opportunity.

Soon after, messmate Bell and I being down striking fish together, I asked him how the affair between him and Owen went on.

'*Oh, swimmingly,*' said he. '*He is as much off the idea now, as on before. You remember the time Owen and I made a march, after the flamingos? It was then when I had him alone from all the rest with me. I began with observing that, "Harry, you said you much wished to be in Jamaica, for there you could soon obtain a white red girl for a wife," but that he was mistaken in that point. "As how?" he said. I told him the women in Jamaica were all white, yellow or as black or old Quamino was; that it was in England where these charming white red girls lived. But there was one great secret I should tell him which, when he knew, would make him not so mad about my countrywomen.*'

That raised his curiosity at once, and he desired to know the secret..

'*Well then, Owen,*' said I, '*it is a thing you would never pass by, I am sure. It is this – should any girl be so mad as to marry you, a black man, the other girls would poison her soon, out of madness that she would disgrace herself so much, because it is what the white women never do at all; and perhaps poison you if they get the opportunity.*'

Upon my saying these last words, he hung down his head with his face to the ground, and said not one word for two or three minutes. When breaking silence as if from a trance, he said, '*My own colour for me, Master Bell. There is enough of them would have me for the love of my dear mother and father. I shall try to love one of them, and make myself as easy*[50] *as I can. I need not go out on the Great Water to look for a wife to get poisoned, for then I would certainly kill the one who did it, and I should not like to do such things.*'

'O ho, my lad,' said I, 'they would hang you for that up to a tree, and leave your flesh for the eagles to devour.'

'Well, say no more, good Norman. I don't want to talk any more upon the matter, and I find he is now quite gone back to his old humour, by Harry's account.'

About this time, I think it was, we had a shock of an earthquake, which lasted fully half a minute, about midnight. It was attended with a noise like that of a cart shooting rubbish; and my wife complained of a sickness in her stomach caused by it. What was very remarkable, all the ducks, geese and fowls began to make a great noise in their different ways, but on a new alarm of a much greater kind, they all became silent. And at this time messmate Bell and Owen came in; they called to know how it went with us. I got up and asked them what had happened, when they said they knew not, except that the old dead Cedar tree had fallen down by the shock of the earthquake, and on going to the place they found it so. It had fallen athwart our way up the hill or lookout, and broke down another tree which stood opposite, of a smaller size. This kept us all awake for the rest of the night; and on the morrow the lads fell to, cutting away all its branches to clear the road up the hill, and to chop it asunder for a pass.

While they were about this work Bell and I went on the look, but such swarms of butterflies of a new sort were to be seen all through the woods, that it was surprising to behold. These were not large; they were pale red, and disappeared in less than a week, so there was not a butterfly to be seen. Our Indians said that it proved there would be a great heat, for the time was coming. This was, as I think, about March.

While we were thinking one day, on the various circumstances of our lives, and how lonely we dwelt, sequestered from the society of Europeans, out of knowledge of all trade and what the busy world was about, our young boys came out of breath from the hill, and told us that all the sea was full of great fish fighting. This took the curiosity of the whole family, and soon the whole of us were on the hill. We found it as the boys reported. We saw a number of grampuses[51] sporting and throwing water up to a great height. While we were viewing them, messmate Bell started a notion that suppose that we should go out and try to catch one of them; it would yield us a fine, large parcel of oil for our burning. I could not help laughing at the proposal, asking him how he would proceed on his whimsical project.

'Have we not got a good length of rope[52],' said he, 'from the poleacre wreck which will serve us for a line? And you know we have a good harpoon. What say you, Harry, are you for a trial?'

'If brother is willing,' said he, so nothing would appease them but out they would go, and Owen one of the foremost, to be sure. But here I chose to interfere and said that he should not go, but that Rory might go with them, and that Owen should absolutely stay at home with me. To work they all three went, and got ready soon, and were off in less than an hour. But I thought it one of the most presumptuous undertakings Bell had ever taken in hand, but his will was for it, and the lads were fully as willing for the sport as he was for the profit. But little did I imagine what dire effects the cursed undertaking would work in the end. Oh, what may not a man prevent, would he give himself five minutes of pure reflection? But Bell was an older man than myself, and as I thought, needed not my precaution. How shortsighted are the young and heedless! Owen became quite crestfallen[53] on being denied going, and retired to his hut.

Much time I kept a constant lookout after them, and saw the boat at length out beyond the bay, in full pursuit of them. By this time it was become evening, and I kept my station until I could see no longer, nor could I for my life devise what was become of

200

them. I came down then from the hill, concluding that they had given them the chase round the Long Key to the southward.

When night had closed in, I gave order that none should go to sleep, but to make up a large fire and wait for their return.

Owen said I need not fear, for they would be back in the morning.

'Well, get me my pipe,' I said, 'and we will sit here until sleep sends us to bed, for I am by no means in that way disposed at present.' I sat musing and smoking until fair daylight, then with fresh ardour mounted the hill with Owen by my side, but could not see the least sign of any canoe, nor was there a fish left on the coast. What to think or imagine we knew not, but that something extraordinary had happened I greatly dreaded.

About nine o'clock Job came running down and said he saw two people with the glass, from the hill. Up I ran, and Owen after me, when out on the Long Key I saw two of them plain enough, but no boat. We waited with impatience to see them put off, but after two hours longer patience we had the grief to see both of them sit down as in no way concerned at all. I then left the children on the hill to keep a good lookout. While I was standing with the women about me, little Somer came down, and told us the men were both gone into the sea to swim over to the other side of the bay. I clasped my two hands together and followed the child up the hill, and by the help of the glass plainly saw them swim for the opposite shore.

On this I bade Owen to run down and get the other canoe ready, and off he went with all speed, leaving the whole family roaring and bellowing. We paddled away as fast as we could lay hands to the paddles, and in about two hours landed opposite the place they swam for. There we waited with eager desires until they landed. I seated myself on the beach, and in a melancholy mood looked on them as they drew towards the shore; but as to describe the condition of my poor heart at that time is beyond my power. When they got aground I sent Owen to meet them, for I could not go myself, being certain that something of a sad consequence had fallen out.

They soon joined me and with all the tokens of unfeigned grief the two poor naked Indians related their dismal story, while I sat looking at the earth with my head on my knees, and my arms clasped around my legs. Owen had his arms clasped together around his neck, which was a custom with him when anything extraordinary happened and was being related. This is what they declared to us as the true circumstances of their misfortunes.

That when they got out about half a mile from the end of Long Key, a large fish came bogueing[54] athwart them, and Harry got the dart in order to strike him, but Mr Bell insisted that he would have the dart and staff out of his hands, and that he gave it up to him as he knew I would have it so. That then Mr Bell advanced forward and sent the dart right into the fish near the tail. On that, the fish flew to the southward with great speed, and they were forced to heave out all the rope they had, with a large piece of wood fastened to the other end. They told me that they never saw Norman in such high spirits before, and that they followed the fish about a mile's distance where they saw him rise again. They came up with the log of wood, and hauled in several fathoms of rope, intending to cut it off lest the fish should carry it all away with him out of their reach again; and while they were doing this Mr Norman said to Harry, 'We will get as much of it as we can, while he is so still.'

He had no sooner spoken than the grampus gave a sudden commotion, and with one stroke of his tail he struck athwart the canoe such a violent sweep that they were all beaten into the sea. That for his part it was some time before he could draw his breath so as to have the power to look round him. He soon discovered Rory's head at about a boat's length from him, but they could not find Mr Bell, although he could swim so well. Thus they were certain that the fish must have killed him with his tail when the canoe was split. For she was split from one end to the other, and one of the ends quite through so that she was of no more use to them, on which they were obliged to swim back for the Key again.

'Say no more,' cried I, 'you have told enough already. When you are rested take me back home again. I have heard enough this day to last me months.' Soon after this we all four put away for home in silence, not a soul speaking until we got to our landing. The whole family soon surrounded us, and on me requesting Owen and Harry not to trouble me until I sent for them, a general howl began. I walked up to my cave with arms folded, and there threw myself at length on my bed.

Soon after this my wife came in to me weeping, and as I refused to speak, she began after the following manner with pushing me: 'Penoly, don't you be mad sorry. You can't break great canoes like great fishes. You won't go away from me and the children like Norman did, because you know you can't kill great fish very well, or else you would have let Owen go with them. I did love Norman, Penoly, indeed, but not as much as you do, because he was foolish mad to take himself away from his wife to go catch what he could not catch, because it was too strong for all men. The great fish has eaten him up, now down his belly for it. You must not kill me and the children because he would go, for you know I did not send him. So, then, get up and eat fish with me, and we will love you as long as we have days.'

'Full well do I know,' said I to her, 'that the man was well esteemed among them all, and I loved him as a brother. Can I then refrain from paying due respects to his memory? After I have subdued my grief a little, I will eat with thee. Until I give liberty then to be visited, I pray keep them all away, as I have some thoughts in my mind which must be composed, before I shall be myself again.' Upon that, she arose and left me in my cogitations, to go and console Janet, as I supposed.

And I fell into a serious rumination. What, thought I, have I to say or think that these things are not as they are permitted by the Great Author of nature, and for causes I know not nor wherefore? Shall I then pine thus because my friend has been removed from me quickly, as I may say, and before I had even reflected that such a time would surely happen to us, as it does to all friends after one way or another. I need not launch out in his praise. He was lent to me for a few years. I loved him, it was returned, he is called as my dear Somer was, and I am left. But why I am spared, or for how long is a profound secret, as it is to what end. Let me be resigned, then. For wherever I am situated on the globe of earth is equal to Him who created me; and sure I am if I live according to the divine ordinances He will enable me to bear up against all sudden alarms and casualties, let them come when they will…

THE TWENTY-FIFTH YEAR – OWEN LOOKS FOR A WIFE
June 15 1771 – June 14 1772

It is now several months since my sincere friend died[55], from which time I have not put pen to paper until now, being May of my 25th year, having rather indulged my melancholy humour too much, and finding nothing worthy recording, the time passing on in a sort of sameness every day. But I shall remark that Bell's wife has determined never to have another husband any more while she lives, as she says, and indeed she seems to be resolved thereon as my wife thinks, too.

My son Owen has been with Harry on a visit among our Indian neighbours for over two months, on the great business of getting him a wife, for his passion for European women has subsided a considerable time past. So that I am at this time of writing, in a situation almost as forlorn as I was twenty years ago, as to my own colour.[56]

I must not forget to observe that Rory the other day found a young faun in the back woods, and brought it home to my wife. She insists on rearing it, although I am not much for it. Yet we have seen no tigers now for years. Nor do I think they frequent our quarter, although our woods are grown almost as ample as ever. But it may be the constant fires and chopping in the wood, which may have caused them to abandon these parts. And indeed, their absence is the best company, as we have goats frequently breeding among us.

CHAPTER IX

THE DEATH OF LEWELLIN PENROSE,
AND THE JOURNAL OF OWEN PENROSE:

Twenty-Sixth to Twenty-Eigth Years

THE TWENTY-SIXTH YEAR – OWEN MARRIES, AND PENROSE
DECLINES WITH ILL-HEALTH
June 15 1772 – June 14 1773

August 20. My son has now been returned about a month, and has brought with him a young Indian girl, by name Bashada.[1] She is the grand-daughter of old Komaloot, and not above fifteen years of age, although so tall that she measures at least five feet four inches; so that if he could not obtain one of the fair ladies of his father's country, he has made it up in length of person, as to one of his own sort. But she seems to be of an agreeable temper and person, so I am at ease on that score – were it not for the misery I undergo as to the agony of my limbs, being so much tormented at times that sleep is a stranger to my nights. Nor can I but seldom hold a pen, or any other light thing in my hand, as such a tremor attends me almost constantly. Yet I can strike fish or do other laborious work as easily as heretofore. And what adds to my sorrow is that I fear I shall soon be past the power of writing unless my disease should abate, which I little expect for the nature of the disorder, which is fish poison; and I am sufficiently confirmed in it, as none tasted it except my girl America and myself, she being touched with the like symptoms but being young, may outgrow it. As for my part, I can take but little joy or comfort nowadays, but if my order continues to gain ground, my days cannot be many more, either here or anywhere else in this world ...

October 30. It is impossible for me to carry on my poor account any farther, being entirely helpless of my right hand and almost of my other, so that what may be wrote from this date must be carried on by my son as I shall direct him, or otherwise my brother Harry as they have both learnt to write tolerably enough. I find my memory much impaired also at times, by my disorder, yet my girl America seems to have but small symptoms of the poison left about her. How many times I have feasted on Red Snappers before, quite clear of all danger. Thus Death has his agents planted in every place, both by sea and land, and when the grand summons comes we must be gone, sooner or later as the Lord wills it. Therefore let me be content. Let me be dumb and patiently bear my pain, as I know that I shall be as surely relieved as that I began first to exist. There must be a last time for every mortal man ...

THE JOURNAL CONTINUED BY OWEN
My dear father has been so bad in all his joints for above six months that we have been forced to feed him like a child. But he is now getting better fast, for the pains begin to

204

leave him. This came about by the good help of our friends, who have been here of late, as they know many kinds of roots, good for several disorders. But my father has lost much of the feeling in his limbs and cannot speak plain enough at times for us to understand his meaning ...

THE TWENTY-SEVENTH YEAR – OWEN'S SON LEWELLIN IS BORN, AND LEWELLIN PENROSE DIES
June 15 1773 – June 14 1774

July 21. I had a son born and we carried him into the cave to my father and mother. My father would have the child in his lap, and asked me what name we intended for it. I said he should call it what he liked best, but that I should like to have him named Lewellin if he pleased.

'*Call him so, son*' said he, '*but yet I think one is enough of the name unless he is more fortunate in regard to his passage through this vale of tears.*'

About the middle of September, as my uncle and I were out in the bay fishing, two ships hove into sight in the east quarter. But as my father was now become quite past all his curiosity or care, for such things, we let them pass to the southward without stirring from our business, or giving ourselves any concern about them, but only told him of them when we got home.

'*I don't think, Owen,*' said he, '*that I shall ever see another sail with my eyes, unless it should happen that I may be carried up the hill by some of you, should another appear before I die. And indeed, Owen,*' said he, '*I cannot think the day of my death is very far off, if any stress may be put on dreams. I dreamed that I was become a very ancient man, and that I lived alone at the old plantation, and as I was walking along the strand by the Whale Point I thought I saw two men going on before me. At last they stopped, as though they were halting until I came up, which I did soon after, and to my surprise found them to be my two old companions Somer and Bell. I thought they were overjoyed at my joining them, and they told me there was a ship waiting for them at Boom Bay bound for Europe, and that if she did not sail that day, they would make interest with the captain to give me my passage – on which they were gone from me in an instant and I was left alone – it awoke me.*'

About three weeks on, early one morning, young Somer came and called me to come with him, for he was sent by my father to fetch me, and his own father (Harry) directly would die if I did not make haste to come. I soon judged what my brother would be at, and ran directly thither, where were my uncle Harry and most of the rest there before me, which grieved me, fearing my father would think I neglected him.

But he turned his eye on me, and said, '*Owen, come by my side,*' which I did, and sat down with him on the right. He then called to uncle Harry and he came, and seated himself on the left. '*Now,*' said he, '*give me your hands, and I have a few words to say to you both.*'

He then began, '*Remember what I am going to deliver to you. Love that woman at my feet, now on her knees, my children, and yourselves. I shall not see another sun arise. Lay me by your mother Luta. Preserve my Journal, and with care deliver it into the hands of the first European or white man who shall chance to touch upon this coast; and pray, pay him to deliver it safe, if possible among my countrymen.*'

We promised truly to observe all his desires and we went out, for we could not refrain our grief. About sunset mother sent for me, and said she believed my father was gone to

England, whereupon I called the whole family. When my uncle came in, he said it was certainly true. And although my father, in his lifetime, had used all the means in his power to wean the whole family of the savage customs, yet directly such a scene of madness and outrageous sorrow began, that the whole place echoed by reason of the crying. The poor dogs howled at a great rate; and I wished that very day would make an end of me also, when I saw how my dear uncle ran about tearing his hair and beating his breast, the women's hair strewed about at a most sad rate, the children screaming and throwing about brands of fire. All was madness and distraction, and it continued the whole night.

In the morning, my uncle came to me and said, 'Owen, come let us be men. We must put our troubles out of our sight. My brother said, "Lay me by Luta." We will do so, and then you shall be as he was among us[2]. But we will let your mother have it all her way, because we must love her, as he charged us before he died.'

The next day, after our hearts had wearied with throbbing, I told my uncle that we all gave up to his direction as he knew best, having lived longest with my father, and he said he would do the best in his power. So Harry showed Rory how to make the grave, and the body of my father was done up in some old cloth we had left among us. Then my uncle ordered that he and Harry would carry the body and that I would walk with my mother[3], the rest to follow after; and thus we proceeded to the grave. When we got there, they laid it down by the side and my uncle told us that he would do as he had learnt off my father, and that we all knew how and must say the same. He then began the Belief and we ended with the Lord's Prayer all together.

My uncle advised me that we ought to let our countrymen know of my father's death, and as Rory no longer seemed to have a desire to remain with us, we took the opportunity to send the news by him overland. He took his leave of us, about a week after, and returned home.

About three months later, there came two canoes of our folks to visit us. We entertained them after the old way my father had used to treat them. We were then asked whether we concluded to break up or to remain as we were. But we had resolved to continue to live after my father's manner before they came, and that was the answer they received.

THE TWENTY-EIGHTH YEAR – THE LAST ENTRY BY OWEN PENROSE
June 15 1774 -

We had not seen one sail for a long time, but about August as Job was on the hill he discovered a fleet of over twenty vessels all standing to the southward. I got the glass, but they were so far out that I could not make much of them, and we lost sight of them towards the evening …

CHAPTER X

Mr. Paul Taylor's Account of the Journal[1]

'Being mate of a large brig, one Captain Smith[2] commander, and lying at Havana[3] anno 1776, it chanced that we lay nigh to a Spanish sloop lately arrived from the Main[4], and as the mate of her happened to get a little acquainted with me by my speaking the Spanish tongue, he one day asked me on board to spend an hour or two, as he had something to show me. Accordingly, the next day being Sunday, and he the only being on board except an old Negro fellow, I went on board to have a little chat with him.

We had not been long together before he unlocked a cedar[5] chest, and got out a bundle of old papers and bade me look at them, saying they were English. After I had looked over a few leaves, I asked him how it came into his hands. He told me that he had it from two Indians who spoke good English, and one of them told him in Spanish that it was wrote by his father who had lived and died there, and that they would give me money enough, if I would swear to give it into the hands of some good English man as soon as I could, after we had taken in what water we wanted. They brought me over 50 pieces of eight, and I swore by the Holy Cross to deliver the papers. Now, as you are the first English man I have met with, if you will take it in charge, you shall have it. Otherwise I shall take it on shore and deliver it to some other, and if not, to the Governor.

I told him he might depend that for my countryman's sake I would put it in the best road for information I could possibly do, upon which he delivered me the Journal, and I offered him the acknowledgment of a doubloon. But he refused it, saying he should think himself a thief to do so; and I have preserved it through many dangers.

You will find when you come to read it, many curious accounts of things which I know to be matters of fact, although I never knew anything of the man. During the time I was out of employ at Charleston[6] I took it into my head to copy it all out and send it to you, as you live at this time in London. I think it may be of some service to you, and if so shall be proud of the little kindness I can render for the former services you have shown me.

If you do not get it soon published I shall dispose of the original at Philadelphia or New York, but not before I heard from you. N.B. You must remember John Waters, who formerly sailed with Captain Dean.[7] It is he who wrote it all out, just as the author spelt it, for I desired him to do so and he has been as careful as possible.'

May 2nd 1783[8] – New York

ADDENDUM

Thomas Eagles saw the manuscript shortly after meeting William Williams in the early 1780's. There is reason to believe that by this date the book was complete and handed over to Williams' benefactor.

The acknowledged *'first American novel'* was a didactic piece of work called *'The Power of Sympathy, or Triumph Founded on Truth'* by William Hill Brown (1765-1793), published in Massachusetts in 1789. It was long thought to have been the work of Sarah Wentworth Morton (1759-1846), and consists of a series of stilted letters recommending rectitude in male-female relationships, not in the type of novel format that we would recognise today. It was based upon fact, Perez Morton's seduction of his wife's sister, Fanny Apthorp, an act that in the 18th century was legally incestuous as well as adulterous. The novel insists that women must be educated to avoid a similar fate. Indeed, one of the advertisements for the book states that it is *'intended to enforce attention to female education, and to represent the fatal consequences of Seduction.'* According to Cowie and others, it was a poor copy of English novels, and noted for *'poor characterisation, loose motivation (and) graceless digressions.'*

The first English novel is Samuel Richardson's *'Pamela: or Virtue Rewarded'* from 1740-1741. Again this is an epistolary novel, told through letters written by the characters, again very unlike the above *'Journal of Penrose.'* *'Pamela'* has a similar storyline to *'The Power of Sympathy'* A maidservant is the object of desire of her master's son, who schemes to seduce her, but she protects her honour. Thus he is forced to propose to her and marry, to achieve his desires.

William Williams lived in America for over 30 years, and thus has a claim that his is the first 'American' novel, written in America by a man who spent the most important part of his life there, and whose descendants remained in the new republic. It is certainly the first American novel of any literary merit. It also seems to be the first anti-slavery book. There was an abolitionist tract in 1733 by Judge Samuel Sewell, *'Selling of Joseph'*, but the first anti-slavery work to reach any sort of audience was by the former slave Equiano, in 1789, *'The Interesting Narrative of the Life of Olauda Equiano.'*

For its pro-Indian and anti-slavery stance alone, Williams' book, *'The Journal of Penrose, Seaman,'* deserves to be widely read in America and Britain. The leading anti-slavery proponents in England were Thomas Clarkson (1760-1846) and William Wilberforce (1759-1833), both from a generation later than that of Williams. Slavery was banned from 1807, but the Slavery Abolition Act was not passed in Britain in 1833. However, in the United States the 13th Amendment was not passed until 1865, after the end of the Civil War, and not raified in Mississippi until 1995.

In the Journal, we see the story of a callow youth maturing into the wise head of an extended family, with ethics and values two centuries in advance of 18th century America and Europe. If we examine the period of the early American novel, it was said that American culture was parochial, and distrustful of any written expression that was not didactic. The great Welsh-American clergyman Jonathan Edwards (1703-1758) preached that reading novels was an indulgence leading to moral decline. If we place Williams' work against his times, it is not surprising that he could not find a publisher in his lifetime in America or England. With this background, the book is all the more a ray of light upon the culture and history of early America.

PART II

THE AUTHOR, THE BOOK, AND
THE LETTERS IN THE WILLIAMS COLLECTION IN THE LILLY LIBRARY

INTRODUCTION

'The amazing William Williams: Painter, Author, Teacher, Musician, Stage Designer, Castaway...The activities of this forgotten genius spread across almost every branch of American culture... he will stand out as a significant figure in the development of American culture' – James Thomas Flexner

'... most undoubtedly had not Williams been settled in Philadelphia I should not have embraced painting as a profession' – Benjamin West, Founder and President of the Royal Academy

This book has been written in two parts. The first part is the lightly edited novel – a fabulous factional story that has been generally ignored by scholars and publishers alike. The second part, the story of the book and its remarkable author, tries to contextualise the novel's value as a wonderful addition to the canon of world literature.

Williams has been called *'amazing'* and *'fascinating'* by previous commentators, and his life has mainly been constructed from four sources. The first is his novel, which Benjamin West averred was based upon Williams' living among the Indians, and contains dozens of contemporaneous references. Secondly we have the recollections of John Eagles as a youngster. Third we have what Williams, as an old man, told John's father Thomas, and finally Benjamin's West's recollections of Williams in America and later in England.

The elusive polymath, William Williams, was an utterly remarkable man, whose immense talents are shown in the following achievements, following his desertion from a ship in Norfolk, Virginia. Williams went to sea as a privateer, and was possibly captured by the Spanish, as recounted in his novel. He built America's first permanent theatre, and was America's first professional theatre scene painter. He had probably lived among the Indians of the Miskito (Mosquito) Coast after being marooned when privateering, perhaps marrying a Rama Indian and having two sons. His two sons by his marriage to a white woman in the American colonies, seem to have died fighting the English crown, possibly at Bunker Hill, in the American War of Independence.

Williams was *'one of the first portraitists of the American colonies'*. He inspired and taught Benjamin West RA[1] to paint, and showed him how to make a camera obscura for greater artistic accuracy. West was one of the founders of the Royal Academy in 1768, and in 1792 succeeded Sir Joshua Reynolds as President of the Royal Academy. West was the greatest painter of the American colonial period, and a close friend of King George III until that Hanoverian's descent into madness. West sympathised with the revolutions in France and America, and George III had been concerned about his democratic principles. Most people will know of West's most famous painting, *The Death of General Wolfe* at the taking of Quebec, and some will know his *The Death of Lord Nelson*.

Williams' son by his second wife Mary Mare was also a painter, and painted the most famous portrait of George Washington, known as *The Masonic Washington* in 1797. This was William Joseph Williams (b. New York 1759, d. Newbern, North Carolina 1823). He was a portraitist and miniaturist who worked in New York City, Virginia, Philadelphia, South Carolina and North Carolina. He added the Joseph upon his conversion to Catholicism in 1821[2]. He also painted the Welsh-American presidents John Adams and Thomas Jefferson. Thus the son of our William Williams painted the first three Presidents of the United States. This Williams also served as a lieutenant in the English army occupying New York City, and had been recommended by Richard Henry 'Light Horse Harry' Lee, Governor of Virginia, to paint Washington. William Joseph Williams also had a son, yet another William Williams, the New York wood engraver, printer and bookseller, (b. Framlingham, Massachusetts in 1787, d. Utaca, New York in 1850).

Our original William Williams taught painting and also musical instruments. According to Flexner, he conducted 'an evening school of the instruction of polite youth in the different branches of drawing, and to sound the hautboy, German and common flutes.' He was a friend of Benjamin Franklin and may have been commissioned by him to paint Benjamin Lay. A poet, he also wrote biographies in the lost manuscript, Lives of the Painters. Williams **wrote America's first novel – The Journal of Penrose, Seaman** before 1780, possibly between 1774 and 1775 or even earlier. (The original claimant was 'The Power of Sympathy' dating from 1789.) As Dickason has conclusively proved, the novel was written during Williams' 30 years in America. According to Jaime Incer (Nicaragua: Viajes, Rutas y Encuentras, 1502-1838), 'Williams was his own protagonist, self-taught, self-sufficient, with talent in the arts as well as letters. As a painter he produced more than two hundred oil paintings, but Penrose is his novel, cynically based on his own real or imagined experience.'

Williams' life has several huge gaps in it, especially during the thirty years or so that he spent in the New World. Dickason, by virtue of Williams' own navigational reckoning, placed Williams-Penrose as being marooned among the Rama Indians of the Miskito Coast. However, experts in the Rama culture and local geography, believe that if he was marooned anywhere, it was more southerly, on the Costa Rica coast. In the book, the Dutch seamen place their landing on the Nicaragua-Costa Rica border. This has more islands and caves such as those described, as well as the same rainforest ecosystem. This is an important caveat to Dickason's work on Williams, and perhaps the places described in the book may yet be definitely found. Even more importantly, the Miskito Coast was almost an English dependency in Williams' lifetime. He may not have been therefore so afraid of the Spanish, who did not penetrate to the eastern coastal strip of modern Nicaragua, whereas the situation was different in Costa Rica. Perhaps the use of the Spanish 'threat' was a device used to increase tension in his novel. Another problem is that the language used does not seem to have Rama connections – perhaps Williams stayed with a tribe which is now extinct, as his list of names does not seem to be replicated in Rama, Bibri or any of the few Caribbean/South American native Indian languages now extant.

However, the book has been left set amongst the Rama Indians, in line with Dickason's work. This is important. The place he named as 'Long Key' has been posited as the crescent-shaped Pigeon Cay[3], just two miles from the shore, an islet of pelicans, 11.47N and 83.40W. It is 15 miles south of Bluefields, the major Rama settlement. There is huge pressure upon the surviving Rama, based around Monkey Point and with the majority now squashed into the tiny Rama Cay, in the Lagoon 15 kilometres south of Bluefields, and just 45 minutes by boat. Pigeon Cay (Isla de Paloma) was a traditional place of shelter for their fishermen, but was recently sold for just $230,000. It was advertised as being the last private island in the area, and had a guest house, electricity, a well, a caretaker's house, 2 piers and a speedboat included in the price. At 7.2 acres, it exactly corresponds to Penrose's description of Long Key. Precious trees are being cut down, and it is being turned into a tourist resort.

The smaller Soap (or Soup) Cay can be seen nearby and seems to be his 'Bird Island'. The mainland beach described by Williams/Penrose with swamps, full of palms and small lagoons matches a site in Green Point (11.8N and 83.7W), 15 miles north of Monkey Point. There is even a small cave there which matches his description of his 'house'. One can contract a cayuco (motorised canoe) from Bluefields to visit Green Point, for $350. Alternatively, at Melvin's Inn in San Juan of the North, one can contract a cayuco to visit Monkey Point, Green Point, Rama Key Island and Bluefields for $450. (Rama Cay/Key is just over a mile from the coast, where Rama buried their dead at the Point of Departure.) The old Rama cemetery at Monkey Point has been disturbed by a land speculator, and high quality artefacts from there and the Torsuani River cemetery have been stolen and sold. Off Monkey Point (24 nautical miles south of Bluefields) is Palmetto Cay, and Monkey Point, at 11.35N is very near Penrose's idea that he was at 11.30N. At Monkey Point, the hills reach down to the sea, matching Penrose's descriptions, otherwise most of the coastline is low and filled with swamps.

Pigeon Cay, Island las Palomas, was advertised for sale on a website, www.tropical-islands.com, and the map on that website is shown in this book. It offered 'the future owner' 'world class fishing for tarpon, jack, snook, yellowtail snapper, kingfish, barracuda ... blue marlin...' and was sold to two Americans from Oregon in 2003. The same website sold Frenchman Island, Cayo French Man of 5.1 acres for $230,000 to a family from Washington DC in 2004. It is 60 minutes south of Bluefields by boat at 11.44N and 83.7W, and 2 miles south of Pigeon Island (see map taken off website). Two miles north of Pigeon Island is Guano Island, Cayo Iguana of 5 acres offered for $240,000 (11.53N, 83.40W). Isla de Venado (Deer Island) is another couple of miles to the north.

Rama territory included all the near-shore Caribbean waters, including Guano Cay, Cayo Paloma (Pigeon Island), Frenchman's Cay, Soap Cay, Booby Cay, Silk Grass Cay, Palmetto Cay, Three Sisters Cays and other small islands. In these waters, islands and mangrove-banked lagoons, turtles, manatees and crustaceans are being systematically wiped out for short-term greed and the ecology is being destroyed. How these islands, used by the Rama for centuries, have come to be sold to non-Nicaraguans, or even sold at all, is a mystery. A man named Peter Tsokos signed papers with the leader of the Rama Cay Community Council and rented the Pigeon Cays (all three islands) for $1500 for 30 years, and has sold those leases. The community knew nothing of the deal. Rama fishermen used to use the cays for shelter and fresh water, but now they are forbidden to land, being chased away by armed guards. Dr Maria Luisa Acosta has been active in trying to protect the rights of Miskito, Rama and Mayagna peoples, and her husband was assassinated by the driver and the bodyguard of Peter Tsokos. (The gun used belonged to Tsokos's lawyer.)

The stream of refreshing water that Penrose/Williams found may be Blackwater Creek. Possibly the incised stones he found could be rediscovered. Penrose also found huge skulls of loggerhead turtles, and the area one of their nesting places. There were English colonists, around 30 miles south of where Williams sets the novel, at the estuary of the Rio Punta Gorda (known as the Rio Rama in the 18th and early 19th centuries), but it appears that he knew nothing of them. (The footnote after Chapter 2 of the

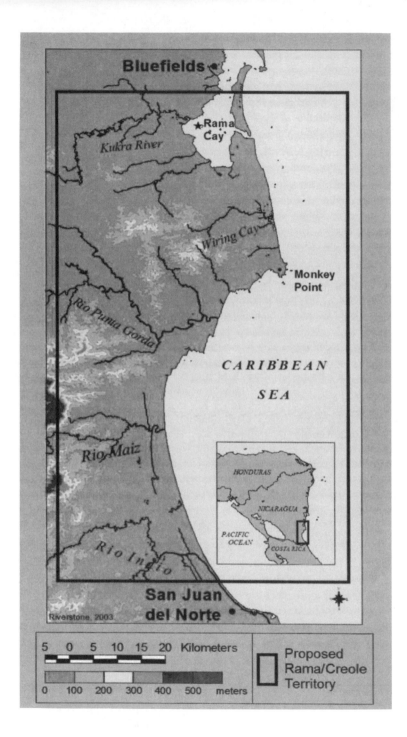

Bluefields

★Rama
Cay

Kukra River

Wiring Cay

Monkey
Point

Rio Punta Gorda

CARIBBEAN

SEA

Rio Maiz

HONDURAS

NICARAGUA

PACIFIC
OCEAN

COSTA RICA

Rio Indio

Riverstone, 2003.

San Juan
del Norte

5   0   5   10   15   20   Kilometers

0   100   200   300   400   500   meters

Proposed
Rama/Creole
Territory

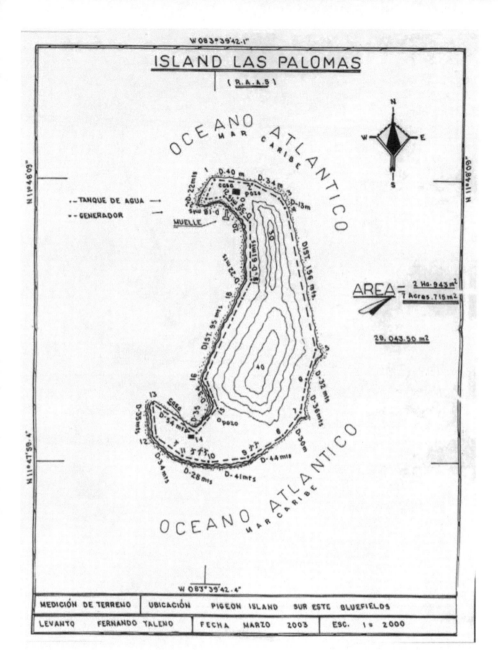

ISLAND LAS PALOMAS

(R.A.A.S)

MEDICIÓN DE TERRENO	UBICACIÓN	PIGEON ISLAND	SUR ESTE BLUEFIELDS	
LEVANTO	FERNANDO TALENO	FECHA MARZO 2003	ESC. 1 = 2000	

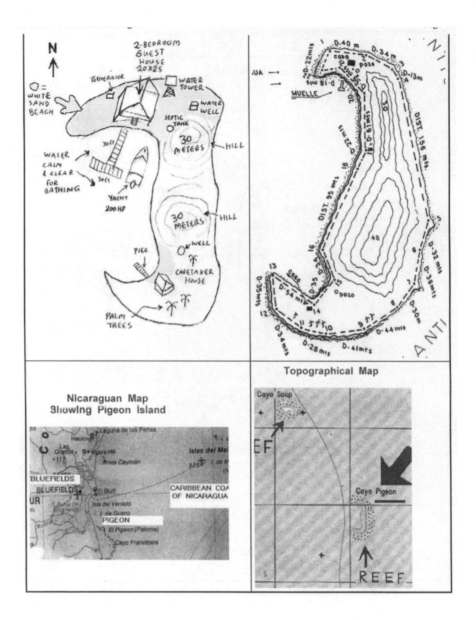

N

2-BEDROOM
GUEST
HOUSE
20×25

GENERATOR

WATER
TOWER

= WHITE
SAND
BEACH

WATER
WELL

SEPTIC
TANK

30
METERS

HILL

30 ft

WATER
CALM
& CLEAR
FOR
BATHING

30 ft

YACHT
200 HP

30
METERS

HILL

PIER

WELL

CARETAKER
HOUSE

PALM
TREES

Nicaraguan Map
Showing Pigeon Island

Topographical Map

Cayo Soup

EF

Cayo Pigeon

REEF

Journal demonstrates Williams' familiarity with Green Point and Pigeon Island).

Less than 60 Rama still speak their language (around 36 fluently), and the tribe is at massive risk of extinction. Hopefully those reading this book will go on to check internet reportage upon their seemingly hopeless plight against the forces of murderous settlers and crooked politicians. If it is the correct tribe, Williams admired the Rama people immensely and this publication may hopefully bring attention to their plight, and that of many other Native American peoples.

From the above, we can make the case for Williams being in Nicaragua for some time. We can also posit him as an enigmatic and enlightened polymath. But how can such an attractive character be forgotten? Is it because William Williams deliberately obscured his past? His life is like a series of Russian dolls. He certainly felt at home in America, but where was he born? Was he Welsh? He proclaimed this inside and outside his book, yet it seems that he was born in Bristol, the son of yet another William Williams, a master mariner. Our Williams died a tragic figure in Bristol, having lost three wives (four if we include the possible 'marriage' to an Indian) and two sons. He had lost contact with his other son, but was still seeking him a couple of years before his death. How old was he when he died? 67 or 81? He died sadly, and unknown, 'not with a bang but a whimper'. The detective story rumbles through the years, from Thomas Eagles through Benjamin West RA in the early 19th century, to Flexner in 1946, who announced that **Williams had changed American culture**, to Dickason in 1969 who published Williams' novel in its original form.

So what keeps attracting interest in this Welsh-American from Bristol? Is there anything more to be said or discovered? The New York Historical Society's 'Dictionary of Artists in America 1564-1860' (Yale University Press, 1957) tersely notes:

WILLIAMS, WILLIAM. *Portrait painter, decorative and scenic artist, drawing and music teacher, novelist. He was an Englishman who went to sea at an early age and after a series of adventures, later described in fictional form in his Defoesque novel "The Journal of Llewellyn Penrose", came to Philadelphia about 1747 and established himself as a portrait painter. Soon after, he gave the young BENJAMIN WEST his first instruction in painting. Williams was one of the builders of the first theatre in Philadelphia in 1759 and also painted scenery for it. In 1763 he returned to Philadelphia from a visit to the West Indies. He was still painting in the colonies as late as 1775, but by 1780 he had gone back to England, where he posed for a figure in WEST'S "The Battle of La Hogue". Not long after, possibly as late as 1790, he died in an almshouse in Bristol, leaving to a patron the manuscript of his novel and an unpublished "Lives of the Painters".*

So there we have it – an unknown privateer, music teacher, art teacher, art critic and collector, painter (whose portraits and landscapes still hang in American and British galleries), poet, biographer, theatre builder, theatre scene painter, socialist egalitarian, marooned on the Mosquito Coast, who wrote America's first novel. Is his story not worth telling?

CHAPTER 1

The Story of the Author

To quote Dylan Thomas, 'to begin at the beginning' is impossible with the life of our subject. William Williams' life is so complicated to unravel, that we can do no better than to begin with the grand picture, as given by Sarah Wadsworth in the *American National Biography* (1999, Oxford University Press). After this extract, we will take a chronological approach to Williams' life, beginning with the curious circumstances of his nationality.

WILLIAMS, WILLIAM (*June 14 1727 – 27 Apr. 1791*), *novelist and painter, was baptised on 14 June 1727 in Bristol, England, the son of William Williams, probably a mariner, and Elizabeth (Belshire?). As a boy Williams attended Bristol Grammar School, but his preferred classroom seems to have been a local artist's studio, where he began to develop his interest in painting as a profession. William's parents had more practical plans for their son, however, and when William was perhaps sixteen or seventeen years old, he was bound as an apprentice to a captain in the Virginia trade. This arrangement proved to be short-lived. Dissatisfied with his appointed career, Williams abandoned his position at the earliest convenience and fled to the West Indies.*

Many years later the renowned artist Benjamin West, who knew Williams intimately, quoted him as saying "After going the second voyage... when in Norfolk, in Virginia – to tell you the truth... I left the ship and sailed for the West Indies, where I hoped to be unknown, that I may make my way to some places - & accomplish my wishes as a Painter." West was of the impression that his friend was "ship-wrecked, & thrown into great difficulties, but Providence... preserved him through a variety of dangers." Although no documentary evidence has surfaced to corroborate this version of Williams' sojourn in the West Indies, the fact that his novel "Mr Penrose: The Journal of Penrose, Seaman" recounts vividly and with apparent fidelity to environmental details the adventures of a castaway on the Mosquito Coast so suggests that Williams may indeed have based the novel on firsthand experience.

In 1747, after two or three years in the Caribbean (of which possibly one or two were spent among the Rama Indians of Nicaragua), Williams journeyed to Philadelphia, where he earned his living as a painter of portraits, landscapes and conversation pieces. There he met West, at that time a precocious nine-year-old boy. Williams, the first professional artist West had ever met, encouraged the boy's interest in painting; lent him some books about the Old Masters, **including his own manuscript "Lives of the Painters"**; *and instructed him over the next decade in the art of painting. So significant was Williams as teacher and mentor to his young protégé that West later remarked that he would not have become a painter had Williams not come to live in Philadelphia.*

In addition to painting, Williams taught drawing and music in an evening school he established for the instruction of "polite youth." Somewhat later, in 1759, he painted scenes for the Southwark Theatre Company, managed by David Douglas, thereby becoming the first known professional scene painter in American theatre. The versatile artist took up pen as well as the brush during these years, composing poetry in addition to his biographical sketches of Old World painters. It was also most likely at this time that he began to write "Mr Penrose."

Shortly after settling in Philadelphia, Williams married "a respectable townswoman" (name unknown), with whom he had two children, but she died within a decade of marriage. In 1757 Williams reportedly wed Mary Mare[1], who added a third child to the family in 1757 (William Williams, Jr., also a painter), but she passed away four years later. In 1760 Williams journeyed to Jamaica and possibly Antigua, where he hoped to commission portraits from wealthy planters. The trip was apparently a success: during 14 months in the West Indies he is thought to have executed some fifty-four paintings. After returning to Philadelphia, Williams resumed his business of "painting in general" and again supplemented his income by teaching. Several of Williams' surviving canvases date from this period, including portraits of William, David and Deborah Hall, children of David Hall[2], Snr., the printing partner of Benjamin Franklin. One of Williams' most profitable undertakings, however, was the painting and ornamentation of ships for Philadelphia shipbuilders Thomas Penrose and James Penrose, quite likely the namesakes of Williams' protagonist Lewellin Penrose.

By 1769 Williams had moved from Philadelphia to New York, where he continued to paint and teach as well as clean and restore paintings. Several portraits from this period survive, including those of Jacob Fox[3], John Wiley[4] and his sisters, and Master Stephen Crossfield[5], as well as his exciting "Imaginary Landscape".[6] With the economic recession of the pre-war years Williams' business declined, however. The Revolutionary War brought additional hardships, including the death in battle of Williams' two sons from his first marriage. (Although Williams was a Loyalist, his sons fought for American independence.) Bereft and financially insecure, Williams returned to England in 1776, accepting an offer of patronage from a gentleman in Bedfordshire (identity unknown). When his patron died after eighteen months of sponsorship, Williams found himself alone and lacking any means of financial support. With only one friend in England, he paid a visit to his former pupil Benjamin West, by this time a prominent artist living in London. Williams declined monetary assistance from West but consented to work for him as a model. (A likeness of Williams appears in West's celebrated painting "Battle of La Hogue.")

Williams moved to Bristol, England, about 1781 and once again set up business as a painter. Among his works from this period are a local river scene titled "Hotwells and Rownham Ferry" and a triptych representing the birth, death and burial of Christ. Williams married a third time, but his new wife, a widow named Esther, died shortly after. Impoverished and by this time quite elderly, the painter, desiring a "place to die in", sought assistance from Thomas Eagles, a wealthy Bristolian merchant and patron of the arts.

Eagles befriended Williams, provided him with discreet but regular financial support, and eventually secured shelter for him at the Merchants' and Sailors' Almshouse of Bristol. Williams was a pensioner of this charitable establishment for five years, during which he continued to paint until his death in Bristol. His fascinating self-portrait dates from this period (intriguingly, X rays reveal that the palette and brush the subject holds are painted over an earlier depiction of a book and pen), and he evidently worked on a painting, now lost, with a theme from Mr. Penrose.

Although Williams' work is not widely known, his contributions to the literature and art of the colonial period are substantial. Williams was one of the first portraitists of the American colonies, and his novel "Mr. Penrose: The Journal of Penrose, Seaman" is **probably the first novel to be written in what was to become the United States of America**. Although only a small proportion of the more than 240 canvases Williams reportedly completed in the American colonies and West Indies have been identified, those that have been positively attributed to him bear witness to a significant artistic talent, characterised by a distinctive sense of theatricality and a penchant for fantastic, dreamlike landscapes. Williams' influence on American literature was minimal due to the fact that his novel was not published until 1815 and then only in England and in a completely restyled form. In fact, Williams was almost wholly unknown to literary scholars until the much belated publication of the original text of "Mr Penrose" in 1969. As a result, literary critics and historians have only recently begun to appreciate this early American tale of a Welsh sailor, "accustom'd," as he says, "to all Vice except Murder and Theft," who learns compassion and tolerance amongst the natives of Central America.

William Williams claimed to be a Welshman on several occasions, but appears to have been born to Welsh parents in Bristol. Dickason records that he was baptised in St Augustine's Church (but born in Wales?) upon June 14 1727, and that he died in Bristol upon April 27 1791. Williams is an extremely common Welsh surname. He could have been born at Penrhos, near Caerffili (Caerphilly) in South Wales. The subject of his factional work, Lewellin Penrose, stated that he came from near Caerphilly (Caerffili). The choice of the name of Lewellin Penrose for the protagonist of his novel is the mixture of an Anglicised version of Llywelyn[7], a traditional Welsh Christian name, and an Anglicised version of the Welsh Penrhos, which means 'top of the moor,' a common name for hamlets and farms across Wales. Strangely, in his version of the book, of which the original title was 'The Journal of Penrose, Seaman,' Thomas Eagles changed Williams' spelling of Lewellin and published it as 'The Journal of Llewellin Penrose, a Seaman.' Because of the relatively small number of surnames and Christian names in Wales, people were often referred to by their occupation or place of origin. Men by the name of David Jones, might be known as Jones the milk(man), Jones the coal(man), Jones the cobbler and so on. Equally a David Jones could be known by his 'bro' (neighbourhood) or address, e.g. Jones Llangatwg, Jones Penrhos, Jones Alltwen and so on. To compound matters, it was common in Wales for boys to have the same Christian names as their fathers, and so our William Williams in actuality seems to have been the son of William Williams, and also sired a son William Williams who also had a son William Williams.

Penrose, Williams' alter-ego in 'The Journal', states 'I was born near Caerphilly, in Glamorganshire, in the month of May 1725.' The farm and hamlet of Penrhos are just on the western outskirts of modern Caerphilly, and a Williams family held the farm as late as the 19th century. Church records for the district are held at Eglwysilan. Dickason claims that Williams was born in Bristol, with the added 'proof' that a search of the Egwysilan (Caerffili) records show no William Williams being born around this time. Dickason noted that 'The faded vellum parish registers in a mountaintop fourteenth-century church in south Wales (Eglwysilan) hold no record of any William Williamses born near Caerphilly between 1700 and 1730.' He used these two base dates, because both the Library of Congress and New York Public Library entries place Williams as being born in 1710, placing him in his mid-30's when he met Benjamin West. A letter by Evan Evans sent to Zoe King in 1857 (in the Lilly Library - see Appendix) reads: 'I was then allowed to make a Search in the Register Book of Eglwysilan in which parish Caerphilly is situated, although the Church is 4 miles distant from it, And also the Register of the adjacent parish of Bedwas, the Church of which is 1/2 mile off (to the east), but without Success. If Williams had reverted to the Scenes of his boyhood in his Journal some clue might have been obtained.'

However, because his father (from Penrose's account) was a mariner, Williams could also have been baptised in St John's in Cardiff, the city and port just 6 miles south of Caerphilly. We have the following potential Welsh claimants to be William Williams:

Father	Baptised	Parish
Robert	Dec 4 1708	Eglwysilan
William	Apr 4 1710	St John Cardiff
James	May 14 1710	St John Cardiff
Robert	Oct 6 1711	Eglwysilan
William	Apr 2 1711	St John Cardiff
John	Sept 6 1713	Llangiwg
Watkin	Jul 25 1714	Eglwysilan
Rev. William	Oct 14 1720	St John Cardiff
David	Dec 9 1726	Eglwysilan
Gronow	Nov 29 1727	Coity
John	Jul 6 1730	St Tydfil, Merthyr

We can see that Evan Evans missed no less than 4 entries for Eglwysilan (and also four potential claimants at Cardiff) for the period in question. Any of the three William Williams baptised in 1708, 1711 and 1714 at Eglwysilan could well have been the established artist who met West when aged 39, 36 or 33 respectively. Equally, the Penrose in the book could have been the William Williams baptised in Bristol in 1726. This final person might well have been born in May 1725, as is Penrose in the book, but not baptised until the following October, although baptisms at this time were often carried out soon after birth because of the risk of infant mortality. Thus Williams could have been born in Caerffili but baptised in Bristol. The earlier attributions of his birth in 1710 may also mean that he was the William, son of William, baptised in Cardiff in 1710. In the text, Williams writes (as Penrose) that his father was named Owen, a particularly Welsh name (originally Owain), like Llywelyn and its derivants, and that his sister was Betty. Williams, as Penrose, calls his children Owen (after his father), Morgan and Rees, all Welsh names, and his daughter, unusually, America. (Is this the earliest occurrence of 'America' as a Christian name?) Perhaps his account in 'The Journal', of running away to sea with his Welsh school friend Howell Gwynne from a new stepfather replicates his life. Williams said he went to Bristol Grammar School, but unfortunately no records of former pupils of this era survive.

Williams first came to Virginia 'on a ship commanded by Captain Hunter' according to Benjamin West... 'Between this time and his appearance in Philadelphia when I first met him (1747) was an interval of more than 20 years, which time I consider him to have passed in adventures related to the Journal.[8] If Williams went to sea as a boy of 12 years of age, and if we go by the age of his protagonist Penrose, born in May 1725, this would have been around 1737. Williams sailed under a Captain Hunter, engaged in the 'Virginia Trade', probably taking slaves from Guinea across to Virginia and returning (perhaps to Bristol) with tobacco. However, on Williams' second voyage, he deserted[9]. This is proven by his meeting almost two decades later, with Captain Hunter in 1755, when he apologised for deserting in Norfolk, Virginia, to sail for the West Indies.

A problem is that the fictional 'Penrose' shipped on the Harrington under Captain Hunter in 1746. Between 1731 and 1741 she made just 4 voyages to the East Indies, not the West Indies. If Williams had shipped on the Harrington as a boy, it would have had to be before 1731, which might take us back to the putative birth date of 1710. If we accept Dickason's birth date of 1727, he may have left home aged 14 in 1742, which gives him around 4 years in the West Indies before we find him as an established painter in Philadelphia, aged just 20. Benjamin West believed that Williams had spent around

20 years in the West Indies. The matter is complex.

Williams claimed to have been shipwrecked in the West Indies. John Eagles believed that he may have left behind him an Indian wife and possibly a half-caste son, as evidenced in his 'The Beggar's Legacy' article, and that the Journal was written to ease Williams' conscience. The years of the book cover the period 1747-1776, mirroring the exact times we know of Williams' residence in Philadelphia and New York.

In 1805, Benjamin West wrote '*From the year 1747 to 1760, my attention was directed to every point necessary to accomplish me for the profession of painting. This often brought me to the house of Williams; and as he was an excellent actor in taking off characters; he often, to amuse me, repeated his adventures among the Carribs and Negro tribes, many of which adventures were strictly the same as related in your manuscript of Penrose... He spoke the Negro and Carrib language, and appeared to me to have lived among them for some years.*'

We must now turn our attention to Benjamin West, who knew Williams for all of his life, and was instrumental in getting his book posthumously published, writing the introduction. West became one of George III's greatest friends, until his 'liberal' ideas and the War of American Independence distanced their relationship. West was a founder of the Royal Academy, and became its second president, succeeding Sir Joshua Reynolds. He is buried in St Paul's Cathedral.

One of the anomalies (of many) in Williams' life appears to be his first meeting with the young Benjamin West. In the *Columbia Encyclopaedia*, part of the entry upon Benjamin West mentions Penrose/Williams: '*West, Benjamin 1738-1820. The farmhouse in which he was born is still standing near Swarthmore, in what is now called Delaware County, Pennsylvania. According to the life by John Galt, which was written from information supplied by West himself, his early life was marked by many remarkable and prophetic circumstances. At seven years old he drew his baby niece in her cradle in red and black chalk. He received his first instructions in art from a Cherokee, and obtained from him his first colours, which were the red and yellow used by the Indians. To these his mother added a stick of indigo, and so completed the chord of what were then called the three primary colours. He shaved a cat to make his brushes, and his early artistic efforts so astonished a merchant named Pennington that he gave him a box of colours. He also gave West some brushes and a piece of canvas on which the boy painted a composition from three engravings by Guercino, also given to him by his admirer. This picture was still in existence, and was exhibited by the side of his large picture of 'Christ Rejected' sixty-seven years after it was painted. **At nine years old he burst into tears at the sight of a landscape by an artist of Philadelphia named Williams, and declared his intention of being a painter.** His father and mother were Quakers, but they and the Society of Friends at Springfield were so convinced of the greatness of the lad's gifts that after solemn deliberations they allowed him to adopt art as a profession. When eighteen years old his mother died, and he set up as a portrait-painter at Philadelphia, and afterwards at Lancaster and New York. Then, with the assistance of £50 from a merchant named Kelly, he went to Italy...*'
Indeed, Williams was the only painter mentioned by West to have 'moulded' him, and Williams' noted use of Romanesque towers and castles in his paintings often also appears in West's works.

However, how was this '*established painter*' only 20, as Dickason states that Williams was born in 1727? Williams was also '*recently married*' to a '*respectable townswoman*'. Where had Williams acquired his library of books and living as a painter, having spent a few years since leaving school as a sailor in the '*Virginia trade*' and in the Caribbean? Williams' '*Self-Portrait*' probably painted in the 1760's, at the height of his powers, shows a man in his 60's, not a man in his 40's. How did he know how to create and use a camera obscura when he first met West? How and where had he written *The Lives of the Painters?* Also, when Williams returned to Britain, he was known to Thomas Eagles, his benefactor, as 'Penrose' for a considerable length of time, not Williams, which makes the story even more confusing. Benjamin West told Eagles the true identity of Williams after Williams' death.

West was born on October 10th, 1738, so upon their first meeting, West would have been 9, and Williams 20 according to Dickason, but West remembers that he thought that Williams had spent around 20 years with the Indians, after coming to Virginia. Assuming Williams went to sea aged 12-14, Williams thus would have been around 34-36 when he first met West. West wrote to John Eagles in 1805, '*Perhaps I am the only person in existence who can give any account of Williams' life and manners. He first came to Virginia on a ship commanded by Captain Hunter. Between this time and his appearance in Philadelphia (1747), when I first met him, was an* **interval of more than twenty years, which time I consider him to have passed in the adventures related in the Journal.**' West had also written to John Eagles' father, Thomas: '*From the year 1747 to 1760, my attention was directed to every point necessary to accomplish me for the profession of painting. This often brought me to the house of Williams, and as he was an excellent actor in taking off character; he often, to amuse me, repeated his adventures among the Indians, many of which adventures were strictly the same as related in your manuscript of Penrose, as was his description of the scenery of the coasts, the birds on them, in particular the Flamingo Birds, which he described, when seen at a distance, as appearing like companies of soldiers dressed in red uniforms. He spoke the language of the savages, and appeared to me to have lived among them for some years. I often asked him how he came to be with them; he replied, he had gone to sea when young, but was never satisfied with that pursuit; that he had been shipwrecked, and thrown into great difficulties, but Providence had preserved him through a variety of dangers. He told me he had imbibed his love for painting at a grammar school in Bristol, where his greatest delight was to go and see an elderly artist who painted heads in oil, as well as small landscapes.'*

In the chapter upon Benjamin West in 'America's Old Masters', a friend of West's father's named Pennington invited Benjamin to visit him in Philadelphia. '*The little boy had no sooner looked at the harbour and seen his first big boats than he demanded some painted and canvas. While his host watched in awe, he slapped off* "*a picturesque view of a river, with vessels on the water and cattle pasturing on the banks.*" *Word of the prodigy of Pennington's sped quickly through the provincial capital; a rich merchant who had just had his portrait commissioned commanded the artist, William Williams, to show it to West. Thus the boy obtained his first view of a painter not himself and a painting not his own.*

The transports of delight he went into before Williams' stiff canvas enchanted the painter into inviting the lad to his studio. It was the most exciting place West had ever seen, for not only did it smell of paints, not only were there canvases against the wall, but Williams was a character to delight any small boy's heart. He had been captured by Indians.... That Williams was an effective storyteller we may be certain, for in his old age he wrote The Journal of Llewellin Penrose, a vivid tale very like Robinson Crusoe but based on his own experiences among the American Indians.

Williams could turn from tales of adventure to another subject just as exciting; he would talk of art. "*He told me that he had imbibed his love of painting when at grammar school at Bristol, where his greatest delight was to go and see an elderly artist who painted heads in oils, as well as small landscapes.*'

From Flexner (Chapter 8, '*Triumphs of Naiveté*'), we read: '*They rushed West off to Philadelphia and introduced him to William Williams, a professional painter. This august personage (aged 20?) joined the conspiracy of enthusiasm. Far from lecturing the child on the complexities of art, he received him as a colleague, and soon the two were chattering about the pictures with the same naïve excitement. Perhaps Williams was trying to make up for the discouragements of his own early career.'...*

'Having lent him books on Old World art, Williams sent his prodigy on his way with his head spinning.'... 'Concerning his childhood visits to Williams' studio, West remembered, "I saw some cattle pieces and admired them, and inquired how he could paint them so accurately." Williams replied by handing West a camera obscura, a device for throwing a miniature image on the back of a darkened box. The lad made one for himself. "My delight was then to go to farmyards, and by means of my camera, draw the cattle, etc." His Landscape with Cow (c.1749-1752) shows the result of such an experiment.'

Another version of Williams' first meeting with West is given by Galt, West's biographer: *'Samuel Shoemaker, an intimate friend of Mr Pennington, one of the principal merchants of Philadelphia, happened to meet in the street with one Williams, a Painter, carrying home a picture. Struck by the beauty of the performance, he enquired if it was intended for sale, and being told that it was already disposed of, he ordered another to be painted for himself. When the painting was finished, he requested the artist to carry it to Mr Pennington's house, in order that it might be shewn to young West. It was very well executed, and the boy was so much astonished at the sight of it, that his emotion and surprise attracted the attention of Williams, who was a man of observation, and judged correctly in thinking that such an uncommon manifestation of sensibility in so young a boy, indicated something extraordinary in his character. He entered into conversation with him, and enquired if he had read any books, or the lives of the great men. The little amateur told him he had read the Bible, and was well acquainted with the history of Adam, Joseph, David, Solomon, and the other great and good men whose actions are recorded in the Holy Scriptures. Williams was much pleased with the simplicity of the answer; and it might have occurred to him that histories more interesting have never been written, or written so well. Turning to Mr Pennington, who was present, he asked if Benjamin was his son; advising him at the same time to indulge him in whatever might appear to be the bent of his talents, assuring him that he was no common boy.'*

Edward Pennington (1726-1796) was the wealthy merchant son of a mayor of Philadelphia. He married into another notable family, wedding the sister of Samuel Shoemaker (1726-1818) the treasurer of Philadelphia who became mayor in 1769-1771. The British occupied Pennington's *'great house'* during the War of Independence from 1777 and 1778. Galt continues: *'The interview was afterwards much spoken of by Williams, who in the mean time lent him (West) the works of Fresnoy and Richardson on Painting, and invited him to see his pictures and drawings. The impression that these books made on the imagination of West finally decided his destination. He was allowed to carry them with him into the country; and his father and mother, soon perceiving a great change in his conversation, were referred to the books for an explanation of the cause.'* Shoemaker was a Loyalist and fled the War of Independence, befriending Benjamin West in London.

A final account of this fateful meeting is given in Alberts' 1978 biography of Benjamin West: *'Before the work (West's landscape) was finished, Samuel Shoemaker, "an intimate friend of Mr. Pennington," came to see the nine-year-old prodigy at work. He said that a few days before he had met a stranger on the street carrying an oil painting. He introduced himself, asked to see it, and found it to be "a landscape of considerable merit, and painted by the person in whose hands the picture was." The artist's name was William Williams. He had recently settled in the city and "appeared to possess a powerful mind and a great love of painting."*

The author William Dunlap recorded that *'Benjamin West remembered him with gratitude, as the first man who put into his hands, when a boy, the first books he had ever read on the subject of painting, and showed him, in specimens from his own pencil, the first oil pictures he had ever seen.'* Intriguingly, William Joseph Williams, the son of William Williams and Mary Mare (More) instructed Dunlap in art from 1781-1782.

Williams seems to have married between 1752 and 1755, but we have at least four men of that name married in Philadelphia in that time. There were marriages in Christ Church to Mary Stewart (August 24, 1752) and Margaret Clare (June 12, 1755), and in the Swedes' Church to Elizabeth Jackson (1754) and Margaret Carns (1755). However, there were two other marriages recorded before Williams met West, one in 1727 to Ann Jones in Christ Church, when Williams would have possibly been 17, and another more feasible upon June 16 1740 to Margaret McGrew. We are assuming that he married in Philadelphia, but this may not be the case. For instance, David Williams was baptised in the Reformed United Dutch Church at Springfield, Pennsylvania upon May 22, 1741, the son of William Williams and Mary Richardson.

In 1755 West set up as a painter in Philadelphia, before moving to Lancaster in Pennsylvania (the oldest inland city in America) and then to New York. *'Philadelphia's pre-eminence extended into the arts. During the decade of the 1750s more than a dozen artists of prominence lived and worked in that city. Benjamin West began his illustrious career there and went on to become president of the Royal Academy in London. Among his contemporaries were James Claypoole, John Meng, Henry Bembridge, Pierre du Simiti`ere, and Charles Willson Peale.'* ('Censorship of the American Theatre in the 20th Century', J.H. Houchin.)

Also in 1755 Captain Hunter visited *'the Williams family'* in Philadelphia, after Williams had told him that he had deserted when a boy. Williams' account is as follows: *'After going on the second voyage… when in Norfolk in Virginia – to tell you the truth – I left the ship and sailed for the West Indies, where I hoped to be unknown, that I might work my way to some places - & accomplish my wishes as a Painter:- and after some years had elapsed I was able to come to this city'.* In 1756, Williams appears on the Philadelphia Tax List as *'William Williams, Painter.'*

It may be that Williams was already in Philadelphia as early as 1746. In *'Philadelphia: Holy Experiment'* (1945) we read *'John Meng, Matthew Pratt, William Williams, Benjamin West's first instructor, were among the earliest of Philadelphia's painters, and presently many more were added to their number.'* We can see from the list of West's contemporaries in Philadelphia above that John Meng was practising in both decades.

Williams would have left Norfolk, Virginia, shortly after deserting his ship, as it was a serious offence, and probably spent some time in the Caribbean before returning to a different state and a city where he would not be known. Williams said he had two sons by his first wife, who he had married possibly around 1747 when aged 20, but she died sometime between 1755 and 1757. These may be the sons which he 'lost' in the American War of Independence. Upon November 16, 1757, *'William Williams, Mariner'* married Mary Mare (born around 1740) in New York City. It is believed that this is our William Williams, although there were other mariners of this name living at the time. Williams and Mary Mare, the sister of the artist John Mare, had a son William upon November 17th, 1759. A daughter Mary seems to have been born some time later but died young, some time after 1761. The fact that their son became a notable artist probably confirms that his father was our William Williams, the Bristol-Welshman. It may be that Williams met Mary through her brother, the painter John Mare (1738-1804), as New York artists would have known each other very well at this time. In his will, Williams left pictures of two wives.

William Williams features in the story of the early theatre, as recounted by William Dunlap in his 1833 'History of the American Theatre.' He tells us that Lewis Hallam and his wife took a company to the New World called 'the American Company' in May 1752. Governor Dinwiddie gave permission for a theatre in Williamsburg, and Hallam's company performed their first play upon September 5th, 'The Merchant of Venice'. There may have been a performance prior to this in Annapolis, on July 13, but from September 17, 1753, the company was performing at Nassau Street in New York. The run closed on March 18th 1754 and the Hallam Company moved to Philadelphia. In April 1754, their programme began with 'The Fair Penitent' before they went to the West Indies, where Lewis Hallam died in Jamaica. David Douglass married Hallam's widow and took over the troupe.

Upon the return of David Douglass's Hallam Company of actors from Jamaica in 1759, Douglass decided to build a new theatre with new scenery in Philadelphia. With a blacksmith named Alexander Alexander, William Williams was contracted to build and decorate what was to become the first permanent theatre in English America. However, the Quakers and conservative elements on the council disapproved vehemently. Alexander had spent £300 on the new building. Flexner tells us: 'Instantly the Quakers, Lutherans and Presbyterians were in an uproar. In a reply to their petition demanding that a law prohibited so immoral a structure, Williams stated that he had painted scenery at a cost of over £100, a large sum for those days. Since he would lose his money if the theatre did not open, he was clearly not so much an employee as a backer of the venture. After the provincial government had ignored his plea and banned the playhouse, the bill was sent to England where it was repealed by King and Council...' Alexander and Williams had petitioned Governor William Denny on June 2nd, that 'unless Douglass were allowed to proceed with his season, he could not pay them and they were faced with ruin' (-Pennsylvania Archives, First Series, III, 659). Denny seemed to know, as he signed the bill which was passed by the Assembly in July, that London would disallow it.

On June 15, 1759, Philadelphia's Southwark Theatre opened. The famous David Douglass, as the manager of the Hallam Company, acted with his troupe, closing the season with 'Hamlet' on December 28th. Williams was the first professional theatre scene painter in America. Williams' scenery was 'probably the finest ever seen in the colonies,'[10] and was probably taken by Douglass on his company's travels, being used until the panels were battered and discarded. They may have even been used in Jamaica by the Hallam Company. Perhaps Williams was inspired to follow the actors to Jamaica, as many wealthy planters would want their portraits painted.

Between 1750 and 1758, Williams painted the anti-slavery campaigner Benjamin Lay (who died in 1759), but the original has been lost. Engravings of Williams' picture, by Henry Dawkins (an English engraver in Philadelphia) exist, however. Lay was a great friend of Benjamin Franklin, and it may be that Franklin commissioned Williams, as addended by Thomas Eagles in his notes on the Williams estate. However, Franklin's letter to his wife from London, June 10 1758, states: 'I wonder how you came by Ben Lay's picture?' Franklin had published an abolitionist tract by Lay in 1737, and perhaps Williams had painted Lay in order to sell it to Franklin or Franklin's wife, rather than being commissioned to paint it. Lay is holding a book entitled 'Trion on Happiness.' Trion was an English Quaker, who in 'The Way to Health, Long Life and Happiness' advocated the rural life, vegetarianism and temperance, and Lay had retreated to a cave to practise this lifestyle.

Robert Proud emigrated from England to Philadelphia in 1759, and was the Headmaster until 1770 at the Public Latin School of Friends. He published his 'History of Pennsylvania' in 1797-1798. In 1852, William F. Cogswell presented a copy of a picture of *Robert Proud* by William Williams, to the Historical Society of Pennsylvania. The note with the portrait states that Williams flourished 1710-1791 (not 1727-1791) and that he operated from 1746-1775. Where did this attribution, in 1852, of his 1710 birth date originate? Proud must have been painted at some time between his arrival in America in 1759 and Williams' leaving for New York around 1769.

In 1760 Benjamin West went to Italy, and Williams went to Jamaica and possibly Antigua in the West Indies for a period of time, given variously as 14 months to 3 years, painting 54 canvases there. Eagles noted '*1760 – Pictures painted in West Indies – 54*'. West moved to London in 1762, and remained there for the rest of his life.

On October 6th 1761, Mary Mare's father left the following will: '*In the name of God, Amen, I, JOHN MORE, of New York, mariner, being in a low state of health, I leave to my son John a lot of land in the out ward, nigh Freshwater, with the buildings, after his mother's death. I leave to my son Henry my other lot, with the buildings, after his mother's death; "And my son John shall pay to Henry as much as his lot is worth more than Henry's." I leave to my daughter, Mary Williams, $5, and the same to my grandson William Williams, and my granddaughter Mary Williams. I leave to my wife Mary all my personal estate, and the use of all lands during widowhood. I make my wife, and Obadiah Wells, executors.*' The witnesses were William Clarke (blockmaker), Charles Lugg and Elias Bonnel, and the will was proved on December 5th, 1766. This must be Mary Mare's father, with a son John, and a daughter Mary married to a Williams, and with grand-children named Williams and Mary Williams. However, in 1761 Mary Mare died, aged around 21, leaving Williams with probably three sons and possibly a daughter to look after.

Around 1761, Williams found regular work in painting and ornamenting ships being built by Thomas and James Penrose, the famous Philadelphia shipbuilders. West believed that the hero of the *Journal* was named after these employers, rather than after Penrhos Farm near Caerphilly.

Not long after arriving in London in 1762, Benjamin West was dining with Colonel (formerly Captain) Hunter from who had then settled with his family from Virginia. Hunter asked West how he came to the art of painting in Philadelphia. West replied '*I told him that it was by the acquaintance of William Williams – who had more enthusiasm for the Art than any person I ever met with. "What a singular event is" replied the Colonel. "I will tell you Mr West, what will surprise you as it did me. – When I went with the Governor of Virginia (Dinwiddie) as one of the Deputies to attend the Governor of Philadelphia in the year 55, to join the Governors from the other Provinces to hold the great treaty at East Town in Pennsylvania with the friendly Indian Chiefs: Mr Williams waited on me while I was at Philadelphia & informed me that when he was a Boy he had been bound to me when I was in the Virginia trade; but not willing to continue in that Service had absented himself from the ship while lying in Norfolk in Virginia, & went to the West Indies from whence he came to this city some years after – that he was married and settled here - & that he had taken the business of painting in general."*

"*I have waited on you Sir*" *said he, "to declare who I am, & if I can make you any recompense for leaving your service, I shall make it to the utmost of my power." "I told him that I had forgot both him, and the circumstance until his narrative brought both to my memory – that I was pleased to see him as well as with the principles of his visit. I frequently called to see him and his family while I stopped at Philadelphia, and introduced him to several of my friends* in that city. When he was on board my ship I often remarked him to be engaged in drawing, & soon distinguished him to be a Boy of no common capacity, and it was my intention had he remained with me to place him in my Counting-house at Norfolk, to better his situation in life. – But I was never more pleased than to find his respectable situation in Philadelphia, except this, which you have told me of being the person who kindled the latent sparks of painting which he then discovered in you, into that blaze with which it now appears in this country."

"I am obliged to you Col." I replied "for the compliment; but it proves how little we are awake to those events which till their development have been the cause of even producing revolutions: for most undoubtedly had not Williams been settled in Philadelphia I should not have embraced painting as a profession."

Mr Williams was a man of quick penetration, but his love of the Fine Arts became his most devout pursuit. Painting he cultivated as a Profession – Music as an amusement, & Poetry he often indulged himself in with considerable power: There was a piece of his Poetry addressed to me in my twelfth year (1750) – It was published in one of the daily papers in Philadelphia, & much admired, tho' no one knew who was the Author. On my preparing to embark for Italy (1760) he wrote me an acrostick on my name, which he sent to me after I had taken my leave of him – in which he predicted my future elevation in painting.'

One wonders if Williams was actually in America when his wife died around 1761[11], because he was only 'lately returned' from the West Indies in January 1763, judging from the advertisement he placed in the Pennsylvania Journal and Weekly Advertiser, January 13th 1763:

WILLIAM WILLIAMS Being lately returned from the West-Indies; desires to acquaint the Publick that he now lives in Loxley's Court, at the Sign of Hogarth's Head, his former place of Residence where he intends to carry out his Business vix (sic), Painting in General. Also an Evening School for the Instruction of Polite Youth, in the different branches of Drawing, and to sound the Hautboy, German and common Flutes, by their humble servant: William Williams.

N.B. Those Gentlemen inclining to learn, may by applying be informed of the conditions.

Also in 1763, on seeing a self-portrait sent home by West from abroad, Williams wrote to him, sending 'a complimentary copy of verses in which he was pleased to compliment me (West) very highly.' So now, according to Flexner, we find Williams was 'a painter and a novelist, a theatrical backer, a teacher and a musician, and that he wrote verses.'

Richardson and others believe that the Williams' Self-portrait was carried out between 1760 and 1770, and it depicts a man aged around 60, which would fit with a 1710 birth date for Williams. (A William Williams was married in Christ Church, Philadelphia in 1740). However, John Eagles and Dickason believe it to be his 'alms-house dress', of 1788-1790. Eagles later confessed that Williams looked younger in the picture than the old man he remembered. This is another crucial piece of evidence in connecting the right William Williams to the correct birth date. According to Richardson, 'Williams in fact wears the informal morning dress of an eighteenth-century gentleman at home: without his wig, he wore a velvet cap to protect his shaven head from the chill; over his shirt a loose, comfortable gown of silk or cotton called a "banyan", which came in with tea, "china", lacquer and other imports of the East India trade. These informal garments became so popular that in 1755 Harvard College had to forbid their use on commencement day, to assure a dignified ceremony. Before the mid-century poets and artists, such as Hogarth and Pope, were painted or sculptured in such informal dress. Following the turn toward informality in portraiture in the sixties, Copley painted several great Boston merchants in velvet cap and banyan; but the fashion seems to have disappeared after the end of the decade. The costume, the man's age, the vigour of the style, all suggest a date in the 60's for this Self-portrait, at the height of William's career, rather *than twenty years later, when he was old and broken in a Bristol alms-house.'* Intriguingly, radiographic analysis shows that he is holding a book in his left hand – perhaps he had originally meant to show himself as an author.

In 1766 Williams painted three full-length portraits of the children of David Hall, William, David Junior and Deborah. They are the earliest full-length portraits extant from colonial Pennsylvania. Hall had been Benjamin Franklin's partner in a printing business for 18 years, until 1766 when the partnership was dissolved because of Franklin's long absence in London. In this year, Hall formed a new printing firm, was publisher of the *Pennsylvania Gazette*, and owned a large bookshop. Williams painted the scenery for the Southwark Theatre again in 1766.

1767 saw Williams painting the companion pictures, *Woman with Book* (representing an Old Testament sybil outside a cave), now in the Deerfield Academy, and the privately owned *Woman with Hour Glass and Skull* (depicting the Magdalene in her cave). Also in 1767, David Douglass's company produced the first tragedy by an American-born playwright, Thomas Godfrey, at the Southwark Theatre. The *Prince of Parthia* was also the first play by an American author to be performed by professional actors. Philadelphia's historians agree that Williams painted the sets.

Around 1767 to 1768 Benjamin West was introduced to George III, who gave him a commission. He was one of four nominated to draw up the plan for the Royal Academy, and was one of its original members nominated by the king. He exhibited *Regulus* at its first exhibition in 1769, and his tremendously popular *The Death of Wolfe* in 1771, and was appointed historical painter to the king in 1772. (He refused a knighthood, and became President of the Royal Academy in 1792, holding the post, with a brief intermission, until his death).

1769 saw Williams settled in Batteaux Street, New York and advertising in the *New York Gazette and Weekly Mercury* (May 8th), offering *'painting in general, viz. History, Portraiture, landskip* (landscape), *sign painting, lettering, guilding* (gilding) *and stewing smalt'* (- a method for colouring substances a cobalt blue.) His trade sign was Rembrandt's Head hanging outside the house - he had used the sign of Hogarth's Head in Philadelphia. There is a note by Thomas Eagles stating *'1769 – Pictures painted in New York 87.'* Of these, four signed and dated in the 1770's are known to survive. Eagles states that he painted 87 canvases in New York and *'amongst 100'* in Philadelphia, with the owner of each specified, plus 54 in the West Indies. If so, he must have been phenomenally busy in Jamaica and thereabouts, unless the tally includes theatre scenes.

In 1771, according to Flexner, *'Williams introduced into America a European fashion which showed even the courts were not immune to the movement of intellectual tides. In France, the aristocrats were playing at being commoners. Great nobles, ostentatiously turning their backs upon the throne room, asked to be depicted with their families in little genre scenes of domestic life. Moved by the same Zeitgeist, English painters, conspicuously John Wootton and Hogarth, produced "conversation pieces." Williams' John Wiley, his Mother and Sisters shows the family sunning themselves in their New York garden, while in the background is a charming landscape said to represent lower Manhattan Island.'* Williams' conversation piece, *The Wiley Family*, measures around 4 by 3 feet. To quote Richardson, *'with the skill of a scenic designer, the artist creates an impression of ancient dignity and gentility.'*

Williams' artistic style has been described by William H. Gerdts as *'although somewhat more primitive than that of his much more prolific contemporaries'* (Blackburn and Wollaston), it is *'a much livelier version of the rococo and far more personal.'* Williams' *Imaginary Landscape* is now in in the Newark Museum. This small oil fantasy on canvas is the earliest extant seascape in the British colonies. Like the Benjamin Lay caricature, it is very different from his other canvases. It may possibly be a representation of the English capture of Havana where Williams/Penrose states he was imprisoned. The sea features in several of Williams' surviving colonial paintings. In *William Hall* there is a ship and lighthouse, and ships feature also in *Jacob Fox*, *The William Denning Family*, *Imaginary Landscape* and *Portrait of an Unidentified Man*. Caves feature in *Mary Magdalene* and *Old Testament Sybil*. *The William Denning Family* of 1772 is included in Eagles' list of Williams' paintings, and in the distance is Lower Manhattan Island, Trinity Church and the buildings of Wall Street, where the Dennings lived[12].

In 1774 *Jacob Fox* was painted and is now in the Colonial Williamsburg Collection. It shows the young Fox holding a flageolet, with ships in the distance. 1775 saw the canvas *A Gentleman and a Lady in a Landscape*, which is either by William Williams or his son William Joseph Williams. From 1775 we have *A Gentleman and his Wife* (now in a private collection), and *Conversation Piece* (now in The Henry Francis du Pont Winterthur Museum). This was possibly painted just before Williams returned to England, but there has been a suggestion that the lady could be the English comedienne Kitty Clive (- in Gerdts' article, posited by Professor Highfill). Kitty Clive (1711-1785) was one of David Garrick's leading ladies.

According to West, Williams' first two sons, '*being born in Philadelphia, they soon became attached to America & took up arms with thousands of other youths to join her Armies, and were killed in some of the battles.*'[13] Williams told Thomas Eagles that they had both been killed at the Battle of Bunker Hill (outside Boston, June 17, 1775), but they are not among the list of known casualties. Two William Williams were among the officers of the Pennsylvania regiments at the battles of Brandytown and Germanstown. Another William Williams was declared a traitor in Philadelphia for aiding General Howe when he occupied the city in 1777. Williams himself remained a Loyalist.

Around 1775, Williams painted *Master Stephen Crossfield*, son of Stephen and Mary Crossfield of New York City. Crossfield was around ten years old at the time. It seems that Williams was now struggling for commissions, as the War of Independence was looming closer. The painting was only acquired and provenanced as late as 1965 by the Metropolitan Museum of Art in New York, and there are probably other paintings by Williams extant or undiscovered in private collections. None of his West India paintings are known from this time.

In 1776, General Howe's army pushed Washington's forces out of New York City, and Manhattan Island became the English headquarters in its attempts to suppress the Revolution, until its forces withdrew in 1783. It seems that Williams' sources of income had dried up by this time. West noted that in 1776 '*Mr Williams finding himself advancing in years - & much dejected at the loss of his sons, & the revolution of families and things... availed himself of a friendly proposition made to him by an English gentleman returning from America, to embark with him for England – to reside under his roof in Bedfordshire, & to paint there for his amusement for the remainder of his life.*' According to Dickason, Williams would have only been 49 years old at this time – would a gentleman take on someone who might live to 90? Also, his son William Joseph Williams was probably about 17 at this time (born November 1759) – why did Williams leave him in a country at war? Arriving in London in 1776, Williams made straight for West's home. He introduced West to his patron, and then headed for Bedfordshire. However, about 18 months later, the gentleman died, so Williams was forced to move to London to make a living. We still are as yet unaware of the name of the Bedfordshire gentleman.

In 1779, matters were improving back in New York, for Williams' 20 year-old son placed the following advertisement upon March 6 in James Rivington's *Royal Gazette:'William Williams, Portrait painter, Acquaints the Ladies and Gentlemen, that he has taken a room at Mr. Griswold's, No. 163, Queen Street, next door to Mr. Joseph Totten's, where he carries on the business of Portrait painting in all its branches, on the most reasonable terms.'* Around 1781-1782 he gave instruction to William Dunlap, as noted earlier. Dunlap (1761-1839) became a noted painter, producer, playwright, writer and actor.

By 1780, Williams was back in London, posing for West's *The Battle of la Hogue,* which was exhibited in that year. He told West that he was collecting 'the heads of *painters.'* When he stopped calling upon West, West made enquiries and found out that Williams had gone to Bristol to claim some provision that he was entitled to, as *'he was very poor and had almost lost his eyesight.'* (This is a compelling reason why his *Self-Portrait* was not painted in Bristol, as Dickason believes). In *The Beggar's Legacy,* Eagles noted that Williams' likeness was extremely accurate. To the author it shows a man nearer to 70 years of age than the 53 posited by Dickason. (However, Eagles was remembering him from the period 1786 to 1791, when Dickason's 'Williams' would have been aging from 59 to 64.)

West noted that Williams' *'greatest wish was to be a Painter; but in that he was disappointed.'* In London, Williams spent *'more than two years in daily pursuit collecting portrait prints of eminent painters',* according to West. It seems that he needed them to illustrate his old manuscript *'Lives of the Artists'.* To this effect he was in constant contact with Nathaniel Smith, at Rembrandt's Head, a specialist in engraved historical portraits. Williams was so close to Smith that West solicited a (seemingly lost) memoir from his son, John Thomas Smith, who when a boy *'saw, & knew more of Williams during his stay in London.'* West noted that soon after painting *The Battle of la Hogue, 'I lost sight of him, & becoming apprehensive he was dead, on my making enquiry of Mr. Smith, what had become of him – he informed me that he was gone to Bristol, but for what purpose he did not know.'*

By the time of his death, Williams had collected enough prints (probably many from Nathaniel Smith) to fill *'two large Folio Volumes entitled Heads of Illustrious Artizans.'* There is a mystery about the lost *'Lives of the Artists'* – had Williams finished it by the time he met West in 1847? If so, he **must** have been born around 1710, not 1727. In 1805 West told Eagles that it was Williams' manuscript of the lives *'of the great Masters of painting'* that determined his ambition to be a painter. *'He first lent me The Lives of the Painters, which lighted up a fire in my breast which has never been extinguished, and confirmed my inclination for the art.'* A footnote by Thomas Eagles reads *'This book, in Williams' handwriting, which was then lent to West, is now in my possession.'* (Author's underlining).

In 1810, Eagles again mentioned the lives *'of the great masters of painting'* that Williams gave him. Did he mean the works by Charles du Fresnoy (*The Art of Painting*) and Jonathan Richardson (*An Essay on the Theory of Painting*), that Williams had given him? In 1857, it was still in the possession of his son, John Eagles. Rather believes that West reinvented himself for his biographer, Galt, by dropping the reference to Williams' *Lives,* much as he did with his information upon the camera obscura. In 1805 West had told Eagles that Williams showed him his *'secret... a small box which prov'd to be a camera... he shewed me the construction of it'* and the 9 year-old West *'went home and was not at peace until I had made one for myself'.* West later told his biographer, Galt, that he had invented it by himself aged 16. Benjamin West had been appointed President of the Royal Academy in 1792. The British Institution was founded in 1805 to promote indigenous art, with West a founding member. He set a precedent in 1811 when patrons spent the enormous sum of £3,000 for his 'Christ Healing the Sick in the Temple' for the British Institution. This was 'considered as the commencement of a national gallery' (Farington Diary, ed. Garlick et al, March 15, 1811).

About 1781, Williams was in Bristol, opening a studio at 29 Clare Street. He painted landscapes and religious subjects, and a business card for William Williams, Portrait & Landscape Painter, is in the Bristol City Archives. The completion date of the 'Journal of Penrose, Seaman' is signed by the alleged carrier of the book, Paul Taylor, upon May 2nd, 1783, in New York. This may well be the date when Williams completed the manuscript, or more likely it was completed before he left New York, and this note was addended in Bristol. The book draws to an inconclusive end – it appears that Williams was unsure how to finish it, and the note is in another hand, probably to give it the appearance of truth. The Journal actually ends in 1776, the year he left New York for London (beginning with the year 1747 when we first trace him in Philadelphia, meeting Benjamin West). It seems to this author, from the internal evidence of the book, with its many parallels to what was happening in the real world, that the book was written in America.

From around 1784, there exists his painting of Bristol's Hotwells and Rownham Ferry. In 1785 the Bristol Journal announced a fee-paying exhibition (in a public house) of three new pictures, and the sale of other paintings by Williams. The other paintings were almost certainly brought over from America and the new ones painted while in Bedfordshire.

To the Lovers of the POLITE ARTS

As it has long been a Custom (and a laudable one too!) by PAINTING AND SCULPTURE to perpetuate the heroic and other deserving Actions of those who died in the Service of their Country, it is presumed it will be an acceptable Remembrance to the Public, to exhibit the Sufferings and death of one, to whom not only this Country but all others have the First of Obligations. Mr. WILLIAMS therefore has, by his great Study and Application, produced three large PICTURES for public

EXHIBITION

Representing the BIRTH, DEATH and BURIAL

of

Our Saviour Jesus Christ

Which will be open'd on WEDNESDAY next the 17th of November, in an excellent Room for the Purpose, at the Mulberry Tree in Round-street, and to continue every Day, for one Week, from Ten in the Morning 'till Three.

N.B There are also Variety of high-finished Pictures and Drawings in History, Landscape, &c. many of which are to be dispos'd of.

There seems to be an acknowledgement of his first two sons he 'lost' in the War of Independence, and also an indication that he was leaving his studio to move into somewhere smaller. However, he now seemingly had fallen into penury, perhaps because of his failing eyesight. He had never accepted any financial assistance from West while in London.

Possibly in 1786, the noted classical scholar and former vicar, Thomas Eagles, met an elderly old man in the city of Bristol, who told him: "I am alone in the world. I have lost my wife and children. My two sons were killed at the battle of Bunker's Hill in the American Civil War. I have nothing to live for. I want a place to die in. Can you get me a pass for St

Peter's Hospital, the old Poorhouse on Castle Park? Will you do that much for me?"

In the course of conversation Eagles found that the aged mariner had travelled afar, was a man of taste and ability and also something of an artist. Eagles finally managed to get him lodgings at the Almshouses and there Williams lived in comparative comfort for some years. However, it appears that Eagles knew the mariner only as Penrose until Williams made his deathbed will. The Merchant Venturers' Almshouse, also known as the Merchants' and Sailors' Almshouse was built around 1560, in King Street, which ran across the Marsh (now Queen Square) from the Welsh Back. Williams had a weekly payment of three shillings a week, and was often invited to Thomas Eagles' house, where he sometimes received extra monies. Eagles' son John remembered '*He was much above want... He was beloved by all our family... He enjoyed several years of tranquillity.*'

Would he be referring in these terms to the William Williams born around 1710 and 76 in 1786, and losing his sight, or to Dickason's 59 year-old? John Eagles was only 2 years old in 1786, and 7 in 1791 when Williams died, so Williams had a great effect on him with his stories and tales. Thomas Eagles was born in 1746 (d. 1812) so would have been 40 years old on first meeting Williams and 45 on Williams' death This is not that much younger than the '*advanced in years*' Williams, who was supposedly 59 when they first met. John Eagles grew up to be a Reverend like his father, and was a noted artist and author. Artists usually have an acute visual acuity, and John Eagles acknowledged that Williams looked older than he did in his *Self-portrait*, allegedly painted around this time.

Some time before 1788, it appears that Williams had married again, as he made a will mentioning his daughter-in-law Mrs Mary Birchmore (presumably a step-daughter), '*the only daughter of my late wife Esther Williams*'. He gave her portraits of his two wives (the unknown first wife and Mary Mare/More, or Mary and Esther?). There is a Hester Williams baptised in 1719, the sister of the William Williams posited by Dickason. Could Williams have married a cousin? Dickason's Williams had 11 siblings (some died very young) – would he have placed his alter-ego Penrose as having just one sister? William also left in his will a portrait of his 'lost' third son, William Joseph Williams. (The Joseph was later added by the son, possibly to distinguish himself from other William Williamses, but also because he later converted to Catholicism.) As this portrait was painted when the boy was in his teens, it is probable that Williams shipped over the portraits of one or two wives, plus his date-disputed *Self-portrait*. If the Self-portrait was shipped rather than painted in Bristol, it is even more likely that Williams was born earlier than the date given by Dickason.

Williams/Penrose was often been invited to Thomas Eagles' house in King's Parade, Bristol for dinner and talked of art and literature, and entertained the family with engrossing tales of his travels and adventures. Eagles remained a friend of Williams until Williams' death in 1791. When he died Williams left all his possessions, a few books and two old manuscripts to his benefactor. Williams' estate included his *Self-portrait*, the manuscript '*Lives of the Artists*', and around 200 books. Two hundred books represented a considerable expense in the 18th century. Williams had desired to be buried in St Augustine's Church Yard, '*which Church, I was baptised in.*' Presumably both his wofe and his step-daughter predeceased him, as Williams' deathbed will left everything to Thomas Eagles.

One of the manuscripts was entitled "*The Journal of Penrose, a Seaman.*" Mr Eagles read it aloud to his sons. It proved so entertaining that one of the boys, John, '*contrived to be too late*' and missed the coach which was to have taken him to school, in order that he might remain at home the next evening to hear the end of Penrose's wonderful adventures. Eagles copied out the manuscript and took it to London. (It appears that this copy of the Williams' manuscript in the Lilly Library has now also been found). John Murray, the famous publisher, offered Thomas Eagles 200 guineas for it. Two well-known artists drew illustrations and the *Journal* was later brought out in book form. Lord Byron, the poet, said of it: *"Penrose kept me up half the night and made me dream the other half. It has all the air of truth – most entertaining and interesting."* Details of its importance and publication are given in the next chapter.

While in Bristol, Williams attempted to find the whereabouts of his remaining son, William Joseph Williams, but he had moved from Philadelphia to Georgetown to Charleston and then New Bern, Craven County, North Carolina where he died in 1823, so it would have been almost impossible to trace him. William Joseph Williams is notable in painting the first three Presidents of the United States when they were in Philadelphia. At this time Washington was president, John Adams was Vice-President and Jefferson was Secretary of State.

A letter to William Williams, Limner[14], No. 24 Merchants Alms House, Bristol from Benjamin Condy[15], (May 26 1788) reveals the sad fact that Williams was trying to find his son: *"Dear Friend, I received yours of Feb 12th, I am glad to hear you are still in the land of the living; as I had concluded you were numbered with the dead…*

I will use the utmost Care & Pains, & make all the enquiry, I can, after your Son, but I am at a loss whom to Enquire of. If you can throw any light on the Affair let me know it, & Nothing Shall be wanting to Serve a Friend whom I have the greatest respect for.' (The full text is appended, with the other letters in the Williams Collection in the Lilly Library, Indiana)

Williams became very ill, and for several weeks was unable to visit Thomas Eagles' mansion, so Eagles sent a servant named Benjamin Pearce to discover *'the cause of our old guest absenting himself.'* Pearce found Williams dying, and a carer in the process of stealing his bed sheets. Williams was pleased to see the servant, because he desired to make his deathbed will, which was effected on April 21st, 1791, witnessed by John Fisher and Benjamin Pearce (see Chapter III). He requested his friends, the glass manufacturers and merchants Richard Vigor Senior and Junior to be his mourners, and gave the younger Vigor his artist's equipment and some books upon painting.

Williams died in 1791, aged according to Flexner about 80 years old and by his own confession going blind, not 64, which Dickason believes. It is possible that Williams assumed the identity of another William Williams, perhaps a cousin, to ensure his place at the Almshouse. The evidence of Benjamin West believing that he had spent 20 years with the Indians after being shipwrecked, aged perhaps 14[16], is compelling. He knew Williams intimately from the age of 9 in 1747 until 22 in 1760, and met him in Williams' old age. Even if at the age of 9 he had mistaken a youth of 20 for a man of 37, surely at his age of 22 he would known that Williams was nearer 50 than 33. The evidence also of the *Lives of the Painters*, or *Lives of the Artists* needs to be taken into account, as does the fact that Williams was an accomplished painter and possessor of books by 1747.

John Eagles, in his *Essays Contributed to Blackwood's Magazine*, states that *'This book, in Williams' handwriting, which was then lent to the youth West, is now in my possession.'* Dickason quotes a 1964 letter from an authority on West, Professor Helmut von Erffa, who *'suggests that this MS, attached to the translation of Dufresnoy, was of greater influence than the book itself.'* It seems fairly clear that the manuscript compendium was in readable form in 1747 – when Williams was just 20 and *'newly arrived in Philadelphia.'* Could a teenager really have compiled it, and from what sources? Also the *Self-portrait* seems to have been painted in the 1760's, not at the alms-house, and the picture of Williams in West's painting of the *Battle of la Hogue* in 1780 appears to be a man closer to 70 than Dickason's 53 years of age.

To this author there are too many loose connections to positively identify Williams as the son of William and Elizabeth Williams (possibly née Belshire) baptised on June 14, 1727, at St Augustine's, Bristol. Williams stated that his mother was buried in the ground pertaining to St Stephen at the Gibb in Bristol. There is a record of an Elizabeth Williams being buried there in 1778, so it may be that Williams returned to Bristol to find her before she died, and even may have lived with her for some time. Williams bequeathed in his will a ring to Ann, his eldest sister. There was an Anne Williams born to William Williams and Ann Belshire in 1710, and an Ann Phillis in 1720, which helps Dickason's case for a birth date of 1727. However, in the *Journal*, Williams' alter-ego Penrose does not mention any family except for missing his mother, and that he left a sister 5 years younger. With 11 living and dead siblings, would Williams have changed family details as much as this?

Addendum:
Was William Williams Welsh?
Williams is a Welsh surname, and he stated to Benjamin West that he was a Welshman *by birth*. Certainly he took on the character of a Welshman in the book. In his *Journal* he stated that he was born near Caerphilly, in Glamorgan, but his mother remarried and went to Worcestershire (on the Welsh border) then to Monmouthshire (officially at that time in England, but predominantly Welsh-speaking), then back to Wales. The choice of his alter ego for the book, Lewellin Penrose, is the corruption of an ancient Welsh name, Llewelyn, or Llywelyn, and the possible corruption of the Welsh pen-rhos (top of the moor), Penrose. Penrose is a common surname in the West Country, and originates from the British-Welsh pen-rhos. (Eagles partially reverted to the Welsh spelling with Llewellin.) Williams certainly told Benjamin West that he was Welsh, and West knew him as Williams, but Thomas Eagles seemed to believe at first that his surname was Penrose.

In the journal Williams expounds the wonders of the Welsh hills of *Penmaenmawr* and *Cader Idris*, and spoke *'in the Welsh tongue'* to his pet bird, *Yellowbill*. He gave his sons the traditional Welsh names of Owen, Morgan and Rees and says that his father's name was Owen. Penrose's son Owen named Penrose's grandson after him, Llewellin. There is the use of the common Welsh idiom *'look you'* in the text, and the reference to a mother as a *'mam'*, the Welsh word for mother. The practice of a *besom*, or *broomstick wedding* was well known in Wales. This author's feeling is that he was born in Wales, of Welsh parents but baptised in Bristol, the greatest seafaring port of the day. However, it may just be possible, because of the age discrepancies noted above, that he was an older man, who took on the identity of a dead relative in Bristol to obtain lodgings in the almshouse. The respect he had from older men as an artist, his possessions and his experience, upon his first meeting with Benjamin West, plus his superb knowledge of the Miskito Coast, makes for a problematical chronology of his life.

There are so many uncertainties involving his birth: we can even posit him as being the William Williams born around 1705, who married in 1731 Ellin (Elinor) Foulke of Gwynedd Twp, Philadelphia, the daughter of Thomas Foulke and Gwen Evans, two Welsh immigrants. They had eleven children born in Philadelphia from 1733 to 1751, only one of whom, Susanna is known to have married (to Evan Meredith).

Williams lost his 'first wife' sometime between 1755 and 1757, and mentions having two sons by her who were killed in the War of Independence. Perhaps the other children, except Susanna, died young. The children were named, from oldest to youngest, Thomas, Elizabeth, Hugh, Susanna, Hannah, Margaret, Elizabeth, Sarah, William, John and Ellin. Ellin was born in 1755 on June 15th.

Merchant Almshouse 1825
by T. L. Rowbottom.
© *Bristol Museums and Galleries Archives*

Old Sailor of the Merchant Venturer's
Almshouse 1823 by H. O'Neill
© *Bristol Museums and Galleries Archives*

The Merchant Almshouse today
Courtesy Francis Greenacre

1726		Baptized in 1726
March	19th	Sannnah Daut. of Moses and Jane Hopkins...
	21	Martha Daut. of Thomas & Alice Jacob

1727		1727
Apr.	—	Not One in this Month
May	2	Hannah Daut. of Robert and Hannah Simes
	14	Mary Daut. of William and Mary Reeves
	17	Robert Son of Edward and Mary Dowding
	18	Ann Daut. of John and Ann Bradshaw
	23	Lathan & Edward Sons of John and Sarah Church
	28	Solamon Son of Patrick and Catharine Penny
June	1	Thomas Son of Pearce and Mary Miles
	6	John Son of Charles and Elizabeth Jones
	11	Daniel Son of Christo: and Mary Baker
	11	Baty Daut. of Morgan and Baty Jou
	13	Ann Daut. of John and Luce Rebits
	14	William Son of William and Eliz. Williams
	18	Mary Daut. of Robert and Susannah Smart
	19	Mary Daut. of George and Ann Bradford
	25	Sofia Daut. of Adam and Margret James
July	2	Martha Daut. of Walter & Mary Wallis
	2	Ann Daut. of Abraham and Mary Sandford
	6	Thomas Son of John and Edith Saunders
	11	William Son of William and Baty Leech
	11	James Son of William and Abigall Walls
	15	John Son of William and Mary Phillips
	30	William Son of Morgan and Alice Thomas

St. Augustine's Church records

235

Buried in the Year 1791

April 4	Margaret Williams	A Child		"	1 —
5	Jane Bunce			"	1 6
10	Thomas Tull	A Child		"	" 6
	John Spencer	do		"	" 6
	Mary Robins	Do		"	" 6
11	John Perry	Do			" 6
14	Edward Gibbins		P	"	"
19	Samuel Pettet			"	1 "
	Jno Thomas	A Child		"	6
	James Slocombe	Do		"	" 6
21	Elizabeth Watkins		P		
24	Thomas Bill	S. P. 16		"	"
26	Margt Thomas			"	2 "
	John Williams	P		"	"
	Carl Witzell	A Dutchman		"	1 "
27	William Williams			"	1 "
28	Revd Mathew Pomphrey, in the Church Ground			"	3 "
				"	7 6
May 3	William Snipe	A Child	P	"	" "
	William Guss			"	1 "
17	John Day	in the Church Ground		"	4 0
				"	7 6
19	Anne Tucker			"	1 "
30	William Taffly			"	1 6
	Mary Deucher		P	"	" "
22	John Cook	A Child		"	" 6
	Carr forwd	£		1	17 —

St. Augustine's Church Records

CHAPTER II

The Story of the Book

*Mr Penrose has every claim to being **America's hitherto unrecognised first novel**. Apart from its historical significance, it is an intrinsically absorbing account of a Caribbean Crusoe's struggle to survive in an alien environment – a highly readable tale which is superior in many ways to Defoe's familiar narrative' –* Dr. D.H. Dickason

'Truth is often stranger than falsehood: + so it is true in this case'
– Robert Southey, writing of *The Journal of Penrose, Seaman*

There are several remarkable circumstances surrounding Williams' book, making it important that a wider public is aware of its literary and historical importance.

Firstly, the novel was the **first piece of 'faction' in the English language** known to this writer. Both Thomas and John Eagles, and Benjamin West believed that the work was semi-autobiographical.

It was also groundbreaking for several reasons mentioned by Dickason. Williams admires the virtues of *the noble savage*, a doctrine Rousseau had expounded between 1756 and 1762. This may be its first use in a work of fiction. It is unknown whether Williams was familiar with Rousseau's work.

The Journal of Penrose, Seaman predates Henry David Thoreau's (1817-1862) exploration of nature and the extraction a principle or moral based upon philosophical observation.

The book may be the first example of the *'South Sea Romance'* genre in the story of Penrose and Luta. Previously it was thought that Herman Melville's small travel narrative *Typee* was the first such narrative, in 1846. *The Journal of Penrose* predates it by around 70 years.

The novel is **anti-slavery** in a time of universal slavery, possibly the **first** such fictional writing of this type. Both Washington and Jefferson were slave-owners at the time of writing the book. This is certainly the first book of fiction in the Americas expounding the abolition of slavery. The horror of the Negro slave Quammino's story and his welcome into Williams 'Utopia' for his final days is a masterful piece of story telling.

The Journal of Penrose, Seaman in 1815 was the first story of buried treasure, copied by Edgar Allan Poe for his first successful story, *The Gold Bug*. It saved Poe from bankruptcy and kick-started his literary career. Without the influence of Williams there may have been no great literary career for Poe. *The Gold Bug* was first published in *The Dollar Newspaper*, Philadelphia, June 1843. It is generally thought that Poe, who died in poverty in 1849, aged 40, was the pioneer of detective story writing, with his masterpiece, *'Tales of Mystery and Adventure'*. An outstanding tale was his account of the recovery of Pirate Captain Kidd's treasure, through the deciphering of a mystically devised parchment (as in *The Journal of Penrose*). When the story was published, it won a prize of $100 and saved Poe's household from near starvation. This was probably the most Poe was paid for a single work, and it was Poe's most widely-read short story in his lifetime. He almost certainly had the idea from Williams' book.

We could even claim that **modern mystery fiction owes its inception** to Williams. Robert Louis Stevenson freely acknowledged that he took the idea of the skeleton and treasure in *Treasure Island* from Poe, so there is another link with Williams' book. One day, Penrose had come upon a rough pyramid of stones. Beneath them were a skeleton and a sealed glass bottle. The skull of the skeleton was fractured, and they inferred from this that it had belonged to *'some poor unfortunate Spaniard, Negro or mulatto',* who had been sacrificed by superstitious pirates in order that his spirit might be a kind of *'guardian to preserve their treasure until their return...In the bottle were three papers. One was inscribed with names in a circle like the points of a compass. There was a drawing of a human head, hands and feet and cross-bones... There were also numerals and an arrow indicating a spot where treasure was buried. They deciphered this cryptic diagram as PAINTER.'*

The *Journal* is an utterly remarkable and truthful account of mammoth bone discoveries (the first recorded instance of the discovery of extinct animal bones), of a possible Mayan Temple (new remains have just been found elsewhere in Nicaragua), of a two-headed snake (known to occur naturally), a two-tailed lizard (again which occurs naturally) and details dozens of exotic species only found on the Miskito Coast. It is almost a natural history of the jungle and coastline in parts, with descriptions of bats, jaguar, ocelot, armadillo, anteaters, humming birds, sharks and the like. Willliams' interest in, and descriptions of natural phenomena, from an albino Indian to a parasitic fig tree are sometimes hauntingly beautiful. His stories about his monkey, hawk, parrots and fawn are extremely early animal stories, a very popular genre around 100 years later.

Williams' use of colloquialisms and dialect for characters is again well in advance of any other American fiction, and the mixture of pathos and sobriety, followed by uplifting philosophy and humour makes the book extremely entertaining.

There are possibly words from the almost extinct Rama language (or its precursor, Voto), and an account of their sayings and habits (they were not man-eaters, etc.) The author cannot trace the etymology of these words – they may have been from the old Voto, or the Carib language, or Kuna (Cuna) in Panama/Colombia, or Bribri or Cabecar in Costa Rica. The Kuna are descendants of the Caribs, and now live on a chain of islands called the San Blas Archipelago, on the Atlantic side of Panama. Interestingly, in regard to the albino Indian in the book, albinos are not uncommon among the Kuna, and are accepted into the community, but encouraged not to marry. If Penrose/Williams was marooned in Costa Rica, the words may well be in Bribri or Cabecar, as Penrose noted in his Journal that it was difficult to spell people's names as *'native words... actually are imperfectly heard by an untrained ear.'* (Remnants of the Guatuso or Maleku Indians survive in Costa Rica and have their own language. In the 19th century they were known as a sub-group of the Rama, and it has been hypothesised that both are descended from the Corobici of Costa Rica's Central Plateau).

Many customs are described, one of the most intriguing being the need to marry again quickly so that one's spouse's soul can pass into your new partner. Harry mentions the *yoho* and *birry* to Penrose, howling at night. This may be a reference to the Rama *yoho* - a gorilla-type man, and the *perry men*, small pale men who hide in the woods. There is a description of a meeting of Rama elders, unrecorded elsewhere in any journals or other factual accounts... *'That after they had weighed the matter well, they called a council and they took him to it, in a large wigwam, and after they all got together he was placed by Owagamy's side. Then a profound silence held for the space of about half an hour, during which time about 12 of them kept smoking. At last an Indian got up and spoke to Bell in Spanish, saying that his people desired Gattaloon (meaning himself) to be the one mouth and voice, through which he was to hear them all. That they all knew of a certainty that he was a fair and true man, and that they saw his heart through his eyes. They knew that he had lost his wife some days before he came to visit them, and they were much satisfied in regard to his coming to them on that account...'*

The Rama Indians, of which there are only 1400 left, are threatened with extinction as loggers and ex-Sandinista guerrillas have taken their territories, and they are still being murdered. (This figure of 1400 has risen because of inter-marriage with other ethnic groups). This book can have an impact upon the future of this wonderful tribe, and other threatened societies in the region. There were only around 200 Rama in existence by 1862, because more powerful Miskitos dominated the coastline. The author has accepted for the present Williams' placing of his stay at 11 degrees 30 north, which is on the Costa Rica border with Nicaragua, near Greytown/San Juan del Norte. There were Miskitu and Rama inhabiting this area. The Miskito Coast extends for 200 miles north from this place to the Bay of Honduras.

The novel was probably completed over several years, prior to 1776, and most if not all of it written in America. As Flexner states, *'it may predate by a few years The Power of Sympathy, the book that is usually considered America's first novel. Furthermore, it is of much higher literary quality than that sprawling sentimental work. Expertly written in a laconic, verisimilitudinous style to Defoe's, the Journal, when published belatedly in London during 1815, was a critical success that inspired Byron to write: 'I have never read so much of a book at one sitting in my life. He kept me up half the night, and made me dream of him the other half... it has all the air of truth, and is most entertaining and interesting in every point of view.'* Thomas Eagles certainly knew of the book before Williams entered the Bristol Almshouse in 1786, and it seems that the short addendum dated 1783 by Paul Taylor was meant *'as a subtle dedication to Thomas Eagles'* according to Dickason. Upon the evidence of parallels with the real world, it seems to have been completed prior to 1780, and probably before 1776 when Williams left New York for Bedford. *The Journal* ends in 1776 when it is finished and handed to Taylor.

William Hill Brown (1765-1793) was thought to be the author of the first American novel, *The Power of Sympathy*, published in 1789, well after the completion of *The Journal of Penrose, Seaman*. He simply copies the English epistolary novel of seduction, giving the reader positive models for imitation and negative ones to avoid, from which one can induce what is right or wrong. The book takes the form of a series of letters. In advertisements for the book, it was *'intended to enforce attention to female education, and to represent the fatal consequences of Seduction.'* However the lessons are not obvious in this poorly written piece of didacticism. The plot is too entangled, and both the main protagonists die. The book was not popular, and it was difficult to discover the moral of the tale. Nowhere is the title explained or its use apparent in the book. A critic blamed its *'poor characterisation, loose motivation (and) graceless digressions'* for its lack of acclaim. There is no sense of closure in this incoherent work, and it bears no comparison with *The Journal of Penrose, Seaman* as a work of literary merit.

Flexner noted that Williams' book did not seem to be *'the first attempt of an amateur. What did Williams write during the 30 years he seems to have practised painting in America? Did the man who as an artist so influenced the painter West, as a writer influence West's friends and contemporaries, the poet Hopkinson and America's first playwright Godfrey? May not this forgotten figure have played a major part on the development of the Philadelphia school of writers? Such questions should make his career as interesting to historians of literature as it is to historians of art.'*

The original, published 25 years after his death, was proof-read by Sir Walter Scott, and approved by Lord Byron and Robert Southey, the leading literary men of the time. Williams also left the manuscript of '*The Lives of the Painters*' as well as Penrose's *Journal*, and it was known to be in the possession of the Rev. John Eagles in 1857, so hopefully it still might resurface in some dusty attic. It was this book that inspired Benjamin West to say it '*lighted up a fire in my breast which has never been extinguished.*'

Upon July 10th 1805, as Flexner recounts, Benjamin West '*is the President of the Royal Academy, an old man full of fame. As he waits in the London lodgings of a Bristol merchant, Thomas Eagles, he picks up an elegantly bound manuscript entitled: The Journal of Llewellin Penrose, a Seaman. Idly he reads this account of the experiences of a castaway, and then a look of amazement enlivens his features. When Eagles enters, West demands impetuously to be told the source of the manuscript. His host replies that some years before he has been accosted on the streets of Bristol by an elderly beggar who asked nothing more than admission to a poorhouse. 'My two sons were killed at Bunker's Hill...' he explained. 'I have been a painter, but am now old and alone, and only want somewhere to end my life.' Although not curious enough to discover anything further about the derelict's history, Eagles was helpful. When the old man died in the Merchants Alms House, he left all his possessions to his benefactor.*

The possessions of a beggar? That did not seem anything to take seriously. Yet investigation revealed that the lost soul had transported about two hundred books to the almshouse, among them two manuscripts: The Lives of the Painters, and the mysterious Journal of Llewellin Penrose.

"Sir", cried West, "I have looked at several parts of this book, and much I have seen I know to be true. I know the man too, and what is more extraordinary, had it not been for him, I should never have been a painter." The manuscript had carried West back to his boyhood. Again he was sitting cross-legged on a chair, breathing in the delightful smell of paints, while his new friend, William Williams, talked excitedly. "As he was an excellent actor in taking off character, he often, to amuse me, repeated his adventures amongst the Indians, many of which adventures are strictly the same as related in your manuscript of Penrose, as were also the description of the scenery of the coasts, the birds on them, particularly the flamingo birds, which he described, when seen at a distance, as appearing like a company of soldiers dressed in red uniforms. He spoke the language of the savages and appeared to have lived among them for some years. I often asked him how he came to be with them. He replied that he had gone to sea when young, but was never satisfied with the pursuit; he had been shipwrecked and thrown into great difficulties." The book West held in his hand was a novelised account of its author's own experiences.'

We also discover that, strangely, Williams was known as Penrose to Thomas Eagles. In '*Artists and their Friends in England, 1700-1799*' by William T. Whitley (1928): '*Galt says that Williams gave West some advice and lent him a book of artists' biographies, but he appears to have been ignorant of the singular later history of the painter; who, after his two sons had been killed at Bunker Hill, came to England and renewed in London his acquaintanceship with West, to whom he sat for one of the figures in the Battle of La Hogue. Williams then disappeared, and West heard nothing of him until 1805 when he happened to call upon Mr Thomas Eagles, the art critic. Mr Eagles was out and West, while awaiting his return, looked over the pages of a book in manuscript that was lying on the table. It was the story of a man who had lived among savages, and ostensibly written by Llewellyn Penrose, but West was amazed to see that the adventures were those of Williams, who had described them to him in*

Philadelphia. Mr Eagles afterwards told West that he met Williams, whom he had always known as Penrose, some years before at Bristol. He was ill and almost destitute, and Mr Eagles befriended him and obtained his admission to the Merchant's Almshouses, where he practised painting for amusement. When the supposed Penrose died he bequeathed to Mr Eagles his book of adventures; and another book, also in manuscript, of lives of artists, which West recognized as the identical volume Williams had lent to him in Philadelphia, the reading of which, he said, "lighted up a fire in my breast that has never been extinguished." The manuscript book of lives of artists was in 1857 still in the possession of the Rev. John Eagles, who had sold The Journal of Llewellyn Penrose many years earlier to Mr John Murray, by whom it was published in 1815.'

Thomas Eagles had read the original Penrose manuscript aloud to his sons, and it proved so interesting that John missed his coach to school in order to hear the end of the adventure. After West had accidentally discovered the Journal in 1805, at Thomas Eagles' London address of 4 Pall Mall, Eagles asked Benjamin West for a foreword and decided to try and publish the manuscript. However, he heavily truncated and bowdlerised the original manuscript, sapping its strength in ways shown by Dickason: (Eagles) 'vitiated its earthly vigour, directness and colour. By regularising its form in what amounted to total paraphrase he did make the manuscript more "correct" and easily readable; but his manipulation of certain details of tones and content was not fair to the original author (who had died twenty-four years before his book was published), not desirable by our contemporary canons.'

Eagles changed Williams' title from *The Journal of Penrose, Seaman* to *The Journal of Llewellin Penrose*, and also altered Williams' original spelling of the Christian name as Lewellin. At last, in 1815, having been read and approved by Walter Scott, the work was accepted in Eagles' bowdlerised version for publication. The Reverend John Eagles received 200 guineas for it. *The Edinburgh Evening Courant* advertised it as 'handsomely printed' for John Murray of Albemarle Street, London and William Blackwood of Edinburgh, on three dates in 1815, at a price of one pound and four shillings for the 4 volume foolscap edition in boards. The advertisement was entitled 'INTERESTING ADVENTURES. This day was published...' There was a Dedication to Benjamin West and an Advertisement in the book, both by John Eagles. The four volumes consisted of 239pp, 217pp, 215ppp and 197pp.

The interest shown in the book is demonstrated by a recent offer by the bookseller Phillip J. Pirages of a copy for $3500. *FIRST EDITION. REALLY LOVELY CONTEMPORARY CITRON STRAIGHT-GRAIN MOROCCO DONE FOR THE EMPRESS MARIE-LOUISE OF FRANCE, SECOND WIFE OF NAPOLEON, covers with wide and animated gilt frame featuring palmette-above-fleuron roll and large roundel cornerpieces, center panel with blind fillets and scrolling cornerpieces just inside the frame, the monogram M. L. surmounted by a crown at center of each board; raised bands, spine panels densely and very attractively gilt in an all-over scrolling foliate design, turn-ins gilt with acorn and oak leaf roll, all edges gilt. One full-page illustration (an encrypted treasure map). Boards with minor spotting, one leaf with small light stain in text, one opening with light marginal soiling, other trifling flaws internally, but A VERY FINE COPY, the especially pretty bindings showing virtually no wear, and the text clean, smooth, and fresh. This intriguing narrative of a castaway, largely fiction but with perhaps some admixture of true reminiscence, was written by William Williams (1727-91), a wanderer who probably came from Wales like his narrator Penrose. Our author lived for some years in Philadelphia, so that this work, allegedly written, though not published, in the 1780s, has been called the first American novel.*

THE

JOURNAL

OF

LLEWELLIN PENROSE,

A

SEAMAN.

IN FOUR VOLUMES.

VOL. I.

———

LONDON:

PRINTED FOR
JOHN MURRAY, ALBEMARLE STREET,
AND WILLIAM BLACKWOOD, EDINBURGH.

1815.

Williams was a painter, and the teacher of Benjamin West, as we learn from the preface, which also tells us that before his death, Williams turned up in England and gave the Penrose tale to the father of our editor, John Eagles (1783-1855). Though some have suspected Eagles as having composed the work himself, most critics accept the veracity of the preface, though Eagles may have reworked the tale considerably. There is a decidedly Utopian cast to this tale that goes Robinson Crusoe one better: Penrose, the castaway, is not only befriended by kindly savages, but he actually marries one and founds a family among them. More castaways arrive—a shipwrecked Dutchman, a Scotsman, and an escaped Black slave—all of whom learn to live in harmony with one another and nature. Penrose dies on his island after 27 years, bequeathing the narrative of his adventures to his son. This set was bound for the Austrian archduchess Marie-Louise, Empress of France, as the second wife of Napoleon.

Again, in the current Rulon-Miller catalogue of recent acquisitions, we read under the heading of:

THE FIRST NOVEL WRITTEN IN AMERICA

123. [WILLIAMS, WILLIAM.] The journal of Llewellin Penrose, a seaman. In four volumes. London: John Murray, and William Blackwood, Edinburgh, 1815. $1,250

First edition, 4 vols., foolscap 8vo, bound without half-titles in contemporary calf-backed pink paste-paper boards; a little bit of rubbing, cracking and flaking of the spines, otherwise a good, sound set, or better. An anonymous narrative, edited by John Eagles, based upon the incidents in the life of the author, whom, according to the preliminary matter, Thomas Eagles, father of the editor, had befriended, and to whom Williams bequeathed the manuscript. In fact, it is a work of fiction. Williams (1727–91), who was a painter and the first tutor of Benjamin West, wrote the novel in America between 1774 and 1775, and it has been consequently claimed as the first novel written in America. The published version of 1815 was much altered by Williams's benefactor in Bristol, Thomas Eagles, and was later re-submitted for publication by his son, the Rev. John Eagles. For an edition based on Williams's original manuscript and a useful introduction describing its publication history, see David Howard Dickason, Mr Penrose: The Journal of Penrose, Seaman (Bloomington: Indiana University Press, 1969).

The Journal was also published as a pirate edition in Germany in 1817, 'Der neue Robinson, oder, Tagebuch Llewellin Penrose, eines Matrosen'. In 1825, there was another, abridged edition, in one volume published by Hessey and Taylor. The advertisement placed in The Morning Chronicle prices it at 7 shillings (boards) or eight shillings (bound) and reads: 'This volume contains the whole of "The Journal of Llewellin Penrose" as originally published in four vols 12mo with some slight corrections, to adapt it the better for the perusal of young persons. The interest of the Narrative, which is not surpassed by any work except "Robinson Crusoe" and the delight it is known to have afforded all classes of readers, but especially the young, are the considerations which have led to the re-publication of it in a compressed form, and at less than one-third of its former price, so as to bring it within the class of works intended for the amusement and instruction of youth.' The advertisement was placed on the 7th of July 1825.

However, this 2007 edition, from the original manuscript, stands highly in any comparison to Robinson Crusoe, which was written by someone with no idea of the traumas of living in a threatening and strange environment. There seems to be no link with Defoe's tale in the pages of The Journal, but it is not known whether Williams had read the book. Dickason's transcript of the original Journal was its first publication, but apart from some paragraph construction, he left it in its original form, so it is difficult to easily read. The present transcriber has amended the Journal slightly, with copious footnotes, to make it far easier for the modern reader to understand and appreciate.

JOURNAL

OF

LLEWELLIN PENROSE,

A

SEAMAN.

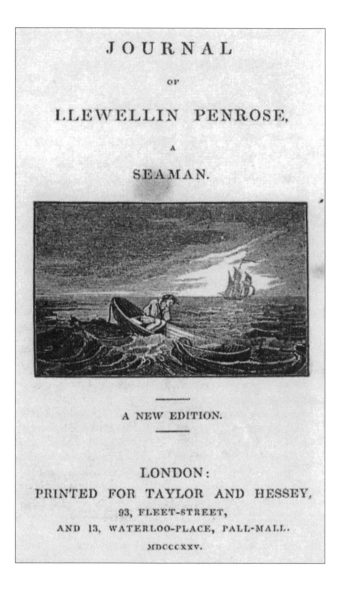

A NEW EDITION.

LONDON:

PRINTED FOR TAYLOR AND HESSEY,

93, FLEET-STREET,

AND 13, WATERLOO-PLACE, PALL-MALL.

MDCCCXXV.

Frontispiece from 1825 edition of Penrose

245

Henri Petter notes Penrose's modernistic religious and philosophical outlook, '*an outlook as enlightened, in the sense of the mid-eighteenth century, as Defoe's was conditioned by late-seventeenth century Dissenting values*' (- *The Early American Novel*, 1971).

Roger B. Stein in an essay entitled *Pulled out of the Bay: American Fiction in the 18th Century* (*Studies in American Fiction*) notes '*The framework of Penrose's first person narrative is vaguely providential, but we have moved far from Bunyan. The voyage of the self leads not towards heaven, but to a New World Eden. The richly detailed flora and fauna of the Nicaraguan coast and the community of noble savages and European refugees whom he has gathered refocus our attention from ultimate goals to an idealised life in this world. Yet any Rousseauistic overtones are offset by the absence of a strong, expansive, and controlling ego.*'

As Sarah Wadsworth summarised in '*Imaginary Landscape? William Williams and the Journal of Penrose, Seaman*': '*Mr. Penrose tells the story of Lewellin Penrose, a British youth who flees an unhappy home to seek his fortune on the high seas. Having learned a sailor's trade, Penrose ventures further to the West Indies, where he falls prey to Spanish privateers, is held prisoner in Havana, recovers his liberty at the cost of impressment to the British (sic, English) Navy, and eventually deserts only to be abandoned by his shipmates off the Mosquito Coast (most likely near the Nicaragua-Costa Rica border). The ensuing history of the castaway, radically divergent from Defoe's shipwreck narrative (Robinson Crusoe), is a tale of survival and human community, enriched by a compassionate but unobtrusive morality and invigorated by a bracing infusion of adventure, romance, and exotic colour. In Mr. Penrose readers will experience vicariously the beauties and wonders of an untrammelled wilderness together with its abundant dangers – wildfires, earthquakes, tempests, wildcats, killer whales, and profligate seafarers. The reader will discover with Penrose an enchanting tropical grotto, a cache of buried pirates' treasure, and, in a remote jungle clearing, a mysterious monolith of enormous height engraved with letters, dates, and assorted pictographs.*

On a more profound level Mr. Penrose is a work that explored the moral and intellectual questions of the author's time, and, indeed, questions that continue to be relevant in our own time. Here, in this American colonial text, the reader will enter the kinds of debates that shaped the political and moral foundation of the United States: debates over human equality, religious tolerance, and the nature of ethical, responsible government. It is this combination of physical adventure and intellectual signification that makes Mr. Penrose as rewarding to scholars and students of literature as it is to readers drawn by its promise to entertain and delight.'

Brief Note on the Book's Publication History
1776 is the key date when Penrose states he completed the book, and the later date of Paul Taylor's appended letter is 1783. This may be the date when the book was first shown to Thomas Eagles, who knew about the book before the date of 1786 when Penrose (as he knew Williams) entered the Bristol almshouse. The manuscript was left to Williams' benefactor, Thomas Eagles, in Williams' will dated 1791. In 1805 Benjamin West accidentally came across the book and vouched for the authenticity of Williams' adventures. In 1807, J.S. Clarke stated in a letter to the publisher John Murray that the manuscript was superior to Robinson Crusoe (first published in 1719).

Thomas Eagles and/or his son John had bowdlerised and altered the book, adding a memorandum by Benjamin West, before the book was eventually published in 1815 in 4 volumes by John Murray, illustrated by Bird, Pocock and John Eagles. Susan Rather has noted that the contribution of Benjamin West has been critical to our understanding of Williams' life – '(West's) *systematic reflection on his early years began not later than 1805, at the height of his troubles in the Royal Academy, after a serendipitous encounter with a* manuscript of castaway adventure. The author was William Williams, a sailor from Bristol who may have based the substantially fictional account on his own youthful experience of Central America. By the late 1740s, Williams had moved to Philadelphia, where he became an artist— and Benjamin West's first instructor. "Had it not been for him," West avowed in 1805, "I should never have been a painter." The owner of the manuscript, hoping to see it published, asked West to write up his recollections of Williams (who died in 1791). The resulting letter of 1810, the most detailed primary source for the fascinating Williams, is also a key document in the life of West, who seized the opportunity to reimagine his own beginnings. Williams's novel, finally published in 1815 as The Journal of Llewellyn Penrose, a Seaman, bore a dedication to West and excerpted extensively from his letter in the preface. With part of his American story in print, West gained a motivation to relate the matter more fully. He was likely released to do so, as well, by the death in 1815 of his American colleague Copley, a constant professional irritant and rival in London and the one man who both could and would have challenged West's American story. With significant encouragement from Galt, West authorized a complete tactical reversal of his insistent claims of Englishness. The biography (by Galt) of 1816 presented instead a remarkable, and at the time quite unfamiliar, account of the famous British painter's formative years—the story of the American West.'

In 1817 a pirated version of Penrose appeared in Germany, 'Der Neue Robinson'. In 1825 a new edition, with more omissions, was printed by Taylor and Hessey, and in 1855 (and also in 1857, posthumously) John Eagles' 'The Beggar's Legacy' was published.

There was another attempt to republish the book in 1857, involving Zoe King. However, it was not until the 1960's that D.H. Dickason rediscovered the manuscript, and the Lilly Library purchased it. The Indiana University Press then republished the original book in 1969, as 'Mr Penrose: The Journal of Penrose, Seaman' by William Williams 1727-1791. The book, as an unamended 18th century document, was intended for the academic market. It is hoped that this edition will reach a far greater proportion of the reading population.

The complicated and posthumous publication process has led to this superb book being ignored, until Dickason had the transcript published in 1969 in a small academic edition. It had been rejected by publishers for being non-authentic, yet we can see that the author must have lived in the Atlantic seaboard rainforest for some considerable time to describe all the details of its flora and fauna. He also mentions pre-Mayan columns and mammoth bones, which have only been found in the last decade in Nicaragua. Yet his book gives us something far deeper than geography, biology, botany and anthropology. This first American novel deals with freedom from religious hatred, the rational autonomy of the self and most importantly equality and democracy in a time of slavery.

CHAPTER III

The Beggar's Legacy

This article, by John Eagles, was first published anonymously in 1855 in *Blackwood's Edinburgh Magazine*, LXXVII (pp 251-272). In 1857, 'The Beggar's Legacy' reappeared posthumously in '*Essays Contributed to Blackwell's Magazine*' (pp 457-502), and attributed to John Eagles. There is a lengthy, generalised and learned polemic about poverty and hypocrisy, but on page 490 Eagles reaches our subject. This following text is from page 490 to the end of the article on page 502. It is interesting that Eagles was only seven or eight years old when Williams died in 1791. Eagles, when writing this article in 1854-55 was aged 71 or 72, yet he constantly refers to Williams as aged and old. If Williams' real birth date was 1727, he would have only been 64 years old at his time of death. The only alteration to the original text is that some indents have been added to form new paragraphs:

'Towards the end of the last century, a gentleman was walking homewards, in the city of Bristol, when he was accosted by a beggar in the street, in these words: "Sir, I have been looking about for a gentleman to whom I might with confidence address myself, and tell my wants. I think I have found him in you." Here, the reader will be at once ready to say – "What an accomplished beggar! This flattery was not learnt in a day." – Reader, if such be your thought, you are mistaken. I verily believe that this was the first day in his life that this poor old man, for old he was, begged, but you shall hear further the nature of his "beggar's petition." It is, however, needful that you know something of him to whom the petition was made. That person was in appearance, what he was thoroughly in character, a *gentleman*; never had any one a kinder, more generous, heart. He was acquainted with the world through intercourse with society, and through extensive literature. He was a ripe scholar, and a man of refined taste. He has been dead more than forty years, yet has the writer of this narrative a remembrance of him never to be erased, for it is made perfect and sanctified by filial veneration, founded upon a rare excellence. Further description would be painful, it would be like the breaking into a sanctuary, and exposing sacred things. If I have given the beggar's words, it is because the whole scene was vividly detailed to me by so truthful an authority.

The beggar paused. After a while he continued, "I am alone in the world, have lost wife and children, my two sons were killed at Bunker's Hill. I have nothing to live for. I want a place to die in. I ask for a pass to St Peter's Hospital[1]. I think you can obtain it for me." He did not ask for money, but a place to die in. Such an address as this was sure to move the person to whom it was made.

He (Thomas Eagles) replied – that the hospital which the man desired was a wretched place, a receptacle for the lowest paupers. "You seem to have seen better days. You would be miserable there. I should be loth to obtain for you that which you desire. You have certainly seen better days."

"I have," replied the beggar, for such I shall continue to call him. "I have been a painter – but am now old and alone, and only want where to end my life."

248

"I must have a further talk with you. Call at my house at -. In the meantime take wherewith to supply your immediate wants, and don't forget to call upon me." And the time was fixed. The man received with hesitation the gift, and they separated. The beggar called at the appointed time, and often repeated his visits. More and more the gentleman became interested in him – was pleased with his conversation – desired him to wait till he could do something better for him – begged him to accept a weekly sum for his maintenance, until he could be better provided for. How long this eleemosynary[2] support continued I am not able to say, whether months, a year, or even years. The result was a comfortable location in the "Merchants' Almshouse"[3], where, with, I have no doubt, some other monthly aids delicately given, the old man enjoyed some years of tranquillity. He said he had been a painter. It was a happy coincidence in this his latter fortune, that he addressed himself to one to whom a scarcely better recommendation could have been offered; for he was passionately fond of the arts, and was himself practically an amateur. The old man must have had an eventful life, for at one time he had been a mariner. There was a book of many events, many cares, many thoughts, and much gathered observation, visibly written in his countenance. I will describe his portrait as it is now before me – painted by himself, and very well painted too, in his Alms-House dress.

THE BEGGAR'S PORTRAIT

First, as to his dress. On his head is a faded red velvet cap, much like that seen in the portraits of authors in Queen Anne's time[4]; a gown of green cloth, somewhat coarse, hangs in loose folds around his person; round the neck a plain white cravat, tied rather loosely. As to features, the shape of the face is square, but within that squareness is a rounded fullness; the features might somewhat resemble those of Hogarth, but the eyes are not so large, the nose not quite so curt, the mouth more compressed, and there is more of decision in the length and firmness of the jaw than in Hogarth. The forehead is broad and open, and more prominent than in the satiric painter, the brow less arched, the eyes remarkably keen and observant. In character, excepting in the point of observation, the resemblance to Hogarth is lost, for there is no expression of combativeness. It is mild, inquiring, experienced, and meditative upon experiences. You would pronounce his a naturalist, as I believe he was. The experienced look is very striking – visible in his eyes and mouth; you might apply to him what was said of Ulysses – take the Latin version of Horace:-

"Qui mores hominum multorum vidit et urbos."

Men, their manners, and their cities, he had soon; but what men and manners? There is nothing of the Grecian hero in his countenance. There is the impression of the world he had seen – not in its best phase of manners, but in its coarser nature; it is without its polish – its varnish. It pictures much that he had felt as well as much that he had seen. It is no ideal, but a commonplace portrait of one whom, at first, most people would call a commonplace man, for it would be difficult to class him of a high grade. But I doubt, if it were in a gallery, and seen a second time, if it would not arrest attention, and something singular be seen in it. There is certainly an indication of that wandering disposition I have spoken of, as of a gentle, scarcely perceptible, unsoundness; but much of this was lost in the look of keen observation which the whole countenance had acquired. I have looked at the portrait so often that I find it one of the most interesting that I have ever seen.

I see a strangeness written in many lineaments[5] – the exact character of which I can not describe; and it is the more strange on that account: sensible, shrewd, inquisitive, patient, unimpassioned – as one cognisant of other men's doings and thoughts – uncommunicative of his own. In age he looks not so old in the picture as I remember him. Do I remember him? it may be asked. Perfectly – and why not? Often, when a boy, have I seen this beggar at his benefactor-friend's table – at the table of a man of polished manners, a scholar, and of refined taste – where he was ever welcomed, unexceptionable as was his whole demeanour, unembarrassed, entertaining, quiet, modest, not from any imposed restraint, but from the sterling, true, simple manliness of his nature. I have described him as I remember him, and as I see now in his portrait, painted by his own hand, the size of life.

I have mentioned the pleasant, and I may say, friendly intercourse between him and his benefactor (*which* deserves best the name of benefactor may yet be seen). It happened that some weeks passed without his making an appearance as was his wont. This created uneasiness – a confidential servant was sent to the alms-house to inquire the cause of our old friend absenting himself. The servant found him ill in his bed, and in a dying state, and one of those human fiends one sometimes reads of, an unfeeling old nurse-tender, was stealing the sheets from under him. The old gentleman was able to express great satisfaction at the arrival of good Benjamin – such was the servant's name. He was glad he had come, for he was desirous to make his will. To make his will! – what could such a one have to bequeath? However, he did make his will, in a few words bequeathing to his patron-friend whatever he might die possessed of. That was his death-bed.

Before this event he had one day asked his friend if he had ever seen his Journal – he would not bring it to him. It may have been opened, or: not, I cannot say; it may have been considered a mere sailor's journal, and not read. At the old man's death, what was the property? I think I have heard not less than a couple of hundred volumes of books. The MS. "Penrose's Journal", a MS. volume of Lives of the Painters, collected by the deceased; some volumes of transcribed poetry; portraits of his two wives, and of himself – that which is now before me, and which I have described. Wherein lay the value of such a legacy? It will be presently seen.

The affectionate interest in the old man's memory eventually led to a remembrance of his journal – the MS. entitled "Journal of Llewellin Penrose, a Seaman."* I have not before advertised the reader that the old man's name was not Penrose, but Williams. I pass on to the narrative. The journal was read, and I well remember with what delight, by every member of the family; and such was its deep interest that I am able to tell an anecdote not very much to my own credit, however it may speak well for the tale of the journal. I was then a boy; I had not finished the manuscript when the last day of my holidays arrived. It is too true, but I must confess it, I *contrived* the next morning to be too late for the coach which was to have conveyed me many miles from home. I was thus able to finish the story.

And what is this story? it may be asked. That is a question I doubt if I should answer. Is it true or fiction? I can no more tell than anyone else who may read it. I can only say, if not true, it is a most ingenious invention, and I should add, that many dates spoken of incidentally in the journal have been inquired into and examined and found correct. But it will be seen, ere I close this account, that one person, who had previously known this "beggar", did believe the story, and asserted that he knew some of the circumstances to have been in the old man's former life. His former life! Then who was he? whence did he come? what had been his life? What was known about him before he came to Bristol, for the strange purpose of dying in the hospital of paupers? The man whom could paint such portraits as his own, and of his deceased wives, it might be thought, might have gained his living.

And then his books – where were they when he sought this miserable refuge, and place of death? Natural questions. No doubt he might have maintained himself. Perhaps there was a delusion in his mind that he could not – perhaps he really could not – from that strange cause I have attributed to that little wandering which becomes the characteristic of some minds, in which misfortune and remembrances that must be shunned have unsettled everything, excepting that root of sanity from which common thoughts and common reasonings and usages of life daily and mechanically proceed.

Certainly no one, in any conversation with him, would for a moment have doubted his perfect sanity; never did he show any tangible symptom – never, that I have heard of, any delusion. If there was one, it was deeply imbedded and out of sight, and no outward spring was visible, or ever touched, that caused a vibration. Perhaps I am wrong in this slightest intimation of a suspicion. But he had been a wanderer; and I have shown my theory, which must be accepted as a general theory. I leave the reader to apply it or reject it, and in any degree, to the individual subject of this memoir.

His patron, whom I should now rather name the legatee, was so much interested in the narrative of Penrose's Journal, that he copied in his own handwriting the whole of it, and had it well bound with blank leaves for illustration of some of its incidents. His friend Nicholas Pocock, the celebrated marine painter, and Edward Bird (subsequently R.A.), made drawings for the book. I was present whenever the latter was at work. The book is now in my sight, with others that belonged to the old man, on my book-shelves. But now, to answer the question as to some further accounts of him. As yet no trace of him had been discovered previous to his coming to Bristol.

But though unknown at the time, there was one man, and probably one man only, who could give any information respecting him. And here I cannot but remark how very curious are coincidences. It was a fortunate coincidence that, on his coming to Bristol, he addressed that particular person, most likely to rescue him from the miserable situation he sought – most likely to appreciate his character, to have sympathy in his tastes and pursuits – most likely to preserve even the little library he had collected, and to value his manuscripts. Without this coincidence everything would, in all probability, have been scattered, utterly lost, and he might have died miserably. There would have been no legacy, and "Penrose's Journal" would have never seen the light.

And here it occurs to mention another coincidence – one of the many that make truth appear more strange than fiction; and which might well cause a suspicion, now and hereafter, to be thrown upon this simple statement I am making. Indeed I know that, though I have so distinctly asserted, and now most distinctly assert the contrary, this work, "Penrose's Journal", has been given to me as its author; and that which I am about to narrate has been treated as a fiction, allowable in novel-making, and as patent an invention as a preface to the *Travels of Lemuel Gulliver*, or any of the numerous impositions which usually amuse the world.

Having so copied out fairly and illustrated this journal of "Penrose, a Seaman", years after the old man's death the copier and legatee, being at his lodgings in London, had taken the manuscript with him. One day, when he was not within, Mr West, President of the Royal Academy,[6] called upon him, and waited his return. On the drawing-room table was the book. Mr West opened it, and, having to wait a considerable time, amused himself by reading a good portion. When the gentleman returned, to his surprise Mr West acquainted him that he knew the author. I find among some papers a memorandum made at the time of this interview with Mr West, of which I here give the substance –

no, I will rather transcribe the memorandum, dated 10th July 1805:-

"He (Mr West) dipped into Penrose's Journal, and read several pages in different parts. I was from home when he came, but returned time enough to give him an account of the author. He seemed very attentive to my history of Williams, and put several questions to me. He said every answer I gave tended to confirm his opinion. 'Sir', said he, 'I have looked at several parts of this book, and much that I have seen I know to be true. I know the man, too; and what is more extraordinary, had it not been for him, I never should have been a painter. It happened thus: I had a relation at Philadelphia, of the name of Pennington, whom I frequently used to visit while there. I saw a person carrying a picture, a landscape, the first, I believe, I had ever seen. I was very much struck with it, and desired him to show it to me. He did; and asked me if I was fond of painting? and, if I was, desired me to come to his house, and he would show me other things. I saw there some cattle-pieces, and admired them, and inquired how he could paint them so accurately? He said he would show me the secret; and took a small box, which proved to be a camera. He showed me the construction of it. I went home, and was not at rest until I had made one for myself; and my father gave me the glass out of an old pair of spectacles to complete it. My delight was then to go out into the farmyards, and, by means of my camera, draw the cattle, &c. I knew that Williams had seen many of the things he describes in the journal; and he gave me the same account of them.

He first lent me *The Lives of the Painters***, which lighted up in my breast a fire which has never been extinguished, and confirmed my inclination for the art. On my return from Italy[7], I sent to my friends in America, as a remembrance of me, my picture, which I had painted whilst abroad. I received a letter from Williams, for that was his name, with a complimentary copy of verses, in which he was pleased to flatter me very highly; but, what is more extraordinary, the lines may be prophetic of my future success in life, which they anticipate. I have his letter and verses by me now somewhere.

I take it, he adopted the name Penrose from a great ship-builder[8] of that name, who was a great friend of his; it being very common for sea-faring men to adopt the names of their particular friends, instead of their own. Williams afterwards came to England. I was of some service to him in London, but of a sudden missed him from town; and on inquiring, I believe of one Smith, an engraver, who knew him well, he told me that he was gone to Bristol, as he was very poor, and had almost lost his eyesight, to claim some provision to which he was entitled from the parish. I was struck with this coincidence with the history of Williams; it induced me to put further questions concerning him, which confirmed my opinion that it was my old friend's composition that was before me; and what you had shown me of *The Lives of the Painters* I knew to be his handwriting." (There is a note here by John Eagles that 'the MS shewn Mr West was copied by my father from the original.')

Again:-

(July) "13th. Saw Mr West again. He said, 'Perhaps I am the only person in existence who could give any account of Williams's life and manners. He first came to Virginia, from London, in a ship commanded by Captain Hunter. Between this time and his appearance in Philadelphia, when I first met him, was an interval of more than twenty years[9]; which time I consider him to have passed in the adventures related in the journal."

I have likewise the following letter from Mr West:

"From the year 1747 to 1760, my attention was directed to every point necessary to accomplish me for the profession of painting. This often brought me to the house of

Williams; and as he was an excellent actor in taking off character, he often, to amuse me, repeated his adventures among the Carribs and Negro tribes in the West Indies - many of which adventures were strictly the same as related in your manuscript of Penrose, as was also the description of the scenery of the coasts, the birds on them, in particular the flamingo birds, which he described, when seen at a distance, as appearing like companies of soldiers dressed in red uniforms. He spoke both the Negro and Carrib tongues, and appeared to have lived among them some years.

I often asked him how he came to be with them; he replied that he had been put to sea when young, that he was never satisfied with that pursuit, & that he took the first opportunity offered to desert it, by making his way for the West Indies, where he was ship-wrecked, & thrown into great difficulties, but Providence had preserved him through a variety of dangers.

He likewise informed me that he was a Welshman by birth; but brought up at a Grammar School in Bristol – where his greatest delight was to go & see an elderly artist who painted heads in oil, as well as small landscapes, and his greatest wish was to be a Painter; but in that he was disappointed, & bound when young to a Virginia Captain who sometimes sailed out of London as well as from Bristol in the Virginia trade."[10]

To this account I can add what I heard from Mr West, that this Williams – so many years having passed since they met in America – surprised him by calling on him in London. He was then painting the battle of La Hogue, and he made Williams sit for a figure in the boat, and whoever wished to see his portrait will see it in this print, and I think, from the description I have given of him, will not miss finding out the man. Mr West further said that he used very frequently to come and smoke his pipe while he (Mr West) was painting; and that he knew him to be collecting prints and heads of painters. That, thinking him poor, he had questioned him, but could never prevail with him to own[11] poverty or to accept money. That he had suddenly missed him, and knew not anything of him till he had read the book at the lodgings in London, and had the interview with the transcriber.

I think that I have shown that this "Beggar" was indeed a singular man. In the midst of poverty, and with perhaps a wounded heart, he wandered, and yet in some way made art his pursuit. He might have had assistance from an able friend, the President of the Academy. He would have none of it; but at an instinct, as it were, yielding to the perverseness of his fortune, he wandered further still, to seek misery, from which, in spite of himself, Fortune, to show her caprice, rescued him, and compelled him to rest at last, and die in peace.

But I have said nothing yet of the value of the legacy. I will speak but of one part of it. I sold to Mr Murray one edition of the "Journal of Penrose, Seaman", for two hundred guineas. It appeared in 1815 in four volumes. Subsequently I received a proposal from Messrs Hessey and Taylor for another edition. It appeared in one volume, but, owing to circumstances relating to that firm, I received no accounts, and cannot speak of its success. Thus ends this narrative, which I have thought so curious, of such strange coincidences and character, that I have specially made it the subject of a paper for Maga.[12] I hope, with the accompanying comments, it has been amusing, if not instructing. At least it may teach, from this example of the fraternity, not to be too hard upon beggars, and think with Mr Bumble[13] that they all deserve whipping.

For neither would any Bumble, nor many of his superiors, were they in my place, as legatee in succession, despise a "Beggar's Legacy". No, let none despise a "beggar", with or without a legacy prospect. Who knows who a beggar may be? Archbishop Usher[14] appeared as a beggar at a curate's gate, and was reproved by the curate's wife for misnumbering the commandments, as being eleven; but it was understood when next morning he preached a sermon in the church, and gave out his text – "A new commandment I give unto you, that ye love one another." By this, said he, it should appear that there are eleven commandments. The good curate's wife would not again say, "for shame, old man", - and there will be some wisdom in all of us, if we be made cautious of casting contempt even on a poor beggar. May we not sometimes even go beyond this forebearance?

Reader, I will give you an example of a beggar worthy (of) your very highest admiration – one neither fabulous nor of a worn-out date, but of this day, at this hour. The last example was of an archbishop, and he in disguise; this shall be of a bishop, and not in any disguise, but in the very dignity of beggary. It is known that Bishop Selwyn[15], when he supposed he was by agreement to receive from the Government £600 per annum, for the expenditure imposed by his Episcopal office, gave up his private fortune, and devoted it to the best purposes. Finding himself, however, deprived of his Parliamentary grant, and altogether without resources, he simply said, "he would dig, or beg, or both"; and indeed pious bishop will not, and need not ever say, "Dig I cannot – to beg I am ashamed".

It may not be difficult to make out pretty clearly that, in some way or other; we are all beggars – all of one fraternity, and requiring aid in some need. Let us then accept willingly the archbishop's eleventh commandment, and look to ourselves, that we do "love one another". We may perhaps, in that case, all receive a "Beggar's Legacy", payable from a never-failing fund, by the hands of those pure celestial executrixes – Faith, Hope and Charity.'

*The Journal of Llewellin Penrose, a Seaman. Four volumes, 8vo. London: Printed for John Murray, Albemarle Street; and William Blackwood, Edinburgh. 1815.

The Same. One volume. With a Print, and Vignette in the Title-page. A New Edition, London: Printed for taylor and Hessey, 93 Fleet Street, and 13 Waterloo Place, Pall Mall. 1825

**This book, in Williams's handwriting, which was then lent to the youth West, is now in my possession.

A NOTE ON THE REVEREND JOHN EAGLES 1783-1855

The Rev. John Eagles was born in St Augustine parish, Bristol in 1783. He was the son of Thomas Eagles (1748-1812), a classical scholar. John Eagles was educated at Winchester College and at Wadham College, Oxford (BA. 1812, MA. 1818). His curacies were at St Nicholas, Bristol; Hambleton, Devon; Winford, Bristol; and Kinnersley, Herefordshire. Eagles was a keen painter, etcher and poet, and from 1831, became a regular contributor of artwork and original or translated poetry to *Blackwood's Magazine*. In 1841, he retired and returned to Bristol. Eagles died in 1855, the year his 'The Beggar's Legacy' article was first published in *Blackwoods*. Eagles also had poetry published in *Felix Farley's Bristol Journal* by its editor and Eagles' friend, John Mathew Gutch. Some of this work was published in Bristol in 1826 under the title *Felix Farley, Rhymes, Latin and English by Themaninthemoon*. The manuscript is held by Nottingham University. In one poem in *Felix Farley's Bristol Journal*, Eagles exposed abuses which had existed in several public bodies in Bristol, especially in the Corporation. A volume entitled *Sonnets* was edited by Zoe King, and published in Edinburgh and London in 1858. Zoe King tried to get *The Journal of Penrose* republished (see letters below). The university also holds watercolour sketches of the English Lake District by the Reverend John Eagles. The paintings are contained in a small sketchbook entitled '*6 Views of The Lakes 1812 by John Eagles*'. Bristol Record Office has acquired his personal papers.

John Eagles was a clergyman, artist and author. His ambition to become a professional landscape artist in the tradition of Poussin was not to be, and after being refused membership by the Old Water-Colour Society in 1809, he decided to take holy orders. A graduate of Oxford, he followed the theories of art outlined in Reynolds's Discourses. In the early nineteenth century, the Bristol School of picturesque landscape painting grew up, patronized by the city's merchant class. It was a rather genteel school of mainly pastoral paintings peopled with, as one of its leading members, John Eagles stated "*beings that are not on the poor's books.*" The Bristol School consisted of a mixture of professional and amateur artists. The amateur painters included George Cumberland (1754-1848), the enthusiastic and influential Reverend Eagles, and John King (1766-1846). The professionals were Edward Bird (1772-1819), Nicholas Pocock (1740-1821) (both of whom illustrated *The Journal of Penrose*), Nathan Cooper Branwhite (1775-1857), Edward Villiers Rippingille (1798-1859), Samuel Colman (1780-1845), George Holmes (1776-c1861), Samuel Jackson (1830-1904), William West (1801-1861) and Francis Danby (1793-1861). Several of Eagles' paintings have come up for sale in the last few years, mainly watercolours, fetching low prices.

By the mid 1820s, there was considerable controversy in the London art world about the point and value of apocalyptic pictures. Eagles, known as '*the Bristol connoisseur*', wrote:

"*... themes sublime – the fiery rain,*
Departing Lot, the blazing plain;
Heaven's vengeance upon Egypt dealt;
Its blood, - its darkness to be felt;...
So DANBY finds, an artist's fame.
Learn this, ye painters of dead stumps,
Old barges, and canals, and pumps."

Danby was a landowner's son and studied art at the Dublin Society. In 1813 he visited London, then worked in Bristol, initially on repetitious watercolours of local scenes: for example *View of Hotwells, the Avon Gorge* (1818), also painted by William Williams. In about 1819 he entered the circle of George Cumberland [1754-1849] and the Rev. John Eagles. Danby's discovery of the '*poetry of nature*' in local scenery and insignificant incident was influenced by the theories of Eagles, published as *The Sketcher* (1856).

In 1831 Bristol suffered the worst civil disturbances in its history during the political reform riots. Most of the city, including Queen Square and the Mansion House fell under mob rule. The New Gaol was attacked by rioters who breached its iron gates after battering them with sledge hammers and crowbars for three-quarters of an hour, allowing a small boy to get inside and draw back its bolts. John Eagles wrote "*The force of the mob was every moment fearfully increasing, a dense mass had collected, and on the other side of the river, wherever the eye could range. Thousands were in motion.*" ('*The Bristol Riots, their Causes, Progress, and Consequences* by A Citizen' i.e Eagles).

Around 170 prisoners were freed and joined the mob, the gaol's treadmill and gallows were set upon and were thrown into the adjacent New Cut. The prison was then set on fire by the mob; the flames could be seen as far away as Wales. Order was eventually restored to the city by troops from Gloucester who opened fire on the mob, killing around 130 of them. In the following days those arrested for their part in the riots were tried before the Bristol Court. Five received the death penalty. Christopher Davies, John Kayes, Richard Vines, Thomas Gregory and William Clarke were all sentenced to be hanged over the entrance of the New Gaol On Friday 27th January 1832, four of the condemned men were led out to the top of the gatehouse where the open-air scaffold had been erected. Despite a petition to King William IV signed by 10,000 Bristolians, "including several merchants of the greatest respectability," there was to be no reprieve.

A Garland of Roses, Gathered from the Poems by John Eagles (& John Mathew Gutch ed.) was privately published in Worcester in 1832. Mr Gutch's own reserved copy was in the sale catalogue of his library sold by Sotheby's in 1858, and was bought for 4 pounds and 6 shillings. 50 copies were printed.

There is also a letter signed by John Eagles dated 15th March 1832, to George Rogers, (14 College Green, Bristol - Attorney) referring to cottages owned by the Dean & Chapter which he lets out to tenants, and complaining of the bad state of repair, *'Should the Dean & Chapter determine to keep them up Mr. Finnimore had better have the work estimated'*. He also refers to *'a Parish School which I am desirous of establishing'*. Eagles was then Curate of Halberton, his rector being Sidney Smith.

From 1833 he had been a regular contributor to *Blackwood's Magazine* on a wide range of subjects, and wrote under the pseudonym of *'The Sketcher'*. Eagles' suggestion, made in 1842, that Blackwood's should publish a periodical entirely devoted to the arts, and which Eagles himself would edit, was accepted. After his death Eagles was described as a *'highly-accomplished old English clergyman and country gentleman"* by Margaret Oliphant reviewing *Modern Painters I* in *Blackwood's Magazine*, December 1855, and by his obituarist as *'a Tory of the old school in matters of both Church and State'* in the same publication.

A dispute between Ruskin and Eagles followed Eagles' critical attack on Turner in 1836, provoking a long-lived animosity which not only coloured the relationship between Ruskin and *Blackwood's*, but developed into a wider dispute between Ruskin and other critics. *'Turner is the exception to all rules, and can be judged by no other standard of art...'* wrote John Ruskin, aged just 17, in reply to an attack on Turner by Eagles, then art critic of *Blackwood's Magazine*, in 1836. Eagles had described Turner's *'Juliet and Her Nurse'* as *'...a composition as from different parts of Venice, thrown higgledy-piggledy together, streaked blue and pink and thrown into a flour tub'*. Eagles aroused Ruskin's passions enough to spur him on to the great heights of art criticism which he eventually achieved, and most importantly for his unequivocal defence of his hero, Turner.

There is a very strange entry on the Wells College, Aurora, New York website: *'Historic portraits: Four 19th century oil paintings by noted artist Charles Loring Elliott have been located and will be restored to hang above the fireplaces on the first floor of the Inn. They depict members of the Eagles family who owned and managed the Inn during the 1840s and 1850s. One of the family members, John Eagles (1783-1855), was a former sea captain (he holds a telescope in his portrait) who ran an inn across Cayuga Lake at Ovid before moving to the Aurora Inn'*. These are the exact dates of the Rev. John Eagles.

CHAPTER IV

Letters in the Williams Collection in the Lilly Library
Letters in the Murray Collection

In Chronological Order

Letter to Mr William Williams, Limner, No. 24 Merchants Alms House, Bristol
Philadelphia May 26th, 1788, from Benjamin Condy (Lilly Library)
Dear Friend,
I received yours of Feb 12th, I am glad to hear that you are still in the land of the living; as I
had concluded that (you) were numbered with the dead. I never could tell what was gone with
you, & what was still worse, I have not been able to see anybody that could. I have frequently
reflected on the agreeable hours we have spent together, and the pleasing conversation in our
little rural excursions. I often think how delightful it was, after the fatigue of the day, to hear
you play on your harmonious flute; but more particularly to hear you tell all the pleasing
anecdotes that were so often introduced between the tunes, and in your attracting conversation
(far too much for a letter to express). But these pleasures are now over, & nothing but the
recollection of them is left. I fear they will never return – I am very sorry to hear of your
misfortunes, & could have wished you a better state. I have not been without my share of
trouble – I have been driven by the war about the country. I have spent a fortune in wandering;
but, thank God! I am now in good circumstances – we must now content ourselves; as we
cannot by the course of nature expect to live much longer, & even if we could it would be a life
of wretchedness and sorrow – Soon must we expect to leave this gaudy world with all its finery
and pleasures, to enjoy one far better, & from which all grief and pain are excluded.
I will use the utmost care, & pains, & make all the enquiry, I can, after your son; but I am at
a loss whom to enquire of. If you can throw any light on the affair let me know ti, & nothing
shall be wanting to serve a friend whom I have the greatest respect for.
I remain Sir
Your fond? friend
Benj. Condy

William Williams' First (Unsigned) Will, April 6 1788,
in the possession of the Graham-Clarke family of Parc Llettis, Abergavenny, Wales
IN THE NAME OF GOD, AMEN. *I William Williams of the parish of St. Augustine in the*
City of Bristol, Mariner and painter being in sound state of Knowledge and Memory, and of the
Age of 61 Years and being truly sensible that every Mortal man must die, according to holy
Ordinance, do make this my last Will and Testament, first I Desire to be privately buried in the
parish Church Yard of St. Augustine, which Church, I was baptiz'd in, otherwise, by my
Mother who was buried in the Ground pertaining to the Church of St Stephen, at the Gibb,
judging what little may be left to Inter me. My Temporal Estate I Bequeath & Dispose of in the

257

following Manner:

Imprimis. To My Daughter in Law Mrs. Mary Byrchmore, the only Daughter of my Late Deceas'd wife Esther Williams, 1 Folio Bible, 1 Folio Josephus, also her Mother's Hymn Book, one Topaz Ring, one Mourning Ring, in Memory of Ann Williams my Eldest Sister also I Bequeath unto her the portraits of my Two Wives, with 5 Volumes of my Own M.S. Writing, on Religious Tracts &c. also I Bequeath unto Thos Eagles Esq. Two large Folio Volumes entitled Heads of Illustrious Artizans, together with my own portrait, with the picture I am attempting on the subject Penrose, God enabling me to finish the same having a hearty Desire thereunto, through a pure spirit of Gratitude, to that Gentleman, — also I give and Bequeath unto Richard Vigor Junr. all Books pertaining to me tending to the Art of painting also 1 Box of Water Colours and all other Appurtenances belonging to the Art, together with what Designs or Prints may be left at the Time of my Decease, save those few which Mr. Eagles may chuse for himself. Also I bequeath unto the said Richd. Vigor, one small Box of medals, with what other books there may be, and now judging what little may be Left will be sufficient to inter me. Hoping that my Faithful Friend will guard my remains against all earthly Rapacious Wolves of what ever Denomination, 'tis my Desire that when that Day shall arrive if Messrs. Richd. Vigor Senr. & Jr. are alive and upon the Spot, that they do attend My Funeral as Mourners, & previous to that Day and on that Day, I beseech my Glorious Redeemer's intercession to his Divine Father for the Remission of all my Sins, — N.B. I appoint my well Experienced Friend Thos. Eagles Esqr. Of Park Street & City aforesaid, to be my only Executor to proceed in Form as above, in due Consideration & Regard of the many Beneficial favours receiv'd from his person, I do with all Love& Regard Acknowledge the same, from him & his Worthy Consort. — I do hereby confirm this, & no other to be my last Will & Testament. In Witness whereof I have hereunto set my Hand & Seal.

Note: A man was sentenced to death by hanging at Newgate, by Bristol Assizes in 1790, for attempting to defraud Richard Vigor with a forged Bill of Exchange.

Letter to Thomas Eagles Esq., 4 Pall Mall
June 9th, 1805, from Richard Phillips (Lilly Library)

Sir,

Since I saw you on Saturday, I have considered & reconsidered of the affair of your Mr P. in every point of view of which I conceive the subject susceptible. I still feel with all its force the embarrassment which hangs over the question of the authenticity of the work & I really feel that it will be impossible to divest it of its apocryphal character.

The letter of Paul Taylor, its date, & the strange circumstances which it narrates are stumbling blocks which I cannot surmount. The obscure account of his birth <u>near</u> Caerphilly, of his residence in Wales, without saying where, & the omission of all those minute details which were calculated to secure the credence and reception of his narrative in England, convince me as fully that the work is a work of fiction as though I had seen the fabricator with his pen in his hand ruminating after new accidents & adventures.

In a word I cannot lend myself to bring out the work as a genuine Narrative, or rather <u>as a</u> genuine narrative I will not give <u>a great price</u>? for it, & in that way count myself on the issue. If you cannot make a better bargain, or one more agreeable to you, I have no objection to bear the expenses of bringing out the work & its contents myself with 10% of the profit, till they have produced to you the sum of 600 guineas, & I will thenceforward divide the profits & the property in the work equally with you, leaving to each the liberty of selling, unless the other will give three years purchase? for it. The amount to be stated every Lady Day & Michaelmas for the sales to Xmas and Midsummer, & the sum due to you to be drawn for 3 months.

A preface must be prefixed? and signed by you, in which you must give an account of Mr P.
I beg these terms may be considered as my ultimatum & I send the Mr P herewith, that you may be a free agent.
With many thanks, as with a grateful sentiment of your urbane and polite consent
I am, Sir, faithfully, yours,
R Phillips, Bridge St.
There is listed on the back of this envelope, in Phillips' writing, the following:
Penrose born (from) Journal May 1725
Taken on his cruise to Spanish Main in 1747 in his 22nd year
Cast away on the continent of S. America same year
Remained there (from) Journal 27 years which makes to the year 1774 when he was in his 49th year
Lived afterwards in America where W. Pocock knew him between 1774 + 82
Came to Bristol about the year 1785 when he appeared to be about 60 years of age
Date of Paul Taylor's letter May 1783
Note: Sir Richard Phillips (1767 - 1840), the publisher, was born in London of a Leicestershire family. His original name was Philip Richard. He worked first as a school-master and subsequently as a hosier. In 1790 he set up as a book-seller in Leicester and founded the Leicester Herald in 1792. 3 years later he was goaled for selling Thomas Paines' *Rights of Man*. He then moved to London and started the Monthly magazine in 1796. He was a sheriff of the City of London in 1807 and was knighted in 1808. A noted vegetarian, in 1823 he retired to Brighton where he died.

Letter to Thomas Eagles, 4 Pall Mall
July 1, 1805, from Richard Phillips, Richmond, London (Lilly Library)
Dear Sir,
I earnestly wished you had related? in your letter to all that has passed between us, & not have partially misrepresented me as you have.
After I had first examined the ms., I decided completely against its authenticity & informed you that I should rather decline it. I returned it. How we came together after, I now forget – but the application was certainly made by you. I was over-persuaded by you; & 500 guineas was agreed on with the condition that I should not feel myself bound till I had slept upon the proposal, nor till I had seen Mr Pocock and learnt from him the extent of his guarantee.
However I did not wait to sleep but having considered fully of the business, I wrote to you the same evening to say that I would not hold myself engaged for more than 400 guineas.
You came the next morning – but my letter had not then reached you. The business was again talked over, the times of payment were altered – & 500 guineas were again reverted to – only however to the same terms, as before – that I would take a night and see Mr Pocock with you in the morning.
I again calculated, & found that 1500 copies would yield £440 profit which sum I offered you definitively.
The next morning you visited me again and £420 was mutually preferred and agreed at an average note? of 12 months, with 200 guineas after the sale of 2500 guineas worth of the work, still subject to the attestation of Mr Pocock which was to be such as I wished – and it was further agreed that the editorship of W. Cheshire? should be secured.
I waited for the closing & ratifying of these terms & have wondered that you have not called on me. I go out of town tomorrow, & of course your letter closes the negotiation.
If I have wavered in my ideas, it has only been in your favour.

If I have demurred & hesitated it has only been because I have not yet been able to persuade myself that the work is genuine.

Believe me, Dear Sir, faithfully, yours, R. Phillips

Letter to Richard Phillips, London
July 2nd 1805, from Thomas Eagles (Lilly Library)

I can assure you that it was with no view to misrepresentation, I omitted to state the whole that had passed between us. Two circumstances which take no colour? from what passed before or after them, strongly impressed themselves upon my mind; To these I wished to call of attention, as on these alone I felt I had some right to complain. I mean the variation of terms on the faith of which, I had actually rejected an advantageous offer & the want of confidence respecting the bills, with the journal in your possession.

The terms which I take from your own writing were Bills @4.8.10.14.20 Months @ 100 Guineas each 1000 guineas @ 6 months after the sale of 2500 copies.

You will please to observe that when these terms were agreed upon between us, there was no reservation of a night's meditation.

I told you that when I left your house, I should immediately act(?) as I had already put off for a day, the giving an answer to the Gentleman I was in treaty, and whose terms, eventually offered me a much fairer prospect of profit than yours. You suffered me to leave your house for this purpose, I went accordingly to Mr Pocock & with him waited on the Gentleman and rejected his proposals.

This is I believe an exact statement of facts. The terms were specifically stated – I did not think myself at liberty to deviate from them in the slightest degree. I cannot give you a stronger proof that such was the impression on my mind, than the conduct I pursued on this occasion, by immediately rejecting the proposals that had been made to me. If I thought myself bound by these terms, I thought you were no less so, or I would not have proceeded to act upon them. Now Sir let me ask you, whether having thus acted on them, in full confidence of the same compliance on your part, I am not justified in complaining of any attempt to violate them.

However unpleasant it may be for me to submit to the conditional payment of the last 100 guineas, having once consented to it, I hold myself bound not to offer it as an objection at this moment. I will abide strictly to the terms of that engagement, to the performance of which, I think, we are equally and honourably bound. I shall not leave town before Monday next; I will retain the Journal in my hand till Friday for your answer. As the terms are precisely those which were dictated by yourself on which, considering myself as bound by them, I have acted; I offer them once more for your consideration, whether you accept them or not, I should not be satisfied in my own mind without making you this offer.

In regard to the authority of the Journal and the testimony you may expect from Mr Pocock, allow me to say a few words that you may know how far either of you can meet your wishes. I have drawn up a short narrative of my connection and acquaintance with W. Williams, the author of the Journal, and the reasons I have for believing it to be a genuine history of his life, veiled with some slight fictions such as his name, birthplace, death & co. & perhaps the concealment of some circumstances which may have happened on the Spanish Main, in which he might have been more an actor than a spectator. My belief is founded on my observation of the character and conduct of the man, and confirmed by many conversations I have held with him, in which subjects connected with the Journal have been incidentally started and discussed & by his words & actions at all times when it was mentioned, as well as when he first put it into my hands. I conjure I think good reasons for I have it in my power to give a more complete and satisfactory account of it. My own mind has been satisfied, how far I may succeed in convincing others I know not – The facts I shall relate, I have no reason to think will be doubted, the inferences from those facts will have weight or not, in proportion as they are fairly deducible from the premises.

Of what use Mr Pocock's testimony may be I cannot gauge. He can only state generally that he knew the man, that frequently seen him at my house whilst he was in Bristol, & that from his conduct, conversation, and opinion of the Journal coincided with mine, though he cannot state that he had any conversation with him on the subject of it, as I am not at all aware whether at the time Mr Pocock knew him in Bristol, the Journal was in my possession. If Mr Pocock's opinion may be thought necessary to bolster up my reputation for veracity; to this he is fully competent, & will, I am sure, give you the most complete satisfaction as to my character, conduct & connections.

Though I cannot bind myself to obtain Mr Clarke's consent to appear as the Editor and to give my narrative in the 3rd person, yet if you agree to the terms, you may mention it as a condition in consequence of his celebrity & I will try all my interest with that of my family to procure it. I have written as fully on the subject as the compass of a letter will permit – whatever be your resolution, you will take this further effort as proof of my respect & (behaviour?)

Letter to Thomas Eagles, 4 Pall Mall
July 3, 1805, from Richard Phillips in Brighton (Lilly Library)
Dear Sir,

I am favoured with your letter which I assure you I consider as a compliment.

I can only confirm my concern that you should have relinquished any of the treaty in consequence of that feuding(?) between you & me. You said you would do so – but I peremptorily desired that you would not, & certainly hold myself in no respect responsible.

I admit that you possess an interesting property in the Journal of Penrose, but its value depends so much on the correct(?) mode in which it is brought forward – that I never felt more anxiety about any literary project which has been submitted to me.

Supported by such a name as that of Mr Clarke, in addition to your Mr Pocock, it may pass comment as a narrative of fact to be generally read – without the aid of such testimony I am not sanguine about it.

If it is to stand on its intrinsic merits as a work of fiction, I confess I am not a competent judge of it, from the cursory view I have taken of it. As a reality, the general facts are sufficient for me to judge from – but as a work of fiction it must be judged, & from its details, its language, and a variety of minute particulars which I have not yet regarded?

If you would do every thing needful to give it currency as a narrative and tract – it is certainly worth what I have offered you: but if it is only half authorated(?) – its credit unpropped by any reputable name known to the world – or is at once admitted like Robinson Crusoe to be but an ingenious fiction – I should consider £100 as enough to give for it with another £100 on the sale of every 1000 copies.

In a world, I have some credit with the world & I should fear to lose it if I sanctioned this work, in any other way than as a reality, not to be lightly questioned, or as an ingenious Romance, published as such, or at least not accompanied by indifferent proofs of reality.

I am sorry my distance is unpropitious to the progress of this negotiation. I hope however that I have made myself intelligible & that you will believe me to be,

Sincerely and faithfully, yours R. Phillips

Note in Thomas Eagles' writing, of the visit of Benjamin West and the journal July 10 1805 (Lilly Library)

Mr Annerley brought Mr West to see Penrose's Journal – he (Mr West) dipped into it and read several pages in different parts. I was from home when he came, but returned (in) time enough to give him an account of the author – he seemed very attentive to my history of Williams & put several questions to me – he said every answer I gave tended to confirm his opinion – "Sir," said he "I looked at several parts of this book, & much that I have seen I know to be true – I knew the man too, & what is more extraordinary, had it not been for him I should never have been a painter – it happened thus – I had a sister married to a person of Philadelphia of the name of Pennington, my father lived in the country & I used frequently to pay my sister a visit. While I was there, I saw a person carrying a picture, a landscape the first I believe I had ever seen, I was very much struck with, and desired the person to show it to me, he did and asked me if I was fond of painting, and if I was, desired me to come to his house.

Then – he showed me other things – I saw there some cattle pieces, admired them and inquired how he could paint them so accurately – he said he would show me the secret & took a small box which proved to be a camera, he showed me the construction of it. I went home and was not at rest until I made one myself – my father gave the glass out of an old pair of spectacles to complete it. My delight then was to go into the farm yards & by means of my camera draw the cattle & co.

I know that he (Williams) had seen many of the things he describes in the Journal & he gave me the same account of them. He first gave me 'The Lives of the Painters'* which confirmed my inclination for the art – On my return from Italy, I sent to my friends in America my picture, (which crossed out) I had painted it whilst abroad – I received a letter from Williams for that was his name, with a complimentary copy of verses in which he was pleased to flatter me very highly, but what is most extraordinary (is that) the lines may be considered as a prophesy of my future success in life, which it anticipates in a most extraordinary manner. I have his letter and the verses by me now somewhere.

I take it he adopted the name Penrose from one of that name at Philadelphia, a great shipbuilder, who was a great friend of his."**

Williams afterwards came to England, & I was of some service to him in London, but of a sudden missed I him from town & upon inquiring, I believe of one Smith, an engraver, who knew him well – he told me he was gone to Bristol, as he was very poor and had almost lost his eyesight, to claim some provision to which he was entitled from the parish. The moment you mentioned that he came to you to claim the assistance of the parish I was struck with this coincidence with the history of Williams & induced me to put further questions concerning him, which confirmed my opinion that it was my old friend's composition that was then before me, & what you have shown me of 'The Lives of the Painters', I know to be in his handwriting.

[The next lines are overwritten on the note, 3 days later]

13ᵗʰ Saw Mr West again. He said perhaps he was the only person in existence who could give any account of Williams' life and manners – he first came to Virginia in a ship commanded by Captain Hunter - between this time and his appearance in Philadelphia, when I first met with him, was an interval of more than twenty years, which time I consider him to have passed in the adventures related in the journal.'

*In the 1855 article 'The Beggar's Legacy', there is a clause here which reads 'which lighted up a fire in my breast which has never been extinguished, and'.

** Ditto another clause appears, reading 'it being very common for sea-faring men to adopt the names of their particular friends, instead of their own'.

Letter from Thomas Eagles to John Murray II.
26 Jan 1807 (Murray Collection)

When I took the pains to copy the journal of Penrose, I was so delighted with the simplicity of the narrative, and so interested with the events of it, that I entertain'd no doubt, if the work should come before the public, that it would be equally a favourite with every class of readers; and in this opinion I was confirmed by the judgment of several literary friends, who did me the favour to peruse the MS. With this expectation, I brought the journal with me to Town. The first person who made me an offer for it was Mr Millar in Albermarle Street, it was his intention to publish it in 4to. in a very handsome manner; we differed only as to the mode and times of payment. It was afterwards shewn to others of the trade, and I was detained in town a considerable time under various pretences, 'till at length I grew quite tired of the business; where I expected openness and candour, I found only intrigue and combination, and I was fully convinc'd that I was not a competent negotiator with such a concern. I therefore left town, and W. Clarke was kind enough to say that he would undertake the disposal of it; this was in July 1805, so much time has elaps'd since, and nothing done, that it has become a kind of dead letter with me. Tho' I feel as much interest as ever in the narrative, I am become quite indifferent as to the publication of it.

If it be your proposal, to take the MS to Scotland, and if approv'd of by your friend Mr Walter Scott then to treat with me for the purchase of it, I object to this mode. I think it better previously to state to you the terms on which I am willing to dispose of the journal; they are as follow Six hundred guineas to be paid in such installments as shall be agreed on To preserve a limited interest in the work, by an engagement to be paid fifty pounds on the appearance of every new edition.// If possible the MS copy and the drawings to be return'd to me after the publication. // If you do not object to these terms, which I wish to have clearly understood previous to your journey to Scotland, I will consent that the journal shall be put into your hands to be submitted to the opinion of Mr Scott, provided that in the six weeks from the delivery of it, you will give me a decisive answer, whether or not you will be the purchaser. [...] The moment I receive your answer, if you approve of the terms, I will write to Mr West and to Mr Clarke. [postscript] I shall be anxious to know Mr Scott's opinion as no one can entertain a higher respect for his genius, judgment and fancy that [sic] I do.

Note a: 'Mr Millar' is William Miller, who occupied premises on Albermarle Street from 1807–11. He was succeeded at those premises in 1812 by John Murray II. According to the timing of the letter, Miller would have been at his old address on Bond Street at the time Eagles first approached him about the novel. W. Clarke is a London publisher, who co-partnered many publications from 1787 to 1813, and eventually set up W. Clarke & Sons at the Shakespeare's Head behind London's Royal Exchange. Eagles' letter of 1 Feb 1807, says that he will have the novel delivered to either Murray or Clarke. Mr West is the painter Benjamin West. West knew William Williams well (see letter of 28 Oct 1807, below). Both Thomas Eagles and his son John were also painters, which could also explain their possible acquaintance with Benjamin West.

Note b: For a time, Edinburgh rivalled London as a centre for British publishing. John Murray was established in 1768 and became a leading British publisher, with an unrivalled galaxy of authors, including Charles Darwin, Jane Austen and Lord Byron.

Letter from Thomas Eagles to John Murray II. 1 Feb 1807 (Murray Collection)
I did not receive your letter in time to answer it by the same post. I am fully satisfied with the

contents of it, and shall at once write to Mr West to deliver the journal either to you or to Mr Clarke.

Note: Mr Clarke is Murray's employee George Rix Clarke.

Letter from Archibald Constable to John Murray II. 14 Mar 1807 (Murray Collection)

[Walter Scott is visiting London and will see Murray when he arrives.] *He is to tell you particularly what he thinks of Penrose's Journal—and in case the M. S. should be wanted I thought it proper to send it you.*

Note: Archibald Constable (1774-1827) began as a bookseller's apprentice in Edinburgh and published *The Edinburgh Review* and the *Encyclopaedia Britannica*. However, it was his partnership with Sir Walter Scott which brought spectacular success to his publishing house.

Letter from John Murray to Archibald Constable & Co. 27 Mar 1807 (Murray Collection)

Mr [Walter] Scott called upon me on Tuesday and we conversed for an hour I mentioned Penrose to him (the MSS) which he thinks very interesting although rather too long—He thinks the price out of all propriety & I shall therefore return the volume with a Letter enquiring if the proprietor be willing to listen to more moderate terms.

Letter from Thomas Eagles to John Murray II. 12 Apr 1807 (Murray Collection)

Early in the month of Feb[uar]y the journal of Penrose was delivered to you for the purpose of being submitted to the judgment of your friend Mr Walter Scott. The terms, on which I was willing to dispose it, you were previously acquainted with, & it was at the same time stipulated, that I was to receive your answer in the course of six weeks. I presume, you are by this time returned to Town; if the work is such, as to induce you to comply with the terms, I am ready to enter into the further necessary arrangements; if not sufficiently approved of to justify your engaging in such an adventure, I will beg you, at once, to return the MS to me by the first coach.

Letter from John Murray II to Thomas Eagles. 21 Apr 1807 (Murray Collection)

The desire which I had of being the Publisher of Penrose's Manuscript has led me to retain it some days since its return to me from Scotland with the hope that I might be able to suggest some arrangement to meet your desire respecting it but upon referring to your former Letter I find the Terms to be too preemptory (i.e. imperative) that if I cannot accord with them I will not affront you by offering you any thing less & I therefore reluctantly return the Book by this Evenings Mail according to the desire expressed in your letter of the 12th. If I might flatter myself that it would not be ungrateful to you to receive other Proposals I shall feel happy to have the pleasure of corresponding with you upon the subject. (Murray plans on visiting Bristol and asks if he might call on Eagles.) *In the mean time anxious to be informed that the M.S. has safely arrived.*

Letter from Thomas Eagles to John Murray II. 23 Apr 1807 (Murray Collection)

I have the pleasure to acquaint you that Penrose is arriv'd perfectly safe, and after so long an absence I am much pleas'd to see it once more in its place in my library. I shall make no further effort to dispose of it ... (postscript) I think Mr Scott must have been pleas'd with Penrose.

Letter from Thomas Eagles to John Murray II. 13 Oct 1807. (Murray Collection)
What is the kind of offer you would make for Penrose's journal if I should be disposed to part with it?
Note: This letter is dated 13 Oct 1807, and seems slightly out of sequence with the above letters. It is possible that Murray and Eagles continued negotiations over the novel, after Murray returned the MS to Eagles in April 1807.

Letter from Thomas Eagles to John Murray II. 28 Oct 1807 (Murray Collection)
I am sorry you do not feel an inducement to make an offer for Penrose, as it is a work that, I think, would be universally read and as universally approv'd of. I intend in a kind of preface to relate all I know concerning the author, with some curious anecdotes from Mr West, who was well acquainted with him, and what is more extraordinary, that gentleman would never have been a painter, had it not been for this man whose real name was Wm. Williams. I have no doubt but that the whole history is founded on facts which actually happen'd to the author, Mr West is of the same opinion, and can account for the time when he met with those adventures, after his first appearance in America. Could I for a moment believe the whole narrative to be fiction, I should consider it as a wonderful effort of the human mind, and look upon the author as a much more extraordinary personage than I have hitherto done. The book is, I think, in merit and interest infinitely superior to that popular fiction Robinson Crusoe [...]. The engravings to Penrose might be made on wood with good effect, which would considerably lessen the expence of publication. Whenever I dispose of this work I shall require a certain sum to be paid down or in short instalments, and reserve a specific interest in every edition after the first.

Undated, incomplete note in Thomas Eagles' handwriting, c.1810 (Lilly Library)
My letter to the Rev. N. Carlisle, Gloucester House – Since I dispatched my letter I have seen by the Court Calendar that the Secretary of State is N. Carlisle Esq. If therefore I do not receive an answer in a few days, I will write again and apologise for the mistake. I presume that my appearance in November may not be dispensed with, I must therefore endure as to obtain permission for that purpose, as the duties of my office are a considerable constraint on my locomotive privileges; Though I may appear somewhat extraordinary, that I have the power of granting a week's leave of absence to any of the subordinate officers, I cannot understand I have no authority to confer that favour upon myself.
When I have a little more command of my time which may be towards the winter, as during the summer months, I am really good for nothing – I shall endeavour to arrange my thoughts and papers on the subject of the poems so generally adjudged to Chatterton, and address them in a letter to you, which if not foreign to the purposes of the society, and you shall approve of it, may be read then. Pray may a complete set of Archaeologia be had of the printer to the society? Can you inform me of what means to pursue them?
X (Penrose)
X It gives me great pleasure to hear that Mr West has determined at length to put pen to paper on the subject of the author of Penrose's Journal. You will have the goodness to hint to him that he cannot be too particular, as it is his first acquaintance with the man, the time he first arrived in Virginia – the many years between his first arrival there and his meeting him at Philadelphia – The letter of Williams from America announcing the arrival of W. Prats(?) portrait, & the lines which appear to have been prophetic of the royal patronage he has since enjoyed – and particularly to state that several incidents in the Journal he had related to him, as truth that had actually happened to him – these several particulars you may have an opportunity of urging to Mr West on your return from Cowbridge, when he shall have leisure to complete this little

narrative, which will be of infinite importance to the work.

I see by the papers that Mr Davis has made a very handsome purchase of the Gun & nets picture, which was in the last exhibition at Somerset House this last summer – By Mr West's very kind attention to the merits of Mr Bird, the Prince has purchased and actually paid 250 guineas for his last picture & Lord Moine has bid for an other at his own price, leaving the choice of subject to him. I am ashamed to think that he has not done what he promised for you, he knows I am displeased at his delay, and whenever I speak on this subject I always promises Arnee(?) to set about it.

Though I do not buy pictures, I have by exchange a few drawings purchased(?) a very fine & undoubted Murillo, and a very sick(?) landscape by Jasper(?) Prussia(?) I wish Mr West could see my bonus(?) in his present state, I could point some particulars that I think would convince him of the originality of the picture, which Mr Barry told me he did not doubt, and its being painted on canvas he said was so objective, as he had seen several painted, and I recollect that no such objection was made to Mt Otley's reported Correggio – my little Gainsborough looks very beautiful.

It is with great satisfaction that I tell you that I am very much....

Benjamin West, Newman Street, London
October 10, 1810 to Thomas Eagles (Lilly Library)

(This is in Eagles' handwriting, a copy of the original letter)

Dear Sir,

The voluminous manuscript under the signature Penrose which I saw in your possession (through the introduction of our respected friend Mr Annesley[1] of Reading) appears to me on the investigation of it to have been written by a William Williams of Philadelphia, & founded on his adventures amongst the uncivilized aborigines in the West India Islands - and not by Penrose.

The following will show you by what circumstance Williams and myself became acquainted, as well as that he was the writer of the above mentioned manuscript. Mr Edward Pennington[2], a gentleman of high respectability, & of the Society of Friends in the City of Philadelphia, was in the habit of annually visiting my father and family in Chester County, Pennsylvania as a relative.

Observing some of my childish attempts at the delineation of domestic objects in colour extracted from roots, herbs and bark of trees; he prevailed upon my parents to take with him to the city his little cousin for some weeks, as he had never seen that place. This happened in the year 1747 in my ninth year – and was a circumstance most grateful to my feelings – indulging the hope of seeing some (paintings is crossed out) pictures in the city.

A few days later I was with Mr Pennington in the city, he bought me colours, & all other materials for making pictures in oil. My first attempt was then a landscape – in which were ships, cattle, & other things which I had been accustomed to see; but before I had finished the picture Samuel Shoemaker[3] (here Eagles inserts at the foot of the page, *quere Shummacher*) *a neighbour of Mr Pennington and a gentleman also of the Society of Friends, came to see the picture I was painting; & in the conversation which took place between these two gentlemen on the subject of Fine Arts, Mr Shoemaker informed his friend Pennington that a few days before he had met a person in the street with a picture; and that he requested the person to favour him with a sight of it, which he found to be a Landscape of considerable merit, & painted by the person in whose hands the picture was.*

I learnt from him, said Mr Shoemaker, that his name was W. Williams (and) that he had been recently married to a respectable townswoman of our City, and settled there, & that he followed the business of painting in general; he appeared to me to possess a powerful mind, and a great love for painting; and tomorrow I find he will have finished the landscape I commissioned him to paint for me: when it is sufficiently dry to be moved with safety, I will, with thy permission friend Pennington, bring both Painter & the picture to thee, & thy little cousin West to see it. The palpitation of joy which this conversation produced in my mind, when I became certain of seeing it, was what I can never forget, nor did hours ever pass slower away than those which intervened until I saw the picture, which in a few days was brought to Mr Pennington's. I believe the blush of joy which overspread my face on the picture first being expose to view attracted the attention of those present even more than the picture itself, although a work of considerable merit: it being the first picture I had seen except the small essays I made in the country, and the one I was then attempting to paint in oil.

The attention of Mr Williams still rested on me – while other persons were beginning to look at this Landscape and to commend it. Soon after Mr Williams addressed himself to Mr Pennington "I am of the opinion, Sir, that this youth has the sensibility proper for the studying of painting" : - he then turned to me, and wished to know if I had ever read any of the lives of any of the great Masters of painting – I replied it was the first time I had ever heard of any such lives for I had never read any account of great men, but those in the Bible and New Testament, which my Parents directed me to read and remember.

"Well, then," said Mr Williams, "if Mr Pennington will give permission, I will lend you Richardson and du Fresnoy on Painting to read at your leisure." He did so, and those two books were my companions by day, and under my pillow by night. This commenced my acquaintance with Mr Williams, which continued without interruption until I embarked for Italy in 1760.

From the year 1747 to 1760, my attention was directed to every point necessary to accomplish me for the profession of painting. This often brought me to the house of Williams; and as he was an excellent actor in taking off character, he often, to amuse me, repeated his adventures among the Carribs and Negro tribes in the West Indies - many of which adventures were strictly the same as related in your manuscript of Penrose, as was also the description of the scenery of the coasts, the birds on them, in particular the flamingo birds, which he described, when seen at a distance, as appearing like companies of soldiers dressed in red uniforms. He spoke both the Negro and Carrib tongues, and appeared to have lived among them some years.

I often asked him how he came to be with them; he replied that he had been put to sea when young, that he was never satisfied with that pursuit, & that he took the first opportunity offered to desert it, by making his way for the West Indies, where he was ship-wrecked, & thrown into great difficulties, but Providence had preserved him through a variety of dangers.

He likewise informed me that he was a Welshman by birth; but brought up at a Grammar School in Bristol – where his greatest delight was to go & see an elderly artist who painted heads in oil, as well as small landscapes, and his greatest wish was to be a Painter; but in that he was disappointed, & bound when young to a Virginia Captain who sometimes sailed out of London as well as from Bristol in the Virginia trade. –

"After going the second voyage with him, when in Norfolk, Virginia – to tell you the truth he said, I left the ship & sailed for the West Indies, where I hoped to be unknown, that I might work my way to some place - & accomplish my wishes as a Painter: - and after some years had elapsed, I was able to come to this city (Philadelphia) – and ever since my arrival, I have studied the science of painting, by collecting the lives of the eminent painters [X] as well as the prints from their works." This I knew to be the truth (Thomas Eagles was left this manuscript, but it appears to have been lost) as it was to his books and prints I was indebted for all the knowledge I possessed of the progress which the Fine Arts had made in the world, & which prompted me to view them in Italy.

The following circumstances came to my knowledge respecting Williams; not long after I arrived in London in the year 1762. Becoming acquainted with a Col. Hunter who had then settled with his family in London from Virginia; one day dining with him, he asked me how I came at the knowledge of painting in the City of Philadelphia. I told him that it was by the acquaintance of a Wm. Williams – who had more enthusiasm for the Art than any person I had ever met with. "What a singular event is this", replied the Col. "I will tell you Mr West, what will surprise you as it did me. – When I went with the Governor (Dinwiddie)[4] of Virginia as one of the Deputies to attend the Governor of Philadelphia in the year 1755, to join the Governors from the other Provinces to hold the great Treaty at East Town[5] in Pennsylvania with the friendly Indian Chiefs: Mr Williams waited on me while I was in Philadelphia & informed me that when he was a boy he had been bound to me when I was in the Virginia Trade: but not willing to continue in that Service had absented himself from my ship lying in Norfolk in Virginia, & went to the West Indies from when he came to this City some years after – that he was married and settled here - & that he had taken the business of painting in general.

"I have waited on you Sir" said he, "to declare who I am, & if I can make any recompense for leaving your service, I shall do it to the utmost of my power."

I told him that I had forgot both him, and the circumstance until his narrative brought both to my memory – that I was much pleased to see him as well as with the principles of his visit. I frequently called to se him in his family while I stopped at Philadelphia, and introduced him to several of my friends in that city. When he was on board my ship I often remarked him engaged in painting and drawing, & soon distinguished him to be a Boy of no common capacity, and it was my intention that he remained with me to place him in my Counting-house in Norfolk (Virginia), to better his situation in life. - But I was never more pleased than to find his respectable situation in Philadelphia, except this, which you have told me of his being the person who kindled the latent sparks of painting which he then discovered in you, into that blaze with which it now appears in this country."

"I am obliged to you Colonel" I replied" for the compliment: but it proves how little we are awake to those events, which till their development, have been the cause of even producing revolutions: for most undoubtedly had not Williams been settled in Philadelphia I should not have embraced painting as a profession."

Mr Williams was a man of quick penetration, but his love of the Fine Arts became his most devout pursuit. Painting he cultivated as a Profession – Music as an amusement, and Poetry he often indulged himself in with considerable power: There was a piece of his Poetry addressed to me in my twelfth year – it was published in one of the daily Papers in Philadelphia, and much admired, though no one knew who was the Author. On my preparing to embark for Italy he wrote me an acrostic on my name, which he sent to me after I had taken my leave of him – in which he predicted my future elevation in painting.'

Soon after my departure from Philadelphia for Italy, Williams had the misfortune to lose his Wife, by whom he had two sons: he was the most devoutly attached to the Mother Country (Britain), but his sons being born in Philadelphia they became attached to America and took up arms with thousands of other youths to join her Armies & were killed in some of the battles. Mr Williams finding himself advancing in years – and much dejected at the loss of his sons, & the revolution of families and things in that Country; availed himself of a friendly proposition made to him by an English gentleman returning for England – to reside under his roof in Bedfordshire, & to paint there for his amusement for the remainder of his life. On their arrival in London, Williams came to me and introduced his friend – They stopped in town about ten days; after which they went into Bedfordshire. In about eighteen months, after his friend died – and Williams once more returned to London. He was frequently at my house, & remained in

268

London more than two years in the daily pursuit of collecting portrait prints of eminent painters – this brought him much into the society of those who collected such prints – in that number was Mr Nathaniel Smith[6], the print seller. His son, the present Thomas Smith saw, and knew more of Williams during his stay in London – and has favoured me with a paper which he has written to oblige me respecting what he knew of Williams while here.

At this time (1778) I was painting my picture of the Battle of la Hogue in which I introduced a likeness of Williams in one of the Boats, next in the rear of Sir George Rooke; & soon after this period I lost sight of him, & becoming apprehensive that he was dead, on my making enquiry of Mr Smith what had become of him – he informed me he was gone to Bristol, but for what purpose he did not know.

Thus good Sir, agreeable to your and Mr Annesley's request, I have given you what knowledge I possess of Mr Williams from the year 1747, to his departure from London to Bristol about the year 1781.-

If you can compile from this account of Williams which I have arranged of him for three and thirty years – one that will be satisfactory to yourself and the World, that he was the Author of the Manuscript in your possession under the signature of Penrose – it is at your service for this purpose.

I have the honour to be with respect

Dear Sir -

Your most obedient humble Servant

Benjamin West

P.S. It has often occurred to me that Williams must have given the name of Penrose to his manuscript in compliment to a very great friend of his in Philadelphia of that name. Mr Penrose Was one of the most elegant ship builders in all America, or I believe, to be found in Europe – And it was the painting, & ornamenting of his ships, that was Williams' last employment, as well as that name Penrose was pleasant to the poetical ear of such a man as Williams.

Thomas Eagles Esq.

Bristol

(The superscript X above refers to this list that Thomas Eagles has added to the letter) X in the Vol of his copying of the Lives of the Painters - at the end is a list of his Paintings – AD 1750 – Pictures painted at Philadelphia amongst 100 – the owner of each is specified – is "Small Portrait of Benjamin Lay[7] for Dr Benjamin Franklin'

1760 – Pictures painted in Jamaica 54 –

1769 – Pictures painted in New York 87 – amongst these is a "small whole length of William Williams Jun[r] Painter" among innumerable portraits are

An Emblematical piece for ye Corsican Club[8]

A small moonlight for Lady Rosehill[9]

A small whole length of Lady Rosehill

A Conversation of Mr Denning & family

A large History of the Good Samaritan for Mr C. Bush (or Buck)

A History piece of the Repose in Egypt for ditto

A small Landskip (landscape) for Mr J. Minshull[10]

A large Tempest for Cap[n] A. Rutgers

Attached to the above copy by Thomas Eagles are the following two notes, one a copy of Williams' 'deathbed' Will, and the other subtitled 'The Letter of Robert Southey'

Copy of the 'Deathbed' Will (Lilly Library)

I William Williams now in the Merchant's Alms House in the Parish of St Stephen in the City of Bristol declare this to be my last Will & Testament.

First I declare Thomas Eagles Esquire in Park Street to be my sole Executor of what little property I have as needed. I would wish this afternoon that all my books be taken to Thomas Eagles & left with him together with several prints, paintings, and other trifling matters, and in case of my decease that the said Mr Eagles will keep what he may think proper and divide any other of my property at his sole direction - Boxes, Chairs &c – having the greatest opinion of Mr Eagles I leave everything I have entirely under his direction – as witness my hand this twenty-first day of April in the year of our Lord one thousand seven hundred and ninety one Signed William Williams

Witness John Fisher, Benjamin Pearce

Letter from Lord Byron to John Murray

November 28 1813 Source *Byron's Letters and Journals*, ed. L.A. Marchand

Dear Sir, Send another copy (if not too much a request) to Lady Holland of the Journal, in my name, when you receive this; it is for Earl Grey – and I will relinquish my own. Also to Mr Sharpe, Lady Holland, and Lady Caroline Lamb, copies of The Bride, as soon as convenient. Ever yours, Biron

Letter from Lord Byron to John Murray

November 28 1813 Source *Byron's Letters and Journals*, ibid

Dear Sir, You shall act as you please upon that point; but whether I go or stay, I shall not say another word on the subject till May – nor then, unless quite convenient to yourself. I have many things I wish to leave to your care, principally papers. The vases need not be sent now, as Mr W(ard) has gone to Scotland. You are right about the Er(rata) page; place it at the beginning. Mr Perry is a little premature in his compliments: these may do more harm by exciting expectation, and I think we ought to be above it – though I see the next paragraph is on the 'journal' which makes me suspect you as the author of both…

Yours very truly, B.

Letter from Lord Byron to John Murray II

December? 1813. Source *Byron's Letters and Journals*, ibid

Will you have the goodness to send me your Buccaneer's Journal for the evening?

Letter from Lord Byron to Henry Fox, third Baron Holland

Dec 2, 1813? Source *Byron's Letters and Journals*, ibid.

I have ordered Mr M (Murray) to send Ly. H (Lady Holland) another copy of ye. Journal - & he will send or I will bring it this day.

Letter from Longman, Hurst, Rees and Orme of Paternoster Row to Orton Smith (in Bristol?)

Feb 4 1814 Source Longmans Letter Books, I, 98, no. 131

The letter shows that the firm was keen to procure this work via the Rev. John Eagles, the son of the author's old benefactor in Bristol, Thomas Eagles, though having previously declined it: 'Some years back we had offered to us a MS entitled "Penrose", which was in the possession of the late Mr Eagles of Bristol. We then declined it. We understand that it is now in the hands of his son, & that he is disposed to part with it. If you are at all acquainted with the present Mr Eagles, we shall feel particularly obliged if you would inquire respecting it, & on what terms he would part with it. [...] We should wish to see the MS before we determine finally respecting [it]' It was presumably at much the same time as this that John Murray was bargaining to publish it, with Walter Scott reading and approving the MS.

Letter from John Murray II to Anne Murray. 15 Aug 1814 (Murray Collection)
I have got at last Mr. Eagle's 'Journal of Penrose, the Seaman,' for which, as you may remember, I am to pay [247/248] £200 in twelve months for 1000 copies: too dear perhaps; but Lord Byron sent me word this morning by letter (for he borrowed the MS. last night): 'Penrose is most amusing. I never read so much of a book at one sitting in my life. He kept me up half the night, and made me dream of him the other half. It has all the air of truth, and is most entertaining and interesting in every point of view.' (Anne Murray is John Murray's wife.)

Letter from John Murray II to John Eagles. 16 Aug 1814 (Murray Collection)
In consequence of your Letter to Mr Townley I have concluded an arrangement with him for an edition of Penrose's Journal to consist of One thousand Copies and for one edition of Atheneus as translated by your Father to consist of Seven Hundred and Fifty Copies agreeing to pay for the first the Sum of Two Hundred Pounds and for the latter the sum of Thirty Pounds by one Note at twelve Months from this date, which I have now the pleasure [367/368] of inclosing & for which I beg the favour of your acknowledgement. I have further agreed to return to you preserved as carefully as the process of Printing from it will Permit the original MSS of Penrose's Journal (in your Fathers Hand writing) The Drawings shall be as well preserved as possible but if at any time I think Proper to have them or any of them engraved it is to be understood that I am to have the use of them I shall determine hereafter what form would be the best for the Journal to appear in & at this time I am wavering between 2 Vol. 8vo & 4 very neat Small volumes such as the Life of Nelson. Mr Townley will write to you either this day or tomorrow ...

Note: A draft version of this letter appears just above this one on p. 367 of the same letter book. The draft letter is crossed out, with a note in margin stating 'This letter was not sent'. The wording of the two versions is different, but the basic details about payment for copyright and edition numbers are the same. It appears from the discarded draft that Murray initially planned on issuing two notes, one for each work, but by the final paragraph he had changed his mind, stating that 'Upon further Consideration I enclose you my note at twelve Months for £230 which includes the amount for both works...' This change in thinking is likely to have prompted Murray to discard this version and write the letter transcribed above. Townley is unidentified and he is possibly one of Murray's clerks. Murray published Robert Southey's *The Life of Nelson* in 1813. No translation of *Athenaeus* published by Murray has been located.

Letter from John Eagles to John Murray II. 18 Aug 1814 (Murray Collection)
I hasten to acknowledge the receipt of your fav(our) 16 Inst(ant). enclosing your bill @ 12 Mos £130 for the Penrose Journal one Edition 1,000 Copies [...]. I hope the MS will not be materially injured. I suppose my friend Townly informed you I was desirous of dedicating Penrose to Mr West, his knowledge of the Author by whom he was induced to profess Painting has excited in him considerable interest for the work, and I think a dedication to him wd be useful. I believe you are already acquainted with the circumstances which brought the MS into my Father's possession. Should you determine to have any of the drawings engraved (which are

by W. Bird and Pocock) I have a portrait of the Author painted by himself and a very good performance, I will shd you so determine with pleasure make you a drawing of it, any size you wish. How far it will be desirable to acquaint the world with the circumstances relating to the author & the manner it came into the possession of my Father I leave you to determine. Townly in his letter to me suggests that the alteration of an expression or two wd be advisable such as the medicine in the spirit bottle working him so fore and aft.

Note (a): The published Dedication by Eagles to West reads as follows: 'To BENJAMIN WEST, ESQ – MY DEAR SIR, I most willingly avail myself of your kind permission, to dedicate to you the Narrative now offered to the Public. I venture to urge this request, not only because (of) your intimate knowledge of the Author, and the circumstance of his having communicated to you many of the facts recorded in it, but also because the respect which the public have long entertained for you virtues and talents, might excite an interest for a work which has the sanction of your name. If I can induce the world to read the following pages, I am not fearful of its judgment. It was a subject of pleasing recollection to my father, that this extraordinary Narrative first led him to your acquaintance; and I am happy that the honour has been extended to myself. From your conversation I have received both pleasure and instruction; and permit me, my dear Sir, to add, that the kindness which I have experienced from you, renders me more devoted to an art which boasts in you a Professor so liberal and enlightened. May you long continue in the enjoyment of the distinction which your merit has obtained. I am, my dear Sir, with great respect and esteem, your most faithful and obedient Servant, JOHN EAGLES.

Note (b): Both Nicholas Pocock (1741–1821) and his son Isaac (1782–1835) were painters with connections to Bristol. In a letter of 1807, Thomas Eagles mentions an artist friend, Edward Bird RA (1772–1819), who settled in Bristol around the turn of the 19th century. W. Bird mentioned above is actually Edward Bird.

Letter from Lord Byron to John Murray II
18 August 1814 Source Byron's Letters and Journals, ibid.
Penrose is most amusing – I never read so much of a book at one sitting in my life – he kept me up half the night and made me dream of him the other half:- it has all the air of truth – and is most entertaining and interesting in my point of view.

Letter from John Eagles to John Murray II. 6 Feb 1815 (Murray Collection)
(Eagles is enclosing an account of the author of Penrose) I leave to you wh(ethe)r you will call it introduction or Preface. As soon as the Work is printed I will thank you to send me 5 copies, as I wish to make presents before the publication to some of my family, you will please to debit me with the amt. A Copy shd likewise be sent to Mr West, & one for Mr Woodforde with whom I believe you are acquainted;— I mentioned a long while ago I had a portrait of the Author, which I wd copy for you engraving, perhaps you do not wish an addition to the work. You mention in yr last you will send me the sheets as they come out, if you will send them to Mr Townly, 59 Welbeck Street Cavendish Square. I shall receive them.

Notes: Samuel Woodforde (1763–1817) was a painter and member of the Royal Academy, with three works in the Tate Gallery. The portion of the letter given above precedes the account of the author; this section of the letter is crossed out, presumably because Murray directly forwarded the text to the printer. The life of the author is given in the 'Advertisement', not an introduction or Preface, to the novel, signed by John

Eagles. The Advertisement is basically the same as the content from Benjamin West in the article 'The Beggar's Legacy' featured above, prefixed by the following in Eagles' own words: 'Some years since an old man, who had apparently seen better days, applied to my father for charitable relief. His language and address bore a character of interest that must have struck the most minute observer. My father was, however, a man of discrimination, as well as feeling, who seeing how ill the superior cultivation of his mind adapted him for the common receptacle of paupers, (which was his object) supplied his immediate wants; which benevolence continuing from time to time, he was so much charmed with his good sense and conversation, that he became much attached to him. He supplied him with the necessities of life, and after some time, was enabled to place him comfortably in the Merchants' Alms House in this city, endowed for the reception of decayed mariners, where, with some weekly addition to the allowance of the charity, he was placed much above want. Here he enjoyed several years of tranquillity. He was beloved by all our family; and such was the kindness with which my father treated him, that I have often, when a boy, seen the old man sit at our table with the familiarity of an old friend. In this asylum he died, and left to my father all he was possessed of. And let not the reader smile at his legacy, for it was not to be despised; it consisted of many volumes of books, collections of prints, MSS., in particular the following narrative. It was not in my father's disposition to make inquiries into the details of private history, especially when it was probably they would excite painful sensations; it is not to be wondered at, therefore, that he did not make himself acquainted with circumstances, the knowledge of which would now be so interesting. It was extraordinary that a man of such a turn of mind, and with property of such a description, should have looked for asylum among paupers. It was fortunate that he met with a person so capable of appreciating his merits, and preserving to the world the Narrative bequeathed to him. But the incident which happily led to a more accurate knowledge of him, was as interesting as it was unexpected. As an account of it, I insert a memorandum found among my father's papers, dated 10th July 1805. "Mr Annesly (sic, this is Francis Annesley) brought Mr West to my lodging; he dipped into Penrose's Journal, and read several pages in different parts...'

Ledger Entries from the Murray Archives, Divide Ledger A:

Divide Ledger Entry, John Murray II. 15 Aug 1814. Paid by note to J Eagles: 200. 0. 0. 16 May 1815. The impression consisted of 1000 copies; it appears that 1026 were actually printed. Murray received 500 copies on 16 May 1815 and a further 526 copies on 20 June 1815. 16 May 1815–1 Feb 1816. Total outlay (excluding payment to Eagles): 1205. 1. 9. 30 May 1816. 7 copies presented by Eagles. [For details, see Notes field below]. 20 June 1815. 1 copy sent to Mr Heber; 10 copies sent to Libraries, 22 Aug 1815.

Notes: The total outlay includes only printing and freight: no details about paper costs are given in the ledger. The Copy Day Book for 1811–17 provides further details about the note to Eagles and the presentation copies. It shows that copies were sent to: Nicholas Pocock, Esq.; W. B. Ellwyn, Esq.; D. Buliard; Ed Bird, Esq.; R. D. Woodforde, Esq.; Gilbert West Esq. (in calf extra binding); 1 copy in boards sent to Eagles himself. No charges were made for these copies. See Murray Archives, Copy Day Book, 1811–17, p. 83. Pocock and Bird were the artist/engravers. No trace can be found of Ellwyn or Bulliard. Thomas Eagles (1746-1812) wrote "Letters on Literature": were copied in manuscript by R.D. Woodforde around 1818. It was a collection of copies of letters received from Eagles and of some of Eagles' replies, 1787-1808; prefaced by a letter addressed to Woodforde's son, Edward Montagu Woodforde, in which Woodforde explains how he became acquainted with the author of The Crier. Gilbert West is presently unknown.

Contemporary Review of The Journal of Llewellin Penrose, from Critical Review, September 1815

We should have treated these volumes merely as an ingenious fiction—a clever piece of book-making—had not the respected name of the President of the Royal Society been used as a kind of vouchee for the very questionable discoveries with which they abound. In perusing them we were frequently reminded of the ingenuity of the author of the 'Isle of Pines, or a late Discovery in Terra Australis incognita,' which was imposed upon the public nearly a century and a half ago; and of its imitators, the writers of the history of the 'Servians'— and of 'Robinson Crusoe.' The journal before us bears the strongest resemblance to the Isle of Pines, with much Crusoe-like adventure sprinkled throughout. The heroes are both cast on shore, though in different ways; Crusoe is shipwrecked, and Penrose driven in the ship's boat alone, and in a state of insensible intoxication on uninhabited shores. Both are mere seaman [sic], informed of nought but naval tactics. Crusoe's character is consistent throughout; but Penrose dips into philosophy and morality.

Penrose entered on board a privateer, among a crew composed of the refuse of several nations; a set of abandoned drunken desperadoes. After one of their disgraceful orgies, Penrose was left in the ship's boat, in so bestial a state of inebriation, that he was driven unconsciously by the tide, and cast upon a sandbank. When the spirituous fumes had partly evaporated, he found himself alone, upon a desolate shore, without food or water, and possessed of no weapon of defence. This unknown region appears to be in South America, but we have neither latitude nor longitude, the objects of a seaman's first inquiry, to guide us to the spot. After much research to satisfy the imperious calls of hunger, he found a few small shell-fish, on which wretched aliment he chiefly subsisted, until fortune grew somewhat kinder. Two young Indians landed from a canoe near the place which he made his miserable dwelling—a male and a female,—brother and sister, who had with them their aged father on the point of death. So soon as the old man's remains were committed to the earth, Penrose set about the work of domiciliating his guests, and he certainly hit upon the most feasible modes—he married the female, and called her brother, his brother. He now enjoyed comparative happiness—his dingy wife was loving—the brother faithful and friendly. The latter, in common with all coast Indians, was expert in fishing, which he exercised with much success, while the hus-[282/283]band laid snares for bird and beast. Here began an establishment which Penrose presided over twenty-eight years, leaving children and grand-children. He had tamed a fawn which he called Miss Doe, his only companion previous to his marriage, a monkey, a hawk, and a couple of parrots. His journal was kept, not in the seaman-like way of Crusoe, by notching a tree, but with shells picked up on the sea-shore, until he obtained materials for writing and many of the good things of this world, from a stranded ship.

Our untutored seaman, settled with his family about him, thus begins to philosophize: 'The world seems to be divided between credulity and scepticism. There are readers who are willing to believe every extraordinary thing related to them; there are others who obstinately refuse to give credit to any, that have not been submitted to the evidence of their senses. There are, however, extremes on both sides. To steer between them requires a cool discriminating judgment. There are few travellers who have not seen things which they are unwilling to relate; not from the slightest doubt in their own minds as to the reality of such objects, but being somewhat of the common order, they are fearful of the imputation of extravagance in their narrations, and would rather suppress a circumstance well worthy to be known, than incur the character of falsehood or weak credulity.

I have been led to these reflections by many extraordinary things which have come under my own observation, of the wonderful economy and management of nature in the animal or vegetable world. An instance or two I shall mention. I will begin with the pudeling wythe, a kind of vine, which, after it has aspired to the top of the proudest tree in the forest, drops down perpendicularly, like a number of bell-ropes, all of a thickness, till within about four feet of the earth; it then sprouts out like the tail of a horse, but on touching the ground takes root afresh, and ascends as before.' Here we were almost inclined to exclaim with Polonius, 'very like a whale,' when behold, our seaman presents one in the very next page. His olfactory nerves were suddenly, and most abominably assailed, and he was scarcely able to support himself.

' "The stench," he observes, "became still more powerful, and came directly into our mouths. I began to suspect the true cause, and made a stretch out in order to weather it. When we got to the windward side, I found it to be a dead whale, lying along on its side. As we drew near to it we saw thousands of birds flying in all directions." ' [283/284]

Among the various topics upon which Mr. Penrose descants, priesthood does not escape his lash. A Father Martin is introduced, in a pretended tale told to our insulated mariner.

'The Padrees were very troublesome with him (the hero of the tale) on the score of religion, trying by every possible means to draw him to their persuasion. He, however, resisted all their importunities, but little thought what a cloud was hanging over his head, and ready to involve him in destruction. He had for some time suspected his wife's fidelity, and one day his suspicions were in a degree confirmed, that Father Martin was somewhat more than confessor to his lady. The high reputation and power of this priest enjoined him to silence from the most prudential motives; however, he took the first opportunity his wife gave him of remonstrating with her, and inveighed against the reverend father for his lewdness and hypocrisy, in no qualified terms. A pretty fellow to think of converting him to the Catholic religion, who made no scruple of violating its most sacred ordinances. The church has enjoined celibacy on the clergy, that their minds, abstracted from all carnal desires, should indulge only in divine contemplations, and their lives be spent in the chaste and pious performance of the duties of their holy function. Under the sanction of their order, they were admitted into families at all times and in all places, from which others of their sex were excluded. To convert this privilege to their purposes of seduction and violation of the marriage bed, was a scandal to the religion they professed, a mockery of God's ordinances, and a contempt of the civil institutions by which society is held together. They deserve to be made severe examples of offended justice; when, instead of teaching others by their precepts and examples, by the purity of their doctrine, and the sanctity of their manners, they became general corrupters, and lived in the open practice of the most abominable vices, in defiance of common decency, above the control of secular authority.'

In order that the reader may be induced to believe the marvellous stories, with which the book abounds, (far exceeding those of any of its predecessors) Penrose solemnly says, returning again to the simple seaman— 'I declare that I have advanced nothing in this book that did not immediately pass under my own eyes; and what interest could such a poor forlorn creature as myself have for imposing falsehoods upon the world, uncertain as I am, whether what I now write may ever fall under the inspection of any civilized being of any nation?'

Then follows an earthquake, the like of which our seaman never felt before. The next sentence is a description of butterflies, 'wild and swift in flight, and seen over the tops of the loftiest trees, full as broad as the palm of my hand, and much larger.' He found pods of the silk worms sticking in crevices of rocks and clefts of trees; and one sort, fixed to the limb of a small twig, five times the size of the ordinary sort, and of a dark brown colour resembling oakum. These pods are so strong, as not to be easily rent asunder. The fly which they produce is as large as a man's hand, of a variety of colours, with a pair of fine yellow feathers in front of its head—another, a brimstone colour, with a circle in each wing, transparent as glass, with the after part of the wings tapering away like a swallow's tail. Then are we told of a brown wasp, which falling head

275

foremost from the trees upon the ground, seems there to take root, a small plant springing up through its body; a humming bird, with two feathers in its tail three times its length; lizards with two tails; a shark without teeth; two-headed snakes, &c. But the most piteous complaint is levelled at the hanging bird.

'As these birds are remarkable, I shall give some description of them. It is about the size of a starling, and called by some the hanger; there are several sorts of them, but all with beautiful plumage: they make their nests to hang down from the outer branch of a tree by a string or strong fibre, the nest is oblong like to a cabbage net. Many times as I have passed near one of them, the bird has at once darted down from a limb, full in my face, fled back, and then returned again in a most furious manner, as if it would pick out my eyes, so that I have been obliged to beat it off. These birds are fond of a particular kind of insect, which is altogether as singular as themselves; they are found on cedar, cyprus, and such kind of trees; they make themselves a kind of house, something in shape resembling a ship's buoy, and of a substance so rough, that it is impossible to break it with the fingers; they fortify this with particles from the same tree in a very curious way. At the upper end of the nest, the insect appears with about half its body out, and is constantly employed in spinning its threads, lowering itself down, then hauling itself up hand over hand, as the sailors term it, with dexterity. I have seen above a thousand of them hanging on one tree, like so many bobbins. It is curious to observe how cunningly the hanging bird catches them as he flies; when he has taken one, he puts it under his feet on a limb of a tree, and then he easily disengages and devours it at his leisure.'

It would seem that the mammoth, or elephant, had formerly been an inhabitant of this terra incognita. Penrose describes a skull which two of his companions could scarcely lift, with teeth which they drew out weighing two pounds each, and a rib [285/286] of great size; but whether the bones were those of a carnivorous or herbivorous animal, he could not determine. In one of their excursions they found an English long-boat bilged—weather-beaten, but not old. He then began to divert himself with his line, and caught two mutton fish, which, with a few shanks and sea pies, and toddy for their beverage, made an excellent repast.—Our party now became rich in precious metals. They discovered, by another wonderful incident, hidden treasures, consisting of various articles of silver, plate, and dollars, which, being useless at present, they melted down (except the dollars), and dug a pit, in which they concealed them. The tide of good fortune sometimes flows rapidly,—it proved so in this case. They found in the boat 'a large lump of ambergrise, differing in colour from that which' they 'had found before.' The same day they found a cask of salted provisions, and saw a vessel standing to the southward, but which did not discover them, as they rowed away from it. During these unexpected events, a strange animal was caught in their trap, which Harry described as subsisting on ants. This new discovered genus of quadrupeds, he said, 'Crept slowly on towards an ant's nest, lay flat on their bellies, then put forth tongues to a great length, which never fails to attract multitudes of these insects upon it. When the beast finds, by their strong biting, that he had got a sufficient freight, he then whips in his tongue, swallows them, and begins the same process again. Harry pulled out the tongue of the dead animal, which was exceedingly long, narrow, and round.'

The reader may aptly inquire, what length? This is left to conjecture; but we think that a narrator, who could give the weight of a tooth, might surely measure the length of a tongue. The next story is certainly very probable, if we except the fire flies, which in Louisiana are the same size as those met with in England.

'I shall now give my reader a sample of my courage when put to the test. My wife and my brother Harry took it into their heads to divert themselves a little at my expense. She knew it to be my custom some times to cut a slice of those hams (the contents of the barrel found upon the sea beach) in an evening, to eat with a plantain. As I was sitting as usual, on a stool without, smoking my pipe, my wife asked me why I did not take a bit of the ham for my supper? I immediately got up, and opening my knife for the purpose, went in to cut a slice. These hams were hung a great way back in the cavern. As I advanced towards the place, whistling as I walked along, I was all at once struck with [286/287] one of the most horrid sights I had ever beheld. I ran back much faster than I had entered, with my hair standing on end. My wife observing me so much alarmed, burst into a fit of laughter. This brought me a little to myself, and she then told me the secret, and rallied me not a little, saying she wondered white men could be frightened at such trifles, who are not afraid of the winds and the great waters. Having now recovered my spirits, I went in again with her to view this tremendous object, for such it really was. Harry having got four fire flies, such as I before mentioned, almost as large as chaffers, had contrived to fix two of them between his teeth, and the other two over his eyes, and thus lighted up, had placed himself in a dark corner. The light thrown upon his face was of a greenish hue, and made him altogether so cadaverous, that I think the stoutest heart would have been daunted at the sight.'

This trick was played off upon another of Mr. Penrose's family, (for it was increased by volunteers from the distant Indian tribe), which threw the terrified person into fits, from which it was long before he recovered. Moralizing upon this mischievous frolic, the seaman says, 'I have been always averse to frolics of this kind, as very idle and very dangerous. Few young people reflect on the consequences that may possibly follow them. Society may be deprived of a very useful member by a sudden fright. Instances of this kind have happened. The nervous system may be thrown into such disorder, as never perfectly to recover from the shock. The gratification which we derive from thus sporting with the feelings of our friends or fellow creatures, is of a malevolent kind; and it would at all times be much better to lose our joke, than endanger our friend's corporeal or mental happiness.'

The ingenious editor of this Journal continues his marvellous accounts in quick succession. The third volume opens with a description of a 'kind of fish called a cuckhold,' which clasped Harry round the leg in wading among the rocks, who, on looking down, saw a monstrous lancksa, as he called it, which was obliged to be cut away by his companion. This animal is said to adhere to a rock or stone, and to expand forth several arms, at the end of each of which is a sort of mouth, which catches all marine insects, and like the proboscis of an elephant, conveys the prey into one great mouth in the centre of the body. It has no eyes, nor can it be removed from the place whereto it is fixed; but should any portion be torn or cut away, the part so torn or separated will soon attach itself to some other spot, and become a new and perfect lancksa. It seizes on every thing within its reach; and if the object be too [287/288] large for deglutition, it will then suck the essential matter, and let the husk or skin drop. For this, however, Mr. Penrose says he has only the ipse dixit of Harry, but supposes the creature to be a kind of polypus. For the existence, however, of the following non-descript marine animal, he himself vouches.

'Through holes in the side of rocks, about four feet down, seemed to grow small tufts of flowers, somewhat resembling our polyanthus, but of a pale rose colour, now and then tinged with yellow; but on my running down a paddle, to shove a bunch of them off, they would instantaneously retire into the rock. This first excited our attention; and finding by repeated trials it evaded all our art, one of them was detached on a piece of rock and beat to pieces, and in a small cell we found a semblance of a thin membraneous sort; but the parts which had expanded like so many flowers had now lost their form. The whole was contracted, and it was shapeless; yet there seemed to be a small palpitation left, which shewed there was life in it. Many of these we had caused to retire, were now expanded again in full beauty; but on offering to touch them, they incontinently withdrew themselves as before.'

We have, next, a description of a variety of tortoises—of a narrow escape from a wild boar—

of piccary hogs, with their navels on their backs, which if not taken out the instant the beast is killed, the carcase will very soon become tainted—of tigers, who first ate up Miss Doe, and then devoured an Indian female, who had become the wife of our seaman's brother, Harry. A cup of pure gold was found containing twenty doubloons, supposed to have been hidden by pirates, but which our worthy mariner lived not to enjoy.

At the conclusion the Editor makes another effort to induce belief in the mind of the reader. He speaks of a Mr. Paul Taylor, mate of a brig lying at the Havannah, who certifies (from New York, in North America) that he became acquainted with the mate of a Spanish sloop—that the mate delivered to him an old bundle of Spanish papers, saying it was entrusted to him by two Indians who spoke English, one of whom told him in Spanish, that the whole was written by his father, with a small addition by himself; and that his father requested that they should be put into the hands of the first person who would promise to deliver them to some trusty good Englishman, to be by him conveyed to his native country.

Penrose contains a fund of entertainment, and, from its moral tendency, may with safety be put into the hands of youth.

Note: Format: 3 vols 8vo; no price. Publisher: Murray.

The Letter of Robert Southey (Lilly Library)

Vol 2. p.410 – There is a book newly published called the Journal of Penrose which I have heard of for twenty years which the Editor and West the painter by a _fortuitous_ want of common sense believe to be true[+] in its main parts – I mention it because there is something about the Buccaneers which very likely is true- a practice they had sometimes of burying treasure, when they did not choose to keep it on board, & burying as prisoner with it so that his spirit might keep guard! In the 2nd Vol. of this book there is the form of a paper said to have been found in such a deposit - & it looks very much as if it were genuine. Eagles (to whom the journal belonged) told me he thought it likely that the man who left it him had at one part of his life been among the Buccaneers.

+ Inserted underneath is the following: _Truth is often stranger than falsehood;_ + so it is in this case – _Williams_ was the author's real name – See – Blackwood's Mag., March 1855. The Beggar's Legacy.

Letter from Zoe King, Frocester, Stonehouse, Gloucestershire
July 25, 1857 to ? (Lilly Library)

My dear Sir,

On comparing the two editions of Penrose, I have no doubt of that in _one_ Volume being the one for you to ILLEG from – Mr Eagles having, as he observed in the introduction, made "some slight corrections to adapt it the better for the perusal of young persons" –

I should much like my 4 Volume copy returned as there are hardly any of the first edition extant. If you will procure me a copy of the Second Edition – One Volume – to be put at Stonehouse's, Paternoster Row, I will set to work, carefully making any corrections and amendments, but I believe _very few_ will be needed, and then I will put together the materials of which I spoke to you for an introduction. I enclose you a list of the drawings made for the original Mr P volume – I need hardly say preserved by the descendants of Mr Eagles as an heirloom.

If you like to introduce them, or any portion of them – Mr Graham Clarke will permit me to have them photographed for the purpose – as I suppose that would be the quickest way of copying them ILLEG. Some of the vignettes are exquisite – and many of them might be used if required for some important plates in (large) size rather than vignette.

I shall remain here until the end of the week and should be obliged if you can let me hear from you before I go away. In comparing the volumes of Penrose, I read with received interest, and think you will have no cause to reject the undertaking with the advantage of your superior mode of executing such works.

The Volume of Essays by Mr Eagles – which contains 'The Beggar's Legacy' is coming out immediately.

Would not Adventures of Penrose – or Penrose the Wanderer – or some such title be appropriate? The family, and I think others also, would not like the name of Penrose to be mentioned in the title? Believe me, Zoe King

I think I could head the paper myself – if you give me a specimen of the way you would like.

Note:

Zoe King is an elusive character. She was born in 1803, the daughter of Emmeline King, who was the daughter of Richard Lovell Edgeworth and the sister of Maria Edgeworth. There is a portrait of Emmeline by Adam Buck in the National Portrait Gallery. There are various letters regarding Zoe in the *Papers of Maria Edgeworth*, held in the National Library of Ireland. In the Coleridge Archives, we also find the following note: *Sara Coleridge, cousin and later wife of H N Coleridge: 'To Zoe King,' Clifton, 1823. f 43.A watercolour drawing (by the Rev Edward Coleridge?) of the Chanter's House, Ottery St Mary, Devon, before reconstruction in 1849, has been laid down inside the front cover (f i). Contemporary blue morocco binding, blind-and gold-tooled. Armorial bookplate of Bernard, Lord Coleridge (f ii).* It therefore appears she lived at Clifton in Bristol in 1823 and would have known of the Eagles family. Regarding the address at Stonehouse, Frocester, there is a Stonehouse Court, now a hotel, which may have been her residence in 1857.

Letter from Evan Evans of Caerphilly
September 9, 1857 to Zoe King? (Lilly Library)
Dear Madam,

I regret that I am not able to furnish you with any information respecting the early history of Williams. My attention was directed some years ago to the subject by seeing an article about it in an old number of the British Review published in 1816.

I was then allowed to make a search on the Register Book of Eglwysilan in which parish Caerphilly is situate, although the Church is four miles distant from it, and also the Register of the adjacent parish of Bedwas, the Church of which is half a mile off, but without success.

If Williams had memories of the scenes of his boyhood, in his Journal some clue might have been obtained.

The account I possess is a condensed one published by Taylor and Hessey in 1825. I believe the first edition, which I have not seen yet, is fuller.

Should I be able jupon further inquiry to obtain any particulars, I shall feel great pleasure in forwarding it to you.

I had the pleasure of seeing Mr Eagles at Southerndown some time before his lamented death. He then told me that Williams' manuscript was in his possession, and that he had written an article under the title of The Beggar's Legacy' – which was published in Blackwell's Magazine of the preceding month of March.

I am, yours faithfully, Evan Evans[11]

CHAPTER V

Characters in order of Appearance

There are over 100 characters mentioned in the Journal, with 26 visits by friendly Indians.

Journal Characters, in order of Appearance	Dates given in book	Sex	Dates in Williams' Life
Penrose born near Caerphilly	May 1725		Williams born 1727? Went to sea aged 12? 1739? Deserted aged 14? 1741? in Norfolk Virginia Williams shipwrecked in West Indies 1742?
Left home for sea with Howell Gwynn	1744		
Shipped aboard the *Harrington* under Captain Hunter. Penrose mentions sailing on the Harrington in convoy with the 'Old *Chatham*'.	1746		Williams would be c.19 Penrose would be just 21 The Harrington was still in service in 1741, and associated with the cause of The War of Jenkins' Ear. The old warship *Chatham* was scrapped in 1749.
Ferdinand VI acceded to throne in August, mentioned by Penrose			Ferdinand VI crowned King of Spain and the Indies
Shipped on the *Recovery*	1747		Williams arrived in Philadelphia, aged 20? after possibly 2-5 years in the Caribbean
Marooned on Mosquito (Miskito) Coast	June 15 1747		Williams (recently married) meets Benj. West, and stays in contact until 1760
Year 1 Sees 3 Indians	June 15 1747– June 14 1748		
Year 2	June 15 1748 – June 14 1749		

Year 3

June 15 1749 – June 14 1750

Williams in Philadelphia

Year 4

June 15 1750 – June 14 1751

Ayasharre (Harry), Penrose's great friend and brother of Yalut-ta	Swift Runner, or Light-Footed Person	M
Yalut-ta (Luta, Penrose's first wife)	Green Grove	F
Codu-uno	Man of Great Strength	M,

Year 5

June 15 1751 – June 14 1752

The Rama word 'kumaa-lut' means 'the women'

Komaloot's first visit	Finder, or Searcher.	M
Futatee	Bald Eagle	M
A third Indian	Unnamed	M
Niuxa, Luta's sister is mentioned – Luta is informed that she is dead		F

Year 6

June 15 1752 – June 14 1753

Komaloot	Again 2nd visit	M
Futatee	Again 2nd visit	M
Vattequeba, Komaloot's brother, brother-in-law of Yalut-ta	Excellent Fisherman	M
Lama-atty, Owa-gamy's wife, sister of Yalut-ta	Transparent Water	F
Owa-gamy, who was the 'principal' in the visiting party	Traveller	M
Dama-sunto	Name not given by Penrose, but *sunto* seems to mean a person	M
Zula-wana	Good Canoe Man	M
Cara-Wouma, or Carrewouma (Patty) who married Ayasharre (Harry)	Beloved Darling	F
Quearuva – this two year old boy was carried by Carrewouma but is not mentioned again	Counsellor	M infant
Owen Penrose born, son of Penrose and Luta	c. September 1752	M

Year 7 – first party

June 15 1753 – June 14 1754

Komaloot	Again 3rd visit	
Owagamy	Again – 2nd visit	
Zula-wana	Again – 2nd visit	
Sama-Lumy (later Toby), fleeing from the Spanish	Mountaineer	M
Matty born to Harry and Patty		F

Year 7 – second party

Komaloot	Again 4th visit	
Owagamy	Again – 3rd visit	
Lama-atty Owagamy's wife	Again – 2nd visit	
Futatee	Again – 3rd visit	
Zula-wana	Again – 3rd visit	
Inna-Tarry, Komaloot's wife	Yellow Flower	F
Quali-rema, Lama-atty's cousin	Tall Vine	M
Nocana-bura	Commander	M
Ina-linca	Mellow Fruit	F
Noonawaiah	The Dreamer	M
Razua-bano	Great Hunter	M
Kona-sove	Basket Maker	M?
Soro-teet, who Penrose has seen when he was first marooned	Crab Catcher	M
Gatto-loon, Gattaloon	Forecaster	M
Latto-gamy	The Returner	M
Shoa-tate	Bird Catcher	M
Nocana-bura	Commander	M
Wayatuza	Comptroller	M
Gayna-sunto	Bewildered Person	M
Faribeed, a boy	Singing Bird	M boy
Muzzo-gayah, a boy	Fighter	M boy
Koura-coon, a boy	Spy	M boy

Williams married to first wife around now, and has 2 sons

282

Vuna-qusta, a girl older than 13	Favourite	F girl
Jasa-wina, a girl about 13, an orphan, Luta (Jessy)	Honey-Sucker	F girl
Matta-linea, whom Toby wished to marry	Red Fruit ·	F
Yova-wan, Toby's brother	Paddle Maker	M
Year 7 – 3rd party		
Toby (Sama-lumy) who has gone to seek a wife	Again	
Yova-wan, Toby's brother	2nd visit	
Noonah-waiah	Again – 2nd visit	
		Capt. (Col.) Hunter visits Williams' Family in 1755
Year 8 – 1st party	**June 15 1754 – June 14 1755**	
Komaloot	Again – 5th visit	
Owagamy	Again – 4th visit	
Futa:ree	Again – 4th visit	
Nocana-Bura	Again – 2nd visit	
Razuabano	Again – 2nd visit	
Gaynasunto	Again – 2nd visit	
Lama-atty	Again – 3rd visit	
Vinniquote, Rava Ccuma's brother	The Smoker	M
Rava Ocuma, Ravacuma, comes to wed Toby, later marries Penrose		F
Luta died in childbirth		
Morgan Penrose born	Breast-fed by Patty, Harry's wife	M
Matty dies, aged about 1	Daughter of Harry and Patty	
Godart Somer arrives – early August 1754	*Dertroost*, en route from Texel to Buenos Aires	M
Captain Meert	Dies on ship	
Verwilt	Drinks to death on sinking ship	
Poersen	Drinks to death on sinking ship	
Jan (John) Brill, bosun		
Jacob Van Tulden, mate		West sets up as painter in Philadelphia
Claus (Claess) Dekker, trouble maker		

Adam Brandt, kills Toby, is killed by Somer
Adam Oest
Harman Byvant
Wouter Meyer
Abert Dubbel
Peter Bylert
Cornelius de Man
Teysen Willems
Davit Oert
Joust van Drill, the ship's boy

Penrose marries Ocuma, Toby's widow (Betty)

Year 8 – 2nd visit   towards end of year
Owagamy   Again – 5th visit
Futatee   Again – 5th visit
Noonawaiah   Again – 3rd visit
Vinnequote   Again – 2nd visit
Selacato   Joyous Person   M

Year 9 – 1st visit   **June 15 1755 – June 14 1756**
Komaloot   Again – 6th visit
Owagamy   Again – 6th visit
Vinnequote   Again – 3rd visit

Year 9 – 2nd visit
Komaloot   Again – 7th visit
Futatee   Again – 6th visit
Lama-atty – Mrs. Owagamy   Again – 4th visit
'Mrs' Komaloot – Inna-tary   2nd visit   F
Mattanany, (Eva, Eve), Somer's bride   Sweet Taste   F
A young girl   F girl
4 more Indians (perhaps inc. Owagamy as his   M

Williams' first wife dies, c.1756

284

wife attended)

Event	M/F	Date	Notes
Job born, son of Harry and Patty Morgan Penrose dies	M	January 7, 1756 January 7, aged .c 18 months	
Year 10 Betty (Ocuma) Penrose loses (Toby's) child Pirate Treasure is found		**June 15 1756 – June 14 1757**	
Year 11 – 1st visit		**June 15 1757 – June 14 1758**	Williams married Mary Mare in New York - Nov 16 1757
Muzogayo	M	Again – 2nd visit	
Damasunto		Again – 2nd visit	
Vattequaba	M	White Shiner	
Erreawa, an albino			
Year 11 – 2nd visit Owagamy and others to announce Komaloot's death Somer's daughter Anauche (Hannah) born	F	7th visit	
Rees Penrose born, a brother to Owen, 3 days after Hannah	M		
Year 12 Captain Dennis Horgan, on a sloop from Santiago del Cuba to Madalena	M	**June 15 1758 – June 14 1759**	
Diego, a Spaniard	M		
Perico, a boy	M		
Rodrigo, a Negro	M		
Pedro Gomez	M	Died on the ship	Williams signed an appeal to Governor Denny of Pennsylvania. Working on Philadelphia's Southwark Theatre, which opened June 25 1759

Event / Person	M/F	Date / Visit	Notes
Martin Galvan	M	Died on the ship	Williams paints Benj. Franklin's friend, Benjamin Lay around now
Year 13 – 1st visit by Indians		**June 15 1759 – June 14 1760**	William Williams jr. born New York November 17, 1759
Gaynasunto	M		
Owasotas, half-brother to Betty	M	Again – 3rd visit	
Another Indian			
Harry and Patty's daughter Luta born, named after Penrose's first wife and Harry's sister – 2nd visit by Indians			Williams also has a daughter, Mary born
Owagamy and 7 others	M	Again – 8th visit	Falconer writes 'The Shipwreck'
Norman Bell	M		
Kayoota			
Year 14 Godart Somer dies		**June 15 1760 – June 14 1761** August 21st, 1760	Williams in West Indies late 1760 with Hallam Theatre Co. Paints 54 pictures in Jamaica
1st visit by Indians			
Gattaloon	M	Again – 2nd visit	
Vattequeba	M	Again – 3rd visit	
Wocozomany			
Outaharry, son of Wocozomany			
Bell marries Somer's widow, Eva			West goes to Italy
America Penrose born, a twin, and sister to	F	February 9th, 1761	
Owen and Rees Somer Penrose born, a twin	M		
Year 14 – 2nd visit by Indians			
Owagamy and another 7 Indians		Again – 9th visit	
Loosoyamy, brother of Eva	M		

Year 15
The burning ship

June 15 1761 – June 14 1762

Williams leaves West Indies after 'fourteen months'.
October 1761 will of father-in-law
Williams 2nd wife dies late 1761
Williams working for the Penrose family shipbuilders

Harnah Godart dies of fever, aged 4

December or January 1762

Year 16
Soroteet – 1st visit by Indians

June 15 1762 – June 14 1763
Again

Williams places ad in Pennsylvania Gazette Jan 13, 1763

Yewarrabaso — M
Kayuza — M

Eva dies in the jungle, eaten by wild beasts, leaving Bell a widower.
Harry and Gaynasunto return from Indians, leaving Bell there
2nd visit by Indians
Owagamy and others

Again – 10th visit

Gattaloon

Again – 3rd visit

Aanora, a widow, to wed the widowed Bell – she is renamed Janet

A Thing Desired (from another tribe or clan)F

Another Indian woman — F

Capt./Col. Hunter meets Benj. West in London and discusses Williams

Year 17
Gattaloon with 10 Indians, all of whom had visited before, with news of Owagamy's death

June 15 1763 – June 14 1764
Again– 4th visit, June or early July

Penrose, Owen and Harry visit the Indians

Year 17 - 2nd visit
They return with Gattaloon
Zulawana and 6 other Indians

Again – 5th visit
Again – 4th visit or more

287

Soroteet (who marries Jessy and stays, and is renamed Rory or Roderick)

Pablo Nunez joins Penrose

Again 3rd visit or more

Year 18
'Fair traders' visit the bay

June 15 1764 – June 14 1765

Gatttaloon
Gaynasunto
8 other Indians

Again – 6th visit
Again – 5th visit

Year 19
Harry and Patty have a girl named Betty, August 10

June 15 1765 – June 14 1766

Williams working on new Philadelphia New Theatre, opened Nov 12, 1766

Williams paints 3 portraits of Benjamin Franklin's partner's children, William, David Jr, and Deborah Hall

Guarda Costa from Carthagena

Captain Zayas
Watty McClintock

Year 20
Hostile Indians seen

June 15 1766 - June 14 1767
July 31 1766

Gaynasunto and 3 Indians
Pablo Nunez died in June

end-December

Year 21
Indians visit with news that Rory (Soroteet) has died of the flux, along with Futaree and others
Sappash comes to marry Jessy

June 15 1767 – June 14 1768

Paints companion pictures.
Paints Southwark Theatre sets.

M

288

Event	Period	Sex	Notes
Year 22 advertisement 1769 Penrose finds Quamino from 1769	**June 15 1768 – June 14 1769**		Williams places New York Gazette Painted 87 pictures in New York
Year 23 Captain Joachim Valdez visits Meets Tady Lort	**June 15 1769 – June 14 1770**		
Year 24 Quamino dies	**June 15 1770 – June 14 1771**		
Finds Poleacre *Isabella*	August		
Attcry	1st visit	M	
Manabo	1st visit	M	
Rabaito	1st visit	M	
Pannee	1st visit	M	
Indian	1st visit	M	
Bell dies			
Year 25 Owen goes to village for a wife	**June 15 1771 – June 14 1772** Around April Penrose falls ill		Painted *The William Denning Family* 1772 Painted *Imaginary Landscape*, the first Seascape painted in any British Colony (Copley's *Watson and the Shark* was not painted until 1778)
Year 26 Bashada married Owen Owen Penrose's Account November onwards Visit by Indians	**June 15 1772 – June 14 1773** c. July 20, 1771 October 30 – Penrose's last entry	F	Painted *Wiley Family* 1772

Year 27
Lewellin born to Owen and Bashada

Penrose dies
Rory leaves
2 canoes of Indians visit

Year 28

Paul Taylor's Account

June 15 1773– August 1774
July 21

c. October 7

c. January 7

June 15 1774 – June 14 1775

1776 – received *Journal*
May 2, 1783 post-script on
The Journal of Penrose, Seaman

Painted *Jacob Fox* 1774

1775 June 17 – Williams claims to lose 2 sons at Bunker Hill. Paints Stephen Crossfield.
1776 Williams leaves New York for Bedford
1778 West paints Williams in London
1781 Williams leaves London for Bristol
1783 Williams' 3rd wife dies?
1786 Williams in alms-houses
1787 Williams' grandson, William Williams born Massachussetts
1788 letter from Benjamin Condy, Philadelphia to Williams, informing him he cannot find his son.
1789 'The Power of Sympathy' published, claimed to be America's first novel
1791 Williams dies 27 April
1792 West becomes President of RA
1815 *Journal* published, and 1825

CHAPTER VI

A note on the Rama Indians and the Tribes of the Atlantic Coast

The Miskito ethnic group begins with the indigenous Bawihka people of northeastern Nicaragua intermarrying with runaway African slaves from the British Caribbean territories. These people are lumped together with the name "Sumu" which include Ulwa and Twaka languages. Other people that the tribe controls are small groups of Rama and Garífuna speakers. By the end of the 19th century, English-speaking Black Creoles inhabited areas around Bluefields and Corn Island. Together all of these people can be considered the Costeños.

Their territory extends from Cape Cameron in Honduras to Rio Grande in Nicaragua. This land is very difficult to enter from inland Nicaragua and was only accessed by boat through the rain forest, rivers and savannas. Due to contact with these slaves and English traders, the Miskito developed a political structure that was heavily influenced by these two peoples. It was a system where the King was the figurehead of the state, but he did not have complete control over the Kingdom. It was broken up between himself, the Governor, the General, and later, around 1759, the position of Admiral was added to the leadership political structure. It was a system that allowed the Miskito Kingdom to be able to enjoy stability for almost 240 years and maintain their independence from Spain, the Federation of Central American States, and Nicaragua until 1894. The first kings of the Miskito were semi-mythical and it was not until 1687 that the first historical account of a Miskito king, Jeremy I, was recorded.

Thanks to English economic interest in the region, Miskito people were able to acquire guns, ammunition, and support from the British Empire that allowed them to secure their independent state. The Miskito-Zambo slave raids in eastern Nicaragua aided the British-Spanish competition. The Miskito found runaway slaves from Providence Island or from Spanish mines or English plantations. It was believed that the raids were started by the Miskito in order to capture those in their surrounding areas to be sold as slaves. Most likely, the buccaneers who were of English, French or Dutch background were assisted by Miskito men on Cape Gracias a Dios. Miskito men made dugouts for transportation, served as guides to interior Nicaragua and gave food to these buccaneers for more guns, ammunition and iron tools.. After buccaneering was outlawed in 1685, many buccaneers settled down with the Indians and blacks in Black River, in Honduras or Cape Gracias and Bluefields, in Nicaragua.

The Miskito men raided many areas according to different documents. The earliest accounts told that Miskito men often captured Indian woman and children of Alboawinney or Oldwawes tribes who lived on the border of their territory because they were considered *wild Indians* to them. The Miskito also raided wild Indians from the border of Costa Rica and the cacao plantations in Matina Valley. Other later sources from Spanish clergy and government officials claimed that Miskito men raided Spanish settlements in central mountains of Honduras and Nicaragua as well as Peten, coast of Yucatan, and more southern regions in Costa Rica. When the Miskito gained more firearms and the demand increased in Jamaica for Indian labour, the slave raids heightened. In the early 18th century, the Miskito had populated the region at an incredible rate because of the offspring from captive women in the slave raids. Because of the excess number of woman, polygamy was practiced and there were more women to do agricultural work. Eventually, Miskito settlements became more permanent with solid agricultural settings. By the late 17th century, the Miskito were introduced to new plants and animals such as pigs, chickens, and rice, which were all added to their diet. Because of their huge growth, other indigenous groups were forced to move or be incorporated into the Miskito culture. Miskito Indians supported British buccaneers in the seventeenth century and continued to raid Spanish colonies well after the British had stopped fighting the Spanish. The Miskito Kingdom signed treaties with British Jamaica and briefly faced an English attempt at greater control in the region, from 1740, with an increased presence of English settlements in Miskito lands.

The reasons why Miskito men participated in the slave raids are interesting. Some researchers claimed that the Miskito did not consider themselves 'wild Indians', and traded with the British because they wanted to have a British identity. The Miskito leaders certainly tried to imitate the British cultural practices of dress, language and customs. All the Miskito kings after Jeremy I in 1687 lived in Bluefields and were Creole, and given names by the British. Eventually the King's residence was moved to Bluefields in 1840 after being in Cape Gracias a Dios, Sandy Bay, and Pearl Lagoon. Even though the kingship stayed within the same lineage the British did not choose the kings. When the Spanish recognized an admiral by the name of Dilson as the leader of the Miskito nation, the Kingdom briefly experienced a divided leadership. With the death of Dilson and his closest ally, Admiral Israel, the Miskito nation was able to once again enjoy stability until the reign of George II. Miskito leaders began siding with the Spanish, which lead to infighting with their kings, political assassinations, and instability. Once the English pulled out, Spanish settlers began to arrive in Miskito land in 1787. However the Miskito showed that they still controlled the land, as many settlers then moved west, and out of the Kingdom. In 1894, President Zelaya ordered the 'reincorporation' of the Miskito Kingdom into Nicragua, and after initial setbacks its army entered Bluefields in August. King Robert Henry Clarence had spent his youth in Rama Cay and was half Rama and half Miskito, and fled to Jamaica. However, the Miskito people have seen themselves as a British and United States protectorate since 1740, so the government of Nicaragua is still in reality considered an 'alien' government.

When the Sandinista revolutionary movement swept Nicaragua in the 1980s, the eastern lands under the Miskito did not support the new government because it was predominately Mestizo in nature and coming from the West. By 1982, the Miskito people were in open revolt against the Nicaragua government until 1985 when the government altered its policies towards the region and allowed the area to be broken into two autonomous regions. The Miskito people are now in the process of once again building their nation independently of the rule of Nicaragua. The Rama refer to Mestizos as 'Spaniards' or 'Nation', reflecting the long period when the Spanish and the Nicaraguan government did not successfully colonise the Atlantic coast, and were seen as outsiders.

After foreign companies left in the in the 1960s, it left the Moravian Church in a financial crisis because the Church was supported by these companies' funding to provide workers. After they left, the economy in the Atlantic Coast suffered and the people could not afford to attend church because they did not have money to give to the required offering. The economic crisis caused the Miskito men to look for alternative sources of income by commercialising their natural resources and agriculture.

The Rama people are the smallest ethnic group living on the Atlantic coast of Nicaragua. There are six ethnic groups in the region, each associated with a different ethnic language. Although the figures given here are from 1982, the relative ranking of the populations has not changed much, and the Rama people remain by far the smallest. Its population is now around 1400 because of inter-marriage with Miskitu, Mestizo and Creole groups, and its main language is a form of English called Rama-Creole. (Another classification of the distinct ethnic communities in Nicaragua as a whole is by URACCAN which names Miskitu, Creole English, Sumu-Mayagna, Sumu-Ulwa and Garifuna.)

Ethnic group	population	language	language family
Mestizos	182,377	Spanish	Indo-European
Miskitus	66,994	Miskitu	Misumalpan
Creoles	25,723	English	Creole (Indo-European)
Sumus	4,851	Sumu	Misumalpan
Caribes	1,487	Garifuna	Arawakan
Ramas	649	Rama	Chibchan

Table Source: Ethnic and Language Composition of the Atlantic Coast (CIDCA 1982)
The assessment of the Rama population was never very high. It was estimated at 500 by 1827 and 285 in 1909, with a lowest citation of 164 by 1865. The total Rama population is now said to be around 1400, with only 36 fluent Rama language speakers. The Ramas may have been relatively latecomers to Nicaragua. The name Rama did not appear in the colonial documents until the eighteenth century. The Ramas are thought to be descendants of the Votos, who at the time of the conquest occupied a territory extending from the Rio Escondido north of Bluefields Lagoon to the Rio San Juan, which forms today the border between Nicaragua and Costa Rica. Traditionally the Ramas lived in small, scattered settlements, moving about and hiding from intruders in the tropical forest. At the turn of the 17th century the Miskitus granted the Ramas a small island in the lagoon of Bluefields in recognition of their help in fighting off Terraba Indians from the south. An estimated 200 Ramas from the coastal area of Punta Gorda moved to the island, which became known from then on as Rama Cay. The island is thirteen kilometres south of Bluefields. (The trip from Rama Cay to the market town of Bluefields takes about four hours on average by dugout canoe, and from an hour and a half to thirty minutes by motor boat.). Today the vast majority of the Rama population lives on Rama Cay. A major problem, apart from illegal logging and lack of government protection, is the dry canal megaproject. This proposed a high speed rail line across Nicaragua from coast to coast (with an associated road infrastructure), a competitor to the Panama Canal, including a new port in the Rama territory of Monkey Point. It may be successful, but there will be uncontrolled colonization of Rama lands, destruction of rainforest and biological diversity, damage to marine resources and violation of indigenous land rights.

In just the decade from 1990, it is estimated that the Rama of south-eastern Nicaragua have lost half of their land (- N.L. Thomas, NicaNet, see references). The worst areas for invasion and deforestation were the supposedly protected 'natural areas' such as the Indio-Maiz Biological reserve, the BOSAWAS and the Cerro Silva Forest reserve. Armed men clear 'grids' of up to 50 acres at a time and take ownership, and the cattle ranches spread inexorably and forever into what used to be virgin rainforest. The soil of the rainforest here is mainly nutrient-poor and thin, stripped by massive rainfalls. When trees are stripped out, the grassland is poor quality, and huge and growing expanses are needed to feed cattle. This is ecological destruction on a massive scale, and is practically irreversible. Not just the Rama of the Atlantic Coast have been evicted and sometimes killed, but also their neighbours, the Sumu, Miskito, Creole and Garifuna. The reserves were meant to protect the largest remaining rainforests in Central America, the domain of the jaguar, puma, macaws, howler monkeys, royal cedar and mahogany that Williams/Penrose described so superbly.

In one year the Nicaraguan government confiscated 7,500 illegal forest extraction permits (– source Ben Gregory), but many of these logging companies are fronts for multinationals with vast economic power and the consequent corporate morality. A Centro Humboldt report noted the huge and irreplaceable losses of mahogany (caoba), pine, two types of tropical cedar, coyote, coralillo, cortez, santa maria, nanciton, balsamo, guayabo, granadillo, palo de agua, quebracho, roble, genizaro, cebo, areno, mora, tamarindo and laurel. The Korean multinational SOLCARSA (now renamed PRADA) has been particularly active in the rainforests, along with MADENSA and PLYNIC, causing deforestation on a terrible scale. Also, trawlers are also depleting valuable fish and shellfish stocks, even in the Bluefields Lagoon, making life even more difficult for the remaining Rama.

The move eastwards of cattle ranching has been inexorable, and settlers wipe out, in days, the forest of ancestral lands that the Rama and other tribes have used for centuries. There is no protection for the Rama, nor the biodiversity of the rainforest and Atlantic coast and rivers. The police seem unable or unwilling to help Rama settlements from Mestizo attacks involving multiple murders and rapes. Riverstone recounts one such attack, among many. 'On February 25, 2001, a group of seven armed and masked Mestizo men showed up at the Rama settlement at Western Hill (Big Hill), 5 kilometres south of Rama Cay on the mainland. This group of bandits is suspected to be the same group that attacked the Wiring Group community a few months before. At Western Hill, Rama from Rama Cay have a community farm, where two families at a time go to work on a two-week rotating basis When the bandits arrived at Western Hill, they rounded up the nine Rama men who were present, and tied them up with barbed wire. The women were raped at gunpoint. One Rama woman was raped in front of her family, including her husband, her parents, and her children. At least one other woman was raped by each of the Mestizo men... (The Rama) say that a least some of the men are local Mestizos... The Rama claim that even though they told this to the police, the police did not pursue the bandits. Many Rama and Monkey point community members suspect that the present violence is part of a larger effort to drive the Rama and Creole from their lands...'

As a result of such continued aggression, perhaps half of the 1400 or so remaining Rama now live on Rama Cay in Bluefields Lagoon. The last surviving Rama speakers seem to live at Cane Creek, and the traditional Rama settlements such as Monkey Point, Pataste and Wiring Cay have been virtually abandoned.

It is instructive that 20 years ago, Uhl and Parkler made the point that beefburger meat used in the USA comes from cleared rainforest in Central America. The low quality beef is ground up and sold to US fast-food chains. The authors calculated that for each beefburger, 55 square feet of rainforest – home to millions of individual rainforest organisms and thousands of species – is lost. Apart from the incursions of chainsaws and

294

armed gangs and multiinationals into indigenous territories, and the activities of Peter Tsokos selling off Rama lands and islands noted above, NicaNet also mentions Americans participating in the land grab (Edward Merrick laying claim to 80,000 acres of indigenous land at Prinzapolka, and John Vogel claiming land around the Rama's Monkey Point).

Nicaragua has the largest tropical rain forest north of Amazonia. It is disappearing ten times faster than the Brazilian rainforest and at the present rate the entire forest will be gone in two decades. In 1960, forest covered 60 percent of Nicaragua but now it only covers 20 percent or roughly 15,000 square miles. During the eight year civil war the deforestation rate declined compared to the steady rate at which trees were being cut down before the war. When the war ended, cutting resumed with a vengeance.

Jaguar, puma, tapir, the harpy eagle, macaws and howler monkeys are becoming regionally extinct in Nicaragua and other parts of Central America, along with species of hardwood. Rainforest takes around a hundred years to regenerate. However, rainforest cannot earn money for politicians and police and army officers. An excerpt from the NicaNet site of an interview with a Rama Elder, Rufino Omier, in June 2000, is instructive:

Q:How long have the Rama been selling shrimp?
Mr. Rufino: *Before 1963, the people never livin by the shrimp. That was bountiful! They doesn't use no kind of cast net. But they just go and side long the dory (canoe) and heel the dory and haul the paddle, make then shrimps jump in the dory. Bountiful!, bountiful! But people never used to buy shrimp then. If you have a net, just one minute and you load the dory with shrimp. Now it's very few, not like once – everything! You see, from that date in 1963, I the first that learn to make cast net in Rama Cay, the first Rama cay man. A man by the name of Professor Eustace Chow learned me to make net. From there everybody learned to make net. So now we used cast net.*

Q: Did you mean that just shrimp were more bountiful then, or other things as well?
Mr. Rufino: *Everything was bountiful in the days past. You found fish, snook, you strike with the harpoon. In those days gillnet never exist. Everything was bountiful, bountiful! You could strike all your snook so much you want. Anywhere you turn you would find, in the river and in the lagoon. In September you go out on the (river) bar and you find when 4 o'clock coming in, when the tide coming in, and you look in the waters, and you see the waters shaking – pure snook. Any way you turn you bring in fish. When the river getting salt you just stand up with your harpoon and your staff and you just strike how much you want. All kind of fish.*

Q: Were animals more bountiful back then, too?
Mr. Rufino: *There in the wild hogs you found all over the place, around the edge, the wild boar them, wari. Bounty. You neither have to go far. You go in the morning and you smell them. When the breeze came from the back you smell them. You just land and you go shoot. Strike them with bow and arrow. People never used no weapons like gun.*

EXTRACTS FROM ORLANDO ROBERTS' 'NARRATIVE OF VOYAGES' OF 1827, PERTAINING TO THE RAMA.

Orlando Roberts, an American seaman and 'resident trader', traveled through Central America to map the east coast, setting up trading relations with native communities. He surveyed between Darien (northern Panama) and the Miskito Coast of Nicaragua, sailing up the San Juan River in Costa Rica and across Lake Nicaragua. His account and maps became the most up-to-date compilation of data on the geography and the indigenous native peoples. He also gives an account of native life, and of the natural environment including descriptions of birds, fish, turtles, manatees, and edible and other useful plants then being considered for commerce. Roberts was the first person use the word creoles in any written text, and also describes the history and politics of the region:

From the Rio de San Juan to Point de Gordo, a distance of between thirty and forty miles, the coast forms a large bay, into which flows the Rio Trigo, (Corn River), Indian River, and several smaller streams… Between Corn River and Point de Gordo, is Grindstone Bay, with anchorage in from four to five fathoms water. At a short distance from the coast the country here rises considerably; and, from the neighbourhood of San Juan to Bluefields, it is occupied by the **Rama** *Indians, whose principal settlement is at* **Rama** *River, or Rio de Punta Gorda, a noble stream, which is said to have a course of about eighty miles, or upwards, from the interior, through a fertile country, and passing between two mountainous ridges at a short distance from the sea-shore. Its mouth may be known by a remarkably high, round, barren islet, laying about four miles distant off its entrance. The bay is shallow, but there is good anchorage under the lee side of Monkey Point, about four miles farther to the northward, a place which may be distinguished by its having several small islands and cays in its vicinity.*

The country from San Juan River to this point abounds in vanilla (Vanilla aromatica) of the finest quality. This plant climbs with ease to the top of the highest tree. At a distance the leaves slightly resemble those of the vine; the flowers are of a white colour, intermixed with red and yellow, when these fall off, they are quickly succeeded by the pods, growing in bunches not unlike the plantain, and generally of the thickness of a child s finger. The pods are green at first, grow yellow, and finally brown; the method used to preserve the fruit, is to gather it when yellow, before the pods begin to open or burst it is then laid in small heaps for the space of three or four days to ferment. The fruit is afterwards spread in the sun to dry; and when about half dried, flattened with the hand, and rubbed over with cocoa, palm, or other oil: it is once more exposed to the sun, to be fully dried, rubbed over with oil a second time, put in small parcels, and closely covered over with the dried leaves of the plantain or Indian reed. Care is taken not to allow the pods to remain upon the stalks too long before they are pulled, as, in that case, they transude a black fragrant balsam, which carries off both the smell and delicate flavour for which alone they are valued. The vanilla plant is also found on most parts of the Mosquito Shore, and in the neighbourhood of Breo del Rero and Chiriqui Lagoons; it requires heat, moisture, and shade, to bring it to perfection, and when used in that state it gives a most delicious flavour to coffee, chocolate, &c., forming an important article of commerce, especially among the Spaniards. In the neighbourhood of the Lagoons and places last mentioned, a very fragrant bean, resembling, if not in reality, the true Tonquin bean, is also found.

The **Rama** *Indians were formerly numerous, but, at present, do not exceed five hundred; they are under subjection to the Mosquito King, to whom they pay an annual tax in tortoise-shell, canoes, hammocks, and cotton lines. The* **Ramas** *are considered mild, and inoffensive; they have little intercourse with other Indians; and, during the fishing season, seldom go to the southward of Matina; they are more expert in the management of canoes and other boats, than* the Mosquito men, and will effect a landing in their barks, where the best European boats would meet certain destruction: their canoes and dories, are much broader, and shallower, than those generally used on the coast; they are also much more buoyant, and better adapted for landing in a heavy surf, or for crossing the bars of rivers. The **Ramas**, when engaged by the English settlers, have always proved very faithful servants. The source of the **Rama** River, is unknown to the settlers at Bluefields ; but some of them have examined it for sixty or seventy miles, and assert that it runs through a country rather level, but having an appearance of very great fertility, and abounding in mahogany, locust, santa maria, and other valuable timber.

The several small cays and islets, which lay off this part of the coast, and that of Bluefields, are, like many places already noticed, much frequented by the Indians from all parts during the season for hawksbill turtle. Bluefields is the next place of importance on the coast, and is said to derive its name from a celebrated English Captain of Buccaniers in the seventeenth century. (N.B. Blauveldt was actually Dutch, and sailed with Henry Morgan). For trading vessels of an easy draught of water, the upper lagoon is perhaps superior to any other harbour on the Mosquito Shore, being completely sheltered from all winds. There are two entrances; that to the southward, through Hone Sound, is very difficult, and dangerous even for small craft; the bar being generally covered with breakers, and having only four to five feet water: but, the principal and only one for ships, is to the northward, close to the Bluff, a high rocky eminence, capable of being easily fortified, completely commanding the entrance, upon the bar of which, extending across to Deer Island, there is never less, but sometimes more, than fifteen feet water. After passing this bar, there is from four to six fathoms water. Close to the shore it continues deep, but it gradually shallows to three, and three and a half fathoms, which is the general depth throughout the upper and lower Lagoons. There are many banks, and shoals, about the entrances, but none of them dangerously situated for shipping ; many of them are dry at low water, and abundance of fine oysters can then easily be procured. The Lower Lagoon is full of small cays, or islets, and is from fifteen to twenty miles in length, having sufficient depth of water for vessels of considerable burthen, but the channels are intricate, and only known to the settlers at Bluefields.

The Upper Lagoon, which is a continuation of the Lower, is not more than a mile broad at its entrance, but its width, farther up, increases to five or six miles; and, into it, the great river of Nueva Segovia of the Spaniards, and several smaller ones, empty themselves. The lands bordering on all these rivers are extremely rich and fertile, capable of growing cotton, cocoa, coffee, sugar, and all the different kinds of produce raised in the British West Indies. The forests abound in cedar of the largest description, mahogany, and many other valuable woods. The pine Savannahs, bordering on Bluefields, and pearl cay lagoons, can furnish an inexhaustible supply of the very finest pitch pine timber, some of it fit for the largest masts.

Colonel Hodgson, the British Superintendent, resided at this place for a number of years, during the time the English held possession of the Mosquito Shore, and he had extensive mahogany works on the banks of the principal river, and a very considerable trade was carried on with the Spaniards and Creoles in the interior. This active and intelligent gentleman, had also extensive grants of land at Black River, and left the Mosquito Shore with much regret, at the time when the extraordinary policy of the British Government compelled their settlers to abandon that country in the year 1786. He spent a great portion of his life on this coast; and the old Indians still speak of their former Governor, with respect, and marks of regret, that no accredited person now resides among them.

Previous to his leaving Bluefields, several of his slaves and people who were established in the interior, refused to leave the place. These people and their descendants, who are Mulattoes and Samboes, are settled at the southernmost extremity of the harbour, about nine miles from its principal entrance, and they have considerably in creased in numbers since Colonel Hodgson s time. They live without fear of molestation from the Indians, none of whom reside within many miles of them; and, although it is not acknowledged as such by the British Government, it may be truly considered a British settlement. It is principally under the influence of two intelligent young men, who claim affinity to the late superintendent. The river of Bluefields, or Rio de Nuevo Segovia, rises in the country possessed by the Spaniards, within fifty or sixty miles of the South Sea, and has a course of several hundred miles ; but few of the present people at Bluefields have ascended its course to any great height. The Cookra and Woolwa tribes of Indians, who are settled on its banks, at a considerable distance in the interior, are a quiet peaceable race of people, on good terms with the **Ramas**, and the people at Bluefields Lagoons. They possess very little energy, and are often enslaved, or murdered, by the Indians resident about Great River, whom I shall afterwards have occasion to notice.

These Indians occasionally descend the river, to the settlements at Bluefields, bringing peccary, warree, iguanas, and other provisions. Bluefields, with its excellent harbour, protected by a rocky, bluff point, capable of being made almost impregnable, is in an excellent situation for opening a communication across the country to the Lakes of Nicaragua, and possesses such other advantages as a commercial station, that, sooner or later, it must become a place of very consider able importance.

From Bluefields, to Pearl Kay Lagoon, the distance is about thirty miles: a moderately elevated headland, named False Bluefields, is the only high land on the coast, until we reach Brangmans, or Branckmans Bluff, called by the Spaniards Monte Gordo; it consists of three or four moderately high hills, of a light red colour, rising almost perpendicularly from the beach; they are composed of stiff clay, and extend along the shore for nearly two miles, falling off at each end with a gentle slope terminating in the savannah. About half a mile to the southward of the bluff, there is good anchorage. The soil in the neighbourhood of the bluff is sandy, yet covered with verdure; and there are several tall pine trees close to them, under the shade of which, a "king s house", similar to those before mentioned, had been erected for the convenience of travellers, there being now no Indian resident here, although at one time there was a small British settlement near it.

The entrance to Pearl Kay Lagoon is little more than a quarter of a mile in width, and is at the bottom, or south end of the bay, over a bar, on which there is about ten feet water. The safest anchorage for vessels is under the north side, off which, there are several small islands, cays, and reefs, on which pearl oysters are said to have been found. Moreover, these places are called the Pearl Cays, but, for what reason, I never could ascertain, as there is certainly no pearl oysters, or oysters of any kind that I could discover, upon them, or on the reefs by which they are surrounded; although, in the Lagoon, there are abundance of good oysters, on banks, many of which are dry at low water. These oysters are in bunches of about eight or ten in each bunch; they are rather larger than the mangrove oyster, but of a different kind from those in the Bay of Panama, and other places producing pearls. I have frequently examined the oysters found in the Lagoon, but never could discover pearls in any of them; and I mention this more particularly, because, since my return to England, I found, that these reports, and the blind zeal of certain ignorant speculators, had induced one of the companies recently formed in London for Foreign Adventure, to determine on sending a vessel, which was in fact ready to depart, to this quarter to fish for pearls; but, on informing them of the truth, they altered her destination...

The country and Lagoon abounds in all the kinds of game and fish peculiar to the country and coast. The Mosquito men, **Ramas**, and other Indians, hire themselves to the settlers at Bluefields, and Pearl Kay Lagoon, as hunters and strikers of fish, at the rate of four or five dollars a month, paid in goods; and they always cover the board of their employer with an ample supply of fish, game, and other provisions ; the **Ramas** or other pure Indians are always preferred, for this purpose, to the mixed breeds. The value of these men, in the capacity above mentioned, was well known to the old Buccaniers, who had always some of them attached to their expeditions, even as far as the South Sea, to which they were frequently guided, by these Indians, across the continent.

Pearl Kay Lagoon is of considerable magnitude; one part of it reaching to within eight miles of Great River, or Rio Grande; its greatest winding length, from north-east, to south-west, cannot be far short of sixty miles, or its breadth from sixteen to twenty. The Indians, in had weather, instead of keeping along the sea-coast, enter Pearl Kay Lagoon by hauling their canoes over the narrow neck of land between it and Bluefields Lagoon ; and, at the upper end of it, they have another haulover of about two hundred yards, into

the ocean...

I may here observe, that the whole of the Indians of these settlements, instigated by the infernal policy of the Mosquito chiefs, used, formerly, to make frequent incursions upon the neighbouring tribes of Cookras, Woolwas, and Toacas, bordering on the Spanish territory, for the sole purpose of seizing and selling them for slaves to the settlers, and chief men on different parts of the Mosquito Shore. Much misery has here resulted to these poor people, who, although now seldom annoyed, have withdrawn themselves far into the interior; and hold very little intercourse with the Indians on the coast. The Cookras are now seldom seen; the Woolwas have also retired from the coast, and their settlements are on the upper branches of the rivers Nuevo Segovia, Rio Grande, and others, at a considerable distance from those of the Coast Indians and Mosquito men. Drummer had, in his early years, been an intolerable scourge to these inland tribes, and, to the Woolwas in particular, some hundreds of whom had been, from first to last, captured by him and his parties, and sold as slaves. His method was, to steal upon, and, if possible, in the absence of the males, surprise the temporary settlements or residences of the small roving parties moving about the heads of the rivers spoken of, seize the women and children, and effect his retreat, if possible, without fighting. In some in stances, these kidnappers have gone as far back as the settlements of the Spaniards and Spanish Creoles, whose wives and children they have not hesitated to carry off, and appropriate to their own use. ...

The Province of Nicaragua, in 1823, was supposed to contain a population of 164,374. The district of Leon, besides the capital of the same name, contains the cities of Granada, and New Segovia; and the towns of Nicaragua, Esteli, Alcoyapa, Villa Nueva and Massaya; to which may he added Monagua, Matares, Nagarotta, and others of less note.

The province of Costa Rica, the most eastern on the Atlantic side, was, at the same time, estimated to contain a population of 37,716. Between Nicaragua and Comayagua are the provinces of Taguzagalpa, Tologalpa, and Matagalpa, peopled by Indians who have not been converted to the Christian religion, and who may be considered entirely independent of the Spaniards, with whom they hold no intercourse. They are called indiscriminately Xicagues, Moscoes, and Samboes. There are also several other tribes inhabiting the country to the eastward and north-westward of the Lakes of Nicaragua and Monagua or Leon. Among which may be reckoned the Valientes or Indios Bravos, the Chilibees, Tiribees, Woolwas, **Ramas**, Cookras, Poyers and various others, who have zealously maintained their liberty, and amongst whom the Spaniards have not been able to establish themselves. All these tribes are favourable to the British, and took the opportunity, on most occasions, of joining the Buccaniers, in their predatory excursions against the Spanish possessions...

The day after we returned to the harbour, some Mosquito men arrived from the Boca de la Tortuga. They had heard of our seizure, and, in common with all the other Mosquito men, had orders from the admiral to furnish me, on my reappearance, with all things necessary to enable me to reach the Cape without delay, there being "a King's order," to supply provisions, men, horses, dories, &c.; and so eager were they to comply with this order, and hear our adventures, that they immediately proceeded for the **Rama** settlement, without waiting to kill manatee, according to their first intention. Accordingly, after taking another view of the place where I had so narrowly escaped death, and having again viewed the entrances to the river in as careful a manner as prudence would admit, I embarked with these Indians, and, at the **Rama** settlement, was received by Pedro, the chief man, with great kindness and attention. He furnished a large canoe to convey us to Bluefields, and from thence to Pearl Cay Lagoon, where we were welcomed with great rejoicing, it having been reported that I had been put to death, and the Indians sold as slaves. At this place I parted with the llamas, and Scipi, the headman, gave us a canoe up the lagoon to the harbour, within eight miles of the great river ; we walked from thence to Drummer's, who provided us with horses, and on the following day, we reached Prinzapulko the native place of my Indians.

By some means or other our approach had been made known, and before we had well entered the savannah leading to the settlement, we were met by a great many of the people, who showed the most lively joy at the safe return of their friends, thus, as it were, restored from death. Brown and his lads were pulled from their horses, and almost devoured by the caresses of their friends and relations, who shed tears of joy at their safe return, venting, at the same time, execrations against the Spaniards; and I could not help shuddering when I thought what might have been my fate, if, through any neglect of mine, these people had periled, and I had afterwards fallen into the hands of their relations. I rode leisurely forward towards the King s house, but was soon rejoined by Brown, and by Para the headman, with other elders, who, having been made aware of the anxiety I had evinced for the safety and comfort of my companions, attributed their deliverance to my exertions, looked upon me as a true friend, and now showed me every mark of respect and kindness. They had, for some weeks past, contemplated an expedition against some of the Spanish settlements nearest to them, with the view of seizing as many Spaniards as possible, to be held as hostages for the safety of Brown and his companions made many inquiries regarding the strength of the Spanish posts, and as my drink was being prepared, we spent the evening of our return in mirth and rejoicing...'

FURTHER NOTES ON THE MANUSCRIPT

The following points of interest were discovered too late to go into the main body of the book, and are added for the reader's interest.

A] Sometime in 1805 or before, James Stanier Clarke saw Eagles' rewritten manuscript, and wrote in 1805 *'This narrative of Penrose ... is fully equal in point of interest, and superior in point of information respecting some parts of Natural history, to the celebrated volumes of Robinson Crusoe.'* (J. S. Clarke, preface to *'Naufragia or Historical Memoirs of Shipwrecks and of the Influential Deliverance of Vessels Volume 1'* published by J. Mawman, London 1805.

Lord Byron knew of *Naufragia*, and quoted it in a letter to John Murray on June 13th, 1813, so he will have been previously aware of the Penrose Journal. Byron suspected John Murray at one stage of writing the Journal, as in the following letter to him.
Nov. 29, 1813, Monday.
Dear Sir,—You will act as you please upon that point; but whether I go or stay, I shall not say another word on the subject till May—nor then, unless quite convenient to yourself. I have many things I wish to leave to your care, principally papers. The vases need not be now sent, as Mr. W. is gone to Scotland. You are right about the Er[rata] page; place it at the beginning. Mr. Perry is a little premature in his compliments: these may do harm by exciting expectation, and I think we ought to be above it—though I see the next paragraph is on the Journal, which makes me suspect you as the author of both...
Yours very truly, B.

B] The Thomas Eagles' copy of Penrose's manuscript, with 23 original illustrations by Edward Bird RA, 4 by Nicholas Pocock and 9 by Eagles, has recently been sold at auction for $30,000 and the pictures are being restored in a museum. Hopefully a future edition of this book could show them. It was hoped that some of Williams' own paintings could have been included in this edition, but the reproduction fees were prohibitive for this publisher.

C] Flexner made the point that Williams possibly contributed to and influenced the Philadelphia school of early American writers, naming Hopkinson and Godfrey. Further research may establish links. Francis Hopkinson (1737-1799) was the first American poet-composer, a friend of Benjamin Franklin like Williams, and signed the Declaration of Independence. Thomas Godfrey (1736-1763) was the dramatist and poet who wrote *'The Prince of Parthia'*, first performed four years after his death in 1767. He was America's first playwright. Williams painted the scenery for *The Prince of Parthia*, the first play by an American author to be performed by professional actors.

D] Apropos of the point that there are 'too many' William Williams, in 1740 a William Williams subscribed to the 'Church Yard Wall' at Old St David's Church, Radnor, Delaware County Pennsylvania, with many other Welsh immigrants. St David is the patron saint of Wales, and Radnor was an old county of Wales.

E] Williams' spelling of Havannah is replicated in the spelling of Havannah Street in Cardiff Bay, the name only remaining of the days when Cardiff was one of the world's major shipping centres.

F] The Indians' practice of speaking during inhalation is difficult to practice and unknown to this author. It is sometimes temporarily used by stammerers.

G] 'Lines by William Williams' are in manuscript group 982 held by the New Jersey Historical Society. These may be by our William Williams, or more likely by the William Williams who was a signatory of the Declaration of Independence, and they come from a collection of verses and notes held by Ann Nicholson (fl. 1819). Her family arrived in New Jersey in 1675.

H] It is beyond the practicalities of time for this author to further research the circumstances of Williams' birth or the 'school' where the mother of Penrose/Williams taught. Most of the early gravestones in the remote Eglwysilan churchyard are in Welsh, including many of those who died in the great Senghenydd mining disaster of 1913. The author has also not been able to access the birth and marriage registers for Bedwas church, where more information may be available.

J] Katherine Hoyt of Nicaragua Network sent me the following article from Nicaragua Network, October 2001, about a remarkable nurse, Pearl Watson, who makes the rather dangerous boat trip to Bluefields local health centre every month for (limited) supplies for her health centre at Monkey Point..

Monkey Point Fights Canal

Q. *We heard that you had a difficult time getting from Monkey Point to Bluefields in order to come on the speaking tour (of the USA).*

A. *Yes, there was a big storm and what is usually a trip of two or three hours turned into six hours of bailing water in a small canoe on a high sea. I thought that we might drown and I had left my life vest in Bluefields. Also, we had a sick woman in the canoe whom we were taking to hospital.*

Q. *Could you tell us something about yourself and your family?*

A. *The story of how my ancestors came to Monkey Point is very interesting. We were Miskito people living further north on Nicaragua's northern coast at Sandy Bay and working as slaves. My ancestor was raped by a white master and she gave birth to a daughter who was very beautiful. When the daughter was grown, she was serving coffee one day to the mistress of the household when a roach ran out of a cup and on to the table. The mistress was so furious that she hit her on the nose with the coffee cup until it broke and she compelled her to eat the roach! After this she fled Nicaragua to the British Cayman Islands where slavery had ended. She married a black African man and they had eight children. Some years later, when they heard that slavery had ended, they decided to return to Nicaragua.*

But when they arrived in Bluefields, they found that there was still slavery there. So they decided to take another boat to Costa Rica where they had heard that slavery was through. But when they were caught by a bad storm they took refuge in a beautiful, enormous bay called Monkey Point where the indigenous peoples took them in. These people were the Rama people and they said my ancestors could stay there and live and farm. So they did, while the rest of the people on the boat sailed south to Costa Rica. That is how black Creole people came to Monkey Point.

I was born in Monkey Point. When I was eight I went to school in Bluefields and came home for vacations. I finished High School, married and worked as a seamstress as I raised my children in Bluefields. During the Revolution, I studied nursing and did my community service in the interior. Then I wanted to return to Monkey Point but the Health Ministry in the new government didn't want to send me. I think that they felt I would stir up trouble in Monkey Point. Finally, I had to threaten to quit in order for them to let me go and set up a clinic there.

Q. *And how has the clinic worked?*

A. *They sent me to Monkey Point without even a boat to get around - with a little food, some sheets and very little medicine. We need outboard motors, medicines and other supplies. Now with the possibility of building a 'dry canal' (high-speed freight railroad) the Aleman government feels that they can push us out of Monkey Point by cutting off public services. We have no public transportation; the school needs repair after Hurricane Mitch and we need police in the community.*

K] The engraver Henry Dawkins, who copied Williams' Benjamin Lay, left London for New York City around 1753. He was in Philadelphia from 1753, and back in New York c.1957. He was imprisoned in 1776 for involvement in counterfeiting.

L] The biographer of Benjamin West, John Galt (1779-1839), also wrote a biography of Lord Byron, who along with West features in the story of the publication of Penrose.

M] Penrose's flag of a two stripes, blue upper and white lower, is similar to that of Nicaragua, which was adopted in 1908 and has a white band between two blue bands. This in turn was based on the flag of the United Provinces of Central America (Guatemala, El Salvador, Honduras, Costa Rica and Nicaragua), which in 1821 became independent of Spain in 1821 and were part of the empire of Mexico from 1822.

N] Williams uses 'truck' several times, meaning 'barter' or 'exchange'. It originally meant any commodities for sale. In Wales, in the early Industrial Revolution, companies had 'truck shops' that accepted the special coinage minted to pay their employees. This ensured the companies received back the wages through 'truck'. They charged extortionate prices for goods, and in sporadic periods of unrest, rioters like the 'Scotch Cattle' often destroyed them. The Truck Act of 1831 abolished these iniquitous entities, hated by workers who had no other outlet for their wages.

O] Zoe King appears to be the sister-in-law of John Eagles, which explains her interest in the manuscript.

P] Many of William Williams' pictures can be seen in Dickason's biography, but it was unfortunately outside the budget of this publication to pay for reproduction rights.

Q] There is a note in the above book, taken from *Bristol Past and Present* (J.F. Nicholls & John Taylor, Bristol, 1881-82): '*Thomas Eagles was, we believe, the author of Llewellyn (sic) Penrose, a charming romance in the style of Robinson Crusoe*'.

R] Another note in Dickason's biography is taken from an article in *Gentleman's Magazine* 45 (Feb. 1846), entitled '*The Eagles' of Bristol, Father and Son*': '*An old literary friend, Mathew Gutch, reminiscences: "It was soon after I was admitted to friendly intercourse with this gentleman (in 1807) and I had obtained his confidence, that I was favoured with the perusal of a manuscript volume which he had transcribed and no doubt improved its language and structure, without altering its details. It took me four nights to read it to an assembled party at a Christmas fireside."* John Mathew Gutch (1776-1861) was a Bristol printer, a colleague and friend of John Eagles. He corresponded with Coleridge and Charles Lamb, and he owned, edited and printed *Felix Farley's Bristol Journal*.

S] The Red Snapper poisoning from which Penrose dies is Ciguatera, caused by reef fish feeding on toxic algae (Ciguatoxin) on the reef.

T] Earl Gray, the Journal and the Abolition of Slavery. Lord George Byron was internationally famous from the publication of *Childe Harolde* in 1812, and was feted in society from that time. From Byron's letters we discover that on November 22nd, 1813, he met Lady Holland and her party at Drury Lane Theatre. Upon November 28th, Byron wrote asking John Murray for a copy of Penrose's Journal for Lady Holland, to give to Earl Grey. Sometime before Christmas, Lady Caroline Lamb burnt effigies of Byron's picture and copies of his letters, with children dancing around the bonfire. On June 18th, 1814, Byron wrote that he had been entertained at Earl Grey's. Earl Grey (1764-1845) was a mature statesman aged around 50 at this time. He later became Prime Minister (1830-1834), when the Reform Act of 1832 sowed the seeds of electoral democracy. He also was responsible for restrictions on the employment of children. Importantly, his Government forced through the abolition of slavery in the British Empire in 1833 – could he have been influenced by his reading of *The Journal of Penrose* two decades earlier?

Notes to Book I Chapter I

1. There was a contemporary ship of this name listed in *Bristol Privateers and Ships of War*, 1930, by Commander J.W. Damer Powell. In late February 1747, Captain William Montague in HMS *Bristol* captured the valuable French ship *Union*, bound from Havana to Cadiz, carrying 360,000 dollars and a rich cargo of cochineal and cocoa. Montague in 1745, in command of the *Mermaid*, had taken part in the capture of Cape Breton and brought home the news of the victory at Louisburg. (He was married a second time, in 1772, to Lucy Smith [nee Lee] in Lancaster County, Virginia, and his will is dated October 21st, 1794). There was a Captain Thomas Williams who may have been known to William Williams, as he captained the *Launceston* and then the *Warwick*, where he served in the Baltic under Admiral Norris. This Captain Williams died in 1752, and as William Williams recounts Norris later in the book, this Thomas Williams could be the actual captain he recalls. Another Captain Thomas Williams was knighted for action off the Scillies in 1796.

2. The *Great Storm* of January 8th, 1734/1735 caused almost as much damage as the one of 1703. There was also one in 1730, which harmed Amsterdam, but it seems that 1734/1735 is the storm referred to. In London, 36 trees were uprooted in St James's Park by a westerly gale, in the '*worst storm since 1703*'. In 1703 the Eddystone Lighhouse has been washed away, half the English fleet was blown to Norway, 10,000 English seamen drowned in the English Channel, HMS *Newcastle* was sunk at Spithead, and HMS *Burlington* had all her masts blown down.

3. A *dogger* is a two-masted ketch-type ship with a blunt prow, and is remembered on today's shipping forecasts for Dogger Bank (a large shoal 60 miles east of Northumbria, noted for herring, cod and dogfish catches). Of Dutch origin, it became the favoured trawler in the North Sea, crewed by '*doggermen*' and catching '*doggerfish*', the origin of dogfish. Holland's waters at Texel now hold the world's largest catamaran race.

4. The *Spanish War* or *War of Jenkins' Ear* (see the author's *The Book of Welsh Pirates and Buccaneers*) began in 1739, and merged into the *War of the Austrian Succession* in 1742. Peace was made by the Treaty of Aix-la-Chapelle in 1748. Howell Gwynn, the name of Penrose's childhood friend, is a typically Welsh name.

5. This appeared to be the small port of Pill, in Newport, Monmouthshire, from whence South Walians made the short crossing over the Severn River to the great slave port of Bristol. Pile is a corruption of Pill, which itself is a corruption of Pillgwenlli, which itself comes from the old Welsh name Pwllgwynlliw. (*The pool, or harbour, of St Gwynlliw*). However, further research proved it to be (Crockham) Pill on the river Avon, next to Hungroad, the largest of many pills (small creeks) off the Avon near its exit to the River Severn and the Bristol Channel. The inn described may have been 'Lamplighters' which was let in 1768 as '*the public house at Passage Leaze opposite Pill, commonly called Lamplighter's Hall*'. Crockham Pill became known as the '*village of pilots*,' so many lived there near Hungroad Anchorage. At Bristol port it was noted in 1717 that the quay wall was extended by 280 feet, as far as 'The Gibb'.

6. Privateers flourished in times of war, being privately commissioned with a letter of commission or a *letter of marque* to fight or loot the enemies of a nation. It was a little like '*outsourcing*' the Royal Navy.

7. Hungroad was the anchorage at the mouth of the Avon River in Bristol where it meets the River Severn in the Bristol Channel. As ships grew larger, it became more and more difficult to use the main port at Bristol, especially with the rapid ebb and flow of the Severn, with the second highest different levels between high and low water in the world. (Only the Bay of Fundy in Newfoundland has a greater differential.) Ships kept getting blocked in or stranded, so the port moved downriver to Hungroad, on a great bend in the Avon between Crockham Pill and Chapel Pill. It is little wonder that Williams/Penrose never saw Howell Gwynn again. Life on merchant ships was short in these times – disease was rife aboard ship, and thirst and hunger were the order of the day under brutal regimes.

8. He '*liked his drink*' so never refused ('flinched') the opportunity to imbibe. Grog is usually rum.

9. To '*curry*' probably means to beat, or bruise, or drub someone in this sense. As a prickly gooseberry branch was used, Williams might be using also the meaning of '*curry*' as applying to preparing a

horse, combing its hide to best effect for show.

10. 'Tars' are sailors, called so because of the prevalence of tar on wooden sailing ships. Sailors smelt of it – it was used to seal the decks and ship's timbers, and to preserve all the ropes and rigging from the effects of salt water. A *sot* is a drunk, so to be '*moored in Sot's Bay*' is to be in a drunken stupor. To '*trip one of their anchors*' would be to waken someone fast asleep, in order for them to move.

11. '*The Champion of Wales*' is one of the 'lost pubs' of Bristol, which was situated on Broad Quay. The incident with the abusive landlord happened in '*The White Lion and Horseshoe*', and there is a 'White Lion' pub on Quay Head, Bristol, which may be the same place. Other lost pubs in Bristol, showing the Welsh conection, many situated on the '*Welsh Back*' are: Cambrian House, Cambrian Tavern, Cardiff Boat, Cardiff Castle (2), Cardigan Arms, Carmarthenshire House, Chepstow Boat, Crown and Leek Tavern, Druid's Head, Druid's Arms, Lord Raglan, Raglan Castle, General Picton, Newport and South Wales Tavern, Pembrokeshire House, Plume of Feathers (7), Prince of Wales (13), St David, Sugar Loaf (6), Swansea Arms, Welsh Harp and Tenby Packet House. Only the *Llandoger Trow* survives. The port of Neath is actually at Briton Ferry (originally in Welsh, Llansawel) in Glamorgan, Wales. Bristol is east of Neath in the Bristol Channel, so an easterly wind was favourable for a fast voyage.

12. A '*snow*' is a small brig-like ship. The name '*Billy Vane*' is an intriguing choice in a work of faction. At this time there lived Charles William Vane, 3rd Marquis of Londonderry (1778-1854) and also William Henry Vane, 1st Duke of Cleveland (1761-1842) who was MP for Totnes in Devon from 1790-92.

13. When a privateer takes a '*prize*', the money from the contents and sale of the ship is shared between the crown, the privateer's owner, the captain and crew.

14. Forcibly '*impressed*' by the Royal Navy – a common hazard for sailors in port. Merchant navy seamen were also 'pressed' into service against their will in times of shortage of crews.

15. Penrose was now nearing 21 years old. The *Harrington* made at least four voyages to the East Indies and India for the East India Company from 1732-1744 according to Dickason, before it sailed in private service to the Caribbean. However, records show that its 4 voyages were made between 1732 and 1741. ('*Lords of the East: the East India Company and its Ships*' – Jean Sutton 1981). It was a huge ship for the times, being variously given at 460 tons and 490 tons. Williams met in real life its Captain Hunter in 1755 and apologised for deserting his ship. Intriguingly, 'A *Biographical Memoir of William Falconer*' notes that Falconer served with Captain Hunter when Hunter was a midshipman on the *Sutherland*, and that they kep in contact until Falconer's death. Falconer was a shipmate of Penrose, so perhaps William Williams served on the *Sutherland*. In March 22, 1741, at St Helena, Lt. Jenkins was reported to be appointed commander of the *Harrington*. (See footnote 8, Chapter IV). From Brooke's *History of St Helena* we learn that was Robert Jenkins, the captain of a Scottish merchant ship which was boarded by the Spanish garda costa off Campeche in 1731, with his ear being torn off. He produced it at the House of Commons in 1738, leading to the War of Jenkins' Ear (1739-1748) which merged into the War of Austrian Succession in 1742. He was later made a commander in the East India Company's service, being made supervisor of St Helena, arriving there in May 1740. His successor Major Lambert arrived in the *Harrington* in March 1741, and Jenkins was given the captaincy of the *Harrington*, distinguishing himself in an action against pirates. However, there is some confusion not only in the dating but also in the geography of this event, as in *The Pirates of Malabar* (1907) by Colonel John Biddulph, we read that Jenkins was master before this time: '*In January, 1740, a gallant action was fought by the Harrington, Captain Jenkins. The Harrington was returning from a voyage to China, and, in coming up the coast, had joined company with the Pulteney, Ceres, and Halifax. Between Tellicherry and Bombay they were attacked by fifteen sail of Angria's fleet. Four grabs ran alongside the Harrington, but were received with such a well-directed fire that they dropped astern. The four Company's ships then formed line abreast, and were attacked from astern by Angria's ships. The brunt of the fight fell on the Harrington. Jenkins had trained his crew, and was prepared for this method of attack. After five hours of heavy firing the Angrian ships drew off, showing confusion and loss. At daylight the next morning they attacked again. The Ceres had fallen to leeward, and three grabs attacked her, while three more bore down on the Harrington to windward. Disregarding his own attackers, Jenkins bore down on the assailants of the Ceres, and drove them off; then, hauling his wind, he awaited the attack of the others. The three leeward grabs were towed up within range, and for the next two or three hours the Harrington engaged all six, almost single-handed. The wind had fallen; the Ceres and Halifax were out of gunshot; the*

Pulteney alone was able to give assistance at long range. So well served were the Harrington's guns that she inflicted more damage than she received, and by ten o'clock four of the grabs gave up the contest and were towed away to windward. The other two grabs continued the action for some time, till they also were towed out of action. The two squadrons, just out of gunshot of each other, consulted among themselves. Jenkins found he had only seven rounds left for his big guns, and his consorts, which were more lightly armed, were in little better plight to renew the combat. Still, he put a good face on it, showing no unwillingness to continue the fight; and, on a breeze springing up, the Angrians drew off, leaving the East Indiamen to pursue their voyage. Only one man on board the Harrington was wounded, though the ship was much knocked about. Jenkins was much commended for his skill and courage, and two years later we find him acting as Commodore of the Company's fleet at Bombay.'

16. Deptford is a dockside area near Greenwich in London. Williams' *Red House* was renamed the Royal Victoria Victualling Yard in 1858.

17. Sometimes known as a '*Scotch tam*', woven in one piece without a seam or binding, a comfortable and larger type of beret to protect the seaman's head against the sun, sometimes with a red tail hanging down the back. The extremely hot Habanera chilli known as the '*Scotch bonnet*' takes its name from its similar appearance, and there is also a '*fairy ring mushroom*' (*marasmus oreades*) known as the 'Scotch bonnet' for the same reason.

18. '*Nearly on one's beam ends*' means that the ship has keeled over and is ready to sink.

19. This 48-gun man of war was built in 1691, rebuilt in 1721 at Deptford, and used as a breakwater at Sheerness in 1749. In the book, Penrose writes about serving on it in 1746, as the '*Old*' *Chatham*, and as having 50 guns. It was a 4th rate ship of the line, and obviously in bad shape in 1746. A new *Chatham*, with 50 guns, was commissioned in 1758 at Portsmouth.

20. Sailors who specialised in rigging the main masts.

21. Near the southwest tip of Haiti, the favourite gathering place for Henry Morgan's buccaneers. Most of the Caribbean islands were Spanish, with few French, Dutch and English possessions.

22. There was an actual Captain William James who dropped dead at his daughter's wedding in 1783, and who had been Commander of the East India Company fleet. Thomas Davers served under Admiral Vernon, became commander-in-chief at Jamaica in 1745, and died there in September 1747. He was captain of the 70-gun *Suffolk* in the Caribbean from 1739-1742, and was at Cartagena with Vernon. He rose to Vice-Admiral, and his death is around a year after Penrose's recollection in the *Journal*. Guns were fired once a minute at the funerals of great people, hence '*minute guns*.'

23. Blewfields was on the southwest tip of Jamaica, and must not be confused with Bluefields in Nicaragua, where the Rama Indians are situated. Bluefields in Jamaica is in Westmoreland parish, and is the third place settled in Jamaica, by the Spanish in 1719-1720, who called it *Oristano*. It was later known as *Oristan*, but renamed Bluefields by 1661, after the British took the island. It was a thriving port in Williams' time, sending sugar, cattle hides, pimento, limejuice and indigo dyewood to England.

24. *Morro* was the term generally used by the Spanish for the forts, which guarded their Caribbean/South American harbours. Williams writes *Moro*, and the passage is confusing as to whether the '*Moro Castle*' is a ship or fort, and if there is a ship ahead, as well as El Fuerte which attacks Penrose's ship from the rear. *Stern chasers* (Williams writes *chases*) are cannon protecting the rear of a ship. There was an Irish goldsmith and painter of miniatures, *John Ramage*, who was an established contemporary of William Williams in New York. Williams variously spells the name as Rammage and Ramage.

25. *El Fuerto* could be the *Fuerte* (*Nuestra Senora de Guadeloupe*), a 60-gun Spanish ship of the line built in 1728 and sold in 1739, which therefore could have been operating as a privateer, especially with an Irish captain. A 64-gun *Conquistador* was originally built in Gloucester, named the *Gloucester*, captured by the French and sold to the Genoese and then the Spanish, being sunk in 1738. It was replaced by the 62-gun *Conquistador*, supposedly deliberately sunk by the Spanish in 1741 during Admiral Vernon's unsuccessful attack on Cartagena, to prevent it falling into English hands. As an unseaworthy hulk, it may well have become a prison ship for Williams/Penrose. (See Chapter 5, footnote 88) The 60-gun *Dragon* (*Santa Rosa de Lima*) was also scuttled by the Spanish during Vernon's attack, according to a letter written to his wife. Vernon actually glossed over what was in actuality an ignominious defeat. The English fleet had landed an army at Playa Grande near Cartagena on 7th March, 1741. The intention was to take Cartagena, cross the Panama Isthmus and take Panama City in conjunction with Anson's Pacific fleet. However, the two-month assault failed

and the fleet returned to Jamaica. Another 60-gun *Dragon* was built in 1742 and wrecked in 1783. The third *Conquistador* was of 64 guns, built in 1745 and captured by the British in 1748. It is therefore possible that Williams/Penrose was actually on one of these ships, the *Fuerte*, *Conquistador* or *Dragon*, as a captive in 1747.

26. 'Horse beans' were fed to slaves on the *'Middle Passage'* from Africa to the Americas. Very large beans, they were used as animal fodder in Europe, and to make them semi-edible for humans, they were pulped then covered with *'slabber sauce'*, made from palm oil, flour, water and red pepper. *Jerked beef* was long strips of beef, slowly dried in the sun and wind.

27. The Spanish still controlled Florida and Texas at this time. However, its possessions traded illegally with smuggled goods from 'interlopers', ships of different nations, which meant that the Spanish used a *costa garda* (coastguard), composed of privateers trying to stop the trade. It seems that ships from the infant English colonies of north-east America were trading also, each time bringing back a few former privateers and naval prisoners from Spanish captitivty.

28. *Oakum* is strands of old hemp rope or manila fibres, soaked in tar, and stuffed in between hull planks to stop leaks. Unpicking old rope into strands was a slow, tedious job, which hurt the thumbs, and fingers, so *'picking oakum'* was a mild punishment in these times. In the Royal Navy, every prisoner had to unpick a pound of oakum every day.

29. To *'cop'* is to receive a punishment, as in to *'cop a good clout'* from someone. *'Puss'* is slang for mouth or face, but it seems here to mean a light hit. A *'barrel stave'* is a narrow plank from the side of a barrel.

30. In July 1746, Ferdinand VI succeeded as King of Spain. Penrose hears the news in 1747.

31. Admiral Vernon had been a scourge of the Spanish, with his attacks on Portobello in 1739 and Cartagena in 1740-41.

32. This *'ship's nurse'* sounds like a special small sail, suitable for slow and careful movement. The sloop seems to have been intended to make an English-for-Spanish prisoner exchange in Jamaica under the flag of truce.

33. The *'weather crutch'* is a problem to define. The *weather* side of a boat, is the direction from which the wind or elements, the weather, is approaching. A *crutch* in nautical terms is a knee, or knee timber, or a forked stanchion or post. The term seems to be unrecorded. *New Providence* is in the Bahamas, now Nassau, and formerly a pirate haven.

34. *Rose Island* is being developed with luxury homes. It lies at the eastern entrance of Nassau Harbour, about 5 miles from Nassau. *Hog Island* is in a small channel near Nassau.

35. *John Tinker* was Governor of the Bahamas from 1740 until he died in 1758, so again Williams has chosen a historical figure to match the chronology in the book, which related to him in 1747.

36. The *'wooden horse'* was a form of punishment and torture, used in the military for dereliction of duty and drunkenness. Two planks about 8 feet long were nailed together at a sharp angle to make an uncomfortable *'horse's back'*. Four pieces of wood were nailed to make the horses legs, and the horse was placed on a stand, on truckles, so it could move. A *'head and tail'* were added. The miscreant was forced to sit on the horse's back, his hands tied behind him and sometimes weighted to make the pain worse. Weights, often 8-pound muskets, were attached to each of his legs, to *'stop the horse kicking him off'*.

37. The *Recovery* was a naval vessel of this time, but there was also a Bristol privateer of this name, first noted in 1758. A *'James Strike'* married Fanny Matthews Oliver in 1802 at Sithney in Cornwall.

38. *'Prize money'* was shared among the crew and consisted of the value of the captured ship (or prize) and its booty (cargo). The ship was often auctioned off.

39. The *east end* of the channel between Hog Island and Nassau.

40. *Andross* is an island noted for its sponges, in the Bahamas east of Miami, Florida. The North and South Bimini Islands almost touch, and are only 50 miles east of Florida.

41. The *'weather'* side of the ship is that which the weather is blowing in from. Being *'under the weather'* has come to mean feeling ill, and anyone under the weather bow will be receiving all the foul weather. The term *'going large'* means that a ship has the wind crossing the direction of its course, in such a way that the sail feels the full force, and the vessel thereby gains the highest speed.

42. The term *'two glasses'* means about an hour. The sandglass of a sailing ship took half an hour to run out, and when it was turned over, the ship's bell was struck. Without the sandglass, it would be impossible to assign the watch on board ship. Later, there were hourglasses, which were turned every

hour. Two of the *shrouds* had been '*shot away*' and were flapping. Shrouds are the set of ropes which stretch from the masthead to the sides of the ship, supporting the mast. The *stoppers* referred to are hitch knots turned on the bitter ends of these ropes to stop them passing through a block or grommet, and thereby securing the mast against various strains.

43. A *round robbin* is also spelt robin, and is a letter or missive signed equally by all, so that no one person can be chosen as responsible.

44. '*Quito* (or Quita) *Sueno*' shoals are in the San Andreas Archipelago, about 150 miles off Nicaragua, between 14 and 14.30 degrees north. Quito Sueno Bank is an elongated carbonate bank structure, and its eastern reef is 37 kilometres long. This forms a dangerous barrier-like formation, partly dry at low tide, upon which the sea swell breaks. In 1981 the US Senate ratified a treaty, which Nicaragua still disputes, giving Colombia these uninhabited islands of Quito Sueno Bank, Roncador Cay and Serrano Bank.

45. *Quondam* means former. *Santa Catalina* is 70km southwest of the Quito Sueno rocks, and was called Old Providence by the early English buccaneers in the Caribbean, twice being taken taken by Admiral Sir Henry Morgan, but a Spanish possession.

46. If there is no time for a full careening, a vessel can be partially careened ('*boot-topped*'), where the upper part of the ship's hull is cleaned of barnacles and weeds, and coated with resins, tallow, sulphur, lime and tar to deter teredos worm, barnacles and weed, as the ship is pulled over onto its side. For a full careening, the ship had to be beached, and dragged over onto its side, by attaching pulleys to the masts, and then turned over so that the other side could be '*paid with pitch*'. Docks as we know today did not exist, but some ports had piers to moor alongside. 'Dry' Docks for repairing a ship out of the water, were invented in the 19th century. A ship comes in on the full tide, and the water is allowed out as the tide recedes, and the sea lock gate closed to prevent water entering on the next full tide.

47. A valid *commission* for privateering gave semi-legitimacy to the cruise, to attack the shipping of an enemy country. Piracy had no such legal claim – pirates would attack anyone, and in turn be attacked by any nation.

48. A league is 3 nautical miles, a nautical mile being about 2000 yards compared to a land mile of 1760 yards.

49. This *tortoise* is a type of turtle, and will be referred to as such throughout the book. Williams refers more specifically to '*land tortoises*' later on.

50. *Grainge* is Williams' spelling of a fish spear or harpoon, possibly formerly called a '*grains*', with two or more '*grains*' used as prongs (tines) to catch a fish. Also known as a *fishgig*.

Notes to Book 1 Chapter 2

1. A *kellick*, as Williams writes, is a killick, a type of small stone anchor, usually in a wooden frame, which allowed a rope to be attached. Killick is used throughout the text. '*Petticoat trousers*' were a kind of kilt used by sailors, made out of blanket or oilskin, which enabled them to climb the rigging more quickly than normal trousers.

2. A *painter* is a rope or line attached to the bow of a boat, to tie up when mooring, docking or being towed.

3. A *belaying* (pin) is the wooden pin on a boat to which ropes can be fastened. Penrose '*spent the day in the doleful dumps*' as he had lost his *painter*, or tow rope. We say today that we are 'in the dumps' when depressed.

4. A *calabash* is an evergreen tree with produces calabash gourds, the dried shells of which were used as water containers, i.e. bottles. The string was attached so that a person could carry many of these lightweight gourds to a source of water.

5. The *creek* was an inlet, not the outlet of a stream.

6. *Maroon Islands* could be anywhere, but in this context are the islands where Penrose was unintentionally marooned. The *maroons* were escaped African slaves who lived in the mountains of Jamaica, with whom the English planters made a treaty in 1738.

7. *Galldings* – it is difficult to recognise this bird – a type of gull? The word '*noddle*' used just previously, means brains or head.

8. Williams/Penrose accidentally omitted the *grainge*, or fish-spear from this list, so it has been added.

9. A *linn* is a common word for a waterfall or cascade in the North of England and Scotland, and there is even a Linn Waterfall in Lanark, to make doubly sure one understands the word.

10. Williams writes this as *Penama* shells. Panama Shells are a class of shells found in the Caribbean and off the South-American coast.

11. *Grunts* are reef fish found all over the world, including the Red Sea and the Indian Ocean, but the species here referred to is one of the four types inhabiting the Nicaragua coast. Grunts shoal in the day to escape predators, so are relatively easy to catch. The most likely grunt caught by Penrose is also known as the *pigfish, pig perch* and *piggy, orthopristis chrysopea*. Apart from French Grunts there are also White Grunts and Tomtate Brown Grunts in the area.

12. If mistaken for a Spaniard, Penrose's life span could have indeed been shortened – these were times of mass genocide of the Indian tribes by the Spanish. However, the Spanish seemed to have no strong presence on this eastern seaboard of Nicaragua.

13. *Popanack* wood may be in German *papayabaum, carico papaya* or *paw-paw*. In French it is the *papayer d'Hawai*, and in Spanish variously known as *papaya, lechosa, fruta bomba* and *melon capote*. The papaya fruit occurs in Nicaragua on the top of the tall and fragile *Carica Papaya* tree. However, Penrose would have possibly mentioned the fruits of the tree. The Nicaraguan rainforest is renowned for hardwoods such as Mahogany, Royal Cedar and Pochote (Kapok), so *popanack* may be a local name for a hardwood tree.

14. A *palm* is a type of large metal and leather thimble, fitting into the palm of the hand, used by sail-makers to mend canvas sails.

15. A *yard* is a horizontal mast.

16. A *'cobbler's knife'* has a 60 degree point, obviously a similar angle to the shark fin.

17. *Punck* seemed to be some sort of fungus. 'Pwnc' is Welsh for a question or riddle, so perhaps Williams did not know what to call it. However, it seems that it is *kapok*, common in the region of the rainforest floor. The Kapok grows to 150 feet tall, and was the sacred tree of Mayan culture. Kapok is the lightweight, silky down used for insulation and stuffing. If dry, the floss is very flammable and an excellent source of tinder, still used today. N.B. wood in the rainforest is often damp, so Penrose would need a plentiful supply of dry Kapok to establish a fire. The Kapok (*the silk-cotton tree, ceiba pentandrada*) is known as the *kapokier* in French and the *pochote* or *bongo* in Spanish. The rainy season on Nicaragua's eastern seaboard last virtually all the year, with heavier rainfall and tropical storms from June to October.

18. The *'woodslave'* is a nocturnal lizard found across the Caribbean and Central America, *'thecadactylus rapicauda'*, but it seems that Williams is describing the *woodslave* known in Jamaica, the gecko *hemidactylus mabouia*. There is a *tropical banded gecko* found in Nicaragua. Geckos seem to have arrived in the Americas on African slave ships and some species such as the *warty gecko* can change colour.

19. It was a problem to identify this *'Fish Hawk'*. The Fish Eagle or Osprey is native to the area. However, the Osprey is not in the eagle family, and it does not have a yellow beak. There are 59 species of true eagle, of which 11 are fish eagles or sea eagles, and none are found in South or Central America. The rainforest's Harpy Eagle is too large. However, the Bald Eagle is a fish eagle, found as far south as Florida at present. Its Latin name, *haliaetus leucocephalus* means *'fish eagle with white head'* and it is found on a Nicaraguan postage stamp. From Williams' description it appears that his yellow-billed fish hawk could only have been a Bald Eagle, and that they were more widely distributed in former times. However, he also mentions later in the text that *'the bald eagles, fish eagles & co. were in greater numbers etc.,'* so he knew what Bald Eagles looked like. There is thus a mystery about the true identity of Mr Yellowbill, although an adventure holiday website ('aventura') affirms that the Rama call the fish eagle *'kwan kwis kwis'*. The *'snuff-box'* shells mentioned just previously in the text are probably those of the Hawksbill Turtle, *'pliis'* in the Rama language. The turtles that nest on many Nicaragua beaches are the *green turtles*, which Williams used to capture for food, and for which the Rama name is *'uuli'*. There is also a *Hicatee* turtle, *'paaruk'* in Rama. The endangered green turtle uses large open beaches for nesting, and the highly endangered hawksbill turtle favours smaller coves. Both are edible, and in the 17th century were the most common form of meat in Caribbean ports. They were kept on pirate ships by flipping them over onto their backs, covering them, and keeping them doused with water, until the cook required them.

20. *Myrmidon* – a hired thug, or henchman (from a band of Achilles' followers in the Trojan Wars.)
21. The Welsh words for this are, not knowing the 18th century dialect, '*Er mwyn dy les di, Meistr Bigfelen*'. This is the 'familiar' Welsh spoken to dear friends, loved ones and pets. '*Er mwyn eich lles chi, Meistr Bigfelen*' would be the formal version.
22. Williams writes '*tacklin*', instead of tackling - the word is used in the sense of instruments of action, e.g. fishing tackling (the origin of *fishing tackle*, i.e. the bits and pieces that one needs, to go fishing).
23. The *Old Man* bird or *rainbird* is in danger of extinction, and the subject of local legend in the San Andreas Archipelago off Nicaragua, also known as the *bearded bellbird* with a white throat and chest, but this bird does not match Penrose's description. In Jamaica, the *chestnut-bellied cuckoo, hyetornis pluvialis*, is known variously as the *old man bird*, the *rainbird*, the *may bird* and the *hunter*, but again does not match the description. There is a '*bearded screech owl*' in Nicaragua, but again this does not seem to be the bird referred to. Could it be a type of bearded heron, bittern or egret?
24. The *Manchineel* tree grows throughout the Caribbean near beaches and has small green apple-like fruits. The sap, fruits and leaves cause severe blistering, and the Carib Indians used to tip their hunting arrows with the poison. Even accidentally bumping into the bark can get sap on a person, which can cause severe blisters. In French it is known as the *arbre-poison (poison-tree)*, and is the species *hippomane mancinella*. This is derived from the Spanish *manzanilla*, little apple. The only creature which can survive eating these '*death apples*' is the *land crab*, and Penrose describes them carrying off the fruits. Previously Penrose mentions the lime, which is native to the area, *citrus auranifolia*.
25. Of the characters inscribed on the stone pillar, Wm. R could be conjectured as William Roberts, one of the principals behind the Royal Africa Company in 1672-73. *Bat S.*[8] could have been the privateer Bartholomew Sharp (c.1650-1690) but the dates do not fit. The letters and marks seem so specific that perhaps Williams has invented a code here to be broken. Slavery of English captives in the Central and South American gold and silver mines is mentioned in the author's '*The Book of Welsh Pirates and Buccaneers*' and '*The Pirate Handbook.*' However, as well as gold and silver, there was local trade in jaguar and ocelot skins, hawksbill turtle shells for jewellery, cacao, sarsaparilla and precious woods like royal cedar and mahogany. (The Spaniard fugitive probably had the surname of Gutierrez, common in Spain and Mexico, and not Williams' spelling of *Guiterez*.)
26. *Plantain* is even now the staple vegetable of Creole Indian cooking. *Corrittoo* is obviously a tree/shrub from which one can make lines of twine, and may be a species of *aloe* – it is not clear from Penrose's narrative. Perhaps it is one of the dominant plant species in the Rama territory, the *Croton Punctatus*. However, it could be also a *liana* species. Thin liana vines are so malleable that one can make sailors' knots in them, to secure logs and branches for rafts or shelters. *Corrittoo* may be *Pita Fibre*. The pita is a relative of the pineapple, harvested in Mexico and Colombia for its long spiky leaves. Juice is scraped from the leaves, fibre pulled out, cleaned and then rolled out into fine thread, used to embroider belts, boots and saddles. A kilogramme can cost $100. It is either the bromeliad *Magdalanae* or the agave *Americana*.
27. *Chigua* – in Richard Hughes' wonderful 'A High Wind in Jamaica' (1929), we read: '*Lame-foot Sam told most stories. He used to sit all day on the stone barbecues where the pimento was dried, digging maggots out of his toes. This seemed at first very horrid to the children, but he seemed quite contented: and when the jiggers got under their own skins, and laid their little bags of eggs there, it was not absolutely unpleasant.*' In Mexico they are called variously '*chiggers*' and '*nigra*'.
28. The urine is temporarily a crimson colour after eating *prickly pear*, which increases the secretion and excretion of urine. It is named the *nopal cactus*, because it was known as *nopalli* by the Aztec Indians. An excess of beetroot has the same, temporarily worrying effect.
29. Fiddler Crabs are very common in Nicaragua, and in the original text someone has added here, in a different script, '*a kind of land crab called by the sailors and West Indian fishermen fiddlers*'. Thus the rustling and scuttling at night during showers is possibly fiddler crabs.
30. All these fish are native to the shores of Nicaragua, most found around the coral reefs. *Marget fish* is *Margate fish*, i.e. *the red mouth grunt, diabasis aurolimentus*. The *porgie, porgy* or *scup* is in the family *sparidae*. The *doctorfish* is a type of grouper and the *schoolmaster* a species of snapper. The *porkfish, anisotremus virginicus* is a type of grunt, and the *squirrelfish* could be the *longjaw* or *Caribbean* variety. It is not known at present what the *Gillambour* fish is, but there is a *Gillambore* Creek in the Turks and Caicos Islands. The *jewfish* is a nearshore grouper, now totally protected in Florida waters. The

old wife is *enoplusus armatus*, and the *hogfish* is probably the *Spanish hogfish, bodianus rufus*.

31. The *Man of War* is the *Frigate Bird*.
32. The sapodilla is spelt *sappodiloo* by Williams, and is known as the *chicle* or *chico*, a type of plum. It is also known as the *Marmalade Tree* and *sapota*. *Mammees* are known as mammee apples, or apricots. Coco plums are spelt *cocoplumbs* by Williams, and are the same family as the *Sea Grape*. *Cassia Fistula* is also known as *Indian Laburnum* and *Golden Shower*, and its fruit used as a laxative. *Sea grapes(coccoloba uvifera)* are vine-like shrubs growing near beaches, and are still very common. The *colliloo* is possibly the palm that dominates Nicaragua's river swamps, the *Raphia Taedigera*, locally known as *yolillo* or *silico*. However, the root vegetable *dasheen* has an edible leaf called *callalloo* (*callalou* in French), and is the species *colocasia esculenta*. The well-known garden flower amaranth is a leaf vegetable known as *callaloo* in Jamaica and *calaloo* in Trinidad, and its leaves (like spinach) are used in cooking a traditional dish also named callaloo. The dasheen bush is also called callaloo in some localities and used in that meal. Another claimant is *coralillo (antigino leptotus)* also known as coral vine or coralina. There was a *coralillo (arctostaphylos uva-ursi)*, which was used as a tobacco substitute by Indians and early settlers in North QAmerica. Edible fruits naturally occurring in Nicaragua are Sapodilla, Banana, Mango, Jocote, Pineapple, Papaya, Orange, Lemon, Tamarind, Breadfruit, Passion Fruit, Pitaya (Dragon Fruit), Mamoncillo, Melon, Avocado, Mammee Apple, Coconut and Sapote.
33. At least 3 species of ground dove are found in nearby Surinam.
34. Either a Brocket Deer or a White-Tailed Deer, both native to the Nicaraguan rain forest. In the Rama language they are '*suula sula*' and '*suula pluma*', and in Creole known as the red deer and white deer.
35. Penroe's information upon whales is intriguing and **original**, as researchers have only recently discovered that humpback whales use an area off the Nicaragua coast in the winter season. They migrate from the north Atlantic to the locality for display and breeding. The preceding term *bushel* refers to a unit of measurement. A bushel is 4 pecks and a peck is 2 gallons, so *half a bushel* is 4 gallons, and refers to the capacity of the basket that Penrose made. The fish mentioned is almost definitely a *sawfish*. The population in Lake Nicaragua has recently suffered a catastrophic decline. Related to sharks, there are probably 7 species of this *Pristidae* family, but no one can ascertain whether there are 4 to 10 remaining species. There are also *swordfish* in the Caribbean, *xiphias gladius*, known as *pez espada* or *emperador* in Spanish.
36. Nothing more confirms the proof of Williams being marooned in Nicaragua more than his description of the flora and fauna. The object of his fear here was the *Howler Monkey*, a native of the rainforest. The Rama word for this monkey is '*uling-uling*'.
37. Now Nassau in the Bahamas.
38. There were regular pardons granted to pirates by the British Crown, to try to stop outbreaks, but the '*Golden Age of Piracy*' had ended in 1722 with the death of '*the last and most lethal pyrate*', Black Bart Roberts. Queen Anne lived from 1702-1713, so the relevant Act of Grace dated from this time.
39. There was a *William Bass* born in Bertie, North Carolina, in 1709, whom Williams might have known, otherwise the origin of the use of this name is unknown. In Caribbean voodoo lore, vampires can only be killed with a silver bullet. Penrose's nocturnal creature can only be killed with a silver bullet, and Williams may have known about such legends from his own time in Jamaica. In 1804, Dessalines became the first ruler of an independent Haiti and believed that he could only be killed by a silver bullet. His officers bayoneted him to death. His successor, King Henri-Cristophe, killed himself with a silver bullet in 1820.
40. The '*wet season*' is an apt description. The climate here is '*humid-tropical*', in southeastern Nicaragua, with an average temperature of 27 degrees Centigrade. It has one of the highest annual rainfalls in the world – up to 6000mm in the wettest inland region. There are year-round rains, with a short drier period from February or March through to April or May. The heaviest rains occur from June to August, with daily torrential downpours.
41. The '*tigre*' is referred to later along with '*wood-cats*'. The Jaguar (*Panthera Onca*), Puma (*Puma Concolor*) and Ocelot (*Leopardus Pardalis*) can still be found in the jungles of southeast Nicaragua, but are now regionally extinct across most of Central America. The jaguar and puma still play central roles in the traditional mythology and shamanic practice of the Rama Indians (as does the *manatee*). The Jaguar is known in Spanish as the '*tigre*' and in Creole as a '*tiger*' and in Rama as '*auma*'. The puma is known as the *leon* in Latin America, and the *cougar* in North America. The

ocelot is 'tigrillo' in Spanish, 'tigercat' in Creole and 'krubu tataara' in Rama. The *jagiarundi* or otter cat (*herpailurus yagouarandi*) is known as the *tigrillo congo* or *negro*, and as the *gato colorado* in Spanish.

42. *Trumpery* signifies objects of no value, worthless items.

43. The canoe was a dugout (*canoa*), hollowed out of a tree trunk, whereas the '*canoe*' of Penrose/Williams was a ship's longboat or tender, probably clinker-built and much larger. Some Rama *canoas* (canoes) are still dugouts. The *matt sail* is probably made of plaited rushes, similar to those noted on war canoes, in Syms Covington's *Journal* of his voyage on Darwin's *Beagle* through the South Seas. There is a mention of Pedro Munez – '*21 de enero de 1620, alegacion de los pintores sobre la aprobacion y confirmacion de las orderanzas de doradores i interrogatorio de Pedro Munoz*', but Pedro Munoz is a far more common name in the Cadiz area.

44. The much-prized *Royal Cedar* (*cedrela odorata*, *cedro*) is probably the cedar which Penrose refers to. After some research, it was discovered that the epiphytic '*fig tree*' is also known in different regions as the *curtain fig tree*, the *Chinese banyan*, the *Malayan banyan* and the *Indian laurel*. It is *ficus microcarpia*, a member of the mulberry family, which slowly strangles and replaces its host tree. Birds and bats in the rainforest disperse its small fruit. In Spanish, it is known as the *matapalo* and *jaguey*. The '*Strangler Fig*' sends down roots to form a living cage around its host, which eventually dies and decays, leaving a hollow surrounded by a latticework of roots reaching up to the rainforest canopy.

45. The top of the rainforest canopy in southeastern Nicaragua is 150 feet to 180 feet above the ground. The Climbing Liana provides the canopy, and in the Amazon reaches up to 250 feet above the ground, or the height of a 21-storey building.

46. The *Yoho* seems actually to be the *Yaohoa* noted above, the Howler Monkey, known as the *hurleur* in French and the *mono alluador* in Spanish. In the Rama language it is known as *uling-uling*, *ulak* or *yahu*, 'monkey monster,' so Penrose seems to be actually using the Rama language on this occasion. However, if we examine the text, we read: *One evening, as Harry and I were walking on the shore I chanced to hear the Yoho's cry. Upon this, I bade him to listen and asked him what he knew concerning it, expecting some odd account or other. But to my no small confusion he laughed as he said, 'That Birry.' 'What is Birry?' said I. 'Bird' said he. 'Go all nights, bite bird little.'* Then, clapping his hand to his mouth, he made exactly the same noise. *That was enough for me. I at once concluded it to be an owl or some such nocturnal bird, and called myself an owl or an ass for implicitly swallowing down such idle tales recited by credulous fools.* In Rama legend, the *yoho* is a dangerous creature resembling a gorilla, who lives in a cave in the mountains (Serrania de Yolaina) from which the Wiring Cay Creek runs. Intriguingly there are also small pale men named '*perry men*' (*Birry*?) who live far up the creeks. They are strong enough to overturn boulders when looking for crabs, their favourite food. Could the *yoho* and *birry* be Harry's understanding of mythological creatures who call in the night? The Rama also have their version of the sasquatch or yeti, the *ulak*.

47. Williams writes this as '*hollowing*'.

48. '*Soldier crab*' is the nickname given to both fiddler crabs and hermit crabs, but from the description '*always singular*' these must be hermit crabs.
A '*peck*' is a measure of 16 pints, or 0.3 cubic feet.

49. The '*ten-pounder*' is a silver herring-like fish, '*elops saurus*', found off the Nicaraguan coast.
The '*Helmet*' fish is a type of conch (*cassidae*).

50. The *chicken turtle* is so named, because of its very long neck, like a chicken's. It is a fresh-water turtle found in the Caribbean and south-west of the USA.

51. The Rama have been persecuted for centuries, sold into slavery by the larger Miskito Indian tribe.

52. These '*crooked sticks*' must have been muskets, and '*crooked*' may have signified the 'lightning' flash from them, which accompanies a clap of thunder. More mundanely, it may be that the large gunstocks made the musket appear crooked.

Additional Footnote to Book 1 Chapter II

The '*Long Key*', where Penrose landed originally, is mentioned later in Part II as being Pigeon Island, Isla de Paloma, a traditional sheltering place for Rama fishermen, and just off Green Point, where Penrose seems to have spent his days. The following coastal information adds to the veracity of Williams having spent some time here:

From Black Bluff, on the northeast extremity of a promontory, the low swampy coast extends 10 miles north, to a ridge of low red cliffs which ends a mile further north at Green Point. A small ridge of low red cliffs is also about a mile south of Green Point. The coast continues 12 miles north from Green Point to El Bluff, on the east side of the main entrance to the Laguna (or Bahia) de Bluefields. A shallow southern entrance lies about 4 miles north of Green Point and leads into Bluefields Lagoon, from which Isla La Venada extends 8 miles to the north entrance. (Rama Cay is in the south of the lagoon). The sea usually breaks heavily on the bar at the south entrance. Breaking reefs lie 3 miles south-east and 2.5 miles east of Green Point.

Cayo de la Paloma (*Pigeon, or Bird Island*) reef-fringed and 33m high, with a saddle-shaped summit, lies 1.5 miles east-north-east of Green Point and is the largest cay in this vicinity. White Rock, 15m high and prominent, is located 0.5 miles north-north-west of Cayo de la Paloma. Trees cover this rock. It seems that Penrose is describing Bird Island as his first landing place, with a small beach and a reef of rocks at the end of the bay. Here he met Indians and made a well in the sand on a point, and described the island as being over two miles long and half a mile across. From here he could see the mainland, at an estimated 5 miles away. He paddled for three quarters an hour in depths of only one to three fathoms to get to a 'small cay' with birds and king conches, which could be White Rock. From there it was another hour of paddling to reach the mainland. Here there were bluffs but he found a creek leading to a lagoon with branches. The cavern he discovered there was 15 feet deep by 10 feet high by 18 feet wide.

From the middle of June through August, the north-east wind is steady and very fresh raising a heavy sea and swell. The strong southerly current causes vessels at anchor to swing across the wind and roll and pitch uncomfortably. Rain is heavy and frequent, coming up in fresh squalls, which follow closely upon one another. From the first of September through October, the weather becomes variable with intervals of calms and frequent offshore winds. During this period heavy thunderstorms from the west-south-west are frequent. From October, the wind begins to blow from the north-east again accompanied by rainsqualls and in early November it becomes stronger from the north with a considerable sea. At this time, the Northers may be expected, which generally attain the greatest violence from morth-west to north. The current usually sets south off the entrance to Bluefields Lagoon at a velocity of 1.5 to 2 knots, but at times it may reverse itself at reduced strength for a day at a time for no apparent reason.

Notes to Book I Chapter III

1. Probably the *Giant Centipede*, a black creature with a needle-sharp bite, capable of eating a *Tarantula Spider*. It grows up to 10 inches long, and the bite causes severe pain, heart palpitations, vomiting and oedema.
2. *Yaluta* is now a widespread female name. Its origin is US Native Indian, meaning '*women talking.*'
3. Of the 16 species of snakes in Nicaragua, 6 are extremely poisonous. The *fer-de-lance* (*Bothops atrox*) is known as *barba amarilla* in Spanish. It is extremely dangerous, and hides in the leaf litter on the forest floor, and around logs, so collecting fuel for a fire can be a hazardous undertaking. The Boa Constrictor and Anaconda inhabit the mangrove swamps, along with Caiman and Crocodiles. (There are 23 species of crocodile across the world.)
4. Also known as the bottle gourd, the edible *calabash*, when mature, can be dried to form a hard wooden shell, used as a drinking vessel.
5. A hundredweight is 112 pounds, so it weighed 28 pounds, or 2 stone.
6. Along the coast, just inland from the beaches, are a series of large and smaller lagoons lined with mangroves, and these '*mangrove swamps*' support fish (especially safe nurseries for the young of larger fish), shellfish, reptiles and birds. They also provide a haven for the endangered *manatee*, which is still being hunted locally and across all its habitats. Nicaragua's Atlantic swamps feature red, white, black and button mangrove, as well as *pelliceria rhizophorae*. There are also many palm swamps in the area. Intriguingly the Spanish word for mangrove is *mangle*. The *whistling duck* referred to by Penrose is either the *black-bellied* or *fulvous* species, both native to Nicaragua.
7. George Needham was a planter on Henrietta Island, from which the Providence Island Company bought his tobacco in 1631. In 1632, planters intending to go to Providence (off Nicaragua) from England were allowed to pay for the passage with the proceeds of their labour. George Needham asked to go on the next ship with six (indentured) servants, giving them a free crossing to his tobacco plantation. They travelled on the *Charity*. The person named in Penrose's Journal could well have been this George Needham, or his son George. A letter dated December 7th 1687 from Lieutenant-

Governor Molesworth of Jamaica records: *'One George Needham, who was sent with my commission after pirates, heard at Providence of some who had burnt their ship and raised a fort of eight guns on a neighbouring island for their security. He accordingly sailed thither, beat them out of it, and brought off the men with their goods, and three or four Portuguese negroes, who were the only witnesses that could be produced against them. It appeared from their account that they had taken a Portuguese ship off Brazil, and on this evidence the men were condemned.'* The Minutes of the Council of Jamaica, April 30, 1688, noted that Captains Spragge and Needham had plundered houses on New Providence, and the captains stated that they had *'pirate instructions'* from Colonel Molesworth to effect this action. Molesworth was a great friend of Captain Henry Morgan, the greatest buccaneer of all time, and also issued him with privateering *'letters of marque'* to attack the Spanish. There was a Captain Needham present when New Amsterdam (New York) was taken from the Dutch in 1664. In 1696 a Captain Fletcher was in charge of the frigate *Hampshire* which escorted 13 merchantmen from Jamaica to Philadelphia. In 1722, a Captain Fletcher and the *Porcupine* were captured by Black Bart Roberts. Importantly, pertaining to this, and other writing found by Penrose in the Towers Field, writing has recently been found on basalt pillars near this area, in the Rio Indio Maiz reservation.

8. These could have been *vampire bats*, which live in vast swarms in Nicaragua's seaside caves. Also half a million *Winklewort Bats* live in individual rainforest cave colonies and emerge at dusk. As Penrose does not note their harming his animals, they are more likely not to have been vampire bats.

9. The plantain and banana are the most common staples of the Rama diet, even today. Other foods cultivated are the root crops *dasheen*, *cassava* and *quequisque/coco*. Some rice, beans and corn are grown, but not much in the southeast. Cultivated fruits include the pineapple, lime, orange and breadfruit. Coconuts and palm seeds (*supa*) are used, and some other crops are sugar cane, cashew, chilli pepper and *achiote*. The yam (*discorea*), or sweet potato, or *ayote*, prized by Penrose, seems to be missing from the modern listings of Rama diet, but it is still grown and eaten in Nicaragua.

10. A *mess* means a quantity of food for a table, or the provision of food, from which the ship's mess gets its name. A *mess of pottage* is a prepared dish of soft food, pottage being a thick soup of vegetables and often meat.

11. The *'great canoe'* is obviously a European ship from over the great water, stuck on the reef. Of the three names, *Komaloot*, *Futatee* and *Niuxa*, allowing for variations in spellings, the only one I found extant today is *Niuxa* in Brazil.

12. *Uncurried* leather is leather that has not been prepared for manufacture by its manipulation, and the dressing and application of tannins, oils and greases. These make the leather more flexible, stronger and water-resistant.

13. A *pet* is an aggravation, annoyance or distress – a bad mood.

14. Using a *grainge*, or fish spear instead of hooks.

15. Tigers and wood cats are jaguars (or pumas), and ocelots.

16. The peccary and the *wari* (spelt by Penrose/Willams as *piccaries* and *warees*) are still hunted by the Rama Indians. The collared peccary is *pecari* in Creole and *muksa* in Rama. *Wari* is the Creole name for a white-lipped peccary, and in Rama it is known as the *ngulkang*. Both are species of pigs. One wonders why Williams/Penrose uses these creole terms in the text, plus the Creole of *'tiger'* for jaguar/puma and *'tigercat'* for ocelot. Wild game is an important part of the diet of the Rama, and a Rama elder from Bluefields Lagoon said in 2000 that *'There in the wild hogs part, you will find all over the place, around the edge, the wild boar – them wari. Bounty. You neither have to go far, You go in the morning and you smell them. When the breeze came from the back, you smell them. You just land and you go shoot. Strike them with bow and arrow. People never used no weapons like gun.'* Some Rama share rifles, but much hunting is still carried out with the bow and arrow, or lances/spears. Arrows and lances are made from the *pejibaye* palm. Lance heads and arrow heads used to be made from sharks' teeth, but now are manufactured from pounded and filed metal. The *wari*, or *white-lipped peccary*, is the most important of the game animals. They occur in droves (herds) of up to 50 animals, and are hunted by groups of men, armed with lances, in the palm forests. The other important wild game are the *collared peccary* and tapir (*ngarbing* in Rama). Sea turtles and manatees are hunted from a dory, with one man paddling slowly and another man standing in the bow with a harpoon. See the list at the end of these Chapter 3 notes, for the animals that are still hunted by the Rama.

17. *'Kettles'* are metal cooking pots, usually with lids, for stewing or boiling.

18. Williams writes *sambraros*. Fish *'gigs'* are a type of three pronged or four pronged fishing trident, made

of metal with barbs on the tines. Mounted on the end of a long pole, they are used by a fisherman standing in the prow of the boat to spear flatfish and bottom feeders. In the 17th century *'Memoirs of a Buccaneer'* by Robert Williams, he mentions the neighbouring Mosquito Indians practising *'throwing the lance, fisgig (sic), harpoon or any manner of dart, being bred to it from their infancy, and never going abroad without one of these weapons in their hand.'* He goes on to describe using the *'fisgig or harpoon'* to kill a young manatee for meat. He also noted that the *Mosquito* (Miskito) went out for fish in single canoes, as more than one would scare the fish, and that they did not like white men to watch them spearing fish.

19. Of course this is the original meaning of *'expedition,'* meaning moving speedily, as when we *'expedite'* something today.

20. *Carthagena*/Cartagena is on the mainland, now in northern Columbia, the main Spanish treasure port on the Caribbean, which Henry Morgan wanted to sack. (See the author's *'The Book of Welsh Pirates and Buccaneers.'*)

21. The place seems to be near San Juan del Norte, but without visiting the area, it is difficult to place it exactly. The Rama used to have far more extended territories, abutting the Miskito Indians at 11 degrees 30 minutes of latitude.

22. Williams spells *'curtsey'* as *'courtesy'*, which was probably the original correct spelling.

23. Williams spells this *'thout'* – a *'thwart'* is a crossbeam spreading from one gunwhale of a boat to the other, used as a seat in a rowing boat.

24. Williams' word is *'lant,'* probably meaning lanky or tall.

25. Williams writes *'sprit.'* The bowsprit is a projecting boom or spar projecting over the bow of a boat to carry a sail forward.

26. These wormholes are those of the *teredos* worm, which is a soft-shelled mollusc and the commonest and worst enemy of ships' hulls in the Caribbean.

27. The wet hull would be subject to *rendering* asunder, or cracking in the high heat and direct sunlight, so was covered by twigs and bunches of leaves to protect it.

28. The *Nicaragua Bull Shark* is extremely common in Lake Nicaragua and along Nicaragua's coasts, and is known variously across the world as the *Zambesi Shark, Van Rooyan's Shark, Swan River Whaler, Square Nosed Shark, Estuary Whaler, Freshwater Whaler, Slipway Grey Shark, Shovel Nose Shark, Ganges River Shark* and the *Cub Shark*. It is the only shark to invade fresh water, and the males grow to 7 feet and 200 pounds, while the females grow to 11.5 feet and 500 pounds. It is the 3rd most aggressive shark in the world, after the *Tiger Shark* and the *Great White Shark*. Experts believe that it was the Bull Shark, not the Great White, responsible for the attacks off New Jersey in 1916, which was the basis for the film *'Jaws'*. Names across the Caribbean for the most common sharks are: *Blue Shark – Requin Bleu (Fr.) – Tiburon Azul (Sp.) – prionace glauca; Bull Shark – Requine Bouledogue or Taureau (Fr.) – Tiburon Sarda or Toro (Sp.) – carcharhinus leucas; Hammerhead Shark – Requin-Marteau (Fr.) – Tiburon Martillo (Sp.) – sphyrna sp.; Mako Shark – Requin Mako (Fr.) – Marrajo (Sp.) – isurus spp.; Whale Shark – Requine-Baline (Fr.) – Tiburon-Ballena (Sp.) – rhiniodon typus;* and *Great White Shark – Grand Requine Blanc (Fr.) – Gran Blanco (Sp.) – carcharodon carcharias*.

29. Williams writes *'paid her bottom,'* which means that Penrose spread preservatives over the hull.

30. *Flambau* is the word in the original text, and a flambeau was a flaming torch which could be used for night processions. Quammino refers to *torchwood*, and the Rama used to fish at night using torches made from the bark of the *silico* palm, mentioned in the text as being plentiful in Rama territory. Thus the torches made by the Indians in Penrose's family seem to be made from the dominant palm of the area, *silico/yolillo (raphia taedigera)*, or from 'candlewood' (West Indian sandalwood).

31. The *snook* is a common fish in Nicaraguan waters, still fished today.

32. This *tiger cat* must be a puma or cougar (*puma concolor*), which feeds principally on deer. It co-exists in the same territory as the jaguar (*panthera onca*), as its food needs are different. The jaguar, with its larger head and stronger jaw can crack armoured reptiles open, and feeds principally on armadillo, caiman, crocodile, turtle, tortoise and snakes. The ocelot, (*leopardus pardalis*), eats agouti, paca, rodents, lizards, small armadillo and birds (incidentally it takes 13 endangered ocelot to make one fur coat).

33. Crayfish are a principal commercial catch today in Nicaragua, along with shrimp.

34. *'Freestone'* is a fine-grained stone like sandstone which can be cut in any direction without breaking, so perhaps a sandy colour is meant here.

35. The *'Doctor Fly'* is like a fast horse fly, with a light green and brown body with yellow wings, which anaesthetises its victims, its sting taking a few seconds to take effect, and which produces a large swollen, painful welt which lasts for hours.

36. A 'scrip' is a small bag or wallet fixed to a girdle. However, in this case, it seems to mean a piece of cloth, as in Robert Williams's description of Mosquitos (Miskitos) in his *'Memoirs of a Buccaneer'* – *'tall, well-made, raw-boned, stern-visaged, hard-favoured, or a dark copper complexion, with lank black hair, each girt about with a small piece of linen tied round the waist and hanging down to the knees.'* The loin-cloth used by the Rama was made of bark cloth (*tunu*) or from bromeliad fibres.

37. *'Burthen'* is a variant of burden, meaning the load or weight that can be carried, and usually applied to ships.

38. Possible confirmation of bald eagles in Nicaragua.

39. This *'fine scene'* reminds one, as later paragraphs in the book, that Williams, as an artist, constantly evaluated the artistic merit of what he was seeing.

40. Williams constantly spells *together* as *'togather'*, which obviously was the original meaning of this word, as things or people gathered.

41. Perhaps the *'cara'* part of this word is borrowed from the Spanish for *'loveable'* or *'dear'*. However, he spells the name Carre-wouma, shortly after in the text.

42. *'Hands'* is a reference to his seafaring days – personnel being ship's hands.

43. The first verse of this popular 1740 air, or march, is: *'Welcome, welcome brother debtor/ To this poor but happy place/ Where no bailiff, dun or gaoler/ Dares to show his dreadful face.'* It was a popular song in early American secular music, of English origin, and part of *'The Prisoner's Opera.'* It is featured on a recent CD entitled *'Marches and Favourite Airs of the American Revolution.'* However, with William Williams' sojourn in Jamaica, he may have come to know of its true author. Francis Williams (c.1720-1770) was the son of John and Dorothy Williams, a free black couple in Jamaica. This in itself was a remarkable event, as free blacks were extremely rare. The Duke of Montague wished to experiment whether a black child, trained at grammar school and at university, could become the equal in literary attainment of white men, and Francis was sent to England to be schooled. In the 1730's Williams returned to Jamaica after spending time in Canbridge University, and set up a school on Spanish Town where he taught reading, writing, Latin and mathematics. It appears that Francis Willams was the author of *'Welcome, welcome brother debtor.'*

44. *'Old fathers'* are ancestors.

45. A *bass rope* is also known as a *bast-rope*, from the Danish *basstorve*, made from basswood, i.e. the inner fibre of the *Lime Tree*, or anything similar.

46. A *peck* is 2 gallons of (liquid or dry) weight. Lima beans are known as *Frijol Lima* in Latin America.

47. These *'rotten oranges'* were for their seeds.

48. Williams writes *retaliation*, not *recompense*. There were sporadic wars with neighbouring tribes, with the Rama captives being sold off into slavery.

49. This wonderful passage is a most remarkable and brave comment upon the genocide carried out in the name of Christianity by the anti-Pelagian authorities of its church. Williams's stance upon the *'savages'*, being his co-equals, his *'family'*, must be understood in the context that slavery was considered normal in these days. George Washington and Thomas Jefferson were among the more prominent slave-owners in these times. Throughout Penrose calls Harry his *'brother'*, for instance.

50. Williams writes *calipash*, meaning the greenish, glutinous part of the turtle found next to the head, but obviously meant *carapace*, the upper shell.

51. 300 pounds or 3 hundredweight (336 pounds). These were probably *green turtle*, as they already had 8 *chicken turtle* in the crawl.

52. *Gravelled* in this sense means perplexed.

53. *Owen* is a Welsh name, the Anglicisation of Owain. Owain Glyndŵr was one of Wales' greatest heroes, who fought the English for 15 years (see *Glyn Dŵr's War*, by G.J. Brough). Penrose's chosen name, Lewellin, is an Anglicisation of LLywelyn, and LLywelyn Fawr (Llywelyn the Great) was probably the greatest of Wales' most notable princes.

54. This humming bird may be a type of *thorntail* or *streamertail* – there are many species in the Nicaragan jungle.

55. The green parrot is still found in the jungle, as is the green macaw. It was possibly the *Great Green (Boffins) Macaw*, now endangered by constant logging of its habitat. They are down to double figures

in Costa Rica, because of the logging of the huge *Almendro* tree, in which it nests. Parrots are still being caught and exported from Nicaragua for the pet trade, among them being the *Red-Lored Amazon, Mealy Amazon, White-Fronted Amazon* and *Yellow-Naped Amazon.*

56. *Goat's pepper* is used to make cayenne and known also as *Scotch Bonnet* in the Bahamas and Jamaica. It may be *capsicum chinense*, sometimes also called the *habanero* pepper. *Bird pepper* is *capsicum frutescens*, used for making Tabasco.

57. *Trapan* seemed to be an old Welsh word for trap, but is defined in the *Dictionary of Thieving Slang* of 1737 as *'he that draws in or wheedles a Cull, and Bites him. Trapan's: sharpn'd, ensnar'd.'* In Webster's 1913 *Dictionary*, It is a snare or stratagem, meaning as a verb to entrap or catch by stratagem. John Bunyan wrote in 1701 *A Book for Boys and Girls*, of which part of verse XXIX reads: *'This rose doth also bow its head to me,/ Saying, Come, pluck me, I thy rose will be;/ Yet offer I to gather rose or bud,/ Ten to one but the bush will have my blood./ Tis looks like a trapan, or a decoy,/ To offer, and yet snap, who would enjoy:'*

58. *Costiveness* means constipation. The *cassia fistula* is renowned today for its laxative use use in bowel disorders, and has other herbal uses. It is also known as the *golden shower tree* and the *Indian laburnum*, and is native to Nicaragua.

59. This *green heart wood* is the hardest wood in the world, with *purple heart wood* found in Guyana, and used in the Manchester Ship Canal. The SS *Great Britain* was the first iron-built ocean ship, but in 1882 was converted to a three-masted sailing ship, and its hull sheathed in green heart wood.

60. The torrential rains are always stripping the soil in Nicaragua, which makes fertile farming difficult.

61. Settling the solids at the bottom of the containers, so clear water could be drawn from the top.

62. The *thornback ray* is a common British flatfish of coastal waters. The stingray is probably the *Southern Stingray*, and the *Giant Whipray* is remembered in the names of Whipray Cay in Belize and Whipray Basin in Florida. The *rasp ray* is as yet unidentified. The skin of shark, dogfish and especially stingray was used by cabinet-makers and artisans in the 18th and 19th centuries as a nodule-laden leather, *shagreen*, a veneer or to embellish small wooden items such as jewellery boxes, tea caddies, candlesticks etc. The Rama Indians traditionally tipped their arrows with pieces of a stingray's backbone.

63. These *sea eggs* are sea urchins, with their painful needles.

64. By *fire works*, Williams means the means by which to make fire. On this trip, in the original text, Toby was accidentally placed on the voyage with Harry, but does not appear in the narrative until the next day.

65. The previous mention of a peccary having its *'navel'* on its back is true. Whether collared or white-lipped, it is sometimes known as the *musk-hog*, because of the strong scent which exudes from a navel-like gland on its back. Peccaries grow to about 70 pounds in weight. The buying of pardons was the classic moneymaking mechanism of the Catholic Church for centuries, allowing all types of sins from murder to rape to be forgiven.

66. Written as *Pickpack* in the text. To 'pick a pack' to carry on one's back must have thus been the origin of '*piggy-back*.'

67. *Daddle* is a synonym for totter, as when infants first walk.

68. A *schooner* is an easily handled, fast, two-masted ship, with all the lower sails rigged fore and aft, popular in the Caribbean, and capable of 11 knots. A *sloop* is a single-masted ship with a very long bowsprit, extremely fast, with a shallow draught.

69. Sometimes the tail grows back wrongly after is has been removed, leaving a large stump and a tail, for example in the case of the Galapagos Lava Lizard. There is also supposed to be a rare two-tailed lizard, which survives on the islet of Filfa off Malta.

70. Williams writes *receipt*, not recipe.

71. *Yabba* seems to be a large pot.

72. *Cader Idris* is one of Wales' highest mountains at almost 3000 feet. In Gwynedd, it is a solitary place of legends, associated with Arthur and said to be haunted. Penmaenmawr means head of great stone, and is spelt *Penmanmour* by Williams. It is in Gwynedd, North Wales, next to the sea and the largest mountain plateau in Great Britain, south of Scotland. The Derbyshire Peak district has waterfalls and caves of the mineral *Blue John* mined by the Romans.

73. The *'Pudeling With'*, or *'Wythe,'* is some sort of liana. A *'with'* is a long, flexible, tender twig used as a band.

74. The *Prickly Pear* Cactus grows in Nicaragua, and its leaves are called *'nopales'* when used in Latino cooking. It will be of the variety *opuntia ficus-indica* or *opuntia tuna-blanca*, and is known as the *higuera chumba* (plant) and *higo chumbo* (fruit) in Spanish.

75. *Hogo* is a strong smell or stench.

76. Penrose put out to sea to approach the whale from the *'weather'* side, i.e. upwind of it, so that the stench would be less.

77. *Cavallos* are horsefish. *'The Commentaries of Governor Alvar Nunez Cabeca de Vaca on his Adventures in the Unknown Interior of America'* notes *'the bay we set out from we gave the name Vaya de Cavallos (Bay of Horses).'* *Horsefish* are any of the silvery fish with flat sides also known as *moonfish, horsehead* or *dollarfish.* Williams spells barracuda throughout the text as *barrowcooters.*

78. *Younckers*, as written by Williams, seems to mean youngsters. In Captain John Smith's *'Seaman's Grammar and Dictionary'* of 1691, however, *'younkers are the young men called Fore-mast-men, to take in the top sails, or Top and Yard, for furling the Sails, or Slinging the Yards, Bousing or Trising, and take their turns at the helm.'* Thus we are talking about the younger and fitter members of the crew. Later in the Journal, it seems that the *youncker* was a young apprentice sailor. A derivant may be the old-fashioned term, common when the author was a child, of *'yukkers'* for fledgling birds in south Wales. Earlier, Williams refers to tradesmen using whalebone – it was used to stiffen bodices in the 16th century and corsets from the 18th century. Williams is correct as whalebone in their gills helps certain whales to strain their food.

79. A *brigantine* is a twin-masted, square-rigged ship, favoured as a general workhorse and for its manoeuvrability. It could hold up to 100 crew and many cannon.

80. *Chimes* – barrels have long wooden chimes to make them easier to handle. They are the ends of staves that project past the top and bottom of the barrel.

81. Williams writes *companion*, not companion-way. *Caboose* is a name for the deckhouse, when used as a galley or kitchen

82. *Burthen* is a variant of burden, the load that a ship could carry.

83. Spelt by Williams as *aguadienta*, and more properly spelt as *aguardiente*. This is Spanish for 'fiery water', a spirit distilled from cane sugar in the Caribbean.

84. *Parbuckleing* is hoisting with a rope loop, in this context. A *bole* is a tree trunk.

85. There are 72 kinds or *rockfish* along the American coastline. The *Jewfish* is now called the *Goliath Grouper* and is a monster of a fish, the largest being recorded at 7 feet 6 inches long and 750 pounds. It is forbidden to fish for them until their stocks build up again.

86. Williams writes this as *'reved'* – it means threaded.

87. The *racoon's tail* hanging from each of Owagamy's ears was that of the *olingo* (probably *bassaricyon gabbii*), a relative of the racoon which lives in the Nicaraguan rainforest. It is a pale brown in colour, with 11-13 dark brown rings on its tail.

88. The *hard green stone* usd for arrowheads could well be *jade*, which is found in Nicaragua and has been used for arrowheads in other societies.

89. These monkeys could be *capuchin, white-faced, spider* or *howler* amongst others.

90. *Indian Corn* is maize. Penrose states that Yova-wan and Noona-waiah have visited before. However, the only Indian who has not been named on previous visits was one on Komaloot's first visit in Penrose's fifth year in the rainforest, and this must have been Noona-waiah as Yova-wan has been mentioned previously.

91. *Pay* here means to clean the canoes of attached sealife and possibly to add pitch to them.

Animals still hunted by the Rama Indians:

English	Spanish	Creole	Rama	Latin
Agouti	Guatuza	Kiaki	Suli	Dasyrocta Punctata
Armadillo	Armadillo	Jacket Man	Kirki	Dasypus sp.
Brocket Deer	Venado Colorado	Red Deer	Suula Sala	Mazama Americana
Brush Rabbit	Conejo	Rabbit	Tukustukus	Sylvilagus Brazilensis
Collared Peccary	Sahino	Pecari	Muksa	Tayassu Tajacu
Crocodile	Crocodrilo	Crocodile	Tuluura	Crocodylus
Currasow	Pavo Real	Carraso	-	Crax sp.
Green Turtle	Tortuga Verde	Turtel	Uuli	Chelnia Mydas

Hawksbill Turtle	Carey	Aksbil	Pliis	Eretmochelys Imbricata
Hicatee Turtle	Bocatora?	Hicatee	Paaruk	Pseudemys sp.
Iguana	Iguana	Guana	Isali or Saliuk	Iguana sp.
Jaguar	Tigre	Tiger	Auma	Panthera Onca
Manatee	Manati	Mananti	Palpa	Trichechus Manatus
Ocelot	Tigrillo	Tigercat	Krubu Tataara	Leopardus Pardalis
Paca	Guardatinaja	Givenot	Puk Sala	Agouti Paca
Spider Monkey	Mico	Red Monkey	Blera	Ateles Geoffroyi
Tapir	Danto/Danta	Mountain Cow	Ngarbing	Tapirus Bairdii
White-lipped Peccary	Chancho de Monte, saino, jabali	Wari	Ngulkang	Tayassu Pecari
White-tailed Deer	Venado cola blanco or coliblanco	White Deer	Suula Pluma	Odocoileus Virginiana

Notes to Book I Chapter IV

1. As mentioned, *bass rope* comes from the Danish *basstorve*, or *bast-rope*, and is made from *bast*, or *bass wood*, the inner fibre of the lime tree, or from a similar fibre. The girl *Vinaquota* is spelt *Vina-qusta* (*favourite*) by Penrose/Williams in the previous visit.

2. *Jumping the broom* is a traditional custom to ward off evil spirits, practised in many parts of the world, including the original North American colonies. However, in this wedding context we are considering an ancient Welsh tradition of the *besom wedding*, a special 'wedding' where a birch besom (broom) was placed aslant in the doorway of a house. The head lay on the step, and the handle on the doorpost. The young man jumped over, and then the bride in the presence of witnesses. If either touched the broom, the marriage would not be recognised. The children of such a union were considered legitimate, and one could divorce by also leaping over the broomstick. The woman kept her own home, and did not become the 'property' of her husband, as in England and other countries. It was called in Welsh 'cyd-fidio', a partnership. The broomstick wedding was known as 'proedas coes ysgub' or 'proedas coes ysgubell' in Welsh. It is called a broomstick because Welsh brushes were made from the broom shrub, as well as thin birch branches.

3. Morgan is a common Welsh Christian name and surname, and comes from the words *mor* (sea) and the mutation of *can*, which is *gan*. *Can* is the abbreviation of the Welsh *cantref*, an old division of land roughly equivalent to the English 'hundred', enough to sustain a hundred families. Thus Morgan is an area of coastal land, made into a name for someone born there. The Welsh county of Glamorgan (which contains the Welsh capital Cardiff) has its roots in *Gwlad Morgan*, the country of Morgan, and legend tells us that Morgan was Arthur's son. The great religious thinker Pelagius had a former name of Morgan, signifying that he was a Briton, possibly from a coastal area. Legend states that he was trained at Bangor-is-Coed, near Chester, the great Welsh monastery sacked by the pagan Saxons in 616.

4. *Mam* is another Welsh word, for mother. *Tad* is Welsh for father, and the mutation to '*dad*' gives us the modern word in the English language.

5. *Ambergris* is a waxy substance found floating at sea, or washed up on beaches, secreted by the Sperm Whale, and of great value in perfume manufacture. Williams writes *ambergrease*, the original spelling signifying its colour and function.

6. 'Ah, poor Man!'... 'Godart Somer, on the ship, speaks English.' There are many people with the surname Somer in the Zeeland area of Holland.

7. *Vrouwen* in the Dutch language means men. However, '*frauen*' in German means women, and '*vrowen*', a semi-archaic word, means womenfolk. It is difficult to find any record of the *Dertroost* – perhaps it was named after Corneli(u)s van der Troost, born in 1656.

8. The *Harrington* was an East Indiaman of 490 tons that made 4 voyages for the East India Company between 1727 and 1736 according to one source, and 1732-1741 according to Sutton. (A brig named the *Harrington* captured the *Estramina* in 1805 off New South Wales.) Dickason states that its last service as an East Indiaman was in 1744, which seems too late. (see footnote 15 to Chapter 1)

9. It was unsure whether Williams means that the ship is 'sewed' into the rocks, or whether the word is 'sough' which means to be discomforted, or in pain. However, Smith's 1691 *Seaman's Grammar* tells us 'When the water is gone and the ship lies dry, we say she is sewed; if her head but lie dry, she is sewed a head but if she cannot all lie dry, she cannot sew there.' *Bilged* means that the ship had taken water into her bilge, and is leaking.

10. 'To a *killick*' means he dropped the stone anchor.

11. A *tinder horn* is an animal horn with a sealed stopper, used to keep tinder dry. Tinder needs to be kindled to start a fire. A *powder horn* kept gunpowder dry.

12. *Jacob van Tulden* – this is a common surname today in Holland and Belgium.

13. The *bo'sun* was in charge of the rigging, sails, cables and anchors, making sure they all work efficiently. He was also usually in charge of stores, and replacement of provisions. In charge of all the work on deck, he translated the captain's orders into operations by the crew. Interestingly, the lower ranks on board, boatswain, coxswain and seaman are all derived from the people's language, Anglo-Saxon. The names of the officers, admiral, captain and lieutenant are all derived from the language of the court in medieval times, French. Incidentally, so many West Countrymen went to sea that they influenced our pronunciation of words like boatswain, which became 'bo'sun'. Similarly, coxswain is pronounced 'cox'n', bowline is pronounced 'bo'lin'; gunwale is pronounced 'gunnel'; leeward is 'loo-wud'; forward is 'forrud', forecastle is 'focs'l', foresail is 'fors'l' and main sail is 'mains'l'. The Spanish equivalent of the boatswain was the '*contramaestre*', superior in rank to all sailors except the '*piloto*'. The *piloto* was the equivalent of the British ship's master.

14. This could have been a 'tabby' cat, needed to keep down the rats endemic on all boats.

15. Too drunk to obey orders.

16. To *chide* is to scold.

17. The *quadrant* (or *cross staff*) was a simple instrument for navigation, basically a quarter circle with a 0 to 90-degree scale, two sights and a plumb line. It was in use from the middle of the 15th century to measure the altitude of heavenly bodies. It was succeeded by the Davis Quadrant, then by Hadley's Quadrant, and finally by Campbell's sextant. John Davis the explorer (1550-1605), designed a new quadrant in 1594 which enabled sailors to find latitude. It was also known as a '*backstaff*' and was a method of finding the angle of the sun above the horizon, without having to sight directly on the sun. It vastly improved navigation and was used for 200 years. John Hadley (1682-1744) invented an improvement in 1731, which was known as an *octant*. This used two mirrors, which allowed for measurements up to 90 degrees, although the device was only 45 degrees (one eighth of a circle). This evolved into the *sextant* around 1757, invented by Captain John Campbell RN. The sextant could measure angles of up to 120 degrees, and with observations of the stars, sun, moon and planets gave the navigator an accurate reading of latitude. Longitude was only enabled by the development of accurate time-keeping devices at sea. The first such device was invented by John Harrison in the 18th century, but they were not commonly available until the 19th century.

18. By '*unhung*', Penrose means that the compass has come off its point, and is easily mended. Barrels were packed with highly salted beef or pork, which became less and less edible as a voyage progressed, especially in the heat of the tropics. Food was served highly spiced to disguise the appearance, smell and taste of it.

19. An *anchor* of brandy was the measurement of transport in the 17th and 18th centuries, and was 25 gallons. Colonists in Virginia and Maryland complained in 1660 about the 5 shillings duty on an anchor of brandy. Gin in these times was the cheap drink of the masses, causing the wonderful cartoons of Hogarth's 'Gin Street.'

20. Portobello, in Panama, is spelt as *Puertobela* by Williams.

21. This latitude is the boundary today between Costa Rica and Nicaragua, 11 degrees and 30 minutes north.

22. Ink powder is still used today to transport ink.

23. A rough translation of Somer's words are 'Well, then, that devil Brandt will say that Toby hid the gin. He said he should not have done it. Then this Hell's son will shoot him in one minute. Out then I runs and blows out his brains, and that is all.'

24. A Dutch court would have probably pronounced the killing as murder, rather than manslaughter, as a 'white man' was considered to be worth more than any 'native.' Somer is afraid that Dekker will inform on him if they return to Holland, so he preferred to remain with Penrose.

25. Merchant seamen provided for their families at home by received an '*advance note*' when they signed on a ship. Their wives and families could cash the note, once they had embarked on the voyage.
26. Williams writes '*protest*'.
27. To *caulk* something was to fill the seams between planks with hot pitch to seal them from leaks.
28. A *pistole* was a gold Spanish coin worth a quarter of a doubloon, so it was worth anywhere between $1 and $4 at the time.
29. Meaning to give a wide berth.
30. The Rama custom was that the widow immediately took a husband, for the deceased's spirit to enter and thus live on. Toby's soul thus moved to Penrose. Toby's spirit also went to Godart Somer, as he had been a '*good friend*' in avenging Toby's death. Whether the soul and spirit are separate or the same, to the Rama, is unknown. Luta's soul moved to Ocuma, as stated later.
31. *Fool-water* is a marvellous description of alcohol.
32. *Old fathers* are ancestors.
33. *Slime* from a *grouper* fish.
34. Ships' surgeons only had alcohol to use when operating upon men, even in amputating limbs.
35. '*Took*' means '*was accepted by*' Harry.
36. *Suckbottle* was naval slang at the time for a drunk.
37. Williams uses naval terms throughout the book, such as '*fore and aft*, and later Harry says '*ay, ay*'. *Fore and aft* in this context means vomiting and diarrhoea.
38. The *turkey buzzard* is common in the Southern USA and Nicaragua. '*Cathartes Aura*' has a naked, warty head.
39. Middleburg is the provincial capital of the municipality of Zeeland, in Holland.
40. Peter Cass could be Dutch and George (Georg, Jorg) Nielsen Danish.
41. Peace was made in 1748. The Treaty of Aix-la-Chapelle ended the War of Austrian Succession, also known as Queen Anne's War.
42. The beetle's provenance is unknown.
43. The cockchafer is known as the *June Bug* in the USA.
44. *Commonwealth* in the sense of '*the common good*' These *white ants* are a species of termite. A recent University of Florida investigation found 37 species in Nicaragua, of which 27 had never been previously recorded there, and 3 are apparently new species.
45. More information upon Falconer is given in Chapter I, footnote 15. William Falconer was the author of '*The Shipwreck, a Poem*,' and was born in Edinburgh about the year 1730 and died in 1769. When young, he became an apprentice on board a ship sailing out of Leith. He afterwards became a servant to Mr Campbell, the author of *Lexiphanes*, who was the purser of this ship, and gave him instruction. Falconer then became second mate in the *Britannia*, a vessel in the Levant trade, which, on her passage from Alexandria to Venice, was shipwrecked off Cape Colonna, on the coast of Greece. Only three of the crew were saved, and Falconer was one of them. This gave him the material for his poem '*The Shipwreck*' where we find the following canto:
Again she plunges! Hark! A second shock
Bilges the splitting vessel on the rock;
Down on the vale of death, with dismal cries,
The fated victims shuddering cast their eyes
In wild despair; while yet another stroke
With strong convulsion rends the solid oak:
Ah Heaven! Behold her crashing ribs divide!
She loosens, parts, and spreads in ruin o'er the tide.
In 1751, aged around 21, he was back in Edinburgh where he published his first known work, a poem, '*Sacred to the Memory of his Royal Highness, Frederick, Prince of Wales.*' Little is known of Falconer during this period of his life, so he could have met Williams/Penrose at sea. Noted above is the fact that he knew and served under Captain Hunter, as did William Williams. '*The Shipwreck*,' was published in 1762, being dedicated to Edward, Duke of York, brother of George III. By this dedication, the poet gained the notice and patronage of the Duke of York, who was also a seaman. Almost immediately after the poem was published, the Duke induced Falconer to leave the merchant service, and procured him the rank of a midshipman in Sir Edward Hawke's ship, the *Royal George*. In 1763, the war ending, Falconer's ship was paid off, before he had completed the period of service,

which could have entitled him to promotion. '*At the peace of 1763, the Royal George was paid off, when Falconer was introduced the gallant brother of his friend, Mr. William Hunter, then midshipman on board the Sutherland.*' He then exchanged the military for the civil department of the naval service, and became purser of the *Glory* frigate of 32 guns. '*The death of the gallant Duke of York at Monacoa, on the 17th of September, 1767, though felt by all the nation, was more precariously a sad loss to Falconer whose welfare, owing to the melancholy event, became again precarious. His literary fame, however, was now established; some few friends, among whom the Hunters took the lead, still remained; and he accordingly endeavoured to dry the tear, which the memory of the royal patron frequently called forth, by indulging in the vision of hope that was still prolonged; nor did Providence in this emergency forsake him. From the Glory, Falconer was appointed to the Swiftsure, at the close of the year*'. He had compiled a '*Universal Marine Dictionary,*' (printed in 1769) which soon became generally used in the navy. Also in 1769, the poet had moved to London, and resided for some time in the former buildings of Somerset House. He was next appointed to the pursership of the *Aurora* frigate, which was ordered to India. The *Aurora* sailed from England on the 30th of September 1769, and, after touching at the Cape, was lost without trace. In '*A Biographical Memoir of William Falconer*' accessed from *The Maritime History Virtual Archives*, ed. Lars Bruzelius, from which the above quotes are taken, the final sentence is '*He often assured Governor Hunter, that his education had been confined merely to reading English, writing, arithmetic, and a little Latin; but notwithstanding, he had by industry and perseverance acquired a tolerable knowledge of most of the modern languages.*' Williams/Penrose had sailed under Hunter, and the Williams family had been visited by Captain Hunter. The identity of 'Captain' or 'Commander' Hunter is a mystery. From the above *Memoir* of Falconer, we find the following references to the Hunter family and Falconer: "*The materials from which the greater part of the following Memoir has been drawn, were first presented to the public in the Royal and Imperial Octavo edition of The Shipwreck, 1804 edited by J.S. Clarke, F.R.S. Vicar of Preston; Chaplain of the Household to the Prince; and author of "The Progress of Maritime Discovery, &c."* "I had long sought in vain," says Mr. Clarke, "to procure any authentic materials, however scanty, for a Biographical Memoir of Falconer, when I fortunately met a shipmate of his, Governor Hunter, at the house of John McArthur, Esq. of York-Place, a literary and naval character of considerable eminence. With the natural cordiality of a seaman, the Governor communicated to me all the information he could remember, and this was also increased by frequent conversations which I enjoyed with that gallant veteran his brother, Lieutenant Hunter of Greenwich Hospital: but for these gentlemen, the little that has survived respecting Falconer, would have perished; and even this, owing to the years that have elapsed since the loss of the Aurora frigate, in which he perished, must necessarily be scanty." …Mr. William Falconer was born about the year 1730, and was the son of a poor but industrious barber at Edinburgh; who like Fielding's celebrated Partridge, possessed considerable talents and humour, and maintained a large family by his industry. It is remarkable that all his children, with the sole exception of William, were either deaf or dumb: Falconer himself mentioned this singular circumstance to Captain Hunter, when they were shipmates together; and, "I had afterwards," adds that officer, "an opportunity of being convinced of its truth; when, long after the commencement of my acquaintance with him, I met two of his family labouring under their infirmities in the Poor-house at Edinburgh, where they continued until their death." … Soon after being wrecked in the Ramillies, it appears Falconer left the Royal Navy, and again entered the merchant-service, as mate on board the Britannia, a ship employed in the Levant trade, in which he also was wrecked, near Cape Colonna; from this melancholy event our poet afterwards drew the outline and characters of one of the finest poems in our language, entitled, "The Shipwreck, in three Cantos by a Sailor," 4to. published by Millar, in 1762 … The Royal Duke, anxious to honour Falconer with some mark if his favour, recommended him to quit the merchant service again for the Royal Navy, where he might be able to serve him: accordingly, before the summer had elapsed, he was rated a midshipman on board Sir Edward Hawke's ship, the Royal George. In this ship Governor Hunter, then a midshipman, commenced an acquaintance with Falconer, which continued until his death: being both of them from the same part of Scotland, their friendship and intimacy soon increased. At the peace of 1763, the Royal George was paid off, when Falconer was introduced to the gallant brother of his friend, Mr. William Hunter, then midshipman on board the Sutherland. Previous to the peace, the Duke of York had embarked on board the Centurion, with Commodore Harrison, for the Mediterranean; on which occasion Falconer published an ode, entitled, 'On the Duke of York's Second Departure from England as Rear-Admiral'. As Falconer had not completed that time of service which is necessary to qualify a midshipman for a lieutenant's commission, his friends advised him to exchange the military, for the civil line in the Royal Navy; and, accordingly, in the* course of the said year 1763, he, through the interest of his patron, was appointed purser of the Glory frigate, 32 guns, afterwards called the Apollo... He soon after this married a young lady of the name of Hicks, daughter of the surgeon of Sheerness yard. Mrs. Falconer is said to have displayed keen abilities; and that it was the lustre of her mind, rather than of her person, which attracted and confirmed the affection of her husband.

Falconer's principal amusement seems always to have consisted in literary pursuits; and when the Glory was laid up in ordinary at Chatham, Commissioner Hanway, brother of the celebrated John Hanway, became delighted with the genius of her purser. The captain's cabin was ordered to be fitted up with a stove, and with every addition of comfort that could be procured; in order that Falconer might thus be enabled to enjoy his favourite propensity, without either molestation or expense. In his retirement he finished his celebrated 'Universal Dictionary of the Marine', 4to; a work that had engaged his utmost application for some years, and to which most of our modern Cyclopædias have been indebted. This alone would have immortalized his name had not his poetical reputation stood foremost. The undertaking was first suggested to him by George Lewis Scott, Esq. and its great utility was acknowledged by Sir Edward Hawke, and other professional men in the navy... The death of the gallant Duke of York at Monacoa, on the 17th of September, 1767, though felt by all the nation, was more particularly a severe loss to Falconer, whose welfare, owing to the melancholy event, became again precarious. His literary fame, however, was now established; some few friends, among whom the Hunters took the lead, still remained; and he accordingly endeavoured to dry the tear, which the memory of his royal patron frequently called forth, by indulging in the vision of hope that was still prolonged: nor did Providence in this emergency forsake him. From the Glory, Falconer was appointed to the Swiftsure,* at the close of that year... 'The Marine Dictionary' was not finally printed till the beginning of 1769; although it appears to have been compiled during his naval retreat at Chatham. Immediately after it was published, he was appointed purser to the Aurora, Captain Lee, when a third edition of The Shipwreck was loudly called for: considerable improvements and additions had been made to it by Falconer; but Mr. Clarke is induced to think, that amidst the agitation of his mind on being appointed purser to that frigate, which was then ordered to carry out to India Henry Vansittart, Esq. Luke Scrofton, Esq. and Colonel F. Forde, officers in the Honourable East India Company's services; that Falconer, who also had the promise of being their private secretary, from the joy of obtaining so lucrative a situation, neglected this edition, and left the last alterations to some friend, as the inferiority of many passages is strikingly evident. Mr. Clarke, however, has endeavoured, with the assistance of the first and second editions, to make the author correct himself, and has thus restored the purity of the original text, which had become strangely impaired. The joy which this appointment gave to the friends of Falconer may easily be imagined; but this, alas! was of short duration: the Aurora sailed from England on the 30th of September, 1769: after touching at the Cape of Good Hope, which she left on the 27th of December following, (she) was lost during the course of the voyage. Thus perished poor Falconer in the bosom of the waves, the occasional fury of which, and consequent disasters, he has so forcibly and elegantly described: thus leaving behind him a work to perpetuate his name, more durable, and far more honourable, than any monument which the artist's hand could erect: a work which affords ample proof of nautical ability, as well a poetical talents. In an interesting little work, entitled, "The Journal of Penrose, a Seaman"; written in 1755, and published by Murray, in 1815, is the following tribute to Falconer's early poetical abilities:— "How often," says he "have I wished to have the associate of my youth, Bill Falconer, with me, to explore these beauties, and to record them in his sweet poetry; but, alas! I parted with him in Old England, never, perhaps, to meet more in this world. His may be a happier lot. Led by a gentler star, he may pass through this busy scene with more ease and tranquillity than has been the portion of his humble friend Penrose." It appears Captain Lee, though a stranger to the navigation of the Mozambique Channel, would not be dissuaded from attempting it; which so much displeased Mr. Vansittart, that if an outward-bound East Indiaman had been at the Cape, it is said he would have quitted the Aurora. To this may be added, that, on the 19th of November, 1773, a Black was examined before the East India Directors, who affirmed, "that he was one of five persons who had been saved from the wreck of the Aurora; that the said frigate had cast away on a reef of rocks off Mocoa; and that he was two years upon an island after he had escaped; and was at length miraculously preserved by a country ship happening to touch at that island." Such are the principal events respecting Falconer, which the Editor has been able to collect. In his person he was about five feet seven inches in height; of a thin light make, with a dark weather-beaten complexion, and rather what is termed hard-featured, being considerably marked with the small-pox: his hair was of a brownish hue. In point of address, his manner was blunt, awkward, and forbidding; but he spoke with great fluency. Though Falconer possessed a warm and friendly disposition, he was fond of controversy, and inclined to satire. In his natural temper he was cheerful, and frequently used to amuse his messmates by composing acrostics on their favourites; in which he particularly excelled. As a professional man, he was a thorough seaman; and like most of that profession, was kind, generous and benevolent. He often assured Governor Hunter, that his education had been confined merely to reading English, writing, arithmetic, and a little Latin; but notwithstanding, he had by industry and perseverance acquired a tolerable knowledge of most of the modern languages.

* Governor Hunter was doubtful whether it was the Swiftsure, or the Warspight; but from MSS. which Mr. Clarke had seen, he prefers the former ship."

There was naval officer Captain John Hunter (1737-1821), born at Leith, the port of Edinburgh, seven years after William Falconer was born in Edinburgh, who may be one of the Hunter family known to Falconer and Williams. He fought for England in the American Revolutionary War of 1775-83, so would have possibly been in New York at this time. He served on the *Sirius*, fought the French, and became Governor of New South Wales, Rear Admiral and Vice Admiral. There was a Captain John Hunter recorded in the Journals of the Continental Congress in 1777 for raising a company for Washington's army, but this cannot be the same man. There was a Captain William Hunter in command when the *Royal Adelaide* was wrecked in Portland harbour in 1787, en route to Australia. Another candidate for Captain Hunter relates to "Hunter's Point" which in early New York was the place of the Hunter homestead, where Jacob Hunter passed the earlier days of his life, a leading New York citizen. He was the eldest and last surviving son of Captain George Hunter, an English gentleman, whose seafaring life brought him to the American colonies some years prior to the Revolution. Captain Hunter was the commander of a vessel sailing between America and England, 'but at the start of the war, being in port, his vessel was ordered out of the city, and harboured in the waters of Newtown Creek. Here he became acquainted with the daughter of Jacob Bennett, a wealthy landholder, who with his family had long owned and occupied as a residence the locality which was afterward so well known as Hunter's Point. After the death of Mr. Bennett the old farm by his will became again an inheritance in the female line, and was given to his daughter Mrs. Anne Hunter and her husband Captain George Hunter, who some time after their marriage had settled in New York city. After some family troubles, arising out of an unsuccessful contest of Mr. Bennett's will by the residue of his heirs, Captain Hunter and his wife returned to the old home, which they occupied for the rest of their lives. Mrs. Hunter died there, March 10th 1833, leaving a family of eight children, three of whom, her sons Jacob, John B., and Richard B., were by her will appointed executors of the estate. Captain Hunter died in October 1825. He was a man greatly admired, esteemed and beloved. He was a model of manly virtues, and when after his marriage he gave up his seafaring vocation, to become a shipping merchant in New York, no name stood higher than his among the mercantile interests and community. In the city and land of his adoption he had thus become a highly honoured citizen, and there is a true legend of his wedding day to the effect that upon that happy occasion the shipping merchants of New York celebrated the event by a universal hoisting of their bunting in the harbour and vicinity. New York City then only covered the lower part of Manhattan Island...' This editor has underlined the date for Penrose's Journal – 1755, which has seemingly been attributed by the Rev. J. S. Clarke, FRS, in 1804.

46. It is unsure what was used as a tobacco substitute, but dried corn (maize) silks have been used by Nicaragua's Nahua Indians for generations, and are still smoked in Central America. Most pipes were clay at this time, but Penrose might have used hardwood more easily.

47. *Mousing* is the nautical rope equivalent of welding metal – it involves turning a small rope to unite the point of a hook with its shank.

48. Williams uses '*sort*' repeatedly instead of the more modern 'matter'.

49. A *yawl* has two masts with fore and aft sails, but the after mast is rather small and very near the stern.

50. *Pay* in the sense of to apply.

51. Not a worm, but a soft-shelled mollusc, and the most common and dreaded attacker of ships' hulls in warm water. The *teredos* bivalves could enter planks through tiny holes, and lay a million eggs a year. The young molluscs bored parallel to the surface, honeycombing planks with no outward signs. Ships were double-planked, with a layer of felt and pitch between them, to try to keep the teredos worm out, as well as other molluscs which attached themselves to the hull and proceeded to devour it layer by layer. If possible, pirates tried to capture brigs and barquentines made from cedar-wood from the Bahamas, which was more resistant to the teredos worm. Not until sailing ships' hulls were copper-sheathed were the problems overcome. Copper-bottoming the Royal Navy before the other

major powers followed suit, led to English hegemony of the seas.

52. *Avast* is *'Be quiet'*, or *'Stop!'* Possibly from the Italian *'basta'*! (*enough!*), or from the Old Dutch words *'houd vast'* meaning to hold fast.

53. A *'slatch'* is a period of a transitory breeze, or an interval of fair weather, and also the slack part of a rope. The meaning here is possibly that Penrose sees a chance to take advantage of a pause in the conversation to make his point.

54. *'There is no bread, no flesh (meat), no other things.'*

55. Williams merely writes *'near her time'* with no other indication that she was pregnant.

56. *Tiger* here means a jaguar or puma.

57. *Gamut* means extent or range, usually referring to emotions.

58. *Quality* seems to mean 'friends' in this context.

59. A *doubloon* is a Spanish gold coin, worth at various times anything between $5 and $15, a pun on 'double' in this context.

60. *Mully grubs* must mean *mealy grubs*, a great source of irritation to sailors as they infested ship's biscuits. It was common practice for sailors to knock the biscuits on the side of a hard surface to dislodge any grubs, while muttering *'ship's biscuits'* as a mark of disapproval.

61. *Grog* is alcohol, usually Jamaica rum. We still say we are *'feeling groggy'* today if we are not very well – this refers to the frequency of pirate hangovers in the seventeenth and eighteenth centuries when pirates used to carouse between and during voyages *'on the account.'* In the Royal Navy, rum replaced brandy as the daily ration because of its cheap availability from newly conquered Jamaica. However, in 1740 Admiral Vernon ensured that the rum was diluted with water, because of drunkenness in the fleet. The daily pint of rum was replaced by adding two pints of water (a quart), and dispensed upon two occasions during the day instead of at one time. As the rum in those days could easily be 60% proof and above, it is no wonder that some crews were incapable of action if they drank a pint quickly. Drunken sailors were punished until the early twentieth century by having *'six water grog'*, their allowance being diluted with six parts water instead of three parts. Grog (in decreasing proportions) was served in the Royal Navy until 1970. Sadly, the last *'grog ration'* - one part rum to three parts water -issued twice a day to sailors in half-pint measures, was drunk on July 30th, 1970. Penrose later improvises when asked what the name *Job* means, saying that it means *patience*. In the Old Testament *Book of Job*, he as a God-fearing man who remains steadfast in his belief even when stripped of his goods, children and health. God rewards him for not succumbing to these tests of his faith. 'The patience of Job' became proverbial and is mentioned in the New Testament in James, 5:11.

62. This is strangely similar to the much later national flag of Nicaragua, which is three stripes, blue on either side of white.

63. *Land crabs* can be brown, red, purple and pink, and move in such masses that an army of them recently forced a road closure in Cuba.

64. To *'crack a bottle'* was the way buccaneers opened captured alcohol, usually with a cutlass, in their anxiety to have a drink.

65. English seamen with a complaint adopted this French practice. All signed their names in a petition, on a piece of paper in a circle. There was more safety in numbers if they wanted something changed, so not one seaman could be pinpointed as the *'ringleader'* of dissent and punished. William Williams was the first to write about the practice in his Journal, with reference to buried treasure. In France, names were signed on the ribbon (*rouban*), which went round (*rond*) the grievance document, hence *rond rouban* and thence *Round Robin*. It is unsure what *'Nimrod's Portion'* refers to in the context of the round robin. Nimrod, in the Old Testament was a mighty warrior, the son of Ham, who ruled Babel and Assyria.

Of the list of names, some have crosses marked against them, but it is difficult to know what this signifies – perhaps they would have a double share of the loot? Or perhaps they were illiterate and their names had been signed for them? Of the names, around 13 could be of Welsh origin. It is uncertain why Williams chose these names, so this author made a quick search to see if any could be a contemporary of Williams. A Richard Quin of the King's Own Regiment of Foot was asked to desert to the rebel army in March 1777 by Peter Brady, a fellow soldier. Brady was court-martialled in April 1777, and sentenced to 1000 lashes of the cat 'o nine tails' on his bare back – effectively a horrific death sentence, and Williams would possibly have known of it. *Cudjoe* is a Ghanaian slave name (like Quamina or Quammino), and an escaped slave named Cudjoe led the Maroons from 1690 in Jamaica in their fight against the English, so the name again would have been known by Williams. *Owen Flinn* bought three slaves in Suffolk, Virginia in 1777. *David Roberson* died in Tennessee in 1821. *Abraham Tobin* was on the tax list of Culpeper County, Virginia in 1822. Cardinal *Giuseppe Renato* was the papal ambassador to Spain, who died in 1737. It may be that a skilled genealogist could cross-reference the names in the list with Williams' known whereabouts over the years. Again, a cryptologist might discover a code in the names, using the crossed names or initials as a key. There seems to be a curious coincidence in *Will Book V* of Augusta County, Virginia, with wills dating mainly between 1772 and 1776. There are 51 signatories to the Round Robbin, and if we discount the two Negroes, *Sambo* and *Cudjoe*, we have 15 men with crosses after their name, and 34 without crosses. Watkins appears in both lists. Of the 15 'crossed men', 5 of their surnames appear in this list of wills (- *Adams*, *McCombe*, *Davis*, *Ruddle*, and *Watkins* [1]). There is also a Richardson, but not a *Richards*, which would have made 6. Of the 34 'uncrossed men', only 3 of their surnames are in the list of wills (*Peters*, *Murphy*, and *Watkins* [2]). Other names in the list are *Williams* and *Needham*, who also appear elsewhere in the Journal.

66. The first clear reference to *Davy Jones's locker* is in Tobias Smollet's *'The Adventures of Peregrine Pickle'* in 1751: *'I'll be damned if it was not Davy Jones himself. I know him by his saucer eyes, his three rows of teeth, and tail, and the blue smoke that came out of his nostrils. This same Davy Jones, according to the mythology of sailors, is the fiend that presides over all the evil spirits of the deep, and is often seen in various shapes, perching among the rigging on the eve of hurricanes, ship-wrecks, and other disasters to which sea-faring life is exposed, warning the devoted wretch of death and woe.'* Davy Jones was a spirit, or sea-devil who lived on the ocean floor. Sending someone to Davy Jones's locker meant despatching them to the ocean's depths. The *'locker'* was the bottom of the sea, the last resting place for sunken ships and bones. How this Welsh name is attached to a sea devil is unknown in dictionaries, but the author believes that it probably refers to a Welsh pirate in the Indian Ocean called David Jones. Serving under Captain William Cobb, then under Captain William Ayres, Jones was in charge of a lightly manned, recently taken prize ship, filled with loot, accompanying Ayres in the *'Roebuck'*. The East India Company ship *'Swan'* under Captain John Proud took Ayres' ship in 1636 off the Comoros Islands. Jones knew he could not escape with his heavily laden ship, so he scuttled it with all its incriminating evidence. *'Old Davy'* was also known as the devil from the 18th century. Another source tells us that David Jones ran a London tavern, with his own press gang which drugged his unwary patrons and stored them in the ale lockers at the back of the inn until they could be taken aboard some departing ship. Phrases from these times include the following: *'I'll see you in Davy Jones's'* (a threat to kill someone); *'He's in Davy's grip'* (he is scared, or close to death); and *'he has the Davys'* or *'he has the Joneseys'* (he is frightened). As regards *'Nimrod's portion'* the meaning is obscure. In *Genesis 10* Nimrod was the great-grandson of Noah and a Mesopotamian king. In later tradition he is the king who built the *Tower of Babel*.

67. The *farthing* was the lowest denomination coin, a quarter of a penny. 240 pennies made a pound. The author remembers saving farthings.

68. One *'awakes with a start'* even today.

69. Caiman or crocodiles were the 'devil creatures'. Penrose has mentioned alligators previously.

70. If this tower actually exists, it could be man-made. South and Central American Indians such and the Maya, Inca and Aztec did not use cement or mortar, and Mayan discoveries are still being made. On the Indio Maiz Reservation in southeast Nicaragua, 62 such towers have recently been found – they are naturally occurring basalt pillars up to 36 feet high. (Penrose's tower is around 40 feet.) However, they were originally thought to be the remnants of an unknown civilization. There is no doubt that such a tower existed for Williams. We must remember that Nicaragua has lost over half of its forests since the 1980's, and unrecorded landmarks across the land have been obliterated in this time. Inland from the coast, at a latitude of 12 degrees 15 minutes (Williams estimated his latitude as 11.30), at Kukra Hill, archaeologists discovered a previously unknown, pre-Mayan civilisation. There seems to be a centre for the production of ceremonial columns (as reported by the BBC's science correspondent Richard Black in May 2003) on the site at El Cascal de Flor de Pino. The town developed around 1700BC and lasted until c.700AD, and there are monuments, petroglyphs and pottery. The most remarkable feature is the area where many huge columns were carved out of rock, presumably for use as burial sites.

71. Williams writes *'launsman'*, meant as an insult, and in reality *'Landsman'* or *'Landlubber'*.

72. A *sheet* is a rope attached to the sail, but in this sense means sail. *Stepped the mast* – it usually takes at least two men to place a mast into its socket. Masts have to sometimes be *unstepped* in a yacht if passing under a bridge.

73. Bristol was the great port for the slave trade, also importing vast quantities of tobacco, sherry and chocolate. Slave ships not only stank, but also could carry disease, so the citizens of the prosperous port would not allow ships to dock until they were cleaned and *'made tidy'* in the way that the Bristol Channel tides are predictable and orderly. Before entering the harbour, the ships were inspected to ensure that they were *'ship shape and Bristol fashion'*. Even when the ship moored, its sailors were not allowed ashore until they had *'slewed'* the yards, swinging them inboard so as not to obstruct other ships or quayside traffic or buildings. Because of the extreme differences between high and low tide in the Bristol Channel (up to 40 feet at Cardiff and Avonmouth), ships entering Bristol had to be of an especially stout construction, as they were left *'high and dry'* at low tide. If not well constructed and properly laden, at low tide they could break their backs or their cargoes could shift and be damaged. The first docks were not constructed until 1804, and the Floating Harbour in the 1830's at The Gibb in Bristol.

74. Nicaragua's rainy season, the *'invierno'* is from around May 15 to November, with the greatest downpour in October. September and October are hurricane months on the Caribbean coast. On this coast, the dry season is virtually unnoticeable as there can still be downpours at any time. The dry season, *vierno*, begins in November. Temperatures range from 27-30C (81-90F) in the rainy season, and 30-35C (86-95F) in the dry season.

75. The fast growing grass must be a species of bamboo. Ernesto Cardenal, in his *'With Walker in Nicaragua'* noted *'the darkness full of fireflies and crickets.'* The *tree toad* is common in Nicaragua – this could be the *Pacific Tree Toad*. A *mark* is a target, and a *butt* is a target range.

76. *'Sail'* in this context means any ship or vessel.

77. An amusing play on words, with Penrose pretending that Somer has said *choking* instead of joking.

78. The *Old Roger* or *Jolly Roger* is the most famous pirate flag, the *'skull and crossbones'*, but most pirates amended this to their own personal banner. Black Bart Robert's main flag had him sharing a glass of wine with the skeleton of the devil, which was holding a burning spear. His personal pennant was a picture of him with a raised sword, standing on two skulls, marked ABH and AMH. These signified a Barbadan's head and a Martinican's head, as the governors of these colonies had both sent vessels to capture Roberts. However, he hung the Governor of Martinique from his yardarm. They were meant to strike fear into the enemy's heart, and when a merchant ship saw Roberts' flags being raised, they did not generally wish to fight *'the great pyrate.'* It may be that the Jolly Roger was named after Black Bart, who took over 400 ships in three years. He always sailed into battle clad in red satin from head to foot, so was known to the French as *'le joli rouge'* – the pretty man in red. This black flag was raised in battle, and if the prize did not strike its colours, the *red flag* would be flown, signifying *'no quarter'*. The first known use of the skull and crossbones was by the Breton pirate Emmanuel Wynne in 1700, where the skull and bones surmounted an hourglass.

79. *Purblind* means partly blind, and also can mean dim-witted.

80. *Calipiver* – the only reference found regarding this fish is in *'Tom Cringle's Cabin'* by Michael Scott (1789-1835) where he refers to *'potted calipiver'*, and for breakfast, *'cold calipiver – our Jamaican salmon'*.

81. *White Poke* – this could be the *Large White Crane*, which is found in the area. *The White Egret* is a Nicaraguan endangered species.

82. In other words, a chamber pot – another aspect of Williams' real sense of humour.

83. A *bason* is a large basin, and also was slang for a prostitute or loose woman. *Cans* are drinking containers, not today's tin cans.

84. *'Cob dollars'* consisted of the clumsy, shapeless Spanish coinage, also commonly called *'cob money'* or *'cobs'* and sometimes *'cross money'* from the figure of a cross, which always characterizes it. The meaning of the word cob is unknown. In Mexico, this currency was termed *'maquina de papalote y cruz'*, that is, *'windmill and cross money'*. The specimens do not appear to have been made by machinery, but seem like lumps of bullion flattened and impressed by the means of a hammer. The figures and inscriptions are extremely rough and imperfect, and sometimes entirely illegible. The largest of these coins were originally made for dollars, and when new were of the lawful standard.

Some of the specimens are what old writers frequently called pieces of eight. The legend which surrounds the exterior, but which is usually mutilated by clipping, was originally '*D-G-HISPANIARVM ET INDIARVM REX*', '*By the Grace of God King of Spain and the Indies*'. Some cob dollars have a date on each side, which generally omits the thousandth and hundredth parts, so that 78 and 82 on the coinage refers to 1678 and 1682.

85. Items aboard ship or for sea transport were often made to be stowed. For instance barrels, when their food contents were exhausted, were '*knocked down*' for better storage capacity on the ship.

86. Of *Isabel Rubiales*, d. 1605, no trace as yet can be found. Rubiales is a town on the Duero River in the Province of Valladolid in Spain. *Lima beans* (also known as *butter beans*) are indigenous to Nicaragua. Williams writes that the lima and guave beans grew up and threw a '*masque*' in front of the treasure site.

87. *Yaspe* is Jasper, as in Jasper Tudor, the great Welsh warrior, and uncle of Henry Tudor in the Wars of the Roses.

88. Hit with a belaying pin, i.e. murdered. So the bones in the treasure pit were of a mulatto, and English privateers or pirates had laid him there.

89. This *Jasper Cary* reminds one of Colonel Cary in Jamaica, a colleague of Sir Henry Morgan around 1672. *Rees* (originally Rhys), is a Welsh name. The Lord Rhys, Rhys ap Gruffudd, *Yr Arglwydd Rhys* was one of the great Welsh lords.

90. A species of diving bird.

91. *Dam* in the sense of mother.

92. A *brake* is a thickly overgrown area of one type of plant. It can also mean an area of large coarse ferns, like bracken.

Notes to Book 1 Chapter V

1. The *Hanger Bird* – possibly a *Nicaraguan Grackle*?

2. This insect is possibly a *rainforest bush cricket*.

3. *Land tortoises* – these could be *red-footed land turtles*, which featured on a 1999 edition of Nicaraguan stamps. Other native fauna featured were the red banded parrot, sloth, porcupine, toucan, howler monkey, anteater, kinkajou, owl monkey, red deer, armadillo, paca, vulture, tarantula, palm viper, ocelot, fighting spider, large fruit bat, jaguar, venomous tree frog, viper, grison, rattlesnake, puma, tapir and caiman.

4. These prehistoric dinosaur, or mammoth, bones must have been recently washed out of the bank by Nicaragua's torrential rains. This is the *first record* by a writer of such a discovery in the Americas. Mammoths ranged the American continent as far south as Nicaragua.

5. Merchant ships for emergencies carried *longboats*, as they could take the entire crew on board. They were big, heavy boats and had to be hoisted by block and tackle into and out of the ship. They had a mast, sail, tarpaulin and banks of rowlocks. The *bilge* in this one refers to a leak in its prow caused by the reef.

6. *Mutton Fish* – this is the '*American Eelpout*' (family *Zoarcidae*), a bottom dweller common off the Nicaragua coastline, with an elongated body and a large head. There is another eelpout, the *burbot* (*lota lota*) but it is a freshwater fish.

7. Williams writes '*scapies*' but probably means *Scaup*, a type of duck. *Lesser scaup* are found in huge numbers in Nicaraguan wetlands. *Redshanks* are waders.

8. *Toddy* – the name is remembered today when we have a '*hot toddy*' – its original 17th – 18th century meaning was a mixed drink of liquor and water, with sugar and spices and served hot.

9. The boat would be extremely heavy to drag up the beach, or to turn on its side for caulking.

10. I presume '*get it off*' means to 'trade' the silver, as there would be no identification marks after melting.

11. This appears to be the *Lesser Sulfur Crested Cockatoo*, still common in Nicaragua. *Auckco* does not seem to occur in the Rama language.

12. The *Great Anteater* (*myrymecophaga tridactyla*) is being seriously threatened with extinction in Nicaragua, because of habitat destruction. Possibly the only land mammal with no teeth, they can weigh up to 70 pounds, and their tongues can protrude up to 24 inches.

13. Williams here has Somer speaking perfect English. Somer's conversations are replicated exactly as

written in the original text, e.g. *'von spook for Brandt'* means Brandt's ghost.

14. This term is an Anglicised form of the Old French *'escoutilles'*, and refers to a small hole cut in a hatch cover, or in the side of a ship, to let in light and air. This latter is commonly called a *'porthole'* by a landlubber and is apparently referred to as a *'scuttle'* by an old seaman. To *scuttle* a ship means to sink her deliberately by opening her seacocks, or by making holes in the bottom of the hull, so that she fills with water. In colloquial English, we use the term scuttle as synonymous with to abandon or destroy.

15. Williams writes *Santiago* as it was written in those times, *St Jago da Cuba*, which was an important Spanish port on Cuba's south coast, just west of Guantanamo.

16. The *partners* is the name given to the heavy timber struts and blocks which support the mast (or capstan or pump) as it comes through the deck.

17. Williams names him *Organ*, but the surname was *Horgan*, which Williams uses later in the original text. Just as with Somer's Dutch accent, Williams usually tries to imitate the Irish accent in the Irishman's speeches. A few lines later, Horgan says that Penrose's family are *'jewels of angels sent from the Holy Powers, to be sure.'* Horgan's ship had been at sea for 29 days, dismasted and helpless for 18 of them.

18. The *yards* are the horizontal spars running from the masts, used to hang sails from. The *jury mast* is a 17th century term, when a temporary mast is made from any available spar, after the mast has broken. The origin may come from *'injury mast'* or from the Old French *'ajurie'* meaning help or relief. *Jury rigged* came to mean assembled in a makeshift manner. To *step* a mast is to erect it in stages.

19. *By your laves* means 'by your leave'.

20. Williams spells the ship *Namure*. The *Namur* was built at Woolwich in 1697, served in the Mediterranean, and was shipwrecked with her 640 crew in the East Indies in 1749. A second *Namur* was built in 1756, and was at Louisburg in 1758. In 1762 it was stationed at Jamaica, the flagship of Sir George Pocock (1706-1792), Admiral of the Blue. The most powerful ship in the fleet, with 90 guns, it was captained by John Harrison when on the Jamaica station.

21. As mentioned previously, *'dudds'* are clothes. *Milling* may mean to steal parts of, as one illegally mills pieces off coins to make new coins. To *pill* is to rob or plunder, from the Old French *'piller'*, and from which we get the word pillage.

22. *Mess* is the seaman's term – From the Anglo-Saxon *mese*, table, the space where the crew ate and slept. A *mess* also means a quantity of food for a table, or the provision of food. A *mess of pottage* is a prepared dish of soft food, pottage or potage being a thick soup of vegetables and often meat.

23. *Barcadera*. This is a puzzle. Barcadera is a small harbour on the west coast of Aruba, a small island at its maximum 20 miles by 6 miles, in the Netherlands Antilles. Offshore there is the Barcadera Reef, so Penrose was probably comparing his little harbour and reef with this port of his acquaintance.

24. *Listed* means wished.

25. *'Sheers'*, are two or more spars rigged as a hoist, so that the mast could be stepped. A *sheer pole* is an iron rod lashed to the *shrouds*, just above the *dead-eyes* and parallel to the *ratlines*. A *sheer strake* is the strake under the gunwale on the top side.

26. In tropical heat, bodies could not be kept on board. Nelson's body was said to have been pickled in a cask of his favourite rum after the Battle of Trafalgar, from which event we get the slang *'Nelson's Blood'* for rum, but actually he was placed in a cask of brandy and 'spirits of wine'.

27. There is a River *Magdalena* in Colombia, but this was probably the smaller Rio Magdalena west of Santiago on the south coast of Cuba (22N 81W). Magdalena is a Colombian Province, with Santa Marta its largest town (population 370,000).

28. *Aaron Manby* – the only record I can find of this name is that of Aaron Manby (1776-1850), who designed the first iron steamship with Captain Napier. This ship was also called the *Aaron Manby*. She first sailed in 1821 and was broken up in 1855.

29. *Flat* here means sure, or certain. We get today's term *'flat broke'*, i.e. certainly with no money, from this meaning of flat.

30. Spanish Town is inland from Kingston, 10 miles to the West. It is Jamaica's second largest town, and originally was its capital. It contains remarkable survivals of 18th century British architecture, with a population today of 18,000.

31. *Old Harbour* is in the southwest of Jamaica, and was renowned for its shipbuilding. It is in St

Catherine Parish. A *mulatto* has one black and one white parent.

32. Williams writes *'ponderate'*. It means to consider, or ponder upon, from the Latin *ponderare*. St *Columb* is St Columba, and the Irish Christian name Colum is a derivant.

33. These books are recorded in Penrose's year June 1758 - June 1759. Williams writes *'Fairy Queen'*, and Edmund Spenser's *Faerie Queene* was first published in 1590. The *Spectator* magazine was founded, as was *The Tatler*, by Sir Richard Steele, and ran from 1711 to the present day. Josephus is Flavius Josephus (37-100AD), a Jewish scholar who became Governor of Galilee and a Roman citizen. Over a dozen editions of his works appeared in the 17th and 18th centuries in England. The book by George Anson was *A Voyage Round the World in the Years 1760-1764*. Allan Ramsay's *Poems* were published in London in 1731. John Foxe's *Actes and Monuments* was known as *The Book of Martyrs*, first published in 1563. The *Spectacle de la Nature* was by Noel Antoine Pluche, translated into English as *Nature Display'd* in 1748. Richard Baxter's *Life and Times* was published in 1696. Cervantes' *Don Quixote* was published in Madrid in 1605, and the most popular English translation was that of 1742. Alexander Pope (1688-1744) wrote essays from 1711, and this publication may be his *Moral Essays* of 1733. Seneca's *Morals by Way of Abstract* was published in England in 1678, and by 1793 had gone through 17 editions.

34. The *shrouds* were the large horizontal ropes fixed to the masts, which latticed with the vertical 'rat lines' that sailors scrambled up to furl and unfurl sails. A *handspike* was a wooden or metal bar used as a lever or obstruction, and sometimes as a weapon.

35. The mainsail had to be cut and trimmed or it would have broken the temporary mast.

36. *'Dizen'd'* was used by Oliver Goldsmith, when he wrote *'like a tragedy queen, she has dizened herself out.'* It means dressed up garishly and tastelessly. Patrick O'Brien mentioned *'black silk Barcelona handkerchiefs'* worn by sailors around their necks in his seafaring novels, and *black Barcelona handkerchiefs* feature as trade goods in the Rockies in 1821. *Worsted Barcelona handkerchiefs* were advertised in the *Virginia Gazette* in 1780.

37. This is remarkably precise accounting. A *pistole* was a quarter of a doubloon, worth about 5 dollars at the time.

38. *Jack Tar* is slang for a sailor. Early sailors wore overalls and hats made of tar-impregnated fabric, which would not rot, and protected the wearer from salt and winds. The hats, as well as the sailors who wore them, became known as *tarpaulins*, shortened to *tars*. Jack is a common name given to men in general, for example *'Jack-of-all-trades'* or *'every man Jack of them'*. It seems to have come from the French synonym for peasant, *Jacques Bonhomme* (Jack the gentleman), which is turn came from *'Jacque'* a leather jerkin. We also see the origin of Jack in the word *'jacket'* today. It somehow also in England became a slang name for someone christened John. *'Jack the Lad'* means someone who does not care what he does, like a sailor on shore leave.

39. The prefix of *'look you'* is an extremely common Welsh idiosyncrasy of speech.

40. *Dross* in this sense means worthless and useless material.

41. The *104th* tune or hymn is the well-known *'Oh, Come All Ye Faithful'*.

42. *Durance* means imprisonment.

43. Bibles were used in Wales to write the births and deaths in a family. As regards the *Shaddon* family, Susannah and Matthew Shaddon were noted in 1766 in Virginia. A coincidence of the two names, *James Rogers* and *Robert Shaddon*, occurs in the 1802 tax list for Roane County, Tennessee. A James Rogers married Mary, the daughter of Tom Paine, in January 1670/1671, at Eastham, Barnstable, Massachusetts, so could have been someone whom Williams knew of, Paine being a seminal figure in early American history.

44. These are probably a species of Lovebirds.

45. The yellow snake could be a form of vine snake, but this small, vividly yellow snake common in Nicaragua is actually called the *'Yellow Snake'* (*Turrialda*).

46. *Athwart* is yet another nautical term, meaning across or transversely.

47. Williams writes *'ranged'*. The wasp species is not identified.

48. The *sweet-scented* beetle is not identified. The *sand wasp* is possibly a variety of hornet.

49. A species of dung-beetle. Williams is a wonderful amateur naturalist.

50. A *'bantling'* is a young or small child; an infant (so called because babies are *bandled*, or bundled, in bands of cloth).

51. The *Jolly Roger* is an adaptation of the *'black flag'*, commonly a black flag with a skull and crossbones,

flown towards the end of the Golden Age of piracy. Other versions showed a whole skeleton with a sword in one hand and an hourglass in the other. Most probably named after Black Bart Roberts, from his habit of dressing up in red silks before battle. He was known as *'le joli rouge'*, the *'pretty man in red'*. In 1700 was the first recorded use of the black flag, used by the Breton pirate, Emanuel Wynne fighting *HMS Poole* off Santiago. It has a skull and crossbones and an hourglass. If an intended victim refused to surrender on the sight of the black flag being raised, a red flag was hoisted, signifying that no quarter would be given. The death's head, and skull and crossbones, were worn as a cap badge in some European regiments in the 17th century

52. A *moidore* is a Portuguese gold coin.

53. Somer means that *'Mother Nature has given us a mountain of money, knowing full well that we are no better off.'* The analogy is of two eunuchs being surrounded by women.

54. *'Mexican Jumping Beans'* come from a small shrub (*sebastiana pavonia*), and are not beans but the carpels of its seed capsules. The movement comes from the actions of a moth larva inside the carpel. If the vine described is not the same shrub, then it appears that Williams is describing a similar phenomenon. The *'royal salute'* is by tradition 21 rounds of cannon fire.

55. Of the two varieties of pigeons, the *bald pate* could be the *Red-Billed Colombian Pigeon*, but the *sprig tail* is more difficult to identify. A *quist* is the name for the the *European ringed dove*, also known as the *collared dove*.

56. This is some racing pigeon – 7 miles a minute is 420 mph. Can racing pigeons travel 1000 miles in a day, as the Indians claimed? The record seems to have been set for 1005 miles, of 1 day, 10 hours, 22 minutes and 20 seconds, so a good pigeon could cover 700 miles. *Rodomontade* means a boastful speech.

57. Changeable colours mean that it is well camouflaged, as by its Indian name of *Deceiver* – perhaps it is the *Buffy-Crowned Wood Partridge*.

58. *Buchanshire* is not a county, but an area around the town of Buchan in Ross-shire in the far north of Scotland. Again the artist in Williams paints the scene here for us.

59. For daylight, Williams writes *'fair day'*.

60. Importantly, an American team has just discovered the skeletal remains of a mammoth near Santa Isabel, halfway between Lake Maracaibo and the Pacific Coast. It is estimated that about 10,000 years ago they emigrated from North to South America, so Williams is right that they were in the area. If his Indian sources were correct, it means that they lingered in Nicaragua long after their supposed extinction. Penrose states that the Indians knew *'those creatures had long white horns as long as an Indian'*, by which he may mean an Indian elephant. The hunter *Waribou* is mentioned as having kept a tusk of a mammoth. If *Kayatoo's* father had seen a mammoth, there may well have been a remnant mammoth population in the rainforest.

61. A *pedlar* is an itinerant trader, selling (peddling) small goods. From this innocent derivation of peddling, we have today's term 'drug-peddling'.

62. Williams taught the flute, and the *'German Flute'* had 8 keys and was also known as the *Transverse Flute*, to distinguish it from recorders or country flutes.

63. A *Merry Andrew* was a person who amused others by ridiculous behaviour, a buffoon or clown like the 'fool' with Morris Dancers.

64. To *rove* is to wander.

65. Williams writes *'Welch'*, as in the Royal Welch Regiment.

66. Williams writes *Leogan*, and this must be the Haitian harbour near Port-au-Prince, and this was by then a French colony, the western part of Hispaniola. Haiti was then known as Saint-Domingue.

67. *Cartagena* is the Spanish treasure port on Colombia's Caribbean coast.

68. *Maracaibo* is in Venezuela.

69. That is, Bell would work on coastal trading ships.

70. *Pantoja's trumpet* – Pantoja is a Spanish surname, but I have no idea of the meaning of this phrase. Isabel Pantoja is a singer referred to on her website as the *Queen of Song*, and Albert Pantoja is a guitar maker of repute. Juan Pantoja de la Cruz (1553-1608) was a noted Spanish painter, who may have featured in Williams' lost manuscript of the lives of the great painters. Intriguingly, he was from Valladolid, as is Rubiales, mentioned in Chapter IV.

71. A *barc*, bark or barque is a smallish, fast-sailing ship with three masts. The foremast and following mast are rigged square and the aftermast (mizzen mast) is rigged fore and aft. It could hold 90 men,

and was a fast ship with a shallow draft. Before the 1700's, the term was applied to any small vessel.

72. Williams writes '*great*', not close.

73. A *hussy* is a loose, common woman, a strumpet.

74. A *pet* is a temper.

75. The Inquisition could investigate, torture and burn non-believers. Bell had only *nine pistoles* with him when he ran away. Pistoles were Spanish gold coins, each worth two escudos.

76. A *slatch* is a period of a transitory breeze, or an interval of fair weather, or the loose or slack part of a rope. Here it seems to mean 'escape' by sea.

77. *Divers* is an old word for many, and *nostrums* are remedies.

78. *Hale* means healthy, and we still use the word today when we say 'hale and hearty'.

79. Henry III chose Deptford on the Thames as the Royal Navy's dockyard, and many famous war ships were built there. The *Red House* was rebuilt in 1685, along with other huge Thames-side storehouses, and there is an engraving of it in 1770. It became the Royal Navy's official victualling yard in 1742, and the hard '*Red House Biscuits*' became the staple diet of sailors – '*hard tack*'. They had '*Give Us This Day Our Daily Bread*' impressed on them.

80. The *Nore* in Kent is an anchorage situated just off the Thames Estuary, just off the entrance to the River Medway (next to the Isle of Sheppey). It was largely protected from easterly winds by the estuary's sandbanks, and was the common point of arrival and departure for vessels proceeding in and out of the Thames, including naval warships. Once they had reached the Nore, ships had to wait until the tide, and the force and direction of the wind, were favourable, to proceed further. Nearby Gravesend is a historic riverside town and former important port with the world's oldest cast iron pier, and is the last resting place of Pocahontas.

81. *Claus* must have been a nickname for Godart. There was a Claus Somer (1675-1731) in Lier, Holland, and at this time the Barbados Islands were known as the Somer (Summer) Islands. A Hans Heinrich Somer, aged 34, sailed on the Jamaica Galley from Rotterdam via Cowes to Philadelphia, arriving February 7th, 1739.

82. The *Main* in this context is the ocean – the Spanish Main was that area of the seas controlled by the Spanish. Often it came to encompass their American land colonies as well.

83. A *snow* is like a brigantine, but smaller, with a mainmast and foremast, and a supplementary sail behind the mainmast.

84. The *Gibb* is the old harbour at Bristol – see endnotes in previous chapters.

85. The *block maker* – sailing ships need blocks and tackles. A block is made of wood, a grooved pulley which has a hook, eye or strap on it to attach to an object, and is used to change the direction and/or rate of motion, or to apply increased force, used in ships' rigging and tackles.

86. The *lodestone* used to sharpen knives is a piece of permanently magnetic iron ore.

87. Sailors signed up for each voyage (some were impressed), to a binding contract. *Younker* was explained in footnote previously, and from Captain Smith in 1691 we read the following: '*The Younkers are the young men called fore-Mast-men, to take in the top sails, or Top and Yard, for furling the sails, Bousing or Tricing, and take their turns at the Helm.*'

88. The *Conquestador*, of 60 guns, was supposedly destroyed in Admiral Vernon's attack on Cartagena in 1741. Perhaps it was severely damaged, a hulk fit only for holding prisoners, or Penrose was imprisoned on its replacement.

89. The *windlass* is a lifting device, usually set in the forecastle and hand-operated. It is a horizontal cylinder, turned by a crank, on which a rope winds, and was often used instead of a capstan for raising the anchor.

90. By this Penrose meant that he had had his *revenge* for Jemmy Fishers inadvertently ousting him from a safe berth. The later reference that Fisher has *fetched* up Penrose *with a wet sail at last* means that he has caught up with him (fetched). In the days of canvas and cloth sails, a wet sail could hold the wind better than a dry sail, so the ship could sail faster.

91. It was the custom of a Rama widow to seek another husband as quickly as possible after the death, probably to re-contact with their husband's spirit, which would pass to the new husband. Later, *Gattaloon* refers to it as '*awakening*' her husband's spirit. When Eva '*hones*', she is whining, or moaning.

92. A *league* is a nautical measurement of about three miles. English nautical leagues in the 17th century were measured at 20 to a degree of latitude, or around 6000 yards. Each league was divided into three

nautical miles. The Spanish used an identical measurement at sea, the *'legua marina'* being 5.57 kilometres. (6,650 Castilian *varas*, to be precise.) A *fathom* is 6 feet (1.83 metres) and measures depth at sea.

93. These vultures are *turkey vultures*, also known as *turkey buzzards*, and this particular species is the *Central American (Ocellated) Turkey Buzzard (Meleagris Ocellata)*, which is more elegantly coloured than the North American Wild Turkey.

94. The *fundament* is the backside of any creature, the fleshy part that humans sit upon.

95. The only meaning of *budget* here can be a *'fund'* of possessions.

96. *Gallitraps* are fairy rings, or mushroom circles, so the meaning here is uncertain. The word has also been applied to a circle of stones.

97. Williams writes *River of Plate*. Hakluyt refers to the River of Plate in 1598, and in 1628, we read in *'The World Encompassed'* that it is near St Mary's Cape, at 38 degrees. In 1711, a pamphlet entitled *'A Proposal for the Humbling of Spain'* stated that Buenos Ayres (sic) was on the River of Plate, so this river must be in modern Argentina, the River Plate we know today. The name comes from the fact that silver could be found in the river.

98. A *farthing* was a quarter of a penny, a 240th of a pound, the lowest denomination of currency at the time.

99. Williams writes *'totus une, tambien'* It seems to mean that *'it's all one and the same.'*

100. We now use the term *'to beat about the bush'* when we wish to obscure our real purpose.

101. The *'dust'* refers to payment in gold dust – Bell was asking to see the money.

102. *'Winnelskews'* means deceives, as Bell explains later in the Journal.

103. This is Bell's Scottish accent, *weel* for well, *onny* for only, *Deel* for Devil etc. A *brae* is the side of a hill.

104. A *horselaugh* is a coarse, mocking laugh, a deep guffaw.

105. To *choose the plantain* might mean to choose one's partner, and the plantain is a staple diet in the area, used in many dishes, and even fried as chips.

106. This is Bell's improvisation upon a long song written in 1733 by William Thomson, *'The Blythsome Bridal'*

    'Fy let us a' to the bridal,
    For there will be lilting there
    For Jock's to be married to Maggie
    The lass wi' the golden hair
    And there will be langkail and porridge
    And bannocks of barley-meal
    And there will be good sawt herring
    O relish a cogue of good ale.'

107. *Buff* means naked, unclothed, as *'in the buff.'*

108. *'Black'* obviously has the same connotations for the Rama as for the British.

109. The snake had sloughed its skin. *Knot* is a collective noun for snakes, and the phenomenon of snakes knotting themselves is often recorded.

Notes to Book I Chapter VI

1. A *narcotic* is a drug that causes numbness and drowsiness, and can cause temporary unconsciousness, so could be used for medicinal reasons. *Styptic* refers to a drug which slows down, stops or prevents bleeding (by contracting the blood vessels or accelerating clotting.) A *diuretic* increased the production of urine. Williams spells the three words as *narcotick, styptick* and *diuretick,* and then word-plays on his suffixes of 'ticks'. In this case, ticks are insects that attach themselves to the skin.

2. *Thumper* must be a name for a type of large tick.

3. The German Flute is the Transverse Flute, first mentioned in the 12th century, and first used in opera in 1677. Boehm changed the position of its keys in 1836, and the Diatonic Flute from 1851 gradually replaced it.

4. Williams offered flute lessons – was Norman Bell the name of the man who taught him? Williams also taught the hautboy in Philadelphia. *Tweedside* was a popular air, the lyrics of which were written by Robert Crawford, who drowned in 1733. *Ettrick Banks* was also a traditional song called *The*

Shepherd's Wedding, first published in 1789 by G. Caw. *Invermay* was written by David Mallet (Malloch) (1700-1765) of Perthshire.

5. *Horse* means to go quickly.
6. A *strake* is a longitudinal plank, making up the sides of a boat. Williams writes '*streake*', and Bell means to higher the sides of the boat with an extra plank, to help keep strong seas from swamping it. The thick strake or plank, which is the highest ridge, is the gunwale.
7. A *cuddy* is a small cabin, galley or pantry on a small ship – a cookhouse like a caboose. Williams writes '*sung*' but he means snug.
8. *Abaft* means aft, towards the rear of the boat.
9. *Account* means end.
10. *Bruited* means told or spread rumours, or noised abroad. Here it means that the only noise, or talk one hears, is of the rich coming home. The poor are forgotten. Later, when Penrose says '*hear by the slant*' he means to hear 'obliquely' or not directly.
11. Williams writes *Havast*. *Avast* means '*Be quiet*', or '*Stop!*' Possibly from the Italian '*basta*'! (enough!), or from the Old Dutch words '*houd vast*' meaning to hold fast. '*Take a turn*' means to start your piece of work and keep quiet, and *belay* here means something similar to '*avast*'. *Belay* was an order to stop doing something, or else something nasty would happen to you. In knotting, belaying is looping the line around the base, under the arms of a cleat, bringing it up and over diagonally, around and over one arm, the one over, around and under the other, in a continuous figure 8, securing *the bitter end* by tucking it under the last crossover.
12. Williams writes '*short eyed*' for '*short sighted*'.
13. A *casuist* is a controversialist, an acute and stubborn disputant.
14. This spaniel is probably the black and white *English Springer Spaniel*, which is larger than the black and white *English Cocker Spaniel*. The largest spaniel is actually the *Irish Water Spaniel* but it is curly-coated and brown, so not the spaniel that Penrose describes.
15. A *lanyard* is essential at sea. Many pirates wore crossed sashes, to hold pistols, daggers, knives and so on, to prevent these being lost overboard. A lanyard was a short line of rope used for making anything fast. Items were fastened by lanyards, to their belts and boots. From the *Ashley Book of Knots*: '*A sailor has little opportunity at sea to replace an article lost overboard, so knotted lanyards are attached to everything moveable that is carried aloft: marling spikes and fids, paint cans and slush buckets, pencils, eyeglasses, hats, snuffboxes, jack-knives, tobacco and money pouches, amulets, bonus's whistles, watches, binoculars, pipes and keys are all made fast around the neck, shoulder, or wrist, or else are attached in a buttonhole, belt or suspender.*'
16. *Fustian* was a strong cotton and linen fabric, with a slight nap, made in Cairo.
17. '*Early one morn a jolly brisk tar*' comes from the English folk song '*The Spanish Lady*', fairly new for the times, being written and published in 1765 by Thomas Hull. Unless it was originally a traditional air, this pushes the date for the Journal back to 1765 at the earliest.
18. The *barber's pole snake* is a type of *Honduran Milksnake*, about 4 feet in length. The *Two-Headed Snake* occurs, according to herpetologists, in 1 in about 10,000 births. A two-headed *Corn Snake* named *Thelma and Louise* was kept at San Diego Zoo and had 15 normal offspring. In 2002 a *Ladder Snake* with two heads was found at Alciranta in Spain, and University of Valencia zoologists said that it could eat using both heads at the same time. Two-headed snakes often occur in the USA, Honduras, Sri Lanka and Argentina. In 2003, in Centertown, Kentucky, a *Black King Snake* with two heads was found.
19. Bell used the word *winnelskewed* earlier, when he was deceived by Penrose showing him '*a*' *that geer*' – all that gear, the silver cache in the *neuck* or nook.
20. Williams writes '*hallier*', and the old spelling of halyard was *halliard*, from the Middle English *halier*. The *halyard* is the rope for raising or lowering a flag or sail. Perhaps the mass of moving ropes and rigging meant that one could be confused in viewing through them.
21. This is fairly conclusive proof that Williams came from a reasonably prosperous family.
22. *Redshanks* are known in Britain, red-legged medium-sized wading birds. The *booby* is the *brown gannet*, '*sula cyanops*', eaten at sea when no other meat at all was available. '*Booby prize*' came to mean something that no one particularly wanted, but had to have. The word comes from the Spanish '*bobo*' meaning foolish or slow-witted, as the birds were easily caught, perceiving no danger from man. They often landed in the ship's rigging and watched passively as a sailor climbed the ropes and

334

caught them.

23. *Red Snappers* (species lutjanus) are known as *'pargo rojo'* in Spanish, and along with coppermouth (cynoscion sp.), jack (caranx hippos) and snook (centropomus sp.) are still the most commonly fished species among the Rama. Other fish caught with nets and harpoons are drum (menticirrhus martinicensis), guapote (cichlasoma sp.), mojarra (cichlasoma sp.), mullet (mugil sp.), mackerel (scomberomus sp.), tarpon (megalops atlanticus) and June fish (epinopaalus sp.).

24. Written as *'Barrowcooter'*, and common in the region.

25. The author is still searching for the meaning of *'feeding on the mineral bank.'* The skeleton has long been known as the 'mineral bank' of the human body, so perhaps Williams means the reef.

26. The *Doctor Fish* could be any one of numerous species of fish, or the family of *Teuthidae* of *Ananthuridae*. They have one or two sharp lance-like spikes on each side of the base of the tail. They are also known as *surgeonfish*, *lancet fish*, *sea surgeons* and *barber fish*. Of course, barbers were the original surgeons, as they have the sharpest instruments, there being a Guild of Barber-Surgeons. It is interesting that Williams states that the spike is *'keen'* (sharp) as a lancet.

27. The *Parrot Fish* lives in tropical reefs, and this fish would be one of the 80 species of the family *Scaridae*.

28. Williams writes *'ruff'*, not roof.

29. Williams may have been referring to 'Old Providence' when he mentions *Providence*, but it is more likely to have been New Providence, which is now Nassau in the Bahamas, which is 60 miles square and called a *'nest of pyrates'* in the 17th century. In Williams' time it was known as Providence Island. Old Providence was sacked by Sir Henry Morgan, being 150 miles east of Nicaragua, and belonging to Spain, but now part of Colombia. This was known as Isla de Providencia or Santa Catalina. The *gillambour* is difficult to trace as a fish, but there is a Gillambore Creek on the main island of Providenciales in the Turks and Caicos Islands. These Caribbean islands were named after the indigenous *Turks Head (Fez) Cactus*, and *'cayo hico'* meaning string of islands. Perhaps Williams/Penrose means Providenciales Island.

30. The *Armadillo* is still fairly common in Nicaragua.

31. *'Tholes'* – from *'The Travels of Captain Smith'* in 1691 we read *'thowls are small wooden pegs put into the gunwale (the highest strake on the boat), against which they bear the oars when they row.'* Williams writes *'thouls.'*

32. A *'muckle'* is a Scottish dialect word meaning a torrent, a large number, a great extent, a deal of trouble, a pile, a lot of money, plenty – here it means *'many'* – *'What sort of many horned Devil is lugging us about now?'* The exclamation *'Hoot, hoot, mon'* may be remembered by some of the older members of society like myself in the record which began *'Hoots mon! It's a braw, bricht, moonlicht nicht'* (*Away with you, man, it's an excellent, bright, moonlit night*) by the late lamented Lord Rockingham's XI. This record *Hoots Mon*, was a massive number one hit in the UK in 1958, and was performed by the house band on Jack Good's seminal pop TV programme *'Oh Boy.'* Of the four sax players in the original line-up, one was the notable jazz musician Benny Greene. Modern writers believe that *hoots mon* is a dismissive term made up by English music-hall comedians, but we can see that its origins are far earlier. *'Mon'* means man, and it is believed that the whole, meaning dismissing someone's opinion, is truncated from the original of *'I hae ma doots, mon'* (*I have my doubts, man*).

33. Williams writes *'hollow'*, as he does throughout the book.

34. There is a snake in Nicaragua known as the *Black Snake* which is non-venomous, but an American website refers to someone having a painful bite from a 4-foot long black snake in the area. This probably was infected, rather than injected with venom.

35. *'Whaap-nab'* seems here to be Gaelic or Scots dialect for the Devil, which Bell refers to throughout also as the *'Deel.'* However, *whaap* or *whaup* is old dialect for the curlew or whimbrel, and *nab* means the summit or head. *Wap* can also mean wasp. Bell is reprimanded by Penrose for telling Harry *'The Devil stick your worm'* and goes on to say *'The Indians would devour the old Devil himself, if he were well cooked, and sup his broth after that.'*

36. Williams writes *'paddocks'* for toads or frogs. The Old English for toad or frog is *padde*. This is possibly the *Nicaraguan Red-Eyed Tree Frog*. *'Muckle'* means troublesome here.

37. Williams writes *'embarqued'*. *Barque* was the original spelling of barc, or bark, a smallish fast-sailing ship with three masts. Before the 1700's, barque or bark was used to describe any small vessel.

38. This may be some variety of parasitic worm – *whipp* in the nautical terms of the time meant a long

pennant (pointed flag) or a small tackle with a single rope used to lift light objects.

39. The *maw* is a mouth, stomach or belly

40. This animal is unknown.

41. The book is full of 'first' written descriptions of flora, fauna and natural phenomena. Williams had a great sense of prescience.

42. Nicaragua is notable for earthquakes – in 2000 there were three over one weekend with the epicentre around the volcano of La Laguna del Apuyo. Another in that year killed 7 people. In 1992, one caused a *tsumani*, with a Richter Scale reading of 7.6. In 2003, west of Nicaragua, just offshore there were two more. Bell was largely correct in stating that Penrose's residence was away from the main areas of earthquake activity and volcanoes in the west of the country. The whole of Central America suffers on average two significant earthquakes a year. Nicaragua's last major earthquake was upon December 23rd, 1972, when the capital Managua was destroyed and over 10,000 died.

43. *'From clew to earring'* means from the lower corner of a square sail, where the *clews* are, to the rope or *earring* attached to the upper edge of the sail, which is used to reef the sail. The sails are attached at their corners by brass rings (*cringles*) sewn into the *clews*. If the clew should become undone, and the vessel *'has no clew'*, it will not sail anywhere until it is *'clewed up'* again. The term *'I haven't a clue'* has this nautical origin. Clew lines are lines running from the corner of the sail, known as the clew, to the yardarm and down to the deck. To clew also means to haul a square sail up to a yard, before furling, by means of clew lines.

44. It is remarkable that the Indians believed that it was a 'sign of heat'. The Caribbean coast Indians were not worried by earthquakes, not experiencing the effects to the west of their domain.

45. The butterflies of Nicaragua are one of its great attractions.

46. By *pod*, Williams means a chrysalis. As regards *oakum*, strands of old hemp rope or manila fibres were soaked in tar, and stuffed in between the planks of a hull to stop leaks. Unpicking old rope into strands was a slow, tedious job that hurt the fingers and thumbs, and this *'picking oakum'* was a regular punishment for minor misdemeanours. In the Royal Navy, each man in a ship's cells had to unpick a pound of oakum every day. The word comes from the Anglo-Saxon *'acumba'*, the coarse part of flax.

47. *Moonlights* are albinos, noted previously. Williams has written previously at the start of the 11th year of an Indian, *white as a horse*, but does not mention the word *albino* in the text.

48. *Diversion* means happiness here, and *younkers* has been altered to youngsters.

49. A *skulker* on board ship has the same meaning as a *'waster.'* Bilge water stank as it lay on the floor of the flat bottom of the ship, and could not be pumped out. Rubbish and waste gathered in it, in the *'waist'* or centre of the bottom of the boat, creating difficulties in steering. *'Waisters'* were older, unfit or forced seamen who were given the unpleasant job of trying to clear up the mess, and prevent the bilge-water becoming too much of a problem. These were useless sailors who could not be trusted in the rigging, and were given other menial tasks like *'swinging the lead'*, casting around to sound out the depth. Spelling over time changed to today's *'wasters'*, people who are a target for derision.

50. Penrose means that he had no worries about security after so many untroubled years in the place.

51. *'The great ugly Spirit'* sums up depression nicely. Interestingly, a *Guardian* obituary of the author William S. Burroughs in 1997 was entitled *'Struggles with the Ugly Spirit.'* Burroughs thought that he was obsessed with the Ugly Spirit, and suffered intense bouts of depression.

52. A *'transport'* is a state of being carried away by heightened emotion, as in a transport of joy.

53. The Rama were often enslaved by neighbouring and larger tribes.

54. This is of socio-anthropological importance – a description of a Rama Council meeting almost 250 years ago. It is doubtful if there is any other such record. The Rama attitude that women must be respected is also a wonderful tribute to a nation that is struggling even now to survive.

55. Penrose was being particularly clever in choosing the Catalan capital of Barcelona, with a different language and dialect to formal Castilian Spanish.

56. Williams spells this *Signior Louis Penalosa*.

57. *Fag ends* are the frayed ends of a rope on ship, possibly corrupted from fatigued, now meaning cigarette butts.

58. Slaves were routinely thrown overboard, if sick or dying. In 1562, John Hawkins removed 300 slaves from a Portuguese vessel, marking the beginning of the English slave trade. It was difficult to get crew for the *'blackbirders'* – their life was short and disease-ridden, and the sailors were sometimes treated worse than the slaves they were transporting to the Indies for work on the sugar plantations, and to

America for the tobacco crops. The Royal African Company, with its monopoly on the slave trade and royal patron, wished to transport healthy slaves who would achieve top prices on the market. However, merchant captains had their profit assessed on the number that arrived alive, and therefore overcrowded their ships, unknown to the Company. Any numbers left over from the official cargo made the captains extra money. Thus the deaths on these voyages, often accelerated by diseases such as smallpox, made the mortality rate for the Atlantic crossing at least 25% in 1679. This was a Royal Africa Company estimate, but it was not in possession of the full facts.

Robert Falconbridge wrote (An *Account of the Slave Trade, 1788*) that between half and two-thirds perished each year, and around 40,000 a year were being transported in the late eighteenth century. Falconbridge describes the disgusting conditions where the slaves were packed on the decks and held in irons by the wrists and legs, lying in their own filth and urine: '*They are frequently stowed so close as to admit of no other disposition than lying on their sides, nor will the height between decks, unless directly under the grating, allow them to stand*'. Brief daily exercise was allowed to keep them mobile, and each morning they were hosed with salt water and the dead thrown overboard. If they did not eat, they were tortured. A Captain Williams used the cat-of-nine tails to keep the slaves fit by making them dance, and '*seemed to find a pleasant sensation in the sight of blood and the sound of their moans.*' His surgeon, James Arnold, gave further evidence to a Parliamentary Committee in 1789 that some of his slaves tried to revolt, and one that could not be removed from the hold had boiling fat poured over him. Two corpses were beheaded, and '*the two gory heads were successively handed to the slaves chained on the deck, and they were obliged to kiss the lips of the bloody heads. Some who refused to obey were unmercifully flogged by the captain and had the bloody part of a head rubbed against their faces.*'

Williams also threw a live slave overboard, and had intercourse with the prettiest of the female slaves. If they refused him, they were flogged until they submitted. Williams also flogged his own crew until they were a '*gory mass of raw flesh*', according to surgeon Arnold. Another captain in 1783 threw 130 sick slaves overboard on the pretext that there was no water for them. This way the insurance underwriters had to pay for the value of the cargo, rather than the owners of the ship lose their profits by the death of the slaves.

59. The *tiger shark* does not appear to have yellow fins, and is more grey than blue, so perhaps this is another species. Along with the *Nicaraguan River Shark* (Bull Shark) and the *Great White*, it is the most dangerous shark in the world, reaching up to 14 feet in length and feeding on anything from sea snakes, stingrays, sea lions and seals to sea turtles. Its teeth seem to have evolved to be able to break through turtle shells. There is a *blue shark*, but it is only one of over 350 species of shark in the oceans.

60. It is difficult to name this animal on the seabed.

61. This could be a type of squid, but more likely a variety of *sea slug*. The sea slug is also known as the sea cucumber because of its shape, and there are numerous varieties across the world. Indeed, a new species has just been found off the Costa Rican coast, *Polycera Manzanilloensis*. As well as *Polycera*, members of another family, *Archidorus*, are known as sea slugs. A sausage-sized variety is eaten raw in Japan as a delicacy. For those with a penchant for this sort of thing, there is an excellent '*Sea Slug Forum*' on the internet.

62. When *Gattaloon* says that he is *Owagamy* now, he seems to be replacing him as the chief, or principal of the group, much as Penrose introduced Owagamy to us at first.

63. We nowadays in Britain sometimes show approval by saying, '*well said, squire,*' or '*well spoken, squire*', but the origin is uncertain. This 18th century usage of *Hardicanute* is puzzling. He was son of King Canute (Cnut), whose legend of trying to hold back the waves was based on the tale of Maelgwn Gwynedd of Wales 500 years previously. Hardicanute, or Knut II was King of Denmark from his father's death in 935, but could not take the kingship of England (Wales was never conquered by the Danes) until 1040 because of an alternative claimant. Hated by his Saxon subjects, he levied an unpopular Fleet Tax, and died of convulsions in a drinking party with his Danish nobles in 1042.

64. The largest and strongest anchor on a sailing ship was the '*sheet anchor,*' which has come to figuratively mean someone who is one's best hope or last refuge in a crisis. It was also known as the *waist anchor* or the *bower anchor*. The '*best bower anchor*' either refers to this, or the larger of two anchors that may be dropped from the bows, the other being the *small bower anchor*.

65. Yet another nautical reference – *skiffs* are small boats, which Williams spells as *skifts*.

66. There is an Aurora Australis, but as the phenomenon is in the north-east, this has to be the Aurora

Borealis. There are several records of this penetrating to the Equator. Bell would have seen it when a boy in the north of Scotland. A legend refers to Quetzacoatl escaping to 'Tlalapan', which means 'where the aurora is born.' This was believed to be near the south-east of the Honduras. The airport at Guatemala City is Aurora Airport. There is a massive dip in magnetic field strengths in Central America, which may increase the chance of the aurora being observed, assisted by the relatively clear and unpolluted air.

67. The *Ballahoo* may originate from *balao*, a type of baitfish species. A class of fast-sailing Bermuda schooners were known as *Ballyhoos* at this time, probably after the lines of this fish. The schooners had elongated bowsprits, and Basseterre's most popular restaurant is *Balahoos*.

68. The *Garr Fish*, or American Garfish is *Lepisoteus Osseus*, with hard scales, long jaws and needle-like teeth. The European Garfish is *Belone Vulgaris*, and it unclear which one Williams is referring to.

69. This fish could be the *South Atlantic Flying Gurnard*, or a species of flying fish (*Exocoetidae* family) that Williams has not seen before. (On the Pacific Coast, the *Californian Flying Fish*, *Cypelurus Californicus* is of a different family, and grows up to 18 inches). In the Atlantic flying fish range from 7 to 12 inches in length, and include the *4-Winged Flying Fish* and the *Bearded Flying Fish*, so called because of its barbels.

70. The *lion lizard* is also known as the *basilisk*, a small, crested tree lizard that can run on its hind legs, of the genus *Basiliscus* and the family *Iguanidae*.

71. A British snake that can sometimes be green is the *adder*, or *viper*. This 'green snake' is probably a *grass snake*.

72. The *galliwasp* can be one of three types of lizard in the region. The *Celestus Occidus* is about a foot long, and 'imagined by the natives to be poisonous.' It could be 'any one of several long-bodied lizards of the genus Diploglossus, native to marshy regions of Central America and the West Indies, especially Diploglossus Monotropus, of the Caribbean family Anguidae.' Again, it could be *Celestus Rozellae* of the family *Anguidae* of the order *Sauria*, found in Belize and Central America.

73. The *satin lizard* cannot be easily identified.

74. Williams writes '*hones*,' meaning complaints or objections.

75. In effect, being to the windward, he had '*taken the wind*' out of his sails. Sailing downwind directly at another ship would take the wind out of its sails, a manoeuvre known as '*overbearing*', and slowing down the enemy to make it easier to capture. The former term *aloof* is also nautical in origin, from the Dutch '*loef*' or windward. On a lee shore, to keep aloof is to keep the vessel's head nearer to the wind to prevent being driven onshore. So '*to keep aloof*' meant to keep your distance from the shore.

76. To *trampoose* is to walk heavily, in a laboured manner, to tramp.

77. This wise woman seems to be the equivalent of the West's '*white witches.*'

78. To *dastardize* means to intimidate.

79. This phrase seems to mean that Penrose had '*drawn trumps*' in a card game, thus being in a more favourable position because he had the information from the Indians.

80. The Biscayans are the Galicians, a Celtic remnant and the same race as the Welsh. In the annual Inter-Celtic Festival at Lorient in Brittany, the 'nations' taking part are Wales, Galicia, Brittany, the Isle of Man, Asturia, Scotland, Cornwall and Ireland. The Welsh, Bretons and Cornish shared the same language, Celtic-P, while the Irish, Scots and Manx share Celtic-C.

81. Jones is another Welsh name. Nunez' words are exactly transcribed, and mean '*Good boy, do you speak English? I speak English also. What's your name, boy?*'

82. Sir John Norris (c.1660-1749) was Admiral of the the fleet serving in the Baltic in 1715, 1716, 1718, 1720 and 1727, and in 1740 he fought off a French fleet in the English Channel. He was known as '*Foul Weather Jack*' as bad weather seemed to follow his command. The *Boyne* (Williams writes *Boyn*) was built at Deptford in 1692 and sailed the Caribbean, Mediterranean and Baltic. Another HMS *Boyne* was a 2nd rate man of war of 80 guns, built at Deptford in 1739, and broken up in 1763. The next *Boyne* was a 70-gun 3rd rate ship of the line, built at Plymouth in 1766 and broken up in 1783. This ship visited Boston in 1777, so could have been known to Williams. The huge 96-gun *Boyne* built in 1790 was in the Caribbean in 1794 and 1794, but destroyed by fire accidentally started by Royal Marines at Portsmouth in 1796. The reference to *Portsmouth Castle* is probably Portchester Castle, which guards the entrance to Portsmouth Harbour.

83. Peter the Great (Peter I of Russia) was in England in 1698, staying at (and almost wrecking) the writer John Evelyn's home, Sayes Court, near Deptford. He came over to study shipbuilding

techniques and communicated in Dutch, having just spent a few months in Holland. Supposedly incognito, his height of 6 feet 7 inches meant that everyone knew who he was. In 1715 he offered Sir John Norris command of the Russian fleet. By 1719, the British government felt the English shipbuilders had effectively helped to create for the Czar a powerful navy, made up of ships that rivalled English ships, and that his navy could present a potential threat to England in the future. In 1715, Admiral Sir John Norris, had pointed out to his superiors that *"It is not unreasonable that you should believe that his Nation by the help of some English builders should have made the Improvement we find. He has three new sixty Gun ships built by them at Petersburg that are in every way equal to the best of that Rank in our Country and are handsomely finished."* The British envoy in St. Petersburg pointed out that, because of the elevated status and high salaries that the English shipbuilders received from Peter the Great, it would be very difficult to persuade them to return to England. The ships that the Englishman Noy and others had built were described *"as good and as well built as any Europe can afford".* The British government became increasingly concerned about the intentions of its former protégée, Peter the Great, especially about the quality and rapid growth of his fast expanding navy and the changing balance of power in the Baltic. In 1719, driven on by this anxiety, Parliament was moved to legislate against English people going abroad to work for foreign powers and passed an Act of Parliament to prevent it. However, it was too late. Noy and others had taught many Russians the English style of shipbuilding and thus the foundations of an independent, native shipbuilding industry had been established. In 1723, Peter the Great in recognition of their work, made Noy, Cozens and Brown *'captains-commodore'.* Indeed, according to Peter's newly established Table of Ranks, the rank of captain-commodore also conferred nobility upon the titleholder. Catherine the Great confirmed this in November 1725, hoping to retain the services of Noy, who may have been thinking of returning to England, on the death of Peter. Peter the Great's high regard for Noy was also highlighted in the funeral ceremony of 1725. Noy had risen to such heights that he was given a privileged position in Peter's funeral procession. Noy remained in Russia until at least the late 1730's, for in 1737, he was rewarded for *"his long and faithful Services"* of forty years as a shipbuilder by the Czarina with a pension of 500 roubles a year. Noy was by now sixty eight and he was becoming unable to do his job properly because of old age and illness. He petitioned Catherine to be allowed to return to England, which she allowed. He spent the last years of his life with his wife in Deptford; where he had originally met up with his employer, Peter the Great. He died in 1753 and was buried in St. Nicholas's church, Deptford. Peter the Great communicated with Sir John Norris on many occasions and met him at Amsterdam in August 1717, so Nunez' recollections may make Nunez' birthdate about 1696.

84. A *pipe* of wine is a large cask of 2 hogsheads, or 136 gallons.
85. Burgos is near Valladolid, the Spain's province of Castille de Leon.
86. *Plata* has two meanings in Spanish. The first is the passage of water where a river's current meets the sea's tide, after which the River Plate may be named. The second meaning of *plata* is silver, so Nunez means that he had no money. As mentioned previously, it may be that the River Plate was named after silver.
87. A southwesterly means that the wind is heading northeast. To *stand away large* is to sail away with the wind, and/or sail away using large sails (-see the author's *The Pirate Dictionary*, published by Pelican USA, or *The Pirate Handbook* published by Glyndwr Publishing, Wales).
88. 'Home is home, be it ever so humble' is the probable proverb here. There is another; 'home is home, though it's never so homely,' and also 'home is home, as the Devil said when he found himself at the Quarter Session.'
89. *Aanora* (Janet) is not mentioned again until much later in the book, in the 24th year. Bell had not been too sure about wanting to marry her. Perhaps at this time she was not sleeping with him.
90. To *mess* in this context is to eat together.
91. *Without control* means without any constraints.

1. *The offing* is a nautical term meaning heading from the shore, and/or out into the sea. *'The ship stands for the offing'* means that the ship sails from the shore to the sea. If a ship keeps in the middle of a channel, and does not near the shore, she is said to *'keep an offing'*. *'Offward'* is contrary to the shore, so if its stern lies to the off-ward, its head faces the shore. *'In the offing'* has come to mean that something is likely to happen, as a ship *in the offing* will either come to land, anchor, send a boat ashore or sail away.

2. *Guardacostas:* Private revenue cutters used by the Spanish to enforce their Caribbean trading monopoly. They were commissioned by local governors, fitted out in Spanish or colonial ports and earned their money by the prizes that they took. An account by Defoe in his *General History* tells us: *'A Guarda del Costa, of Porto Rico, commanded by one Matthew Luke, an Italian, took four English vessels, and murdered all the crews. He was taken by the Lanceston Man of War, in May 1722, and brought to Jamaica, where they were all but seven deservedly hanged. It is likely the man-of-war might not have meddled with her, but she blindly laid the Lanceston on board*, thinking that she had been a Merchant Ship, who thereupon catched a Tartar. Afterwards, in rummaging, there was found a Cartridge of Powder which was made up of an English journal, belonging, I believe, to the Crean snow; and upon this examination, at last, it was discovered that they had taken this vessel and murdered the crew; and one of the Spaniards, when he came to die, confessed that he had killed twenty Englishmen with his own hands.'* (* to lay aboard is to draw alongside a ship to board it). These 17th century *'Spanish'* coastguard boats tried to stop all foreign trade to the West Indies. They regularly tortured English, Dutch and French merchant seamen and handed them over to the Inquisition. They were privateers, including Irish and English captains, commissioned by Spanish crown officials, and were restricted in peacetime, but from the 1670's had almost free rein to protect the Spanish West Indies and mainland from pirate, smuggling and logwood raids. They complemented the activities of the Armada de Barlovento, the Spanish royal squadron that patrolled the Caribbean. Guardacostas were given authority to patrol a particular stretch of coastline, and based in a specific port. Their crews were therefore fresh and ready for action, and had to be successful, for they were mercenaries who lived off the prizes they took. Acting Governor Molesworth of Jamaica complained in 1684 that *'these galleys and piraguas are mostly manned by Greeks, but they are of all nations, rogues culled out for the villainies they commit. They never hail a ship; and so they can but master her, she is a certain prize. They lurk in the bushes by the shore, so that they can see every passing vessel without being seen. When our sloops are at anchor they set them by their compasses in the daytime, and steal on them at night with so little noise that they are aboard before they are discovered.'* The previous year, Governor Lynch had written to London that the Spanish had armed some small craft and *'ordered them to take all ships that have on board any "frutos de esas Indias" (fruits of these Indies), whereby they make all fish that come to net. They have committed barbarous cruelties and injustices, and better cannot be expected, for they are Corsicans, Slavonians, Greeks, mulattoes, a mongrel parcel of thieves and rogues that rob and murder all that come into their power without the least respect to humanity or common justice.'*

3. 1763 saw the end of The Seven Years War, with the *Treaty of Paris* on February 10th. There was another treaty at Fontainebleu in November. It is now June 1764, so Nunez has known about it for some time. (The news would take around 6 – 10 weeks to reach the Americas.) England received Florida from Spain and Canada from France and emerged as the world's leading colonial empire. Britain returned Cuba and the Philippines to Spain, having captured Havana and Manila in 1762. Previously 'The War of Jenkins' Ear' of 1739 had melded into 'The War of the Austrian Succession' in 1740, which ended in 1748.

4. *Doused their colours* means lowered their flag(s).

5. A *jack* is a small flag flown at the bow, denoting nationality. The Cross of St George denoted an English ship, and the Union Jack is the flag of the United Kingdom.

6. A *sloop* was much favoured by pirates and privateers, being fast and manoeuvrable and easily handled in shallow waters. It had one mast and a fore-and-aft rig, a long bowsprit and could carry 10 to 32 guns.

7. Penrose refers to *guns*, which to us are cannon. The sloop must have been recently careened, so it was ready for evasive action from the coastguards.

8. *Charge* means order.

9. Henry Purcell wrote an air named *Gillicrankie*, also known as *Killiecrankie*, a place in Perthshire in

Scotland, where 'Bonny Dundee' was killed in battle in 1689. When hailed, ships always gave their port of origin, which made Bell extremely suspicious (of an inland port, Perthshire being a landlocked county in Scotland).

10. They were smugglers or 'interlopers' – the 'fair trade' that avoided penal taxes in the colonies. Colonists welcomed such trade, which the guarda costas tried to prevent. Piracy was called 'the sweet trade' by its participants.

11. This is Williams's version of Spanish – it should be 'mucha plata' – 'much silver (money) for certain.'

12. To truck is to exchange or barter commodities, and also small commodities used for barter. The notorious 'truck shops' in Britain's Industrial Revolution, belonging to the employers, kept the workers permanently in debt.

13. An adze is an edged tool, used to cut and shape wood, a hatchet.

14. Pottage or potage is vegetables and meat boiled in water to make a soft, thick soup.

15. Osnabrigs is a type of coarse linen, originally made in Osnaburg, Germany. In the narrative we are now in 1764, and there was an advertisement in the Virginia Gazette, upon June 16, 1768, appealing for the capture of three indentured servants, all of whom were wearing shirts made from this rough fabric: 'Ran away from the subscribers, living on Seneca, in Frederick County, Maryland, the three following convicted servant men, viz. James Dobby, about 40 years of age, 5 feet 8 or 9 inches high; had on and took with him, two cotton and one broadcloth waistcoats, a pair of old cotton breeches, black yarn stockings, oznabrigs shirts, country made shoes, and a new felt hat. He is a shy, artful fellow, and very talkative; has black hair tied behind, a very large beard, and somewhat grey, he is also pitted with the small pox, and is a sailor.' After a description of two other men, a reward of £10 is offered. The hardwearing Oznabrigs could also be used as tablecloths and towels, and the material was specified for the pockets, staying and sleeve linings of the uniforms of the 1st New Hampshire Regiment in 1775. George Washington mentioned it in 1761 in an advertisement for runaway slaves, who wore 'osnabrigs' shirts. It was used most in sacking and bagging, like the coarse German Hessian, and was also made in Lancashire and Scotland. 'In truck' means in exchange.

16. 'Under the rose' was an 18th century term for something carried out privately or in secret, a translation of the Latin 'sub rosa'. The rose has always been a symbol of secrecy; it was formerly hung up at entertainments as a token that nothing should be divulged. The round house was the captain's cabin, according to Smith in 1691, situated at the very aft of the vessel. It was on deck to be cooler and more hygienic than below decks. In the context of the book, Penrose suspected that a plot hd been hatched in the captain's cabin to pay much less than his treasure was worth.

17. Raven duck, or Raven's-Duck is fine quality sailcloth, from the German ravenstuch.

18. A serving mallet is a nautical term for a wooden instrument shaped like a mallet, used in serving ropes.

19. As regards marlin spikes, 'Marling is a small line of untwisted hemp, very pliant and well tarred, to cease the ends of ropes from ravelling out, or the sides of the blocks at their arses, or if the sail rent out of the bolt-ropes, they will make it fast with marlin until they have leisure to mend it. The marling spike is but a small piece of iron to splice ropes together, or open the boltrope when you sew the sail.' – Smith, 1691. As merchant crews had no weapons, the marling spike was often the chosen weapon for a mutiny of would-be pirates

20. Small wooden blocks which have a grooved pulley to enable hoisting or leveraged pulling, as in block and tackle.

21. Ratlines are the small ropes attached to the shrouds, by which men go aloft to trim the sails. Marline is mentioned as marling in note 19 and is a light rope of two loose strands used for lashing.

22. 'You red-powdered? brute, she is now remarking you to be the most ill-faced devil she ever beheld with her two eyes!' Possibly 'pow'd' is an abbreviation of powdered, as wigs used to be powdered white at this time, and it was a jibe at the red-haired seaman.

23. Blackguard – to curse and slander

24. Captain Sawney was a pirate of the time, but this may be a reference to the famous Cherokee chief Sawny, also known as Captain Sawny and Big Sawny, from the Middle Towns, who was well known around 1760. Perhaps as Penrose was tanned and had an Indian wife, it was an attempt at sarcasm.

25. A crawthumper was 18th century Dublin slang, which must have passed to the USA, which meant a 'holy Joe'. It was someone who was ostentatiously pious or religious, a sanctimonious person looked upon with distaste and suspicion.

26. Close-hauled means that the sails and boom are pulled in tightly, allowing the boat to sail as near as

possible to the direction the wind is coming from.

27. *Purchase* here means '*prize*', as in the privateer term, '*no purchase, no pay.*'

28. *Owyooks* – the etymology of this term is unknown.

29. To *whelve* is from the Old English, to overturn or capsize, which came to mean to hide, or cover with an upturned vessel.

30. Called variously the *Sea Hedgehog, Porcupine Fish* or *Globefish*, this is a spinose *plectognath* fish, of the genus *Diodon*. It is studded with tough, sharp quills. It is said that when it is attacked and swallowed by a 20-foot shark, it sucks in air or water and inflates itself enormously inside the shark's belly. Its quills rip a hole through the body of the shark so it can escape, leaving the shark to die. Williams writes '*Hedg Hog or Globfish.*'

31. '*Soundings*' were those inshore areas, and above reefs and shoals, where a seaman sounded out the depth of the water *by swinging the lead*, to ensure that a carefully moving ship did not ground herself.

32. The *Amber Fish* flourishes on the Southern Atlantic coasts, *Seriota Carolensis*.

33. There is a *Coffin Fish*, also known as the *Cow Fish* or *Trunk Fish*, but this is possibly not the black fish described. If any reader can elucidate upon this fish, or any of the other flora and fauna described, the author will attribute and include this assistance in any future editions of this book. The cow fish occurs widely in the area, known as the *coffre* in French and the *chapin* or *cofre* in Spanish, a species of *lactophrys*.

34. A *cat's paw* is a warm, light wind on the surface of the sea, also known as a *cat's skin*.

35. The first *moray* is possibly the *Green Moray*, which often reaches 5-6 feet and even rarely 8 feet. The second is possibly the *Spotted Moray*, which reaches 2-4 feet in length. There are 200 species of Moray Eel, in 5 genera. They are typically around 5 feet in length, but some reach up to 13 feet.

36. A *squib* is an old name for a firework, a tube filled with combustibles that acts as a firecracker. This tube was directed at the nest from the fire, pouring smoke into it and killing all the bees, which were in the nest for the night. Squibs and smoke bombs were in common use amongst pirates and privateers, often called '*stinkpots*', and were thrown onto the deck of the ship to be boarded. They were often crockery jars filled with sulphur, gunpowder and other combustibles, with a fuse. They were also sometimes filled with plant gum and rotting fish, and were a crude and early form of tear gas. A popular method was for the pirates to suspend them from their yardarms, and when the ships closed together, to light and cut them so they dropped onto the deck of the intended prize. From Falconer's '*Marine Dictionary*' of 1771 we have the following description: '*The fuses of the stinkpot being lighted, they are immediately thrown on the deck of the enemy, where they burst and catch fire, producing an intolerable stench and smoke, and filling the air with tumult and distraction. Amidst the confusion occasioned by this infernal apparatus the (boarding) detachment rush aboard sword in hand, under cover of smoke, on their antagonist.*'

37. The author fully remembers this gamekeepers' practice of hanging dead vermin. On one estate near Osmotherley in North Yorkshire, a line had been strung along a gap in the woodland, from which hung magpies, crows, stoats, weasels and anything else which threatened the local grouse and pheasant populations. They were called '*gamekeepers' gibbets*'.

38. The practice of using a poison to relieve pain is a principle in homeopathy and some medicinal cures today. New species of spiders are still being discovered in Central America. The previous mention of a scorpion is noted in that the neighbouring Miskito Indians have a wonderful folk tale about *Mother Scorpion Country*.

39. Instead of concealed, Williams writes '*perdue*', meaning hidden, or lost from sight, from the French '*perdu*' or lost.

40. The *poop* is the afterdeck of a sailing vessel.

41. *Close quarters* is a nautical term, meaning a small wooden fortress or barricade erected on the deck of a merchant ship when attacks by pirates were expected. Small openings, loop-holes, enabled sailors to fire weapons with some protection. Wooden partitions in the quarters below decks also had loopholes pierced in them, to allow defenders to thrust pikes and cutlasses through, and fight off boarders.

42. *Theobroma cacao* and *coffea arabica* both grow wild in Nicaragua. These canoes seemed to have taken some months to hollow out of suitable tree-trunks, and are similar in length to those used by the Rama today.

43. The sentence containing *Agogo* and *Manoluvy (Manolubee)* is exactly transcribed from Williams'

script. These words seem not to occur in the Rama language.

44. *Maracaibo* is in Venezuela, and was sacked by the Welsh buccaneer Sir Henry Morgan in 1668.

45. There were some silver mines in Nicaragua, but tens of thousands of Nicaraguans were sold by the Spanish into the huge silver mines of Peru and Bolivia.

46. Hermits – Williams' spelling is *'Anchorets.'*

47. *Bono* is Spanish (masculine) for good. Williams writes *'Bon Catholicks.'*

48. *'Star'* is *'Esta'*, meaning *'that is.' 'Esta bien'* means *'that's good.'*

49. The *Cuckold Fish* is shown in an 1804 hand engraving sold at the British Museum, and is not the same class that the French call *cuckoldfish*, which are squid of the family *disbranchia* of the class *cepaloda*.

50. *'Lancksa'* is some species of octopus.

51. Either a type of coral, or a sea anemone.

52. A *switch* is a small cane or rod. This 'sensitive grass' can be seen in Hawai, but seems from pictures to be a dwarf fern. Various ferns, moonworts and spleenworts have these similar characteristics, as do two leguminous herbs, *cassia chamcrita* and *cassia nictitans*, which are known as *'wild sensitive plant.'* Available in garden shops is *'The Sensitive Plant'*, *mimosa pudica*, which grows up to two feet tall, and it is native in Nicaragua.

53. This beach vine is native to Central American beaches, and its beans sold as *'Mary's Beans'* by Costa Rica street vendors. It is a member of the Morning Glory family (*convolulacacae*), and is *meremia diresidesperma*. Beach morning glory (*ipomoea pes-caprae*) is common on beaches in Rama territory. Other dominant beach species are sea-grape (*coccoloba uvifera*), icaco (*chrysobalanus icaco*), *sporobulus* and *paspalum* grasses and coconut palm (*cocos nucifera*).

54. The *'ship's stern fast'* or sternfast was a nautical term for the rope used to tie the stern of the vessel to a wharf, jetty, another ship or buoy. *Turgid* is used in the sense of being swollen. Williams spells taut as *tought*. Elephants 'hear' through their feet, so perhaps deer have the same capability.

55. Williams prefixes *'There'* with *'Similarity:'* which I have omitted.

56. This fruit sounds like an aubergine, *solanum melongena*, known as *berenjena* by the Spanish settlers in Central America. There is a *'Yellow Green Finch'* in Nicaragua, but I am uncertain if it is the bird described.

57. *'Tiberoon'* – *'tiburon'* is Spanish for shark. In these waters, the bull shark (cub shark, ground shark, Nicaraguan River Shark) was *Tiburon sarda* or *toro*; the blue shark was *Tiburon azul*; the hammerhead was *Tiburon martillo*; the mako (blue pointer) was *marajo*; the whale shark the *tiburon-ballena*; and the great white shark was the *jaqueton blanco* or *gran blanco*. This shark, as the lagoon is a mixture of fresh water and seawater, is probably the Nicaragua River Shark. There is a Cape Tiberoon in Haiti, and a Point Tiberoon in San Francisco Bay.

58. It seems that this is a locally occurring shrub, the *Castor Oil Tree*, *ricinus communis*, called by the Spanish *higuera infernal* or *higuera del Diablo*.

59. Of the 6 species of sea turtle, four nest on Nicaragua's beaches. *Kemp's Ridley turtle* is now confined to a single site in Mexico. All and endangered and threatened with extinction. 2.5 million turtles are hatched in Nicaragua every year, but are subject to the predations of man and turkey buzzards. They are still being hunted. 20 were found recently tipped onto their backs in a hut on Nicaragua's Corn Island. Until recently the Japanese were importing 20 tons of *'tortoiseshell'* from the *Hawksbill Turtle* every year. (Japan is not the only nation in the world which is endangering species, but along with its needless slaughter of dolphins and whales, it sets the worst ecological example of all the developed nations). The *Green Turtle* was a listed species in 1978, the *Hawksbill* in 1978, the *Leatherback*, which Williams calls the *Trunck* turtle, in 1970, and the *Loggerhead* in 1978. The fifth turtle Penrose mentions is one of several species of *Freshwater Turtle*. The sixth appears to be the *Diamondback Terrapin*. Green turtles next from July to mid-October, and Leatherbacks from March to May, so they do not compete for nesting sites. Williams' seventh animal, the *Land Turtle*, is in fact the *Box Tortoise*. In the Spanish Caribbean, the land tortoise is the *tortuga*, after which the island was named, as its shape resembles that of a tortoise. The green turtle is the *tortuga verde* or *branca*; the hawksbill turtle is the *tortuga carey* or *de concha*; the leatherback is the *tortuga laud* or *barriguda*; the loggerhead is the *tortuga caguama* or *boba*; and the ridley turtle is the *lora*. Up to 11,000 Green Turtles are caught every year in Nicaragua, for their meat. It grows to 180kg, does not reach sexual maturity until it is 20-50 years old, and is an endangered species. All the other turtles in Nicaragua also have problems from egg poaching on a massive scale. Penrose mentioned thinking that the skulls of

Loggerheads resembled those of humans, and their name derives from their exceedingly large heads. They grow up to 115kg and are an exceptionally endangered species. The Hawksbill turtle, like many whale species, is subject to a danger created by the Japanese. That nation imports huge quantities of its shell for decoration. It grows to 80kg and is critically endangered. The Leatherback is the largest turtle, growing to 700kg and is critically endangered.

60. A *savannah* is flat grassland found in tropical and sub-tropical areas.

61. From the 1530's onwards, Europeans had formed small settlements on the coasts of Jamaica, Cuba and especially Hispaniola. The few surviving Indians, those not wiped out by the Spanish, showed them how to cure long strips of meat on a *barbecue* over a slow fire, in a hut called a *'boucan'*. The Spanish had seen the Taino Indians using a framework suspended from forked sticks, for cooking over charcoal or wood. When they asked what it was, the Indian word sounded like *'barbacoa.'* European fugitives from the Spanish caught wild cattle and pigs, and exchanged the hides, meat and tallow for guns, clothes, provisions and alcohol. These butchers evolved a system of living where the past was not mentioned, and were only known to each other by Christian names. Excellent sharpshooters, their favourite food was the warm marrow from the bones of newly slaughtered animals. In retaliation against Spanish attacks on their settlements, these *'boucaniers'* or *buccaneers* attacked Spanish shipping in *'pirogues'* or *'piraguas'*, hollowed-out tree-trunks that served as canoes. The Spanish tried to massacre their herds, and this turned the *'Brethren of the Coast'* even more to piracy and buccaneering, and from 1630 the island of Tortuga became their unofficial headquarters.

62. Today some people refer to small immature apples as *codling* apples, but it is an old apple variety more suitable for cooking than eating. A traditional English folk air begins: *'As I was going to Banbury/I saw a fine codling apple tree.'*

63. A *bombshell* was thrown or fired onto the decks of ships to be boarded.

64. *Vent* means a fissure – it was the touch-hole on a ship's cannon, so it means a void or space.

65. Literally, *'I am a great knight'* – a *caballero* is literally a horse-rider, and only knights could ride horses.

66. *Gillarandy* is Harry's attempt to say *Gillicranky* (*Killiecrankie*), the supposed port of origin of the *'fair trader'*.

67. The *weather gauge* is the position of a ship to the windward of another, literally *'taking the wind out of its sails'* and rendering it powerless. It meant therefore to have a position of advantage or superiority.

68. A *schooner* is a small fast vessel, with two masts, rigged fore and aft.

69. The meaning of *dips or casts* is as follows. A dip is slang for a pickpocket, and cast is shortened from a cast-off, someone worthless, a reject. To *cast off* is a nautical term for letting something go, and this is its origin. Bell thus does not have a good opinion of this crew.

70. *Carthagena*, or *Cartagena* was the treasure port between Panama and Venezuela, and is now part of Colombia. It was one of only three treasure ports visited by the annual Spanish treasure fleet, the *flota*. Pearls were shipped from Margarita Island, as well as precious woods, gold, silver and emeralds. Founded in 1533, it was heavily defended and was the only major Spanish port never taken by the buccaneers, although Henry Morgan had wanted to attack it. The French took it in 1689.

71. A *loon* is Scottish dialect for a worthless lazy fellow, a rogue and waster.

72. The Treaty of Seville, 1729, prevented English trade with the Spanish colonies, and the Spanish severely treated any English seamen captured in 'their' waters in the New World. Resentment simmered, and Edward Vernon (1684-1757) was an MP who said in Parliament that he could take Porto Bello *'with 6 ships only.'* He was made an admiral and given 9 men-of-war and a sloop to sail to the Caribbean in 1739. He took on supplies and another 240 men in Jamaica, and headed for the Isthmus of Darien and Portobelo. He kept his promise of taking 6 ships only, in line of battle into Porto Bello's harbour, chasing some costa guardas into it. Vernon had 370 cannon and 2735 men, and the Spanish were amazed that he would dare to sail into the range of the fort of San Felipe. HMS *Hampton Court* fired over 400 cannon ball from its 70 guns into the fort in 25 minutes, as the fleet was becalmed in the harbour, then she was joined in the bombardment by the 50-gun *Norwich*, the 60-gun *Worcester* and the 70-gun *Burford*. The fire was so intense that the Spanish could not approach their 100 cannon to fire back. The *Burford* was hit, but put covering fire onto the lower shore for a party of marines to take the fort. The *Hampton Court* was also engaged in gunfire, from its lower tier of guns, with the fort across the channel, El Castillo Santiago, until nightfall. The next morning, with the English fleet still becalmed, the Castillo Santiago raised a white flag, and the Spanish governor and the commander of the guarda costa brought a surrender document. Spanish

ships and Porto Bello were plundered, and the fortifications destroyed. Ammunition was taken, along with the best cannon. Other cannon were destroyed. Members of the South Sea Company were released from dungeons. After a few weeks, the fleet sailed back to Jamaica. In February 1740, Vernon bombarded Cartagena and took Porto Bello again. He bombarded the Castillo de San Lorenzo for a day at the mouth of the Chagres River. It was the key to taking Panama, and Henry Morgan had taken it before his sack of Panama. The castle was blown up, and the fleet next ranged along the coast. In 1741, Vernon set off again with a huge fleet from Jamaica, consisting of 30 ships of the line, 90 support vessels, 15000 sailors and 12000 soldiers. His intention was to cross the Isthmus of Panama, to meet up with Admiral Anson's Pacific fleet and take the city. First he wanted to take Cartagena, to allow Anson time to sail around Cape Horn to reach Panama. The 70-gun Spanish admiral's ship, the *Gallicia* was taken. Other Spanish ships, the 80-gun *St Felipe*, and the *Carlos, Africa, Conqestadore* and *Dragon*, all with 60 guns, were sunk or scuttled. However, the fort was so heavily defended that Vernon lost many men through malaria and dysentery, as well as in action. The Spanish surrendered Cartagena, but Vernon's force was too depleted to march to Panama and take it. In Vernon's absence, Anson went on to circumnavigate the world. In July 1741, Vernon attacked Cuba's coastal towns, and tried again in 1742 to take Panama, but the rainy season, sickness and mortality caused him to return to Jamaica. Thus McLintock must have deserted Vernon between 1739 and 1742, over 20 years before he met Bell in March 1766.

73. This clause makes no sense in the original so has been altered from: *'when he told him he had found it before it was lost on a Maroon Key some few months ago.'* The guarda costa made their only source of income from taking 'fair traders'. They might have stripped the fair trader and sunk it – naturally Bell and Penrose were suspicious.

74. The *Remora* is any of several fishes of the family *echenidae*, having on the head a sucking disk, which attaches to sharks, sea turtles, swordfish, whales or the hulls of ships. They are also called suckerfish, suckfish and shark suckers.

75. Possibly the *Crested Bulbul*, also known as the *Red-Whiskered Bulbul* or the *Persian Nightingale*, *pycnonotus jocosus*.

76. *Sancoodas* – *sancudas* are horseflies in Mexico, and herons in the Altamura district of Spain.

77. The Miskito Indians were friendly to the English and hated the Spanish – see the introduction to Part II of this book. However, they enslaved weaker tribes.

78. It is suspicious that both the Spaniard Nunez and the faux-Italian Bell wished to avoid the Spanish authorities. Both had been living with Indians, rather than among the Spanish. Britain and Spain were at peace at this time. This is another pointer to the author's belief in the semi-autobiographical nature of the book. Williams has no idea of the reason – in a work of fiction, this could have been explained.

79. *Studding posts* - the first verse of a poem by Charles Bruce, 'Nova Scotia Fish Hut' is the only reference I can find for this term: *'Rain and blown sand, and southwest wind/ Have rubbed these shingles crisp and paper-thin. / Come in: Something has stripped these studding-posts/ And pinned time to the rafters. / Where the woodworm ticked shick shick shick shick, / Steady and secretive, his track is plain: The fallen bark is dust; the beams are bare.'*

80. *Heave to* – this meant that sails were set to counteract each other, so that the vessel stayed almost motionless in the water.

81. *Tittle* – this means a very tiny amount, a shred, an iota.

82. Williams writes *fish'd*, not fixed, perhaps meaning fetched.

83. *Durance* means duration.

84. Ball lightning?

85. A *Dover Court* must mean what Williams says, but the author can find no other reference.

86. A surmise is that *qats* means quarts or quarters in Scots dialect, and that it is an old term for fourths. As a man has four limbs, Owen had no use of his limbs, i.e. his legs.

87. Swinging a boom (*gybeing*) when changing course can lead to someone being hurt, or damage sail or rigging. *Gybes* came to mean unwelcome actions, and are the origin of today's jibes.

88. It was probably of no effect to throw out the flag as it could not be seen from the lagoon.

89. Williams writes the Indian word for dawn as *Sunrising*.

90. Williams writes 'massy' for *massive*.

1. These he calls *White Pokes* earlier on – either Great White Egrets or White Herons. *Poak* is an old name for a type of duck called a widgeon. However it is also a folk name for a poacher, so perhaps this refers to the heron being a poacher of fish.
2. A *churl* is a surly, bad-tempered person, unwilling to give ground.
3. *Fry* are the young of any fish, and here the word means children. The term '*small fry*' comes from this word, meaning persons of little significance (-fish only useful for throwing back into the water.)
4. *Primus* is a Latin name, meaning first. Williams says that he comes from *Ginny*, meaning Guinea. Williams writes that he comes from the *Ebo* country, which is inland Angola, but must have meant Ibo, as Quamino came from the coast of Guinea, now part of southern Nigeria. The English rarely picked up slaves from Angola – it was a Portuguese territory. Ebo Landing in Georgia is named after the Ebo, or Ibo (formerly Igbo), who walked into the sea in their chains rather than disembark as slaves. An Ibo called Olaudah Equiano bought his freedom in 1746 and wrote a wonderful autobiography. The Ibo were involved in a bitter civil war in Biafra from 1967-1970, when between 500,000 and 2,000,000 Ibo civilians died from starvation. Quamino's story of his wife being beaten and thrown overboard replicates what went on in Spanish colonial times. The precious ore and jewel deposits in Mexico, Peru and Colombia needed slaves to work in the mines. However, war, disease, overwork and suicide caused the native Indian population to plummet, in one of the worst genocides in history. In the Antilles alone the native population dropped from 300,000 in 1492 to 14,000 in 1514, and millions died on the South American mainland. On the eve of the Conquest, the Mexican population was 24 million. By the middle of the 16th century there were only 1 million Indians left. To save the Indians from extinction, a former explorer, Bartolome de Las Casa, proposed that the King of Spain introduced Negroes to save them from extinction, as '*the labour of one Negro is more valuable than that of four Indians*'. Thus in 1517, the first '*asiento*' was agreed, enabling 4000 Negroes to be imported into the West Indies over the following 8 years. By 1540, an estimated 30,000 men, women and children had been transplanted from Africa to Hispaniola alone. From the 1560's, Hawkins, Drake and others were trafficking slaves to Spanish America. Around the time that the Welsh pirate captain Howell Davis was trading on the Slave Coast with '*Old Crackers*' we have a merchant captain's bill for dealing with him. In 1721, the price for a male slave was 8 guns, a wicker bottle, 2 cases of spirits and 28 sheets of cloth. A woman cost 9 gallons of brandy, 6 iron bars, 2 pistols, a bag of powder and 2 strings of beads. A boy cost 7 large kettles, an iron bar, a length of cotton and 5 lengths of blue and white cloth. The merchant at the same time would have to pay the Royal Africa Company £15 for a man, and £12 for a woman, so their forts were always potentially full of money to attract pirates. The price was £60 for a man and £48 for a woman in the West Indies, partially because a 25% death rate on the Atlantic crossing was factored in. From this coast, the Royal Africa Company sold around 18000 slaves a year, and the private traders around 75000, but still could not meet demand. By 1820, Guinea slaves could be bought for a few beads, or $30 at the most, and sold in the Americas for $700, and American captains were said to make a million dollars from each voyage. The hold on slave ships was usually 6-7 feet high, and was divided halfway up by a platform to double the number of slaves that could be transported. Slaves were chained in pairs at the ankle, and allowed a space of around 6 feet in length, 1 foot 6 inches wide and 3 foot six inches high. They could not stand up in the dark, and lay in their own excrement and vomit. They were daily taken to the open air so that the slave decks could be hosed down. The stench was so bad that the ships could be smelt a mile away, and candles could not be lit in the foetid air on the slave decks. Only the strongest Africans survived the Atlantic Crossing. Much of the investment capital of the wonderful buildings in Bath came from the Bristol slave trade. The town, possibly the first in the world built solely for pleasure, relied on the arms and cloth sent to Africa, the slaves sent from Africa to the colonies, and the tobacco, rum, sugar and raw cotton that came from the colonies. This *triangular trade* in described in books by this author upon pirates and buccaneers. As a result, Beau Nash himself noted '*Bath is become a mere sink of profligacy and extortion. Every article of house-keeping is raised to an enormous price…I have known a Negro-driver, from Jamaica, pay overnight, to the master of one of the rooms, 65 guineas for tea and coffee to the company, and leave Bath the next morning, in such obscurity, that not one of the guests had the slightest idea of his person, or even made the least enquiry about his name.*' (From the entry upon Beau Nash in '*100 Great Welshmen*' by T.D. Breverton). Genocide

and the rape of the Spanish Main and South American mainland likewise financed the wonderful Spanish and Portuguese cathedrals. We gaze at these magnificent works without realising the horrors that paid for their construction. Even in the West Indies, the life of a good, strong slave was reckoned to be no more than 10 years in the brutal conditions of the sugar plantations. Thus, apart from new slaves for new plantations where the land had been cleared by the slaves, and for the tobacco plantations in America, there was also a 10% attrition and replacement rate each year to satisfy. Just to replace dead slaves created a demand in Jamaica for 10,000 slaves a year, and in the Leeward Islands for 6000, and for Barbados 4000 slaves. The surgeon John Atkins, on board the HMS *Swallow's* expedition to destroy the *'murderous Captain Bart Roberts'*, interestingly noted the differences in the sales of manufactured goods along the slave coast of north-east Africa: *'The windward and leeward parts of the coast are as opposite in their demands as is their distance. Iron bars, which are not asked for to leeward, are a substantial part of windward cargoes. Crystals, oranges, corals and brass-mounted cutlasses are almost peculiar to the Windward coast; as are brass pans from the Rio Sethos to Appollonia (the Gold Coast) and cowries... at Whydah, copper sheets and iron bars at Calabar; but arms, gunpowder, tallow, old sheets, Indian cottons ... and English spirits (whisky) are everywhere called for. Sealing wax and pipes are necessary in small quantities...'*

5. Willams variously spells the name Quameeno, Quammeno etc. A 'Negro' called Quammino was listed in the 1755 tax list at Granville County, North Carolina. In Belize there are islands named Quamino Cay and Quamina Cay, and also Quamino Creek on the mainland. In 1771 there were several slaves called Quamino at Cape Coast Castle in Guinea, including a 14 year-old cook, a 22 year-old male, and a 63 year-old hall servant named Quamino Dick. Quamino, A North Carolina runaway who spoke no English, may have escaped with success. Only 4 feet, 10 inches tall, this thirty-year-old African with filed teeth and country marks fled in August 1774, with "*a Collar about his Neck with Two Prongs, marked P.G. [Public Gaol], and an iron on each leg*." Ten months later Henry Young of Wilmington gave up hope that Quamino would be captured, and placed an advertisement in the *North Carolina Gazette*. New Englanders preferred to acquire young slaves and train them to their liking. Quamino was possibly an Akan name; but it is could be from West Africa in what today is Ghana. The name means *'a male child born on Saturday'*. Quamino's African name was a rare survivor in a culture which usually re-named slaves. Thus there were plenty of opportunities for Williams to have known of a slave called Quamino or the like. In Newport, Rhode Island, the Quamino family are buried in God's Little Acre on Farewell Street. In December 1778, an elderly black slave named Quamino Dolly led the British troops on a hidden path through a swamp, to allow them to take Savannah, Georgia, from the Americans – perhaps his exploit inspired Williams to use the name. Although Williams' sons fought and died for the Americans, Williams remained a loyalist.

6. Queen Anne (Williams writes Ann) died on August 1st, 1714. Born in 1655, she was the last of the Stuarts, and married Prince George of Denmark. Leaving no issue, she was succeeded by a minor princeling, George, from Hanover, a tiny state smaller than the Isle of Wight, beginning the Germanic line of the current royal family. As this is late 1778 in the book, Penrose is saying that Quamino's memory of the English queen was of at least 64 years ago. If Quamino married at 18 and was immediately captured by slavers, this would place him at 82 years of age. Bell and Penrose surmised that he was at least 80 years old.

7. A *thrumb mop* was used on ships, and was made up from ends of rope yarn, to swab the decks. *Thrumb*, or *thrum* mats were absorbent mats made of canvas and tufts of yarn, and used at sea. Thrum was the old name for the ends of weavers' threads.

8. Quamino's wife was young, and probably allowed more freedom than other slaves because she was being 'used' by the captain or crew. The literature upon slave rape, and slave revolts at sea, is quite horrifying.

9. Williams writes *'the Bridgtown.'* Bridgetown in Barbados is its only town, capital and major port. The most easterly of the Caribbean islands, it was settled by the British in 1627 after the Spanish and Caribs had wiped out the native Arawak Indians. Barbados was a British colony until recently. Of course, apart from some small French (Antilles) and Dutch possessions (Surinam), nearly all of the West Indies was controlled by the Spanish except England's Barbados and Jamaica.

10. Williams writes *'vamus'* – in Spanish *vamos* means *'we go'*.

11. A *picaroon* is a pirate, or one who plunders, a common term dating from the 17th century, from the Spanish *picaro*, meaning rogue or rascal.

12. Williams writes *St Jago da Cuba*, the original name of *Santiago*.
13. *Benneba* seems to have been a common name for female slaves in Jamaica. In 1765, in Jamaica, Isaac Teale wrote an ode called 'The Sable Venus' in 26 stanzas. It ends with his declaration of utter love to her, in different personae as she appears as a Phibba, Mimba, Cuba, Quasheba and Benneba, all names of female black slaves in Jamaica at this time, and found in Edward Long's 'The History of Jamaica' and Orlando Patterson's 'The Sociology of Slavery', an analysis of slavery in Jamaica. Williams may have picked the name Benneba from this poem as he was in Jamaica around this time, and Quasheba is mentioned shortly later in this text. (See footnote 16)
14. Slave stocks and Spanish stocks were different to those in England and America. In traditional Anglo-Saxon stocks one sat, or stood, in them.
15. *Hernan* was the Christian name of the genocidal explorer, Hernan Cortez. (Neil Young's record *Cortez Killer* is an excellent evocation). *Vera Cruz* was an extremely important centre for the Spanish bullion fleet, the outlet for the treasures of Mexico. All the major silver and gold production centres were all located far inland, and so were the cities where the silver and gold was stored, relatively safe from privateers and pirates. Since this main threat to Spain's interests was from the sea, only the ports from where cargoes were shipped to Spain, were considered as important enough to fortify. The silver produced in Nueva España (Mexico) was mined in Zacatecas, Guanajuato and other locations across the country. The Mexico City Mint produced *cob*-type coins, especially pieces of eight, which Penrose had discovered. It was shipped to Spain from the city of Vera Cruz, in the Gulf of Mexico. Silver was also mined in Potosi, Peru, and Peru Mint also produced cob-type coins, which were shipped to Panama for transport to Nombre de Diós and Porto Bello (Portobelo), waiting for transport to Spain. It would take over two months to ship the silver from the ports of Arica and Callao in Peru to Panama. Panama City had a poor harbour and a terrible climate. However it was located on the Pacific side of the Isthmus and there were roads across the Isthmus, passable by mule trains in some seasons. The silver and gold was stored in Panama until the Treasure Fleet was scheduled to arrive in Nombre de Diós or Porto Bello. Then it was transported by mule train, via the Las Cruces Trail to the fortified town and castle of Chagres, on the Chagres River. Two great convoys were organized to transport the treasure. The Tierra Firme fleet would visit Cartagena and Nombre de Diós. The Nueva España fleet would go to Vera Cruz. These fleets would depart from Spain, once a year, loaded with supplies needed by the colonists. These trips were scheduled to take the maximum advantage of winds, currents, and to avoid the hurricane season. Each fleet travelled separately, just in case they were lost to pirates or storms, so that the Spanish Crown would not lose everything. The America-bound fleets first sailed to the Canary Islands to take on supplies. From there, they sailed west, using the trade winds. The fleet bound to Nueva España left during the spring and made about four knots, and took nearly two months to reach Vera Cruz. When the officials at Mexico City learned that the fleet was arriving in Vera Cruz, they would transport all of the silver by wagons to Vera Cruz. When the fleet arrived, there would be a large fair, where the Spanish merchants that were part of the fleet, would trade their goods for silver. These fairs generally lasted from one to two months. After the fair was over, all of the silver was loaded on the ships for the return trip to Spain. For the first part of the journey back to Spain, because of the winds and currents, the flota sailed along the coast of the Gulf of Mexico, until it reached the safety of Havana in Cuba. The fleet that was bound to Tierra Firme, left Spain in the late summer. It sailed from Sevilla to Cartagena. This trip took from 4 to 6 weeks and had the job of picking up the gold and silver from the southern colonies. When the fleet arrived in Cartagena, word was sent to Panama City advising officials, to start sending the treasure, by road and riverboats, over the Kings Highway to Nombre de Diós. The silver from Peru was sent to Panama City, on the South Sea Fleet. This fleet was smaller and not as heavily armed as the Atlantic Fleet. This was because the Spanish believed that it was much more difficult for pirates to transverse the Straits of Magellan, and prey on the South Sea Fleet. It would take about two months to move the silver from the ports of Arica (Chile) and Callao (Peru) to Panama, for storage. Nombre de Diós, like Vera Cruz, was very unhealthy forcing the inhabitants to abandon the cities, and only came to life when the treasure fleets, came to port. Once the Fleet arrived, there was great fair, just like in Vera Cruz, for the merchants to exchange silver and gold for merchandise from Europe. When the Fleet was fully loaded with treasure, it sailed to Havana, to begin its trip across the Atlantic to Spain. The Spanish used the town of Nombre de Diós as their shipping port, until 1596, when they switched to Porto Bello. Porto Bello had a much better port,

and it was easy to defend, unlike Nombre de Diós.

16. Quasheba – see footnote 13. The strong female slave was often caricatured in Jamaican publications in the early nineteenth century with a character named '*Quasheba*' who was known as an independent, outspoken troublemaker. '*The Sable Venus*', for example, referred to the '*pleasure*' and '*raptures*' the poet would seek in '*gentle Phibia…artful Benneba…wanton Mimba…sprightly Cuba…or grave and sober Quasheba I still shall find thee out*'. This unsubtle threat to rape the least willing '*Sable Queen*' alludes to her spirit of resistance, and the name was adopted to mean an unwilling, recalcitrant female slave.

17. It would be possible to sail from Cuba to the Miskito Coast in 5 days.

18. *Poppanack* is possibly papaya wood. However, common in the palm swamps is *poponjoche (pachira aquatica)*, which is variously described as a fruit tree and a palm, and also ascribed to the genus *huberodenrum alleni*.

19. *Huzza* was the 18th century equivalent of, and replaced by, 'Hooray!' It meant a shout of joy, a cheer, a hurrah.

20. *Campeche*, called by Williams and British privateers of the time *Campechy*, is the most thoroughly restored colonial city in Mexico, in the Yucatan, and was plagued by pirates and privateers.

21. Williams writes *Valdes*. Valdez is an extremely common name in the Yucatan.

22. Even today this author has to say on international travel that he is English, as few people seem to know Wales or the Welsh. This Celtic race of Britons was pushed out to Wales by the Angles and Saxons from Germany (the English) in the 5th to 7th centuries. The French Normans then overcame the English in 1066-1067, but the Normans did not control full mastery of Wales, with its own language, until the failure of the War of Owain Glyndŵr around 1415. 70 years later a largely Welsh army, headed by a Welshman, Henry Tudor, defeated Richard III and gave Britain its greatest line of kings and queens, the Tudors. Wales still has its own language, one of the oldest in the world, and some measure of devolved political power.

23. *Finn MacCoul* (Fionc mac Cumhail) is a legendary Irish warrior, the greatest leader of the Fianna, the 4th century military elite in Leinster.

24. This phrase reminds one of the great Yogi Bear's '*Yabba Dabba Doo*,' and may have been an Irish saying. Teddy would have sounded like *Tady* in an Irish dialect. Lort was on board a Spanish ship, which was not unusual. After the ceasing of hostilities between France, Britain and Spain in 1763, there were thousands of former naval men seeking berths on ships. It caused a surge in piracy, as unemployed sailors could not find any other work.

25. Lewellin, properly spelt LLewelyn or LLywelyn in Welsh, is a notoriously difficult name to say for other nationalities, and would have been abbreviated to Lew, or Welly or somesuch. 'LL' is a consonant, so both letters are capitalised in Welsh. The 1815 posthumous publication, edited by Thomas Eagles, names the protagonist Llewellin, but the original manuscript in the Lilly Library has *Lewellin*.

26. The *Oxford* was Henry Morgan's flagship, accidentally blown up in 1669. There seems to have been no '*Flying Oxford*'. HMS *Oxford* was a 4th rate ship of the line, a man of war with 50 guns built by Bailie of Bristol in 1674. At some time it patrolled the James River in Virginia. '*Official Dockyard models*' or '*Admiralty models*' were made of such expensive ships, to demonstrate the design and construction details before they were commissioned. The model of the *Oxford* was given by the Napier family to the city of Glasgow, and is now in its transport museum. It was enlarged in 1702 at Deptford and rebuilt in 1727 at Portsmouth, so will have been a famous ship in Williams' time.

27. There was an Edward (Teddy) Lort born in 1785 in Virginia, the son of William Lort of Birmingham, Warwickshire, but Penrose's Lort was Irish – see footnotes 24, 28 and 29. The Lort family occupied Stackpoole Court in Pembrokeshire until 1754.

28. '*Daddle*' obviously means hand, but no reference can be found to its source. It might be a word-play upon 'paddle.'

29. Williams writes '*agrah*', which seems to mean '*begorrah*.'

30. '*Run up the cable*' means to hoist up the anchor cable. The schooner was obviously towing Penrose's boat.

31. Williams writes '*gabb*', and here it means unnecessary talking. *Gab* usually means light, informal conversation, and one can be blessed with '*the gift of the gab.*'

32. *Proved* means tested, and shown to be of quality.

33. The use of *crater* for alcohol confirms Lort to be Irish or Scots – it is an old dialect word for whisky – see footnotes 24, 27, 28 and 29. He begins a sentence here with *'sure'*, a common Irish prefix in conversation, but then mentions *'ould acquaintance.'* *'Should auld acquaintance be forgot'* is the first line of the Scots song *'Auld Lang Syne.'*

34. *'Making his leg to the captain'* sounds as if Lort is making a sort of curtsey or bow to interrupt the conversation. As a *'foremast man'* he would have been a normal seaman, with responsibility for the rigging on the foremast. We next find that he is definitely from Ireland, in Penrose's acceptance of sharing grog.

35. *Grog* was alcohol, usually Jamaica rum, mentioned in earlier footnotes.

36. *'Ads Flesh'* is the same as *Odds Flesh*, a mild curse adapted from *'God's Flesh'*, much like *God Blind Me* was ameliorated to *Cor Blimey*, and *God's truth* to *strewth*.

37. The island of *Surinam* was a Dutch colony, notable for trading across the West Indies and with Europe.

38. Williams writes *'speak.'*

39. Owen was born soon in September 1752.

40. *Edification* means enlightenment, receiving moral instruction, in this context.

41. *'White and Red'* is an engaging way of expressing the pink skin of 'white' people.

42. A *poleacre* was a fast ship with three masts, with no tops or cross-trees, usually found in the Mediterranean, and rarely in the Caribbean. Williams calls it a *polacre*. Strangely, a fast ship was sent from Spain to the New World in 1756 on a special mission. Hernan(do) Cortez (Cortes) had conquered the Aztecs and Mexico in 1519. Cortez had looted a huge emerald of 964 carats in cut shape, meant as a wedding gift for his second wife, Dona Juana de Zuniga. Queen Isabella of Portugal, the wife of Emperor Charles V, desperately wanted the jewel. A ship was sent shortly before his death to retrieve it for the crown, but was wrecked in 1757. The emerald has since been found, along with carved Aztec crystal skulls and 25,000 carats of cut emeralds. There is also gold and silver jewellery, and the emerald has been valued at $20 million. It is a strange coincidence with Penrose's sunken ship, the *Isabella*, and this other shipwreck of 13 years previously. Incidentally, this is the first instance of a *'message in a bottle'* that this author can find. The *Isabella Emerald* is the largest ever discovered, worth 20 million dollars.

43. The choice of Lopez as a surname for this captain is intriguing. Because of persecution, the Portuguese Jewish family of Lopez escaped to Newport, Rhode Island. Moses Lopez was naturalised in New York in 1741, but Newport refused Aaron Lopez nationality, and he obtained it in Massachusetts. Aaron Lopez concentrated on the slave trade from 1764, bringing across at least one ship a year, and from 1767 focussed on the Jamaica trade, sending his son Moses to work there. He used the *Cleopatra* as his slave ship. He became Newport's leading merchant, buying molasses in the West Indies to make rum for Newport, to export to Africa in exchange for slaves, which he then exchanged in Jamaica for molasses. By 1775 he was sending at least 4 slave ships to Africa each year. At the outbreak of the Revolutionary War, he was the pre-eminent merchant in all of New England, and would have been known to Williams, developing Newport for almost 30 years and eventually owning 30 transatlantic vessels and many more coastal ships. It is an imperfect lesson to us all that someone who is chased by the Inquisition for not being 'perfect', should follow their example and enrich his family by persecuting his 'inferiors.'

44. *'God wat'* is an old expression, probably coming from *God knows (what)*, or from the Dutch/German.

45. The *Old Men* are the village elders, or council. Williams did not record the 5th Indian's name. Rama villages consisted of two or three large oval or rectangular houses, with palm thatched roofs. Houses often had no walls or floors, and they lived in multiple-generation extended family groups known as *kwima* or *kwinbalut*.

46. This is possibly the only really racist remark of Penrose in the book. However, we must remember that there were rare mixed marriages of white men and Indian women, and many more 'forced' or 'paid' relationships, but for a white woman to marry or liase with an Indian or Negro was absolutely unheard of at this time. Only in the latter half of the 20th century were mixed relationships generally accepted as normal in American and European society.

47. To make a landing, i.e. *touch the shore*

48. Williams writes *'Oh, let the whole be to me,'* etc.

49. Meaning that Owen had given up his dreams of going to Jamaica to search for a wife.

50. Meaning at ease, content.
51. These grampuses (spelt *grampuss's* by Williams) are probably young Humpbacks, migrating north with their mothers in spring.
52. Williams writes '*stuff*' instead of rope.
53. Williams writes *chapfallen*, which means the same as crestfallen, to be brought low in spirit, dejected and downcast. It has a 16th century origin of '*chops*' meaning jaw, and fallen, similar to today when one's *jaw drops* on hearing bad news.
54. To *bogue* is to fall off a wind in nautical terms, and a *bogue* is a boat which is difficult therefore to handle.
55. It is difficult to ascertain when the 25th year began – Penrose certainly seems to have been affected by Bell's death.
56. Possibly Penrose means that he will be the only white man in the extended family – he is still missing the company of Bell and Somer.

Notes to Book I Chapter IX

1. The use of *Bashada* as a name is interesting – there seems to be no Central American equivalent, but there is a tribe of 3000 Bashada still living in Ethiopia, in the Omo Valley near Kenya. It has thus far been difficult to find the names that Williams assigns to his Indians in the Rama or Sumu or Miskito languages.
2. Leadership of the family would pass to Owen.
3. Williams writes '*his wife*' not '*my mother*', but I assume he is referring to Penrose's wife, who was not Owen's real mother, but accepted by him as such. Otherwise the sentence reads as if Owen is leading the procession with Harry's wife.

Notes to Book I Chapter X

1. This chapter is written in a slightly larger handwriting, and the page has been creased and folded as if to post it, being worn through in one place. It is far more damaged on the periphery than the rest of the Journal. It seems that it has been added at a later date. The preceding page is only two-thirds full, the only page in the *Journal* with any blank space on it.
2. There was a Captain A. Smith and a Captain John Smith who were noted in the 1776 Lloyd's Register as sailing brigs in the Caribbean, trading between New England and Bermuda, Tobago and other islands. In 1774 and 1777, Thomas Smith captained the '*Jamaica Packet*' (a brig of 80 tons built in Massachussets in 1772, and registered at Kirkcaldy, Scotland) around Jamaica. It featured in a 1774 book, '*The Journal of a Lady of Quality – The Voyage to the West Indies.*' Upon April 8th, 1767, an unnamed ship under another Captain Smith was shipwrecked off Sandy Hook, New Jersey on its way to St Kitts. In 1794, a French privateer captured Captain Smith's '*Friends*' en route from Jamaica to North Carolina, and in 1797 another Captain Smith was captured en route from St Vincents to New York. Thus it is impossible to pin down this Captain Smith.
3. Williams writes, as usual, '*the Havannah*'.
4. Here, Williams means the Spanish mainland of Central and South America.
5. *Cedar* wood repels moths and insects and so was used for storing papers and clothes.
6. *Charleston* is spelt in its original form as *Charlestown*, (from King Charles' Town) in South Carolina, a wonderful and evocative city.
7. Captain Stewart Dean (1748-1836) was Albany, New York's most famous navigator. His voyage from Albany to China and back during the mid-1780s represents a pioneering effort to connect the emerging city of Albany with the outside world. In 1771, he captained the sloop *Beaver* to the West Indies with flour and timber. With the outbreak of the Revolutionary War, Dean offered his services to the American cause and was commissioned as a privateer with the *Beaver* in June 1776. During the next three years, he cruised the Caribbean Atlantic - taking prizes and loading cargoes to aid the American war effort. In January 1782, he had the privateer schooner *Nimrod* built in Philadelphia, which he took to the West Indies, but he was captured by the British at St Kitts, taken to Antigua and later released. In 1784 Dean began to build a new sloop, the *Experiment*, and left Albany on the first leg of a voyage to China. By the summer of 1787, Dean was back in Albany, re-establishing his

merchant business and took several more voyages abroad. In 1833, he was granted a pension for his services during the American Revolution. He died in New York in 1836.

Notes to Book II Introduction

1. William Dunlap called Benjamin West's effect on American art 'incalculable' (History of the Rise and Progress of the Arts of Design of the United States, 1834). In 1939, James Flexner stated that West was 'incontrovertibly the father of American painting.' In 1760, West left America for Europe, and after touring Italy spent 57 years in England, becoming known as the 'American Raphael'. Upon seeing his 'Death of Wolfe', George III allowed West to call himself 'Historical Painter to the King', and he became the second President of the Royal Academy after Reynolds' death in 1792. From Susan Wadsworth's article we read: 'The artist's systematic reflection on his early years began not later than 1805, at the height of his troubles with the Royal Academy, after a serendipitous encounter with a manuscript of castaway adventure. The author was William Williams, a sailor from Bristol who may have based the substantially fictional account on his own youthful experience of Central America. By the late 1740's, Williams had moved to Philadelphia, where he became an artist – and Benjamin West's first instructor. "Had it not been for him," West avowed in 1805, "I should never have been a painter." The owner of the manuscript, hoping to see it published, asked West to write up his recollections of Williams (who died in 1791). The resulting letter of 1810, the most detailed primary source for the fascinating Williams, is also a key document in the life of West, who seized the opportunity to re-imagine his own beginnings. Williams' novel, finally published in 1815 as The Journal of Llewellyn (sic) Penrose, a Seaman, bore a dedication to West and excerpted extensively from his letter in the preface. He was likely released to do so, as well, by the death in 1815 of his American colleague Copley, a constant professional irritant and rival in London and the one man who could and would have challenged West's American story. With significant encouragement from Galt, West authorized a complete tactical reversal of his insistent claims of Englishness. The biography of 1816 presented a remarkable, and at the time quite unfamiliar, account of the famous British painter's formative years – the story of the American West.' An interesting amendment to his story was made concerning Williams. Formerly Williams had been credited with showing West how to make a camera obscura, but in Galt's work, West claimed to have invented it himself.

2. Source: Williams Family of Craven County website information from Jerome Williams 'My 3x great Grandfather was William Joseph Williams 1759-1823 He lived his last years in New Bern and is buried in Cedar Grove Cemetery. William Joseph Williams came to New Bern from Charleston, S.C. around 1804. He'd been a regular visitor to New Bern for about 25 years before that. He was born in New York City the Son of William Williams 1727-1791 (Artist, Musician, Author of the first American novel, "Penrose", friend of Benjamin Franklin, tutor of Benjamin West, etc.) and Mary Mare - Sister of John Mare, Jr. 1738-1804, (Artist, Merchant, moved to Edenton, member of first North Carolina Cabinet with Governor Caswell, co-founder of UNC, organised NC Masons, etc.) Mare served as a Lieutenant in the British Army occupying New York City and during that time Williams taught Art (to among others William Dunlap, author of "the Rise of the Arts, etc. in America" 1826). Thereafter Williams painted the portraits of George Washington (to whom he was recommended by his friend and patron, Richard Henry "Light Horse Harry" Lee, who was Governor of Virginia at the time), John Adams, Thomas Jefferson and other Revolutionary figures. (Washington, Adams and Jefferson were painted at Philadelphia when they were President, Vice-President and Secretary of State respectively). His paintings are partially listed in SIRIS at the Smithsonian and are found in private collections and in museums including the Pennsylvania Academy of Fine Arts, The Adams National Historic Site, The Rockefeller Museum at Williamsburg, The DuPont Museum at Winterthur and The Museum of Southern Decorative Arts at Old Salem. He lived in Philadelphia, Georgetown and Charleston before settling in New Bern. While living in New Bern (roughly 1804-1823) he returned to New York for a while and served as a Quartermaster Officer in the United States Sea-Fensibles during the War of 1812. At this time, he was nearly blind. His Son, Joseph Augustus Williams was a New Bern Merchant. His son, David published a Newspaper in New Bern. His painting of the "Crucifixion" hangs over the altar at Old St. Pauls Roman Catholic Church in New Bern. The painting was gifted to the Church by my family and was recently restored by the Conservators of the North Carolina Museum of Art. He had been an Episcopal Clergyman and converted to Roman Catholicism. He was instrumental in founding St. Pauls. Joseph Augustus Williams took his family to Charlotte during the Union bombardment of New Bern in the Spring of 1862...'

As regards William Joseph Williams, the son of our William Williams, he was around 19 when he started giving art lessons to William Dunlap (1766-1839). These lessons had been arranged by Dunlap's father, and Dunlap described Williams as 'the third best painter in New York.' He said that Williams had been conscripted by the British so was serving in a Loyalist unit at this time. Also, Williams was described as a drunkard, and an unreliable teacher, and had been allowed to live with his 'mother' at the family home on Mott Street, Lower Manhattan. Rather than his mother, this could have been his sister Mary. Williams had been conscripted when the English took New York, which they held until 1783, and he painted several Loyalist officers in these years. His mother's brother, John Mare, supported the Revolution. Williams joined his uncle John Mare in 1783, and subsequently painted Washington, Adams and Jefferson when they were in government in Philadelphia. Dunlap later went to England and studied under Benjamin West. When William Joseph Williams was serving as a quartermaster in the Sea Fensibles in 1812, Dunlap met him again, and Williams claimed to be 'the best painter in America'. Williams was back in New York with his family, living on Spring Street, Manhattan at this time. He made an income from painting miniatures, and inspired many to paint, including the Lake Sisters.

William Dunlap, in his 'History of the Rise and Progress of the Arts of Design in the United States' of 1834 noted of our William Williams that 'This gentleman would have escaped our notice, but that Benjamin West remembered him with gratitude, as the man who put into his hand, when a boy, the first books he had ever read on the subject of painting, and showed him, in specimens from his own pencil, the first oil pictures he had seen. Mr Williams was an Englishman, and was employed by the inhabitants of Penn's city, in 1746-47, and perhaps after. That he sought knowledge in his art we know, or he would not have lent to the boy, West, the works of Fresnoy (of course the translation) and of Richardson; of his attainments as exemplified in his pictures, we know nothing. The information that Benjamin West received from his conversation, his book and his paintings, entitles him to a place among those who assisted in forwarding the progress of art in our country.'

One of the problems of researching Americans of this time is that are just too many 'William Williams'. A William Williams was born around 1705 and married Gwen Foulke of Gwynedd Twp, Philadelphia County, Pennsylvania, the daughter of Welsh immigrants. William and Gwen had 11 children, including a William and a Gwen, all born in Philadelphia, and their daughter Susannah married another Welshman Evan Meredith. Pennsylvania was absolutely full of Welsh immigrants at this time. A notable William Williams signed the Declaration of Independence. Back in Bristol, if Dickason's 'Williams' had remained there, in his time a Captain William Williams was named as a resident, along with a William Williams (cooper) in 1775. In 1768 the sloop Relief sailed from Bristol for Guadeloupe with William Williams as captain. In 1754-1755 the Carnation tavern in Old King Street, Bristol was run by yet another William Williams.

3. Cayo Pigeon, Cayo Pingeon or Isla de Paloma is c. 30 metres high and c. 400 metres long, crescent-shaped, with a white sandy beach and a water supply. The much smaller Soup Cay (Cayo Soup or Cayo Sopa or White Rock) can be seen from its central hill. Measuring 7.2 acres, Pigeon Island is 11 degrees 47 minutes north and 83 degrees 40 minutes west. It is around 15 miles south of Bluefields, or 45 minutes by motorboat, and two miles from the mainland. There are at least two deer on it. A few miles north is Isla de Guano (5 acres) and a few miles south is Cayo Franceses (Frenchman's Island). All of these Nicaraguan islands were sold to Americans, for around a quarter of a million dollars each, from 2003 to 2005.

Notes to Book II - Chapter I - The Story of the Author

1. Mary Mare was the sister of the painter John Mare, who was born in 1738 and died in1804. John Mare was born in New York City, and worked as a portraitist in Albany in 1759, and then in New York from 1760 to 1772 painting many prominent citizens, and a portrait of George III for the city. A prominent Freemason and politician, there are 13 extant canvases by him, out of the 20 documented.

2. David Hall (1717-1772) was born in Scotland and entered business in printing with Benjamin Franklin in 1747-48 in Philadelphia. As Franklin and Hall, they printed Pennsylvania bills of credit, amongst other items. In 1765, Franklin sold out to Hall. On David Hall's death, his sons David (junior) and William merged with the printer William Sellers to form the printer Hall and Sellers.

3. Jacob Fox was born in 1750 in Philadelphia, the son of Philip Fuchs and Amelia Catherine (Rosenbaum?) who had emigrated from Germany three months previously. He lived with his parents and later in Bucks County. With his father he is said to have fought for the Revolutionaries, and he married Martha Huddleston (born 1756) whose parents owned a nearby farm in Bucks County. In the early 1780's they moved to North Carolina and Fox died in 1834. There was also a Jacob Fox (or Fuchs) who served in the Pennsylvania Germans of von Heer's Provost Corps, policing the American Continental Army. He was from Reading, Pennsylvania, and was recorded as being in Shenandoah County, Virginia, in 1825. This is probably the same Jacob Fox. There was another Jacob Fox, who died in Philadelphia in 1785, and had immigrated around 1740. He farmed at Bedminster Twp in Bucks County.

4. John Wiley may have been of Scottish origin, with his surname spelt variously as Wyley, Wylie and Wilie.

5. The 1775? portrait of young Stephen Crossfield holding a racquet and battledore shuttlecock may be the first picture of anyone with badminton equipment. He was the son of Stephen Crossfield the shipwright, who married Hannah Disbrow in 1778 after the death of his wife Mary. With fellow shipwright Joseph Totten, Stephen Crossfield senior negotiated the purchase of 1,150,000 acres from the Mohawk Indians in 1771, on behalf of George III. The land around the Central Andirondacks is now in New York State. Intriguingly, William Willams had painted 'a small whole length of William Williams Junr painter', his son when he was a teenager and an aspiring painter. When Williams had returned to Britain, his 20-year-old son set up in business next to a Joseph Totten. Williams Junior placed an advertisement in the *Royal Gazette* in New York: '*William Williams, Portrait Painter, Acquaints the Ladies and Gentlemen, that he has taken a room, at Mr Greshwold's, No. 163, Queen Street, next door to Mr. Joseph Totten's, where he carries on the business of Portrait Painting in all its branches, on the most reasonable terms.*' This was in 1784. In 1767 Joseph Totten, a ships' carpenter was the executor of the rigger James Lovey's will in New York. The Joseph Totten who purchased land with Crossfield appears to have become a wealthy Loyalist merchant, who as a refugee bought Bailey House in Annapolis Royal, Nova Scotia in 1793, moving there with his wife, six children and four slaves.

6. This is America's **first seascape**, predating Copley, who previously held that claim. Copley knew Williams, and was much younger than him. Another famous portrait was of Benjamin Lay, the Quaker reformer and abolitionist (1681-1759), and a friend of Benjamin Franklin.

7. LLywelyn was the name of the last of the princes of Gwynedd, murdered in an entrapment by the Mortimer family and Gruffudd ap Gwenwynwyn. LL is a single letter in Welsh, and thus should be doubly capitalised.

8. Hunter and the *Harrington* might hold the key to Williams' early life. The 490-ton *Harrington* was in the service of the East India Company for 4 voyages from 1732-1741, but it is not known if she was built before this date. She was certainly in service after 1741, in which case it is feasible that Williams served on her from 1741, after she was assumedly re-decked to cope with carrying slaves across the Atlantic. Williams could then be 14 and born in 1727. A Captain Hunter was in charge of the *General Wolfe* carrying Irish immigrants from Londonderry to Hampton Road in 1772. A Captain Hunter was also involved in the early exploration of Australia, writing 'Voyage to Botany Bay', published 1793. A James Hunter owned a counting house, plantation and properties in Stafford, Virginia in 1785. It is not known if any of these are related to our Captain/Colonel Hunter.

9. Slave ships were terrible places to be, with a short life expectancy for the crew. (see note 58 to Book 1, Chapter VI).
Even in the West Indies, the life of a good, strong slave, was reckoned to be no more than 10 years in the brutal conditions of the sugar plantations. Thus, apart from new slaves for new plantations where the land had been cleared by the slaves, and for the tobacco plantations in America, there was also a 10% attrition and replacement rate each year to satisfy. Just to replace dead slaves created a demand in Jamaica for 10,000 slaves a year, and in the Leeward Islands for 6000, and for Barbados 4000 slaves.
The surgeon John Atkins, on board the HMS *Swallow's* expedition to destroy the '*murderous Captain Bart Roberts*', interestingly noted the differences in the sales of manufactured goods along the slave coast of north-east Africa: '*The windward and leeward parts of the coast are as opposite in their demands as is their distance. Iron bars which are not asked for to leeward are a substantial part of windward cargoes.*

Crystals, oranges, corals and brass-mounted cutlasses are almost peculiar to the Windward coast; as are brass pans from the Rio Sethos to Appollonia (the Gold Coast) and cowries... at Whydah, copper sheets and iron bars at Calabar; but arms, gunpowder, tallow, old sheets, Indian cottons ... and English spirits (whisky) are everywhere called for. Sealing wax and pipes are necessary in small quantities...'

10. *'David Douglass and the Beginnings of American Theatre Architecture'* – Brooks McNamara, *Winterthur Portfolio 3* (1967).

11. It may well be that Williams' wife died in Jamaica, when travelling with him and her son and perhaps her two step-sons.

12. William Denning is noted in the *New York City Directory* of 1796 as an original underwriter for the New York Insurance Company. He lived from 1740-1719, and owned a house on Wall Street which still exists. A landowner, the town of Denning, in Ulster County, New York, is named after him. There is a 1770 Colonial-style 'William Dennings House' in Salisbury Mills, New York.

13. Dickason refers us to *History of Philadelphia 1609-1884*, J Thomas Scharf and Thompson Westcott, 1884. Also to the *Encyclopaedia of Philadelphia*, Joseph Jackson, 1933.

14. A *limner* is an 18th century term for a painter or drawer of portraits, a portraitist.

15. Benjamin Condy was a navigational instrument maker in Philadelphia. He was a witness to the will of John Hopkins, a Philadelphia merchant in 1754. He was an executor of the will of David James Dove in 1769, and was a witness to the will of Joseph Graisbury, a tailor in 1783. Graisbury died in 1796 and Condy in 1798. Condy was making instruments as early as 1763, and seems to have finished working in 1792. One of his signed octants is in the Smithsonian, dated 1778. In September 1776, the Pennsylvania Council of Safety ordered a Mr Nesbitt to pay Condy £2 5s for a spy-glass delivered to a Lieutenant Christee.

16. The date Penrose was marooned in the Journal was the same year that Williams seems to have arrived in Philadelphia, 1747. In the Journal, Williams states that he left home at the age of 19, but surely he went to sea in real life before this age, as West said that *'he had been put to the sea when young.'*

Notes to Book II Part III - The Beggar's Legacy:

1. Behind St Peter's Church was a timbered, gabled mansion called St Peter's Hospital, which was destroyed in the Blitz in 1940. For a short time part of the building was the Bristol Mint, but its main claim to fame was as the paupers' workhouse, first known as the Mint Workhouse and then as St Peter's Hospital. The whole of this blitzed area was transformed into Castle Park. St Peter's would have been a terrible place for Williams to end his days, so he was lucky that Eagles intervened to find him a home in the almshouses. A 1795 account informs us: *'The Poor are managed by the Corporation of the Poor, and are partly supported in a Workhouse called St Peter's Hospital, and partly by a parish allowance at home. The number of inmates is 350, of whom 63 are in a pest house belonging to the Workhouse. In 1794 the total was 390. The only work at present is picking oakum by which very little is earned. A few years ago a factory for spinning wool was set up, but after 3 years £600 was lost, and it was discontinued. The master says that the house was not built with a view to its present use and is therefore not one of the most convenient. There are 12 or 15 beds, principally of flocks, in each apartment, for which reason probably, and on account of the number of old and diseased persons in it, the house is infested with vermin, particularly bugs. To a visitor there appears on the whole to be a want of cleanliness. Bill of fare: Breakfast—Sunday, Monday, Tuesday, Thursday, water gruel; Wednesday, Friday, broth; Saturday, gruel. Dinner—Sunday, soup made of bullocks' head; Monday, Friday, pease soup; Tuesday, Thursday, meat and potatoes; Wednesday, Saturday, bread and cheese. Supper—every day, bread and cheese. 1lb. of meat and the same quantity of bread are allowed to each person on meat days. On Sundays, Wednesdays and Saturdays, 6oz. of cheese are allowed for the two meals, and on other days 3oz. The Poor eat their victuals in their lodging rooms. The master of the Workhouse says 1,010 poor persons are on the out-pay bill, but he does not know what they receive.'*

2. *Eleemosynary* means dependent on charity.

3. In 1553 the Merchant Venturers took over the almshouse in Marsh Street, and the present building was built in King Street in 1696 by the Merchant Venturers as the Merchants' Almshouse, for sick and elderly sailors. It now provides sheltered housing for seven residents.

4. Queen Anne (born 1655) reigned from 1702-1714, dying aged 49.

5.   *Lineaments* are distinctive shapes, contour or lines, especially of the face, distinctive features.
6.   The (c.1778) painting of *The Battle of La Hogue* is in the National Gallery of Art, Washington DC, and from the gallery's literature we read: '*Benjamin West sailed from colonial Philadelphia to Rome in 1760. Visiting London three years later, the American artist decided to stay in England, where he soon became principal history painter to King George III. A London newspaper's review of the 1780 Royal Academy exhibition stated that The Battle of La Hogue "exceeds all that ever came from Mr. West's pencil." In 1692, Louis XIV of France had mounted an ill-fated attempt to restore James II, a fellow Catholic, to the throne of England. In response, Britain and her Protestant allies, the Dutch, massed their fleets and engaged the enemy for five days off the northern French coast near La Hogue. Nine decades later, West employed much artistic license to devise this patriotic scene that is almost entirely propaganda. Standing in a boat at the left, for instance, Vice Admiral George Rooke embodies heroic command with his raised sword. Yet he undoubtedly gave orders far from the thick of battle. At the right, a Frenchman deserts his craft with its fleur-de-lis motif. Having lost his wig, he becomes an object of ridicule. West parted the foreground's thick smoke to reveal the French flagship beached in the center distance. Actually sunk a few days before this encounter, the Royal Sun is here imaginatively refloated — only to be run against the cliffs so that West might better symbolize the French defeat.*'
7.   Benjamin West (1738-1820), when aged 20 had become a portraitist in New York City. In 1760 he sailed to Italy to study, and completed his first major work there. One of the leading exponents of Neo-Classicism, West then went to London in 1763.
8.   The founder of the family of Penroses in America was Bartholomew Penrose, who came to Philadelphia in the latter part of the 17th century, and with his brother James became a leading ship builder in William Penn's colony, William Penn being a partner in the enterprise. His son, Thomas Penrose, was born in 1709 and by his wife, Sarah Coats, became the father of James Penrose, born Feb. 3, 1737. This James Penrose married Sarah Biddle on March 15, 1766, and became the father of the Hon. Clement Biddle Penrose. The shipyard founded by Bartholomew Penrose (1674-1711) was one of the most important in Philadelphia. His family and Penn's family had been friends in England. By the time Penrose was 24 years old he wanted to go to Pennsylvania. Not only had he inherited sufficient money to be certain that the enterprise would be a successful one, but he also had investors such as William Penn Jr., James Logan (secretary to Penn), and William Trent. Penrose was a capable man who started acquiring land on the waterfront. It is likely at first that he built very small boats and started acquiring a stock of oak and other special lumber needed in his yard. The first ship of major importance was launched on 4 May 1707. In spite of the fact that Bartholomew Penrose died when he was only thirty-six, he started a dynasty of Penrose shipbuilders who continued for the next 200 years as one of the most outstanding in the field. The cost factor has a great deal to do with the huge success of the Philadelphia shipyards. A ship could be built in America for about $24 per ton, while such a ship could not be built anywhere in Europe for less than $60 per ton. This was partially due to the fact that the oak in America was not only superior to that in Europe, it was also much more plentiful. There were not many virgin forests left in Europe at this time. One third of the total tonnage of Great Britain was of colonial origin. From the time of the arrival of William Penn in 1682 until the start of the Revolution in 1776, more than 900 major ships were built in the Delaware River yards. Joshua Humphreys, who became known as the '*Father of the American Navy*' was born in 1751 and moved with his parents to Philadelphia in 1765. He was apprenticed to the shipbuilder Jonathan Penrose, who was described as "*a gentleman of the highest respectability.*" Humphreys had not served his full term when Penrose died, but he knew the business of ship construction so well that the widow turned to him as the best man available to complete a ship on the stocks. In 1785, Thomas and Samuel Penrose were operating as shipbuilders on Water Street, between Almond and Catharine Street.
9.   According to Dickason, Williams was born in 1727 and therefore only 20 when he first met West in 1747. If we accept an alternative Williams born in 1710, not 1727, this would fit far more easily with the recollections of West, John Eagles and the evidence of the *Self-Portrait* and the old man in West's *The Battle of La Hogue.*
10. The full text of this letter is shown below in the letter to Thomas Eagles dated October 10, 1810.
11. In the sense to *own* up to poverty, to admit it.
12. *Maga* here seems to mean Blackwells Magazine, for which he was the art critic.
13. *Mr Bumble* was the pompous, hypocritical beadle in '*Oliver Twist*' professing to be a Christian but the

exact opposite.

14. James Usher (1581-1656) was the Archbishop of Armagh and Primate of Ireland who famously published the chronology of Creation dating from 4004BC. There are many versions of this event, and C.H. Spurgeon writes in *'Christ's New Commandment'*:

    'A new commandment I give unto you, that ye love one another; as I have loved you, that ye also love one another. By this shall all men know that ye are My disciples, if ye have love one to another."—John xiii. 34, 35

    Many of you, I do not doubt have heard the story of Archbishop Usher and Mr. Rutherford; It is so appropriate to this subject that I cannot but help telling it again. The archbishop had heard of the wondrous power of Rutherford's devotion, and of the singular beauty of the arrangement of his household, and he wished to witness it himself; but he could not tell how to do so until it occurred to him that he might disguise himself as a poor traveler. Accordingly, at nightfall, he knocked at the door of Rutherford's house, and was received by Mrs. Rutherford. He asked if he could find lodgings there for the night, to which she answered Yes," for they entertained strangers. She placed him in the kitchen and gave him something to eat.

    It was a part her regular family discipline, on Saturday eve to catechize the children and the servants; and, of so, the poor man in the kitchen came in among them. Mrs. Rutherford put to all of them some questions concerning the commandments, and to this poor man she put the question, "How many commandments are there?" and he answered, "Eleven."

    "Ah!" she said, "what a sad thing that a man of your age, whose hair is sprinkled with grey, should not even know how many commandments there are, for there is not a child, above six years old, in our parish, who does not know that."

    The poor man said nothing in reply, but he had his oatmeal porridge, and went to bed. Later, he rose, and listened to Rutherford's midnight prayer. He was charmed with it; made himself known to him, borrowed a better coat from him, preached for him on the Sunday morning, and surprised Mrs. Rutherford by taking as his text, "A new commandment I give unto you," and by commencing with the observation that this might very properly be called the eleventh commandment.

    By-and-by, the archbishop went on his way, and he and Rutherford had been refreshed together. It is the eleventh commandment; and if, the next time we are asked how many commandments there are, we answer "Eleven", we shall reply rightly enough'.

15. The Rev. George Augustus Selwyn (1809-1878) from Hampstead was the first Bishop of New Zealand (1841-58) and first Primate of New Zealand (1858-1868), and became Bishop of Lichfield from 1868 until his death in 1878. Selwyn College, Cambridge is named after him.

Notes to Book II Part IV:

1. This appears to be Sir Francis Annesley, Fellow of All Souls, (1734-1812), who was MP for Reading.

2. Edward Pennington is known as Penington in the American National Biography. He lived from 1726-1790, and his family was related to the Welsh-American family of William Penn. Edward's grandfather had been one of the Welshmen who accompanied Penn on his second voyage to America in 1698, ostensibly to set up The Welsh Tract, an independent nation in what is now Pennsylvania. In 1754, Pennington married Sarah Shoemaker, the daughter of Benjamin Shoemaker. Pennington was one of the 'ruling elite' of Philadelphia.

3. Samuel Shoemaker was a local merchant who served two terms as mayor of Philadelphia from 1769-1771. His sister married Edward Pennington. Samuel married Rebecca Rawle, a widow, of Laurel Hill, Philadelphia and their mansion was seized for supporting the British in the War of Independence, but later regained. He was introduced by Benjamin West at Windsor to the king as an American Loyalist. Samuel's father was Benjamin Shoemaker of Germantown, Philadelphia, of German stock, who was also Mayor of Philadelphia, in 1743, 1752 and 1760.

4. Robert Dinwiddie (1693-1770) was Governor of Virginia from 1751 to 1758. Colonel Hunter is mentioned elsewhere in this book.

5. There is little information upon this Indian Conference held in East Town, or 'Easton', Pennsylvania in 1756, not 1755 as in the letter. The *Virginia Trade* is essentially the slave trade.

6. Nathaniel Smith, operating under the sign of Rembrandt's Head, was followed by his son Charles Smith as a printer based in Newgate Street, London, around the late 1750's to late 1760's.

7. Benjamin Lay (1681-1760) was a noted philanthropist, born in Colchester, England, but who lived

and died in Pennsylvania. Only four feet high, he earned the dislike of many people for his strong abolitionist views, views which paralleled those of William Williams and Mr. Penrose. Williams knew Benjamin Franklin also.

8. There was a Corsican Club opened in Dublin to celebrate liberty and the patriot Paoli.
9. Lady Rosehill would have been one of the Carnegie Family, of whom the Earl of Northesk is a descendant. Lord Rosehill is the title of the Earl's eldest son. The last Lord Rosehill appears to have killed himself in 2001.
10. There was a John Minshull, who wrote 'The Sprightly Widow' in 1803. A Captain Rutgers served in the New York Provincial Congress and on the New York Committee of Safety, giving a dissenting opinion on exports of livestock, March 22, 1776, the year that Williams returned to England.
11. This is a strange letter – there definitely was a William Williams registered at Eglwysilan in 1726 (December 9), the son of David Williams. Why would Evan Evans contradict this fact? This Evan Evans may have been the person born at Llanwonno, Glamorgan in 1812, who died at the Star Inn, Ystradyfodwg, Glamorgan in 1857, the year of this letter.

REFERENCES TO PART II

William Williams' original manuscript – *The Journal of Penrose, Seaman* – c. 1760? – courtesy of The Lilly Library, Indiana University, Bloomington, Indiana.

Robert C. Alberts – *'Benjamin West'* – Houghton Mifflin, Boston 1978
Joshua Berman and Randy Wood – *Moon Handbook to Nicaragua* – Avalon Travel Publishing 1993
Helen Burr Smith – *The Two William Williamses* – The New York Historical Society Quarterly XXXV 1951
CIDCA (Centro de Investigacion y Documentacion de la Costa Atlantica) – *Diccionario Elemental Rama* - 1987
Nick Cole and Dennis Smith – *The Naked Feet of Nicaragua* – Hodder and Stoughton 1997
Cathy Davidson – *Revolution and the Word: The Rise of the Novel in America* –OUP New York 1986
D.H. Dickason - *William Williams: Novelist and Painter of Colonial America* – Indiana University Press 1970
D.H. Dickason – Introduction and Notes to Mr. *Penrose: The Journal of Penrose, Seaman* – Indiana University Press 1969
D.H. Dickason – *Benjamin West on William Williams* – *A Previously Unpublished Letter* – Winterthur Portfolio 1970
William Dunlap – *History of the American Theatre* – Oxford University 1833
William Dunlap – *History of the Rise and Progress of the Arts of Design in the United States* – G.P. Scott & Co. 1834
Thomas Eagles (ed.) William Williams – *The Journal of Lewellin Penrose, A Seaman,* in four volumes - John Murray 1815
John Eagles – *The Beggar's Legacy* – Essays contributed to Blackwell's Magazine 1857
James Thomas Flexner – *Benjamin West's American Neo-Classicism* –New York History Society Quarterly - 1952
James Thomas Flexner – *History of American Painters* – *First Flowers of our Wilderness* – *American Painters of the Colonial Period* – Houghton Mifflin 1947
James Thomas Flexner – *America's Old Masters* – Dover Publications 1994
James Thomas Flexner – *The Amazing William Williams* – *Author, Teacher, Musician, Stage Designer, Castaway* – Magazine of Art XXXVII 1944
John Galt – *Life and Studies and Works of Benjamin West* - 1816
William H. Gerdts – *William Williams: New American Discoveries* – Winterthur Portfolio 4 1968
Ben Gregory – *Caribbean Coast under Siege* – Latin America Solidarity Centre's Publication Enlace
Svein Jentoft – *The Poverty Trap: Defending Indigenous Peoples' Resource Rights in Nicaragua* – draft paper presented at the COASTFISH meeting in Merida, Yucatan, Mexico 4-8 October 2004
Richard Leonardi – *Nicaragua – Footprint Handbook* – Footprint Handbooks 2001
Tim L. Merrill (editor) – *Nicaragua – A Country Study* – Federal Research Division, Library of Congress 1993
Wayne O'Neill – *Diccionario Elemental Rama* – 1987 Centro de Investigacion y Documentacion de la Costa Atlantica
Hazel Plunkett – *In Focus Nicaragua: A Guide to the People, Politics and Culture* - Interlink Books 2002
Susan Rather – *Benjamin West's Professional Endgame and the Historical Conundrum of William Williams* – The William and Mary Quarterly Vol. 59, issue 4 October 2002
Susan Rather – *Benjamin West, John Galt and the Biography of 1816* – The Art Bulletin June 2004
E.P. Richardson – *William Williams* – *A Dissenting Opinion* –The American Art Journal 1972
Gerald Riverstone – *Living in the Land of Our Ancestors: Rama Indian and Creole Territory in Caribbean Nicaragua* – ASDI, Managua 2004
John Roach – *The Surprizing Adventures of John Roach, Mariner of Whitehaven* – 1784 – reprint by La Tienda el Quetzal, Conway, New Hampshire 1986
Orlando W. Roberts – *Narrative of Voyages and excursions on the East Coast and in the Interior of Central America* – 1827 – Edinburgh, reprinted by the Southport Press 2003
William Sawitzky – *William Williams, First Instructor of Benjamin West* – Antiques, 31 May 1937
William Sawitzky – *Further Light on the Work of William Williams* – New York History Society Quarterly Bulletin, XXV 1941

N.L. Thomas – *Defending Indigenous Land Rights in Nicaragua*- Nicaragua Network News – The People's Voice, September 19 2000 - copyright Nicanet 2000
C. Uhl & G. Parker – *Our Steak in the Jungle'* – Bioscience 36, 642 1986
Sarah Wadsworth – *Imaginary Landscape? William Williams and 'The Journal of Penrose, Seaman'* – paper presented at a University of Minnesota conference, 'Snapshots from Abroad.'
Ernest Walls – *The Bristol Avon* 1927
John Francis Williams – *The Ancestor – The World of William Williams* – Dorrance & Co. 1971

The Secret Vale of Glamorgan ISBN 190352900X 230pp (Terry Breverton 2000) Millennium Award – 'shows a local man's pride in the history and culture of his native patch, combined with a historian's delight in tracing the past and relating it to the present.' (OUT of PRINT) £13.99

The Book of Welsh Saints ISBN 1903529018 606pp hardback (Terry Breverton 2000) – 'this book is a really extraordinary achievement: a compilation of tradition, topography and literary detective work that can have few rivals. I have enjoyed browsing it immensely, and have picked up all sorts of new lines to follow up' – Rowan Williams, Archbishop of Canterbury; 'an enormous work of research'. £24.99

100 Great Welshmen ISBN 1903529034 376pp (Terry Breverton 2001) Welsh Books Council 'Book of the Month' – 'a revealing volume illustrating the great and good with Welsh connection… painstaking research'; 'a veritable goldmine of a book'. (OUT of PRINT) £17.99

The Dragon Entertains – 100 Welsh Stars ISBN 1903529026 230pp (Alan Roderick 2001) ' a celebration of Welsh talent in all its vibrany variety', 'this is the book to reach for the next time someone tells you that Wales has not nurtured any great talent in the worlds of entertainment or show-biz.' £5.99 (Special Offer, from £11.99)

A Rhondda Boy: The Memoirs of Ivor Howells edited by Owen Vernon Jones ISBN 1903529050 144pp (Ivor Howells 2001) 'a charming evocation of the childhood of a 93 year old Welshman. Son of a miner, Rhondda born and bred, Rhondda educated apart from his degree years at Aberystwyth, Ivor Howells spent all his professional life as teacher and headmaster in Rhondda schools.' £6.99

100 Great Welsh Women ISBN 1903529042 304pp (Terry Breverton 2001) – 'this book is an absolute must for all those who value their Welsh heritage, and for all those who wish to see women accorded their rightful place in history.' £16.99

The Welsh Almanac ISBN 1903529107 320pp hardback (Terry Breverton 2002) Welsh Books Council Book of the Month – 'a tremendous undertaking, and a very worthwhile and absolutely fascinating addition to the library of Welsh history'; 'It will take its place on the bookshelf with other works of reference.' £6.99 (special offer, from £16.99)

From Wales to Pennsylvania: The David Thomas Story ISBN 1903529085 112pp (Dr Peter N. Williams 2002) 'the story of the man who emigrated from Ystradgynlais, to transform the American iron industry and make America an economic superpower… Dr Peter Williams takes us back to the days of mass emigration to the United States. The terrible conditions at home, which sparked the Chartist Riots, are described, to put into context the reasons for this difficult transatlantic flight. Through Dr Thomas's correspondence with Wales, Dr Williams shows us the Welshman's immense contribution to the industrialisation and economic growth of America.' £8.99

Glyn Dŵr's War: The Campaigns of the Last Prince of Wales 238pp ISBN 1903529069 (Gideon Brough 2002) 'The Great Liberation War is THE defining moment of our nation's history. Had it not been for Owain Glyndŵr and the men and women who stood at his side against overwhelming odds, there would be no Welsh nation today. You will find all the details here,' 'A massive undertaking indeed for a 30 year old, first-time author, but one which Brough, who himself boasts an impressive militart background, has tackled with immense confidence and success.' £13.99 (OUT OF PRINT)

The Path to Inexperience ISBN 1903529077 160pp (Terry Breverton 2002) – 'magnificent, compassionate and moving' Special offer £3.99

Glamorgan Seascape Pathways – 52 Walks in the Southern Vale of Glamorgan ISBN 1903529115 144pp (Terry Breverton 2003) ARWAIN Award - 'fascinating… useful to anybody interested in the topography, geography and history of the southern Vale of Glamorgan.' Special Offer £6.99

The Book of Welsh Pirates and Buccaneers ISBN 1903529093 388pp (Terry Breverton 2003) <u>Welsh Books Council Book of the Month</u> – 'an immense work of great scholarship… effectively, a study of the whole genre of piracy… exemplary, yet the writing is light and accessible… wonderful, fascinating detail and essential reading.' (OUT of PRINT) £17.99

The Man from the Alamo : Why the Welsh Chartist Uprising of 1839 Ended in a Massacre ISBN 190352914X 332pp (John Humphries 2004) 'one of the fastest-selling books in Welsh publishing history', 'the remarkable story of two men sentenced to hanging, drawing and quartering. Zephaniah Williams ended up a respectable businessman after being transported to hard labour in Tasmania. John Rees ('Jack the Fifer' escaped from the Alamo to probably fire the first shot at the Westgate Hotel, before escaping back to join the great California Gold Rush', 'an amazing story, full of meticulously researched new facts, from the former editor of the Western Mail.' <u>W.H. Smith Welsh Book of the Month.</u> £9.99

Black Bart Roberts – The Greatest Pirate of Them All ISBN1903529123 254pp (Terry Breverton 2004) 'a must read for anyone interested in pirates', 'the true story of John Robert, the most successful pirate of all time, who captured over 400 ships, and brought Atlantic shipping to a standstill', 'a fascinating story of piratical history on the High Seas', 'he basically declared war against the world.' £10.99

The Pirate Handbook- A Dictionary of PirateTerms and Places ISBN1903529131 388pp <u>Welsh Books Council Book of the Month</u> (Terry Breverton 2004) – 'this wonderful sourcebook is an absolute must for all those interested in nautical matters', 'the amount of detail and depth is phenomenal', 'a vitally important addition to the canon of literature about naval history'. £11.99

Heroic Science: Swansea and the Royal Institution of South Wales 1835-1865 ISBN1903529166 258pp – (Ron Rees 2005) – Who knows that at one time Swansea's scientists were at the centre of the Scientific Revolution, and the great men of the day made their way by carriage and boat to its Royal Institution? £9.99

Gringo Revolutionary: The Amazing Story of Carel ap Rhys Price ISBN1903529182 - John Humphries (2005) – 'the former editor of the Western Mail has done it again, following the amazing success of his The Man from the Alamo' – this is the true story of a Welsh anarchist who fought with Zapata and Pancho Villa, was Hollywood's first all-action hero, and a World War I hero. £9.99

100 Great Welshmen (New Edition) ISBN1903529157 432pp – (Terry Breverton 2005) 'a fascinating compendium', 'this book is great fun', 'a massive treasure-chest of facts and figures which no collector of books on Wales can overlook.'£14.99

Admiral Sir Henry Morgan: the Greatest Buccaneer of Them All ISBN1903529174 174pp <u>Welsh Books Council Book of the Month</u> – (Terry Breverton 2005) – what more is there to say? Breverton has recently given an academic paper at Gregynog to an international conference, pointing out the little-known fact that Morgan was one of the greatest 'generals' in history, a genius at defeating overwhelming odds. £11.99

Welsh Sailors of the Second World War ISBN 1903529190 448pp <u>WH Smith Book of the Month</u> – Phil Carradice and Terry Breverton 2007 – 'One can only wonder at the mystery of human courage, in the face of what must have seemed overwhelming odds against survival… An account worthy of the pen of Xenophon.'

Other Books from Terry Breverton
An A to Z of Wales and the Welsh, 2000, Christopher Davies ('the first Welsh encyclopaedia!')
Contributions to *A Song for Owain: Poems in Praise of Owain Glyndwr*, 2004 ed. Rhys Parry, Y Lolfa

Forthcoming books by Terry Breverton
A Historical Companion to Wales, 2008 Tempus Publishing
'The Pirate Diaries' 2008 Collins (USA).

Where to Buy

All of the Above Books are Available from The Welsh Books Council, Unit 16, Parc Menter Glanyrafon, Llanbadarn Fawr, Ceredigion SY23 3AQ, or from its **website** *www.gwales.com*, or from **any good bookseller**. If your bookseller states that it cannot get any of these books, they are on all the relevant ordering databases. Alternatively, send a cheque with order to Wales Books (Glyndŵr Publishing) at PO BOX 68, Cowbridge, Vale of Glamorgan CF71 9AY. There is no postage on orders in the British Isles, but £6 per book is charged for overseas orders. Visit our **website** *www.walesbooks.com* to download an order form, if you wish. The web pages feature a Welsh Quiz, addresses for over 400 Welsh Societies around the world, and reviews on all our books. Please let us know any additions or alterations to societies.

Our American Publishing Partners are Pelican Publishing Company, PO Box 3110, Gretna, New Orleans LA 70054, with the website *www.pelicanpub.com*. In 2004-5 Pelican published Terry Breverton's 'Black Bart Roberts' , 'The Pirate Dictionary', 'Admiral Sir Henry Morgan', and John Humphries' 'The Man from the Alamo' , and it is hoped that all of Glyndŵr Publishing's output will be available in the USA via Pelican over the forthcoming years.